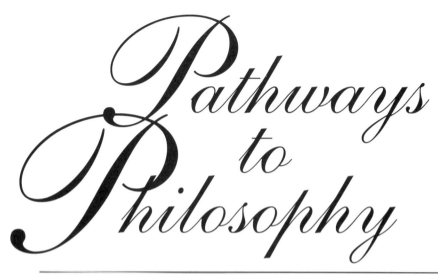

Pathways to Philosophy

A Multidisciplinary Approach

Douglas W. Shrader

Ashok K. Malhotra

State University of New York
College at Oneonta

Prentice Hall, Upper Saddle River, New Jersey 07458

Library of Congress Cataloging-in-Publication Data

Shrader, Douglas W.
    Pathways to philosophy : a multidisciplinary approach / Douglas W.
Shrader ; Ashok K. Malhotra.
        p.   cm.
    Includes bibliographical references.
    ISBN 0-02-410191-5
    I. Malhotra, Ashok Kumar, 1940-   . II. Title.
    B72.S55   1996   95-40431
    100—dc20   CIP

Editorial/production supervision: Patricia V. Amoroso/Jean Lapidus
Interior and cover design: Anne Bonanno Nieglos
Creative design director: Leslie Osher
Editorial assistant: Meg McGuane
Editor-in-chief: Charlyce Jones Owen
Manufacturing buyer: Lynn Pearlman
Photo editor: Lorinda Morris-Nantz
Photo researcher: Rona Tuccillo
Cover art: Profile in a Collage. Courtesy of The Stock Illustration
    Source, Inc. Photographer: Fred Otnes.

©1996 by Prentice-Hall, Inc.
Simon & Schuster/A Viacom Company
Upper Saddle River, NJ 07458

For Barbara, Callie, and Sterling.
DWS

For Nina, Raj, and Ravi.
AKM

Printed in the United States of America

10   9   8   7   6   5   4   3   2   1

ISBN   0-02-410191-5

Prentice-Hall International (UK) Limited, *London*
Prentice-Hall of Australia Pty. Limited, *Sydney*
Prentice-Hall Canada Inc., *Toronto*
Prentice-Hall Hispanoamericana, S.A., *Mexico*
Prentice-Hall of India Private Limited, *New Delhi*
Prentice-Hall of Japan, Inc., *Tokyo*
Simon & Schuster Asia Pte. Ltd., *Singapore*
Editora Prentice-Hall do Brasil, Ltda., *Rio de Janeiro*

CONTENTS

PREFACE   IX

INTRODUCTION   A Guidebook for Students   1

PART ONE

THE HUMAN CONDITION: KNOWING THYSELF

CHAPTER 1   The Meaning of Life   14

INTRODUCTORY ESSAY   The Meaning of Life   17
Douglas W. Shrader

PHILOSOPHICAL READINGS   My Confession from *My Confession* (1884)   23
Leo Tolstoy

The Meaning of Life from *Good and Evil* (1984)   31
Richard Taylor

SCIENTIFIC READING   Love, the Answer to the Problem of Human Existence
from *The Art of Loving* (1956)   38
Erich Fromm

LITERARY READING   Total Perspective Vortex from *The Restaurant at the End
of the Universe* (1981)   44
Douglas Adams

REVIEW AND REFLECTION   45
SUGGESTIONS FOR FURTHER STUDY   45

CHAPTER 2   Death and Beyond   46

INTRODUCTORY ESSAY   Death and Beyond   49
Douglas W. Shrader

PHILOSOPHICAL READINGS   The Death of Socrates from *The Apology* and *Phaedo*
(circa 399 B.C.)   55
Plato

The Myth of Immortality from *Forum*, vol. 80 (October 1928)   59
Clarence Darrow

SCIENTIFIC READING   Stages from *On Death and Dying* (1969)   63
Elisabeth Kübler-Ross

LITERARY READING   The Myth of Er from *The Republic* (circa 375 B.C.)   72
Plato

REVIEW AND REFLECTION   79
SUGGESTIONS FOR FURTHER STUDY   79

CHAPTER 3   Existentialism   80

INTRODUCTORY ESSAY   Existentialism   83
Ashok K. Malhotra

PHILOSOPHICAL READING   The Far Side of Despair from *An Existentialist Ethics* (1967)   87
Hazel Barnes

SCIENTIFIC READING   Taking Charge of Yourself from *Your Erroneous Zones* (1976)   96
Wayne Dyer

LITERARY READINGS   The Myth of Sisyphus from *Le Mythe de Sisyphe* (1942)   102
Albert Camus

On The Three Metamorphoses from *Thus Spoke Zarathustra* (1954)   105
Friedrich Nietzsche

REVIEW AND REFLECTION   107
SUGGESTIONS FOR FURTHER STUDY   107

PART TWO
VALUES AND SYSTEMS: LIVING WITH OTHERS

CHAPTER 4   Ethics   110

INTRODUCTORY ESSAY   Choices   113
Douglas W. Shrader

PHILOSOPHICAL READINGS   The Ring of Gyges from *The Republic* (circa 375 B.C.)   122
Plato

The Prisoner's Dilemma from *The Expanding Circle* (1981)   126
Peter Singer

SCIENTIFIC READING   Anthropology and the Abnormal from *The Journal of General Psychology* 10 (1934)   128
Ruth Fulton Benedict

LITERARY READING   A Good Man is Hard to Find from *A Good Man is Hard to Find* (1953/5)   133
Flannery O'Connor

REVIEW AND REFLECTION   142
SUGGESTIONS FOR FURTHER STUDY   142

CHAPTER 5   Social and Political Philosophy   143

INTRODUCTORY ESSAY   It's Just Not Fair!   145
Douglas W. Shrader

PHILOSOPHICAL READING   Abortion and the Concept of a Person from the *Canadian Journal of Philosophy* 5.2 (October 1975)   155
Jane English

SCIENTIFIC READING   I'm Black, You're White, Who's Innocent? from *Harper's Magazine* (June 1988)   163
Shelby Steele

LITERARY READING   Crime and Punishment from *The Prophet* (1923)   169
Kahlil Gibran

REVIEW AND REFLECTION   171
SUGGESTIONS FOR FURTHER STUDY   171

CHAPTER 6   Technology and Human Values   172

INTRODUCTORY ESSAY   The Power Button   175
Douglas W. Shrader

PHILOSOPHICAL READING   The Growing Danger from Gene-Spliced Hormones from *Discover* (1987)   185
Thomas H. Murray

SCIENTIFIC READING   Harvesting the Dead from *Harper's Magazine* (September 1974)   189
Willard Gaylin

LITERARY READING   Brave New World from *Brave New World* (1932)   196
Aldous Huxley

REVIEW AND REFLECTION   207
SUGGESTIONS FOR FURTHER STUDY   207

PART THREE
TRUTH AND BEING: EXPLORING THE LIMITS

CHAPTER 7   Philosophy of Science   210

INTRODUCTORY ESSAY   Matters of Theory   213
Douglas W. Shrader

PHILOSOPHICAL READINGS   Historical Structure of Scientific Discovery from *Science* 136 (June 1, 1962)   220
Thomas S. Kuhn

Feminism and Science from *Signs* 7.3 (Spring 1982)   228
Evelyn Fox Keller

SCIENTIFIC READING   Bathybius Meets Eozoon from *Natural History* 87.4
(April 1978)   238
Stephen Jay Gould

LITERARY READINGS   Scientific Hypotheses from *Zen and the Art of Motorcycle
Maintenance* (1974)   243
Robert M. Pirsig

Poincaré and the Development of Non-Euclidean Geometry
from *Zen and the Art of Motorcycle Maintenance* (1974)   248
Robert M. Pirsig

REVIEW AND REFLECTION   253
SUGGESTIONS FOR FURTHER STUDY   253

CHAPTER 8   Metaphysics: Reflections on Reality   254

INTRODUCTORY ESSAY   If a Tree Falls . . .   257
Douglas W. Shrader

PHILOSOPHICAL READINGS   The Allegory of the Cave from *The Republic* (circa 375 B.C.)   265
Plato

Meditations from *Meditations on First Philosophy* (1641)   269
René Descartes

SCIENTIFIC READING   The Dynamic Universe from *The Tao of Physics* (1991)   276
Fritjof Capra

LITERARY READING   The Metaphysician's Nightmare from *Nightmares of
Eminent Persons* (1954)   285
Bertrand Russell

REVIEW AND REFLECTION   288
SUGGESTIONS FOR FURTHER STUDY   288

PART FOUR
OF ULTIMATE CONCERN: A HIGHER CONSCIOUSNESS

CHAPTER 9   The Existence of God   290

INTRODUCTORY ESSAY   The Ontological Argument   293
Douglas W. Shrader

PHILOSOPHICAL READINGS   Why I Am Not A Christian (1927 lecture and monograph)   300
Bertrand Russell

Symbols of Faith from *Dynamics of Faith* (1957)   309
Paul Tillich

SCIENTIFIC READING   Why Women Need the Goddess from *Womanspirit Rising* (1979)   315
Carol P. Christ

LITERARY READINGS   A Conversation with God from *The Tao is Silent* (1977)   325
Raymond M. Smullyan

Demons and Devils from *The Screwtape Letters* (1941/3)   327
C. S. Lewis

REVIEW AND REFLECTION   334
SUGGESTIONS FOR FURTHER STUDY   334

CHAPTER 10   Wisdom of India   335

INTRODUCTORY ESSAY   Hinduism   339
Ashok K. Malhotra

Buddhism   345
Ashok K. Malhotra

PHILOSOPHICAL READINGS   *Two Vedic Hymns* from the *Rig Veda*   349
Māndūkya Upanishad   352
The Fourth Noble Truth from *What the Buddha Taught* (1979)   354
Walpola Rahula

SCIENTIFIC READING   The Cosmic Dance from *The Tao of Physics* (1991)   358
Fritjof Capra

LITERARY READINGS   The Way of Renunciation from The *Bhagavad Gītā*   361
translated by Ashok K. Malhotra

Some Buddhist Parables and Legends from *The Gospel of Buddha*   363
Paul Carus

REVIEW AND REFLECTION   366
SUGGESTIONS FOR FURTHER STUDY   367

CHAPTER 11   Wisdom of the Orient   368

INTRODUCTORY ESSAY   Taoism   371
Ashok K. Malhotra

Zen Buddhism   376
Ashok K. Malhotra

PHILOSOPHICAL READINGS   Selections from the *Tao Te Ching*   380
Lao Tzu

The Technique of Zen from *The Spirit of Zen* (1958)   384
Alan Watts

SCIENTIFIC READING   Zen in the West from *Zen Action/Zen Person* (1981)   391
Thomas P. Kasulis

LITERARY READING   Stories of Chuang Tzu and Hui Tzu from *Three Ways of Thought
in Ancient China* (1956)   397
Arthur Waley

REVIEW AND REFLECTION   402
SUGGESTIONS FOR FURTHER STUDY   402

CHAPTER 12   Yoga and Meditation   404

INTRODUCTORY ESSAY   The Philosophy and Psychology of Yoga   407
Ashok K. Malhotra

PHILOSOPHICAL READINGS Selections from the *Yoga Sūtras* (circa 500 B.C.,
translated by Ashok K. Malhotra)   412
Patañjali

Mysticism from *The Varieties of Religious Experience* (1902)   415
William James

SCIENTIFIC READING   Meditation in Daily Life from *Yoga Psychology* (1977)   422
Swami Ajaya

LITERARY READING   With the Samanas from *Siddhartha* (1951)   430
Hermann Hesse

REVIEW AND REFLECTION   435
SUGGESTIONS FOR FURTHER STUDY   435

EPILOGUE   436

GLOSSARY   439

SUGGESTIONS FOR FURTHER STUDY   449

PREFACE

Pathways is a playful, imaginative introduction to the art of philosophical reflection and wonderment. Original essays are combined with classical and contemporary readings from philosophy, science, and literature. Both structure and content emphasize the wide-ranging nature of the field, its relevance to other disciplines, and the interrelatedness of seemingly disparate areas of study.

There are four main sections divided into a total of twelve chapters held together by a common thread: analysis and exploration of various concepts and dimensions of the Self. The text covers Eastern as well as Western traditions and includes selections by women as well as men.

All material is carefully chosen, edited, and coordinated to insure that it is accessible to and appropriate for introductory students. The overall effect is a presentation which is sure to be engaging, exciting, provocative, and fun.

Distinctive Features

1. The text is structured so as to reveal and explore interconnections between Philosophy, Science, and Literature. Among the many benefits of this approach we believe the following to be worthy of special note:

    (i) The approach helps demonstrate the relevance of philosophy to other disciplines (and thus helps counter the all-too-common misperception of philosophy as an isolated and self-perpetuating series of puzzlements with little if any practical importance).

    (ii) The approach provides multiple paths to difficult concepts and issues. Students who have difficulty with traditional philosophical presentations may find the scientific and/or literary readings especially illuminating. More generally, multiple perspectives help to add dimension and clarity to what may otherwise be a rather shallow or limited understanding.

    (iii) The approach facilitates exploration of disciplinary boundaries. The text can be used to highlight differences as well as similarities between various fields, to explore ways in which some research cuts across traditional boundaries, or to investigate historical connections between what may now seem to be conceptually distinct areas.

    (iv) The approach encourages development of conceptual tools and perspectives which should benefit students in other classes as well. Specifically, performance in literature and/or science classes may be enhanced as a consequence of the contextual understanding facilitated by the text's multidisciplinary approach.
    Example: Chapter 4 examines ethical and cultural obligation through the lenses of philosophy (Plato), science (Ruth Fulton Benedict), and literature (Flannery O'Connor).

2. The text is organized around concepts of the Self (beginning rather narrowly then progressively expanding in ever-widening circles of concern). Focus on the Self captures and maintains the interest of the reader. It also results in an investment at a personal level which in turn results in more diligent class preparation, attendance, etc. Additionally, this unifying focus provides the conceptual connections necessary to move from a series of isolated inquiries to a somewhat more comprehensive vision of the philosophical terrain.
   Example: Chapter 1 focuses on the meaning of life. Chapter 2 examines death and the possibility of life after death. Chapter 6 investigates technology and human values. Chapter 10 explores Hindu concepts of Ātman and Brahman. Chapter 12 explores Yoga and Meditation. Etc.

3. The text covers Eastern as well as Western Philosophical traditions. This not only facilitates understanding of the diverse traditions, but encourages evaluation of concepts and ideas according to a larger, more global context than most texts provide.
   Example: In addition to readings which explore the work of Western philosophers such as Plato and Aristotle, the text includes chapters devoted to Hinduism, Buddhism, Taoism, Zen, and Yoga.

4. The text covers contemporary issues and thinkers as well as the rich historical tradition for which Philosophy is known. In addition to benefits which arise from the intrinsic value of the material, the approach helps maintain student interest and paints a vibrant picture of Philosophy as a discipline which has not forgotten the past, ignored the present, nor forsaken the future.
   Example: Readings by recognized masters stand alongside contributions by contemporary, and sometimes controversial, thinkers (Albert Camus, Jane English, Stephen Jay Gould, Elisabeth Kübler-Ross, Thomas Kuhn, Robert M. Pirsig, Bertrand Russell, Richard Taylor, *et al*).

5. The text incorporates perspectives and contributions by both men and women. These include, but are not restricted to, presentation and defense of what is sometimes termed "The Feminist Position". The overall effect is a text which is more inclusive than most of its competitors. Given increased social and political concern over the changing roles of men and women, the readings provide much-needed perspective as well as more than ample occasion for debate.
   Example: Female authors include Hazel Barnes, Ruth Benedict, Carol P. Christ, Jane English, Evelyn Fox Keller, Elisabeth Kübler-Ross, and Flannery O'Connor.

6. *Pathways* presents a multiplicity of perspectives which cannot be achieved in a single-author text, but avoids the disjointed smorgasbord effect often associated with an anthology. Self-contained original essays by the authors provide a sense of cohesiveness and serve as an occasion for the development of viewpoints which span several chapters.
   Example: The interwoven dialogues and readings in chapters 4-*Ethics*, 5-*Social and Political Philosophy*, and 6-*Technology and Human Values* combine to produce a fabric of human relationship and concern.

7. The layout of the text provides organization and structure without limiting professional choice regarding what to assign or when. Professors may adjust assignments according to their own needs and temperaments, as well as those of the students. The structure also facilitates rereading selected assignments.

    Example: A professor may restrict assignments according to type (e.g. making all literary readings optional), subject matter (e.g. skipping one or more particular chapters), or any other standard which seems particularly appropriate (e.g. skipping this or that reading for more personal reasons). Assigning just the introductory essays would produce the effect of a short but nonetheless complete overview of philosophy (accompanied by a series of optional readings).

8. Each chapter is preceded by a brief organizational preview. Each reading begins with a short biographical or historical introduction. In general, students are not asked to read materials presented in an intellectual vacuum. Nor are they presumed to have an extensive knowledge of the history of philosophy, etc.

    Example: A selection from Plato is preceded by a brief introduction which helps students understand who Plato was, when he lived, the types of problems with which he wrestled, etc.

9. *Pathways* contains chapters on a number of topics which, though important, remain comparatively rare in introductory texts. Of particular note are chapters on The Meaning of Life, Death, Existentialism, Yoga, Philosophy of Science, and Technology and Human Values. *Pathways* thus succeeds in capturing some of the richness of Philosophy which eludes other texts.

    Example: In the 60's and 70's when Existentialism was sexy and hot (intellectually speaking) many texts focused too heavily on the movement (as though it constituted the whole field of Philosophy). Now many texts have gone to the opposite extreme of ignoring the movement. *Pathways* strikes a balance between the two, devoting one chapter to Existentialism and presenting it in the social, historical, and intellectual climate which it deserves.

10. Many concepts and issues recur, from slightly different perspectives, throughout the text. Students are thereby given opportunity to develop a greater depth of understanding of these concepts and issues, as well as a greater appreciation for the complex web of philosophical interconnection.

    Example: The question, "What is a Person?", is examined in chapters 2-*Death and Beyond*, 5-*Social and Political Philosophy*, and 8-*Metaphysics*. Other chapters (e.g. Hinduism, Taoism, and Yoga) provide additional dimension.

Acknowledgments

This text began as a project between three professors of different philosophical perspective, cultural heritage, and pedagogic temperament. Due to unfortunate circumstances and reasons of health, Dr. Anthony Roda was unable to serve as a co-author. He nonetheless helped shape content as well as structure. His influence can be felt throughout the text.

Much of the inspiration for *Pathways* belongs to Nina J. Malhotra. She helped simplify language so that readings may appeal to students who have no background in philosophy. She spent many hours helping select content for chapters on Hinduism, Buddhism, Taoism, and Zen. And she helped edit the chapters on Existentialism and Yoga. Ironically, Nina did not live to see completion of the text which, without her support and inspiration, might never have been completed.

Barbara Shrader, Majorie Holling, and Alane Strong provided clerical assistance as well as moral support. The following individuals provided useful feedback and encouragement concerning various portions of the manuscript: Lewis E. Hahn, Southern Illinois University at Carbondale; Joseph C. Pitt, Virginia Polytechnic Institute; James E. Faulconer, Brigham Young University; and Thomas F. Pyne, California State University-Sacramento.

Finally, we wish to acknowledge the patience and assistance of Maggie Barbieri, Ted Bolen, Patricia Amoroso, and their capable staff at Macmillan and Prentice Hall. Together they helped transform an abstract idea into a tangible reality.

INTRODUCTION

A Guidebook for Students

Fasten your imaginary seat belt, for you are about to embark on a journey as exciting, challenging, and full of unexpected adventure as anything you have ever encountered. The study of philosophy can be daunting and difficult, especially for a first-time student. It can also be a time of immense intellectual reward, conceptual growth, and personal empowerment. Philosophy will challenge your perceptions and beliefs concerning your self, those around you, the political and social systems that guide and discipline your life, even the universe itself. You will encounter concepts, cultures, and people who will sometimes seem foreign and strange, but often vaguely familiar as well.

Imagine yourself seated in an airplane of the mind. The pilot has turned off the "No Thinking" sign. You recline your seat and begin reading a standard guidebook which your travel agent suggested to help establish your bearings and give you some sense of the terrain you will be exploring. It covers in a brief and clearly inadequate way a little bit about the language, history, and customs of the land you are about to visit. Just as guidebooks for geographic travel often begin with a brief history of the area and/or description of some of the more colorful locals, this material begins with a tale of Thales, often regarded as the first Western philosopher.

Beginnings

On May 28, 585 B.C., a solar eclipse darkened the skies in the area surrounding the Mediterranean Sea, interrupting a battle between the ancient communities of Media and Lydia. As often happens in war, many of the soldiers may have believed they were participating in a historic event. In this case, they were. But the primary historic occurrence of that day did not depend on their heroics, the bloodshed of their enemies, or the political differences between their communities. For the day belonged not to Media or Lydia, but to Thales of Miletus.

Solar eclipses were rare and poorly understood. Yet Thales had accomplished what few would have even dreamed possible: he had successfully predicted the temporary darkening of that fateful day. What had once seemed a mysterious supernatural phenomenon was suddenly shown to depend not upon whether human behavior found divine approval or disapproval, but rather upon a simple mathematical equation. Thales' discovery opened the heavens, the very domain of the gods themselves, to the systematic observation, investigation, and reasoning of mere mortals.[1]

With these simple tools of observation and reason, Thales probed the secrets of the universe. He is said to have diverted the course of a river to allow an army to cross it in either direction. His study of the stars provided principles of navigation. In mathematics, he discovered a method for computing the distance of a ship at sea based on observations from two land points. In chemistry, he hypothesized that what appears to be an enormous array of diverse, unconnected substances is in fact a series of localized manifestations of a single, uniform, primordial fluid. Thales' fluid is commonly called "water," but in so naming it one should recognize that even this paper is "water." He is also widely known for his rather cryptic saying that all things are full of gods.[2]

It is perhaps fitting that Thales was the brunt of what may well have been the first absent-minded professor story. He is said to have been walking along, observing the heavens. Not minding his feet, he fell headlong into a well. A servant who witnessed the spectacle laughed and chided him at length. As Plato noted 200 years later, the image of the philosopher as an individual with his head in the clouds, unconcerned with the practical affairs of day-to-day life, is as old as the discipline of philosophy itself.[3]

Perhaps because he had been reproached for his impracticality and poverty, Thales devised a simple but effective get-rich-quick scheme. From his observations of the heavens he predicted that the olive harvest for the coming year would be especially rich and abundant. During the winter, when no one else thought to bid against him, Thales purchased options on all the olive presses in the region (used to procure precious olive oil, which in turn was used for cooking, lighting, and other practical purposes). Then, when demand for the presses was high, he lent them out on his own terms, making a fortune from those who had previously reproached him.

As Aristotle was later to observe, Thales' scheme worked because he established an economic monopoly and manipulated the market accordingly.[4] In the process, he also demonstrated an interconnectedness of seemingly disassociated parts of reality: studying the heavens (so distant, remote, and ethereal) can have direct consequences for agriculture, the olive press industry, and other human affairs. On a more individual level, Thales' scheme shows that the cultivation of reason can be used to serve a vast array of purposes, including worldly success and personal aggrandizement. It is perhaps instructive to note that Thales used the funds to construct a public monument rather than a mansion for his own private use. The true philosopher is motivated by a love of wisdom and understanding, not a promise of monetary reward.

A Tapestry of Many Threads

In Greek mythology, Athena (the Goddess of Wisdom) sprang full-grown from the head of Zeus. Pretty impressive; very convenient. If you like melodrama and ease of classification you will perhaps be tempted to consider the eclipse of 585 B.C. as the Athenian origin of philosophy. As long as you recognize that it is only a rough and approximate measure, there is no great harm in doing so.[5] For whatever else we make of his work, it is clear that Thales was a foundational figure. Others continued his line of questioning concerning the substance and structure of the universe. They shared his belief in a world characterized by mathematical regularity, governed by natural law rather than supernatural whim, predictable, and accessible to human reason. Like him, they came to believe that events and phenomena are to be understood, controlled, and manipulated on the basis of empirical experience and disciplined reasoning.

If Thales seems strange and difficult to the modern mind, think how much more so he must have seemed to his contemporaries, who were accustomed to the stories and explanations of poets like Homer and Hesiod. These influential poets presented an image of the world as a magical place, ruled by gods and goddesses who bickered among themselves and were more frequently concerned with their own power and prestige than with the welfare of humans. It was a strangely personal yet chaotic and unpredictable world.

Thales' commitments and contributions mark him not only as one of the first Western philosophers, but one of the first scientists as well. Such is as it should be. He and his followers did not draw the same sharp separations we sometimes do between philosophy, science, and other academic fields. Their thought was more holistic. It moved freely across boundaries that seem obvious and possibly even impassible to us.

It has been over 2500 years since Thales walked the shores of the Mediterranean Sea. In his footsteps have followed not only Socrates, Plato, and Aristotle, but also Copernicus, Galileo, Einstein, and a host of others. Together they have woven a tapestry which records an ongoing attempt to understand ourselves and the universe in which we live. It is a rich complex tapestry of many colors, threads, and patterns: some threads and segments we now identify as mathematics, some as philosophy, some as physics, some as poetry, and so on.

The primary purpose of this text is to exhibit and allow you to explore some of the portions of the fabric we typically regard as philosophy. As you will see, philosophy is a wide-ranging field: its presence and influence can be felt throughout the entire fabric. Thus to fully appreciate the nature and contributions of philosophy, it is important that one also develop an appreciation of the relationships between philosophy and other disciplines. To help develop a broad-based understanding and sense of the fabric as a whole, each chapter begins with an introductory essay, then presents a series of interconnected readings from philosophy, science, and literature.

You will find that the distinctions between fields are sometimes clear, but other times murky and difficult to discern. Some readings even cut across traditional boundaries. It is not always a question of whether something is philosophy *or* science *or* literature; some studies are best regarded as philosophy *and* science, philosophy *and* literature, and so on. The distinctions, roughly, are as follows:

- Philosophy is concerned with articulation, analysis, and evaluation of concepts and ideas. Confronted with a problem, the philosopher responds: "Let's think about it."
- Science places a premium on empirical study and investigation. While the philosopher thinks about concepts, the scientist plots an experiment. Tugging at the philosopher's sleeve, the scientist urges: "Let's go look and see."
- Like science, literature prefers concrete images to abstract concepts. But whereas science is restricted to empirical observation, literature has at its disposal the full range of human cognition and imagination. The author creates a series of images that explore the consequences of various concepts and ideas, then entreats philosopher and scientist alike: "Let's look at the possibilities and imagine what the world could be like."

Philosophy, science, and literature combine to produce a richer, more vibrant vision of the universe than any of the three could accomplish on its own. To accommodate a broad range of perspective and opinion, including materials which defy conventional classification, this text uses terms like *philosophy, science,* and *literature* as general indicators of domain rather than strict, mutually exclusive categories. Thus "philosophical" readings include selections by Leo Tolstoy (the novelist) and Clarence Darrow (the defense attorney). "Scientific" readings include selections by Carol P. Christ (a contemporary feminist theologian) and Swami Ajaya (a student of yoga). "Literary" readings include dialogues by Plato as well as legends drawn from the oral traditions of Buddhism and Taoism.

What Is This Thing Called Philosophy?

When I was six, my parents gave me a Mickey Mouse watch (the kind that is now a rather valuable collector's item). I was overjoyed. I disappeared into my room, then reemerged after an hour or so with a shoebox full of gears, springs, and other assorted pieces. I showed the box triumphantly to my father. Then, in my childlike innocence, I said the words he dreaded perhaps more than any others: "Now show me how to put it back together!" Alas, such was not to be. I learned that day that there are some things even my father could not do. I also learned that the various parts of a watch, even when arranged according to size and shape in a shoebox, are not quite the same thing nor have the same value as a complete, functioning watch. One keeps track of time; the other does not.

I wish I still had the watch. But the experience was not, as my parents may have believed, a complete waste. As misguided as my deconstruction of the watch may have seemed to those who scrimped and saved to purchase it, there was also something fundamentally correct about my methodology of disassembly. Even though I destroyed much of the utility of the watch, I learned far more about what a watch is and how it works than if I had just strapped it to my wrist and gone on about the everyday affairs of a six-year-old.

The lessons are simple, but they hold true for a wide range of human endeavor. Because individual parts are typically simpler and easier to examine than the composite entity taken in its entirety, separation and division facilitate both research and understanding. Thus, as indicated in the previous section, scholars have focused on smaller and smaller pieces of the cosmic puzzle. Such is both right and good. But if we are to end up with anything more than a shoebox full of disjointed and unconnected pieces, it is imperative that we remember that the parts are not the whole; even a complete knowledge of each and every part is not yet knowledge of the whole. As each generation of scholars adds new and smaller pieces to the puzzle, tracking and integration become increasingly more difficult.

Given its traditional status as a guardian of unity, it may seem ironic that even philosophy is subject to specialization and division. As with other fields, however, the distinctions can be both convenient and instructive; they assist the work of the philosopher as well as the understanding of the student. The discipline is simply too all-encompassing and complex to be digested in a single meal: there is more than enough for a feast to last an entire lifetime. To provide you with a multiplicity of perspectives, and also to discourage you from identifying any as *the* (one and only) correct set of distinctions, the next few pages present four different ways in which philosophy can be disassembled into a series of component parts. In each case, please remember:

1. none of the parts, taken individually, should be identified as philosophy any more than an arm, heart, or liver should be identified as a human being, and

2. most instances of philosophy use or involve several, of not all, parts (just as most activities of a human being use or involve several different body parts).

1. Animal, Vegetable, or Mineral? Like most words, *philosophy* is a term with several distinct if related meanings. It can refer to:

a. the complex activity of questioning, conceptualizing, analyzing, evaluating, puzzling, wondering, and reflecting,

b. the academic discipline based on that activity, or

c. any of a number of specific answers or approaches to thorny problems and issues (the philosophy of Plato, Oriental philosophy, and so on).

The order of primacy is as given (activity, academic discipline, and specific answers). Philosophy is first and foremost something that one does.

2. Basic Anatomy. Some questions, issues, and concerns are so distinctive as to form subfields which have lasted the test of time:

a. Metaphysics. Aristotle (fourth century B.C.) wrote on a wide variety of topics, many of which we would now consider science rather than philosophy. Andronicus (first century A.D.) was attempting to catalog Aristotle's work. One particularly problematic set of writings he simply placed *meta ta physika* (after the work on physics). Perhaps because no better term existed, the name stuck. But it was a fortunate choice as well, for metaphysics is an attempt to understand the basic nature and structure of reality, going above and beyond the limitations of natural science. Thales' assertion that all is water (that there is an underlying physio-chemical identity of all things) is a classic example of a metaphysical thesis. Typical metaphysical questions include the following: What is real? What is not? Does God exist? Does this book exist if you put it in a drawer and forget about it? Do you exist? Do I?

b. Epistemology. If you are going to ask questions as difficult as the ones just listed, you had better discover some standards by which to evaluate the various answers you are liable to get. Such is the domain of epistemology: the study of belief, opinion, knowledge, and related concepts. Philosophy moves from metaphysics to epistemology when we begin asking questions like: How do you know? What is your evidence? How could we go about determining which thesis is more likely to be true?

c. Logic. Logic, sometimes regarded as a part of epistemology, is nothing more mysterious than the disciplined effort to think and reason clearly. Logicians have discovered rules and principles that enhance our ability to guard against error, confusion, and deception when moving from one set of beliefs or assumptions to a second, related set. The rules and principles are similar to those you may have previously encountered in mathematics. By themselves they tell us very little, but when the going gets tough and truth becomes a matter of serious concern, there is no matching the power or importance of logical principles.

d. Axiology. Axiology is the study of values and value judgments. The term comes from the Greek words *axios* (worth, worthy) and *logos* (the study or understanding of—cf. *logic*). Primary divisions in axiology include **ethics** (the study of moral values and judgments) and **aesthetics** (the study of values and judgments concerning beauty, taste, and related concepts).

Ethical questions include the following: What is the nature of right and wrong? Are moral principles innate or learned? Are there any moral standards that are not simply reflections of individual or cultural preferences? Is abortion immoral? What responsibilities, if any, do we have to other humans? To nonhumans?

Aesthetic questions include: What is art? What makes one painting better than another? Do Beethoven's compositions have more aesthetic value than those of the Grateful Dead, The Rolling Stones, or the Doors? Why? If I agree that they have more aesthetic value, does it follow that I like them better? If not, what?

3. Philosophy of This and That. What do philosophers philosophize about when philosophers philosophize? Anything and everything. There is no sacred ground which philosophers dare not tread. Absolutely nothing is off limits. As a result, we create a series of identifiable fields of inquiry simply by using the tools and techniques of philosophy to investigate other fields or areas of concern. In some cases these fields parallel traditional academic disciplines: Philosophy of Science, Philosophy of Literature, Philosophy of Art, Philosophy of Religion, and so on. In other cases the fields cut across or fall outside traditional disciplines: Philosophy of Life, Philosophy of Love, Philosophy of Mind, and so on. Some perennial issues and concerns merit labels all their own: the Mind/Body Problem and the Free-Will/Determinism Issue, for example.

4. A Family of Traditions. With all these questions floating around, someone must have come up with some answers. Indeed they have—whole sets of different and sometimes incompatible answers and approaches (cf. *1.iii*). Although the distinctions are somewhat rough and incomplete, it may help to divide this way of classifying philosophy into four general groupings:

a. Geographic Divisions. Philosophy developed differently in different cultures. Thus we distinguish Eastern from Western philosophy. More specifically, Chinese philosophy differs from that which developed in India; European Continental philosophy differs from its American counterpart; and so on.

b. Historical Divisions. As the field has progressed, so too have the questions, answers, and techniques of its practitioners. We generally recognize a minimum of four historical periods: Ancient, Medieval, Modern, and Contemporary Philosophy.

c. Schools. Great thinkers tend to attract followers. They may, as did Plato and Aristotle, set up actual schools. In other cases the term *school* is used in a more general sense, referring to those who practice philosophy according to the manner or standards of some particular master(s). Thus we speak of Platonic philosophy, Aristotelian philosophy, Kantian philosophy, and so on.

d. -isms. Some answers and approaches cut across not only time and geography, but even the individual identities of their authors and practitioners. These typically become -isms: Hinduism, Buddhism, and existentialism, for example.

The chapters in this text provide a representative sampling of each of these ways of dividing philosophy into its component parts. Chapters 4 ("Ethics") and 8 ("Metaphysics") cover major segments of the field's traditional anatomy. Chapter 7 ("Philosophy of Science") is a good example of what happens when the philosophical lens is used to examine another academic discipline. Chapters 1 ("The Meaning of Life") and 6 ("Technology and Human Values") illustrate philosophical concerns for which there is no readily identifiable academic discipline. Chapters 10 ("Wisdom of India") and 11 ("Wisdom of the Orient") provide counterbalance to the Western philosophy that dominates most of the text. There, as in Chapter 3 ("Existentialism"), you will encounter systems of thought that cut across barriers of time and space. In all cases you will be asked to participate in the activity as you learn about the academic discipline and the answers various philosophers give.

Philosophy and You

Remember the airplane of the mind I asked you to think about at the beginning of this essay? Suppose you touch down in what appears to be a strange and foreign land, only to find that the people there have built monuments to you and spent centuries preparing for your arrival. Their most eminent scholars have formulated theories about you and your relations to others. Since they speak different languages and sometimes express themselves in ways that are unfamiliar to you, you may wander about for a period of time before realizing that everyone is talking about you. Some of their ideas and concepts may seem strange and difficult to understand. You may even encounter some skeptics who have doubted your existence.

Preposterous? Perhaps. But odd as it may seem, it is true. This book is about you. It is, if you wish, a philosophical biography.

Before your ego becomes too enlarged, you should note that the book is also about me, your mother, and your roommate, among others. It is about all people. It is about God (including the possibilities that there may be none, or many). It is about the Universe—and beyond.

How, you may wish to ask, can it be about *all* of these things? Easy—it is a philosophy text. As noted above, philosophers examine any and everything that presents itself as a topic to the human mind. So as not to overwhelm you more than is absolutely necessary—and also to provide focus, continuity, and a sense of intrinsic interest—the entire text is centered around concepts concerning the Self.

Part 1 initiates the investigation with a series of questions concerning the meaning of life, the importance of your eventual death, and the possibility that you have the freedom to choose your own being. Part 2 explores the ethical and sociopolitical context of our investigations, asking not simply about the Self but about our relationships to others as well. Part 3 expands the focus once more, this time investigating our relationship to the world of sensation and empirical experience. In the final expansion (Part 4) we will extend our concern to the farthest reaches of the universe, examining various concepts of the divine and the possibility that there is a cosmic dimension to human life.

Sometimes we will attempt to focus directly on the Self, but it is not a focus that is easily sustained. Thus, more often than not we will come at the Self from an oblique angle, trying to catch a sidewise glimpse. For the Self is like an entity you can almost see out of the corner of your eye—if you turn to focus on it you find that it has moved faster than your glance, or simply dissipated into a wispy and indiscernible form.

You Can't Make Me Care

The study of philosophy can be extremely interesting and rewarding, but it is not easy. It requires careful thought, reflection, and a willingness to follow the directive of reason and rationality wherever it may lead. Philosophical essays are often densely packed entities with numerous concepts and ideas which may be new and unfamiliar to you. They are not the sorts of things you can read once, mark off a little box labeled "done," and place on the top shelf of your bookcase. I have read many of the essays in this text twenty or thirty times—perhaps even more. Yet each time I find something new, something I missed in each of my previous encounters. Be prepared not only to read, but to reread as well. Do not allow temporary setbacks or discouragement to dampen your sense of excitement and exploration. Approach each reading as an opportunity to encounter a new horizon, vision, or perspective. Remember, it is almost impossible to learn anything truly worthwhile from something you read "because it was assigned."

Be prepared to talk about these materials with your friends, family, and classmates. Perhaps you will find some of their views and perspectives rather dull and uninteresting. Be assured that they may form a similar judgment concerning some of your thought. But you can also bet that some of your discussions will be provocative and rewarding. The introductory essays in Part 2 are designed to give you a sense of how a study group might proceed, and how each member of the group can benefit from the contributions of others.

Above all, philosophy requires involvement. We have put together a text that we think you will find exciting and challenging. Now it is up to you. No one can give you knowledge, wisdom, or understanding; these you must earn as a return from your own investment.

In keeping with the general approach of the text, we conclude this introduction with a literary selection from Kahlil Gibran's *The Prophet*. Its meaning and importance should be fairly evident.

Then said a teacher, Speak to us of Teaching.

And he said:

No man can reveal to you aught but that which already lies half asleep in the dawning of your knowledge.

The teacher who walks in the shadow of the temple, among his followers, gives not of his wisdom but rather of his faith and his lovingness.

If he is indeed wise he does not bid you enter the house of his wisdom, but rather leads you to the threshold of your own mind.

The astronomer may speak to you of his understanding of space, but he cannot give you his understanding.

The musician may sing to you of the rhythm which is in all space, but he cannot give you the ear which arrests the rhythm nor the voice that echoes it.

And he who is versed in the science of numbers can tell of the regions of weight and measure, but he cannot conduct you thither.

For the vision of one man lends not its wings to another man.

And even as each one of you stands alone in God's knowledge, so must each one of you be alone in his knowledge of God and in his understanding of the earth.

Notes

1. To better appreciate Thales' discovery for what it was, neither overrating nor understating its importance, please note the following points:

   a. Babylonian thinkers had developed techniques for predicting lunar eclipses with a fair degree of accuracy. Thales probably knew of their work and success, but prediction of a solar eclipse had eluded all comers, including the Babylonians.

   b. Thales' success was due in some measure to luck and happenstance. While he may have realized that solar eclipses are visible in limited regions, it is unlikely that he knew anything of the mechanisms that determine the region of visibility.

   c. That the eclipse occurred during a major battle between two ancient civilizations provided greater visibility and rich symbolic dimension to Thales' accomplishment, but there is little reason to believe that the conjunction of the two events was anything more than a fortuitous coincidence.

   d. Records from this period are sketchy. There is much we will probably never know (for example, exactly when and how Thales made his prediction).

   e. Thales' prediction was not, and could not have been, very precise according to present-day standards. It is fairly certain that he did not establish the hour or even the day on which the eclipse would occur. Scholars are divided as to whether he identified the season. He may have done "little more" than predict that an eclipse would occur within a particular year.

2. Greater detail concerning the accomplishments of Thales and his contemporaries, including various interpretations of the phrase "All things are full of gods," can be found in the following works:

    G. S. Kirk and J. E. Raven. *The Presocratic Philosophers.* New York: Cambridge University Press, 1957.

    Bertrand Russell. *A History of Western Philosophy.* New York: Simon & Schuster, 1945.

3. Plato, *Theaetetus*—174a.

4. Aristotle, *Politics*—Book 1, Chapter 11, 1259a.

5. Perhaps because we attach special importance to being first, humans are often fascinated by questions like "Who discovered *x*?" and "Who was the first person to do *y*?" Some questions are relatively clear and straightforward ("Who was the first person to walk on the moon?"), but others, while they may appear similar in form, are extraordinarily complex and difficult. The question "Who was the first philosopher?" belongs to this latter group. It is particularly problematic for the following reasons:

    a. Philosophy originated and developed somewhat differently in different cultures. For convenience and ease of introduction I have focused here on the origins of Western philosophy. Details concerning the beginnings of Indian and Oriental philosophy are provided in the introductory essays of Chapters 10 and 11.

    b. Even within a particular culture, an academic discipline like philosophy emerges from the creative labors of a great many people. It is not, as the Athenian legend might suggest, the brainchild of a single heroic sage. Contemporary studies show that even a comparatively simple question such as "Who discovered oxygen?" is far more complex and difficult to answer than we might at first imagine (see Chapter 7).

PART 1

The Human Condition: Knowing Thyself

CHAPTER 1   The Meaning of Life
CHAPTER 2   Death and Beyond
CHAPTER 3   Existentialism

The parts of the text radiate, like ripples in a pond of consciousness, from a central, deceptively simple query: *Who am I?*

The three chapters in Part 1 concern the innermost circle: the discovery, analysis, and exploration of individual being. Specific points of focus include the meaning of life, the significance of death, and the possibility of human freedom, dignity, and responsibility.

Spiritual Being

Physical Being

Social Being

Individual Being

Who Am I

Part One

Part Two

Part Three

Part Four

CHAPTER 1

The Meaning of Life

The imaginary plane you boarded in the Introduction: A Guidebook for Students has landed near an open forum where an assortment of scholars have gathered to debate one of the most intensely personal of all philosophical questions:

What is the meaning of life?

Introductory Essay

The **Introductory Essay** presents and clarifies some of the basic issues. Questions about the meaning of life often reflect concerns which differ significantly from one individual to the next—concerns about the nature and source of human values, the quality of life, the possibility of happiness, and the inevitability of our own mortality. A partial framework for clarification and analysis of the various issues and concerns is provided by a schematized example of reasoning called *The Transient Argument*. Basic philosophical positions include nihilism, existentialism, and others that are more traditionally associated with religion. Final reflections concern human frailty, loneliness, the interconnectedness of human lives, the importance of love, and the fear of isolation and rejection.

Philosophical Readings

The selection by **Leo Tolstoy** describes a condition that he called "an arrest of life." Despite financial and social success, life seemed empty and void of purpose. He searched without success for a solution from the intellectuals and social theorists of his day (late nineteenth century). He considered suicide, but could not bring himself to accept such a final and irreversible action. Finally, when all other avenues had been explored and rejected, Tolstoy turned to the simple life and religious faith of the Russian peasants. For although he regarded their faith as uneducated and irrational, he came to believe that it possessed the power to imbue their lives with more meaning and purpose than was otherwise possible.

Richard Taylor uses the myth of Sisyphus to explore two related but conceptually in-dependent sources of meaning. Viewed from a detached, external perspective, our lives may seem repetitious and pointless. Yet viewed from within, according to our own in-ternal state of mind and feeling, those same lives may have a rich sense of purpose and value. In the final analysis, Taylor argues, it is the internal standard that matters most.

Scientific Reading

Erich Fromm argues that the existential awareness that separates us from other life forms produces a complex set of psychological needs and dispositions. Coupled with anxiety, shame, and guilt is an intense need to reach out and unite with others. Although partial answers may be found in orgiastic states, group conformity, or creative activity, Fromm argues that the only full answer is love. He distinguishes mature love from mere symbiotic union and offers a series of reflections concerning personal integrity, individu-ality, care, responsibility, respect, and knowledge.

Literary Reading

The two short selections by **Douglas Adams** form part of his *Hitchhiker's Guide to the Galaxy*. Both stories illustrate, in a comic yet piercing fashion, the narrowminded vision which has often characterized the human race. If the universe is as vast as contemporary science suggests, we may need to temper our sense of self with a sense of humor.

The Meaning of Life

DOUGLAS W. SHRADER

"Know Thyself"

Socrates

The word *philosophy* is said to have been coined by Pythagoras (sixth century B.C.). It means, literally, "love of wisdom." A philosopher, accordingly, is anyone with a love of wisdom—that is, anyone genuinely devoted to the pursuit of learning and understanding. As the various chapters of this text demonstrate, philosophy is a wide-ranging discipline. Philosophers have concerned themselves with everything from art and literature to religion and ethics, from science and technology to politics and poetry. Perhaps most stereotypical of philosophy is a concern with what is often called "the Meaning of Life."

I recall, as an undergraduate, asking a professor why none of his courses dealt with the Meaning of Life. He replied, "If you want to know the meaning of the word *life*, consult a dictionary. If you want to know something else, rephrase your question." I thought at the time that he was playing dumb, being difficult just for the sake of being difficult. But as I struggled to rephrase the question I realized just how nebulous and unclear my concerns were, even to myself.

Years have passed. Although I do not profess to have all the answers, and perhaps not even a clear understanding of all the questions, I have nonetheless managed to sort through and settle many of the issues to my own personal satisfaction. Do not treat my answers as though they were carved in stone. As a general rule, you should be critical and suspicious of everything in this, or any, text. Philosophers often give very different answers to the same question. We cannot all be right; perhaps none of us are. Pathways to philosophy are often controversial. Ultimately, it is each individual who must answer, "What is the Meaning of Life?"

FIRST STEPS: PRELIMINARY CLARIFICATIONS AND DISTINCTIONS

What are people looking for when they express a concern or ask a question about "the Meaning of Life"? I suppose some, as my former professor suggested, are simply looking for clarification about the proper usage of the term. At the simplest level those concerns can be cleared up with the help of a good dictionary. At a somewhat higher level there are interesting philosophical and biological questions regarding the nature of the phenomenon we call *life*. Wrapped up with the general question, "What is life?," are subsidiary questions about the origin of life, the conditions that are required to support life, the possibility of alternative life forms, and the sometimes thin and fuzzy dividing line between living and nonliving. This final set includes questions about the transition from life to death (which we will explore in Chapter 2) as well as questions about the possibility of "machine life" (could we make a machine so complex or autonomous that an unbiased rational observer would judge it to be alive?).

To ask whether a machine could ever be alive invites the further question, "What, if anything, distinguishes us from machines?" This question concerns our own nature as much as it does that of machines. It requires us to ask: "What am I?" Am I purely a physical being—the biological organism whose hands and feet I see with ease, whose nose and mouth I glimpse only with difficulty, and whose eyes and ears I see but indirectly in a mirror or similar device? Am I, as some suggest, a spiritual being (soul, mind, etc.) which inhabits or pilots the body as a captain pilots a ship, but which may survive its destruction to take up residence in another body or ethereal realm? Is the truth perhaps somewhere in between? Am I a composite of body and soul, joined together in an inexplicable union called "me"? Or is my "self" perhaps an irreducible basic, too elementary to be classed as either body or spirit?

Although I have never encountered anyone whose concern with "the Meaning of Life" was exhausted by a mind-body analysis, it does seem that a lot of people's confusions and difficulties start or pass through here in one way or another. Most people who are seriously looking for "the Meaning of Life" are engaged in a fairly hefty amount of self-questioning. "What am I?" is one such question. "Who am I?" is another.

People sometimes express themselves with phrases like, "I am searching for myself." I have known people who traveled to California, India, or New York City to "find themselves." I even have students tell me they came to college or enrolled in my philosophy courses to find out who they are. I usually find myself wondering what they are really looking for, how they would recognize their "self" if they did somehow "find it," and whether they would be satisfied with it if they did. I frequently find their concerns more specific and pragmatic than their initial questions might suggest. Oftentimes their concerns are more accurately represented by asking: What should I do with my life? Should I continue my education and try to become a doctor or lawyer, or should I drop out and work at Pizza Hut? Should I get married? Have children? Would I make a good father/mother? Would I feel fulfilled? How much money will I need to be "truly happy"? How important is social position?

These questions are serious and difficult, but they may point the way toward a deeper understanding of "the Meaning of Life." Note first that the questions have a strong value component: How important is professional success, money, social relations, or a family? People who express concern about "the Meaning of Life" usually wind up talking about values, including the possible shallowness or absence thereof. "What is the Meaning of Life?" can be at least partially paraphrased as "What is the sig-nificance of life?," "What is the purpose of life?," or "What goals are really worth pursuing?" Those who express doubts about the Meaning of Life often say things like, "Nothing matters," "Nothing is truly worthwhile," or "Nothing I/we/you do will make any real difference."

Note next that values are inherently relative. Nothing is valuable in and of itself. It is valuable only if it is valuable to someone or something. In general, this means only that someone values the item or activity in question. To say that something is or is not valuable without saying to whom or to what it is or is not valuable is worse than incomplete; it is obscuring and unintelligible. It may lead us to think that we are saying something profound, or that we disagree with one another about fundamental matters, when in fact we can claim nothing more interesting than a certain elementary misuse of the language.

Someone who says "Nothing matters" has not made a complete intelligible claim. We should neither agree nor disagree. If they mean "Nothing matters *to anyone,*" the claim is clearly false. A wide variety of things matter to me as well as to others. If they mean that nothing matters *to them,* the claim is problematic since apparently telling us "Nothing matters" matters a great deal to them. More likely they mean something like, "Nothing matters *to the cosmos*—that is, the cosmos is value-neutral or indifferent to human existence, affairs, concerns, or behavior." I tend to agree, but do not see the dire consequences others often find in the value-neutrality of the cosmos. Differences here are often deep and thus potentially instructive. Many of the most basic disagreements about the Meaning of Life can be understood in terms of what I call the *Transient Argument.*

THE TRANSIENT ARGUMENT

There are two premises, each of which may be stated or argued in a variety of ways. The first is that (human) life is meaningless when viewed from a cosmic perspective or evaluated on the infinite scale of eternity. This may be expressed by saying that the cosmos is value-neutral or indifferent to human existence (above), or by lamenting the shortness of a human life, the haste with which most of us will be forgotten even by our own descendants, and our inability to "leave a mark in the world" which time will not quickly erase. In short, our lives have no eternal or lasting significance. They are not of cosmic importance.

The second premise tells us that life cannot be *really* meaningful unless it has *cosmic* meaning; that nothing *ever* matters unless it *always* matters. This, together with the first premise, leads to the conclusion that life is meaningless. Since both premises admit of alternative formulations, the conclusion should be expected to show variation as well. Construed strongly, the implication is that life is *totally* meaningless. A slightly weaker version "merely" asserts that life cannot be meaningful *in any real sense*—it may have some slight measure of a grossly inferior form of meaning, but nothing worthy of notice.

The Transient Argument

1. Life does not have cosmic significance.
2. Without cosmic significance, life is meaningless.

Life is meaningless.

People who accept both premises, and with them the conclusion of the Transient Argument, are called *nihilists*. Nihilism can be a depressing position. Taken to the extreme, it would lead to behavioral paralysis or randomness. One would simply have no reason to move rather than to remain still (or to remain still rather than to move), to eat rather than not, etc. Choosing to do one thing rather than another is an expression of preference, and preference is a function of values. If nihilism truly eliminates values, it eliminates purposive behavior.

Nihilism is a swirling black hole of nothingness, strangely attractive but also terribly frighten-

ing to those who struggle to find "the Meaning of Life." More than a few have found themselves teetering on its edge, peering into the darkness. To avoid the nihilistic conclusions of the Transient Argument, we must reject either or both of the premises.

Religions typically accept the second premise but reject the first. They agree that true meaning must have a cosmic or eternal dimension but, contrary to the first premise, preach the immortality of the soul or the existence of a "grand plan" in which everyone's life has (or can have) extraordinary, incalculable, perhaps even infinite value. Whereas the first premise spoke of a value-neutral or indifferent universe, religions preach cosmic law and divine love. The suggestion has an obvious sort of appeal. We all like to think we are somewhat special. We like to be loved and to be told how important we are. Jews consider themselves "the chosen people." Christians speak of becoming "children of God." Some even talk of "becoming one with God." Hinduism teaches that Ātman (the self) is Brahman (ultimate reality).[1]

Many people, especially in modern times, have tried to beat the Transient Argument on opposite grounds: they accept the first premise, but reject the second. They argue that life can be meaningful in a subjectively satisfying sense even if our lives (and values) quickly fade into an indifferent nothingness, unnoticed by the cosmos. Their approach is usually that of existentialism.

Existentialism is a complex, interesting philosophy which is treated at length in Chapter 3. For our purposes here it will suffice to note a few elementary points.

The central concept is expressed in a memorable phrase by Jean-Paul Sartre: for human beings, existence precedes essence. We are given, without choice or consultation, existence and various biological characteristics. What we are not given is an essence or identifying nature. The laws of nature suffice to give us life and even constrain and direct our behavior in certain ways: we cannot fly without mechanical assistance; we naturally begin looking for food when we get hungry; and so forth. But human life is more complex than walking and foraging. The more interesting parts of our lives are intimately bound up with what we call human values or priorities (including but not limited to ethics and aesthetics). These, the existentialist suggests, come not from nature, but from ourselves. They are not cosmic, but human concerns.

For example: if social position is important, it is important only because people attach importance to it. If everyone ceased to value it, it would cease to be important. Recall my earlier remarks about value-relativity. To meaningfully ask whether social position is important, we must specify a relevant object class. It seems somehow inappropriate to ask whether social position is important to the cosmos. To the extent to which the question makes sense, the answer seems to be an obvious "no." If we ask whether social position is important to people in general, the answer seems to be a somewhat qualified "yes." If we ask whether it is important to our family, friends, or spousal prospects, the answer clearly depends on the values of the people in question. If I ask whether it is important to me, individually, existentialism answers: "Only if you make it so."

Relativistic Considerations

Almost all questions about "the Meaning of Life" require clarification and analysis similar to that indicated in the above example. First, we must be clearer about "life." Do we mean to ask about all life, life in general, human life, our own individual lives, or perhaps something else entirely? Next, we must specify a reference class. Do we want to know "the Meaning of Life" to the cosmos, to God (or gods), to other people, or to our own individual selves? As we vary the questions we can expect correspondingly different answers. It is entirely possible that my life will be extremely important and meaningful to me, but of absolutely no interest or consequence to Alexander the Great, KGB or CIA agents, space-shuttle stewards in the year 2050, the cosmos, or God.

These considerations should make us uneasy with talk about "*the* Meaning of Life." Since different people often value different things, we should not expect everyone's life to have "the same meaning." I value an assortment of different things: family relationships, semi-mystical experiences of natural phenomena (sunsets, the crisp air of autumn, and the warm sun of summer), teaching, and philosophical discussions, to name a few. It is these things that give meaning to my life (make my life meaningful, pleasing, or satisfying to me). Since other people may and do have different values (they may be bored silly by sunsets and philosophical discussions, but attach far greater value than I do to wealth and social position), it seems only reasonable to expect that "the" meaning(s) of their lives (to them) will be corrrespondingly different from that of mine (to me).

Even talk about "the" meaning of *my* life is problematic. It makes sense to say that I value quiet times with my wife and the laughter of my children. It makes sense to say that these are some of the things which make my life subjectively worthwhile or meaningful. It may even make sense to say that they are the most meaningful things in my life, or that I would crumble without them. But it seems silly to call them "the" meaning of my life for the simple reason that there are other things which contribute to the subjective worth or meaning of my life.

There is also an element of temporal relativity. Some values seem to stay relatively constant over long periods of our lives, but others come and go or change markedly in intensity. As my values change, so too must "the" (subjective) meaning of my life. Such change does not negate the earlier periods or make them silly, absurd, or meaningless. It would be ridiculous to expect a six-year-old to have the same values as an eighteen-year-old, to expect the things that matter most to an eighteen-year-old to be of similar importance to someone in her forties, or to think the concerns that occupy us in our forties will make a similar claim on our being when we are seventy. Accordingly, "the" meaning of my life to me is different now from what it was when I was a child. And although I do not expect radical change in the near future, I will be surprised if reflection a few years after retirement does not show some significant changes to have occurred. I think in some sense I should even be disappointed. Be that as it may, the present meaningfulness of my life is not diminished by the anticipation that my values may one day change. If anything, it is enhanced in an odd sort of way. Realizing that I do not have lifelong title to the conditions that make my life meaningful and satisfying even at present causes me to appreciate those things all the more. Similarly, the present meaningfulness of my life is not diminished by the fact or realization that I will one day die. Like a vacationer who rents a cottage at the beach for a week, I choose not to waste the time I have wishing I did not have to leave so soon.

BRIDGING THE GAPS

"No man is an island, entire of itself."

John Donne,
Devotions Upon Emergent Occasions

The relativism of the preceding section is essential. The egocentrism is nothing more than a convenient starting point. Talking about "the" meaning of *my* life does not rule out the possibility of talking about the meaning of someone else's life, of human life, or of "life" in general. Similarly, talking about "the" meaning of my life *to me* does not rule out the possibility that my life has meaning to someone else as well. Moreover, it may be meaningful to them on different grounds (for different reasons) than it is to me. Such is not necessarily demeaning, nor need it be a point of contention. I suspect that "the" meaning of my life to my wife may be quite different from "the" meaning of my life to me. I am sure that "the" meaning of her life to me is different than it is to her. Our differences arise partially from simple differences of perspective or vantage point (Whose life is it anyway?) and partially from differences in value orientation.

Try as we might, we cannot actually live anyone's life other than our own, and in the final analysis that is a life which must be lived and judged by our own values and standards. We cannot look to anyone else to make our lives meaningful or satisfying to us, and we cannot take it upon ourselves to make someone else's life meaningful to them. But individualism does not require social isolation, nor does it deny the possibility of interdependence. People's lives often become intertwined with one another in a thick, tangled web of meaning and importance. This is why we can feel so happy and secure in the company of our family and special friends, and why the loss of someone dear can leave such a void in our life.

The interconnectedness of human lives may create responsibilities some of us would rather not have. Love requires a risk some would rather not take. Where there is potential for great happiness, there is also much room for heartache and despair. People who have been hurt in love often vow never to love again, yet somehow they usually do. We are drawn to one another by forces most of us do not understand. We seem to have a need for other people. We may even have a need to be needed. For many people there is no worse imaginable fate than a totally anonymous existence, where no one cares whether you live or die and nothing you do matters to anyone other than yourself. Perhaps it is this fear of loneliness and isolation, even more than the obvious pride or arrogance, that fuels the quest for cosmic meaning. Just as we do not wish to be ignored while we are alive, we do not wish to be forgotten when we die. We hate the thought that, within just a few years of our death, it might be "as though we had never lived at all."

Does life have cosmic meaning? I would like to think so, but find little reason to believe that it does beyond my own wishful thinking. For the most part, I have chosen to place my bets on the human relations and experiences I find in this life. As far as I can rationally ascertain, it is the only life I have. Is it enough? Yes—at least for the time being.

Notes

1. Do not worry if the example concerning Ātman and Brahman is not clear. Basic concepts of Hinduism, including these, will be treated at greater length in Chapter 10, "Wisdom of India."

My Confession

LEO TOLSTOY

Born of a prominent Russian family, Leo Tolstoy (1828–1910) lived a life of luxury. Novels like *War and Peace* (1869) and *Anna Karenina* (1877) increased his wealth and brought him widespread literary renown. He was, by the standards of the world, immensely successful. Yet he regarded writing as a trivial endeavor and, in the fall of 1879, came to believe that his life was worthless and absurd. He searched for the Meaning of Life in science, philosophy, and society before turning to religion and the simple life of the Russian peasants. The selection below is edited from *My Confession* (first published in 1884).

Although I regarded authorship as a waste of time, I continued to write during those fifteen years. I had tasted of the seduction of authorship, of the seduction of enormous monetary remunerations and applauses for my insignificant labour, and so I submitted to it as being a means for improving my material condition and for stifling in my soul all questions about the meaning of my life and life in general.

In my writings I advocated, what to me was the only truth, that it was necessary to live in such a way as to derive the greatest comfort for oneself and one's family.

Thus I proceeded to live, but five years ago something very strange began to happen within me: I was overcome by minutes at first of perplexity and then of an arrest of life, as though I did not know how to live or what to do, and I lost myself and was dejected. But that passed and I continued to live as before. Then those minutes of perplexity were repeated oftener and oftener, and always in one and the same form. These arrests of life found their expression in ever the same questions: "Why? Well, and then?"

At first I thought that those were simply aimless, inappropriate questions. It seemed to me that that was all well known and that if I ever wanted to busy myself with their solution, it would not cost me much labour, that now I had no time to attend to them, but that if I wanted to I should find the proper answers. But the questions began to repeat themselves oftener and oftener, answers were demanded more and more persistently, and, like dots that fall on the same spot, these questions, without any answers, thickened into one black blotch.

There happened what happens with any person who falls ill with a mortal internal disease. At first there appear insignificant symptoms of indisposition, to which the patient pays no attention; then these symptoms are repeated more and more frequently and blend into one temporally indivisible suffering. The suffering keeps growing, and before the patient has had time to look around, he becomes conscious that what he took for an indisposition is the most significant thing in the world to him—his death.

The same happened with me. I understood that it was not a passing indisposition, but something very important, and that, if the questions were going to repeat themselves, it would be necessary to

Leo Tolstoy, "My Confession" translated by Leo Weiner (London: J. M. Dent, 1905). [First published in 1884.] Reprinted with the permission of the publishers.

find an answer for them. And I tried to answer them. The questions seemed to be so foolish, simple, and childish. But the moment I touched them and tried to solve them, I became convinced, in the first place, that they were not childish and foolish, but very important and profound questions in life, and, in the second, that, no matter how much I might try, I should not be able to answer them. Before attending to my Samára estate, to my son's education, or to the writing of a book, I ought to know why I should do that. So long as I did not know why, I could not do anything. I could not live. Amidst my thoughts of farming, which interested me very much during that time, there would suddenly pass through my head a question like this: "All right, you are going to have six thousand desyatínas of land in the Government of Samára and three hundred horses—and then?" And I completely lost my senses and did not know what to think farther. Or, when I thought of the education of my children, I said to myself: "Why?" Or, reflecting on the manner in which the masses might obtain their welfare, I suddenly said to myself: "What is that to me?" Or, thinking of the fame which my works would get me, I said to myself: "All right, you will be more famous than Gógol, Púshkin, Shakespeare, Molière, and all the writers in the world— what of it?" And I was absolutely unable to make any reply. The questions were not waiting, and I had to answer them at once; if I did not answer them, I could not live.

I felt that what I was standing on had given way, that I had no foundation to stand on, that that which I lived by no longer existed, and that I had nothing to live by. . . .

All that happened with me when I was on every side surrounded by what is considered to be complete happiness. I had a good, loving, and beloved wife, good children, and a large estate, which grew and increased without any labour on my part. I was respected by my neighbours and friends, more than ever before, was praised by strangers, and, without any self-deception, could consider my name famous. With all that, I was not deranged or mentally unsound; on the contrary, I was in full command of my mental and physical powers, such as I had rarely met with in people of my age: physically I could work in a field, mowing, without falling behind a peasant; mentally I could work from eight to ten hours in succession, without experiencing any consequences from the strain. And while in such condition I arrived at the conclusion that I could not live, and, fearing death, I had to use cunning against myself, in order that I might not take my life.

This mental condition expressed itself to me in this form: my life is a stupid, mean trick played on me by somebody. Although I did not recognize that "somebody" as having created me, the form of the conception that some one had played a mean, stupid trick on me by bringing me into the world was the most natural one that presented itself to me.

Involuntarily I imagined that there, somewhere, there was somebody who was now having fun as he looked down upon me and saw me, who had lived for thirty or forty years, learning, developing, growing in body and mind, now that I had become strengthened in mind and had reached that summit of life from which it lay all before me, standing as a complete fool on that summit and seeing clearly that there was nothing in life and never would be: And that was fun to him—

But whether there was or was not that somebody who made fun of me did not make it easier for me. I could not ascribe any sensible meaning to a single act, or to my whole life. I was only surprised that I had not understood that from the start. All that had long ago been known to everybody. Sooner or later there would come diseases and death (they had come already) to my dear ones and to me, and there would be nothing left but stench and worms. All my affairs, no matter what they might be, would sooner or later be forgotten, and I myself should not exist. So why should I worry about all these things? How could a man fail to see that and live—that was surprising! A person could live only so long as he was drunk; but the moment he sobered up, he could not help seeing that all that was only a deception, and a stupid deception at that! Really, there was nothing funny and ingenious about it, but only something cruel and stupid.

Long ago has been told the Eastern story about the traveller who in the steppe is overtaken by an infuriated beast. Trying to save himself from the animal, the traveller jumps into a waterless well, but at its bottom he sees a dragon who opens his jaws in order to swallow him. And the unfortunate man does not dare climb out, lest he perish from the infuriated beast, and does not dare jump down to the bottom of the well, lest he be devoured by the dragon, and so clutches the twig of a wild bush growing in a cleft of the well and holds on to it. His hands grow weak and he feels that soon he shall have to surrender to the peril which awaits him at either side; but he still holds on and sees two mice, one white, the other black, in even measure making a circle around the main trunk of the bush to which he is clinging, and nibbling at it on all sides. Now, at any moment, the bush will break and tear off, and he will fall into the dragon's jaws. The traveller sees that and knows that he will inevitably perish; but while he is still clinging, he sees some drops of honey hanging on the leaves of the bush, and so reaches out for them with his tongue and licks the leaves. Just so I hold on to the branch of life, knowing that the dragon of death is waiting inevitably for me, ready to tear me to pieces, and I cannot understand why I have fallen on such suffering. And I try to lick that honey which used to give me pleasure; but now it no longer gives me joy, and the white and the black mouse day and night nibble at the branch to which I am holding on. I clearly see the dragon, and the honey is no longer sweet to me. I see only the inevitable dragon and the mice, and am unable to turn my glance away from them. That is not a fable, but a veritable, indisputable, comprehensible truth.

The former deception of the pleasures of life, which stifled the terror of the dragon, no longer deceives me. No matter how much one should say to me, "You cannot understand the meaning of life, do not think, live!" I am unable to do so, because I have been doing it too long before. Now I cannot help

seeing day and night, which run and lead me up to death. I see that alone, because that alone is the truth. Everything else is a lie.

The two drops of honey that have longest turned my eyes away from the cruel truth, the love of family and of authorship, which I have called an art, are no longer sweet to me.

"My family—" I said to myself, "but my family, my wife and children, they are also human beings. They are in precisely the same condition that I am in; they must either live in the lie or see the terrible truth. Why should they live? Why should I love them, why guard, raise, and watch them? Is it for the same despair which is in me, or for dullness of perception? Since I love them, I cannot conceal the truth from them—every step in cognition leads them up to this truth. And the truth is death.

"Art, poetry?" For a long time, under the influence of the success of human praise, I tried to persuade myself that that was a thing which could be done, even though death should come and destroy everything, my deeds, as well as my memory of them; but soon I came to see that that, too, was a deception. It was clear to me that art was an adornment of life, a decoy of life. But life lost all its attractiveness for me. How, then, could I entrap others? So long as I did not live my own life, and a strange life bore me on its waves, so long as I believed that life had some sense, although I was not able to express it, the reflections of life in every description in poetry and in the arts afforded me pleasure, and I was delighted to look at life through this little mirror of art; but when I began to look for the meaning of life, when I experienced the necessity of living myself, that little mirror became either useless, superfluous, and ridiculous, or painful to me. I could no longer console myself with what I saw in the mirror, namely, that my situation was stupid and desperate. It was all right for me to rejoice so long as I believed in the depth of my soul that life had some sense. At that time the play of lights—of the comical, the tragical, the touching, the beautiful, the terrible in life—afforded me amusement. But when I knew that life was meaningless and terrible, the play in the little mirror could no longer amuse me. No sweetness of honey could be sweet to me when I saw the dragon and the mice that were nibbling down my support. . . .

In my search after the question of life I experienced the same feeling which a man who has lost his way in the forest may experience.

He comes to a clearing, climbs a tree, and clearly sees an unlimited space before him; at the same time he sees that there are no houses there, and that there can be none; he goes back to the forest, into the darkness, and he sees darkness, and again there are no houses.

Thus I blundered in this forest of human knowledge, between the clearings of the mathematical and experimental sciences, which disclosed to me clear horizons, but such in the direction of which there could be no house, and between the darkness of the speculative sciences, where I sunk into a deeper darkness, the farther I proceeded, and I convinced myself at last that there was no way out and could not be.

By abandoning myself to the bright side of knowledge I saw that I only turned my eyes away from the question. No matter how enticing and clear the horizons were that were disclosed to me, no matter how enticing it was to bury myself in the infinitude of this knowledge, I comprehended that these sciences were the more clear, the less I needed them, the less they answered my question.

"Well, I know," I said to myself, "all which science wants so persistently to know, but there is no answer to the question about the meaning of my life." But in the speculative sphere I saw that, in spite of the fact that the aim of the knowledge was directed straight to the answer of my question, or because of that fact, there could be no other answer than what I was giving to myself: "What is the meaning of my life?"—"None." Or, "What will come of my life?"—"Nothing." Or, "Why does everything which exists exist, and why do I exist?"—"Because it exists."

Putting the question to the one side of human knowledge, I received an endless quantity of exact answers about what I did not ask: about the chemi-

cal composition of the stars, about the movement of the sun toward the constellation of Hercules, about the origin of species and of man, about the forms of infinitely small, imponderable particles of ether; but the answer in this sphere of knowledge to my question what the meaning of my life was, was always: "You are what you call your life; you are a temporal, accidental conglomeration of particles. The interrelation, the change of these particles, produces in you that which you call life. This congeries will last for some time; then the interaction of these particles will cease, and that which you call life and all your questions will come to an end. You are an accidentally cohering globule of something. The globule is fermenting. This fermentation the globule calls its *life*. The globule falls to pieces, and all fermentation and all questions will come to an end." Thus the clear side of knowledge answers, and it cannot say anything else, if only it strictly follows its principles.

With such an answer it appears that the answer is not a reply to the question. I want to know the meaning of my life, but the fact that it is a particle of the infinite not only gives it no meaning, but even destroys every possible meaning.

Those obscure transactions, which this side of the experimental, exact science has with speculation, when it says that the meaning of life consists in evolution and the cooperation with this evolution, because of their obscurity and inexactness cannot be regarded as answers.

The other side of knowledge, the speculative, so long as it sticks strictly to its fundamental principles in giving a direct answer to the question, everywhere and at all times has answered one and the same: "The world is something infinite and incomprehensible. Human life is an incomprehensible part of this incomprehensible *all*. . . ."

I lived for a long time in this madness, which, not in words, but in deeds, is particularly characteristic of us, the most liberal and learned of men. But, thanks either to my strange, physical love for the real working class, which made me understand it and see that it is not so stupid as we suppose, or to the sincerity of my conviction, which was that I could know nothing and that the best that I could do was to hang myself, I felt that if I wanted to live and understand the meaning of life, I ought naturally to look for it, not among those who had lost the meaning of life and wanted to kill themselves, but among those billions departed and living men who had been carrying their own lives and ours upon their shoulders. And I looked around at the enormous masses of deceased and living men—not learned and wealthy, but simple men—and I saw something quite different. I saw that all these billions of men that lived or had lived, all, with rare exceptions, did not fit into my subdivisions,[1] and that I could not recognize them as not understanding the question, because they themselves put it and answered it with surprising clearness. Nor could I recognize them as Epicureans, because their lives were composed rather of privations and suffering than of enjoyment. Still less could I recognize them as senselessly living out their meaningless lives, because every act of theirs and death itself was explained by them. They regarded it as the greatest evil to kill themselves. It appeared, then, that all humanity was in possession of a knowledge of the meaning of life, which I did not recognize and which I condemned. It turned out that rational knowledge did not give any meaning to life, excluded life, while the meaning which by billions of people, by all humanity, was ascribed to life was based on some despised, false knowledge.

The rational knowledge in the person of the learned and the wise denied the meaning of life, but the enormous masses of men, all humanity, recognized this meaning in an irrational knowledge. This irrational knowledge was faith, the same that I could not help but reject. That was God as one and three, the creation in six days, devils and angels, and all that which I could not accept so long as I had not lost my senses.

My situation was a terrible one. I knew that I should not find anything on the path of rational knowledge but the negation of life, and there, in faith, nothing but the negation of reason, which was still more impossible than the negation of life. From the rational knowledge it followed that life was an evil and men knew it; it depended on men whether they should cease living, and yet they lived and continued to live, and I myself lived, though I had known long ago that life was meaningless and an evil. From faith it followed that, in order to understand life, I must renounce reason, for which alone a meaning was needed.

There resulted a contradiction, from which there were two ways out: either what I called rational was not so rational as I had thought; or that which to me appeared irrational was not so irrational as I had thought. And I began to verify the train of thoughts of my rational knowledge.

In verifying the train of thoughts of my rational knowledge, I found that it was quite correct. The deduction that life was nothing was inevitable; but I saw a mistake. The mistake was that I had not reasoned in conformity with the question put by me. The question was, "Why should I live?" that is, "What real, indestructible essence will come from my phantasmal, destructible life? What meaning has my finite existence in this infinite world?" And in order to answer this question, I studied life.

The solutions of all possible questions of life apparently could not satisfy me, because my question, no matter how simple it appeared in the beginning, included the necessity of explaining the finite through the infinite, and vice versa.

I asked, "What is the extra-temporal, extra-causal, extra-spatial meaning of life?" But I gave an answer to the question, "What is the temporal, causal, spatial meaning of my life?" The result was that after a long labour of mind I answered, "None."

In my reflections I constantly equated, nor could I do otherwise, the finite with finite, the infinite with the infinite, and so from that resulted precisely what had to result: force was force, matter was matter, will was will, infinity was infinity, nothing was nothing—and nothing else could come from it.

There happened something like what at times takes place in mathematics: you think you are solving an equation, when you have only an identity.

The reasoning is correct, but you receive as a result the answer: *a = a*, or *x = x*, or *0 = 0*. The same happened with my reflection in respect to the question about the meaning of my life. The answers given by all science to that question are only identities.

Indeed, the strictly scientific knowledge, that knowledge which, as Descartes did, begins with a full doubt in everything, rejects all knowledge which has been taken on trust, and builds everything anew on the laws of reason and experience, cannot give any other answer to the question of life than what I received—an indefinite answer. It only seemed to me at first that science gave me a positive answer—Schopenhauer's answer: "Life has no meaning, it is an evil." But when I analyzed the matter, I saw that the answer was not a positive one, but that it was only my feeling which expressed it as such. The answer, strictly expressed, as it is expressed by the Brahmins, by Solomon, and by Schopenhauer, is only an indefinite answer, or an identity, *0 = 0*, life is nothing. Thus the philosophical knowledge does not negate anything, but only answers that the question cannot be solved by it, that for philosophy the solution remains insoluble.

When I saw that, I understood that it was not right for me to look for an answer to my question in rational knowledge, and that the answer given by rational knowledge was only an indication that the answer might be got if the question were differently put, but only when into the discussion of the question should be introduced the question of the relation of the finite to the infinite. I also understood that, no matter how irrational and monstrous the answers might be that faith gave, they had this advantage that they introduced into each answer the relation of the finite to the infinite, without which there could be no answer.

No matter how I may put the question, "How must I live?" the answer is, "According to God's law." "What real result will there be from my life?"— "Eternal torment or eternal bliss." "What is the meaning which is not destroyed by death?"—"The union with infinite God, paradise."

Thus, outside the rational knowledge, which had

to me appeared as the only one, I was inevitably led to recognize that all living humanity had a certain other irrational knowledge, faith, which made it possible to live.

All the irrationality of faith remained the same for me, but I could not help recognizing that it alone gave to humanity answers to the questions of life, and, in consequence of them, the possibility of living.

The rational knowledge brought me to the recognition that life was meaningless, my life stopped, and I wanted to destroy myself. When I looked around at people, at all humanity, I saw that people lived and asserted that they knew the meaning of life. I looked back at myself: I lived so long as I knew the meaning of life. As to other people, so even to me, did faith give the meaning of life and the possibility of living.

Looking again at the people of other countries, contemporaries of mine and those passed away, I saw again the same. Where life had been, there faith, ever since humanity had existed, had given the possibility of living, and the chief features of faith were everywhere one and the same.

No matter what answers faith may give, its every answer gives to the finite existence of man the sense of the infinite—a sense which is not destroyed by suffering, privation, and death. Consequently in faith alone could we find the meaning and possibility of life. What, then, was faith? I understood that faith was not merely an evidence of things not seen, and so forth, not revelation (that is only the description of one of the symptoms of faith), not the relation of man to man (faith has to be defined, and then God, and not first God, and faith through him), not merely an agreement with what a man was told, as faith was generally understood—that faith was the knowledge of the meaning of human life, in consequence of which man did not destroy himself, but lived. Faith is the power of life. If a man lives he believes in something. If he did not believe that he ought to live for some purpose, he would not live. If he does not see and understand the phantasm of the finite, he believes in that finite; if he understands the phantasm of the finite, he must believe in the infinite. Without faith one cannot live. . . .

In order that all humanity may be able to live, in order that they may continue living, giving a meaning to life, they, those billions, must have another, a real knowledge of faith, for not the fact that I, with Solomon and Schopenhauer, did not kill myself convinced me of the existence of faith, but that these billions had lived and had borne us, me and Solomon, on the waves of life.

Then I began to cultivate the acquaintance of the believers from among the poor, the simple and unlettered folk, of pilgrims, monks, dissenters, peasants. The doctrine of these people from among the masses was also the Christian doctrine that the quasi-believers of our circle professed. With the Christian truths were also mixed in very many superstitions, but there was this difference: the superstitions of our circle were quite unnecessary to them, had no connections with their lives, were only a kind of an Epicurean amusement, while the superstitions of the believers from among the labouring classes were to such an extent blended with their life that it would have been impossible to imagine it without these superstitions—it was a necessary condition of that life. I began to examine closely the lives and beliefs of these people, and the more I examined them, the more did I become convinced that they had the real faith, that their faith was necessary for them, and that it alone gave them a meaning and possibility of life. In contradiction to what I saw in our circle, where life without faith was possible, and where hardly one in a thousand professes to be a believer, among them was hardly one in a thousand who was not a believer. In contradistinction to what I saw in our circle, where all life passed in idleness, amusements, and tedium of life, I saw that the whole life of these people was passed in hard work, and that they were satisfied with life. In contradistinction to the people of our circle, who struggled and murmured against fate because of their privations and their suffering, these people accepted diseases and sorrows without any perplexity or opposition, but with the calm and firm conviction that it was all for good. In contradistinction to the fact that the more intelligent we are, the less do we understand the meaning of life and the more do we see a kind of a bad joke in our suffering and death, these people live, suffer, and approach death, and suffer in peace and more often in joy. In contradistinction to the fact that a calm death, a death without terror or despair, is the greatest exception in our circle, a restless, insubmissive, joyless death is one of the greatest exceptions among the masses. And of such people, who are deprived of everything which for Solomon and for me constitutes the only good of life, and who withal experience the greatest happiness, there is an enormous number. I cast a broader glance about me. I examined the life of past and present vast masses of men, and I saw people who in like manner had understood the meaning of life, who had known how to live and die, not two, not three, not ten, but hundreds, thousands, millions. All of them, infinitely diversified as to habits, intellect, culture, situation, all equally and quite contrary to my ignorance knew the meaning of life and of death, worked calmly, bore privations and suffering, lived and died, seeing in that not vanity, but good.

I began to love those people. The more I penetrated into their life, the life of the men now living, and the life of men departed, of whom I had read and heard, the more did I love them, and the easier it became for me to live. Thus I lived for about two years, and within me took place a transformation, which had long been working within me, and the germ of which had always been in me. What happened with me was that the life of our circle—of the rich and the learned—not only disgusted me, but even lost all its meaning. All our acts, reflections, sciences, arts,—all that appeared to me in a new light. I saw that all that was mere pampering of the appetites, and that no meaning could be found in it; but the life of all the working masses, of all humanity, which created life, presented itself to me in its real significance. I saw that that was life itself and that the meaning given to this life was truth, and I accepted it.

Notes

1. Editor's note: Tolstoy had previously identified four responses to the apparent meaninglessness of life:

   a. ignorance: "not understanding that life is evil and meaningless,"

   b. Epicureanism: "knowing the hopelessness of life, one should in the meantime enjoy such good as there is, without looking at either the dragon or the mice, but licking the honey in the best manner possible,"

   c. suicide: "having comprehended that life is evil and meaningless, one should set out to destroy it," and

   d. resignation: "comprehending the evil and the meaninglessness of life, one continues to drag it out, knowing in advance that nothing can come of it."

The Meaning of Life

RICHARD TAYLOR

Richard Taylor is a distinguished contemporary American philosopher and educator. A Phi Beta Kappa scholar who has also been named to the Academy of Humanism, Dr. Taylor received his Ph.D. from Brown University in 1951. His teaching career included appointments at Brown, Columbia, Ohio State, Cornell, and the University of Rochester. Now largely retired, he continues to teach occasional courses at the University of Rochester and Hartwick College. His books include *Action and Purpose* (1965), *Freedom, Anarchy and the Law* (1973), *With Heart and Mind* (1973), *Having Love Affairs* (1982), *Reason, Faith and Ethics* (1984), and *Metaphysics* (1992). The following selection is the concluding chapter of his popular and influential *Good and Evil* (1970).

The question whether life has any meaning is difficult to interpret, and the more one concentrates his critical faculty on it the more it seems to elude him, or to evaporate as any intelligible question. One wants to turn it aside, as a source of embarrassment, as something that, if it cannot be abolished, should at least be decently covered. And yet I think any reflective person recognizes that the question it raises is important, and that it ought to have a significant answer.

If the idea of meaningfulness is difficult to grasp in this context, so that we are unsure what sort of thing would amount to answering the question, the idea of meaninglessness is perhaps less so. If, then, we can bring before our minds a clear image of meaningless existence, then perhaps we can take a step toward coping with our original question by seeing to what extent our lives, as we actually live them, resemble that image, and draw such lessons as we are able to from the comparison.

MEANINGLESS EXISTENCE

A perfect image of meaninglessness, of the kind we are seeking, is found in the ancient myth of Sisyphus. Sisyphus, it will be remembered, betrayed divine secrets to mortals, and for this he was condemned by the gods to roll a stone to the top of a hill, the stone then immediately to roll back down, again to be pushed to the top by Sisyphus, to roll down once more, and so on again and again, *forever*. Now in this we have the picture of meaningless, pointless toil, of a meaningless existence that is absolutely *never* redeemed. It is not even redeemed by a death that, if it were to accomplish nothing more, would at least bring this idiotic cycle to a close. If we were invited to imagine Sisyphus struggling for awhile and accomplishing nothing, perhaps eventually falling from exhaustion, so that we might suppose him then eventually turning to something having some sort of promise, then the meaninglessness of that chapter of his life would not be so stark. It would be a dark and dreadful dream, from which he eventually awakens to sunlight and reality. But he does not awaken, for there

Richard Taylor, "The Meaning of Life" from *Good and Evil: A New Direction*, pp. 256–268. Copyright © 1984 by Richard Taylor. Reprinted with the permission of Prometheus Books.

is nothing for him to awaken to. His repetitive toil is his life and reality, and it goes on forever, and it is without any meaning whatever. Nothing ever comes of what he is doing, except simply, more of the same. Not by one step, nor by a thousand, nor by ten thousand does he even expiate by the smallest token the sin against the gods that led him into this fate. Nothing comes of it, nothing at all.

This ancient myth has always enchanted men, for countless meanings can be read into it. Some of the ancients apparently thought it symbolized the perpetual rising and setting of the sun, and others the repetitious crashing of the waves upon the shore. Probably the commonest interpretation is that it symbolizes man's eternal struggle and unquenchable spirit, his determination always to try once more in the face of overwhelming discouragement. This interpretation is further supported by that version of the myth according to which Sisyphus was commanded to roll the stone *over* the hill, so that it would finally roll down the other side, but was never quite able to make it.

I am not concerned with rendering or defending any interpretation of this myth, however. I have cited it only for the one element it does unmistakably contain, namely, that of a repetitious, cyclic activity that never comes to anything. We could contrive other images of this that would serve just as well, and no myth-makers are needed to supply the materials of it. Thus, we can imagine two persons transporting a stone—or even a precious gem, it does not matter—back and forth, relay style. One carries it to a near or distant point where it is received by the other; it is returned to its starting point, there to be recovered by the first, and the process is repeated over and over. Except in this relay nothing counts as winning, and nothing brings the contest to any close, each step only leads to a repetition of itself. Or we can imagine two groups of prisoners, one of them engaged in digging a prodigious hole in the ground that is no sooner finished than it is filled in again by the other group, the latter then digging a new hole that is at once filled in by the first group, and so on and on endlessly.

Now what stands out in all such pictures as oppressive and dejecting is not that the beings who enact these roles suffer any torture or pain, for it need not be assumed that they do. Nor is it that their labors are great, for they are no greater than the labors commonly undertaken by most men most of the time. According to the original myth, the stone is so large that Sisyphus never quite gets it to the top and must groan under every step, so that his enormous labor is all for nought. But this is not what appalls. It is not that his great struggle comes to nothing, but that his existence itself is without meaning. Even if we suppose, for example, that the stone is but a pebble that can be carried effortlessly, or that the holes dug by the prisoners are but small ones, not the slighest meaning is introduced into their lives. The stone that Sisyphus moves to the top of the hill, whether we think of it as large or small, still rolls back every time, and the process is repeated forever. Nothing comes of it, and the work is simply pointless. That is the element of the myth that I wish to capture.

Again, it is not the fact that the labors of Sisyphus continue forever that deprives them of meaning. It is, rather, the implication of this: that they come to nothing. The image would not be changed by our supposing him to push a different stone up every time, each to roll down again. But if we supposed that these stones, instead of rolling back to their places as if they had never been moved, were assembled at the top of the hill and there incorporated, say, in a beautiful and enduring temple, then the aspect of meaninglessness would disappear. His labors would then have a point, something would come of them all, and although one could perhaps still say it was not worth it, one could not say that the life of Sisyphus was devoid of meaning altogether. Meaningfulness would at least have made an appearance, and we could see what it was.

That point will need remembering. But in the meantime, let us note another way in which the image of meaninglessness can be altered by making only a very slight change. Let us suppose that the gods, while condemning Sisyphus to the fate just described, at the same time, as an afterthought, waxed perversely merciful by implanting in him a strange and irrational impulse; namely, a compulsive impulse to roll stones. We may if we like, to make this more graphic, suppose they accomplish this by implanting in him some substance that has this effect on his character and drives. I call this perverse, because from our point of view there is clearly no reason why anyone should have a persistent and insatiable desire to do something so pointless as that. Nevertheless, suppose that is Sisyphus' condition. He has but one obsession, which is to roll stones, and it is an obsession that is only for the moment appeased by his rolling them—he no sooner gets a stone rolled to the top of the hill than he is restless to roll up another.

Now it can be seen why this little afterthought of the gods, which I called perverse, was also in fact merciful. For they have by this device managed to give Sisyphus precisely what he wants—by making him want precisely what they inflict on him. However it may appear to us, Sisyphus' fate now does not appear to him as a condemnation, but the very reverse. His one desire in life is to roll stones, and he is absolutely guaranteed its endless fulfillment. Where otherwise he might profoundly have wished surcease, and even welcomed the quiet of death to release him from endless boredom and meaninglessness, his life is now filled with mission and meaning, and he seems to himself to have been given an entry to heaven. Nor need he even fear death, for the gods have promised him an endless opportunity to indulge his single purpose, without concern or frustration. He will be able to roll stones *forever*.

What we need to mark most carefully at this point is that the picture with which we began has not really been changed in the least by adding this supposition. Exactly the same things happen as before. The only change is in Sisyphus' view of them. The picture before was the image of meaningless activity and existence. It was created precisely to be an image of that. It has not lost that meaninglessness, it has now gained not the least shred of mean-

ingfulness. The stones still roll back as before, each phase of Sisyphus' life still exactly resembles all the others, the task is never completed, nothing comes of it, no temple ever begins to rise, and all this cycle of the same pointless thing over and over goes on forever in this picture as in the other. The *only* thing that has happened is this: Sisyphus has been reconciled to it, and indeed more, he has been led to embrace it. Not, however, by reason or persuasion, but by nothing more rational than the potency of a new substance in his veins.

THE MEANINGLESSNESS OF LIFE

I believe the foregoing provides a fairly clear content to the idea of meaninglessless and, through it, some hint of what meaningfulness, in this sense, might be. Meaninglessness is essentially endless pointlessness, and meaningfulness is therefore the opposite. Activity, and even long, drawnout and repetitive activity, has a meaning if it has some significant culmination, some more or less lasting end that can be considered to have been the direction and purpose of the activity. But the descriptions so far also provide something else; namely, the suggestion of how an existence that is objectively meaningless, in this sense, can nevertheless acquire a meaning for him whose existence it is.

Now let us ask: Which of these pictures does life in fact resemble? And let us not begin with our own lives, for here both our prejudices and wishes are great, but with the life in general that we share with the rest of creation. We shall find, I think, that it all has a certain pattern, and that this pattern is by now easily recognized.

We can begin anywhere, only saving human existence for our last consideration. We can, for example, begin with any animal. It does not matter where we begin, because the result is going to be exactly the same.

Thus, for example, there are caves in New Zealand, deep and dark, whose floors are quiet pools and whose walls and ceilings are covered with soft light. As one gazes in wonder in the stillness of these caves it seems that the Creator has reproduced there in microcosm the heavens themselves, until one scarcely remembers the enclosing presence of the walls. As one looks more closely, however, the scene is explained. Each dot of light identifies an ugly worm, whose luminous tail is meant to attract insects from the surrounding darkness. As from time to time one of these insects draws near it becomes entangled in a sticky thread lowered by the worm, and is eaten. This goes on month after month, the blind worm lying there in the barren stillness waiting to entrap an occasional bit of nourishment until. . . . Until what? What great thing awaits all this long and repetitious effort and makes it worthwhile? Really nothing. The larva just transforms itself finally to a tiny winged adult that lacks even mouth parts to feed and lives only a day or two. These adults, as soon as they have mated and laid eggs, are themselves caught in the threads and are devoured by the cannibalist worms, often without having ventured into the day, the only point to their existence having now been fulfilled. This has been going on for millions of years, and to no end other than that the same meaningless cycle may continue for another millions of years.

All living things present essentially the same spectacle. The larva of a certain cicada burrows in the darkness of the earth for seventeen years, through season after season, to emerge finally into the daylight for a brief flight, lay its eggs, and die— this all to repeat itself during the next seventeen years, and so on to eternity. We have already noted, in another connection, the struggles of fish, made only that others may do the same after them and that this cycle, having no other point than itself, may never cease. Some birds span an entire side of the globe each year and then return, only to insure that others may follow the same incredibly long path again and again. One is led to wonder what the point of it all is, with what great triumph this ceaseless effort, repeating itself through millions of years, might finally culminate, and why it should go on and on for so long, accomplishing nothing, getting nowhere. But then one realizes that there is no point to it at all, that it really culminates in nothing,

that each of these cycles, so filled with toil, is to be followed only by more of the same. The point of any living thing's life is, evidently, nothing but life itself.

This life of the world thus presents itself to our eyes as a vast machine, feeding on itself, running on and on forever to nothing. And we are part of that life. To be sure, we are not just the same, but the differences are not so great as we like to think; many are merely invented, and none really cancels the kind of meaninglessness that we found in Sisyphus and that we find all around, wherever anything lives. We are conscious of our activity. Our goals, whether in any significant sense we choose them or not, are things of which we are at least partly aware and can therefore in some sense appraise. More significantly, perhaps, men have a history, as other animals do not, such that each generation does not precisely resemble all those before. Still, if we can in imagination disengage our wills from our lives and disregard the deep interest each man has in his own existence, we shall find that they do not so little resemble the existence of Sisyphus. We toil after goals, most of them—indeed every single one of them— of transitory significance and, having gained one of them, we immediately set forth for the next, as if that one had never been, with this next one being essentially more of the same. Look at a busy street any day, and observe the throng going hither and thither. To what? Some office or shop, where the same things will be done today as were done yesterday, and are done now so they may be repeated tomorrow. And if we think that, unlike Sisyphus, these labors do have a point, that they culminate in something lasting and, independently of our own deep interests in them, very worthwhile, then we simply have not considered the thing closely enough. Most such effort is directed only to the establishment and perpetuation of home and family; that is, to the begetting of others who will follow in our steps to do more of the same. Each man's life thus resembles one of Sisyphus' climbs to the summit of his hill, and each day of it one of his steps; the difference is that whereas Sisyphus himself returns to push the stone up again, we leave this to our children. We at one point imagined that the labors of Sisyphus finally culminated in the creation of a temple, but for this to make any difference it had to be a temple that would at least endure, adding beauty to the world for the remainder of time. Our achievements, even though they are often beautiful, are mostly bubbles; and those that do last, like the sand-swept pyramids, soon become mere curiosities while around them the rest of mankind continues its perpetual toting of rocks, only to see them roll down. Nations are built upon the bones of their founders and pioneers, but only to decay and crumble before long, their rubble then becoming the foundation for others directed to exactly the same fate. The picture of Sisyphus is the picture of existence of the individual man, great or unknown, of nations, of the race of men, and of the very life of the world.

On a country road one sometimes comes upon the ruined hulks of a house and once extensive buildings, all in collapse and spread over with weeds. A curious eye can in imagination reconstruct from what is left a once warm and thriving life, filled with purpose. There was the hearth, where a family once talked, sang, and made plans; there were the rooms, where people loved, and babes were born to a rejoicing mother; there are the musty remains of a sofa, infested with bugs, once bought at a dear price to enhance an ever-growing comfort, beauty, and warmth. Every small piece of junk fills the mind with what once, not long ago, was utterly real, with children's voices, plans made, and enterprises embarked upon. That is how these stones of Sisyphus were rolled up, and that is how they became incorporated into a beautiful temple, and that temple is what now lies before you. Meanwhile other buildings, institutions, nations, and civilizations spring up all around, only to share the same fate before long. And if the question "What for?" is now asked, the answer is clear: so that just this may go on forever.

The two pictures—of Sisyphus and of our own lives, if we look at them from a distance—are in outline the same and convey to the mind the same image. It is not surprising, then, that men invent

ways of denying it, their religions proclaiming a heaven that does not crumble, their hymnals and prayer books declaring a significance to life of which our eyes provide no hint whatever.[1] Even our philosophies portray some permanent and lasting good at which all may aim, from the changeless forms invented by Plato to the beatific vision of St. Thomas and the ideals of permanence contrived by the moderns. When these fail to convince, then earthly ideals such as universal justice and brotherhood are conjured up to take their places and give meaning to man's seemingly endless pilgrimage, some final state that will be ushered in when the last obstacle is removed and the last stone pushed to the hilltop. No one believes, of course, that any such state will be final, or even wants it to be in case it means that human existence would then cease to be a struggle; but in the meantime such ideas serve a very real need.

THE MEANING OF LIFE

We noted that Sisyphus' existence would have meaning if there were some point to his labors, if his efforts ever culminated in something that was not just an occasion for fresh labors of the same kind. But that is precisely the meaning it lacks. And human existence resembles his in that respect. Men do achieve things—they scale their towers and raise their stones to their hilltops—but every such accomplishment fades, providing only an occasion for renewed labors of the same kind.

But here we need to note something else that has been mentioned, but its significance not explored, and that is the state of mind and feeling with which such labors are undertaken. We noted that if Sisyphus had a keen and unappeasable desire to be doing just what he found himself doing, then, although his life would in no way be changed, it would nevertheless have a meaning for him. It would be an irrational one, no doubt, because the desire itself would be only the product of the substance in his veins, and not any that reason could discover, but a meaning nevertheless.

And would it not, in fact, be a meaning incomparably better than the other? For let us examine again the first kind of meaning it could have. Let us suppose that, without having any interest in rolling stones, as such, and finding this, in fact, a galling toil, Sisyphus did nevertheless have a deep interest in raising a temple, one that would be beautiful and lasting. And let us suppose he succeeded in this, that after ages of dreadful toil, all directed at this final result, he did at last complete his temple, such that now he could say his work was done, and he could rest and forever enjoy the result. Now what? What picture now presents itself to our minds? It is precisely the picture of infinite boredom! Of Sisyphus doing nothing ever again, but contemplating what he has already wrought and can no longer add anything to, and contemplating it for an eternity! Now in this picture we have a meaning for Sisyphus' existence, a point for his prodigious labor, because we have put it there; yet, at the same time, that which is really worthwhile seems to have slipped away entirely. Where before we were presented with the nightmare of eternal and pointless activity, we are now confronted with the hell of its eternal absence.

Our second picture, then, wherein we imagined Sisyphus to have had inflicted on him the irrational desire to be doing just what he found himself doing, should not have been dismissed so abruptly. The meaning that picture lacked was no meaning that he or anyone could crave, and the strange meaning it had was perhaps just what we were seeking.

At this point, then, we can reintroduce what has been until now, it is hoped, resolutely pushed aside in an effort to view our lives and human existence with objectivity; namely, our own wills, our deep interest in what we find ourselves doing. If we do this we find that our lives do indeed still resemble that of Sisyphus, but that the meaningfulness they thus lack is precisely the meaningfulness of infinite boredom. At the same time, the strange meaningfulness they possess is that of the inner compulsion to be doing just what we were put here to do, and to go on doing it forever. This is the nearest we may hope to get to heaven, but the redeeming side of that fact is that we do thereby avoid a genuine hell.

If the builders of a great and flourishing ancient civilization could somehow return now to see archaeologists unearthing the trivial remnants of what they had once accomplished with such effort—see the fragments of pots and vases, a few broken statues, and such tokens of another age and greatness—they could indeed ask themselves what the point of it all was, if this is all it finally came to. Yet, it did not seem so to them then, for it was just the building, and not what was finally built, that gave their life meaning. Similarly, if the builders of the ruined home and farm that I described a short while ago could be brought back to see what is left, they would have the same feelings. What we construct in our imaginations as we look over these decayed and rusting pieces would reconstruct itself in their very memories, and certainly with unspeakable sadness. The piece of a sled at our feet would revive in them a warm Christmas. And what rich memories would there be in the broken crib? And the weed-covered remains of a fence would reproduce the scene of a great herd of livestock, so laboriously built up over so many years. What was it all worth, if this is the final result? Yet, again, it did not seem so to them through those many years of struggle and toil, and they did not imagine they were building a Gibraltar. The things to which they bent their backs day after day, realizing one by one their ephemeral plans, were precisely the things in which their wills were deeply involved, precisely the things in which their interests lay, and there was no need then to ask questions. There is no more need of them now—the day was sufficient to itself, and so was the life.

This is surely the way to look at all of life—at one's own life, and each day and moment it contains; of the life of a nation; of the species; of the life of the world; and of everything that breathes. Even the glow worms I described, whose cycles of existence over the millions of years seem so pointless when looked at by us, will seem entirely different to us if we can somehow try to view their existence from within. Their endless activity, which gets nowhere, is just what it is their will to pursue. This is its whole justification and meaning. Nor would it be any salvation to the birds who span the globe every year, back and forth, to have a home made for them in a cage with plenty of food and protection, so that they would not have to migrate any more. It would be their condemnation, for it is the doing that counts for them, and not what they hope to win by it. Flying these prodigious distances, never ending, is what it is in their veins to do, exactly as it was in Sisyphus' veins to roll stones, without end, after the gods had waxed merciful and implanted this in him.

A human being no sooner draws his first breath than he responds to the will that is in him to live. He no more asks whether it will be worthwhile, or whether anything of significance will come of it, than the worms and the birds. The point of his living is simply to be living, in the manner that it is his nature to be living. He goes through his life building his castles, each of these beginning to fade into time as the next is begun; yet, it would be no salvation to rest from all this. It would be a condemnation, and one that would in no way be redeemed were he able to gaze upon the things he has done, even if these were beautiful and absolutely permanent, as they never are. What counts is that one should be able to begin a new task, a new castle, a new bubble. It counts only because it is there to be done and he has the will to do it. The same will be the life of his children, and of theirs; and if the philosopher is apt to see in this a pattern similar to the unending cycles of the existence of Sisyphus, and to despair, then it is indeed because the meaning and point he is seeking is not there—but mercifully so. The meaning of life is from within us, it is not bestowed from without, and it far exceeds in both its beauty and permanence any heaven of which men have ever dreamed or yearned for.

Notes

1. A popular Christian hymn, sung often at funerals and typical of many hymns, expresses this thought:

   Swift to its close ebbs out life's little day;
   Earth's joys grow dim, its glories pass away;
   Change and decay in all around I see:
   O thou who changest not, abide with me.

Love, the Answer to the Problem of Human Existence

ERICH FROMM

Erich Fromm is a well-known psychoanalyst. His books include *Escape From Freedom, Man for Himself, The Sane Society,* and *The Art of Loving,* from which the following selection is edited. Originally published in 1956, *The Art of Loving* has been translated into seventeen languages. Sales in English alone exceed 1.5 million copies.

Any theory of love must begin with a theory of man, of human existence. While we find love, or rather, the equivalent of love, in animals, their attachments are mainly a part of their instinctual equipment; only remnants of this instinctual equipment can be seen operating in man. What is essential in the existence of man is the fact that he has emerged from the animal kingdom, from instinctive adaptation, that he has transcended nature—although he never leaves it; he is a part of it—and yet once torn away from nature, he cannot return to it; once thrown out of paradise—a state of original oneness with nature—cherubim with flaming swords block his way, if he should try to return. Man can only go forward by developing his reason, by finding a new harmony, a human one, instead of the prehuman harmony which is irretrievably lost.

When man is born, the human race as well as the individual, he is thrown out of a situation which was definite, as definite as the instincts, into a situation which is indefinite, uncertain and open. There is certainty only about the past—and about the future only as far as that it is death.

Man is gifted with reason; he is *life being aware of itself;* he has awareness of himself, of his fellow man, of his past, and of the possibilities of his future. This awareness of himself as a separate entity, the awareness of his own short life span, of the fact that without his will he is born and against his will he dies, that he will die before those whom he loves, or they

before him, the awareness of his aloneness and separateness, of his helplessness before the forces of nature and of society, all this makes his separate, disunited existence an unbearable prison. He would become insane could he not liberate himself from this prison and reach out, unite himself in some form or other with men, with the world outside.

The experience of separateness arouses anxiety; it is, indeed, the source of all anxiety. Being separate means being cut off, without any capacity to use my human powers. Hence to be separate means to be helpless, unable to grasp the world—things and people—actively; it means that the world can invade me without my ability to react. Thus, separateness is the source of intense anxiety. Beyond that, it arouses shame and the feeling of guilt. This experience of guilt and shame in separateness is expressed in the Biblical story of Adam and Eve. After Adam and Eve have eaten of the "tree of knowledge of good and evil," after they have disobeyed (there is no good and evil unless there is freedom to disobey), after they have become human by having emancipated themselves from the original animal harmony with nature, i.e., after their birth as human beings—they saw "that they were naked—and they were ashamed." Should we assume that a myth as old and elementary as this has the prudish morals of the nineteenth-century outlook, and that the important point the story wants to convey to us is the embarrassment that their genitals were visible? This can hardly be so, and by understanding the story in a Victorian spirit, we miss the main point, which seems to be the following: after man and woman have become aware of themselves and of each other, they are aware of their separateness, and of their difference, inasmuch as they belong to different sexes. But while recognizing their separateness they remain strangers, because they have not yet learned to love each other (as is also made very clear by the fact that Adam defends himself by blaming Eve, rather than by trying to defend her). *The awareness of human separation, without reunion by love—is the source of shame. It is at the same time the source of guilt and anxiety. . . .*

Man—of all ages and cultures—is confronted with the solution of one and the same question: the question of how to overcome separateness, how to achieve union, how to transcend one's own individual life and find at-onement. The question is the same for primitive man living in caves, for nomadic man taking care of his flocks, for the peasant in Egypt, the Phoenician trader, the Roman soldier, the medieval monk, the Japanese samurai, the modern clerk and factory hand. The question is the same, for it springs from the same ground: the human situation, the conditions of human existence. . . .

As soon as one ignores smaller differences which belong more to the periphery than to the center, one discovers that there is only a limited number of answers which have been given. . . .

The history of religion and philosophy is the history of these answers, of their diversity, as well as of their limitation in number.

The answers depend, to some extent, on the degree of individuation which an individual has reached. In the infant I-ness has developed but little yet; he still feels one with mother, has no feeling of separateness as long as mother is present. . . .

Similarly, the human race in its infancy still feels one with nature. The soil, the animals, the plants are still man's world. He identifies himself with animals, and this is expressed by the wearing of animal masks, by the worshiping of a totem animal or animal gods. But the more the human race emerges from these primary bonds, the more it separates itself from the natural world, the more intense becomes the need to find new ways of escaping separateness.

One way of achieving this aim lies in all kinds of *orgiastic states*. These may have the form of an auto-induced trance, sometimes with the help of drugs. Many rituals of primitive tribes offer a vivid picture of this type of solution. In a transitory state of exaltation the world outside disappears, and with it the feeling of separateness from it. Inasmuch as these rituals are practiced in common, an experience of fusion with the group is added which makes this solution all the more effective. Closely related to, and often blended with this orgiastic solution, is the sexual experience. The sexual orgasm can produce a state similar to the one produced by a trance, or to the effects of certain drugs. Rites of communal sexual orgies were a part of many primitive rituals. It seems that after the orgiastic experience, man can go on for a time without suffering too much from his separateness. Slowly the tension of anxiety mounts, and then is reduced again by the repeated performance of the ritual.

As long as these orgiastic states are a matter of common practice in a tribe, they do not produce anxiety or guilt. To act in this way is right, and even virtuous, because it is a way shared by all, approved and demanded by the medicine men or priests; hence there is no reason to feel guilty or ashamed. It is quite different when the same solution is chosen by an individual in a culture which has left behind these common practices. Alcoholism and drug addiction are the forms which the individual chooses in a non-orgiastic culture. In contrast to those participating in the socially patterned solution, such individuals suffer from guilt feelings and remorse. While they try to escape from separateness by taking refuge in alcohol or drugs, they feel all the more separate after the orgiastic experience is over, and thus are driven to take recourse to it with increasing frequency and intensity. Slightly different from this is the recourse to a sexual orgiastic solution. To some extent it is a natural and normal form of overcoming separateness, and a partial answer to the problem of isolation. But in many individuals in whom separateness is not relieved in other ways, the search for the sexual orgasm assumes a function which makes it not very different from alcoholism and drug addiction. It becomes a desperate attempt to escape the anxiety engendered by separateness, and it results in an ever-increasing sense of separateness, since the sexual act without love never bridges the gap between two human beings, except momentarily.

All forms of orgiastic union have three characteristics: they are intense, even violent; they occur in the total personality, mind *and* body; they are transitory and periodical. Exactly the opposite holds true for that form of union which is by far the most frequent solution chosen by man in the past and in the present: the union based on *conformity* with the group, its customs, practices and beliefs. Here again we find a considerable development.

In a primitive society the group is small; it consists of those with whom one shares blood and soil. With the growing development of culture, the group enlarges; it becomes the citizenry of a *polis*, the citizenry of a large state, the members of a church. Even the poor Roman felt pride because he could say *"civis romanus sum"*; Rome and the Empire were his family, his home, his world. Also in contemporary Western society the union with the group is the prevalent way of overcoming separateness. It is a union in which the individual self disappears to a large extent, and where the aim is to belong to the herd. If I am like everybody else, if I have no feelings or thoughts which make me different, if I conform in custom, dress, ideas, to the pattern of the group, I am saved; saved from the frightening experience of aloneness. . . .

. . . Man becomes a "nine to fiver," he is part of the labor force, or the bureaucratic force of clerks and managers. He has little initiative, his tasks are prescribed by the organization of the work; there is even little difference between those high up on the ladder and those on the bottom. They all perform tasks prescribed by the whole structure of the organization, at a prescribed speed, and in a prescribed manner. Even the feelings are prescribed: cheerfulness, tolerance, reliability, ambition, and an ability to get along with everybody without friction. Fun is routinized in similar, although not quite as drastic ways. Books are selected by the book clubs, movies by the film and theater owners and the advertising slogans paid for by them; the rest is also uniform: the Sunday ride in the car, the television session, the card game, the social parties. From birth to death, from Monday to Monday, from morning to evening—all activities are routinized, and prefabricated. How should a man caught in this net of routine not forget that he is a man, a unique individual, one who is given only this one chance of living, with hopes and disappointments, with sorrow and fear, with the longing for love and the dread of the nothing and of separateness?

A third way of attaining union lies in *creative activity*, be it that of the artist, or of the artisan. In any kind of creative work the creating person unites himself with his material, which represents the world outside of himself. Whether a carpenter makes a table, or a goldsmith a piece of jewelry, whether the peasant grows his corn or the painter paints a picture, in all types of creative work the worker and his object become one, man unites himself with the world in the process of creation. This, however, holds true only for productive work, for work in which *I* plan, produce, see the result of my work. In the modern work process of a clerk, the worker on the endless belt, little is left of this uniting quality of work. The worker becomes an appendix to the machine or to the bureaucratic organization. He has ceased to be he—hence no union takes place beyond that of conformity.

The unity achieved in productive work is not interpersonal; the unity achieved in orgiastic fusion is transitory; the unity achieved by conformity is only pseudo-unity. Hence, they are only partial answers to the problem of existence. The full answer lies in the achievement of interpersonal union, of fusion with another person, in *love*.

This desire for interpersonal fusion is the most powerful striving in man. It is the most fundamental passion, it is the force which keeps the human race together, the clan, the family, society. The failure to achieve it means insanity or destruction—self-destruction or destruction of others. Without love, humanity could not exist for a day. Yet, if we call the achievement of interpersonal union "love," we find ourselves in a serious difficulty. Fusion can be achieved in different ways—and the differences are not less significant than what is common to the various forms of love. Should they all be called love? Or should we reserve the word "love" only for a specific kind of union, one which has been the ideal virtue in all great humanistic religions and philosophical systems of the last four thousand years of Western and Eastern history?

As with all semantic difficulties, the answer can only be arbitrary. What matters is that we know what kind of union we are talking about when we speak of love. Do we refer to love as the mature answer to the problem of existence, or do we speak of those immature forms of love which may be called *symbiotic union*? In the following pages I shall call love only the former. I shall begin the discussion of "love" with the latter.

Symbiotic union has its biological pattern in the relationship between the pregnant mother and the foetus. They are two, and yet one. They live "together" (*symbiosis*), they need each other. The foetus is a part of the mother, it receives everything it needs from her; mother is its world, as it were; she feeds it, she protects it, but also her own life is enhanced by it. In the *psychic* symbiotic union, the two bodies are independent, but the same kind of attachment exists psychologically.

The *passive* form of the symbiotic union is that of submission, or if we use a clinical term, of *masochism*. The masochistic person escapes from the unbearable feeling of isolation and separateness by making himself part and parcel of another person who directs him, guides him, protects him; who

is his life and his oxygen, as it were. The power of the one to whom one submits is inflated, may he be a person or a god; he is everything, I am nothing, except inasmuch as I am part of him. As a part, I am part of greatness, of power, of certainty. The masochistic person does not have to make decisions, does not have to take any risks; he is never alone—but he is not independent; he has no integrity; he is not yet fully born. . . .

The *active* form of symbiotic fusion is domination or, to use the psychological term corresponding to masochism, *sadism*. The sadistic person wants to escape from his aloneness and his sense of imprisonment by making another person part and parcel of himself. He inflates and enhances himself by incorporating another person, who worships him.

The sadistic person is as dependent on the submissive person as the latter is on the former; neither can live without the other. The difference is only that the sadistic person commands, exploits, hurts, humiliates, and that the masochistic person is commanded, exploited, hurt, humiliated. This is a considerable difference in a realistic sense; in a deeper emotional sense, the difference is not so great as that which they both have in common: fusion without integrity. . . .

In contrast to symbiotic union, mature *love* is *union under the condition of preserving one's integrity*, one's individuality. *Love is an active power in man;* a power which breaks through the walls which separate man from his fellow men, which unites him with others; love makes him overcome the sense of isolation and separateness, yet it permits him to be himself, to retain his integrity. In love the paradox occurs that two beings become one and yet remain two.

. . . In the most general way, the active character of love can be described by stating that love is primarily *giving*, not receiving.

What is giving? Simple as the answer to this question seems to be, it is actually full of ambiguities and complexities. The most widespread misunderstanding is that which assumes that giving is "giving up" something, being deprived of, sacrificing. The person whose character has not developed beyond the stage of the receptive, exploitative, or hoarding orientation, experiences the act of giving in this way. . . .

For the productive character, giving has an entirely different meaning. Giving is the highest expression of potency. In the very act of giving, I experience my strength, my wealth, my power. This experience of heightened vitality and potency fills me with joy. I experience myself as overflowing, spending, alive, hence as joyous. Giving is more joyous than receiving, not because it is a deprivation, but because in the act of giving lies the expression of my aliveness. . . .

In the sphere of material things giving means being rich. Not he who *has* much is rich, but he who *gives* much. The hoarder who is anxiously worried about losing something is, psychologically speaking, the poor, impoverished man, regardless of how much he has. Whoever is capable of giving of himself is rich. . . .

The most important sphere of giving, however, is not that of material things, but lies in the specifically human realm. What does one person give to another? He gives of himself, of the most precious he has, he gives of his life. This does not necessarily mean that he sacrifices his life for the other—but that he gives him of that which is alive in him; he gives him of his joy, of his interest, of his understanding, of his knowledge, of his humor, of his sadness—of all expressions and manifestations of that which is alive in him. In thus giving of his life, he enriches the other person, he enhances the other's sense of aliveness by enhancing his own sense of aliveness. He does not give in order to receive; giving is in itself exquisite joy. But in giving he cannot help bringing something to life in the other person, and this which is brought to life reflects back to him; in truly giving, he cannot help receiving that which is given back to him. Giving implies to make the other person a giver also and they both share in the joy of what they have brought to life. In the act of giving something is born, and both persons involved are grateful for the life that is born for

both of them. Specifically with regard to love this means: love is a power which produces love; impotence is the inability to produce love. . . .

Beyond the element of giving, the active character of love becomes evident in the fact that it always implies certain basic elements, common to all forms of love. These are *care, responsibility, respect* and *knowledge.*

That love implies *care* is most evident in a mother's love for her child. No assurance of her love would strike us as sincere if we saw her lacking in care for the infant, if she neglected to feed it, to bathe it, to give it physical comfort; and we are impressed by her love if we see her caring for the child. It is not different even with the love for animals or flowers. If a woman told us that she loved flowers, and we saw that she forgot to water them, we would not believe in her "love" for flowers. *Love is the active concern for the life and the growth of that which we love.* Where this active concern is lacking, there is no love. . . .

Care and concern imply another aspect of love; that of *responsibility.* Today responsibility is often meant to denote duty, something imposed upon one from the outside. But responsibility, in its true sense, is an entirely voluntary act; it is my response to the needs, expressed or unexpressed, of another human being. . . .

Responsibility could easily deteriorate into domination and possessiveness, were it not for a third component of love, *respect.* Respect is not fear and awe; it denotes, in accordance with the root of the word (*respicere* = to look at), the ability to see a person as he is, to be aware of his unique individuality. Respect means the concern that the other person should grow and unfold as he is. Respect, thus, implies the absence of exploitation. I want the loved person to grow and unfold for his own sake, and in his own ways, and not for the purpose of serving me. If I love the other person, I feel one with him or her, but with him *as he is,* not as I need him to be as an object for my use. It is clear that respect is possible only if *I* have achieved independence; if I can stand and walk without needing crutches, without having to dominate and exploit anyone else. Respect exists only on the basis of freedom: "l'amour est l'enfant de la liberté" as an old French song says; love is the child of freedom, never that of domination.

To respect a person is not possible without *knowing* him; care and responsibility would be blind if they were not guided by knowledge. Knowledge would be empty if it were not motivated by concern. There are many layers of knowledge; the knowledge which is an aspect of love is one which does not stay at the periphery, but penetrates to the core. It is possible only when I can transcend the concern for myself and see the other person in his own terms. I may know, for instance, that a person is angry, even if he does not show it overtly; but I may know him more deeply than that; then I know that he is anxious, and worried; that he feels lonely, that he feels guilty. Then I know that his anger is only the manifestation of something deeper, and I see him as anxious and embarrassed, that is, as the suffering person, rather than as the angry one.

Knowledge has one more, and a more fundamental, relation to the problem of love. The basic need to fuse with another person so as to transcend the prison of one's separateness is closely related to another specifically human desire, that to know the "secret of man." While life in its merely biological aspects is a miracle and a secret, man in his human aspects is an unfathomable secret to himself—and to his fellow man. We know ourselves, and yet even with all the efforts we make, we do not know ourselves. We know our fellow man, and yet we do not know him, because we are not a thing, and our fellow man is not a thing. The further we reach into the depth of our being, or someone else's being, the more the goal of knowledge eludes us. Yet we cannot help desiring to penetrate into the secret of man's soul, into the innermost nucleus which is "he."

There is one way, a desperate one, to know the secret: it is that of complete power over another person; the power which makes him do what we want, feel what we want, think what we want; which transforms him into a thing, our thing, our possession. The ultimate degree of this attempt to know lies in the extremes of sadism, the desire and ability to make a human being suffer; to torture him, to force him to betray his secret in his suffering. . . .

In children we often see this path to knowledge quite overtly. The child takes something apart, breaks it up in order to know it; or it takes an animal apart; cruelly tears off the wings of a butterfly in order to know it, to force its secret. The cruelty itself is motivated by something deeper: the wish to know the secret of things and of life.

The other path to knowing "the secret" is love. Love is active penetration of the other person, in which my desire to know is stilled by union. In the act of fusion I know you, I know myself, I know everybody—and I "know" nothing. I know in the only way knowledge of that which is alive is possible for man—by experience of union—not by any knowledge our thought can give. Sadism is motivated by the wish to know the secret, yet I remain as ignorant as I was before. I have torn the other being apart limb from limb, yet all I have done is to destroy him. Love is the only way of knowledge, which in the act of union answers my quest. In the act of loving, of giving myself, in the act of penetrating the other person, I find myself, I discover myself, I discover us both, I discover man.

Total Perspective Vortex

DOUGLAS ADAMS

Douglas Adams is the author of several popular, wacky, yet often philosophical science fiction novels. He is especially known for a successful and innovative trilogy that includes *The Hitchhiker's Guide to the Galaxy, The Restaurant at the End of the Universe,* and *Life, the Universe and Everything.* The short selection that follows is edited from the second book of the trilogy.

The Universe, as has been observed before, is an unsettlingly big place, a fact which for the sake of a quiet life most people tend to ignore.

Many would happily move to somewhere rather smaller of their own devising, and this is what most beings in fact do.

For instance, in one corner of the Eastern Galactic Arm lies the large forest planet Oglaroon, the entire "intelligent" population of which lives permanently in one fairly small and crowded nut tree. In which tree they are born, live, fall in love, carve tiny speculative articles in the bark on the meaning of life, the futility of death and the importance of birth control, fight a few extremely minor wars and eventually die strapped to the underside of some of the less accessible outer branches.

In fact the only Oglaroonians who ever leave their tree are those who are hurled out of it for the heinous crime of wondering whether any of the other trees might be capable of supporting life at all, or indeed whether the other trees are anything other than illusions brought on by eating too many Oglanuts.

Exotic though this behavior may seem, there is no life form in the galaxy which is not in some way guilty of the same thing, which is why the Total Perspective Vortex is as horrific as it is.

For when you are put into the Vortex you are given just one momentary glimpse of the entire unimaginable infinity of creation, and somewhere in it a tiny little market, a microscopic dot on a microscopic dot, which says "You are here." . . .

The Total Perspective Vortex derives its picture of the whole Universe on the principle of extrapolated matter analyses.

To explain—since every piece of matter in the Universe is in some way affected by every other piece of matter in the Universe, it is in theory possible to extrapolate the whole of creation—every sun, every planet, their orbits, their composition and their economic and social history from, say, one small piece of fairy cake.

The man who invented the Total Perspective Vortex did so basically in order to annoy his wife.

Trin Tragula—for that was his name—was a dreamer, a thinker, a speculative philosopher or, as his wife would have it, an idiot.

And she would nag him incessantly about the utterly inordinate amount of time he spent staring out into space, or mulling over the mechanics of safety pins, or doing spectrographic analyses of pieces of fairy cake.

"Have some sense of proportion!" she would say, sometimes as often as thirty-eight times in a single day.

Douglas Adams, excerpt from *The Restaurant at the End of the Universe*, pp. 71–72 and 78–79. Copyright © 1981 by Douglas Adams. Reprinted with the permission of Harmony Books, a division of Crown publishers, Inc. and Pan Books, Ltd.

And so he built the Total Perspective Vortex—just to show her.

And into one end he plugged the whole of reality as extrapolated from a piece of fairy cake, and into the other end he plugged his wife: so that when he turned it on she saw in one instant the whole infinity of creation and herself in relation to it.

To Trin Tragula's horror, the shock completely annihilated her brain; but to his satisfaction he realized that he had proved conclusively that if life is going to exist in a Universe of this size, then the one thing it cannot afford to have is a sense of proportion.

Review and Reflection

1. Present, as clearly as you can in your own words, the premises and conclusion of the Transient Argument. Do you believe the argument is a good one? Do you accept its conclusion? Why?

2. Compare and contrast the assumptions of Nihilism with those of Judaism, Christianity, or other religions with which you may be familiar.

3. Why did Leo Tolstoy seek out the simple life and religious faith of the Russian peasants? Do you agree with his approach? His conclusions? Why?

4. What, in your opinion, can we learn from the myth of Sisyphus? To what extent does your interpretation agree with the one presented by Richard Taylor?

5. What, according to Erich Fromm, distinguishes mature love from its less-developed forms? Do you agree?

6. Try to imagine the experience of Trin Tragula's wife when her husband exposed her to his extrapolation of reality based on a small piece of fairy cake. What would she have seen? How might she have felt?

Suggestions for Further Study

ALBERT CAMUS. *The Myth of Sisyphus and Other Essays.* New York: Alfred A. Knopf, 1955.

VICTOR FRANKL. *Man's Search for Meaning.* New York: Washington Square Press, 1959.

WALKER PERCY. *Lost in the Cosmos: The Last Self-Help Book.* New York: Farrar, Straus and Giroux, 1983.

STEVEN SANDERS AND DAVID CHENEY. *The Meaning of Life.* Englewood Cliffs, NJ: Prentice-Hall, 1980.

RICHARD TAYLOR. *Good and Evil: A New Direction.* New York: Macmillan, 1970.

LEO TOLSTOY. *My Confession.* Translation by Leo Wiener. London: J. M. Dent and Sons, 1905.

CHAPTER 2

Death and Beyond

Jacques Louis David, "The Death of Socrates." Courtesy of The Metropolitan Museum of Art.

As we saw in the preceding chapter, many people's concerns about the meaning of life are connected to the realization that one day, we too will die. Thus, to facilitate better understanding of life, the present chapter examines several faces of the phenomenon we call "death."

Introductory Essay

The **Introductory Essay** presents a series of reflections concerning three distinct but related areas: the analysis of death, the phenomenon known as near-death experiences, and the possibility of life after death. It is argued that developments in medical technology have outpaced our ability to deal with the ethical issues and dilemmas that sometimes result. The attempt to formulate a socially responsible yet philosophically and medically sensitive definition of death leads to a conceptual dualism in which death of the person is distinguished from that of the biological organism. While such dualism does not guarantee near-death experiences or life after death, it nonetheless invites serious discussion of people's experiences and beliefs about such matters.

Philosophical Readings

Two short selections from **Plato** paint a picture of Socrates during his final days. It is argued that death is either annihilation of consciousness or migration of the soul from this place to another. Although Socrates claims that mere annihilation of consciousness is nothing to be feared, it is clear that he hopes for a transmigration in which his consciousness may commune with others. Inasmuch as philosophy prepares one for such communion of consciousness, he tells Simmias, it may be asserted that philosophy serves as a preparation for death.

    Clarence Darrow, basing his analysis on his understanding of biology and the evolution of life, rejects Socrates' notion of an immortal and imperishable soul. He similarly considers and dispenses with the doctrine of resurrection and the possibility that we may somehow acquire immortality via the supposed indestructibility of matter and force. In the end, he believes, if we can accept the brevity of life and the finality of death, we can develop greater compassion and sensitivity for our fellow travelers along the way.

Scientific Reading

The selection by **Elisabeth Kübler-Ross** presents and explains her theory that people prepare for and accept death in five distinct stages:

1. Denial and Isolation,
2. Anger,
3. Bargaining,
4. Depression, and
5. Acceptance.

She clarifies the stages, as well as her interpretation of them, via a series of sometimes poignant and touching stories of the patients she has known.

Literary Reading

"The Myth of Er" is a story told by **Plato** in his most famous dialogue, *The Republic.* Er, it is said, was killed in battle but arose from the funeral pyre with a tale of having visited the realm of the dead. It is a tale of heaven and hell, of reward and punishment, of justice and reincarnation. Although it concerns the afterlife, the story's message is clearly intended for the living. Er was allowed to return so that we might learn, with a minimum of pain and suffering, the importance of wisdom and proper cultivation of the human soul.

Death and Beyond

DOUGLAS W. SHRADER

"Death is a black camel, which kneels at the gates of all."

Abd-el-Kadar, *Rappel a' l'Intelligent*

Death. Even the word may be enough to invoke a cold shiver. Our palms may begin to sweat. Our hearts may beat a little faster. Our psychological and physical beings quickly bring forth defense mechanisms, built up over the years to shield against this phenomenon which threatens not simply the meaning of life, but our very existence itself.

Philosophy holds no monopoly on death. From early childhood to old age, death confronts, challenges, and puzzles us all.

But what is death? Is it, as many believe, simply the cessation of life? Or is it, as many others believe, a transition to a new stage of being?

THE ANALYSIS OF DEATH: COMPETING DEFINITIONS AND STANDARDS[1]

Because death is a phenomenon with wide-ranging implications and effects, the seemingly simple question, "What is death?" requires a complex, multifaceted analysis. Even the multiple-choice question, "Alive or dead?," is problematic when asked with respect to someone in an irreversible coma. Cases such as those of Karen Ann Quinlan and Nancy Cruzan have become relatively commonplace. Somewhat less common, but even more intriguing and of greater philosophical and social significance, are cases such as the following.

Born of a corpse: On March 29, 1983, a California woman gave birth, via Caesarean section, to a slightly premature but reasonable healthy baby boy. Across the nation, news media carried headlines like "Brain-dead Woman Gives Birth to Healthy Baby," "Infant Is Born 63 Days After Death of Mother," and "Out of Death, a New Life Comes." On January 24 the unidentified woman had suffered cardiac arrest and seizures believed to have been caused by a cerebral cyst. The following day, January 25, she was pronounced dead on the basis of "brain death," but was nonetheless placed on a respirator to supply oxygen while her heart continued to pump blood to vital organs and, of special concern, the placenta nourishing the fetus.

The doctors were faced with a dilemma. At 22 weeks of development the fetus weighed approximately one pound. They could perform an emergency C-section, but the child's chances of survival would be slim. Even if it did survive, the probability of mental or physical retardation would be enormous. With the husband's consent the decision was made to sustain the vital functions of the woman artificially so that the fetus might continue its growth and development.

After two weeks in an intensive care unit in a northern California hospital, the woman was airlifted to the perinatal unit of the University of California's Moffitt Hospital in San Francisco. There she and her fetus were monitored around the clock. The respirator required frequent adjustment. Intravenous infusions of amino acids, vitamins, sugars, and fats provided nourishment. Damage to the pituitary gland necessitated that the woman be treated for a type of diabetes caused by a lack of hormones. Because damage to the brain affected the body's ability to regulate temperature, the woman's body had to be periodically warmed or cooled with special blankets. Antibiotics were used to combat infection. Perhaps equally important, nurses attempted to make up for the lack of prenatal stimulation. As reported by *Newsweek*:

They stroked the mother's abdomen and murmured soothing words. They placed a tape recorder nearby and played music the mother had enjoyed. Occasionally they could see the baby's heartbeat increase on the monitor in response to outside sounds. "We were trying to simulate the environment that would be normal," says nurse Pat Willever. (April 11, 1983, p. 65)

When tests revealed that the fetus had stopped growing after 31 weeks of development, Dr. Robert K. Creasy removed the 3 lb., 3 oz. infant by Caesarean section. An hour later they disconnected the mother's "life support" systems. Twenty-seven minutes thereafter the woman stopped breathing and may even have been pronounced dead a second time.

Although the infant suffered mild respiratory distress and was thus placed on a respirator for a few days, no further difficulties were reported. Dr. Creasy assessed his chances of survival as "excellent."

Brain death and the concept of personhood: How do we decide who is alive and who is not? If we use traditional heart-lung standards we will have to insist that the unidentified California woman did not die until March 29. If on the other hand, as has become increasingly more commonplace, we focus upon the activity of the brain, we may find ourselves arguing that the woman died on January 24 when she suffered seizures, cardiac arrest, and massive brain damage. The appeal of heart-lung standards should be fairly evident at a gut, experiential level. Brain-based criteria require a little more sophisticated argument.

As explained by Robert Veatch, "The task of defining death is not a trivial exercise in coining the meaning of a term. Rather it is an attempt to reach an understanding of the philosophical nature of man and that which is essentially significant to man which is lost at the time of death."[2] Since many capacities, functions, and even bodily parts are commonly held to be more important than others in the determination of who or what we are, many philosophers have developed concepts of personhood.

These thinkers usually acknowledge that we are biological organisms. But, they continue, we are more than that. Unlike amoebas or pine trees, which are also biological organisms, we are *persons.* Those who place great value on our spiritual capacities develop concepts of personhood in which the ability to "respond to the divine" is given central billing. Others who place greater value on our cognitive abilities, aesthetic sensibilities, emotions, or capacity for social interaction develop correspondingly different concepts of personhood.

Since certain parts of the body are more indispensable than others to some of these "essential" characteristics, irreversible loss of function in that/those bodily part(s) may be judged to signal, if not constitute, death of the person. Thus, if the heart is truly the seat of the emotions, as Aristotle and many others have believed, cessation of heartbeat implies cessation of emotion.

If, as is more common in modern times, the brain is taken to be the seat of all thought processes, governing not only consciousness but perhaps emotions, aesthetic sensibilities, capacity for social interaction, and even spiritual awareness as well, then irreversible loss of brain function may be taken to signal/constitute death of the person. If only a portion of the brain (the neocortex, for example) is believed to be the seat of these functions, then irreversible damage to that part of the brain may be judged sufficient to signal or constitute death of the person. Thus it is that brain death, whether whole or partial, begins to serve as a standard of Death.

Beyond personhood: If indeed the capacity for consciousness and associated phenomena is seated in the neocortex, and if, as seems likely, the California woman's neocortex was completely and irreversibly destroyed on January 24, 1983, then there is excellent reason for maintaining that the *person* in question died on that date, and thus excellent reason for making a pronouncement of death (of the person) the following day. Yet there is still something grotesquely amiss about the claim that the *entire* entity in question (the woman) died on either of those dates.

We will perhaps do better to regard a *human being* (man, woman, or child) as a composite of two intimately related but conceptually distinguishable components. We are, on the other hand, biological entities (homo sapiens) and, on the other hand, persons. Thus construed, human beings may be subject to more than one death. As biological entities, humans are subject to the biological processes of death and decay. As persons, we may be subject to a somewhat different sort of death.

Under "normal" circumstances, our death as a person and our death as a biological organism will be closely crowded together in space and time. With technological intervention, however, the death of the person may occur at one place and time, and the death of the biological organism at some distant place and time. Thus, in the extraordinary case presented above, we may reasonably assert that the woman—insofar as she was a person—died January 24, 1983, in a northern California hospital, but that as a biological organism she did not die until March 29, 1983, in San Francisco. We may further maintain that the neeeds of the unborn fetus justified keeping the woman *qua* biological organism alive (note: *not* just maintaining a semblance of life) even though the woman *qua* person had died. Still further, we can hold the doctors to have acted correctly in allowing the biological organism to die on March 29, on the grounds that the person associated with that biological organism had died nine weeks earlier.

In general, by *biological death* we mean "cessation of the processes of biological synthesis and replication." Inasmuch as different organs or parts of the body may cease to function at different times, physicians distinguish between local death (death of a part of the body), somatic death (death of the organism as a whole), and molecular death (death of the tissues). With these distinctions we can judge a biological organism to have died (as an organism), even though its fingernails and hair may continue to grow for a period of hours, days, or even weeks, and even though its heart, kidneys, or other organs may continue to function in a different biological organism for several years. Someone who says that their daughter has died, but that part of her still lives through organ donation, is not, as it might otherwise seem, speaking simple nonsense.

Turning now to the other side of the division, *death of the person* is the phenomenon whereby a body ceases to be, encase, or be uniquely associated with a person. This may be taken to constitute loss of essence, departure of soul or spirit, or simply permanent loss of consciousness. An essentialist who believes that rationality, or some similar candidate, constitutes the essence of personhood is apt to identify the loss of that ability with the loss of personhood, and thus to treat the point of that loss as the death of the person.

If on the other hand one conceives the person to be a complex entity with many potentially separable capacities and activities (roughly *parts*), it may be difficult in some cases to say just when the person died. Thus, if someone loses the capacity for meaningful social interaction, ability to do abstract mathematics, and language ability, but is still able to plant and tend a garden, I would hesitate to say that the (entire) person has died. It may be best to parallel the biological distinction between local and somatic death and say sometimes simply that part of the person has died (with appropriate specification as the occasion warrants).

The importance of distinctions: In the past few pages I have introduced a sizable number of distinctions and divisions, all in an attempt to get a better handle on questions like "What is death?" and "When is death?" I have distinguished between biological death and death of the person, and allowed for a fair diversity of opinion and subdivision within each of those areas.

As a rule, philosophers draw a lot of distinctions. It may sometimes seem as though we draw distinctions simply for the sake of doing so, but such is rarely the case. A pathway to philosophy is rather like a frontiersman's trail into an uncharted wilderness. The distinctions and divisions drawn by philosophers can perhaps best be seen as attempts to draw conceptual maps of the wilderness. Different philosophers may draw radically different maps of much the same territory. The ultimate test of such a map is whether or not it provides conceptual guidance. Do the distinctions and divisions I have suggested enable us to better comprehend, understand, and deal with cases such as that of the unidentified California woman? If not, we must back up and try a different tack. This may involve rethinking the same case through a different set of distinctions or, as in the present essay, moving on to a different vantage point.

NEAR-DEATH EXPERIENCES: A GLIMPSE OF WHAT LIES BEYOND?

What is it like to die? Does it hurt? Is it perhaps like drifting off into a deep, peaceful sleep? Do guardian spirits or ancestors come to guide you to a new life?

In 1975 Dr. Raymond Moody breathed new life into these age-old questions with the publication of *Life After Life*. Dr. Moody, who also holds a Ph.D. in philosophy, described the experiences of people who had been "near death." Some simply had a close brush with death, while others had suffered genuine cardiac arrest. No two people reported exactly the same experience, and many reported no experience at all, but when a number of cases are examined a distinctive pattern begins to emerge.

The experiences fall into three general groups. Some people continue to experience the earthly events (the car crash, the emergency room, and so on), albeit from a somewhat unusual perspective. Some people have a sort of dreamlike netherland experience. And most suggestively, some report experiences of a transcendent "otherworldly" realm.

Those who report a continued but altered perception of earthly events usually report what is called an "out-of-body experience." The "self" seems to leave the body and view the happenings from above or off to one side. It sometimes happens that the separated self can see, but not hear; though

many report increased acuity of both sight and sound. There is of course a sense of detachment, and usually a floating sensation. Many people report that there is no pain or feeling, but simply peace and tranquillity. And a number of people are most impressed with being able to view their own physical self from this altered perspective.

Those who report a dreamlike netherland experience may similarly report a floating sensation, sense of detachment, and absence of pain. They may further report that they seem to be in total darkness, or alternatively a gray mist or even an all-pervasive light. Some report clarity of thought, while others report uncertainty and confusion. And although some report loud, unpleasant noise, others report soft, pleasant sounds (especially music) or total silence.

Those who report an experience of a transcendent otherworldly realm often report meeting others, who may or may not serve as guides. These beings may be deceased ancestors, friends, angels, demons, deities, or simply "beings of light." Some communicate with these beings through ordinary language, some through telepathy or instantaneous understanding, some through signs and gestures, and some not at all. Many report passing through a tunnel or narrow passageway toward a boundary or destination interpreted as a threshold which, if only they could reach, they would be allowed to "stay dead."

It also happens that a person's experience may cover two or even all three of these groups. Thus one may begin with an altered perception of earthly events, drift away into a dreamlike netherland experience, and finally find oneself "in the midst of a heavenly realm."

Conclusions: What conclusions can we draw from these experiences? Do they, as many believe, afford good grounds for belief in an afterlife? Or do they simply represent a last-ditch effort of the human psyche to deny death?

First, the experiences do give us some idea of what it may be like to die. Since not everyone who suffers cardiac arrest or other critical conditions reports a near-death experience, we cannot guarantee that you will have an experience of this sort when you die. But since a large number of people do report experiences of this sort, and since the vast majority report a positive, pleasant experience, we can be fairly sure that death will not be the horrible, painful experience which many fear.

The out-of-body experiences and the experiences of an otherworldly realm strongly suggest, but cannot guarantee, an afterlife. The self seemed to leave the body, and may even have seemed to have been transported to an otherworldly realm, but what seems to be the case and what actually happens are often two different things. The world is not really out to get the paranoic, and dreaming that you fall off a cliff does not require a visit to the doctor.

Finally, and perhaps most importantly, it must be remembered that these are the experiences of people who were dying or believed they were dying, not the experiences of people who died (and stayed dead). As such, as much as they may be able to tell us about the experience of dying, they can only hint at the experience (if there is any) of being dead.

DEATH SURVIVAL POSSIBILITIES: WHO, WHAT, WHERE, WHEN, AND WHY?

What is it like to be dead? If you do not believe in life after death, you will of course respond, "There is no such experience." But even those who believe in life after death often disagree about the specifics of that existence. There is the well-known question of happiness versus misery (heaven versus hell). I would not particularly wish to survive death only to find that I had been condemned to an eternity of suffering. Equally important, if somewhat less frequently discussed, are questions of who, what, where, when, and why.

First, *who* survives death? Do all life forms survive, or just a select few? Are there dogs in heaven? Flowers? Trees? Bacteria? For that matter, do all humans survive, or is it again a matter of a select few? For any possible answer you come up with, there is likely to be a group of people who believe just that.

What is it that survives death? Is it our total being, physical body and all, or just a disembodied spirit? If the latter, do we continue to survive as a pure spirit or do we somehow acquire a new body? If we acquire a new body, is it a standard physical body (as in the doctrine of reincarnation) or is it a nonphysical, astral body (as the Apostle Paul seems to have taught)?

Where do we "live" after death? Do we continue to inhabit this world (as with ghosts or reincarnated spirits) or do we take up residence in some new ethereal realm (like heaven or hell)?

Next is the question of *when*. Do we pass into this afterlife immediately upon death, or do we (as the doctrine of resurrection holds) have to wait till "the final days"? Further, how long does the afterlife last? Is it forever (eternity), or will this new life eventually give way to a new death?

Finally, *why* should there be an afterlife? Is it, as most religions have believed, to reward the just and punish the wicked? Is it, as Christianity has often taught, so that the righteous may "walk with God"? Or is it, as others have believed, simply so we may have time to develop and realize the fullness of our own complex self?

Different religions answer each of these questions in different ways. The afterlife beliefs of a Hindu only vaguely resemble those of a Christian. Saying "I believe in life after death" raises the question of what lies beyond the grave. It does not even begin to answer it.

Notes

1. For more extensive discussion of the material presented in this section, see Douglas Shrader, "On Dying More Than One Death," *Hastings Center Report* 16.1 (February 1986), pp. 12–17.

2. Robert Veatch, "Brain Death: Welcome Definition or Dangerous Judgment?," *Hastings Center Report* 2 (November 1972), pp. 10–13.

The Death of Socrates

PLATO

Because free thought threatens the status quo, it sometimes happens that a philosopher must pay a price for freedom of thought. One of the best-known philosophers of all time, Socrates (469–399 B.C.), was brought to trial in his native Athens on charges of heresy and corrupting the youth. In the speech that follows, recreated by his disciple Plato[1] (428–348 B.C.), Socrates addresses the jury which has just found him guilty and sentenced him to death.

. . . I suspect that this thing that has happened to me is a blessing, and we are quite mistaken in supposing death to be an evil. . . . Death is one of two things. Either it is annihilation, and the dead have no consciousness of anything; or, as we are told, it is really a change: a migration of the soul from this place to another. Now if there is no consciousness but only a dreamless sleep, death must be a marvellous gain. I suppose that if anyone were told to pick out the night on which he slept so soundly as not even to dream, and then to compare it with all the other nights and days of his life, and then were told to say, after due consideration, how many better and happier days and nights than this he had spent in the course of his life—well, I think that the Great King himself, to say nothing of any private person, would find these days and nights easy to count in comparison with the rest. If death is like this, then, I call it gain; because the whole of time, if you look at it in this way, can be regarded as no more than one single night. If on the other hand death is a removal from here to some other place, and if what we are told is true, that all the dead are there, what

greater blessing could there be than this, gentlemen? . . .

It would be a specially interesting experience for me to join them there, to meet . . . heroes of the old days who met their death through an unfair trial, and to compare my fortunes with theirs—it would be rather amusing, I think—; and above all I should like to spend my time there, as here, in examining and searching people's minds, to find out who is really wise among them, and who only thinks that he is. What would one not give, gentlemen, to be able to question the leader of that great host against Troy, or Odysseus, or Sisyphus, or the thousands of other men and women whom one could mention, to talk and mix and argue with whom would be unimaginable happiness? At any rate I presume that they do not put one to death there for such conduct; because apart from the other happiness in which their world surpasses ours, they are now immortal for the rest of time, if what we are told is true.

You too, gentlemen of the jury, must look forward to death with confidence, and fix your minds on this one belief, which is certain: that nothing can

[1] Details concerning the life and accomplishments of Plato precede the selection titled "The Myth of Er" (Literary Reading for Chapter 2).

harm a good man either in life or after death, and his fortunes are not a matter of indifference to the gods. This present experience of mine has not come about mechanically; I am quite clear that the time had come when it was better for me to die and be released from my distractions. That is why my sign never turned me back. For my own part I bear no grudge at all against those who condemned me and accused me, although it was not with this kind intention that they did so, but because they thought that they were hurting me; and that is culpable of them. However, I ask them to grant me one favour. When my sons grow up, gentlemen, if you think that they are putting money or anything else before goodness, take your revenge by plaguing them as I plagued you; and if they fancy themselves for no reason, you must scold them just as I scolded you, for neglecting the important things and thinking that they are good for something when they are good for nothing. If you do this, I shall have had justice at your hands, both I myself and my children.

Now it is time that we were going, I to die and you to live; but which of us has the happier prospect is unknown to anyone but God.

* * *

The death penalty was usually carried out at once, but the absence of key officials kept Socrates in prison for about a month. During this time he must have discoursed with his disciples about death on several different occasions. In the dialogue that follows, again recreated by Plato, Socrates discusses the matter with Simmias.

* * *

. . . 'If I did not expect to enter the company, first, of other wise and good gods, and secondly of men now dead who are better than those who are in this world now, it is true that I should be wrong in not grieving at death. As it is, you can be assured that I expect to find myself among good men; I would not insist particularly on this point, but on the other I assure you that I shall insist most strongly: that I shall find there divine masters who

are supremely good. That is why I am not so much distressed as I might be, and why I have a firm hope that there is something in store for those who have died, and (as we have been told for many years) something much better for the good than for the wicked.' . . .

'Ordinary people seem not to realize that those who really apply themselves in the right way to philosophy are directly and of their own accord preparing themselves for dying and death. If this is true, and they have actually been looking forward to death all their lives, it would of course be absurd to be troubled when the thing comes for which they have so long been preparing and looking forward.'

Simmias laughed and said 'Upon my word, Socrates, you have made me laugh, though I was not at all in the mood for it. I am sure that if they heard what you said, most people would think—and our fellow-countrymen would heartily agree—that it was a very good hit at the philosophers to say that they are half dead already, and that they, the normal people, are quite aware that death would serve the philosophers right.'

'And they would be quite correct, Simmias; except in thinking that they are "quite aware." They are not at all aware in what sense true philosophers are half dead, or in what sense they deserve death, or what sort of death they deserve. But let us dismiss them and talk among ourselves. Do we believe that there is such a thing as death?'

'Most certainly,' said Simmias, taking up the rôle of answering.

'Is it simply the release of the soul from the body? Is death nothing more or less than this, the separate condition of the body by itself when it is released from the soul, and the separate condition by itself of the soul when released from the body? Is death anything else than this?'

'No, just that.'

'Well then, my boy, see whether you agree with me; I fancy that this will help us to find out the answer to our problem. Do you think that it is right for a philosopher to concern himself with the nominal pleasures connected with food and drink?'

'Certainly not, Socrates,' said Simmias.

'What about sexual pleasures?'

'No, not at all.'

'And what about the other attentions that we pay to our bodies? do you think that a philosopher attaches any importance to them? I mean things like providing himself with smart clothes and shoes and other bodily ornaments; do you think that he values them or despises them—in so far as there is no real necessity for him to go in for that sort of thing?'

'I think the true philosopher despises them,' he said.

'Then it is your opinion in general that a man of this kind is not concerned with the body, but keeps his attention directed as much as he can away from it and towards the soul?'

'Yes, it is.'

'So it is clear first of all in the case of physical pleasures that the philosopher frees his soul from association with the body (so far as is possible) to a greater extent than other men?'

'It seems so.' . . .

'Now take the acquisition of knowledge; is the body a hindrance or not, if one takes it into partnership to share an investigation? What I mean is this: is there any certainty in human sight and hearing, or is it true, as the poets are always dinning into our ears, that we neither hear nor see anything accurately? Yet if these senses are not clear and accurate, the rest can hardly be so, because they are all inferior to the first two. Don't you agree?'

'Certainly.'

'Then when is it that the soul attains to truth? When it tries to investigate anything with the help of the body, it is obviously led astray.'

'Quite so.'

'Is it not in the course of reflection, if at all, that the soul gets a clear view of facts?'

'Yes.'

'Surely the soul can best reflect when it is free of all distractions such as hearing or sight or pain or pleasure of any kind—that is, when it ignores the body and becomes as far as possible independent, avoiding all physical contacts and associations as much as it can, in its search for reality.'

'That is so.'

'Then here too—in despising the body and avoiding it, and endeavouring to become independent—the philosopher's soul is ahead of all the rest.'

'It seems so.' . . .

'All these considerations,' said Socrates, 'must surely prompt serious philosophers to review the position in some such way as this. It looks as though this were a bypath leading to the right track. So long as we keep to the body and our soul is contaminated with this imperfection, there is no chance of our ever attaining satisfactorily to our object, which we assert to be Truth. In the first place, the body provides us with innumerable distractions in the pursuit of our necessary sustenance; and any diseases which attack us hinder our quest for reality. Besides, the body fills us with loves and desires and fears and all sorts of fancies and a great deal of nonsense, with the result that we literally never get an opportunity to think at all about anything. Wars and revolutions and battles are due simply and solely to the body and its desires. All wars are undertaken for the acquisition of wealth; and the reason why we have to acquire wealth is the body, because we are slaves in its service. That is why, on all these accounts, we have so little time for philosophy. Worst of all, if we do obtain any leisure from the body's claims and turn to some line of inquiry, the body intrudes once more into our investigations, interrupting, disturbing, distracting, and preventing us from getting a glimpse of the truth. We are in fact convinced that if we are ever to have pure knowledge of anything, we must get rid of the body and contemplate things by themselves with the soul by itself. It seems, to judge from the argument, that the wisdom which we desire and upon which we profess to have set our hearts will be attainable only when we are dead, and not in our lifetime. If no pure knowledge is possible in the company of the body, then either it is totally impossible to acquire knowledge, or it is only possible after death, because it is only then that the soul will be separate and independent of the body. It seems that so long as we are alive, we shall continue closest to knowledge if we avoid as much as we can all contact and association with the body, except when they are absolutely necessary; and instead of allowing ourselves to become infected with its nature, purify ourselves from it until God himself gives us deliverance. In this way, by keeping ourselves uncontaminated by the follies of the body, we shall probably reach the company of others like ourselves and gain direct knowledge of all that is pure and uncontaminated—that is, presumably, of Truth. . . .

The Myth of Immortality

CLARENCE DARROW

There are certain times and occasions on which almost everyone becomes something of a philosopher. Clarence Darrow (1857–1938) is best known as a brilliant defense lawyer.[1] But in the following selection, written when he was seventy-one, he reflects philosophically on the nature of a human being and the prospects for immortality. Whereas Socrates had believed that a human being is a composite of perishable body and immortal soul, Darrow rejects the idea of the soul and, with it, Socrates' belief in immortality. Darrow also considers and rejects the concept of resurrection, which is sometimes presented as an alternative to the Socratic concept.

. . . The belief in immortality expresses itself in two different forms. On the one hand, there is a belief in the immortality of the "soul." This is sometimes interpreted to mean simply that the identity, the consciousness, the memory of the individual persists after death. On the other hand, many religious creeds have formulated a belief in "the resurrection of the body"—which is something else again. It will be necessary to examine both forms of this belief in turn.

The idea of continued life after death is very old. It doubtless had its roots back in the childhood of the race. In view of the limited knowledge of primitive man, it was not unreasonable. His dead friends and relatives visited him in dreams and visions and were present in his feeling and imagination until they were forgotten. Therefore the lifeless body did not raise the question of dissolution, but rather of duality. It was thought that man was a dual being possessing a body and a soul as separate entities, and that when a man died, his soul was released from his body to continue its life apart. Consequently, food and drink were placed upon the graves of the dead to be used in the long journey into the unknown. In modified forms, this belief in the duality of man persists to the present day.

But primitive man had no conception of life as having a beginning and an end. In this he was like the rest of the animals. Today everyone of ordinary intelligence knows how life begins, and to examine the beginnings of life leads to inevitable conclusions about the way life ends. If man has a soul, it must creep in somewhere during the period of gestation and growth.

All the higher forms of animal life grow from a single cell. Before the individual cell can begin its development, it must be fertilized by union with another cell; then the cell divides and multiplies until it takes the form and pattern of its kind. At a certain regular time the being emerges into the world.

Clarence Darrow, "The Myth of Immortality," *Forum*, vol. 80 (October 1928).

[1] Readers will perhaps find it instructive to recall Darrow's role in the famous Scopes trial in Tennessee concerning the teaching of Darwin's Theory of Evolution. Regarded by some as a mockery of the judicial system, the trial is heralded by others as a landmark victory and unequivocal precedent regarding the proper relationship between science, religion, and public education.

During its term of life millions of cells in its body are born, die, and are replaced until, through age, disease, or some catastrophe, the cells fall apart and the individual life is ended.

It is obvious that but for the fertilization of the cell under right conditions, the being would not have lived. It is idle to say that the initial cell has a soul. In one sense it has life; but even that is precarious and depends for its continued life upon union with another cell of the proper kind. The human mother is the bearer of probably ten thousand of one kind of cell, and the human father of countless billions of the other kind. Only a very small fraction of these result in human life. If the unfertilized cells of the female and the unused cells of the male are human beings possessed of souls, then the population of the world is infinitely greater than has ever been dreamed. Of course no such idea as belief in the immortality of the germ cells could satisfy the yearnings of the individual for a survival of life after death.

If that which is called a "soul" is a separate entity apart from the body, when, then, and where and how was this soul placed in the human structure? The individual began with the union of two cells, neither of which had a soul. How could these two soulless cells produce a soul? I must leave this search to the metaphysicians. . . .

The beginnings of life yield no evidence of the beginnings of a soul. It is idle to say that the something in the human being which we call "life" is the soul itself, for the soul is generally taken to distinguish human beings from other forms of life. There is life in all animals and plants, and at least potential life in inorganic matter. This potential life is simply unreleased force and matter—the great storehouse from which all forms of life emerge and are constantly replenished. It is impossible to draw the line between inorganic matter and the simpler forms of plant life, and equally impossible to draw the line between plant life and animal life, or between other forms of animal life and what we human beings are pleased to call the highest form. If the thing which we call "life" is itself the soul, then cows have souls; and, in the very nature of things, we must allow souls to all forms of life and to inorganic matter as well.

Life itself is something very real, as distinguished from the soul. Every man knows that his life had a beginning. Can one imagine an organism that has a beginning and no end? If I did not exist in the infinite past, why should I, or could I, exist in the infinite future? "But," say some, "your consciousness, your memory may exist even after you are dead. This is what we mean by the soul." Let us examine this point a little.

I have no remembrance of the months that I lay in my mother's womb. I cannot recall the day of my birth nor the time when I first opened my eyes to the light of the sun. I cannot remember when I was an infant, or when I began to creep on the floor, or when I was taught to walk, or anything before I was five or six years old. Still, all of these events were important, wonderful, and strange in a new life. What I call my "consciousness," for lack of a better word and a better understanding, developed with my growth and the crowding experiences I met at every turn. I have a hazy recollection of the burial of a boy soldier who was shot toward the end of the Civil War. He was buried near the schoolhouse when I was seven years old. But I have no remembrance of the assassination of Abraham Lincoln, although I must then have been eight years old. I must have known about it at the time, for my family and my community idolized Lincoln, and all America was in mourning at his death. Why do I remember the dead boy soldier who was buried a year before? Perhaps because I knew him well. Perhaps because his family was close to my childish life. Possibly because it came to me as my first knowledge of death. At all events, it made so deep an impression that I recall it now.

"Ah, yes," say the believers in the soul, "what you say confirms our own belief. You certainly existed when these early experiences took place. You were conscious of them at the time, even though you are not aware of it now. In the same way, may not your consciousness persist after you die, even though you are not now aware of the fact?"

On the contrary, my fading memory of the events that filled the early years of my life leads me to the opposite conclusion. So far as these incidents are concerned, the mind and consciousness of the boy are already dead. Even now, am I fully alive? I am seventy-one years old. I often fail to recollect the names of some of those I knew full well. Many events do not make the lasting impression that they once did. I know that it will be only a few years, even if my body still survives decay, when few important matters will even register in my mind. I know how it is with the old. I know that physical life can persist beyond the time when the mind can fully function. I know that if I live to an extreme old age, my mind will fail. I shall eat and drink and go to my bed in an automatic way. Memory—which is all that binds me to the past—will already be dead. All that will remain will be a vegetative existence; I shall sit and doze in the chimney corner, and my body will function in a measure even though the ego will already be practically dead. I am sure that if I die of what is called "old age," my consciousness will gradually slip away with my failing emotions; I shall no more be aware of the near approach of final dissolution than is the dying tree. . . .

There are those who base their hope of a future life upon the resurrection of the body. This is a purely religious doctrine. It is safe to say that few intelligent men who are willing to look obvious facts in the face hold any such belief. Yet we are seriously told that Elijah was carried bodily to heaven in a chariot of fire, and that Jesus arose from the dead and ascended into heaven. The New Testament abounds in passages that support this doctrine. St. Paul states the tenet over and over again. In the fifteenth chapter of First Corinthians he says: "If Christ be preached that he rose from the dead, how say some among you that there is no resurrection of the dead? . . . And if Christ be not risen, then is our preaching vain. . . . For if the dead rise not, then is not Christ raised." The Apostles' Creed says: "I believe in the resurrection of the body." This has been carried into substantially all the orthodox creeds; and while it is more or less minimized by neglect and omission, is still a cardinal doctrine of the orthodox churches.

Two thousand years ago, in Palestine, little was known of man, of the earth, or of the universe. It was then currently believed that the earth was only four thousand years old, that life had begun anew after the deluge about two thousand years before, and that the entire earth was soon to be destroyed. Today it is fairly well established that man has been upon the earth for a million years. During that long stretch of time the world has changed many times; it is changing every moment. At least three or four ice ages have swept across continents, driving death before them, carrying human beings into the sea or burying them deep in the earth. Animals have fed on man and on each other. Every dead body, no matter whether consumed by fire or buried in the earth, has been resolved into its elements, so that the matter and energy that once formed human beings has fed animals and plants and other men. As the great naturalist, Fabre, has said: "At the banquet of life each is in turn a guest and a dish." Thus the body of every man now living is in part made from the bodies of those who have been dead for ages.

Yet we are still asked to believe in the resurrection of the body. By what alchemy, then, are the individual bodies that have successfully fed the generations of men to be separated and restored to their former identities? And if I am to be resurrected, what particular *I* shall be called from the grave, from the animals and plants and the bodies of other men who shall inherit this body I now call my own? My body has been made over and over, piece by piece, as the days went by, and will continue to be so made until the end. It has changed so slowly that each new cell is fitted into the living part, and will go on changing until the final crisis comes. Is it the child in the mother's womb or the tottering frame of the old man that shall be brought back? The mere thought of such a resurrection beggars reason, ignores facts, and enthrones blind faith, wild dreams, hopeless hopes, and cowardly fears as sovereign of the human mind.

Some of those who profess to believe in the immortality of man—whether it be of his soul or his body—have drawn what comfort they could from the modern scientific doctrine of the indestructibility of matter and force. This doctrine, they say, only confirms in scientific language what they have always believed. This, however, is pure sophistry. It is probably true that no matter or force has ever been or ever can be destroyed. But it is likewise true that there is no connection whatever between the notion that personal consciousness and memory persist after death and the scientific theory that matter and force are indestructible. For the scientific theory carries with it a corollary, that the forms of matter and energy are constantly changing through an endless cycle of new combinations. Of what possible use would it be, then, to have a consciousness that was immortal, but which, from the moment of death, was dispersed into new combinations so that no two parts of the original identity could ever be reunited again?

These natural processes of change, which in the human being take the forms of growth, disease, senility, death, and decay, are essentially the same as the process by which a lump of coal is disintegrated in burning. One may watch the lump of coal burning in the grate until nothing but ashes remains. Part of the coal goes up the chimney in the form of smoke; part of it radiates through the house as heat; the residue lies in the ashes on the hearth. So it is with human life. In all forms of life nature is engaged in combining, breaking down, and recombining her store of energy and matter into new forms. The thing we call "life" is nothing other than a state of equilibrium which endures for a short span of years between the two opposing tendencies of nature—the one that builds up and the one that tears down. In old age, the tearing-down process has already gained the ascendancy, and when death intervenes, the equilibrium is finally upset by the complete stoppage of the building-up process, so that nothing remains but complete disintegration. The energy thus released may be converted into grass or trees or animal life; or it may lie dormant until caught up again in the crucible of nature's laboratory. But whatever happens, the man—the *You* and the *I*—like the lump of coal that has been burned, is gone, irrevocably dispersed. All the King's horses and all the King's men cannot restore it to its former unity.

The idea that man is a being set apart, distinct from all the rest of nature, is born of man's emotions, of his loves and hates, of his hopes and fears, and of the primitive conceptions of undeveloped minds. The *You* or the *I* which is known to our friends does not consist of an immaterial something called a "soul" which cannot be conceived. We know perfectly well what we mean when we talk about this *You* and this *Me:* and it is equally plain that the whole fabric that makes up our separate personalities is destroyed, dispersed, disintegrated beyond repair by what we call "death." . . .

And after all, is the belief in immortality necessary or even desirable for man? Millions of men and women have no such faith; they go on with their daily tasks and feel joy and sorrow without the lure of immortal life. The things that really affect the happiness of the individual are the matters of daily living. They are the companionship of friends, the games and contemplations. They are misunderstandings and cruel judgments, false friends and debts, poverty and disease. They are our joys in our living companions and our sorrows over those who die. Whatever our faith, we mainly live in the present—in the here and now. Those who hold the view that man is mortal are never troubled by metaphysical problems. At the end of the day's labor we are glad to lose our consciousness in sleep; and intellectually, at least, we look forward to the long rest from the stresses and storms that are always incidental to existence.

When we fully understand the brevity of life, its fleeting joys and unavoidable pains; when we accept the fact that all men and women are approaching an inevitable doom: the consciousness of it should make us more kindly and considerate of each other. This feeling should make men and women use their best efforts to help their fellow travellers on the road, to make the path brighter and easier as we journey on. It should bring a closer kinship, a better understanding, and a deeper sympathy for the wayfarer who must live a common life and die a common death.

Stages

ELISABETH KÜBLER-ROSS

There is no other researcher in the field of thanatology (the study of death and dying) whose visibility or influence can compare with that of Dr. Elisabeth Kübler-Ross. A psychiatrist by training, she is best known for her theory that people come to terms with death (either their own or that of others) over a protracted period of time and that the process usually involves passing through five distinct stages. The following selection is edited from her classic *On Death and Dying* (1969).

FIRST STAGE:
DENIAL AND ISOLATION

Man barracades against himself.

> Tagore, from *Stray Birds,* LXXIX

Among the over two hundred dying patients we have interviewed, most reacted to the awareness of a terminal illness at first with the statement, "No, not me, it cannot be true." This *initial* denial was as true for those patients who were told outright at the beginning of their illness as it was true for those who were not told explicitly and who came to this conclusion on their own a bit later on. One of our patients described a long and expensive ritual, as she called it, to support her denial. She was convinced that the X-rays were "mixed up"; she asked for reassurance that her pathology report could not possibly be back so soon and that another patient's report must have been marked with her name. When none of this could be confirmed, she quickly asked to leave the hospital, looking for another physician in the vain hope "to get a better explanation for my troubles." This patient went "shopping around" for many doctors, some of whom gave her reassuring answers, others of whom confirmed the previous suspicion. Whether confirmed or not, she reacted in the same manner; she asked for examina-

tion and reexamination, partially knowing that the original diagnosis was correct, but also seeking further evaluations in the hope that the first conclusion was indeed an error, at the same time keeping in contact with a physician in order to have help available "at all times" as she said.

This anxious denial following the presentation of a diagnosis is more typical of the patient who is informed prematurely or abruptly by someone who does not know the patient well or does it quickly "to get it over with" without taking the patient's readiness into consideration. Denial, at least partial denial, is used by almost all patients, not only during the first stages of illness or following confrontation, but also later on from time to time. Who was it who said, "We cannot look at the sun all the time, we cannot face death all the time"? These patients can consider the possibility of their own death for a while but then have to put this consideration away in order to pursue life. . . .

SECOND STAGE: ANGER

We read the world wrong and say that it deceives us.

Tagore, from *Stray Birds*, LXXV

If our first reaction to catastrophic news is, "No, it's not true, no, it cannot involve me," this has to give way to a new reaction, when it finally dawns on us: "Oh, yes, it is me, it was not a mistake." Fortunately or unfortunately very few patients are able to maintain a make-believe world in which they are healthy and well until they die.

When the first stage of denial cannot be maintained any longer, it is replaced by feelings of anger, rage, envy, and resentment. The logical next question becomes: "Why me?" As one of our patients, Dr. G., put it, "I suppose most anybody in my position would look at somebody else and say, 'Well, why couldn't it have been him?' and this has crossed my mind several times. . . . An old man whom I have known ever since I was a little kid came down the street. He was eighty-two years old, and he is of no earthly use as far as we mortals can tell. He's rheumatic, he's a cripple, he's dirty, just not the type of a person you would like to be. And the thought hit me strongly, now why couldn't it have been old George instead of me?" (extract from interview of Dr. G.).

In contrast to the stage of denial, this stage of anger is very difficult to cope with from the point of view of family and staff. The reason for this is the fact that this anger is displaced in all directions and projected onto the environment at times almost at random. The doctors are just no good, they don't know what tests to require and what diet to prescribe. They keep the patients too long in the hospital or don't respect their wishes in regards to special privileges. They allow a miserably sick roommate to be brought into their room when they pay so much money for some privacy and rest, etc. The nurses are even more often a target of their anger. Whatever they touch is not right. The moment they have left the room, the bell rings. The light is on the very minute they start their report for the next shifts of nurses. When they do shake the pillows and straighten out the bed, they are blamed for never leaving the patients alone. When they do leave the patients alone, the light goes on with the request to have the bed arranged more comfortably. The visiting family is received with little cheerfulness and anticipation, which makes the encounter a painful event. They then either respond with grief and tears, guilt or shame, or avoid future visits, which only increases the patient's discomfort and anger.

The problem here is that few people place themselves in the patient's position and wonder where this anger might come from. Maybe we too would be angry if all our life activities were interrupted so prematurely; if all the buildings we started were to go unfinished, to be completed by someone else; if we had put some hard-earned money aside to enjoy a few years of rest and enjoyment, for travel and pursuing hobbies, only to be confronted with the fact that "this is not for me." What else would we do with our anger, but let it out on the people who are most likely to enjoy all these things? People who rush busily around only to remind us that we cannot even stand on our two feet anymore. People who order unpleasant tests and prolonged hospitalization with all its limitations, restrictions, and costs, while at the end of the day they can go home and enjoy life. People who tell us to lie still so that the infusion or transfusion does not have to be restarted, when we feel like jumping out of our skin to be doing something in order to know that we are still functioning on some level!

Wherever the patient looks at this time, he will find grievances. He may put the television on only to find a group of young jolly people doing some of the modern dances which irritates him when every move of his is painful or limited. He may see a movie western in which people are shot in cold blood with different onlookers continuing to drink their beer. He will compare them with his family or the attending staff. He may listen to the news full of reports of destruction, war, fires, and tragedies—far away from him, unconcerned about the fight and plight of an individual who will soon be forgotten.

So this patient makes sure that he is not forgotten. He will raise his voice, he will make demands, he will complain and ask to be given attention, perhaps as the last loud cry, "I am alive, don't forget that. You can hear my voice, I am not dead yet!"

A patient who is respected and understood, who is given attention and a little time, will soon lower his voice and reduce his angry demands. He will know that he is a valuable human being, cared for, allowed to function at the highest possible level as long as he can. He will be listened to without the need for a temper tantrum, he will be visited without ringing the bell every so often because dropping in on him is not a necessary duty but a pleasure.

The tragedy is perhaps that we do not think of the reasons for patients' anger and take it personally, when it has originally nothing or little to do with the people who become the target of the anger. As the staff or family reacts personally to this anger, however, they respond with increasing anger on their part, only feeding into the patient's hostile behavior. They may use avoidance and shorten the visits or the rounds or they may get into unnecessary arguments by defending their stand, not knowing that the issue is often totally irrelevant. . . .

THIRD STAGE: BARGAINING

The woodcutter's axe begged for its handle from the tree. The tree gave it.

Tagore, from *Stray Birds*, LXXI

The third stage, the stage of bargaining, is less well known but equally helpful to the patient, though only for brief periods of time. If we have been unable to face the sad facts in the first period and have been angry at people and God in the second phase, maybe we can succeed in entering into some sort of an agreement which may postpone the inevitable happening: "If God has decided to take us from this earth and he did not respond to my angry pleas, he may be more favorable if I ask nicely." We are all familiar with this reaction when we observe our children first demanding, then asking for a favor. They

may not accept our "No" when they want to spend a night in a friend's house. They may be angry and stamp their foot. They may lock themselves in their bedroom and temporarily express their anger by rejecting us. But they will also have second thoughts. They may consider another approach. They will come out eventually, volunteer to do some tasks around the house, which under normal circumstances we never succeeded in getting them to do, and then tell us, "If I am very good all week and wash the dishes every evening, then will you let me go?" There is a slight chance naturally that we will accept the bargain and the child will get what was previously denied.

The terminally ill patient uses the same maneuvers. He knows, from past experiences, that there is a slim chance that he may be rewarded for good behavior and be granted a wish for special services. His wish is most always an extension of life, followed by the wish for a few days without pain or physical discomfort. A patient who was an opera singer, with a distorting malignancy of her jaw and face who could no longer perform on the stage, asked "to perform just one more time." When she became aware that this was impossible, she gave the most touching performance perhaps of her lifetime. She asked to come to the seminar and to speak in front of the audience, not behind a one-way mirror. She unfolded her life story, her success, and her tragedy in front of the class until a telephone call summoned her to return to her room. Doctor and dentist were ready to pull all her teeth in order to proceed with the radiation treatment. She had asked to sing once more—to us—before she had to hide her face forever.

Another patient was in utmost pain and discomfort, unable to go home because of her dependence on injections for pain relief. She had a son who proceeded with his plans to get married, as the patient had wished. She was very sad to think that she would be unable to attend this big day, for he was her oldest and favorite child. With combined efforts, we were able to teach her self-hypnosis which enabled her to be quite comfortable for several hours. She had made all sorts of promises if she could only live long enough to attend this marriage. The day preceding the wedding she left the hospital as an elegant lady. Nobody would have believed her real condition. She was "the happiest person in the whole world" and looked radiant. I wondered what her reaction would be when the time was up for which she had bargained.

I will never forget the moment when she returned to the hospital. She looked tired and somewhat exhausted and—before I could say hello—said, "Now don't forget I have another son!"

The bargaining is really an attempt to postpone; it has to include a prize offered "for good behavior," it also sets a self-imposed "deadline" (e.g., one more performance, the son's wedding), and it includes an implicit promise that the patient will not ask for more if this one postponement is granted. None of our patients have "kept their promise"; in other words, they are like children who say, "I will never fight my sister again if you let me go." Needless to add, the little boy will fight his sister again, just as the opera singer will try to perform once more. She could not live without further performances and left the hospital before her teeth were extracted. The patient just described was unwilling to face us again unless we acknowledged the fact that she had another son whose wedding she also wanted to witness.

Most bargains are made with God and are usually kept a secret or mentioned between the lines or in a chaplain's private office. In our individual interviews without an audience we have been impressed by the number of patients who promise "a life dedicated to God" or "a life in the service of the church" in exchange for some additional time. Many of our patients also promised to give parts of or their whole body "to science" (if the doctors use their knowledge of science to extend their life).

Psychologically, promises may be associated with quiet guilt, and it would therefore be helpful if such remarks by patients were not just brushed aside by the staff. If a sensitive chaplain or physician elicits such statements, he may well wish to find out if the patient feels indeed guilty for not attending church more regularly or if there are deeper, unconscious hostile wishes which precipitated such guilt. It is for this reason that we found it so helpful to have an interdisciplinary approach in our patient care, as the chaplain often was the first one to hear about such concerns. We then pursued them until the patient was relieved of irrational fears or the wish for punishment because of excessive guilt, which was only enforced by further bargaining and more unkept promises when the "deadline" was past.

FOURTH STAGE: DEPRESSION

The world rushes on over the strings of the lingering heart making the music of sadness.

Tagore, from *Stray Birds,* XLIV

When the terminally ill patient can no longer deny his illness, when he is forced to undergo more surgery or hospitalization, when he begins to have more symptoms or becomes weaker and thinner, he cannot smile it off anymore. His numbness or stoicism, his anger and rage will soon be replaced with a sense of great loss. This loss may have many facets: a woman with a breast cancer may react to the loss of her figure; a woman with a cancer of the uterus may feel that she is no longer a woman. Our opera singer responded to the required surgery of her face and the removal of her teeth with shock, dismay, and the deepest depression. But this is only one of the many losses that such a patient has to endure.

With the extensive treatment and hospitalization, financial burdens are added; little luxuries at first and necessities later on may not be afforded anymore. The immense sums that such treatments and hospitalizations cost in recent years have forced many patients to sell the only possessions they had; they were unable to keep a house which they built for their old age, unable to send a child through college, and unable perhaps to make many dreams come true.

There may be the added loss of a job due to many absences or the inability to function, and mothers and wives may have to become the bread-winners, thus depriving the children of the attention they previously had. When mothers are sick, the little ones may have to be boarded out, adding to the sadness and guilt of the patient.

All these reasons for depressions are well known to everybody who deals with patients. What we often tend to forget, however, is the preparatory grief that the terminally ill patient has to undergo in order to prepare himself for his final separation from this world. If I were to attempt to differentiate these two kinds of depressions, I would regard the first one a reactive depression, the second one a preparatory depression. The first one is different in nature and should be dealt with quite differently from the latter.

An understanding person will have no difficulty in eliciting the cause of the depression and in alleviating some of the unrealistic guilt or shame which often accompanies the depression. A woman who is worried about no longer being a woman can be complimented for some especially feminine feature; she can be reassured that she is still as much a woman as she was before surgery. Breast prosthesis has added much to the breast cancer patient's self-esteem. Social worker, physician, or chaplain may discuss the patient's concerns with the husband in order to obtain his help in supporting the patient's self-esteem. Social workers and chaplains can be of great help during this time in assisting in the reorganization of a household, especially when children or lonely old people are involved for whom eventual placement has to be considered. We are always impressed by how quickly a patient's depression is lifted when these vital issues are taken care of. . . .

The second type of depression is one which does not occur as a result of a past loss but is taking into account impending losses. Our initial reaction to sad people is usually to try to cheer them up, to tell them not to look at things so grimly or so hopelessly. We encourage them to look at the bright side of life, at all the colorful, positive things around them. This is often an expression of our own needs, our own inability to tolerate a long face over any ex-

tended period of time. This can be a useful approach when dealing with the first type of depression in terminally ill patients. It will help such a mother to know that the children play quite happily in the neighbor's garden since they stay there while their father is at work. It may help a mother to know that they continue to laugh and joke, go to parties, and bring good report cards home from school—all expressions that they function in spite of mother's absence.

When the depression is a tool to prepare for the impending loss of all the love objects, in order to facilitate the state of acceptance, then encouragements and reassurances are not as meaningful. The patient should not be encouraged to look at the sunny side of things, as this would mean he should not contemplate his impending death. It would be contraindicated to tell him not to be sad, since all of us are tremendously sad when we lose one beloved person. The patient is in the process of losing everything and everybody he loves. If he is allowed to express his sorrow he will find a final acceptance much easier, and he will be grateful to those who can sit with him during this stage of depression without constantly telling him not to be sad. This second type of depression is usually a silent one in contrast to the first type, during which the patient has much to share and requires many verbal interactions and often active interventions on the part of people in many disciplines. In the preparatory grief there is no or little need for words. It is much more a feeling that can be mutually expressed and is often done better with a touch of a hand, a stroking of the hair, or just a silent sitting together. This is the time when the patient may just ask for a prayer, when he begins to occupy himself with things ahead rather than behind. It is a time when too much interference from visitors who try to cheer him up hinders his emotional preparation rather than enhances it. . . .

FIFTH STAGE: ACCEPTANCE

I have got my leave. Bid me farewell, my brothers! I bow to you all and take my departure.

Here I give back the keys of my door—and I give up all claims to my house. I only ask for last kind words from you.

We were neighbours for long, but I received more than I could give. Now the day has dawned and the lamp that lit my dark corner is out. A summons has come and I am ready for my journey.

Tagore, from *Gitanjali*, XCIII

If a patient has had enough time (i.e., not a sudden, unexpected death) and has been given some help in working through the previously described stages, he will reach a stage during which he is neither depressed nor angry about his "fate." He will have been able to express his previous feelings, his envy for the living and the healthy, his anger at those who do not have to face their end so soon. He will have mourned the impending loss of so many meaningful people and places and he will contemplate his coming end with a certain degree of quiet expectation. He will be tired and, in most cases, quite weak. He will also have a need to doze off or to sleep often and in brief intervals, which is different from the need to sleep during the times of depression. This is not a sleep of avoidance or a period of rest to get relief from pain, discomfort, or itching. It is a gradually increasing need to extend the hours of sleep very similar to that of the newborn child but in reverse order. It is not a resigned and hopeless "giving up," a sense of "what's the use" or "I just cannot fight it any longer," though we hear such statements too. (They also indicate the beginning of the end of the struggle, but the latter are not indications of acceptance.)

Acceptance should not be mistaken for a happy stage. It is almost void of feelings. It is as if the pain had gone, the struggle is over, and there comes a time for "the final rest before the long journey" as one patient phrased it. This is also the time during which the family needs usually more help, understanding, and support than the patient himself. While the dying patient has found some peace and acceptance, his circle of interest diminishes. He wishes to be left alone or at least not stirred up by news and problems of the outside world. Visitors are often not desired and if they come, the patient is no longer in a talkative mood. He often requests limitation on the number of people and prefers short visits. This is the time when the television is off. Our communications then become more nonverbal than verbal. The patient may just make a gesture of the hand to invite us to sit down for a while. He may just hold our hand and ask us to sit in silence. Such moments of silence may be the most meaningful communications for people who are not uncomfortable in the presence of a dying person. We may together listen to the song of a bird from the outside. Our presence may just confirm that we are going to be around until the end. We may just let him know that it is all right to say nothing when the important things are taken care of and it is only a question of time until he can close his eyes forever. It may reassure him that he is not left alone when he is no longer talking and a pressure of the hand, a look, a leaning back in the pillows may say more than many "noisy" words.

A visit in the evening may lend itself best to such an encounter as it is the end of the day both for the visitor and the patient. It is the time when the hospital's page system does not interrupt such a moment, when the nurse does not come in to take the temperature, and the cleaning woman is not mopping the floor—it is this little private moment that can complete the day at the end of the rounds for the physician, when he is not interrupted by anyone. It takes just a little time but it is comforting for the patient to know that he is not forgotten when nothing else can be done for him. It is gratifying for the visitor as well, as it will show him that dying is not such a frightening, horrible thing that so many want to avoid.

There are a few patients who fight to the end, who struggle and keep a hope that makes it almost impossible to reach this stage of acceptance. They are the ones who will say one day, "I just cannot make it anymore," the day they stop fighting, the fight is over. In other words, the harder they struggle to avoid the inevitable death, the more they try to deny it, the more difficult it will be for them to reach this final stage of acceptance with peace and dignity. The family and staff may consider these patients tough and strong, they may encourage the fight for life to the end, and they may implicitly communicate that accepting one's end is regarded as a cowardly giving up, as a deceit or, worse yet, a rejection of the family.

How, then, do we know when a patient is giving up "too early" when we feel that a little fight on his part combined with the help of the medical profession could give him a chance to live longer? How can we differentiate this from the stage of acceptance, when our wish to prolong his life often contradicts his wish to rest and die in peace? If we are unable to differentiate these two stages we do more harm than good to our patients, we will be frustrated in our efforts, and will make his dying a painful last experience. The following case of Mrs. W. is a brief summary of such an event, where this differentiation was not made.

Mrs. W., a married fifty-eight-year-old woman, was hospitalized with a malignancy in her abdomen which gave her much pain and discomfort. She had been able to face her serious illness with courage and dignity. She complained very rarely and attempted to do as many things as possible by herself. She rejected any offer of help as long as she was able to do it herself and impressed the staff and her family by her cheerfulness and ability to face her impending death with equanimity.

Briefly after her last admission to the hospital she became suddenly depressed. The staff was puzzled about this change and asked for a psychiatric consultation. She was not in her room when we looked for her and a second visit a few hours later found her still absent. We finally found her in the hallway outside of the X-ray room where she lay uncomfortably and obviously in pain on a stretcher. A brief interview revealed that she had undergone two rather lengthy X-ray procedures and had to wait for other pictures to be taken. She was in great discomfort because of a sore on her back, had not had any food or drink for the past several hours, and most uncomfortable of all, needed to go to the bathroom urgently. She related all

this in a whispering voice, describing herself as being "just numb from pain." I offered to carry her to the adjacent bathroom. She looked at me—for the first time smiling faintly—and said, "No, I am barefoot, I'd rather wait until I am back in my room. I can go there myself."

This brief remark showed us one of the patient's needs: to care for herself as long as possible, to keep her dignity and independence as long as it was possible. She was enraged that her endurance was tested to the point where she was ready to scream in public, where she was ready to let go of her bowel movements in a hallway, where she was on the verge of crying in front of strangers "who only did their duty."

When we talked with her a few days later under more favorable circumstances, it was obvious that she was increasingly tired and ready to die. She talked about her children briefly, about her husband who would be able to carry on without her. She felt strongly that her life, especially her marriage, had been a good and meaningful one and that there was little left that she could do. She asked to be allowed to die in peace, wished to be left alone—even asked for less involvement on the part of her husband. She said that the only reason that kept her still alive was her husband's inability to accept the fact that she had to die. She was angry at him for not facing it and for so desperately clinging on to something that she was willing and ready to give up. I translated to her that she wished to detach herself from this world and she nodded gratefully as I left her alone.

In the meantime, unbeknown to the patient and myself, the medical-surgical staff had a meeting which included the husband. While the surgeons believed that another surgical procedure could possibly prolong her life, the husband pleaded with them to do everything in their power to "turn the clock back." It was unacceptable to him to lose his wife. He could not comprehend that she did not have the need to be with him any longer. Her need to detach herself, to make dying easier, was interpreted by him as a rejection which was beyond his comprehension. There was no one there to explain to him that this was a natural process, a progress indeed, a sign perhaps that a dying person has found his peace and is preparing himself to face it alone.

The team decided to operate on the patient the following week. As soon as she was informed of the plans she weakened rapidly. Almost overnight she required double the dose of medication for her pains. She often asked for drugs the moment she was given an injection. She became restless and anxious, often calling for help. She was hardly the patient of a few days before; the dignified lady who could not go to the bathroom because she was not wearing slippers!

Such behavioral changes should make us alert. They are communications of our patients who try to tell us something. It is not always possible for a patient to openly reject a life-prolonging operation, in the face of a pleading, desperate husband and children who hope to have mother home once more. Last but not least, we should not underestimate the patient's own glimpse of hope for a cure in the face of impending death. As outlined earlier, it is not in human nature to accept the finality of death without leaving a door open for some hope. It is therefore not enough to listen only to the overt verbal communications of our patients.

Mrs. W. had clearly indicated that she wished to be left in peace. She was in much more pain and discomfort after the announcement of the planned surgery. Her anxiety increased as the day of the operation approached. It was not in our authority to cancel the operation. We merely communicated our strong reservations and felt sure that the patient would not tolerate the operation.

Mrs. W. did not have the strength to refuse the operation nor did she die before or during the procedure. She became grossly psychotic in the operating room, expressed ideas of persecution, screamed and carried on until she was returned to her room minutes before the planned surgery was to take place.

She was clearly delusional, had visual hallucinations and paranoid ideas. She looked frightened and bewildered and made no sense in her communications to the staff. Yet, in all this psychotic behavior, there was a degree of awareness and logic that remained impressive. As she was returned to her room, she asked to see me. When I entered the room the following day, she looked at her bewildered husband and then said, "Talk to this man and make him understand." She then turned her back to us, clearly indicating her need to be left alone. I had my first meeting with her husband, who was at a loss for words. He could not understand the "crazy" behavior of his wife who had always been such a dignified lady. It was hard for him to cope with her rapidly deteriorating physical

illness, but incomprehensible what our "crazy dialogue" was all about.

Her husband said with tears in his eyes that he was totally puzzled by this unexpected change. He described his marriage as an extremely happy one and his wife's terminal illness as totally unacceptable. He had hopes that the operation would allow them once more to be "as close together as they had been" for the many happy years of their marriage. He was disturbed by his wife's detachment and even more so by her psychotic behavior.

When I asked him about the patient's needs, rather than his own, he sat in silence. He slowly began to realize that he never listened to her needs but took it for granted that they were the same. He could not comprehend that a patient reaches a point when death comes as a great relief, and that patients die easier if they are allowed and helped to detach themselves slowly from all the meaningful relationships in their life.

We had a long session together. As we talked, things slowly began to clear and came into focus. He gave much anecdotal material to confirm that she had tried to communicate her needs to him, but that he could not hear it because they were opposing his needs. Mr. W. felt obviously relieved when he left and rejected an offer to return with him to the patient's room. He felt more capable of talking with his wife frankly about the outcome of her illness and was almost glad that the operation had to be canceled because of her "resistance" as he called it. His reaction to her psychosis was, "My God, maybe she is stronger than all of us. She sure fooled us. She made it clear she did not want the operation. Maybe the psychosis was the only way out of it without dying before she was ready."

Mrs. W. confirmed a few days later that she was not able to die until she knew that her husband was willing to let go. She wanted him to share some of her feelings rather than "always pretend that I am going to be all right." Her husband did make an attempt to let her talk about it, though it came hard and he "regressed" many times. Once he clung to the hope for radiation, at another time he tried to put pressure on her to come home, promising to hire a private nurse for her care.

During the following two weeks he often came to talk about his wife and his hopes but also about her eventual death. Finally he came to accept the fact that she would become weaker and less able to share the many things that had been so meaningful in their life.

She recovered from her psychotic episode as soon as the operation was permanently canceled and her husband acknowledged the impending death and shared this with her. She had less pain and resumed her role of the dignified lady who continued to do as many things as her physical condition allowed. The medical staff became increasingly sensitive to the subtle expressions to which they responded tactfully, always keeping in mind her most important need: to live to the end with dignity.

Mrs. W. was representative of most of our dying patients, though she was the only one I have seen to resort to such an acute psychotic episode. I am sure that this was a defense, a desperate attempt to prevent a life-prolonging intervention which came too late.

As stated earlier, we have found that those patients do best who have been encouraged to express their rage, to cry in preparatory grief, and to express their fears and fantasies to someone who can quietly sit and listen. We should be aware of the monumental task which is required to achieve this stage of acceptance, leading towards a gradual separation (decathexis) where there is no longer a two-way communication.

We have found two ways of achieving this goal more easily. One kind of patient will achieve it with little if any help from the environment—except a silent understanding and no interference. This is the older patient who feels at the end of his life, who has worked and suffered, raised his children and completed his tasks. He will have found meaning in his life and has a sense of contentment when he looks back at his years of work.

Others, less fortunate ones, may reach a similar state of body and mind when they are given enough time to prepare for their death. They will need more help and understanding from the environment as they struggle through all the previously described stages. We have seen the majority of our patients die in the stage of acceptance, an existence without fear and despair. It is perhaps best compared with what Bettelheim describes about early infancy: "Indeed it was an age when nothing was asked of us and all that we wanted was given. Psychoanalysis views earliest infancy as a time of passivity, an age of primary narcissism when we experience the self as being all."

And so, maybe at the end of our days, when we have worked and given, enjoyed ourselves and suffered, we are going back to the stage that we started out with and the circle of life is closed.

The Myth of Er

PLATO

Plato was born in Athens in 427 B.C. His heritage was impressive: on his father's side he was descended from Codrus, Athens' last king, and on his mother's from Solon, an esteemed poet and legal reformer. When Plato's father died his mother married Pyrilampes, a prominent statesman who had been a close friend and supporter of Pericles (d. 429 B.C.).

Plato's life was thus aristocratic, but also deeply troubled. The Peloponnesian War began four years before his birth and continued until he was twenty-three. He fought in three battles and was decorated for bravery.[1] At the end of the war a commission was established to frame a new Athenian constitution.

The commission (known as "the Thirty") was led by Critias, Plato's mother's cousin. Plato was invited to join the commission, but declined. It was a wise decision. In practice the Thirty operated as a oligarchy, settling old scores and perpetuating personal wealth. Within eight months they had been deposed and killed.

Following the downfall of the Thirty, Plato contemplated an active role in the reconstituted democracy. But in 399 B.C. the new government executed Socrates on charges of impiety and corrupting the youth.[2] Plato had apparently known Socrates from an early age and had developed a deep admiration and respect for the man and his teaching. Plato left Athens, traveling to Italy, Sicily, Cyrene, Egypt, and perhaps Phoenicia.

Socrates left behind a legacy of students, but no writings. Determined that he would not be forgotten, Plato began to create dialogues portraying conversational exchanges between Socrates, his students, and critics. Scholars generally agree that these early dialogues are reasonably faithful representations of the historical Socrates.

At about the age of forty (circa 387 B.C.) Plato returned to Athens and founded the Academy, the first institution of higher education in the Western world. His goal was relatively simple and

---

[1] The individual we know as "Plato" was in fact named "Aristocles." "Plato" is but a nickname given to him by his wrestling coach. To appreciate these many dimensions of Plato's life, simply think of "Hulk" Hogan as (a) the son of John F. Kennedy and (b) the most influential social and political theorist of our time.

[2] See "The Death of Socrates" (Philosophical Reading for Chapter 2).

straightforward: to create a better world by educating the leaders of tomorrow. A few years later (circa 375 B.C.) he composed his most famous dialogue, *The Republic.*

The Republic begins with an exchange about wealth, happiness, and morality.[3] Cephalus and his son Polemarchus argue that morality is a simple matter of telling the truth and paying one's debts. With slight sophistication, the definition becomes one of "giving each his due." When Socrates criticizes the definition, Thrasymachus proposes a new one: morality in the individual is simply self-interested behavior; in the state it is nothing more than the interest of the stronger party.

Socrates argues against Thrasymachus' position, attempting to show connections between morality, human excellence, and happiness. Adeimantus and Glaucon (Plato's older brothers and sole respondents for the remainder of the dialogue) restate the case for immoral behavior, challenging specifically Socrates' contention that morality brings happiness in this life.[4]

Presupposing a parallelism of individual and state, Socrates proceeds to answer the challenge by examining first the larger entity (the state), and only subsequently the smaller one (the individual). In the process he discusses the foundations of society, education, censorship, the status of women, the conduct of war, and the regulation of commerce. The result is a vision of an ideal society in which each individual plays a role commensurate with his/her own talents.[5] The rulers, Socrates argues, would be the people with the keenest vision of the greatest good (i.e., philosophers).[6] The relationship, of course, is between that which is good and that which is in the interest of a well-constructed society.

If we could see clearly, he continues, we would recognize that the same is true on an individual level as well. A proper understanding of the human self allows us to appreciate the intimate interconnections between morality and happiness. But such understanding may take us beyond the realm of the literal and the ordinary, and Socrates concludes his defense with a story known as "The Myth of Er." It is a story of reincarnation and karmic justice, with striking similarities to Hinduism and

---

[3] The term that Plato most frequently uses, δικαιοσύνη, is sufficiently broad to encompass individual, social, and religious behavior. Commonly translated as "justice," it may also be rendered as "doing right," "righteousness," or as here, "morality." The dialogue is subtitled περὶ δικαίου (Concerning Morality.)

[4] See "The Ring of Gyges" (Philosophical Reading for Chapter 4).

[5] Further discussion of Plato's views on these issues is included in the Introductory Essays for Chapters 4 and 5.

[6] It is in this context that Socrates presents "The Allegory of the Cave" (Philosophical Reading for Chapter 8).

Buddhism, as well as to the tales of people who have had near-death experiences in modern times.

'What I have to tell won't be like Odysseus' tale to Alcinous,'[1] I continued, 'but the story of a brave man, Er, son of Armenius, a native of Pamphylia. He was killed in battle, and when the dead were taken up on the tenth day the rest were already decomposing, but he was still quite sound; he was taken home and was to be buried on the twelfth day, and was lying on the funeral pyre, when he came to life again and told the story of what he had seen in the other world. He said that when his soul left his body it travelled in company with many others till they came to a wonderfully strange place, where there were, close to each other, two gaping chasms in the earth, and opposite and above them two other chasms in the sky. Between the chasms sat Judges, who having delivered judgment, ordered the just to take the right-hand road that led up through the sky, and fastened the evidence for the judgment in front of them, while they ordered the unjust, who also carried the evidence of all that they had done behind them, to take the left-hand road that led downwards. When Er came before them, they said that he was to be a messenger to men about the other world, and ordered him to listen to and watch all that went on in that place. He then saw the souls, when judgment had been passed on them, departing some by one of the heavenly and some by one of the earthly chasms; while by the other two chasms some souls rose out of the earth, stained with the dust of travel, and others descended from heaven, pure and clean. And the throng of souls arriving seemed to have come from a long journey, and turned aside gladly into the meadow and encamped there as for a festival; acquaintances exchanged greetings, and those from earth and those from heaven inquired each other's experiences. And those from earth told theirs with sorrow and tears, as they recalled all they had suffered and seen on their underground journey, which lasted a thousand years, while the others told

of the delights of heaven and of the wonderful beauty of what they had seen. It would take a long time to tell you the whole story, Glaucon, but the sum of it is this. For every wrong he has done to anyone a man must pay the penalty in turn, ten times for each, that is to say, once every hundred years, this being reckoned as the span of a man's life. He pays, therefore, tenfold retribution for each crime, and so for instance those who have been responsible for many deaths, by betraying state or army, or have cast others into slavery, or had a hand in any other crime, must pay tenfold in suffering for each offence. And correspondingly those who have done good and been just and god-fearing are rewarded in the same proportion. He told me too about infants who died as soon as they were born or who lived only a short time, but what he said is not worth recalling. And he described the even greater penalties and rewards of those who had honoured or dishonoured gods or parents or committed murder. For he said that he heard one soul ask another where Ardiaeus the Great was. (This Ardiaeus was the tyrant of a city in Pamphylia some thousand years before, who had killed his old father and elder brother and done many other wicked things, according to the story). "He has not come, and he never will," was the reply. "For this was one of the terrible things we saw. We were near the mouth of the chasm and about to go up through it after all our sufferings when we suddenly saw him and others, most of them tyrants, though there were a few who had behaved very wickedly in private life, whom the mouth would not receive when they thought they were going to pass through; for whenever anyone incurably wicked like this, or anyone

Plato, from *The Republic*, Third Revised Edition, translated by Desmond Lee, pp. 448–455. Copyright 1953, © 1974, 1987 by H. D. P. Lee. Reprinted with the permission of Penguin Books Ltd.

who had not paid the full penalty, tried to pass, it bellowed. There were some fierce and fiery-looking men standing by, who understood the sound, and thereupon seized some and led them away, while others like Ardiaeus they bound hand and foot and neck, flung them down and flayed them, and then impaled them on thorns by the roadside; and they told the passers-by the reason why this was done and said they were to be flung into Tartarus." And Er said that the fear that the voice would sound for them as they went up was the worst of all the many fears they experienced; and when they were allowed to pass in silence their joy was great.

'These, then, are the punishments and penalties and the corresponding rewards of the other world.'

*   *   *

The paragraph which follows gives, in brief and allusive form, a picture of the structure of the universe, in which the rings on the spindle-whorl are the orbits of the planets and the sphere of the fixed stars.

*   *   *

'After seven days spent in the meadow the souls had to set out again on the eighth and came in four days to a place from which they could see a shaft of light stretching from above straight through[2] earth and heaven, like a pillar, closely resembling a rainbow, only brighter and clearer; this they reached after a further day's journey and saw there in the middle of the light stretching from the heaven the ends of the bonds of it;[3] for this light is the bond of heaven and holds its whole circumference together, like the swifter of a trireme. And from these ends hangs the spindle of Necessity, which causes all the orbits to revolve; its shaft and its hook are of adamant, and its whorl a mixture of adamant and other substances. And the whorl is made in the following way. Its shape is like the ones we know; but from the description Er gave me we must suppose it to consist of a large whorl hollowed out, with a second, smaller one fitting exactly into it, the second being hollowed out to hold a third, the third a fourth, and so on up to a total of eight, like a nest of

bowls. For there were in all eight whorls, fitting one inside the other, with their rims showing as circles from above and forming the continuous surface of a single whorl round the shaft, which was driven straight through the middle of the eighth. The first and outermost whorl had the broadest rim; next broadest was the sixth, next the fourth, next the eighth, next the seventh, next the fifth, next the third, and last of all the second. And the rim of the largest and outermost was many-coloured, that of the seventh was the brightest, the eighth was illuminated by the seventh, from which it takes its colour, the second and fifth were similar to each other and yellower than the others, the third was the whitest, the fourth reddish and the sixth second in whiteness. The whole spindle revolved with a single motion, but within the movement of the whole the seven inner circles revolved slowly in the opposite direction to that of the whole, and of them the eighth moved fastest, and next fastest the seventh, sixth and fifth, which moved at the same speed; third in speed was the fourth, moving as it appeared to them with a counter-revolution; fourth was the third, and fifth the second. And the whole spindle turns in the lap of Necessity. And on the top of each circle stands a siren, which is carried round with it and utters a note of constant pitch, and the eight notes together make up a single scale. And round about at equal distances sit three other figures, each on a throne, the three Fates, daughters of Necessity, Lachesis, Clotho, and Atropos; their robes are white and their heads garlanded, and they sing to the sirens' music, Lachesis of things past, Clotho of things present, Atropos of things to come. And Clotho from time to time takes hold of the outermost rim of the spindle and helps to turn it, and in the same way Atropos turns the inner rims with her left hand, while Lachesis takes inner and outer rims with left and right hand alternately.

'On their arrival the souls had to go straight before Lachesis. And an Interpreter first marshalled them in order and then took from the lap of Lachesis a number of lots and patterns of life and, mounting on a high rostrum, proclaimed: "This is the word of Lachesis, maiden daughter of Necessity. Souls of a day, here you must begin another round of mortal life whose end is death. No Guardian Spirit will be allotted to you; you shall choose your own. And he on whom the lot falls first shall be the first to choose the life which then shall of necessity be his. Excellence knows no master; a man shall have more or less of her according to the value he sets on her. The fault lies not with God, but with the soul that makes the choice." With these words he threw the lots among them, and each picked up that which fell beside him, all except Er himself, who was forbidden to do so. And as each took up his lot he saw what number he had drawn. Then the Interpreter set before them on the ground the different patterns of life, far more in number than the souls who were to choose them. They were of every conceivable kind, animal and human. For there were tyrannies among them, some life-long, some falling in mid-career and ending in poverty, exile and beggary; there were lives of men famed for their good looks and strength and athletic prowess, or for their distinguished birth and family connections, there were lives of men with none of these claims to fame. And there was a similar choice of lives for women. There was no choice of quality of character since of necessity each soul must assume a character appropriate to its choice; but wealth and poverty, health and disease were all mixed in varying degrees in the lives to be chosen.

'Then comes the moment, my dear Glaucon, when everything is at stake. And that is why it should be our first care to abandon all other forms of knowledge, and seek and study that which will show us how to perceive and find the man who will give us the knowledge and ability to tell a good life from a bad one and always choose the better course so far as we can; we must reckon up all that we have said in this discussion of ours, weighing the arguments together and apart to find out how they affect the good life, and see what effects, good or ill, good looks have when accompanied by poverty or wealth or by different dispositions of character, and what again are the effects of the various blends of birth and rank, strength and weakness, cleverness

and stupidity, and all other qualities inborn or acquired. If we take all this into account and remember how the soul is constituted, we can choose between the worse life and the better, calling the one that leads us to become more unjust the worse, and the one that leads us to become more just the better. Everything else we can let go, for we have seen that this is the best choice both for living and dead. This belief we must retain with an iron grip when we enter the other world, so that we may be unmoved there by the temptation of wealth or other evils, and avoid falling into the life of a tyrant or other evil-doer and perpetrating unbearable evil and suffering worse, but may rather know how to choose the middle course, and avoid so far as we can, in this life and the next, the extremes on either hand. For this is the surest way to the highest human happiness.

'But to return. Er told us that the Interpreter then spoke as follows: "Even for the last comer, if he chooses wisely and lives strenuously, there is left a life with which he may be well content. Let him who chooses first look to his choice, and him who chooses last not despair." When he had spoken, the man with the first lot came forward and chose the greatest tyranny he could find. In his folly and greed he chose it without examining it fully, and so did not see that it was his fate to eat his children and suffer other horrors; when he examined it at leisure, he beat his breast and bewailed his choice, ignored the Interpreter's warning, and forgot that his misfortunes were his own fault, blaming fate and heaven and anything but himself. He was one of the souls who had come from heaven, having lived his previous life in a well-governed state, but having owed his goodness to habit and custom and not to philosophy; and indeed, broadly speaking, the majority of those who were caught in this way came from heaven without the discipline of suffering, while those who came from earth had suffered themselves and seen others suffer and were not so hasty in their choice. For this reason and because of the luck of the draw there was a general change of good for evil and evil for good. Yet it is true also that anyone who, during his earthly life, faithfully seeks wisdom and whose lot does not fall among the last may hope, if we may believe Er's tale, not only for happiness in this life but for a journey from this world to the next and back again that will not lie over the stony ground of the underworld but along the smooth road of heaven.

'And to see the souls choosing their lives was indeed a sight, Er said, a sight to move pity and laughter and wonder. For the most part they followed the habits of their former life. And so he saw the soul that had once been Orpheus[4] choose the life of a swan; it was unwilling to be born of a woman because it hated all women after its death at their hands. The soul of Thamyris[5] chose the life of a nightingale, and he saw a swan and other singing birds choose the life of a man. The twentieth soul to choose chose a lion's life; it was the soul of Ajax,[6] son of Telamon, which did not want to become a man, because it remembered the judgment of the arms. It was followed by Agamemnon,[7] who also because of his sufferings hated humanity and chose to be an eagle. And Atalanta's[8] turn came somewhere about the middle, and when she saw the great honours of an athlete's life she could not resist them and chose it. After her he saw Epeius[9] son of Panopeus, taking on the role of a skilled craftswoman, and right among the last the buffoon Thersites[10] putting on the form of an ape. And it so happened that it fell to the soul of Odysseus to choose last of all. The memory of his former sufferings had cured him of all ambition and he looked round for a long time to find the uneventful life of an ordinary man; at last he found it lying neglected by the others, and when he saw it he chose it with joy and said that had his lot fallen first he would have made the same choice. And there were many other changes from beast to man and beast to beast, the unjust changing into wild animals and the just into tame in every kind of interchange.

'And when all the souls had made their choice they went before Lachesis in the order of their lots, and she allotted to each its chosen Guardian Spirit, to guide it through life and fulfil its choice. And the Guardian Spirit first led it to Clotho, thus ratifying beneath her hand and whirling spindle the lot it had chosen; and after saluting her he led it next to where Atropos spins, so making the threads of its destiny irreversible; and then, without turning back, each soul came before the throne of Necessity and passing before it waited till all the others had done the same, when they proceeded together to the plain of Lethe through a terrible and stifling heat; for the land was without trees or any vegetation.

'In the evening they encamped by the Forgetful River, whose water no pitcher can hold. And all were compelled to drink a certain measure of its water; and those who had no wisdom to save them drank more than the measure. And as each man drank he forgot everything. They then went to sleep and when midnight came there was an earthquake and thunder, and like shooting stars they were all swept suddenly up and away, this way and that, to their birth. Er himself was forbidden to drink, and could not tell by what manner of means he returned to his body; but suddenly he opened his eyes and it was dawn and he was lying on the pyre.

'And so, my dear Glaucon, his tale was preserved from perishing, and, if we remember it, may well preserve us in turn, and we shall cross the river of Lethe safely and shall not defile our souls. This at any rate is my advice, that we should believe the soul to be immortal, capable of enduring all evil and all good, and always keep our feet on the upward way and pursue justice with wisdom. So we shall be at peace with the gods and with ourselves, both in our life here and when, like the victors in the games collecting their prizes, we receive our reward; and both in this life and in the thousand-year journey which I have described, all will be well with us.'

Notes

1. *Odyssey,* ix–xii, where Odysseus tells his adventures to Alcinous, king of Phaeacia. Proverbial of a long story. But there is also a play on words: Alci-noos means "stout-hearted," "brave," as Er was.

2. Perhaps "across."

3. Probably of the heaven, but possibly of the light: the Greek is ambiguous.

4. Singer and religious teacher, torn in pieces by Maenads, women followers of Dionysus.

5. Another singer, blinded because he challenged the Muses.

6. After the death of Achilles the Greeks adjudged his arms to Odysseus, in preference to Ajax. Ajax committed suicide in disappointment.

7. Victor of Troy, murdered by his wife Clytemnestra on his return.

8. Arcadian princess and huntress. Her suitors had to race with her and were killed if defeated.

9. Maker of the Trojan horse.

10. From the *Iliad.*

Review and Reflection

1. When, in your opinion, did the unidentified woman discussed in the Introductory Essay actually die? What was the cause of death? Defend your answer in terms of some of the concepts and positions presented in the various essays.

2. Do near-death experiences provide evidence of life after death? Why or why not?

3. What do you think Socrates might have had in mind when he suggested that the study of philosophy prepares a person for their own death? Do you agree? Why?

4. Represent, in your own words, Clarence Darrow's arguments concerning the possibility of death survival. Do you find the arguments convincing? Why?

5. Discuss, in order, Elisabeth Kübler-Ross's five stages of "death work." What sorts of things might we learn from listening to people who are confronting death?

6. Retell, in contemporary terms, Plato's Myth of Er. Do you find the story plausible? Are there valuable lessons for the modern mind?

Suggestions for Further Study

T. BEAUCHAMP and S. PERLIN. *Ethical Issues in Death and Dying.* Englewood Cliffs, NJ: Prentice-Hall, 1978.

VICTOR FRANKL. *Man's Search for Meaning.* New York: Washington Square Press, 1959.

ELISABETH KÜBLER-ROSS. *On Death and Dying.* New York: Macmillan, 1969.

RAYMOND MOODY. *Life After Life.* New York: Bantam, 1975.

RAYMOND MOODY. *Reflections on Life After Life.* New York: Bantam, 1977.

WALKER PERCY. *The Thanatos Syndrome.* New York: Farrar, Straus and Giroux, 1987.

PLATO. *The Last Days of Socrates [Euthyphro, The Apology, Crito, and Phaedo].* Translation by Hugh Tredennick. New York: Penguin, 1954.

MICHAEL SABOM. *Recollections of Death: A Medical Investigation.* Philadelphia: Harper and Row, 1982.

CHAPTER 3

Existentialism

Existentialism is a popular philosophical movement of the nineteenth and twentieth centuries which emphasizes human existence, freedom, and responsibility. It challenges traditional views concerning religion, purpose, and the meaning of life. In the process it reveals and explores the interconnectedness of epistemology, ontology, and value.

Introductory Essay

The **Introductory Essay** summarizes some of the basic ideas of Jean-Paul Sartre. This choice of focus was motivated by the following considerations: first, Sartre was the first philosopher to openly use the term "existentialism" in reference to his own views; second, his many contributions to philosophy, literature, and politics have made him one of the most studied philosophers of the twentieth century; and third, he offers one of the clearest and most concise statements of the position. According to Sartre, a human being is a unique creature. Humans, and humans alone, possess a special kind of consciousness that is the source of all meanings and values. Sartre accepts no god-given essence of a human being, but argues instead that a person may live an authentic life through the continuous performance of existential acts.

Philosophical Reading

The selection by **Hazel Barnes** builds upon, complements, and extends the philosophical position of Jean-Paul Sartre. Specifically, she attempts to delineate the assumptions and conditions of an existentialist ethics. Central to such a system is the notion that each person is a creator or chooser of values. Each moral decision is unpredictably unique. Thus, Barnes argues, moral decisions must be made by individuals without the assistance of objective rules or guarantees. As a result, existentialist ethics is necessarily hypothetical and based upon choice. It can be neither categorical nor *a priori.*

Scientific Reading

The selection by **Wayne Dyer** demonstrates clearly the empirical consequences associated with the philosophy of existentialism. Specifically, Dyer applies Sartre's concept of freedom to the analysis and understanding of human emotions. He reiterates Sartre's position from *Being and Nothingness:* human beings can control their emotions, rather than be controlled by them. We are happy or sad according to our own choosing. Moreover, emotional behavior is but one of the available choices. One has the freedom to choose a different response.

Literary Readings

Albert Camus uses the myth of Sisyphus to address philosophical issues of freedom, absurdity, meaninglessness, and futile toil. Sisyphus is an existential hero whose life represents the human predicament. His life may appear absurd and pointless. There does not seem to be any way in which his situation can be substantially improved. Nonetheless, Camus argues, there is hope: even the life of Sisyphus can be made worthwhile.

The selection by **Friedrich Nietzsche** is a poetic expression of his philosophical solution to the existential dilemma. Nietzsche believes that all meanings disappear when a person realizes that "God is dead." Something must be invented to fill this vacuum. Nietzsche's answer to the meaninglessness of existence concerns the creation of a superman. To do this, a human must go through three metamorphoses: the camel (hard work), the lion (courage), and the child (innovation).

Existentialism

ASHOK K. MALHOTRA

Søren Kierkegaard, a nineteenth-century Danish philosopher, tells the story of a man so absent-minded and unaware of his own existence that he awakens one morning to find that he is dead. What does Kierkegaard wish to convey through his story? Is it possible for us to "wake up" and find ourselves dead? Like this "man," most of us are so caught up in fulfilling roles assigned to us by family, religion, and society that we never exercise our human freedom to choose our own goals or direct our own lives. By unreflectively following society's values, we may discover too late that we have been "dead" all along, never having experienced our human existence or knowing what it means to be a human being.

Although various thinkers have contributed to existentialism, it is Jean-Paul Sartre, a French philosopher and playwright, who popularized the movement in Europe and America. While Sartre was not the first philosopher to be concerned with the nature of human existence, he was the first to label his philosophy "existentialism." The present chapter will follow the basic outline developed by Sartre, but it is important to note that different thinkers develop even similar ideas in radically different ways. For Kierkegaard, Jaspers, and Marcel, existentialism is a *theistic* position (i.e., it includes a concept of God as well as various assumptions about the implications for human life). For Heidegger, Merleau-Ponty, Camus, and Sartre, existentialism is an *atheistic* position (i.e., it is built on a foundation that deliberately excludes divine beings and other external sources of value and meaning).

Sartre's Existentialism: A Summary

1. Philosophy is anthropocentric: its central concern is human existence.

2. A human being is a special kind of *consciousness* (being-for-itself). Everything else is *matter* (being-in-itself).

3. A human being has no God-given essence: a human being first exists and then creates his/her essence. Therefore, in a human being, existence precedes essence.

4. A human being is absolutely free and absolutely responsible.

5. Anguish is the result of this absolute freedom and absolute responsibility. Most human beings avoid anguish by falling into bad-faith or self-deception.

6. Human existence is absurd and unjustified. Therefore, the goal of a human being is to justify his/her existence.

Philosophy Is Anthropocentric

The focus of all existential philosophy is the careful study of the human being. Existentialists regard human existence as infinitely rich, dense, and mysterious. In fact, they insist that human existence and its meaning constitute everything worth discussing in philosophy. Questions that relate to the physical world, God, or society are regarded as "games" that make sense only in the context of the human condition.

Human Beings Are Unique

This special focus on human existence is justified in terms of the unique place that humans occupy in the universe. Everything else makes sense only in reference to a human being. Sartre created the phrase *being-for-itself* to designate being of a human person. He contrasts *being-for-itself* with *being-in-itself* (i.e., the material world). The universe (reality) manifests itself through these two aspects of *being-for-itself* and *being-in-itself.*

It will be helpful to think of *being-in-itself* as the nonconscious physical world. Sartre claims that this nonconscious material universe is uncreated by God, is absurd, and is eternally superfluous: It exists without intrinsic or extrinsic purpose. It is there for absolutely no reason. Sartre uses minimalist phrases to describe what he perceives as the purposelessness of *being-in-itself:* "it is," "it is in itself," and "it is what it is." These descriptions of *being-in-itself* tell us that it is nothing more than an enormous presence. You cannot deny that it is there, but there is nothing special or unique about it. This description of reality is a direct attack on the Christian view, which regards existence as something special. Sartre is telling us that there is nothing sacred about the physical universe. *Being-in-itself* functions merely as a point of contrast to the being of a human, that is, *being-for-itself.*

The *for-itself* that characterizes a human's being is identified with consciousness. Sartre describes *being-for-itself* as: "it is not," "it is not in itself," and "it is not what it is and it is what it is not." The phrases are clearly intended as contrasts to the descriptions of *being-in-itself.* These apparently strange descriptions imply that human consciousness is a non-substantial being that lacks self and is in constant pursuit of a self. Sartre calls our inherent lack of self "nothingness." This identification of our being with negativity is of fundamental importance, for in it lies the individual's uniqueness. Because a human being is burdened neither with essence nor self, that being is free to fashion from its existence any life it chooses. A human's intrinsic nothingness, therefore, is the creative source or wellspring from which all human possibilities can be realized. What is implied in the preceding discussion is that humans are the only beings in the universe in whom existence comes before essence.

EXISTENCE PRECEDES ESSENCE

Sartre clarifies his phrase "existence precedes essence" by critiquing the positions of philosophers who believe that each human is born with an innate self. He considers first the notion that a human is an idea realized by God's intelligence. According to this view, when a human comes into being, his/her essence has already been defined by God. Like an artist, God constructs a human person from a predetermined concept or idea. Those who hold this view maintain that a human is a being with a divine essence.

The second target of Sartre's criticism are eighteenth-century philosophers who argued for the existence of a universal human nature. They assumed that each of us is born with similar qualities and may be described in like terms.

In sharp contrast to these views, which have been the prevailing ones in Western philosophy, Sartre asserts that a person is a being for whom existence comes before essence. As an atheist, Sartre rejects the notion that a human has divine essence. He also rejects the idea that a human shares a universal nature with other human beings. If a human then is a mere existence devoid of essence, his/her reality can be correctly characterized as a "nothingness." It is only through its consciousness that a human being can come to understand itself, and through its acts that it can create a self. Thus it is only the totality of a person's acts which constitutes his/her essence. Since humans are free to choose to be other than what they are at any given moment, one's essence is always a "becoming"; it is never complete.

A HUMAN BEING IS FREEDOM

For Sartre, freedom is inseparable from the being of a human. He describes this freedom as *openness, separation, nihilation, projection, transcendence,* and *choice.* These terms convey two complementary meanings: *Openness, separation,* and *nihilation* refer to the fact that a human being lacks an essence or self, while *projection, transcendence,* and *choice* indicate the human desire for a substantial self. Human freedom is never identical with a self, but is capable of projecting and realizing an essence in the future. Thus a human being unencumbered by a predetermined nature is free to choose what he/she wishes to become.

Moreover, human reality is a condemned freedom: an individual is *not free not to be free.* Because of this paradoxical nature of human reality, no one can escape from his/her freedom. Moreover, human beings are *absolutely* free. This rather radical notion implies that a human's freedom is unrestricted.

Sartre's view is a direct challenge to the traditional belief that human freedom is limited by internal hindrances (e.g., emotions and motives) and by external obstructions (e.g., social and political institutions).

Consider first the internal hindrances. Many psychologists regard emotions and motives as restrictions to freedom. Specifically, they regard emotions and motives as psychic entities that determine a person's actions and thus dictate behavior over which an individual has little or no control.

Sartre mounts a two-tiered attack against this deterministic model. First, he replaces this materialistic concept of the mind with his concept of the *for-itself.* Since the *for-itself* is nothingness, it can have no psychic content. Thus, emotions and motives must lie outside the subjectivity of human consciousness. Second, Sartre reinterprets the nature of the emotions, arguing that they are not subjective entities but merely "ways of behaving."

Suppose, for example, that we have been fired from a high-paying job. As a result, we face a situation in the social world which requires an immediate response or action. We are free to adopt one of the three responses: emotional, rational, or indifferent. Whatever we choose constitutes a form of coping behavior, and it is we alone who have chosen it. When we choose to respond emotionally we discriminate even further by reacting to the occasion with joy, fear, or sadness. The loss of our job as a situation in the world has no meaning beyond that which we impart to it. Our emotional behavior, like other behaviors, has significance only within the framework of our projected goals. Our goals are freely chosen, and our emotions are just as freely adopted by us as modes of behavior. Therefore, Sartre concludes, there exist no internal hindrances to freedom.

Turning now to external restrictions, it is generally believed that past occurrences or other people may constitute hindrances to our freedom. When we are labeled, for example, as shy, intellectual, or ugly by others, it may appear that our freedom is curtailed. But Sartre argues that it is we ourselves who weigh and accept "the other's" opinion though we are equally free to disregard these judgments. It is therefore our freedom which ultimately decides to accept, reject, or ignore "the other's" evaluation. Hence a human's freedom is unrestricted; consequently, human reality is absolutely free.

FREEDOM AND RESPONSIBILITY

If there exist no psychological or social barriers to freedom, who then is responsible for our way of being? Since we alone choose for ourselves, it is we alone who are responsible for everything we become. Whether we are cowardly or heroic, optimistic or pessimistic, it is we who choose these behaviors and are responsible for our lifestyle. Thus a human being is a creature without excuses.

But our responsibility extends far beyond this personal dimension; it reaches other human beings as well. No act is isolated. Each has repercussions for the entire human race, for when we choose to act in response to our unique situation we create an image of man/woman that we desire to have universally accepted. By deciding a particular course of action, though it arises out of our own special situation, we set an example that we want others to approve and perhaps follow. Not only are we responsible for our own individuality, but for the totality of humankind as well. Such awesome and total responsibility, however, is more than an individual is usually ready to bear. Most people try to avoid the painful anguish that awareness of their responsibility entails, by falling into some kind of *bad-faith* or *self-deception.*

FREEDOM AND SELF-DECEPTION

To escape freedom and responsibility, a human being in *bad-faith* lies to him/herself. One convinces oneself that one is unfree by citing God, heredity, environment, or upbringing as determinants of one's actions and way of being. By using these as excuses, the individual attempts to shift the burden of responsibility to something other than him/herself. Sartre criticizes those philosophers, psychologists, and theologians who, by positing some form of determinism—whether Freudian, Marxist, religious, or scientific—hide the painful truth that the individual alone is responsible for his/her actions. Belief in God, like belief in a universal human nature, is little more than yearning for an essence underlying existence. To live a life of *non-self-deception,* on the other hand, is to recognize that human reality is free, that existence precedes essence, and that human actions cannot be excused by rationalization.

JUSTIFICATION OF EXISTENCE

What further consequences arise from the realization of freedom? For the existentialists, freedom is both a curse and a blessing. Human life has no inherent justification. We confront our lives like an empty script whose destiny is yet to be written. Although we face life without God, abandoned and alone in the universe, we realize that our absolute freedom can be the creative source of all values. With no intrinsic meaning in life, the human being is free to create his/her own destiny. The justification of existence then becomes the primary focus of an individual's endeavor.

Attempts to justify human existence can take both erroneous and authentic forms. An incorrect attempt is made by those who believe, for example,

that they are born with a special purpose and therefore have a *right* to exist. For them, this sense of right is so strong that the meaninglessness of their existence is quickly forgotten. They regard themselves as having been created by God. Once their essence is thus established, their right to exist becomes sacred. Moreover, this arrogant faith succeeds in convincing them that their lives are part of a rational scheme, and are therefore essential and justified. Since this attempt to justify one's life presumes that essence precedes existence, it is regarded by Sartre as *inauthentic.*

What then can we do to make sense of our lives? Sartre's existentialism does not give us a solution, but brings us to the awareness of our unique creative potential. The awareness of one's freedom and its total engagement in action can be conducive to the achievement of an authentic or meaningful life. *Authenticity* is neither a part nor an essence of an act, nor a number of special acts. It should be understood rather in terms of conditions which *any* act must satisfy to be considered authentic: awareness of freedom, respect for the freedom of others, total commitment to a particular cause or action, and the acceptance of responsibility by the performer. An action that satisfies these conditions may be regarded as authentic. A person who lives a life performing actions fulfilling such conditions lives an authentic or meaningful life. Sartre's existentialism does not commend a special class of acts that are authentic by nature, but leaves us free to choose our own acts which we as individuals can make authentic.

Much has been written about the dehumanizing influence of modern technology and the impersonal character of many of society's religious, political, economic, and educational institutions. This dehumanization is challenged by Sartre's existentialism, for his is a view that helps us look at ourselves not as machines or objects, but as free creative beings, capable of individual commitment. Sartre's existentialism compels us to reflect upon our human condition and, ultimately, invites us to regain our lost human dignity.

The Far Side of Despair

HAZEL BARNES

Hazel E. Barnes is distinguished Professor Emerita of Philosophy at the University of Colorado. Her many influential writings concerning existentialism include *Sartre and Flaubert* and *An Existentialist Ethics,* from which the present selection is edited. Additionally, she is known for her translations of Jean-Paul Sartre's *Being and Nothingness* and *Search for a Method.*

It is generally assumed that a lack of higher meaning or over-all purpose in the Universe is a terribly bad thing. Even Sartre has remarked that it would be much better if God the Father existed. Our forlornness is due to our discovery that He is not there. It is worthwhile to ask ourselves just what this hypothesis of higher meaning and purpose really does and has meant to man and why he has felt the necessity to project it. Most of the time I believe it has been bound up with the hope for immortality. Certainly in traditional Christianity, as in any religion which promises a personal afterlife, the significant part of the idea of historical development is not that God and His Universe are infinitely good and eternal but that the individual shares in this destiny. Most important of all for our present selves is the thought that the specific role we play in this far future is determined by the way we conduct ourselves here and now. This life on earth is our trial and test, and the grade we receive indicates the eternal class we go into. The undeniable positive element here is the conviction that what we do matters forever. If taken literally—or as near to literally as today's fundamentalist is willing to take it—the pragmatic value of this doctrine is overwhelming. Meaning, purpose, and progress toward some definite destination are clearly defined and omnipresent. The catch is that the more concrete and specific the positive promise, the darker the negative side. The Medieval Heaven gains part of its shining light from the contrast with the smoky darkness of the Hell which lies below it. "Here pity or here piety must die," says Dante; and I, for one, would at this point bid piety a hasty adieu. A God who would for eternity subject even one person to horrors surpassing those of Buchenwald, a Creator who would create souls capable of deserving such punishment seems to me to echo man's ignoble desire for vengeance more than his aspirations for an understanding Justice. Of course very few people today believe in everlasting punishment, and it is easy to see why. Only the most hardened sinner could bear to live with this sort of anticipation for any of his acquaintances—let alone the fear of being condemned himself.

In a more acceptable form, Christianity for today's average believer stresses the mercy of God. Although it may not be put in quite this way, the idea seems to be that since God views each life from within, He sees each man's good intentions. "*Tout comprendre, c'est tout pardonner.*" Hell isn't left quite empty, but like the Greeks' realm of Hades, it is reserved for the really great sinners—like Hitler, perhaps—who are condemned by almost everybody and sufficiently remote so as not to concern us. Heaven and Hell are less concrete and precisely located than they used to be. If one gets liberal enough in his Christian commitment, he may think

Hazel Barnes, "The Far Side of Despair" from *An Existentialist Ethics,* pp. 102–118. Reprinted with the permission of the author and The University of Chicago Press.

of Heaven as simply the eternal consciousness of God's presence and Hell as the painful awareness of His absence. At this point, even if individual immortality is not lost, we are in danger of floating off into a vague pantheism which is no longer specifically Christian. In itself, this makes no difference for our present discussion. The issue is not specifically between existentialism and Christianity. Yet we may note that the more the old idea of Heaven and Hell is subjected to ethical purification and intellectual criticism, the feebler becomes any specific hypothesis as to the meaning and ultimate goal of the individual life. If Christianity reaches the point of no longer postulating any afterlife for the specific person, then we may well ask what remains of what centuries have found most valuable—the infinite value of every human soul, its eternal existence, and its freedom of choice to determine the quality of that existence.

Not all hypotheses of the existence of a higher meaning necessarily postulate eternal life for the individual consciousness, whether separate or absorbed in some ultimate Unity. Aristotelianism does not—despite the First Cause, the Unmoved Mover which thinks itself and by its very presence draws all other forms upward toward pure Thought. The Hebrew prophets, too, speak of no future life for man. It is in the present that man must walk humbly and righteously in the sight of the Just God, who will champion those whose cause is right. These interpretations of reality are not oriented toward any eternal Future, but they do serve as some sort of absolute guarantee and point of reference. If the Universe is rationally organized, whether ordered by a Deist Creator, or simply sustained by an Unmoved Mover, it at least serves as a mirror for man wherein he can find himself and his proper place. If the order of the Universe both corresponds to human reason and exists independently of it, one may conclude, at the very least, that Reason is our essence and guide, that to develop it to its greatest extent is our highest good. It is an easy step from there to the notion that Reason may discover absolutes in the ethical sphere as well and that

the ultimate attainment of rationality will be a culmination of all that is best in ourselves and a steadfast bond between us and the outside world. Similarly, the belief that the structure of things is permeated with the spirit of Justice offers a sustenance and guarantee to man which come from outside himself. Not only will God reward the Just. He furnishes the assurance that we *ought* to be just and that we may know what Justice is.

Existentialism rejects all of these blandishments. In the early writing of French existentialists, man's recognition that he stood alone in an irrational world without God was expressed in an attitude in which revolt and despair were equally mingled. Things ought not to be this way, was the cry. We will never accept our fate with resignation, but we will live it—in our own way—against the Universe. At the end of *The Flies*,[1] Orestes declares: "On the far side of despair, life begins." But the life which was to start involved no change in the view of things which precipitated Orestes' self-chosen exile. Camus said that his thought had gone beyond what he formulated early in *The Myth of Sisyphus,* but he added that he had never renounced the vision of the absurd which led him to ask, "Can I live without appeal? Can Thought live in this desert?" It is important not to forget this tragic vision of man against the Universe. Humanistic existentialism finds no divine presence, no ingrained higher meaning, no reassuring Absolute. At the same time, no humanistic existentialist will allow that the only alternative is despair and irresponsibility. Camus has pointed out the fallacy involved in leaping from the premise "The Universe has no higher meaning" to the conclusion, "Therefore my life is not worth living." The individual life may have an intrinsic value, both to the one who lives it and to those in the sphere of his influence, whether the Universe knows what it is doing or not.

Merleau Ponty has remarked, "Life makes no sense, but it is ours to make sense of." In a popular lecture, Sartre expressed somewhat the same idea, explaining in simple terms both what he means by creating or "inventing" values and by value itself.

To say that we invent values means nothing except this: life has no meaning a priori. Before you live it, life is nothing, but it is for you to give it a meaning. Value is nothing other than this meaning which you choose.[2]

In *Being and Nothingness* Sartre defined the ontological status of value as "beyond being" and as "the lacked." "Value is the self insofar as the self haunts the heart of the for-itself as that for which the for-itself is."[3] This definition sounds more negative, but it is not really so. Or if it is negative, it is the same sort of negativity which allowed Plato to describe love as the reaching out toward what one does not possess—even if the desire is only for the continued future possession of what is already within one's grasp. Value for Sartre corresponds to the ideal full moon by which one judges the present form of light to be only a crescent. Value is "the missing totality toward which a being makes itself be."[4] Sartre in these passages makes no clear distinction between "meaning" and "value." In other contexts, it seems that he would have to do so. When it comes to the reasons and motives for living, he is probably right in recognizing that value and meaning become inextricable. Both are included in our word "significance." Value and meaning are subjective structures which one imposes upon the world. They cannot, of course, exist independently of the world.

In contrasting traditional and existentialist attitudes toward the question of the meaning of life, I should like to use a homely example as an illustration. Let us imagine reality to have the shape of a gigantic Chinese checkerboard—without even the logically arranged spacing of the regularly shaped holes as in the usual game board, and with various-sized marbles, only some of which will fit into the spaces provided. The traditional attitude of religion and philosophy has been that we faced two alternatives. Theological and rational positions have assumed that there exists some correct pattern, impressed into the board itself, which can be discovered and which will then show us how we may satisfactorily and correctly arrange the piles of mar-

bles near us. They have assumed—and so have the Nihilists—that if there is no such pattern, then there is no reason to play at all. If there is no motive for making a particular pattern, they have concluded that one might as well destroy the patterns set up by others or commit suicide. Existentialism holds that there is a third possibility. There is no pre-existing pattern. No amount of delving into the structure of the board will reveal one inscribed there in matter. Nor is it sensible to hope for some nonmaterial force which might magnetically draw the marbles into their correct position if we put ourselves in touch with such a power by prayer or drugs or any other device which man might think of. But while this lack deprives man of guide and certain goal, it leaves him free to create his own pattern. It is true that there is no external model according to which one may pronounce the new pattern good or bad, better or worse. There are only the individual judgments by him who makes it and by those who behold it, and these need not agree. If the maker finds value in his own creation, if the process of making is satisfying, if the end result compares sufficiently favorably with the intention, then the pattern *has* value and the individual life has been worthwhile. I must quickly add that no such pattern exists alone. Although its unique form and color remain distinctly perceptible, it is intermeshed with the edges of the patterns of others—like the design of a paisley print. The satisfaction in a life may well result in large part from the sense that these intermeshings have positive significance for the individual pattern. There is another kind of satisfaction—that which comes from the knowledge that other persons have declared one's pattern good. Still a third derives from the realization that what one has done has helped make it easier for others to live patterns intrinsically satisfying to them.

That a positive value is present in experiencing a delight in what one has created and in the approval of others cannot be denied. For many people this is not enough. The sense that there is something missing is sufficient to undermine any quiet content with what one has. We hear most frequently three basic complaints, and these refer respectively to (1) the starting point, (2) the here and now, and (3) the farther on. First, there is the feeling that we need some sort of external archetype or measuring stick. Existentialism admits that there is nothing of the sort and that life is harder without it. Yet we may well ask whether the privilege of having such an authority would not come at too high a price, and cost more than it is worth. Pragmatically, the over-all destiny and purpose of the Universe play a small part in the daily projects of Western man—with the possible exception of those remaining fundamentalists who still take the promise of Heaven and Hell quite literally. Mostly it is there as a kind of consolation at moments of failure, cheering our discouragement with the idea that things may be better sometime in a way that we cannot begin to comprehend. I do not deny the psychic refreshment of such comfort. But if the belief in any such authority and plan is sufficiently specific to be more than a proud hope, it must be restrictive as well. If man can be sure that he is right by any nonhuman standard, then his humanity is strictly confined by the nonhuman. He is not free to bring anything new into the world. His possibilities are those of the slave or the well-bred child. Higher meaning is itself a limitation for a being-who-is-a-process. Such a future is not open but prescribed. Man as a tiny being in an impersonal world may be without importance from the theoretical but nonexistent point of view of an omniscient objective observer. Man in the theological framework of the medieval man-centered Universe has only the dignity of the child, who must regulate his life by the rules laid down by adults. The human adventure becomes a conducted tour. It is in this sense that I seriously question the sincerity or the wisdom of Sartre's statement that it would be better if God the Father existed. The time has come for man to leave his parents and to live in his own right by his own judgments.

The second disturbing aspect of a life of self-created patterns emerges when we compare ourselves with our fellow man. Obviously some people are satisfied with patterns which others regard as deplorable. Can we allow this chaos of judgments and still cling to the belief in the positive value of whatever patterns we ourselves have made? Is the result not such an anarchy of the arbitrary that to speak of pattern at all is nonsense? Here existentialism begins by saying that up to a point, arbitrariness, inconsistency, and the simultaneous existence of divergent value systems are not to be lamented but welcomed. The creative freedom to choose and structure one's own pattern would be worthless if we were to agree that we would all work in the same way toward the same end. Just as we expect persons to differ in their specific projects, so we should allow for those individual over-all orientations which bestow upon the project its significance and which are, in turn, colored by it. Sartre has declared that the creation of a value system by which one is willing to live and to judge one's life is man's most important creative enterprise. This means more than the working out of standards of right and wrong and the regulation of one's own demands in the light of our relations with others. It involves the whole context of what we might call "the style" of a life—not just the moral but the aesthetic, the temperamental—everything which goes to make up the personality which continues, with varying degrees of modification, until death and which even then will leave behind it an objectified "Self for Others." Every such life is unique, no matter how hard the one who lives it may have tried to mold himself after the pattern of his contemporaries. Existentialism prizes this uniqueness and resists all attempts to reduce it to the lowest possible minimum. Existentialism recognizes and exults in the fact that since everyone *is* a point of view, there is no more possibility of all persons becoming the same than there is of reducing to one perspective the views of two people looking at a landscape from different spots.

Someone will object that this is exactly what is wrong with existentialism—that it is nothing but a chaos of arbitrary outlooks and that if uniqueness is cherished and justified, then no ethics or supraindividual value system can exist. This book is, of course, an attempt to show that chaotic relativism is not the only alternative. Let us admit, however, that an existentialist ethics is chosen, that it is not a priori. Is this any reason for finding it untenable? As we have seen, any ethics is hypothetical, not categorical. So are most human activities. The man who values freedom of movement does not insist that everyone must go where he goes. It is the possibility of choice which he holds as the absolute, not the specific choice himself.

The most difficult aspect of the problem comes when we ask whether this conclusion justifies our waiving those fundamental principles which we have discovered to be the conditions of an existentialist ethics. Could our ethics, for example, allow the choice of an individual value system which attached positive values to bad faith? Or action based on the premise that we are not free and responsible? Or that we may consider and treat the Other as being merely object, not subject? Or that people *are* to be identified with the accidents of their situations?

No. No, quite simply because both types of self-realization, which must be the culminating value embracing all values, depend upon the recognition that man is a free consciousness. The other premises follow as corollaries. At first thought there might appear to be one exception. I don't think that we need to argue again the claim that an existentialist ethics cannot accept bad faith or the attempt to deny one's responsibility for one's own life. Is the same true with regard to our attitude toward others? In the chapter on guilt, I tried to show that respectful acknowledgment for other people as free subjects and recognition of our responsibility for them is an inevitable part of good faith and that guilt stems from the attempt to deny it. In that discussion, I associated ethical responsibility with self-realization in the over-all pattern of a life, i.e., with self-realization in being. It seems, however, that in the spontaneous realization of oneself as free consciousness there might easily be an assertion which would affront this Other's freedom as the result of a deliberate realization that one did not have to be ethical, that one was free not to act by any regula-

tive, temporal demand. Even more probably, one's fullest realization of freedom might involve the deliberate choice to demonstrate its power over the Other taken as object. One cannot deny that there is a positive immediate value for the acting consciousness at this point. Can the ethical category apply at all in an experience which involves a separation from the usual temporal considerations? Moreover, if we allow that this kind of bad faith may still be called ethical, we seem to undermine the entire structure of an ethics in good faith.

Depending on the situation, we find either an easy answer or a hard one. In some instances there is merely a conflict of ethical principles such as we are used to encounter in any traditional ethics. We may find an analogy in the lie. I do not see how any ethics could—abstractly or universally—classify a lie as anything but a disvalue. Ethical systems always claim to have some firm connection with reality (regardless of what, specifically, reality is taken to be). The lie tends to undermine such connections. To lie is wrong because it is calculated to promote a disvalue which undermines the ethical system itself. Yet we are all aware that there are innumerable occasions when the lie, even if it does blur connections with reality, is nevertheless the ethical choice; for in certain specific cases, the lie results in promoting other and more intense vital values. I would maintain here that some sort of hedonistic calculus is inevitable. The lie retains its minus quality as disvalue. The sum of the resulting value may pragmatically be possible only because of the lie. It would be greater if it could be effected by a method not involving the lie.

We have observed already that some degree of Original Sin is inevitable in human relations. Even in a clear ethical choice, there may be a conflict of values which can be resolved only by acting against the freedom of someone else. Obviously there are many instances when one's own freedom seems to exert the greater claim. In these situations there is no bad faith. One does not pretend that the Other is not a free subject or that one is not responsible for one's own actions. One realizes only that in pursuing the greater good, lesser values are sacrificed. The choice is impure ethically but justifiable. An example would be the killing of a guard in order to save a dozen prisoners condemned by an enemy tribunal in wartime. Such ethical choices involve what Camus called "calculated culpability." The term suggests that it would find a place only in reflective self-realization, but I believe that such acts can be performed nonreflectively; it is the later judgment of them which is reflective.

When Sartre says that we cannot describe the authentic man inasmuch as he freely makes himself, we can agree only with reservations. It is true that we cannot predict in advance the unique style of his life or the specific ordering of his freely created hierarchy of values. Yet we can declare in advance certain limits within which he must choose if his life is to remain authentic. We are on still firmer ground if we move from "authentic" to "ethical."

Despite these qualifications, I do not want to play down the dangerous aspect of the existentialist view that each one is a creator as he is a chooser of values. It is perilous as is any resolve to venture upon new ways of thinking and acting. To put everything into question is always a risk, no matter how firmly we determine that our answers will be responsible ones. It may be interesting to note that the New Theologians have arrived at a position which, while radically different in its foundation, places fully as much emphasis on the unpredictable uniqueness of each moral decision which the individuals must make and on the necessity of choosing without objective rules or guarantees. Bishop Robinson says of his "theonomous" ethics (in contrast to "heteronomous" or "autonomous"), "It is, of course, a highly dangerous ethic and the representative of supranaturalist legalism will, like the Pharisees, always fear it. Yet I believe it is the only ethic for 'man come of age.' "[5] Theonomous ethics takes its point of departure from St. Augustine's directive, "Love God, and do as you will." As Robinson points out, these words "were never safe." Tillich speaks of an "ethics of kairos," an "existential" or "situational" ethics, in which a person, secure in

that external Love which is his relation to Being, mediates "the meeting with the eternal in the temporal." The New Theologians are in complete harmony with humanistic existentialism in declaring that there are no rules, codes, or commandments which may not be set aside by the authentic choice of an individual who judges in the light of his vision of new and greater possibilities for human freedom in-the-world. The New Theologian's reliance on Love and man's ability to *know* that this love is of God purports to introduce an assurance that one is right, albeit a subjective one. To my mind it is even more open to self-deception than the humanistic appeal to the authentic ethical choice without God. The New Theologian's choice is certainly no more objective, and it seems to rest finally on an irrationalism which makes its own claim to being absolute.

The absence of any discernible higher meaning in the Universe takes on a new and special significance when we confront the future, not merely my own but that of the world as a whole. What difference does it make, some will ask, whether I fashion one kind of pattern rather than another or none at all? All patterns will be blotted out as though they had never been. If this world is all, how can one attach any significance whatsoever to the individual life in the face of the immensity of space, the staggering infinity of Time? "We are sick with space!" cries Robert Frost. The French keep reminding us of the futility of all endeavor "from the point of view of Sirius." Again, I feel that we suffer still from Christianity's insistence that all of us together and the Universe with us are going somewhere definite and that the destination bestows its meaning on the present mile of the journey. Deprived of this forward voyaging, we find no delight in the nonpurposeful development of an impersonal cosmos which has no prearranged destination. Whether this drifting Universe will eventually become cold and lifeless, or whether there will occur once again—or many times—the coming together of organized matter and the appearance of other forms of consciousness, it seems unlikely that man will be remembered any more than we have reason to think that all of this present world of matter was put here for his express benefit.

Is there any reason *why* we should try to adopt the point of view of Sirius? We should realize that observation of a dead planet through a telescope is neither more or less true as a vision of the Universe than is the examination of living organisms through a microscope. To see the big without the small is to exclude much of reality just as surely as to stay within the limits of the microscopic. If there is a falsification of boundaries at the one end, there is a blurring of details and elimination of foreground at the other. William James has commented that inasmuch as death comes at the end to cut off all human projects, every life is finally a failure. The point of view of Sirius reveals the same message on the cosmic scale. Yet if it were possible for one to stand on Sirius at the instant before the final disappearance of all life, that moment of conclusion would be no more real or significant than any one of the moments preceding it. If there is an absolute negative quality in the absence of what will not be, then there is a corresponding positive value in what will have been. This last awareness might just as well take pride in what had been there as despair in the knowledge that it will no longer be. One does not choose to eat something bitter today simply because tomorrow it will make no difference which food one has chosen. The addition of positive moments does not add up to zero even if the time arrives when nothing more is added to the series. One might say that there is never any adding up of the sum, but this is not quite true. The new digits carry the weight of those which have gone before.

It is illogical to conclude that human values and meanings are unreal and of no importance simply because they do not originate in the structure of the nonhuman Universe. It is enough that the world serves to support these subjective structures for the consciousness which lives them. At the same time it is only natural that an individual man, whose being is a self-projection, should rebel at the prospect of seeing his projects suddenly brought to a stop. If the patterns and meanings which a consciousness creates were restricted to those experiences which we can live directly, then despair would in truth seem to be our only proper response. But man's being is that of a creature who is always about-to-be. In a peculiar sense also, he is, in his being, always outside or beyond himself, out there in the objects of his intentions or—more accurately—in his projects in the world. An impersonal Universe cannot sustain these subjective structures. But we do not exist in an impersonal Universe. We live in a human world where multitudes of other consciousnesses are ceaselessly imposing their meanings upon Being-in-itself and confronting the projects which I have introduced. It is in the future of these intermeshed human activities that I most fully transcend myself. In so far as "I" have carved out my being in this human world, "I" go on existing in its future.

What sort of world future does humanistic existentialism envision as the framework of its projections? Confronting the present scientific interpretations of the Universe, an existentialism which will not appeal to God may consistently follow either of two alternatives. Each rests upon a hypothesis. While the distant future may confirm one or the other, contemporary man must recognize that his rational choice is necessarily accompanied by some degree of faith or what William James calls "over-belief." We must live by a view of things which goes beyond our confirmable knowledge since our choice involves to some degree an attempt to predict the future.

The first alternative assumes that the human condition will not be significantly altered. By "human condition" I refer to those circumstances of man's being which—at least at this stage of the evolution of *Homo sapiens*—are inseparable from any human existence: man's finiteness and his mortality, the fact that his mind is dependent upon a body, that his nervous system responds to stimuli in terms of both physical and mental pain and pleasure. These are but a few of the obvious factors. On this hypothesis, we would include certain things which perhaps are more debatable: that the possibilities of communication between consciousness are forever fixed, that the quantity of man's knowledge will increase but not the definition of what we call "knowing." To call the human condition immutable is to state that man will undergo no further existential changes. Its corollary is the view that while science may be expected to continue to develop both theoretically and technologically, future discoveries will not essentially alter our appraisal of the Universe so far as man's relations with it are concerned. This is the position which until now existentialist philosophers have all assumed, at least implicitly. We must be careful not to restrict it too narrowly or make it too wholly negative. For while the *human condition* will never change, the view still holds that there is no fixed *human nature*. Sartre and de Beauvoir explicitly deny the existence of any human nature. Camus, to be sure, suggests in a passage to which critics have attached undue importance, that perhaps, after all, the Greeks may have been right in ascribing reality to some sort of underlying idea of man. But aside from the tentative and incomplete quality of this remark, Camus makes no use of the concept of human nature in any way which would constitute of it a determining force. For him it is an idea of what "humanity" is which serves to explain why men will revolt, placing a higher value on an ideal to be attained than on life itself. It is the basis also for the sense of human solidarity. To my mind, this is only another way of saying that man transcends himself in his projects—or, more accurately, man *is* his projects. Be that as it may, neither Camus nor any other existentialist philosopher holds that man's moral traits are predetermined or determining. Such a position means that we must give up both the belief in inevitable progress and the gloomy predictions of decline. Along with the latter must go those old saws which claim that war is inevitable, that human life is and always will be merely a more subtle manifestation of the tooth-and-claw struggle for survival, that man is essentially selfish, lawless, and cruel—in short, that "you can't change human nature."

None of the existentialists seem to me to have made even a fair beginning at developing the posi-

tive implications of this position. De Beauvoir in her novel *All Men Are Mortal* affirms her belief in the continuing sameness of man and his institutions, an attitude which I find to be inconsistent with her basic philosophy. Incredibly she uses the moon as a symbol for the futility of human aspirations, assuming that man can never reach that cold and shining sphere. Camus, who employs almost the same moon symbolism in his play *Caligula,* does not, any more than de Beauvoir, envision any significant changes in human attitudes. Friedrich Duerrenmatt, admittedly neither a philosopher nor an avowed existentialist, nevertheless writes fiction in which the existentialist view of man seems omnipresent. He, too, in *Traps* and in *The Visit,* appears bent on demonstrating the cynical notion that everyone is guilty and has his price, and that this is the way things always have been and will be. Only Sartre, as I have shown in his prediction of the "philosophy of freedom" which is to come, allows for the possibility of there being a society so far in advance of anything we have known that we cannot now imagine its "open spaces." Sartre himself has so far limited himself primarily to explanation of the failures of historical Marxism and to the philosophical analysis of the emersion and collapse of a We-Group as it has been observed in France, in the Soviet Union, and in North Africa. His efforts toward a future have been cast in terms of direct political action or in sketching out a "progressive-regressive method" to be used in interpreting events in history and in the biographies of famous individuals. But Sartre is at least theoretically aware that both the social structure and the so-called "human character" are open to such willed modification that the life of man in the future may well be as different from that of our contemporary as ours is from that of the Neolithic inhabitants. It will not necessarily be better or worse. What it will be and the extent to which it develops beyond our present concepts depends on us. Thus, in choosing for ourselves, we are indeed choosing for mankind.

The second alternative goes further. It envisions not only a life for creatures like ourselves which satisfies in ways we have never known or thought possible. It proffers the hypothesis that future human beings may be very much unlike ourselves. Without going so far as to postulate the evolution of a creature one could no longer call human, we may accept the idea that there may be thrusts forward as significant as the discovery of writing or even the development of language. And of course there is no reason to exclude the further development of man as a species as the result of a consciously controlled evolution such as has certainly never happened before on earth. For this view, the future is not only open but unlimited. Space exploration, for instance, may be allowed, at least hypothetically, to change life essentially, not merely to increase the geographical scope of familiar conflicts.

There are, then, two possible ways in which to respond to the challenge to create meaning in a Universe where we have found none already inscribed. The first looks toward founding a society in good faith, to changing the external life of man in such a way as to give the fullest possible scope to his creative freedom. The second is more profoundly a self-creative process. It seeks self-transcendence of a kind which might well transform the very concept of meaning and purpose and the possible ways of satisfying our demand for them.

Notes

1. A play by Jean-Paul Sartre.

2. Sartre, *L'Existentialisme est un humanisme*, pp. 89–90.

3. Sartre, *Being and Nothingness*, p. 93.

4. Ibid., p. 94.

5. John A. T. Robinson, *Honest to God* (Philadelphia: Westminster Press, 1963), p. 117.

Taking Charge of Yourself

WAYNE DYER

Wayne Dyer is a practicing therapist and counselor whose work has been influenced by existentialist philosophy. The present selection, taken from his popular book, *Your Erroneous Zones,* demonstrates clearly the empirical consequences associated with the existential approach to being. Dr. Dyer reiterates Jean-Paul Sartre's position from *Being and Nothingness*: human beings can control their actions rather than be controlled by them. Do not be deceived by the apparent simplicity or commonplace nature of the advice. Taking charge of yourself may be more difficult, and have greater consequence, than you realize.

Look over your shoulder. You will notice a constant companion. For want of a better name, call him *Your-Own-Death.* You can fear this visitor or use him for your personal gain. The choice is up to you.

With death so endless a proposition and life so breathtakingly brief, ask yourself, "Should I avoid doing the things I really want to do?" "Should I live my life as others want me to?" "Are *things* important to accumulate?" "Is putting it off the way to live?" Chances are your answers can be summed up in a few words: Live . . . Be You . . . Enjoy . . . Love.

You can fear your death, ineffectually, or you can use it to help you learn to live effectively. Listen to Tolstoy's Ivan Ilych as he awaits the great leveler, contemplating a past which was thoroughly dominated by others, a life in which he had given up control of himself in order to fit into a system.

"What if my whole life has been wrong?" It occurred to him that what had appeared perfectly impossible before, namely that he had not spent his life as he should have done, might after all be true. It occurred to him that his scarcely noticeable impulses, which he had immediately suppressed, might have been the real thing, and the rest false. And his professional duties and the whole arrangement of his life and of his family, and all his social and official interests, might all have been false. He tried to defend all those things to himself and suddenly felt the weakness of what he was defending. There was nothing to defend. . . .

The next time you are contemplating a decision in which you are debating whether or not to take charge of yourself, to make your own choice, ask yourself an important question, "How long am I going to be dead?" With that eternal perspective, you can now make your own choice and leave the worrying, the fears, the question of whether you can afford it and the guilt to those who are going to be alive forever.

If you don't begin taking these steps, you can anticipate living your entire life the way others say you must. Surely if your sojourn on earth is so brief, it ought at least to be pleasing to you. In a word, it's your life; do with it what *you* want.

HAPPINESS AND YOUR OWN I.Q.

Taking charge of yourself involves putting to rest some very prevalent myths. At the top of the list is the notion that intelligence is measured by your ability to solve complex problems; to read, write and compute at certain levels; and to resolve abstract equations quickly. This vision of intelligence predicates formal education and bookish excellence as the true measures of self-fulfillment. It encourages a kind of intellectual snobbery that has brought with it some demoralizing results. We have come to believe that someone who has more educational merit badges, who is a whiz at some form of scholastic discipline (math, science, a huge vocabulary, a memory for superfluous facts, a fast reader) is "intelligent." Yet mental hospitals are clogged with patients who have all of the properly lettered credentials—as well as many who don't. A truer barometer of intelligence is an effective, happy life lived each day and each present moment of every day.

If you are happy, if you live each moment for everything it's worth, then you are an intelligent person. Problem solving is a useful adjunct to your happiness, but if you know that given your inability to resolve a particular concern you can still choose happiness for yourself, or at a minimum refuse to choose unhappiness, then you are intelligent. You are intelligent because you have the ultimate weapon against the big N.B.D. Yep–*Nervous Break Down.*

Perhaps you will be surprised to learn that there is no such thing as a nervous breakdown. Nerves don't break down. Cut someone open and look for the broken nerves. They never show up. "Intelligent" people do not have N.B.D.'s because they are in charge of themselves. They know how to choose happiness over depression, because they know how to deal with the *problems* of their lives. Notice I didn't say *solve* the problems. Rather than measuring their intelligence on their ability to *solve* the problem, they measure it on their capacity for maintaining themselves as happy and worthy, whether the problem gets solved or not.

You can begin to think of yourself as truly intelligent on the basis of how you choose to feel in the face of trying circumstances. The life struggles are pretty much the same for each of us. Everyone who is involved with other human beings in any social context has similar difficulties. Disagreements, conflicts and compromises are a part of what it means to be human. Similarly, money, growing old, sickness, deaths, natural disasters and accidents are all events which present problems to virtually all human beings. But some people are able to make it, to avoid immobilizing dejection and unhappiness despite such occurrences, while others collapse, become inert or have an N.B.D. Those who recognize problems as a human condition and don't measure happiness by an absence of problems are the most intelligent kind of humans we know; also, the most rare.

Learning to take total charge of yourself will involve a whole new thinking process, one which may prove difficult because too many forces in our society conspire against individual responsibility. You must trust in your own ability to feel emotionally whatever you choose to feel at any time in your life. This is a radical notion. You've probably grown up believing that you can't control your own emotions; that anger, fear and hate, as well as love, ecstasy and joy are things that happen to you. An individual doesn't control these things, he accepts them. When sorrowful events occur, you just naturally feel sorrow, and hope that some happy events will come along so that you can feel good very soon.

CHOOSING HOW YOU'LL FEEL

Feelings are not just emotions that happen to you. Feelings are reactions you choose to have. If you are in charge of your own emotions, you don't have to choose self-defeating reactions. Once you learn that you can feel what you choose to feel, you will be on the road to "intelligence"—a road where there are no bypaths that lead to N.B.D.'s. This road will be new because you'll see a given emotion as a choice rather than as a condition of life. This is the very heart and soul of personal freedom.

You can attack the myth of not being in charge of your emotions through logic. By using a simple syllogism (a formulation in logic, in which you have a major premise, a minor premise and a conclusion based upon the agreement between the two premises) you can begin the process of being in charge of yourself, both thinkingly and emotionally.

Logic—Syllogism

MAJOR PREMISE: Aristotle is a Man.
MINOR PREMISE: All men have facial hair.
CONCLUSION: ARISTOTLE HAS FACIAL HAIR.

Illogic—Syllogism

MAJOR PREMISE: Aristotle has facial hair.
MINOR PREMISE: All men have facial hair.
CONCLUSION: ARISTOTLE IS A MAN.

It is clear that you must be careful as you employ logic that your major and minor premises agree. In the second illustration, Aristotle could be an ape or a mole. Here is a logical exercise that can forever put to rest the notion that you cannot take charge of your emotional world.

MAJOR PREMISE: I can control my thoughts.
MINOR PREMISE: My feelings come from my thoughts.
CONCLUSION: I can control my feelings.

Your major premise is clear. You have the power to think whatever you choose to allow into your head. If something just "pops" into your head (You choose to put it there, though you may not know why), you still have the power to make it go away, and therefore you still control your mental world. I can say to you, "Think of a pink antelope," and you can turn it green, or make it an aardvark, or simply think of something else if you so choose. You alone control what enters your head as a thought. If you don't believe this, just answer this question, "If you don't control your thoughts, who does?" Is it your spouse, or your boss, or your mamma? And if *they* control what you think, then send them off for therapy and *you* will instantly get better. But you really know otherwise. You and only you control your

thinking apparatus (other than under extreme kinds of brainwashing or conditioning experimentation settings which are not a part of your life). Your thoughts are your own, uniquely yours to keep, change, share, or contemplate. No one else can get inside your head and have your own thoughts as you experience them. You do indeed control your thoughts, and your brain is your own to use as you so determine.

Your minor premise is hardly debatable if you examine the research as well as your own common sense. You cannot have a feeling (emotion) without first having experienced a thought. Take away your brain and your ability to "feel" is wiped out. A feeling is a physical reaction to a thought. If you cry, or blush, or increase your heartbeat, or any of an interminable list of potential emotional reactions, you have first had a signal from your thinking center. Once your thinking center is damaged or short-circuited, you cannot experience emotional reactions. With certain kinds of lesions in the brain you cannot even experience physical pain, and your hand could literally fry on a stove burner with no sensation of pain. You know that you cannot bypass your think-center and experience any feelings in your body. Thus your minor premise is lodged in truth. Every feeling that you have was preceded by a thought, and without a brain you can have no feelings.

Your conclusion is also inescapable. If you control your thoughts, and your feelings come from your thoughts, then you are capable of controlling your own feelings. And you control your feelings by working on the thoughts that preceded them. Simply put, you believe that things or people make you unhappy, but this is not accurate. You make yourself unhappy because of the thoughts that you have about the people or things in your life. Becoming a free and healthy person involves learning to *think* differently. Once you can change your thoughts, your new feelings will begin to emerge, and you will have taken the first step on the road to your personal freedom.

To look at the syllogism in a more personal light, let's consider the case of Cal, a young executive who spends most of his time agonizing over the fact that his boss thinks he is stupid. Cal is very unhappy because his boss has a low opinion of him. But if Cal didn't know that his boss thought he was stupid, would he still be unhappy? Of course not. How could he be unhappy about something he didn't know? Therefore, what his boss thinks or doesn't think doesn't make him unhappy. What Cal thinks makes him unhappy. Moreover, Cal makes himself unhappy by convincing himself that what someone else thinks is more important than what he thinks.

This same logic applies to all events, things and persons' points of view. Someone's death does not make you unhappy; you cannot be unhappy until you learn of the death, so it's not the death but what you tell yourself about the event. Hurricanes aren't depressing by themselves; depression is uniquely human. If you are depressed about a hurricane, you are telling yourself some things that depress you. This is not to say that you should delude yourself into enjoying a hurricane, but ask yourself, "Why should I choose depression? Will it help me to be more effective in dealing with it?"

You have grown up in a culture which has taught you that you are not responsible for your feelings even though the syllogistic truth is that you always were. You've learned a host of sayings to defend yourself against the fact that you do control your feelings. Here is a brief list of such utterances that you have used over and over. Examine the message they send.

- "You hurt my feelings."
- "You make me feel bad."
- "I can't help the way I feel."
- "I just feel angry, don't ask me to explain it."
- "He makes me sick."
- "Heights scare me."
- "You're embarrassing me."
- "She really turns me on."
- "You made a fool of me in public."

The list is potentially endless. Each saying has a built-in message that you are not responsible for how you feel. Now rewrite the list so it is accurate, so it reflects the fact that you are in charge of how you feel and that your feelings come from the thoughts you have about anything.

- "I hurt my feelings because of the things I told myself about your reaction to me."
- "I made myself feel bad."
- "I can help the way I feel, but I've chosen to be upset."
- "I've decided to be angry, because I can usually manipulate others with my anger, since *they* think *I* control them."
- "I make myself sick."
- "I scare myself at high places."
- "I'm embarrassing myself."
- "I turn myself on whenever I'm near her."
- "I made myself feel foolish by taking your opinions of me more seriously than my own, and believing that others would do the same."

Perhaps you think that the items in List 1 are just figures of speech, and that they really don't mean very much, but are simply figures of speech that have become clichés in our culture. If this is your rationale, then ask yourself why the statements in List 2 did not evolve into clichés. The answer lies in our culture, which teaches the thinking of List 1, and discourages the logic of List 2.

The message is crystal clear. You are the person responsible for how you feel. You feel what you think, and you can learn to think differently about anything—if you decide to do so. Ask yourself if there is a sufficient payoff in being unhappy, down, or hurt. Then begin to examine, in depth, the kind of thoughts that are leading you to these debilitating feelings.

LEARNING NOT TO BE UNHAPPY: A TOUGH ASSIGNMENT

It is not easy to think in new ways. You are accustomed to a certain set of thoughts and the debilitating thoughts that follow. It requires a great deal of work to unlearn all of the habits of thought you have assimilated until now. Happiness is easy, but learning not to be unhappy can be difficult.

Happiness is a natural condition of being a person. The evidence is plainly visible when you look at young children. What is tough is unlearning all of the "shoulds" and "oughts" that you've digested in the past. Taking charge of yourself begins with awareness. Catch yourself when you say things like, "He hurt my feelings." Remind yourself what you're doing at the moment you're doing it. New thinking requires awareness of the old thinking. You have become habituated in mental patterns that identify the causes of your feelings as outside of yourself. You have put in thousands of hours of reinforcement for such thinking, and you'll need to balance the scale with thousands of hours of new thinking, thinking that assumes responsibility for your own feelings. It is tough, damn tough; but so what? That certainly is no reason to avoid doing it.

Think back to the time you were learning to drive a stick shift automobile. You were faced with what seemed to be an insurmountable problem. Three pedals but only two feet to make them work. You first became aware of the complexity of the task. Let the clutch out slow, ooops too fast, jerky business, gas pedal down at the same rate as you release the clutch, right foot for the brake, but the clutch must go in, or you jerk again. A million mental signals: always thinking, using your brain. What do I do? *Awareness,* and then after thousands of trials, mistakes, new efforts, the day comes when you step into your car and drive away. No stalling, no jerking and *no thinking.* Driving a stick shift has become second nature, and how did you do it? With great difficulty. Lots of present-moment thinking, reminding, working.

You know how to regulate your mind when it comes to accomplishing physical tasks, such as teaching your hands and feet to coordinate for driving. The process is less well-known but identical in the emotional world. You've learned the habits you now have by reinforcing them all of your life. You get unhappy, angry, hurt and frustrated automatically because you learned to think that way a long time ago. You have accepted your behavior and

never worked at challenging it. But you can learn to not be unhappy, angry, hurt, or frustrated just as you learned to be all those self-defeating things.

For example, you've been taught that going to the dentist is a nasty experience, and one that is associated with pain. You've always felt that it is unpleasant and you even say things to yourself like, "I hate that drill." But these are all learned reactions. You could make the whole experience work for rather than against you by choosing to make it a pleasant, exciting procedure. You could, if you really decided to use your brain, make the sound of the drill signal a beautiful sexual experience and each time the brrrrrr sound appeared, you could train your mind to envision the most orgiastic moment of your life. You could think something different about what you used to call pain, and choose to feel something new and pleasurable. How much more exciting and fulfilling to take charge and master your own dental world environment than to hang on to the old images and just endure.

Perhaps you're skeptical. You may say something like, "I can think all I want, but I still get unhappy when he starts to drill." Think back to the stick shift. When did you *believe* that you could drive it? A thought becomes a belief when you've worked on it repeatedly, not when you simply try it once and use your initial ability as the rationale for giving up.

Taking charge of yourself involves more than simply trying on new thoughts for size. It requires a demonstration to be happy and to challenge and destroy each and every thought that creates a self-immobilizing unhappiness in you.

CHOICE—YOUR ULTIMATE FREEDOM

If you still believe that you don't choose to be unhappy, try to imagine this course of events. Each time you become unhappy you are subjected to some treatment you find unpleasant. Perhaps you are locked in a room alone for long periods of time or, conversely, forced into a crowded elevator where you must stand for days. You may be deprived of all food and forced to eat some dish you find particularly distasteful. Or perhaps you will be tortured—

physically tortured by others, rather than mentally tortured by yourself. Imagine that you were subjected to any one of these punishments until you made your unhappy feelings go away. How long do you think you would continue to hold on to them? Chances are you would take control rather quickly. So the issue is not whether you can take control of your feelings, but whether you will. What must you endure before you'll make such a choice? Some people choose to go insane rather than take control. Others merely give up and succumb to a life of misery because the dividend of pity received is greater than the reward of being happy.

The issue here is your own ability to choose happiness or at least not to choose unhappiness at any given moment of your life. A mind-blowing notion perhaps, but one that you should consider carefully before rejecting, since to discard it is to give up on yourself. To reject it is to believe that someone else instead of you is in charge of you. But choosing to be happy might seem easier than some things which daily confound your life.

Just as you are free to choose happiness over unhappiness, so in the myriad events of everyday life you are free to choose self-fulfilling behavior over self-defeating behavior. If you drive in this day and age, chances are you find yourself frequently stuck in traffic. Do you become angry, swear at other drivers, berate your passengers, take your feelings out on anyone and anything in range? Do you justify your behavior by saying that traffic always sends you into a snit, that you simply have no control in a traffic jam? If so, you are accustomed to thinking certain things about yourself and the way you act in traffic. But what if you decided to think something else? What if you chose to use your mind in a self-enhancing kind of way? It would take time but you could learn to talk to yourself in new ways, to become accustomed to new behavior which might include whistling, singing, turning on a tape recorder to write several letters, even timing yourself with thirty-second postponements of your anger. You have not learned to like the traffic but you have learned to practice, very slowly at first, new thoughts. You have decided not to be uncomfortable. You have chosen to substitute in slow, progressive steps healthy new feelings and habits for old self-defeating emotions.

You can choose to make any experience enjoyable and challenging. Dull parties and committee meetings are fertile territory for choosing new feelings. When you find yourself bored, you can make your mind work in exciting ways, by changing the subject with a key observation, or writing the first chapter of your novel, or working on new plans which will help you to avoid these settings in the future. Using your mind actively means assessing the people and events which give you the greatest difficulty and then deciding on new mental efforts to make them work for you. In a restaurant, if you typically get upset over poor service, think first of why you should not choose to be upset because someone or something is not going the way you would like it to go. You're too worthy to be upset by someone else, especially someone who is so unimportant in your life. Then devise strategies to change the setting, or leave, or whatever. But don't just get perturbed. Use your brain to work for you, and eventually you'll have the terrific habit of not being upset when things go wrong.

The Myth of Sisyphus

ALBERT CAMUS

Albert Camus was born in Algeria in 1913. A year later his father was killed in World War I, and Camus was raised in poverty by his deaf and illiterate mother. He first achieved prominence as a member of French resistance during World War II, publishing an underground newspaper (*Combat*) and two books: *The Stranger* and *The Myth of Sisyphus,* from which the following selection is taken. Later works include *The Rebel, The Plague, The Fall, Caligula,* and *The Possessed.* In 1957 he was awarded the Nobel Prize for literature. Camus died in an automobile accident in 1960.

Like Richard Taylor (Chapter 1), Albert Camus interpreted the myth of Sisyphus as an allegory for the human condition. Compare the lessons that struck Camus in 1942 with those presented by Professor Taylor in 1970.

The gods had condemned Sisyphus to ceaselessly rolling a rock to the top of a mountain, whence the stone would fall back of its own weight. They had thought with some reason that there is no more dreadful punishment than futile and hopeless labor.

If one believes Homer, Sisyphus was the wisest and most prudent of mortals. According to another tradition, however, he was disposed to practice the profession of highwayman. I see no contradiction in this. Opinions differ as to the reasons why he became the futile laborer of the underworld. To begin with, he is accused of a certain levity in regard to the gods. He stole their secrets. Ægina, the daughter of Æsopus, was carried off by Jupiter. The father was shocked by that disappearance and complained to Sisyphus. He, who knew of the abduction, offered to tell about it on condition that Æsopus would give water to the citadel of Corinth. To the celestial thunderbolts he preferred the benediction of water. He was punished for this in the underworld. Homer tells us also that Sisyphus had put Death in chains. Pluto could not endure the sight of his deserted, silent empire. He dispatched the god of war, who liberated Death from the hands of her conqueror.

It is said also that Sisyphus, being near to death, rashly wanted to test his wife's love. He ordered her to cast his unburied body into the middle of the public square. Sisyphus woke up in the underworld. And there, annoyed by the obedience so contrary to human love, he obtained from Pluto permission to return to earth in order to chastise his wife. But when he had seen again the face of this world, enjoyed water and sun, warm stones and the sea, he no longer wanted to go back to the infernal darkness. Recalls, signs of anger, warnings were of no avail. Many years more he lived facing the curve of the gulf, the sparkling sea, and the smiles of earth. A decree of the gods was necessary. Mercury came and seized the impudent man by the collar and, snatching him from his joys, led him forcibly back to the underworld, where his rock was ready for him.

You have already grasped that Sisyphus is the absurd hero. He *is,* as much through his passions as through his torture. His scorn of the gods, his hatred of death, and his passion for life won him that unspeakable penalty in which the whole being is exerted toward accomplishing nothing. This is the price that must be paid for the passions of this earth. Nothing is told us about Sisyphus in the underworld. Myths are made for the imagination to breathe life into them. As for this myth, one sees merely the whole effort of a body straining to raise the huge stone, to roll it and push it up a slope a hundred times over; one sees the face screwed up, the cheek tight against the stone, the shoulder bracing the clay-covered mass, the foot wedging it, the fresh start with arms outstretched, the wholly human security of two earth-clotted hands. At the very end of his long effort measured by skyless space and time without depth, the purpose is achieved. Then Sisyphus watches the stone rush down in a few moments toward that lower world whence he will have to push it up again toward the summit. He goes back down to the plain.

It is during that return, that pause, that Sisyphus interests me. A face that toils so close to stones is already stone itself! I see that man going back down with a heavy yet measured step toward the torment of which he will never know the end. That hour like a breathing-space which returns as surely as his suffering, that is the hour of consciousness. At each of those moments when he leaves the heights and gradually sinks toward the lairs of the gods, he is superior to his fate. He is stronger than his rock.

If this myth is tragic, that is because its hero is conscious. Where would his torture be, indeed, if at every step the hope of succeeding upheld him? The workman of today works every day in his life at the same tasks, and this fate is no less absurd. But it is tragic only at the rare moments when it becomes conscious. Sisyphus, proletarian of the gods, powerless and rebellious, knows the whole extent of his wretched condition: it is what he thinks of during his descent. The lucidity that was to constitute his torture at the same time crowns his victory. There is no fate that cannot be surmounted by scorn.

If the descent is thus sometimes performed in sorrow, it can also take place in joy. This word is not too much. Again I fancy Sisyphus returning toward his rock, and the sorrow was in the beginning. When the images of earth cling too tightly to memory, when the call of happiness becomes too insistent, it happens that melancholy rises in man's heart: this is the rock's victory, this is the rock itself. The boundless grief is too heavy to bear. These are our nights of Gethsemane. But crushing truths perish from being acknowledged. Thus, Œdipus at the outset obeys fate without knowing it. But from the moment he knows, his tragedy begins. Yet at the same moment, blind and desperate, he realizes that the only bond linking him to the world is the cool hand of a girl. Then a tremendous remark rings out: "Despite so many ordeals, my advanced age and the nobility of my soul make me conclude that all is well." Sophocles' Œdipus, like Dostoevsky's Kirilov, thus gives the recipe for the absurd victory. Ancient wisdom confirms modern heroism.

One does not discover the absurd without being tempted to write a manual of happiness. "What! by such narrow ways—?" There is but one world, however. Happiness and the absurd are two sons of the same earth. They are inseparable. It would be a mistake to say that happiness necessarily springs from the absurd discovery. It happens as well that the feeling of the absurd springs from happiness. "I conclude that all is well," says Œdipus, and that remark is sacred. It echoes in the wild and limited universe of man. It teaches that all is not, has not been, exhausted. It drives out of this world a god who had come into it with dissatisfaction and a preference for futile sufferings. It makes of fate a human matter, which must be settled among men.

All Sisyphus' silent joy is contained therein. His fate belongs to him. His rock is his thing. Likewise, the absurd man, when he contemplates his torment, silences all the idols. In the universe suddenly restored to its silence, the myriad wondering little voices of the earth rise up. Unconscious, secret calls, invitations from all the faces, they are the necessary reverse and the price of victory. There is no sun without shadow, and it is essential to know the night. The absurd man says yes and his effort will henceforth be unceasing. If there is a personal fate, there is no higher destiny, or at least there is but one which he concludes is inevitable and despicable. For the rest, he knows himself to be the master of his days. At that subtle moment when man glances backward over his life, Sisyphus returning toward his rock, in that silent pivoting he contemplates that series of unrelated actions which becomes his fate, created by him, combined under his memory's eye and soon sealed by his death. Thus, convinced of the wholly human origin of all that is human, a blind man eager to see who knows that the night has no end, he is still on the go. The rock is still rolling.

I leave Sisyphus at the foot of the mountain! One always finds one's burden again. But Sisyphus teaches the higher fidelity that negates the gods and raises rocks. He too concludes that all is well. This universe henceforth without a master seems to him neither sterile nor futile. Each atom of that stone, each mineral flake of that night-filled mountain, in itself forms a world. The struggle itself toward the heights is enough to fill a man's heart. One must imagine Sisyphus happy.

On the Three Metamorphoses

FRIEDRICH NIETZSCHE

Friedrich Nietzsche (1844–1900) challenged the assumptions and beliefs of Christianity. As an alternative to the idea of God, he presented the concept of an übermensch (superman). Through works like *The Joyful Wisdom, Thus Spoke Zarathustra, Beyond Good and Evil, The Genealogy of Morals,* and *Twilight of the Idols,* Nietzsche influenced the development of the atheistic branch of the twentieth-century existentialism.

The present selection is taken from Part I of *Thus Spoke Zarathustra*. Zarathustra is a rebel sage who comes down the mountain to tell the masses that God is dead. He tells people that the death of God takes away all significance from their lives. People are forlorn and abandoned; their fate is in their own hands. His message is to find the meaning of life, not in God, but through the creation of a superman. This will require hard work (symbolized by the camel), courage (symbolized by the lion), and creative innovation (symbolized by the child).

Of three metamorphoses of the spirit I tell you: how the spirit becomes a camel; and the camel, a lion; and the lion, finally, a child.

There is much that is difficult for the spirit, the strong reverent spirit that would bear much: but the difficult and the most difficult are what its strength demands.

What is difficult? asks the spirit that would bear much, and kneels down like a camel wanting to be well loaded. What is most difficult, O heroes, asks the spirit that would bear much, that I may take it upon myself and exult in my strength? Is it not humbling oneself to wound one's haughtiness? Letting one's folly shine to mock one's wisdom?

Or is it this: parting from our cause when it triumphs? Climbing high mountains to tempt the tempter?

Or is it this: feeding on the acorns and grass of knowledge and, for the sake of the truth, suffering hunger in one's soul?

Or is it this: being sick and sending home the comforters and making friends with the deaf, who never hear what you want?

Or is it this: stepping into filthy waters when they are the waters of truth, and not repulsing cold frogs and hot toads?

Or is it this: loving those who despise us and offering a hand to the ghost that would frighten us?

All these most difficult things the spirit that would bear much takes upon itself: like the camel that, burdened, speeds into the desert, thus the spirit speeds into its desert.

In the loneliest desert, however, the second metamorphosis occurs: here the spirit becomes a

Friedrich Nietzsche, "On the Three Metamorphoses" from Walter Kaufmann, editor and translator, *The Portable Nietzsche*, pp. 137–139. Copyright 1954 by The Viking Press, renewed © 1982 by Viking Penguin Inc. Reprinted with the permission of Viking Penguin, a division of Penguin Books USA Inc.

lion who would conquer his freedom and be master in his own desert. Here he seeks out his last master: he wants to fight him and his last god; for ultimate victory he wants to fight with the great dragon.

Who is the great dragon whom the spirit will no longer call lord and god? "Thou shalt" is the name of the great dragon. But the spirit of the lion says, "I will." "Thou shalt" lies in his way, sparkling like gold, an animal covered with scales; and on every scale shines a golden "thou shalt."

Values, thousands of years old, shine on these scales; and thus speaks the mightiest of all dragons: "All value of all things shines on me. All value has long been created, and I am all created value. Verily, there shall be no more 'I will.' " Thus speaks the dragon.

My brothers, why is there a need in the spirit for the lion? Why is not the beast of burden, which renounces and is reverent, enough?

To create new values—that even the lion cannot do; but the creation of freedom for oneself for new creation—that is within the power of the lion. The creation of freedom for oneself and a sacred "No" even to duty—for that, my brothers, the lion is needed. To assume the right to new values—that is the most terrifying assumption for a reverent spirit that would bear much. Verily, to him it is preying, and a matter for a beast of prey. He once loved "thou shalt" as most sacred: now he must find illusion and caprice even in the most sacred, that freedom from his love may become his prey: the lion is needed for such prey.

But say, my brothers, what can the child do that even the lion could not do? Why must the preying lion still become a child? The child is innocence and forgetting, a new beginning, a game, a self-propelled wheel, a first movement, a sacred "Yes." For the game of creation, my brothers, a sacred "Yes" is needed: the spirit now wills his own will, and he who had been lost to the world now conquers his own world.

Of three metamorphoses of the spirit I have told you: how the spirit became a camel; and the camel, a lion; and the lion, finally, a child.

Review and Reflection

1. Present, as clearly as possible, Jean-Paul Sartre's "two aspects of being." Do you agree with Sartre's analysis? Why?

2. Explicate and discuss Sartre's concept of freedom. Why does he regard it as absolute? How is it related to the concepts of responsibility and bad-faith?

3. What, according to Hazel Barnes, are the basic conditions of an existentialist ethics? How does her position differ from those of Sartre and Camus?

4. Can one control one's emotions? Is there a real choice? Are we responsible for our way of being? How do your answers differ from those of Wayne Dyer? In what ways are they similar?

5. In what respects does Sisyphus represent the existential predicament of a human being? What propels him to go on?

6. What meaning does Nietzsche assign to the three metamorphoses? What do they signify to you?

Suggestions for Further Study

WILLIAM BARRETT. *Irrational Man.* New York: Anchor Books, 1962.

ALBERT CAMUS. *The Myth of Sisyphus and Other Essays.* New York: Alfred A. Knopf, 1955.

ASHOK MALHOTRA. *Jean-Paul Sartre's Existentialism in Nausea and Being and Nothingness.* Calcutta, India: Writers Workshop, 1978.

L. NATHAN OAKLANDER. *Existentialist Philosophy: An Introduction.* Englewood Cliffs, NJ: Prentice Hall, 1992.

JEAN-PAUL SARTRE. *Existentialism Is a Humanism.* New York: Philosophical Library, 1957.

JEAN-PAUL SARTRE. *Nausea.* New York: New Directions, 1964.

ROBERT C. SOLOMON. *Introducing the Existentialists.* Indianapolis: Hackett Publishing Co., 1981.

PART 2

Values and Systems: Living with Others

CHAPTER 4   Ethics
CHAPTER 5   Social and Political Philosophy
CHAPTER 6   Technology and Human Values

Part 2 continues our exploration of the conceptual circles that emanate from the question: *Who am I?* Whereas the three chapters in Part 1 focused largely on the private, individual aspects of being, those in Part 2 concern that dimension of self which depends upon an inclusive community. Specific points of focus include the nature of ethical obligation and responsibility, the foundations of society, and the impact of modern technology.

CHAPTER 4

Ethics

Ethics is the study of moral values and judgments. Principal concepts include right and wrong, good and evil, should and ought, duty and obligation.

Introductory Essay

The **Introductory Essays** in Part Two are not essays as such, but rather interconnected dialogues between participants in a hypothetical study group. The device allows us to explore a diversity of opinions in a more realistic context than might otherwise have been achieved. Additionally, students who have been unsure about how to respond to the multiplicity of material presented in previous chapters may find an appropriate model for their own reflection, analysis, and discussion. The first study session explores the concept of choice, the distinction between intrinsic and extrinsic values, and various puzzles concerning the language of ethics. Basic positions include *eudemonism*, Aristotle's doctrine of the Golden Mean, Socrates' position that no one knowingly does wrong, Relativism (including Individual Relativism, Cultural Relativism, and the Divine Will Theory), Consequentialism (including Egoism, Altruism, and Utilitarianism), and Deontological Theories (including Immanuel Kant's categorical imperative and William David Ross's concept of *prima facie* duties).

Philosophical Readings

The selection by **Plato** presents a story known as "The Ring of Gyges." What, we are challenged to imagine, would you do if you could act with complete impunity (if you knew you would never get caught)?

The selection by **Peter Singer** is focused on a hypothetical situation known as "The Prisoner's Dilemma." The dilemma effectively asks whether the interest of the individual (Egoism) is sometimes best served via a pattern of altruistic action (action performed for the sake of others). Based in part on his views concerning sociobiology (the study of evolutionary pressures on the behavior of biological organisms), Singer answers "yes."

Scientific Reading

The selection by **Ruth Fulton Benedict** is a classic example of Cultural Relativism. Rejecting the notion that human behavior is defined according to abstract ethical principles, she focuses discussion on two societies in which standards of expectation and approval differ markedly from our own.

Literary Reading

In the short story by **Flannery O'Connor** we encounter human nature at its most blunt, unadorned, and unprincipled level. In the process we encounter the society in which we live, the religious beliefs by which we abide, and the phenomenon which we often simply label *evil*.

Choices

DOUGLAS W. SHRADER

A human life is a complex web of conditions, choices, and consequences. Each moment presents far more opportunity, and responsibility, than is commonly realized. It is not always easy to know what to do. In fact, it is often very difficult.

If we ask advice from a number of friends we are apt to get a series of conflicting, incompatible suggestions. There are many different views and opinions about right or wrong, and about the things which we ought or ought not to do. How then do we choose? What standards do we use? How can we ever be sure that we have made the "right" choice?

This diversity of perspective and opinion is both the source of, and need for, many of the distinctions and theories we find in the study of ethics. Ideally, ethical theories provide clear behavioral and conceptual guidance, helping us to choose between a multiplicity of confusing alternatives and possible consequences. Yet all too often a set of distinctions becomes just that: a set of distinctions. Worse, as Alexander Pope observed, a little learning may be a dangerous thing.[1] Improperly understood distinctions and theories may actually prove counterproductive, adding to the confusion rather than pointing the way toward its dissolution.

Thus I find myself confronted by a perplexing situation. I need to introduce you to a number of distinctions and theories concerning human values and behavior. Experience confirms that they can in fact clarify rather than confuse. But experience also confirms the obstacles and dangers to which I alluded in the previous paragraph. If only we could just sit down and talk about these things. Then you could ask questions and I could offer clarifications, examples, or whatever else may prove useful.

Unfortunately I cannot, as a practical matter, hope to have a conversation of that sort with each person who reads this book. But I can invite you to join with me in an imaginative dialogue with a small study group of students who, it is hoped, look and sound a little like some of your own classmates. To give them something to talk about, we will begin with a few simple questions and observations about human behavior, and our reasons for doing what we do.

Why Do You Do the Things You Do?

Why are you reading this book? More specifically, why are you reading this chapter—this page—this sentence? There are some who will pause to reflect upon these questions, some who will continue reading without giving much thought to the matter, and others will perhaps close the book and put it away, firm in their conviction that philosophy is a waste of time.

Which response did you make? Did you have a choice? Most of us take for granted that no matter what our response may have been, we could have done otherwise. Yet pressed for an explanation of why we responded in this way rather than that, we may find ourselves reduced to a series of stammers and hypotheses which even we do not fully believe.

"Hey, this is great!" yelled Callie, the fastest reader and one of the most active participants in class discussions. "Everybody stop reading as soon as you've finished the first two paragraphs of the section titled 'Why do you do the things you do?'"

Not everyone shared Callie's enthusiasm. Bo, a popular and usually pleasant student, expressed obvious annoyance: "What now? Can't we just read this and get it over with? I promised a couple of friends that I would meet them at ten. We're going to check out some of those downtown bars. . . . "

"Yeah, yeah. You and those downtown bars. Seems like that's all I ever hear about," interrupted

Caitlin. "Why don't you just go meet your friends now and spare us the grief?"

Bo was surprised by Caitlin's remarks. The two had dated briefly and he had always thought they got along reasonably well. Now he was not so sure. "It's not exactly like I have a *choice* in the matter," he retorted. "I would far rather be partying, but the professor assigned this stupid chapter for tomorrow's class!"

"Like you do everything the professor says?" asked Caitlin. "I've known you to blow off classes, assignments, even midterms! Anything for the sake of a party!"

"Yeah, I know," Bo admitted. "But I got placed on probation last semester and I've already fallen behind in several classes this term. I can't afford anything less than a B."

"I'm sorry I got you two started," apologized Callie. "Forget I ever mentioned it. It is just that I've been thinking a lot about things like this lately and I thought it might be neat to discuss some of my ideas with you."

"No need to apologize," consoled Martha. She glared at Bo and Caitlin. "If anyone should apologize, it's those two. I, for one, would like to hear your ideas."

"Count me in," chimed Sterling. "I love a good debate. Besides, it seems to me that Bo has already given us everything we need to understand the whole chapter."

"Whatever do you mean?" asked Callie.

"Well, consider the claim he made a few minutes ago," continued Sterling, "when he said he didn't have any choice in the matter. Surely that is just plain false. As Caitlin pointed out, he could be out partying with his friends right now if he really wanted to."

Bo chuckled. "Are you trying to say that I'd rather be studying philosophy than partying? You must not know me very well." Bo seemed almost proud of his poor study habits and lack of academic commitment. The whole group laughed—a little too long and a little too loud—but friendly laughter nonetheless. The uncomfortable tension that had

developed in the previous exchange between Caitlin and Bo dissipated in a series of smiles and chuckles.

Still laughing softly, Sterling continued: "Yes, Bo. Given what you said about the importance of your grade in this class, I really do think you'd rather be here studying philosophy than partying. You may not *want* to study philosophy, but you do want a good grade—and I think you want a good grade more than you want to have a good time."

"I think we spend too much time worrying about grades," Martha interjected. "What good are grades, anyway?"

"Well, I can't answer for you," responded Bo, "but for me this grade is very serious business. If I don't get a B in this class I may be thrown out of school. If that happens my parents will have an absolute fit: no more free ride. Worse, if I don't get a college degree I'll never get a high-paying executive-level position. I'd probably wind up washing dishes for the rest of my life: no sports car, no custom home in the 'burbs, no winters in the Bahamas. . . . My whole life would be ruined."

"So," Martha said, "the grade is only important to you because you think it will help you get a better job—things like that. You don't really think a grade has any importance of its own."

"Right," Bo said. "And if I didn't think studying this material would help improve my grade I'd be out of here in an instant."

Callie's eyes sparkled as the significance of the conversation began to sink in. "I see what Sterling means," she exclaimed. "This is just what the professor was talking about in class yesterday. You know: the distinction between intrinsic and extrinsic values."

"No," Martha confessed. "That part went right over my head. I hate all those terms our professors use."

"It's really quite simple," Sterling explained. "There are many things we do for the sake of some future reward, many things we value because we think they will help us get something else. If Bo is right, studying this assignment will help him get a better grade; a better grade will help him get a better job; a better job will help him earn more money, which in turn will let him buy sports cars, a custom home, exotic vacations, or whatever else he may happen to want. Anything that derives its value from something else is called an *extrinsic* value. An *intrinsic* value, on the other hand, is anything we value for its own sake—something we would value even if it brought no additional advantage."

"It sounds like the distinction between means and ends," Caitlin observed. "I also heard some students comparing it to the difference between a path and a destination."

"I've heard those comparisons too," Sterling responded. "And while I agree that the distinctions are similar, I think there are important differences as well. For example, we could say that Bo's reading this chapter is a means to improving his grade in this class. Improving his grade is thus an end, but it is not thereby an intrinsic value. As Bo explained earlier, he does not regard grades as anything other than means to further goals."

"It reminds me of the steps on a ladder," said Caitlin. "But what I want to know is: Where is the ladder going? I can't believe Bo is willing to make himself miserable just so he can buy a sports car."

"I agree," echoed Martha. "What good is a sports car if it just sits in the garage? Who wants to take an exotic vacation with someone they hate? Money can't buy happiness, and neither can sports cars!"

"You two sound like Aristotle," chuckled Sterling.

"Now I know you are nuts," groaned Martha. "I didn't understand any of that mumbo jumbo about Aristotle! I quit paying attention as soon as I found out he was one of Plato's students. If I can't understand Plato, I know I can't understand Aristotle."

"Don't be so hard on yourself," said Sterling. "I may have been a bit hasty, but it seemed to me that you were going to say that happiness is the only thing that is really worthwhile."

"I was," Martha acknowledged. "But what has that got to do with Aristotle?"

"Everything! That's what *eudemonism* means," explained Sterling.

"You . . . what?" stammered Bo.

"*Eudemonism* [yōō-dēʹmə-nĭzʹəm]," Sterling hung on each syllable as though he were reveling in Bo's puzzlement. "According to Aristotle, the morality of an action depends on its ability to produce happiness. The Greek term for happiness is *eudemonia* [yōōʹdĭ-mōʹnē-ə]; hence the system is called *eudemonism.*"

Bo moaned, "You sound like a dictionary. I'll never remember all that."

"It's really not that hard," encouraged Sterling. "Just remember that a *demon* is a *spirit* and that *eu* is a prefix meaning *good*. *Eudemonia* is a matter of having a good spirit."

"Well, it does make better sense when you explain it that way," conceded Bo. "But why do we need all these terms, anyway?"

"Ideally the terms help us express our thoughts more clearly, to ourselves and to others. If, as Aristotle believed, our behavior is based on those thoughts and judgments, it may even make a difference in the types of things we do and the lives we lead." Sterling paused, then lowered his voice and leaned closer to Bo. "But if you need a more immediate reason for learning some terms, just remember that they may be on our exam."

"I get it," said Bo. "Even if I don't assign any intrinsic importance to these terms, I should recognize that they have extrinsic value in terms of the things I said before about getting a good grade."

"Precisely," answered Sterling. "Although personally I think there are better reasons for expanding your vocabulary."

"Enough already with the language lesson," interrupted Caitlin. "I thought Aristotle was the guy who kept going on and on about the Golden Mean."

"He was," Sterling replied. "And that concept is fairly easy too. In any circumstance where we have to choose, Aristotle encourages us to use our reason to avoid extremes of both excess and deficiency. It is not simply a question of 'What?,' but 'How much?' "

"Like Bo's drinking," inserted Caitlin.

"Right," Sterling continued. "Aristotle does not simply ask, 'Should I drink?,' but rather, 'How much should I drink?' And the correct answer to that depends upon the circumstances, your body weight, and any number of other factors. For Aristotle the *right* action is one that correctly weighs these factors and adjusts behavior accordingly, drinking neither too much nor too little."

"Before Bo gets the wrong idea," cautioned Callie, "you had better point out that for some people and in some circumstances—if you are studying for an important exam, or getting ready to drive a car, or if you can't control your actions once you've started drinking—the correct answer might be 'None.' Any amount would be too much."

"I like that analysis," reflected Martha. "Maybe I am an Aristotelian after all."

"Well, I'm not so sure," Caitlin said, "that this ethics business isn't just so much nonsense. When you come right down to it, it's all a matter of individual choice. If you think something is right, then it *is* right, for you. And if you think something is wrong, then it *is* wrong, for you. Everyone should just do their own thing and leave everyone else alone."

Up until this point one member of the study group, Wesley, had sat quietly listening to the exchange between his classmates. At Caitlin's last statement he sat upright and spoke with uncharacteristic firmness: "Now you've gone too far. In fact, you've contradicted yourself. After telling us that right and wrong are a matter of individual choice, you proceeded to tell us what everyone else should do."

"Well, that's just my opinion," defended Caitlin. "What do you think people should do?"

"What I think doesn't matter," Wesley responded, "any more than what you or Aristotle thinks. What matters is what God thinks. We are righteous (or good) when we act in conformity with God's plan, and sinful (or evil) when we do not. All of these philosophical distinctions just cloud the issue."

"How do you know what God's plan is?" asked Callie.

"Easy," answered Wesley. "I just read the Bible."

"Do you believe everything you read in the Bible?" asked Callie. "Doesn't it contain some contradictions or something?"

"Well," Wesley responded, "I admit there are parts I don't understand. That's why I continue to study it. But it says it is the Word of God and I believe it. The so-called contradictions just reflect the difficulty humans have in trying to understand the ways of God."

"Wait a minute," said Callie. "Do you mean to tell me that you believe the Bible because the Bible says you should believe it? Would you believe everything in this philosophy book if it had a sentence in it that said you should?"

"Well," confessed Wesley, "it is a little more complicated than that. My parents taught me to believe in the Bible, not in a Philosophy text. Besides, I pray a lot and my experience confirms that I am happier when I trust the Bible than when I try to go against it."

"It seems to me," mused Callie, "that you value your own happiness more than you do following the will of God."

"Fortunately," Wesley countered, "I don't have to choose. God would never want me to do something that would make me unhappy."

"Then why don't you just follow your own desires?" asked Caitlin. "Just do those things that make you happy and, if you are right, you will be doing the will of God."

"Because," Wesley explained, "as my Creator, God knows better than I do the things that will make me happy. Without the Bible as my guide I would be like a blind person at a banquet: I might find enough food to eat but I would never manage the balanced diet which would bring both health and culinary satisfaction."

"Then you admit," Callie asked, "that you sometimes make mistakes about the will of God."

"Of course," Wesley answered. "It is important to distinguish God's will from what we *believe* to be God's will. I confess, to my shame, that I often confuse my own selfish desires with the will of God. But that is a defect in my behavior, not my views."

"What do you mean?" asked Callie.

Wesley continued: "Do you remember Caitlin's statement a few minutes ago, the one that annoyed me so? She said if you *think* something is right, then it *is* right, at least for you. According to such a system, we could never make mistakes. Anything we did would *automatically* be right. There would be no reason to think about the consequences: how it would affect others, or even ourselves."

"Didn't you ever do something you knew was wrong, but you did it anyway?" Callie asked.

"No one knowingly does wrong," replied Wesley.

"What?" asked Callie.

Wesley explained: "It's a quote from Socrates: 'No one knowingly does wrong.' What he was trying to say, I think, is that people always act in a manner that they believe to be good. You don't have to keep telling them, 'Be good. Be good.' You just have to teach them how to tell right from wrong."

"I'm willing to concede that point," inserted Caitlin. "But your remark about never having any reason to think about the consequences of an action is too strong. Bo seems to have thought a lot about the consequences of his actions: studying will result in a better grade, which will result in a better job, etcetera. But suppose he is wrong. Suppose all this studying confuses him and he ends up with a worse grade than if he had just tried to get through on his good looks and natural charm. We would all agree that he had made a mistake, but it would not be an *ethical* mistake, just a mistaken judgment about the consequences of a particular plan of behavior."

"Why does everybody keep picking on me?" asked Bo, with a grin. Turning to Sterling, he asked: "Well, Mr. Terminology, Caitlin's skepticism notwithstanding, I think I'm learning a lot from this discussion. Is there a name for Wesley's position?"

"There are several," Sterling answered. "It is usually called the *Divine Will Theory*, though I've also heard it called the *Divine Command Theory*. Like Caitlin's position, it is a form of Relativism."

"What?" asked Wesley in amazement.

Sterling continued: "Caitlin and Wesley agree with one another that right and wrong are matters of approval and/or disapproval. Caitlin defines them relative to the individual agent: as long as I ap-

prove of my own behavior then I am doing the right thing. Wesley uses a different standard: the approval of a divine being."

"It's an important difference," observed Wesley wryly.

"Yes, it is," answered Sterling. "But the similarities are important as well."

"There is one other form of Relativism," volunteered Callie, "in which right and wrong are defined in terms of the approval or disapproval of the social group."

"Right," said Sterling. "It is usually called *Cultural Relativism*, because the focus is usually on the laws, norms, or customs of an entire culture. But there is no reason you can't apply the same principles to a subculture, family unit, or even an informal study group such as this one."

"It sounds like it is halfway between Caitlin's position and that of Wesley," observed Bo.

"It is, at least in some ways," agreed Sterling. "I suppose that is part of the position's appeal. It isn't as anything-goes as Caitlin's position, but it doesn't require you to decipher the mind of a Divine Being as Wesley's does. It is a lot easier to figure out social norms and customs than it is to determine the will of God."

Callie added: "It seems also to have gained some popularity from the study of anthropology. As we come to know more about different cultures, it becomes harder and harder to insist that ours is right and theirs are wrong."

"Do you mean to say," asked Martha, "that incest and cannibalism are morally right if you happen to live in a culture which approves of or even expects that kind of behavior?"

"I'm not sure," Callie answered. "I don't approve of incest or cannibalism, but then I don't live in a culture which approves of them. I'd hate to judge someone simply because he or she happened to grow up in a different culture."

"We judge the behavior, not the person," Sterling remarked. "To answer your question, Martha, Cultural Relativists are typically uncomfortable with examples like incest and cannibalism; but if they are consistent they will acknowledge that, in some cultures, these are the right things to do. Depending upon the level of social expectation, they may even have to acknowledge that it would be wrong *not* to commit incest or cannibalism!"

"I never cared much for the judgments of society," groaned Martha. "It seems to me that we should be focusing on the consequences of our actions, not the manner in which they may be judged or perceived. If we do something that makes other people happy, then that is right and good, even if the whole world says we are wrong."

"What if making some people happy makes other people unhappy?" Callie asked. "I'll bet Caitlin would be happy if I took away your candy bar and gave it to her, but then you would be unhappy."

"Actually," Martha responded, "I don't think that would make Caitlin happy. But I do see your point. We can't always please everyone, and some of our actions may generate unhappiness as well as happiness."

"Precisely," Callie said.

Martha continued: "I think of a giant adding machine. You put all the happiness your action will cause in one column, and all the unhappiness in another. Then add them up. If the happiness is greater than the unhappiness, then the action is good. If the unhappiness is greater, the action is bad."

"What if you are confronted with a no-win situation?" Callie asked. "You know, a choice between the lesser of two evils, where each option generates more unhappiness than not."

"Hopefully those situations are few and far between," Martha remarked. "At any rate, I think you should do the best you can. If the best you can do generates more unhappiness than not, it does not become good simply because you could have done worse. But it may be, as you termed it, the lesser of two evils."

"I suppose the same logic applies," Callie observed, "to a situation in which two options produce more happiness than unhappiness, but one produces a greater quantitative difference?"

"That's right," Martha said. "In such a situation you ought to try to do the action that produces the greatest amount of happiness (minus any unhappiness, of course)."

"Then if I understand you correctly," Callie continued, "there will be times when what you should do is bad, and others when there is something good that you should not do?"

"I'm getting confused!" complained Bo.

"Callie is just picking through the logical consequences of Martha's position," Sterling explained, "sort of like Socrates does in his discussions with people in the Platonic dialogues."

"I am quite capable of explaining my own actions," Callie interjected. "I am not trying to play Socrates. But I am trying to clarify our use of the language, which, at least in some cases, he may have been trying to do as well. Sometimes we think we know what we are talking about, but then get misled simply because we do not have a firm handle on our own terms."

"Which terms didn't you understand?" asked Martha.

"It's not so much the terms as it is the relationship between the terms," Callie answered. "There are several sets of terms we use when we talk about ethics. Some are valuative terms like *good* and *bad, right* and *wrong.* Others are prescriptive terms like *should* and *ought.* These are closely related to terms of obligation, like *duty* and *responsibility.* We also sometimes find ourselves talking about the *rights* of this or that person or group. I've been wondering lately whether we have obligations simply because other people have rights, or if we have rights because they have obligations . . ."

". . . or if there are ever times when we ought to do something bad," finished Martha. "Now I see what you were getting at: as I've used the terms, *should* and *ought* are stronger than *good* and *bad.* I've agreed that there are some situations in which more than one option is *good,* and argued that we *should* pick the better of the two."

"Right," Callie said. "Similarly in the lesser-of-two-evils case. You argued that we *should* pick the lesser of the two evils, but did not thereby conclude that the evil was *good.*"

"Is that a problem?" asked Martha.

"I don't think so," Callie replied. "In fact, I agree with you. That is one of those things I've been thinking about and I was somewhat surprised to find you arguing a similar position."

"Time out!" called Bo. "I'm still confused. Sterling, are there names for these things?"

Sterling thought a moment, then said, "Well, much as I hate to admit it, Callie has done just about as good a job as I can do with this last set of distinctions. But I think it has gotten a little confusing because she has pressed Martha for the detail of her view before we had a chance to see the broad stroke. If we back up to where Martha objected to being bound by the judgments of society, we may get a closer picture of the matter."

"I'm all for that," commented Bo.

Sterling continued: "Just as Caitlin's and Wesley's views form part of a set called *Relativism,* Martha's view is part of a set known as *Consequentialism.*"

"Because I've focused on the consequences of our behavior," observed Martha.

"Exactly," said Sterling. "People who focus on the consequences for the individual self are called *Egoists.* According to *Egoism,* I ought to do whatever is best for me, no matter how it may affect someone else."

"Well, that's not my view!" exclaimed Martha.

"I didn't say it was," Sterling responded. "But like your view, it focuses on the consequences of behavior and is thus a form of Consequentialism. *Altruism,* like Egoism, separates the self from the rest of the society. But whereas Egoism favors the self to the exclusion of others, Altruism favors others to the exclusion of the self: I ought to do whatever is best for others, no matter how it may affect me."

"That's dumb!" remarked Bo.

"Perhaps," Sterling replied. "At any rate, it is not a particularly popular view. Far more common is the middle ground known as *Utilitarianism.* A Utilitarian considers the effects on the self as well as the other members of the group, and prefers the action that has the optimal effect for the unit as a whole."

"I never meant to exclude myself from the group," Martha commented. "But given the choice between making myself happy or others happy, I think I have a little more obligation to make the others happy."

"Don't get hung up over a label," Sterling advised. "These terms represent pure types to help locate ourselves in an otherwise confusing environment, sort of like the lines on a highway. Most of us drive somewhere between the lines. You seem to be expressing a preference for a position somewhere between Utilitarianism and Altruism. There are others who would choose a position between Utilitarianism and Egoism. With these terms we can find not only the differences, but the similarities between your positions as well."

"That makes sense," Martha said.

"Good," Sterling replied, "because there is also a distinction between *Act* versus *Rule* versions of Consequentialist Theories. The version you presented is act oriented. Your imaginary adding machine adds up all the happiness and unhappiness produced by each individual action."

"Right," said Martha. "What does the rule version do?"

"Well," Sterling continued, "it tries to simplify the situation a little by using the adding machine to evaluate rules rather than individual actions. Individual actions are then gauged in terms of how well they conform to the rules."

"Can you give an example?" asked Bo.

"Sure," Sterling replied. "Consider the rule: 'Do not steal.' Is this a good rule or not? A *Rule Utilitarian* would use an adding machine much like Martha's to calculate whether our society would be better if we followed this rule than if not. If so, then it is a good rule and we should adjust our behavior accordingly."

"That seems much easier than Martha's way," Bo remarked. "Why would anybody bother with the more complicated approach of *Act Utilitarianism?*"

"Because all rules admit of exceptions," Sterling replied. "Besides, there are situations in which even good rules conflict with one another. 'Do not steal' is a good rule. But then so is 'Do not let your children starve.' Rule Utilitarianism will not be able to provide guidance if a person has to choose between stealing and allowing their children to starve."

"Unless of course we have other rules about what to do when the rules break down," observed Bo.

"Right," conceded Sterling. "It could also be that our rules have lots of exceptions clauses built into them: Do not steal *unless* your children are starving and you need food to feed them, or *unless* . . . some other such condition. Either way, we complicate the situation and lose the simplicity you thought you found in Rule Utilitarianism."

"Can we perhaps steer between the two," Bo asked, "sort of like you were saying about Martha choosing a course between the pure forms of Utilitarianism and Altruism?"

"Of course," said Sterling. "In fact, I think that is what most Consequentialists do. They develop general rules that suffice to guide most behavior, then dredge out their imaginary adding machine when confronted with a truly tough or novel situation."

"Must we always justify rules in reference to their consequences?" asked Callie. "Isn't it just sort of obvious that lying and stealing are wrong, and that being friendly and helping other people are right?"

"You mean," Sterling probed, "that we ought *never* to lie or steal, even if doing so would result in some personal or social advantage?"

"I guess that depends," Callie responded, "on the measure and importance of the personal or social advantage. I agree that we have obligations to ourselves and to others. It is, I suppose, possible that those obligations would sometimes outweigh our obligations to tell the truth, not to take things to which we do not have a proprietary right, and so on."

"Like lying to a lunatic with a knife, or stealing bread to keep your children from starving," volunteered Martha.

"Sure," Callie said. "But I don't think all situations are that obvious. Suppose your children aren't starving, just hungry. Stealing bread might bring them more benefit than it would cause harm to the grocer; but I don't think that automatically makes it the *right* thing to do. You have to remember that it is still *stealing*!"

"Your view sounds similar to that of William David Ross," Sterling remarked.

"Who?" Bo asked.

"William David Ross," Sterling repeated. "He was a British philosopher (1877–1970) who developed a theory of duty and obligation. Like Callie, he believed the consequences of our actions are important, but did not think they sufficed to provide a complete account of ethical obligation. Because his view contains ethical assumptions that cannot be reduced to matters of human preference or behavioral consequence, it is known as a *Deontological Theory*."

"I don't suppose it is the only Deontological Theory," muttered Bo.

"No," Sterling replied. "The Divine Will Theory is sometimes considered a Deontological Theory. There are others as well, one of the most famous of which was developed by the German philosopher Immanuel Kant (1724–1804). Kant based his theory on the principle that we should never act in a way we would not be willing for others to act as well."

"Yes, yes," interrupted Callie. "Kant's principle was called the *Categorical Imperative*. It reminds me of Christianity's Golden Rule: do unto others as you would have them do unto you. I think both the principle and the rule are valuable, but I also think you are getting sidetracked. You started to tell us about Ross's theory, remember?"

"Right," Sterling said. "Recall our earlier discussion about intrinsic versus extrinsic values. Professor Ross believed there are four intrinsic values: pleasure, virtue, knowledge, and distributive justice (that is, the distribution of pleasure and pain according to merit). Since none of the four can be reduced to any of the others, situations may arise in which we must balance or choose between them."

"Like wanting a doctor to tell you the truth about your medical condition, even though you know it may cause you pain or unhappiness?" asked Callie.

"Yes," said Sterling. "In that example, you've expressed a preference for knowledge over pleasure. But it's not always easy to tell which you should prefer. Thus, when it came to human behavior, Ross distinguished a theoretical abstract called *actual duty* from a set of specific obligations called *prima facie duties*."

"More terminology," moaned Bo. "I can figure

out pretty well what *actual duty* means. But what are these *prima facie duties?*"

"*Prima facie* is a Latin term meaning *at first sight,*" Sterling explained. "It is not too hard to think of *prima* as *prime* (first) and *facie* as *face* (appearance). Ross distinguished seven prima facie duties that he believed to be intuitively obvious to an unbiased moral agent. In the absence of conflict, the duties would suffice to guide behavior."

"You're right," said Callie. "That does sound a lot like what I was saying about lying and stealing. The rules seem intuitively right, but some situations are just too complex for them to work correctly. Sometimes, what you ought to do is break the rule!"

"Now I see why you were grilling Martha so mercilessly before about the varieties of ethical discourse," Sterling said. "You want to be able to say that lying and stealing are *bad*, but that nonetheless there are some situations in which that is precisely what you *ought* to do."

"You've got it," said Callie with a smile. "But now tell me, what are these seven prima facie duties Ross claimed to have found?"

"The first one," Sterling said, "is similar to your rule about lying. Ross called it *fidelity*: you ought to tell the truth, keep your promises, and so on. The second is *reparation*: if you tear something up, you should fix it. The third is *gratitude*: if someone does something nice for you, you should do something nice for them—things like that. The fourth prima facie duty is *justice*: we should not imprison innocent people, etcetera. The fifth is *beneficence*: we should assist those in need, help the homeless, and so on.

The sixth is *self-improvement*: this is like beneficence toward one's self; we should develop our talents and potential, etcetera. The final prima facie duty, *non-maleficence,* Ross considered most important of all: we should harm neither ourselves nor others."

"It sounds like Ross has a little of everything," remarked Bo. "That fifth rule reminded me of Altruism and Utilitarianism. And the sixth sounded like a pretty fair statement of Egoism."

"Very perceptive," congratulated Sterling. "Ross accepted the basic values promoted by Altruists, Utilitarians, and Egoists, but criticized their philosophical positions for elevating one or two prima facie duties above all the rest. According to his account, any such theory makes the mistake of oversimplifying complex ethical situations."

"Which brings us back to the question you were discussing earlier," observed Callie. "What do we do when conflicts arise?"

"That," Sterling answered, "is the toughest question of all. Somewhat like Aristotle, Ross advises us to examine the situation carefully, weigh all the factors as objectively as possible, then make the best decision we can. Even if we later come to believe a different course of action would have been better, we will at least know that we acted in good faith to the best of our abilities. And that, when all is said and done, may be the most you can expect from any human being."

"I agree," said Bo. "And I think we've gotten through about as much material as you could expect from a study group like this. What do you say we take a break?"

Notes

1. *Essay on Criticism,* 1709. It should be noted that Pope's meaning is substantially different from the one I have intended here.

The Ring of Gyges

PLATO

The following selection is excerpted from *The Republic* (circa 375 B.C.). As we join the dialogue, Socrates has just convinced Thrasymachus to abandon the view that morality is a simple matter of adjusting one's behavior according to the interests of the stronger party (that might makes right). Plato's brother, Glaucon, refuses to accept Thrasymachus' withdrawal and presents Socrates with a classic challenge: demonstrate some reason, other than threat of punishment or similar social penalty, that people should restrict self-interested behavior according to legal and/or ethical principles.[1]

I thought, when I said this, that the argument was over; but in fact, as it turned out, we had only had its prelude. For Glaucon, with his customary pertinacity, characteristically would not accept Thrasymachus' withdrawal, but asked: 'Do you want our conviction that right action is in all circumstances better than wrong to be genuine or merely apparent?'

'If I were given the choice,' I replied, 'I should want it to be genuine.'

'Well, then, you are not making much progress,' he returned. 'Tell me, do you agree that there is one kind of good which we want to have not with a view to its consequences but because we welcome it for its own sake? For example, enjoyment or pleasure, so long as pleasure brings no harm and its only result is the enjoyment it brings.'

'Yes, that is one kind of good.'

'And is there not another kind of good which we desire both for itself and its consequences? Wisdom and sight and health, for example, we welcome on both grounds.'

'We do,' I said.

'And there is a third category of good, which includes exercise and medical treatment and earning one's living as a doctor or otherwise. All these we should regard as painful but beneficial; we should not choose them for their own sakes but for the wages and other benefits we get from them.'

'There is this third category. But what is your point?'

'In which category do you place justice and right?'

'In the highest category, which anyone who is to be happy welcomes both for its own sake and for its consequences.'

'That is not the common opinion,' Glaucon replied. 'It is normally put into the painful category, of goods which we pursue for the rewards they bring and in the hope of a good reputation, but which in themselves are to be avoided as unpleasant.'

Plato, from *The Republic*, Third Revised Edition, translated by Desmond Lee, pp. 102–108. Copyright 1953, © 1974, 1987 by H. D. P. Lee. Reprinted with the permission of Penguin Books Ltd.

[1]A sketch of Plato's answer to his brother's challenge is provided in the Introductory Essay to Chapter 5 ("Social and Political Philosophy": "It's Just Not Fair!"). Details concerning Plato's life and philosophical commitments precede the selection titled "The Myth of Er" (Literary Reading for Chapter 2). A third selection from *The Republic*, "The Allegory of the Cave," is included in Chapter 8.

'I know that is the common opinion,' I answered; 'which is why Thrasymachus has been criticizing it and praising injustice. But it seems I'm slow to learn.'

'Listen to me then, and see if I can get you to agree,' he said. 'For you seem to have fascinated Thrasymachus into a premature submission, like a snake charmer; but I am not satisfied yet about justice and injustice. I want to be told what exactly each of them is and what effects it has as such on the mind of its possessor, leaving aside any question of rewards or consequences. So what I propose to do, if you agree, is this. I shall revive Thrasymachus' argument under three heads: first, I shall state the common opinion on the nature and origin of justice; second, I shall show that those who practise it do so under compulsion and not because they think it a good; third, I shall argue that this conduct is reasonable because the unjust man has, by common reckoning, a better life than the just man. I don't believe all this myself, Socrates, but Thrasymachus and hundreds of others have dinned it into my ears till I don't know what to think; and I've never heard the case for the superiority of justice to injustice argued to my satisfaction, that is, I've never heard the praises of justice sung simply for its own sake. That is what I expect to hear from you. I therefore propose to state, forcibly, the argument in praise of injustice, and thus give you a model which I want you to follow when your turn comes to speak in praise of justice and censure injustice. Do you like this suggestion?'

'Nothing could please me better,' I replied, 'for it's a subject which all sensible men should be glad to discuss.'

'Splendid,' said Glaucon. 'And now for my first heading, the nature and origin of justice. What they say is that it is according to nature a good thing to inflict wrong or injury,[1] and a bad thing to suffer it, but that the disadvantages of suffering it exceed the advantages of inflicting it; after a taste of both, therefore, men decide that, as they can't evade the one and achieve the other, it will pay to make a compact with each other by which they forgo both.

They accordingly proceed to make laws and mutual agreements, and what the law lays down they call lawful and right. This is the origin and nature of justice. It lies between what is most desirable, to do wrong and avoid punishment, and what is most undesirable, to suffer wrong without being able to get redress; justice lies between these two and is accepted not as being good in itself, but as having a relative value due to our inability to do wrong. For anyone who had the power to do wrong and was a real man would never make any such agreement with anyone—he would be mad if he did.[2]

'This then is the account they give of the nature and the origins of justice; the next point is that men practise it against their will and only because they are unable to do wrong. This we can most easily see if we imagine that a just man and an unjust man have each been given liberty to do what they like, and then follow them and see where their inclinations lead them. We shall catch the just man red-handed in exactly the same pursuits as the unjust, led on by self-interest, the motive which all men naturally follow if they are not forcibly restrained by the law and made to respect each other's claims.

'The best illustration of the liberty I am talking about would be if we supposed them both to be possessed of the power which Gyges, the ancestor of Gyges the Lydian, had in the story. He was a shepherd in the service of the then king of Lydia, and one day there was a great storm and an earthquake in the district where he was pasturing his flock and a chasm opened in the earth. He was amazed at the sight, and descended into the chasm and saw many astonishing things there, among them, so the story goes, a bronze horse, which was hollow and fitted with doors, through which he peeped and saw a corpse which seemed to be of more than human size. He took nothing from it save a gold ring it had on its finger, and then made his way out. He was wearing this ring when he attended the usual meeting of shepherds which reported monthly to the king on the state of his flocks; and as he was sitting there with the others he happened to twist the bezel of the ring towards the inside of his hand. Thereupon he became invisible to his companions, and they began to refer to him as if he had left them. He was astonished, and began fingering the ring again, and turned the bezel outwards; whereupon he became visible again. When he saw this he started experimenting with the ring to see if it really had this power, and found that every time he turned the bezel inwards he became invisible, and when he turned it outwards he became visible. Having made his discovery he managed to get himself included in the party that was to report to the king, and when he arrived seduced the queen, and with her help attacked and murdered the king and seized the throne.

'Imagine now that two such rings existed and the just man put on one, the unjust the other. There is no one, it would commonly be supposed, who would have such iron strength of will as to stick to what is right and keep his hands from taking other people's property. For he would be able to steal from the market whatever he wanted without fear of detection, to go into any man's house and seduce anyone he liked, to murder or to release from prison anyone he felt inclined, and generally behave as if he had supernatural powers. And in all this the just man would differ in no way from the unjust, but both would follow the same course. This, it would be claimed, is strong evidence that no man is just of his own free will, but only under compulsion, and that no man thinks justice pays him personally, since he will always do wrong when he gets the chance. Indeed, the supporter of this view will continue, men are right in thinking that injustice pays the individual better than justice; and if anyone who had the liberty of which we have been speaking neither wronged nor robbed his neighbour, men would think him a most miserable idiot, though of course they would pretend to admire him in public because of their own fear of being wronged.

'So much for that. Finally, we come to the decision between the two lives, and we shall only be able to make this decision if we contrast extreme examples of just and unjust men. By that I mean we make each of them perfect in his own line, and do not in any way mitigate the injustice of the one or the justice of the other. To begin with the unjust man. He

must operate like a skilled professional—for example, a top-class pilot or doctor, who know just what they can or can't do, never attempt the impossible, and are able to retrieve any errors they make. The unjust man must, similarly, if he is to be thoroughly unjust, be able to avoid detection in his wrongdoing; for the man who is found out must be reckoned a poor specimen, and the most accomplished form of injustice is to seem just when you are not. So our perfectly unjust man must be perfect in his wickedness; he must be able to commit the greatest crimes[3] perfectly and at the same time get himself a reputation for the highest probity, while, if he makes a mistake he must be able to retrieve it, and, if any of his wrongdoing comes to light, be ready with a convincing defence, or when force is needed be prepared to use force, relying on his own courage and energy or making use of his friends or his wealth.

'Beside our picture of the unjust man let us set one of the just man, the man of true simplicity of character who, as Aeschylus says, wants 'to be and not to seem good.'[4] We must, indeed, not allow him to seem good, for if he does he will have all the rewards and honours paid to the man who has a reputation for justice, and we shall not be able to tell whether his motive is love of justice or love of the rewards and honours. No, we must strip him of everything except his justice, and our picture of him must be drawn in a way diametrically opposite to that of the unjust man. Our just man must have the worst of reputations for wrong-doing even though he has done no wrong, so that we can test his justice and see if it weakens in the face of unpopularity and all that goes with it; we shall give him an undeserved and lifelong reputation for wickedness, and make him stick to his chosen course until death. In this way, when we have pushed the life of justice and of injustice each to its extreme, we shall be able to judge which of the two is the happier.'

'I say, Glaucon,' I put in, 'you're putting the finishing touches to your own pictures as vigorously as if you were getting them ready for an exhibition.'

'I'm doing my best,' he said. 'And these being our two characters, it is not, I think, difficult to describe the sort of life that awaits each. And if the description is somewhat brutal, remember that it's not I that am responsible for it, Socrates, but those who praise injustice more highly than justice. It is their account that I must now repeat.

'They will say that the just man, as we have pictured him, will be scourged, tortured, and imprisoned, his eyes will be put out, and after enduring every humiliation he will be crucified, and learn at last that one should want not to be, but to seem just. And so that remark which I quoted from Aeschylus could be more appropriately applied to the unjust man; for he, because he deals with realities and does not live by appearances, really wants not to *seem* but to *be* unjust. He

Reaps thought's deep furrow, for therefrom
Spring goodly schemes[5]

—schemes which bring him respectability and office, and which enable him to marry into any family he likes, to make desirable matches for his children, and to pick his partners in business transactions, while all the time, because he has no scruples about committing injustice, he is on the make. In all kinds of competition public or private he always comes off best and does down his rivals, and so becomes rich and can do good to his friends and harm his enemies. His sacrifices and votive offerings to the gods are on a suitably magnificent scale, and his services to the gods, and to any man he wishes to serve, are far better than those of the just man, so that it is reasonable to suppose that the gods care more for him than for the just man. And so they conclude, Socrates, that a better life is provided for the unjust man than for the just by both gods and men.'

Notes

1. *Adikein*: The Greek word translated as 'doing right' is *dikaiosunē*, commonly translated as 'justice,' which is the main theme of the *Republic*, whose subtitle is 'about *dikaiosunē*'. But 'justice' is, as Cross and Woozley say (p. vi), 'a thoroughly unsuitable word to use as a translation of the Greek word.' *Dikaiosunē* has a less legal and more moral meaning than 'justice'; it is in fact the most general Greek word for 'morality', both as a personal quality and as issuing in right action. So Liddell and Scott translates the corresponding epithet *dikaios* as 'observant of duty to god and man, righteous'. Normally in this translation the two words are rendered by 'justice', 'right action', and 'just', 'right'. But the Greek meaning is uncomfortably wide and occasional variants are used, indicated when appropriate by footnotes. Similar remarks apply to words of opposite meaning—*adikia* 'injustice', 'wrong-doing', *adikos* 'unjust', 'wrong'. But here there is the further complication of a verb *adikein*, 'to do wrong' or 'injustice' (intrans.) or to 'wrong' or 'injure' (trans.).

2. This paragraph has been seen as a form, or anticipation, of the Social Contract theories of the 17th/18th centuries. But there are differences as well as similarities. Both have a historical element (not perhaps to be taken too seriously): in both the basis of social arrangements is a contract, explicit or implicit (though this contractual element is not much stressed by Glaucon). But whereas the 17th/18th centuries were interested in the problem of sovereignty—why should I obey the political authorities?—Glaucon is concerned to find a basis for *moral* (rather than political) obligation, which he founds on mutual agreement.

3. *Adikein—dikaiosunē.*

4. *Septem contra Thebas,* l. 592.

5. These two lines follow immediately that quoted above from the *Septem:* ll. 593–4.

The Prisoner's Dilemma

PETER SINGER

Peter Singer is a professor of philosophy and director of the Centre for Human Bioethics at Monash University in Victoria, Australia. The following selection is taken from *The Expanding Circle: Ethics and Sociobiology* (1981). Other books by Professor Singer include *Animal Liberation* (1975), *Practical Ethics* (1980), *Should the Baby Live?* (1985), and *Applied Ethics* (1986).

In the cells of the Ruritanian secret police are two political prisoners. The police are trying to persuade them to confess to membership in an illegal opposition party. The prisoners know that if neither of them confesses, the police will not be able to make the charge stick, but they will be interrogated in the cells for another three months before the police give up and let them go. If one of them confesses, implicating the other, the one who confesses with be released immediately but the other will be sentenced to eight years in jail. If both of them confess, their helpfulness will be taken into account and they will get five years in jail. Since the prisoners are interrogated separately, neither can know if the other has confessed or not.

The dilemma is, of course, whether to confess. The point of the story is that circumstances have been so arranged that if either prisoner reasons from the point of view of self-interest, she will find it to her advantage to confess; whereas taking the interests of the two prisoners together, it is obviously in their interests if neither confesses. Thus the first prisoner's self-interested calculations go like this: "If the other prisoner confesses, it will be better for me if I have also confessed, for then I will get five years instead of eight; and if the other prisoner does not confess, it will still be better for me if I confess, for then I will be released immediately, instead of being interrogated for another three months. Since we are interrogated separately, whether the other prisoner confesses has nothing to do with whether I

confess—our choices are entirely independent of each other. So whatever happens, it will be better for me if I confess." The second prisoner's self-interested reasoning will, of course, follow exactly the same route as the first prisoner's, and will come to the same conclusion. As a result, both prisoners, if self-interested, will confess, and both will spend the next five years in prison. There was a way for them both to be out in three months, but because they were locked into purely self-interested calculations, they could not take that route.

What would have to be changed in our assumptions about the prisoners to make it rational for them both to refuse to confess? One way of achieving this would be for the prisoners to make an agreement that would bind them both to silence. But how could each prisoner be confident that the other would keep the agreement? If one prisoner breaks the agreement, the other will be in prison for a long time, unable to punish the cheater in any way. So each prisoner will reason: "If the other one breaks the agreement, it will be better for me if I break it too; and if the other one keeps the agreement, I will still be better off if I break it. So I will break the agreement."

Without sanctions to back it up, an agreement is unable to bring two self-interested individuals to the outcome that is best for both of them, taking their interests together. What has to be changed to reach this result is the assumption that the prisoners are motivated by self-interest alone. If, for instance, they are altruisic to the extent of caring as much for the interests of their fellow prisoner as they care for their own interests, they will reason thus: "If the other prisoner does not confess it will be better for us both if I do not confess, for then between us we will be in prison for a total of six months, whereas if I do confess the total will be eight years; and if the other prisoner does confess it will still be better if I do not confess, for then the total served will be eight years, instead of ten. So whatever happens, taking our interests together, it will be better if I don't confess." A pair of altruistic prisoners will therefore come out of this situation better than a pair of self-interested prisoners, *even from the point of view of self-interest.*

Altruistic motivation is not the only way to achieve a happier solution. Another possibility is that the prisoners are conscientious, regarding it as morally wrong to inform on a fellow prisoner; or if they are able to make an agreement, they might believe they have a duty to keep their promises. In either case, each will be able to rely on the other not confessing and they will be free in three months.

The Prisoner's Dilemma shows that, paradoxical as it may seem, we will sometimes be better off if we are not self-interested. Two or more people motivated by self-interest alone may not be able to promote their interests as well as they could if they were more altruistic or more conscientious.

The Prisoner's Dilemma explains why there could be an evolutionary advantage in being genuinely altruistic instead of making reciprocal exchanges on the basis of calculated self-interest. Prisons and confessions may not have played a substantial role in early human evolution, but other forms of cooperation surely did. Suppose two early humans are attacked by a sabertooth cat. If both flee, one will be picked off by the cat; if both stand their ground, there is a very good chance that they can fight the cat off; if one flees and the other stands

and fights, the fugitive will escape and the fighter will be killed. Here the odds are sufficiently like those in the Prisoner's Dilemma to produce a similar result. From a self-interested point of view, if your partner flees your chances of survival are better if you flee too (you have a 50 percent chance rather than none at all) and if your partner stands and fights you still do better to run (you are sure of escape if you flee, whereas it is only probable, not certain, that together you and your partner can overcome the cat). So two purely self-interested early humans would flee, and one of them would die. Two early humans who cared for each other, however, would stand and fight, and most likely neither would die. Let us say, just to be able to put a figure on it, that two humans cooperating can defeat a sabertooth cat on nine out of every ten occasions and on the tenth occasion the cat kills one of them. Let us also say that when a sabertooth cat pursues two fleeing humans it always catches one of them, and which one it catches is entirely random, since differences in human running speed are negligible in comparison to the speed of the cat. Then one of a pair of purely self-interested humans would not, on average, last more than a single encounter with a sabertooth cat; but one of a pair of altruistic humans would on average survive ten such encounters.

If situations analogous to this imaginary sabertooth cat attack were common, early humans would do better hunting with altruistic comrades than with self-interested partners. Of course, an egoist who could find an altruist to go hunting with him would do better still; but altruists who could not detect—and refuse to assist—purely self-interested partners would be selected against. Evolution would therefore favor those who are genuinely altruistic to other genuine altruists, but are not altruistic to those who seek to take advantage of their altruism. We can add, again, that the same goal could be achieved if, instead of being altruistic, early humans were moved by something like a sense that it is wrong to desert a partner in the face of danger.

Anthropology and the Abnormal

RUTH FULTON BENEDICT

Ruth Fulton Benedict (1887–1948) was one of the leading anthropologists of the early twentieth century. She taught at Columbia University, conducted field work on a variety of cultures, and influenced generations to come with publications like *Patterns of Culture* (1935). In the following selection, edited from an article that originally appeared in *The Journal of General Psychology* (1934), she argues that ethical values and social standards are culturally determined.

Modern social anthropology has become more and more a study of the varieties and common elements of cultural environment and the consequences of these in human behavior. For such a study of diverse social orders primitive peoples fortunately provide a laboratory not yet entirely vitiated by the spread of a standardized worldwide civilization. Dyaks and Hopis, Fijians and Yakuts are significant for psychological and sociological study because only among these simpler peoples has there been sufficient isolation to give opportunity for the development of localized social forms. In the higher cultures the standardization of custom and belief over a couple of continents has given a false sense of the inevitability of the particular forms that have gained currency, and we need to turn to a wider survey in order to check the conclusions we hastily base upon this near-universality of familiar customs. Most of the simpler cultures did not gain the wide currency of the one which, out of our experience, we identify with human nature, but this was for various historical reasons, and certainly not for any that gives us as its carriers a monopoly of social good or of social sanity. Modern civilization, from this point of view, becomes not a necessary pinnacle of human achievement but one entry in a long series of possible adjustments.

These adjustments, whether they are in mannerisms like the ways of showing anger, or joy, or grief in any society, or in major human drives like those of sex, prove to be far more variable than experience in any one culture would suggest. In certain fields, such as that of religion or of formal marriage arrangements, these wide limits of variability are well known and can be fairly described. In others it is not yet possible to give a generalized account, but that does not absolve us of the task of indicating the significance of the work that has been done and of the problems that have arisen.

One of these problems relates to the customary modern normal-abnormal categories and our conclusions regarding them. In how far are such categories culturally determined, or in how far can we with assurance regard them as absolute? In how far can we regard inability to function socially as diagnostic of abnormality, or in how far is it necessary to regard this as a function of the culture? . . .

The most spectacular illustrations of the extent of which normality may be culturally defined are those cultures where an abnormality of our culture is the cornerstone of their social structure. It is not possible to do justice to these possibilities in a short discussion. A recent study of an island of northwest Melanesia by Fortune describes a society built upon

Ruth Benedict, "Anthropology and the Abnormal," *Journal of General Psychology* 10 (1934), pp. 59–82 (edited). Copyright 1934. Reprinted with the permission of Heldref Publications.

traits which we regard as beyond the border of paranoia. In this tribe the exogamic groups look upon each other as prime manipulators of black magic, so that one marries always into an enemy group which remains for life one's deadly and unappeasable foes. They look upon a good garden crop as a confession of theft, for everyone is engaged in making magic to induce into his garden the productiveness of his neighbor's; therefore no secrecy in the island is so rigidly insisted upon as the secrecy of a man's harvesting of his yams. Their polite phrase at the acceptance of a gift is, "And if you now poison me, how shall I repay you this present?" Their preoccupation with poisoning is constant; no woman ever leaves her cooking pot for a moment unattended. Even the great affinal economic exchanges that are characteristic of this Melanesian culture area are quite altered in Dobu since they are incompatible with this fear and distrust that pervades the culture. . . . They go farther and people the whole world outside their own quarters with such malignant spirits that all-night feasts and ceremonials simply do not occur here. They have even religiously enforced customs that forbid the sharing of seed even in one family group. Anyone else's food is deadly poison to you, so that communality of stores is out of the question. For some months before harvest the whole society is on the verge of starvation, but if one falls to the temptation and eats up one's seed yams, one is an outcast and a beachcomber for life. There is no coming back. It involves, as a matter of course, divorce and the breaking of all social ties.

Now in this society where no one may work with another and no one may share with another, Fortune describes the individual who was regarded by all his fellows as crazy. He was not one of those who periodically ran amok and, beside himself and frothing at the mouth, fell with a knife upon anyone he could reach. Such behavior they did not regard as putting anyone outside the pale. They did not even put the individuals who were known to be liable to these attacks under any kind of control. They merely fled when they saw the attack coming

on and kept out of the way. "He would be all right tomorrow." But there was one man of sunny, kindly disposition who liked work and liked to be helpful. The compulsion was too strong for him to repress it in favor of the opposite tendencies of his culture. Men and women never spoke of him without laughing; he was silly and simple and definitely crazy. Nevertheless, to the ethnologist used to a culture that has, in Christianity, made his type the model of all virtue, he seemed a pleasant fellow.

An even more extreme example, because it is of a culture that has built itself upon a more complex abnormality, is that of the North Pacific Coast of North America. The civilization of the Kwakiutl, at the time when it was first recorded in the last decades of the nineteenth century, was one of the most vigorous in North America. It was built up on an ample economic supply of goods, the fish which furnished their food staple being practically inexhaustible and obtainable with comparatively small labor, and the wood which furnished the material for their houses, their furnishings, and their arts being, with however much labor, always procurable. They lived in coastal villages that compared favorably in size with those of any other American Indians and they kept up constant communication by means of sea-going dug-out canoes.

It was one of the most vigorous and zestful of the aboriginal cultures of North America, with complex crafts and ceremonials, and elaborate and striking arts. It certainly had none of the earmarks of a sick civilization. The tribes of the Northwest Coast had wealth, and exactly in our terms. That is, they had not only a surplus of economic goods, but they made a game of the manipulation of wealth. It was by no means a mere direct transcription of economic needs and the filling of those needs. It involved the idea of capital, of interest, and of conspicuous waste. It was a game with all the binding rules of a game, and a person entered it as a child. His father distributed wealth for him, according to his ability, at a small feast or potlatch, and each gift the receiver was obliged to accept and to return after a short interval with interest that ran to about 100 per cent a year. By the time the child was grown, therefore, he was well launched, a larger potlatch had been given for him on various occasions of exploit or initiation, and he had wealth either out at usury or in his own possession. Nothing in the civilization could be enjoyed without validating it by the distribution of this wealth. Everything that was valued, names and songs as well as material objects, were passed down in family lines, but they were always publicly assumed with accompanying sufficient distributions of property. It was the game of validating and exercising all the privileges one could accumulate from one's various forebears, or by gift, or by marriage, that made the chief interest of the culture. Everyone in his degree took part in it, but many, of course, mainly as spectators. In its highest form it was played out between rival chiefs representing not only themselves and their family lines but their communities, and the object of the contest was to glorify oneself and to humiliate one's opponent. On this level of greatness the property involved was no longer represented by blankets, so many thousand of them to a potlatch, but by higher units of value. These higher units were like our bank notes. They were incised copper tablets, each of them named, and having a value that depended upon their illustrious history. This was as high as ten thousand blankets, and to possess one of them, still more to enhance its value at a great potlatch, was one of the greatest glories within the compass of the chiefs of the Northwest Coast. . . .

Every contingency of life was dealt with in . . . two traditional ways. To them the two were equivalent. Whether one fought with weapons or "fought with property," as they say, the same idea was at the bottom of both. In the olden times, they say, they fought with spears, but now they fight with property. One overcomes one's opponents in equivalent fashion in both, matching forces and seeing that one comes out ahead, and one can thumb one's nose at the vanquished rather more satisfactorily at a potlatch than on a battlefield. Every occasion in life was noticed, not in its own terms, as a stage in the sex life of the individual or as a climax of joy or

of grief, but as furthering this drama of consolidating one's own prestige and bringing shame to one's guests. Whether it was the occasion of the birth of a child, or a daughter's adolescence, or of the marriage of one's son, they were all equivalent raw material for the culture to use for this one traditionally selected end. They were all to raise one's own personal status and to entrench oneself by the humiliation of one's fellows. A girl's adolescence among the Nootka was an event for which her father gathered property from the time she was first able to run about. When she was adolescent he would demonstrate his greatness by an unheard-of distribution of these goods, and put down all his rivals. It was not as a fact of the girl's sex life that it figured in their culture, but as the occasion for a major move in the great game of vindicating one's own greatness and humiliating one's associates.

In their behavior at great bereavements this set of the culture comes out most strongly. Among the Kwakiutl it did not matter whether a relative had died in bed of disease, or by the hand of an enemy; in either case death was an affront to be wiped out by the death of another person. The fact that one had been caused to mourn was proof that one had been put upon. A chief's sister and her daughter had gone up to Victoria, and either because they drank bad whiskey or because their boat capsized they never came back. The chief called together his warriors, "Now, I ask you, tribes, who shall wail? Shall I do it or shall another?" The spokesman answered, of course, "Not you, Chief. Let some other of the tribes." Immediately they set up the war pole to announce their intention of wiping out the injury, and gathered a war party. They set out, and found seven men and two children asleep and killed them. "Then they felt good when they arrived at Sebaa in the evening."

The point which is of interest to us is that in our society those who on that occasion would feel good when they arrived at Sebaa that evening would be the definitely abnormal. There would be some, even in our society, but it is not a recognized and approved mood under the circumstances. On the

Northwest Coast those are favored and fortunate to whom that mood under those circumstances is congenial, and those to whom it is repugnant are unlucky. This latter minority can register in their own culture only by doing violence to their congenial responses and acquiring others that are difficult for them. The person, for instance, who, like a Plains Indian whose wife has been taken from him, is too proud to fight, can deal with the Northwest Coast civilization only by ignoring its strongest bents. If he cannot achieve it, he is the deviant in that culture, their instance of abnormality.

This head-hunting that takes place on the Northwest Coast after a death is no matter of blood revenge or of organized vengeance. There is no effort to tie up the subsequent killing with any responsibility on the part of the victim for the death of the person who is being mourned. A chief whose son has died goes visiting wherever his fancy dictates, and he says to his host, "My prince has died today, and you go with him." Then he kills him. In this, according to their interpretation, he acts nobly because he has not been downed. He has thrust his back in return. The whole procedure is meaningless without the fundamental paranoid reading of bereavement. Death, like all the other untoward accidents of existence, confounds man's pride and can only be handled in the category of insults. . . .

These illustrations, which it has been possible to indicate only in the briefest manner, force upon us the fact that normality is culturally defined. An adult shaped to the drives and standards of either of these cultures, if he were transported into our civilization, would fall into our categories of abnormality. He would be faced with the psychic dilemmas of the socially unavailable. In his own culture, however, he is the pillar of society, the end result of socially inculcated mores, and the problem of personal instability in his case simply does not arise.

No one civilization can possibly utilize in its mores the whole potential range of human behavior. Just as there are great numbers of possible phonetic articulations, and the possibility of language depends on a selection and standardization of a few of these in order that speech communication may be possible at all, so the possibility of organized behavior of every sort, from the fashions of local dress and houses to the dicta of a people's ethics and religion, depends upon a similar selection among the possible behavior traits. In the field of recognized economic obligations or sex tabus this selection is as nonrational and subconscious a process as it is in the field of phonetics. It is a process which goes on in the group for long periods of time and is historically conditioned by innumerable accidents of isolation or of contact of peoples. In any comprehensive study of psychology, the selection that different cultures have made in the course of history within the great circumference of potential behavior is of great significance.

Every society, beginning with some slight inclination in one direction or another, carries its preference farther and farther, integrating itself more and more completely upon its chosen basis, and discarding those types of behavior that are uncongenial. Most of those organizations of personality that seem to us most incontrovertibly abnormal have been used by different civilizations in the very foundations of their institutional life. Conversely the most valued traits of our normal individuals have been looked on in differently organized cultures as aberrant. Normality, in short, within a very wide range, is culturally defined. It is primarily a term for the socially elaborated segment of human behavior in any culture; and abnormality, a term for the segment that that particular civilization does not use. The very eyes with which we see the problem are conditioned by the long traditional habits of our own society.

It is a point that has been made more often in relation to ethics than in relation to psychiatry. We do not any longer make the mistake of deriving the morality of our own locality and decade directly from the inevitable constitution of human nature. We do not elevate it to the dignity of a first principle. We recognize that morality differs in every society, and is a convenient term for socially approved habits. Mankind has always preferred to say, "It is morally good," rather than "It is habitual," and the fact of this preference is matter enough for a critical science of ethics. But historically the two phrases are synonymous.

The concept of the normal is properly a variant of the concept of the good. It is that which society has approved. A normal action is one which falls well within the limits of expected behavior for a particular society. Its variability among different peoples is essentially a function of the variability of the behavior patterns that different societies have created for themselves, and can never be wholly divorced from a consideration of culturally institutionalized types of behavior.

Each culture is a more or less elaborate working-out of the potentialities of the segment it has chosen. In so far as a civilization is well integrated and consistent within itself, it will tend to carry farther and farther, according to its nature, its initial impulse toward a particular type of action, and from the point of view of any other culture those elaborations will include more and more extreme and aberrant traits.

Each of these traits, in proportion as it reinforces the chosen behavior patterns of that culture, is for the culture normal. Those individuals to whom it is congenial either congenitally, or as the result of childhood sets, are accorded prestige in that culture, and are not visited with the social contempt or disapproval which their traits would call down upon them in a society that was differently organized. On the other hand, those individuals whose characteristics are not congenial to the selected type of human behavior in that community are the deviants, no matter how valued their personality traits may be in a contrasted civilization. . . .

The problem of understanding abnormal human behavior in any absolute sense independent of cultural factors is still far in the future. The categories of borderline behaviors which we derive from the study of the neuroses and psychoses of our civilization are categories of prevailing local types of instability. They give much information about the stresses and strains of Western civilization, but no final picture of inevitable human behavior. Any conclusions about such behavior must await the collection by trained observers of psychiatric data from other cultures. Since no adequate work of the kind has been done at the present time, it is impossible to say what core of definition of abnormality may be found valid from the comparative material. It is as it is in ethics; all our local conventions of moral behavior and of immoral are without absolute validity, and yet it is quite possible that a modicum of what is considered right and what wrong could be disentangled that is shared by the whole human race. When data are available in psychiatry, this minimum definition of abnormal human tendencies will be probably quite unlike our culturally conditioned, highly elaborated psychoses such as those that are described, for instance, under the terms of schizophrenia and manic-depressive.

A Good Man Is Hard to Find

FLANNERY O'CONNOR

Flannery O'Connor (1925–1964) was born in Savannah, Georgia. She grew up, lived, and died in the small town of Milledgeville. Her frank, powerful fiction uses the backdrop of the South to explore the human condition. The literary pictures she painted are often dark and disturbing: violence and evil are confronted as bare facts of human existence—without excuse, reason, or explanation.

The grandmother didn't want to go to Florida. She wanted to visit some of her connections in east Tennessee and she was seizing at every chance to change Bailey's mind. Bailey was the son she lived with, her only boy. He was sitting on the edge of his chair at the table, bent over the orange sports section of the *Journal.* "Now look here, Bailey," she said, "see here, read this," and she stood with one hand on her thin hip and the other rattling the newspaper at his bald head. "Here this fellow that calls himself The Misfit is aloose from the Federal Pen and headed toward Florida and you read here what it says he did to these people. Just you read it. I wouldn't take my children in any direction with a criminal like that aloose in it. I couldn't answer to my conscience if I did."

Bailey didn't look up from his reading so she wheeled around then and faced the children's mother, a young woman in slacks, whose face was as broad and innocent as a cabbage and was tied round with a green head-kerchief that had two points on the top like rabbit's ears. She was sitting on the sofa, feeding the baby his apricots out of a jar. "The children have been to Florida before," the old lady said. "You all ought to take them somewhere else for a change so they would see different parts of the world and be broad. They never have been to east Tennessee."

The children's mother didn't seem to hear her but the eight-year-old boy, John Wesley, a stocky child with glasses, said, "If you don't want to go to Florida, why dontcha stay at home?" He and the lit-tle girl, June Star, were reading the funny papers on the floor.

"She wouldn't stay at home to be queen for a day," June Star said without raising her yellow head.

"Yes and what would you do if this fellow, The Misfit, caught you?" the grandmother asked.

"I'd smack his face," John Wesley said.

"She wouldn't stay at home for a million bucks," June Star said. "Afraid she'd miss something. She has to go everywhere we go."

"All right, Miss," the grandmother said. "Just remember that the next time you want me to curl your hair."

June Star said her hair was naturally curly.

The next morning the grandmother was the first one in the car, ready to go. She had her big black valise that looked like the head of a hippopotamus in one corner, and underneath it she was hiding a basket with Pitty Sing, the cat, in it. She didn't intend for the cat to be left alone in the house for three days because he would miss her too much and she was afraid he might brush against one of the gas burners and accidentally asphyxiate himself. Her son, Bailey, didn't like to arrive at a motel with a cat.

She sat in the middle of the back seat with John Wesley and June Star on either side of her. Bailey and the children's mother and the baby sat in the front and they left Atlanta at eight forty-five with the mileage on the car at 55890. The grandmother wrote this down because she thought it would be interesting to say how many miles they had been when they got back. It took them twenty minutes to reach the outskirts of the city.

The old lady settled herself comfortably, removing her white cotton gloves and putting them up with her purse on the shelf in front of the back window. The children's mother still had on slacks and still had her head tied up in a green kerchief, but the grandmother had on a navy blue straw sailor hat with a bunch of white violets on the brim and a navy blue dress with a small white dot in the print. Her collar and cuffs were white organdy trimmed with lace and at her neckline she had pinned a purple spray of cloth violets containing a sachet. In case of an accident, anyone seeing her dead on the highway would know at once that she was a lady.

She said she thought it was going to be a good day for driving, neither too hot nor too cold, and she cautioned Bailey that the speed limit was fifty-five miles an hour and that the patrolmen hid themselves behind billboards and small clumps of trees and sped out after you before you had a chance to slow down. She pointed out interesting details of the scenery: Stone Mountain; the blue granite that in some places came up to both sides of the highway; the brilliant red clay banks slightly streaked with purple; and the various crops that made rows of green lace-work on the ground. The trees were full of silver-white sunlight and the meanest of them sparkled. The children were reading comic magazines and their mother had gone back to sleep.

"Let's go through Georgia fast so we won't have to look at it much," John Wesley said.

"If I were a little boy," said the grandmother, "I wouldn't talk about my native state that way. Tennessee has the mountains and Georgia has the hills."

"Tennessee is just a hillbilly dumping ground," John Wesley said, "and Georgia is a lousy state too."

"You said it," June Star said.

"In my time," said the grandmother, folding her thin veined fingers, "children were more respectful of their native states and their parents and everything else. People did right then. Oh look at the cute little pickaninny!" she said and pointed to a Negro child standing in the door of a shack. "Wouldn't that make a picture, now?" she asked and they all turned and looked at the little Negro out of the back window. He waved.

"He didn't have any britches on," June said.

"He probably didn't have any," the grandmother explained. "Little niggers in the country don't have things like we do. If I could paint, I'd paint that picture," she said.

The children exchanged comic books.

The grandmother offered to hold the baby and the children's mother passed him over the front seat to her. She set him on her knee and bounced him and told him about the things they were passing. She rolled her eyes and screwed up her mouth and stuck her leathery thin face into his smooth bland one. Occasionally he gave her a faraway smile. They passed a large cotton field with five or six graves fenced in the middle of it, like a small island. "Look at the graveyard!" the grandmother said, pointing it out. "That was the old family burying ground. That belonged to the plantation."

"Where's the plantation?" John Wesley asked.

"Gone With the Wind," said the grandmother. "Ha. Ha."

When the children finished all the comic books they had brought, they opened the lunch and ate it. The grandmother ate a peanut butter sandwich and an olive and would not let the children throw the box and the paper napkins out the window. When there was nothing else to do they played a game by choosing a cloud and making the other two guess what shape it suggested. John Wesley took one the shape of a cow and June Star guessed a cow and John Wesley said, no, an automobile, and June Star said he didn't play fair, and they began to slap each other over the grandmother.

The grandmother said she would tell them a story if they would keep quiet. When she told a story, she rolled her eyes and waved her head and was very dramatic. She said once when she was a maiden lady she had been courted by a Mr. Edgar Atkins Teagarden from Jasper, Georgia. She said he was a very good-looking man and a gentleman and that he brought her a watermelon every Saturday afternoon with his initials cut in it. E. A. T. Well, one Saturday, she said, Mr. Teagarden brought the watermelon and there was nobody at home and he left it on the front porch and returned in his buggy to Jasper, but she never got the watermelon, she said, because a nigger boy ate it when he saw the initials, E. A. T.! This story tickled John Wesley's funny bone and he giggled and giggled but June Star didn't think it was any good. She said she wouldn't marry a man that just brought her a watermelon on Saturday. The grandmother said she would have done well to marry Mr. Teagarden because he was a gentleman and had bought Coca-Cola stock when it first came out and that he had died only a few years ago, a very wealthy man.

They stopped at The Tower for barbecued sandwiches. The Tower was a part stucco and part wood filling station and dance hall set in a clearing outside of Timothy. A fat man named Red Sammy Butts ran it and there were signs stuck here and there on the building and for miles up and down the highway saying, TRY RED SAMMY'S FAMOUS BARBE-CUE, NONE LIKE FAMOUS RED SAMMY'S! RED SAM! THE FAT BOY WITH THE HAPPY LAUGH. A VETERAN! SAMMY'S YOUR MAN!

Red Sammy was lying on the bare ground outside The Tower with his head under a truck while a gray monkey about a foot high, chained to a small chinaberry tree, chattered nearby. The monkey sprang back into the tree and got on the highest limb as soon as he saw the children jump out of the car and run toward them.

Inside, The Tower was a long dark room with a counter at one end and tables at the other and dancing space in the middle. They all sat down at a broad table next to the nickelodeon and Red Sam's wife, a tall burnt-brown woman with hair and eyes lighter than her skin, came and took their order.

The children's mother put a dime in the machine and played "The Tennessee Waltz," and the grandmother said that tune always made her want to dance. She asked Bailey if he would like to dance but he only glared at her. He didn't have a naturally sunny disposition like she did and trips made him nervous. The grandmother's brown eyes were very bright. She swayed her head from side to side and pretended she was dancing in her chair. June Star said play something she could tap to so the children's mother put in another dime and played a fast number and June Star stepped out onto the dance floor and did her tap routine.

"Ain't she cute?" Red Sam's wife said, leaning over the counter. "Would you like to come be my little girl?"

"No I certainly wouldn't," June Star said. "I wouldn't live in a broken-down place like this for a million bucks!" and she ran back to the table.

"Ain't she cute?" the woman repeated, stretching her mouth politely.

"Aren't you ashamed?" hissed the grandmother.

Red Sam came in and told his wife to quit lounging on the counter and hurry with these people's order. His khaki trousers reached just to his hip bones and his stomach hung over them like a sack of meal swaying under his shirt. He came over and sat down at a table nearby and let out a combination sigh and yodel. "You can't win," he said. "You can't win," and he wiped his sweating red face off with a gray handkerchief. "These days you don't know who to trust," he said. "Ain't that the truth?"

"People are certainly not nice like they used to be," said the grandmother.

"Two fellers come in here last week," Red Sammy said, "driving a Chrysler. It was a old beat-up car but it was a good one and these boys looked all right to me. Said they worked at the mill and you know I let them fellers charge the gas they bought? Now why did I do that?"

"Because you're a good man!" the grandmother said at once.

"Yes'm, I suppose so," Red Sam said as if he were struck with the answer.

His wife brought the orders, carrying the five plates all at once without a tray, two in each hand and one balanced on her arm. "It isn't a soul in this green world of God's that you can trust," she said. "And I don't count anybody out of that, not nobody," she repeated, looking at Red Sammy.

"Did you read about the criminal, The Misfit, that's escaped?" asked the grandmother.

"I wouldn't be a bit surprised if he didn't attact this place right here," said the woman. "If he hears about it being here, I wouldn't be none surprised to see him. If he hears it's two cent in the cash register, I wouldn't be a tall surprised if he . . ."

"That'll do," Red Sam said. "Go bring these people their Co'Colas," and the woman went off to get the rest of the order.

"A good man is hard to find," Red Sammy said. "Everything is getting terrible. I remember the day you could go off and leave your screen door unlatched. Not no more."

He and the grandmother discussed better times. The old lady said that in her opinion Europe was entirely to blame for the way things were now. She said the way Europe acted you would think we were made of money and Red Sam said it was no use talking about it, she was exactly right. The children ran outside into the white sunlight and looked at the monkey in the lacy chinaberry tree. He was busy catching fleas on himself and biting each one carefully between his teeth as if it were a delicacy.

They drove off again into the hot afternoon. The grandmother took cat naps and woke up every few minutes with her own snoring. Outside of Toombsboro she woke up and recalled an old plantation that she had visited in this neighborhood once when she was a young lady. She said the house had six white columns across the front and that there was an avenue of oaks leading up to it and two little wooden trellis arbors on either side in front where you sat down with your suitor after a stroll in the garden. She recalled exactly which road to turn off to get to it. She knew that Bailey would not be willing to lose any time looking at an old house, but the more she talked about it, the more she wanted to see it once again and find out if the

little twin arbors were still standing. "There was a secret panel in this house," she said craftily, not telling the truth but wishing that she were, "and the story went that all the family silver was hidden in it when Sherman came through but it was never found . . ."

"Hey!" John Wesley said. "Let's go see it! We'll find it! We'll poke all the woodwork and find it! Who lives there? Where do you turn off at? Hey Pop, can't we turn off there?"

"We never have seen a house with a secret panel!" June Star shrieked. "Let's go to the house with the secret panel! Hey, Pop, can't we go see the house with the secret panel!"

"It's not far from here, I know," the grandmother said. "It wouldn't take over twenty minutes."

Bailey was looking straight ahead. His jaw was as rigid as a horseshoe. "No," he said.

The children began to yell and scream that they wanted to see the house with the secret panel. John Wesley kicked the back of the front seat and June Star hung over her mother's shoulder and whined desperately into her ear that they never had any fun even on their vacation, and that they could never do what THEY wanted to do. The baby began to scream and John Wesley kicked the back of the seat so hard that his father could feel the blows in his kidney.

"All right!" he shouted, and drew the car to a stop at the side of the road. "Will you all shut up? Will you all just shut up for one second? If you don't shut up, we won't go anywhere."

"It would be very educational for them," the grandmother murmured.

"All right," Bailey said, "but get this: this is the only time we're going to stop for anything like this. This is the one and only time."

"The dirt road that you have to turn down is about a mile back," the grandmother directed. "I marked it when we passed."

"A dirt road," Bailey groaned.

After they had turned around and were headed toward the dirt road, the grandmother recalled other points about the house, the beautiful glass over the front doorway and the candle-lamp in the hall. John Wesley said that the secret panel was probably in the fireplace.

"You can't go inside this house," Bailey said. "You don't know who lives there."

"While you all talk to the people in front, I'll run around behind and get in a window," John Wesley suggested.

"We'll all stay in the car," his mother said.

They turned onto the dirt road and the car raced roughly along in a swirl of pink dust. The grandmother recalled the times when there were no paved roads and thirty miles was a day's journey. The dirt road was hilly and there were sudden washes in it and sharp curves on dangerous embankments. All at once they would be on a hill, looking down over the blue tops of trees for miles around, then the next minute, they would be in a red depression with the dust-coated trees looking down on them.

"This place had better turn up in a minute," Bailey said, "or I'm going to turn around."

The road looked as if no one had traveled on it in months.

"It's not much farther," the grandmother said and just as she said it, a horrible thought came to her. The thought was so embarrassing that she turned red in the face and her eyes dilated and her feet jumped up, upsetting her valise in the corner. The instant the valise moved, the newspaper top she had over the basket under it rose with a snarl and Pitty Sing, the cat, sprang onto Bailey's shoulder.

The children were thrown to the floor and their mother, clutching the baby, was thrown out the door onto the ground, the old lady was thrown into the front seat. The car turned over once and landed right-side-up in a gulch on the side of the road. Bailey remained in the driver's seat with the cat—gray-striped with a broad white face and an orange nose—clinging to his neck like a caterpillar.

As soon as the children saw they could move their arms and legs, they scrambled out of the car, shouting. "We've had an ACCIDENT!" The grandmother was curled up under the dashboard, hoping she was injured so that Bailey's wrath would not come down on her all at once. The horrible thought she had had before the accident was that the house she had remembered so vividly was not in Georgia but in Tennessee.

Bailey removed the cat from his neck with both hands and flung it out the window against the side of a pine tree. Then he got out of the car and started looking for the children's mother. She was sitting against the side of the red gutted ditch, holding the screaming baby, but she only had a cut down her face and a broken shoulder. "We've had an ACCIDENT!" the children screamed in a frenzy of delight.

"But nobody's killed," June Star said with disappointment as the grandmother limped out of the car, her hat still pinned to her head but the broken front brim standing up at a jaunty angle and the violet spray hanging off the side. They all sat down in the ditch, except the children, to recover from the shock. They were all shaking.

"Maybe a car will come along," said the children's mother hoarsely.

"I believe I have injured an organ," said the grandmother, pressing her side, but no one answered her. Bailey's teeth were clattering. He had on a yellow sport shirt with bright blue parrots designed in it and his face was as yellow as the shirt. The grandmother decided that she would not mention that the house was in Tennessee.

The road was about ten feet above and they could see only the tops of the trees on the other side of it. Behind the ditch they were sitting in there were more woods, tall and dark and deep. In a few minutes they saw a car coming some distance away on top of a hill, coming slowly as if the occupants were watching them. The grandmother stood up and waved both arms dramatically to attract their attention. The car continued to come on slowly, disappeared around a bend and appeared again, moving even slower, on top of the hill they had gone over. It was a big black battered hearse-like automobile. There were three men in it.

It came to a stop just over them and for some minutes, the driver looked down with a steady expressionless gaze to where they were sitting, and didn't speak. Then he turned his head and muttered something to the other two and they got out. One was a fat boy in black trousers and a red sweat shirt with a silver stallion embossed on the front of it. He moved around on the right side of them and stood staring, his mouth partly open in a kind of loose grin. The other had on khaki pants and a blue striped coat and a gray hat pulled down very low, hiding most of his face. He came around slowly on the left side. Neither spoke.

The driver got out of the car and stood by the side of it, looking down at them. He was an older man than the other two. His hair was just beginning to gray and he wore silver-rimmed spectacles that gave him a scholarly look. He had a long creased face and didn't have on any shirt or undershirt. He had on blue jeans that were too tight for him and was holding a black hat and a gun. The two boys also had guns.

"We've had an ACCIDENT!" the children screamed.

The grandmother had the peculiar feeling that the bespectacled man was someone she knew. His face was as familiar to her as if she had known him all her life but she could not recall who he was. He moved away from the car and began to come down the embankment, placing his feet carefully so that he wouldn't slip. He had on tan and white shoes and no socks, and his ankles were red and thin. "Good afternoon," he said. "I see you all had a little spill."

"We turned over twice!" said the grandmother.

"Oncet," he corrected. "We seen it happen. Try their car and see will it run, Hiram," he said quietly to the boy with the gray hat.

"What you got that gun for?" John Wesley asked. "Whatcha gonna do with that gun?"

"Lady," the man said to the children's mother, "would you mind calling them children to sit down by you? Children make me nervous. I want all you all to sit down right together there where you're at."

"What are you telling us what to do for?" June Star asked.

Behind them the line of woods gaped like a dark open mouth. "Come here," said their mother.

"Look here now," Bailey began suddenly, "we're in a predicament! We're in . . ."

The grandmother shrieked. She scrambled to her feet and stood staring. "You're The Misfit!" she said. "I recognized you at once."

"Yes'm," the man said, smiling slightly as if he were pleased in spite of himself to be known, "but it would have been better for all of you, lady, if you hadn't of reckernized me."

Bailey turned his head sharply and said something to his mother that shocked even the children. The old lady began to cry and The Misfit reddened.

"Lady," he said, "don't get upset. Sometimes a man says things he don't mean. I don't reckon he meant to talk to you thataway."

"You wouldn't shoot a lady, would you?" the grandmother said and removed a clean handkerchief from her cuff and began to slap at her eyes with it.

The Misfit pointed the toe of his shoe into the ground and made a little hole and then covered it up again. "I would hate to have to," he said.

"Listen," the grandmother almost screamed, "I know you're a good man. You don't look a bit like you have common blood. I know you must come from nice people!"

"Yes mam," he said, "the finest people in the world." When he smiled he showed a row of strong white teeth. "God never made a finer woman than my mother and my daddy's heart was pure gold," he said. The boy with the red sweat shirt had come around behind them and was standing with his gun at his hip. The Misfit squatted down on the ground. "Watch them children, Bobby Lee," he said. "You know they make me nervous." He looked at the six of them huddled together in front of him and he seemed to be embarrassed as if he couldn't think of anything to say. "Ain't a cloud in the sky," he remarked, looking up at it. "Don't see no sun but don't see no cloud neither."

"Yes, it's a beautiful day," said the grandmother. "Listen," she said, "you shouldn't call yourself The Misfit because I know you're a good man at heart. I can just look at you and tell."

"Hush!" Bailey yelled. "Hush! Everybody shut up and let me handle this!" He was squatting in the position of a runner about to sprint forward but he didn't move.

"I pre-chate that, lady," The Misfit said and drew a little circle in the ground with the butt of his gun.

"It'll take a half a hour to fix this here car," Hiram called, looking over the raised hood of it.

"Well, first you and Bobby Lee get him and that little boy to step over yonder with you," The Misfit said, pointing to Bailey and John Wesley. "The boys want to ask you something," he said to Bailey. "Would you mind stepping back in them woods there with them?"

"Listen," Bailey began, "we're in a terrible predicament. Nobody realizes what this is," and his voice cracked. His eyes were as blue and intense as the parrots in his shirt and he remained perfectly still.

The grandmother reached up to adjust her hat brim as if she were going to the woods with him but it came off in her hand. She stood staring at it and after a second she let it fall to the ground. Hiram pulled Bailey up by the arm as if he were assisting an old man. John Wesley caught hold of his father's hand and Bobby Lee followed. They went off toward the woods and just as they reached the dark edge, Bailey turned and supporting himself against a gray naked pine trunk, he shouted, "I'll be back in a minute, Mamma, wait on me!"

"Come back this instant!" his mother shrilled but they all disappeared into the woods.

"Bailey Boy!" the grandmother called in a tragic voice but she found she was looking at The Misfit squatting on the ground in front of her. "I just know you're a good man," she said desperately. "You're not a bit common!"

"Nome, I ain't a good man," The Misfit said after a second as if he had considered her statement carefully, "but I ain't the worst in the world neither. My daddy said I was different breed of dog from my brothers and sisters. 'You know,' Daddy said, 'it's some that can live their whole life out without asking about it and it's others has to know why it is, and this boy is one of the latters. He's going to be into everything!'" He put on his black hat and looked up suddenly and then away deep into the woods as if he were embarrassed again. "I'm sorry I don't have on a shirt before you ladies," he said, hunching his shoulders slightly. "We buried our clothes that we had on when we escaped and we're just making do until we can get better. We borrowed these from some folks we met," he explained.

"That's perfectly all right," the grandmother said. "Maybe Bailey has an extra shirt in his suitcase."

"I'll look and see terrectly," The Misfit said.

"Where are they taking him?" the children's mother screamed.

"Daddy was a card himself," The Misfit said. "You couldn't put anything over on him. He never got in trouble with the Authorities though. Just had the knack of handling them."

"You could be honest too if you'd only try," said the grandmother. "Think how wonderful it would be to settle down and live a comfortable life and not have to think about somebody chasing you all the time."

The Misfit kept scratching in the ground with the butt of his gun as if he were thinking about it. "Yes'm, somebody is always after you," he murmured.

The grandmother noticed how thin his shoulder blades were just behind his hat because she was standing up looking down at him. "Do you ever pray?" she asked.

He shook his head. All she saw was the black hat wiggle between his shoulder blades. "Nome," he said.

There was a pistol shot from the woods, followed closely by another. Then silence. The old lady's head jerked around. She could hear the wind move through the tree tops like a long satisfied insuck of breath. "Bailey Boy!" she called.

"I was a gospel singer for a while," The Misfit said. "I been most everything. Been in the arm service, both land and sea, at home and abroad, been twict married, been an undertaker, been with the railroads, plowed Mother Earth, been in a tornado, seen a man burnt alive oncet," and he looked up at the children's mother and the little girl who was sitting close together, their faces white and their eyes glassy; "I even seen a woman flogged," he said.

"Pray, pray," the grandmother began, "pray, pray . . ."

"I never was a bad boy that I remember of," The Misfit said in an almost dreamy voice, "but somewheres along the line I done something wrong and got sent to the penitentiary. I was buried alive," and he looked up and held her attention to him by a steady stare.

"That's when you should have started to pray," she said. "What did you do to get sent to the penitentiary that first time?"

"Turn to the right, it was a wall," The Misfit said, looking up again at the cloudless sky. "Turn to the left, it was a wall. Look up it was a ceiling, look down it was a floor. I forgot what I done, lady. I set there and set there, trying to remember what it was I done and I ain't recalled it to this day. Oncet in a while, I would think it was coming to me, but it never come."

"Maybe they put you in by mistake," the old lady said vaguely.

"Nome," he said. "It wasn't no mistake. They had the papers on me."

"You must have stolen something," she said.

The Misfit sneered slightly. "Nobody had nothing I wanted," he said. "It was a head-doctor at the penitentiary said what I had done was kill my daddy but I know that for a lie. My daddy died in nineteen ought nineteen of the epidemic flu and I never had a thing to do with it. He was buried in the Mount Hopewell Baptist churchyard and you can go there and see for yourself."

"If you would pray," the old lady said, "Jesus would help you."

"That's right," The Misfit said.

"Well then, why don't you pray?" she asked trembling with delight suddenly.

"I don't want no hep," he said. "I'm doing all right by myself."

Bobby Lee and Hiram came ambling back from the woods. Bobby Lee was dragging a yellow shirt with bright blue parrots in it.

"Throw me that shirt, Bobby Lee," The Misfit said. The shirt came flying at him and landed on his shoulder and he put it on. The grandmother couldn't name what the shirt reminded her of. "No, lady," The Misfit said while he was buttoning it up. "I found out the crime didn't matter. You can do one thing or you can do another, kill a man or take a tire off his car, because sooner or later you're going to forget what it was you done and just be punished for it."

The children's mother had begun to make heaving noises as if she couldn't get her breath. "Lady," he asked, "would you and that little girl like to step off yonder with Bobby Lee and Hiram and join your husband?"

"Yes, thank you," the mother said faintly. Her left arm dangled helplessly and she was holding the baby, who had gone to sleep, in the other. "Hep that lady up, Hiram," The Misfit said as she struggled to climb out of the ditch, "and Bobby Lee, you hold onto that little girl's hand."

"I don't want to hold hands with him," June Star said. "He reminds me of a pig."

The fat boy blushed and laughed and caught her by the arm and pulled her off into the woods after Hiram and her mother.

Alone with The Misfit, the grandmother found that she had lost her voice. There was not a cloud in the sky nor any sun. There was nothing around her but woods. She wanted to tell him that he must pray. She opened and closed her mouth several times before anything came out. Finally she found herself saying, "Jesus, Jesus," meaning Jesus will help you, but the way she was saying it, it sounded as if she might be cursing.

"Yes'm," The Misfit said as if he agreed. "Jesus thrown everything off balance. It was the same case with Him as with me except He hadn't committed any crime and they could prove I had committed one because they had the papers on me. Of course," he said, "they never showed me any papers. That's why I sign myself now. I said long ago, you get you a signature and sign everything you do and keep a copy of it. Then you'll know what you done and you can hold up the crime to the punishment and see do they match and in the end you'll have something to prove you ain't been treated right. I call myself The Misfit," he said, "because I can't make what all I done wrong fit what all I gone through in punishment."

There was a piercing scream from the woods, followed closely by a pistol report. "Does it seem right to you, lady, that one is punished a heap and another ain't punished at all?"

"Jesus!" the old lady cried. "You've got good blood! I know you wouldn't shoot a lady! I know you come from nice people! Pray! Jesus, you ought not to shoot a lady. I'll give you all the money I've got!"

"Lady," The Misfit said, looking beyond her far into the woods, "there never was a body that give the undertaker a tip."

There were two more pistol reports and the grandmother raised her head like a parched old turkey hen crying for water and called, "Bailey Boy! Bailey Boy!" as if her heart would break.

"Jesus was the only One that ever raised the dead," The Misfit continued, "and He shouldn't have done it. He thrown everything off balance. If He did what He said, then it's nothing for you to do but throw away everything and follow Him, and if He didn't, then it's nothing for you to do but enjoy the few minutes you got left the best way you can— by killing somebody or burning down his house or doing some other meanness to him. No pleasure but meanness," he said and his voice had become almost a snarl.

"Maybe He didn't raise the dead," the old lady mumbled, not knowing what she was saying and feeling so dizzy that she sank down in the ditch with her legs twisted under her.

"I wasn't there so I can't say He didn't," The Misfit said. "I wisht I had of been there," he said, hitting the ground with his fist. "It ain't right I wasn't there because if I had of been there I would of known. Listen lady," he said in a high voice, "if I had of been there I would of known and I wouldn't be like I am now." His voice seemed about to crack and the grandmother's head cleared for an instant. She saw the man's face twisted close to her own as if he were going to cry and she murmured, "Why you're one of my babies. You're one of my own children!" She reached out and touched him on the shoulder. The Misfit sprang back as if a snake had bitten him and shot her three times through the chest. Then he put his gun down on the ground and took off his glasses and began to clean them.

Hiram and Bobby Lee returned from the woods and stood over the ditch, looking down at the grandmother who half sat and half lay in a puddle of blood with her legs crossed under her like a child's and her face smiling up at the cloudless sky.

Without his glasses, The Misfit's eyes were red-rimmed and pale and defenseless-looking. "Take her off and throw her where you thrown the others," he said, picking up the cat that was rubbing itself against his leg.

"She was a talker, wasn't she?" Bobby Lee said, sliding down the ditch with a yodel.

"She would of been a good woman," The Misfit said, "if it had been somebody there to shoot her every minute of her life."

"Some fun!" Bobby Lee said.

"Shut up, Bobby Lee," The Misfit said. "It's no real pleasure in life."

Review and Reflection

1. Explicate and evaluate Aristotle's distinction between intrinsic and extrinsic values, his doctrine of the Golden Mean, and his commitment to the position known as *eudemonism*.

2. Explicate and evaluate the following positions: Egoism, Utilitarianism, Cultural Relativism, and Divine Will Theory.

3. Suppose you somehow acquired Plato's mythical Ring of Gyges. Would it change your behavior? If so, how? Why?

4. Retell, in your own words, the Prisoner's Dilemma. Do you agree with Peter Singer's analysis? Why?

5. What impressed you most about the Kwakiutl society? What conclusions does Ruth Fulton Benedict draw from her study of cultures such as these? Do you agree? Why?

6. Does Flannery O'Connor paint an accurate picture of the human condition? What opinions did you form concerning The Misfit? What is his nature? What does he symbolize?

Suggestions for Further Study

ARISTOTLE. *Nicomachean Ethics.* Translated by M. Ostwald. New York: Macmillan, 1962.

LISA H. NEWTON. *Ethics in America: Source Reader.* Englewood Cliffs, NJ: Prentice Hall, 1989.

PLATO. *The Republic.* Translated by Desmond Lee. New York: Penguin, 1955.

PETER SINGER. *The Expanding Circle: Ethics and Sociobiology.* New York: Farrar, Straus, and Giroux, 1981.

CHRISTINA HOFF SOMMERS. *Right and Wrong: Readings in Ethics.* New York: Harcourt Brace Jovanovich, 1986.

CHAPTER 5

Social and
Political Philosophy

$\mathbb{T}$he chapter combines presentation of basic theories and perspectives (Plato, Aristotle, Mill, Rawls, and Nozick) with reflection concerning complex and controversial social issues (such as world hunger, abortion, racial relations, crime and punishment).

Introductory Essay

The **Introductory Essay** continues the dialogue between members of a hypothetical study group. They exchange ideas concerning issues like world hunger, homelessness, and cultural diversity. They debate the rights of the individual versus those of the state, the role of education versus social indoctrination, political correctness, censorship, taxation, and the distribution of wealth. They wrestle with concepts like justice, equality, friendship, and civic responsibility. Along the way they encounter the philosophical perspectives of Plato, Aristotle, Mill, Rawls, and Nozick.

Philosophical Reading

The selection by **Jane English** concerns abortion and the concept of a person. Rejecting conservative as well as liberal extremes, she seeks a middle ground which recognizes a wide latitude of permissibility without sacrificing basic obligation. She discusses the views of Mary Anne Warren, Judith Jarvis Thomson, John Rawls, and Michael Tooley. Although much of the article concerns the concept of a person, Professor English repeatedly dismisses it as too vague and imprecise to provide clear conceptual or behavioral guidance concerning the issue of abortion.

Scientific Reading

The selection by **Shelby Steele** offers a historical perspective as well as a series of personal reflections concerning racial integration, innocence, power, the civil rights movement, and the assorted difficulties we sometimes face when trying to learn to live together.

Literary Reading

Kahlil Gibran challenges some of our most common views concerning crime, justice, and punishment. Instead of isolating and distancing ourselves from the criminal, Gibran suggests, we must seek to understand that part of our being which somehow participates in the crime. Until we accept joint responsibility, he argues, we will be unable to appreciate our common destiny.

It's Just Not Fair!

DOUGLAS W. SHRADER

Martha pushed her tray away and complained, "It's just not fair!"

"What's not fair?" asked Callie.

"We have so much while others have so little," Martha explained.

"We can't be responsible for everyone," said Bo as he stuffed a final bite of mystery meat *du jour* in his mouth. "If you don't want that, I'll take it," he said, gesturing toward Martha's tray.

"Go ahead," Martha sighed. "I can't eat when I think about all those starving children in Africa."

"Why is it," Wesley asked, "that we seem always to be worrying about the starving children in Africa, or China, or Bosnia—anywhere but here? Do you even know any children in Africa? Have you been downtown lately? There are people living in cardboard boxes right here in the good ol' U.S. of A."

"Have you *seen* them?" Caitlin asked. "Most of those people are just bums. They could make something of themselves if they wanted. If they weren't so lazy they could get jobs and find decent places to live. But it's easier for them to clutter up the streets and try to make us feel sorry for them. I'm scared to go downtown alone anymore. You never know what a person like that might do."

"I don't think you're being fair," protested Wesley.

"Not fair?" Caitlin retorted sharply. "I'll tell you what's not fair. It's not fair that our hard-earned tax money goes to support people who do nothing to contribute to our society. The welfare program is a joke. Rather than helping people get back on their feet and become self-sufficient, the system simply encourages abuse and laziness. I'm working twenty hours a week washing dishes here in the dining hall just to afford books and other school supplies. It is not fair that the government takes nearly a third of my money to support people who don't do a darned thing except sit under a bridge and stick a tin can in the face of everyone who walks by."

"We all know there is abuse," Callie said. "We probably could, and should, manage social service programs more efficiently. But that doesn't mean everyone receiving public assistance is a lazy cheat. Some are just down on their luck—like being fired after twenty years with the same company. Others never had the same opportunities we do. I don't envy you your job washing dishes, but you shouldn't act like you're paying for your education all by yourself. I know for a fact that your uncle left a trust fund to help pay the tuition. Besides, not all your taxes are used to help feed the poor. Without government support, this college might not even be here."

"You're right," Caitlin said, shaking her head softly. "Sometimes I forget to look at the good part. I don't mean to make excuses, but I've been under a lot of stress lately, I've got some important tests coming up, I've been feeling very tired after work, and sometimes when I sit in class I feel like the dumbest person in the whole world."

Tears began to well up in Caitlin's eyes. Stillness hung over the table for what seemed an unbearable eternity. Then Callie reached over, gave Caitlin a hug and a kiss on the cheek, and consoled: "You're not dumb, not by any means. College can be tough. Fate dealt you a rotten hand in some ways; I don't know how I would have taken being bounced around from foster home to foster home. But you've got smarts, and more resourcefulness and determination than anyone I've ever seen. And you've got us; if there is something we can do to help, just let us know."

"Thanks," Caitlin muttered softly, still fighting to hold back the tears.

"Life is not always fair," Callie continued. "It is an uphill climb for people who have never known anything but poverty. It can be especially challenging for people of a disadvantaged race. If you happen to be a woman or a child the situation is just that

145

much worse. And imagine how much harder it would be if you had a severe mental or emotional handicap, or suffered from a debilitating physical condition. What if you had been a victim of persistent child abuse or grew up in a rat-infested drug-ridden ghetto?"

"Can't we talk about something else?" asked Bo. "This is depressing."

"No," Callie replied firmly. "If we are ever to become responsible members of this society we had better learn to deal with situations and issues that make us uncomfortable. It is far too easy to turn our heads and look the other way. Martha raised an important issue. Wesley's point is a valid one as well: we tend to forget about the needs of people in our own community. I don't think any of us realized Caitlin was having so much trouble."

"We all take each other a little too much for granted," Martha observed. "When someone asks, 'How are you?' we don't stop to give a litany of our troubles. We may have the flu and feel terrible, but still we will answer, 'Just fine.' It's like we don't think anyone really wants to know."

"Perhaps," mused Wesley, "that's why we tend to focus on problems in distant countries. We're used to the street people. We see them all the time. Eventually we become numb to their plight and deaf to their pleas. We move from compassion to annoyance to a point where the people become almost invisible, just another featureless feature of our everyday environment."

"I agree that's part of it," said Callie, "but I think there is more. When we hear of injustice and suffering in distant countries we express outrage and compassion, but only at a comfortable distance. There is always a little voice that consoles us, saying: 'It's not your problem. You didn't create their society or its difficulties. You don't live there. You don't know anyone who does. If only they would use birth control, or stop cutting down the rain forests, or eat the cows instead of worshipping them or using them as currency.' If the problem is distant we can give a few dollars to a relief fund, feel better, and assuage our conscience. If the problem is closer to

home it becomes harder to do that; so we try to ignore it, give lame excuses, or possibly even blame the people themselves—like Caitlin did a few minutes ago. In fact, I think we sometimes concentrate on distant problems just so we don't have to face those in our own front yard."

"Well spoken," said Martha. "But I don't think we can turn our backs on the rest of the world simply because we have troubles at home. Look at all the multinational corporations and shifting political boundaries. We are not just a bunch of isolated little countries anymore. There is, I believe, a world community and a brotherhood (and sisterhood) of all people of every race, religion, and socioeconomic class."

"Apparently," Bo interjected, "there are lots of areas that haven't heard about your enlightened world community. I don't see the point of sending food to countries torn apart by civil war. In fact, I think it is wrong to keep someone alive just so they can be shot by a soldier or, worse still, so they can shoot others. If people are bent on destroying each other, we should either find a way to stop them or let them get it over with as quickly as possible."

"I was talking about feeding children, not soldiers," Martha retorted.

"Even if the country is not at war," Bo continued, "sending food may be one of the worst things you can do. If the country does not have the economy or agricultural base to support a burgeoning population, feeding children just so they can grow up to live in poverty and watch their own children die of malnutrition seems positively cruel. If the country cannot develop self-sufficiency, the people will never develop a sense of pride or cultural identity. Even if we provide enough food to feed them well, their lives will be little better than those of animals in a cage, always depending on a handout from another source which keeps them alive for its own purpose, not theirs."

"I didn't mean to say that *all* we should send is food," Martha replied. "We should also help them build houses and schools. If population control is a problem, we should help them find solutions compatible with their cultural heritage as well as with the economic conditions of their country. If their agricultural techniques are inadequate, we should help develop new techniques or teach them to plant new crops. It is like the old adage about giving a man a fish: If you give a man a fish every day for a year, next year he will still be hungry. But if you teach him to fish, he need never be hungry again."

"Provided there are enough fish to be had," remarked Bo. "Some of these countries are little more than sand."

"And some of that sand covers a lot of oil," returned Martha. "You don't have to take everything so literally."

"I wasn't," Bo said with the smile of a child who had been caught in his own cleverness. "But you have some pretty idealistic notions. You seem to think we can create a utopia in which everybody has enough to eat, nobody takes advantage of anybody else, and we all sit around and talk philosophy for want of anything else to do."

"I don't know about the philosophy part," Martha said, "but I do think the world has riches to spare if we just learn to share. Have you all heard the story of the dying man who was given the opportunity to visit both heaven and hell?"

"No," responded Callie, eager to ease the tensions developing around the table. "Please tell us."

"First the Devil took him on a guided tour of the underworld," said Martha. "It wasn't nearly as hot as he had expected, more like a day at the beach than anything else. After a while they came to a great dining hall where everyone was sitting around a huge table filled with every imaginable food. There were fresh vegetables, steaming casseroles, scrumptious cakes and pies, and everything you could have wanted. But when the man looked at the people's faces, he found not happiness, but terrible anguish. And when he looked at their bodies, he found little more than skin and bones. Here they were sitting at a feast of a lifetime, and they were all starving. The reason, he discovered, was that each person had a six-foot fork strapped to their right hand and a six-foot spoon strapped to their left.

They could reach the food, but they couldn't get it to their mouths.

"Watching this sight, the man's pain was almost too much to bear. Finally, an angel came to take him on a tour of heaven. The temperature was much the same as it had been below, but there was a cool breeze blowing somewhere in the distance. He didn't realize how much difference such a simple thing could make. When they came to the banquet hall he found a scene similar to what he had seen in hell. Everyone was sitting around a huge table filled with all the same foods as the one below. Here too, everyone had a six-foot fork strapped to their right arm and a six-foot spoon strapped to their left. But these people were happy, laughing, and joking. They weren't starving; if anything, they might have been just a little too plump. The difference, he soon realized, is that they had discovered something that would never have occurred to their counterparts: they were feeding *each other*."

After a brief silence Bo said, "It's a pretty story. But that is all it is: just a story. Those are not real people. I'm not sure whether there is a heaven or a hell, but I am sure people don't sit around feeding each other with six-foot forks and spoons."

"It is not *just* a story," Martha replied. "It is a metaphor for the human condition. None of us can make it on our own. But if we cooperate with one another instead of always thinking about our own individual selves, it would actually be much better for all of us. We can't change the length of the forks and spoons, but we can change what we do with them."

"Wake up and smell reality," chided Bo. "There have always been poor people; there always will be. People die of starvation every day and there is nothing you can do to make any real difference. Do you know what *utopia* means? It means *nowhere*. It just isn't possible to create the kind of world you envision. I wish it were, but it isn't. I'm not going to throw away my happiness just because someone somewhere is starving. And if the situation were reversed I wouldn't expect them to feel any differently than I do. It's a jungle out there. We can't all be happy, but that doesn't mean none of us can. Don't throw your life away chasing an impossible dream. And don't make yourself miserable with a bunch of misplaced guilt for all the sins of the world. It's not fair, but it's not your fault."

"I agree with you about the guilt part," noted Callie, "but Martha has a point too. It used to take weeks or months to get from one place to another. Now you can fly anywhere in the world in a matter of hours. We're just not as isolated and independent as we used to be. And it is time we realized that. We can't go on burning fossil fuels as though it were a purely personal matter. If we destroy the ozone layer it is bad news for *all* of us."

"Martha's story reminds me of the Prisoner's Dilemma we read about last week," added Wesley. "The suspects will probably mistrust each other and try to gain some advantage at the other person's expense. As a result, they will both do more time than if they had been a little less self-centered."

"Does that seem so strange?" asked Martha. "I don't think a group of selfish people would be as happy as one in which people took a genuine interest in one another, helped each other out in times of trouble and things like that."

"Maybe that's what my uncle meant when he said, 'The hardest way to find happiness is by looking for it,' " mused Caitlin.

Bo moaned: "All this talk of cooperation reminds me of *Sesame Street*."

"Good," Martha retorted. "Perhaps you learned something from watching television after all. Children are the future. If we can teach them to respect and cooperate with one another, there may be hope for all of us. Education is the key."

"Education?" responded Bo. "Sounds more like indoctrination. Education is teaching kids two plus two equals four. Teaching them that everybody is equal, that diversity is valuable, or that we ought to cooperate with one another is indoctrination. That stuff is nothing more than a bunch of propaganda designed to keep the masses in line."

"You're far too cynical," commented Callie. "I suppose you think education is learning a set of facts to regurgitate on a test sometime?"

"That's about the size of it," said Bo. "Every once in a while you get a course where they teach you something that may come in handy later on, when you get a job. But those times are few and far between."

"*Déjà vu*," groaned Callie. "I guess I forgot we had this conversation before."

"You mean about being here just for the grade," Bo replied. "Hey, at least I don't lie about it like some people do. Besides, I'm also here to have a good time. Haven't you heard? These are the best years of your life!"

"You speak of learning something useful," observed Martha. "Don't you think cooperation is useful? Suppose you land an executive-level job with a multinational corporation. You may have to travel all over the world, meeting with workers and clients in many different countries. They won't all look like you, talk like you, or have the same values and beliefs as you. Don't you think it would be of benefit to cultivate some understanding and skills concerning all that diversity with which you may have to deal?"

Bo sat silently for a moment, then countered: "I admit I hadn't thought of it in quite that way. But I still say a lot of what they try to teach us in just a bunch of political propaganda. Like that crap about everybody being created equal; we all know that's not true. But if you dare say it, everybody acts like you committed the worst sin imaginable. You might as well announce to the world that you have AIDS; people wouldn't treat you any worse."

"We may not all be the same, but we *are* equal," protested Martha.

"Oh, come off it," replied Bo. "Some kids are born with almost no brain. Others have terrible physical handicaps. Some people are just naturally more intelligent than others. Some are more attractive. Some have greater physical prowess. We don't all start on a level playing field. No matter how long or how loud politicians may say it, we don't all have equal opportunity. As Callie pointed out when we first started talking about all this, a person born into poverty, or someone whose skin doesn't happen to be the 'right' color, may not enjoy the same advantages as someone else. Equality is a myth."

For a while, no one spoke. Finally Sterling said, "Bo, I'm proud of you."

"What?" Callie gasped. "You can't mean to say that you agree with him!"

"I didn't say I agreed with Bo," said Sterling, "just that I'm proud of him. He has stated his beliefs very clearly and forcefully, even though he knew we would probably disapprove. That takes courage and honesty. He also did a pretty fair job of defending his position against your attacks. That means he has probably thought about it quite a bit. Not bad for a guy who's 'just here for the grade.'"

"Some things are more important than grades," noted Bo.

"Indeed they are," said Sterling, "and you have given us a focus on some very important issues, things like the nature and possibility of justice, social and political equality, the function of education in a political system, even the role of myth. Your conversation with Martha also brought out some fairly interesting points about fairness, world hunger, happiness, and obligation."

"I did all that?" asked Bo, suppressing a grin.

"Sure," replied Sterling. "And even though your remarks about equality weren't very popular with your classmates here, your viewpoint is at least similar to the one developed by Plato and Aristotle."

"Really?" asked Bo. "Those guys thought like I do?"

"In some ways," cautioned Sterling. "Plato sketched a plan for an ideal society in a dialogue called *The Republic.* He argued that since people have different talents and abilities, the best society is one where each person is performing the task to which he or she is best suited. Each person should be treated according to their needs, abilities, and contributions."

"That makes sense to me," commented Bo.

"He divided people into three basic groups," continued Sterling, "corresponding to what he believed to be the three basic parts of the human psyche. One group, corresponding to reason, would be the most insightful and intelligent. Naturally, Plato argued, they should rule."

"Naturally," agreed Bo.

"The next group," Sterling went on, "corresponded to what he called *spirit* or *virtue.* These people would be faithful, courageous, and willing to put the good of the community ahead of any personal glory or gain."

"They sound kind of like cops," remarked Bo.

"Right," said Sterling. "Together with the rulers they constitute the guardians of the community, defending it against injustice from within as well as aggression from without. The final group of people is of course the largest. These are the merchants and consumers, corresponding to the human appetite. Only they would be allowed to own property and acquire wealth."

"Correct me if I am wrong," observed Wesley, "but this analysis of the human psyche sounds an awful lot like Freud. You know: ego, superego, and id."

"Freud developed the ideas a little differently," Sterling said, "but the influence is still pretty easy to see. According to Plato, a person is most happy when reason is in control, guiding the two motive forces of spirit and appetite. According to Freud, our mental and emotional health is best when the ego can successfully mediate the two counterpoising forces of superego and id."

"I thought the superego was socially determined," remarked Wesley.

"Freud thought so," replied Sterling. "But he did not thereby argue that it is unimportant or that it can be ignored. Inasmuch as we are communal animals, living in social groups, a properly developed superego is extremely important to personal adjustment, well-being, and happiness."

"What does any of this have to do with justice?" asked Caitlin.

"It is really pretty simple," Sterling responded. "Just think of the state as though it were a giant person. Plato believed the best government is one that is knowledgeable and enlightened, corresponding to an individual whose decisions are based on reason. A government controlled by economic interests is similar to an individual who is always at the mercy of his or her appetite. One controlled by the military, or a special-interest group representing a particular religion or moral agenda, is like an individual who sacrifices all in blind obedience to something which she or he neither understands nor desires."

Caitlin shook her head. "I still don't get it," she said.

Sterling tried again: "There is a place for each of these: reason, appetite, and spirit. Justice, whether in the individual or the state, is a matter of each performing its own proper function. The parts work together for the sake of a better whole. Appetite does not try to take the place of reason. Reason does not expect to be treated in the same manner as appetite. Each is treated as a unique and valuable part of the larger unit."

"And despite their differences, Aristotle pretty much agreed with that analysis," commented Callie. "A person is a *politikon zōon* a political animal. Only in a community of others is it possible for us to realize our full being or develop our full potential. As you pointed out in our previous discussion, Aristotle's views on ethics concentrate on happiness (or well-being) and the use of reason to guide behavior in accordance with the principle of the golden mean."

"And as you pointed out," returned Sterling, "the golden mean is not the same in all situations, or for all people. Like Plato, Aristotle believed people are neither equal nor identical. To treat them as though they were interchangeable parts is like treating a screwdriver as though it were a hammer. Doing so would ignore the unique qualities and potential contributions of a screwdriver, probably break it in the process, and result in a more poorly crafted product than if we had simply used a hammer from the start."

"Why must we equate diversity and difference with equality?" asked Martha.

"I don't," Callie said. "But Plato and Aristotle grew up in societies where slavery was common. Women were not accorded the same status or social privilege we currently have. They were progressive

thinkers relative to their own culture, but some of their views would probably cause us to shudder if we fail to remember those differences in time and place."

"Those cultural differences are indeed important," Sterling remarked. "But remember the examples Bo used. He wasn't claiming that we should have slaves or that women are somehow innately inferior to men. He was objecting to the way in which the concept of universal equality blinds us to differences in people's abilities, needs, and social opportunity. And that, all other differences aside, is much the same thing that Plato and Aristotle were getting at."

"Then we will just have to educate people to celebrate difference and diversity," commented Martha.

"How are you going to do that?" asked Bo.

"We'll start by telling them the right kind of stories when they are very little," she said. "We will teach them that the rainbow is beautiful because the different colors exist peacefully, one alongside the other. When they get old enough, they can participate in discussions like this one. And of course we will have to make sure that there are some good movies, television programs, plays, and songs to reinforce these ideas."

"What about freedom of speech?" asked Bo. "Will you suppress the views of those who disagree? Will you insist that university professors observe politically correct speech or risk losing their positions of influence? You speak of difference and diversity, but it sounds to me like you want everyone to have the same attitude and opinions as you. I bet Plato wouldn't have allowed censorship in his ideal society!"

"Surprise!" Sterling said. "Plato's *Republic* described an educational process almost exactly like the one Martha just enunciated. According to his arguments, even the best society requires a carefully controlled system of education to ensure its future. I don't think he liked the idea of censorship; after all, he was mortified when his teacher Socrates was executed on charges of impiety and corrupting the youth. But if necessary, Plato was willing to support enlightened government control of the media—funding and/or commissioning some things, censoring others. He even describes the creation of a Foundation Myth: a story that would promote the idea that all members of the society are parts of a larger whole, while at the same time explaining the existence and importance of their natural differences."

"Both Plato and Aristotle recognized education as a powerful political and social tool," Callie added. "Plato founded the Academy to educate the future statesmen of Athens. Aristotle founded his own school, the Lyceum. His pupils included the son of Philip of Macedonia, a young man who eventually came to be known as Alexander the Great."

"Though I think Alexander may have taken about the same attitude toward his studies as Bo does," remarked Sterling.

"I'll accept that comparison," boasted Bo, feigning a regal posture.

Somewhat despite herself, Martha laughed. "Say what you will, but education is the key to a better tomorrow. That's why I support better education for everyone. In the long run it will benefit us as well. They may gripe about our attitudes and study habits, but I think even our college professors believe they are doing something socially worthwhile."

"They just gripe because we don't treat it as seriously as they do," Caitlin remarked. "If only they could see us now. They'd never believe it. Here we are talking about Plato and Aristotle, justice and equality, homelessness and world hunger. What's come over us, anyway?"

"Part of the difference," observed Bo, "is that we are sitting and talking with one another. This is a far cry from sitting in a classroom listening to a professor read from a bunch of notes on a lectern."

"Good," said Martha, "because I'm not ready to give up on the idea that everyone is equal. Surely there must have been some philosophers willing to disagree with Plato and Aristotle, difficult as that may seem."

"Of course there were," Sterling said. "Some of the most influential ones lived in Europe during the seventeenth, eighteenth, and nineteenth centuries: Thomas Hobbes, John Locke, David Hume, John

Stuart Mill, and others. They examined the differences between themselves and others, concluded that the differences were less important than Plato and Aristotle had believed, and thus argued for a system of social and political equality."

"I remember Mill," Martha remarked. "He was one of the founders of Utilitarianism."

"Right," Sterling said. "As a utilitarian, Mill came to believe that justice is primarily a matter of social utility. If punishing someone benefits the society as a whole, the punishment is just. If not, then it is not."

"Doesn't it even matter whether they committed a crime?" asked Caitlin.

"Not unless you add some assumptions about negative social consequences of punishing people who did not commit crimes," replied Sterling. "Even then, there might be cases where the benefit (deterrence, for example) would outweigh the negative consequences."

"I find that difficult to believe," commented Callie. "Why would anyone want to live in a society where you might be put in jail for something you didn't do?"

"What if the chance of *your* being imprisoned was very small?" asked Sterling. "Would that make a difference?"

"It might, as a practical matter," replied Callie. "But it wouldn't make it fair. I believe everybody has certain basic rights. And I don't think it is fair to punish an innocent person just because it happens to benefit someone else, no matter how great that benefit might be."

"Have you ever read anything by the contemporary American philosopher John Rawls?" asked Sterling.

"No," confessed Callie. "Why?"

"Like you," Sterling explained, "Rawls is concerned that Utilitarianism may disadvantage some groups for the sake of others. If we are ever to have a stable society, one in which dissatisfaction and unrest are minimized, the governing principles must be acceptable to everyone. But principles that are perceived as unfair to some members of the society will not be acceptable to everyone. Thus Rawls uses principles of fairness as a basis for his concept of justice."

"That makes sense," agreed Callie. "But how does he determine which principles are fair and which are not?"

"Rawls's theory is a version of what is called *Social Contract Theory*," answered Sterling. "He asks us to imagine a fictional time, which he calls the *original position*, in which all members of the society participate in choosing the principles according to which their society will be governed. To guard against unfair advantage, they choose these principles under what he calls the *veil of ignorance*: no one know what race, gender, or socioeconomic class to which she or he will belong. They don't know whether they will be tall or short, fat or skinny, or even the generation into which they will be born. Since no one knows what their fate in the natural lottery might be, Rawls believes they would establish principles to maximize their position if perchance they should end up on the short end of the stick, so to speak."

"So the system will take care of them," Callie observed, "if they happen to be born with disabilities, or members of a disadvantaged class, and so on. If some happen to be rich and enjoy social position, no one would be able to complain since all agreed (hypothetically) to the principles."

"Wouldn't they just agree to distribute the wealth equally?" asked Martha.

"Not necessarily," Sterling replied. "It might be to everyone's advantage to allow an unequal distribution. For example, a free market system might foster greater economic productivity, create more satisfying jobs, and raise the standard of living for the entire community."

"I suppose that is possible," Martha conceded.

Sterling continued: "Rawls presents two principles of justice which he believes people would choose in the original position under the veil of ignorance. The first, the *Principle of Equal Basic Liberty for All*, guarantees everyone the same fundamental rights and freedoms. Everyone has the maximum amount of liberty compatible with everyone else having that same amount. His second principle, the *Difference Principle*, governs social and economic inequalities. Such inequalities are just, argues Rawls, only if they benefit all members of the society, especially the least advantaged."

"I take it the first principle would protect us from false imprisonment," speculated Callie.

"Right," replied Sterling. "Rawls doesn't claim to give a complete list of rights and freedoms, but does mention things like the right to vote and run for public office, the right to own personal property, liberty of thought and speech, freedom of assembly, and freedom from arbitrary arrest and seizure."

"I don't object to people having rights like that," commented Caitlin, "but his Difference Principle concerns me. Does he really mean that everything should be divided equally unless an unequal distribution benefits *everybody*? You can't go around taking things away from people just because a different distribution would benefit someone else."

"Sure you can," inserted Wesley. "That's what taxes and social welfare programs do."

"Well, of course you *can*," replied Caitlin, "but that doesn't make it *fair*. If Rawls wants to see social unrest, just let him try taking away *my* stuff. I got what I have fair and square, and I intend to keep it. I am not working my way through college to support some bum who doesn't have the gumption to . . . " Unable to find the right word, Caitlin slumped back in her chair and sighed. Her thought trailed away unfinished.

"It sounds like Rawls is going to need a pretty big social welfare program," Callie observed. "I like his ideas about basic rights, but I share some of Caitlin's reservations as well. I don't want to turn my back on people who are socially or economically disadvantaged, but I don't want to live in a welfare state, either. There must be some sort of in-between."

"Suppose we do away with taxes altogether," suggested Bo, "and support everything with a national lottery. That would be fair; if you didn't want to play, you wouldn't have to."

"Lotteries aren't fair," Wesley objected. "They prey unfairly on the poor, encourage false hope, and promote an unrealistic and socially detrimental image of happiness, success, and personal well-being."

"Oh, come on," protested Bo. "Buying a few lottery tickets never hurt anyone. Besides, it's fun."

"Gambling is a sickness," Wesley replied. "It's not always a question of buying a *few* lottery tickets. People become addicted. You say it is fun, but the lottery is far more than a game. People see it as their ticket out, their chance at the big time."

"So?" asked Bo.

"So people take less and less responsibility for their own success or failure," explained Wesley, "and blame it more and more on fate, luck, or 'the system.' They lose sight of the fact that they are responsible for their own lives. Our lives are something we create, not just something that happens to us as a result of a bunch of random events."

"It was only a suggestion," defended Bo.

"Well, it was a terrible suggestion," responded Wesley. "Do you know what's wrong with this country? There is a declining commitment to the Protestant Work Ethic. I remember my grandfather telling me, 'It's not what you have, but how you got it.' He would have starved to death rather than eat stolen bread. How many people do you see like that anymore? I'll tell you: not very many. Almost everyone I see is standing in line for a handout. I agree with my grandfather: the world doesn't owe you a living—and the sooner people realize that, the happier they will be."

Bo glanced about the table, then turned to Sterling and pleaded, "I could use your help about now."

Sterling smiled, patted Bo on the shoulder, and said: "Wesley has some good points. Since the temptation to play the lottery is far greater for poor people than it is for those who already have a lot of money, lotteries generate a disproportionate share of their revenue from those who have the least to give."

"Aargh!" groaned Bo. "I'm surrounded by bleeding-heart liberals."

Sterling continued: "Wesley's remarks about the Protestant Work Ethic, and the phrase he quoted from his grandfather, are worth our attention as well. They remind me somewhat of the criticisms of Rawls's theory advanced by his colleague at Har-vard, Robert Nozick. Rather than concentrating on fairness, as did Rawls, Nozick bases his system of justice on principles of entitlement."

"Principles of what?" asked Caitlin.

"Principles of entitlement," repeated Sterling. "You know: things to which you are entitled. It is a lot like you were saying before: you got what you have fair and square; it would be unjust for the government to take it away just because someone else has less."

"Anyone can see that," remarked Bo. "Caitlin has had a rough life. She deserves better. But she never asks anybody for anything. She has always worked hard, and she has developed more personal integrity and self-reliance than anyone I've ever known. We would all be better off if we had less government and more respect for the rights of individuals."

"Like Bo," Sterling noted, "Nozick places far more value on the rights of individuals than he does on abstract principles like equal distribution of wealth. Thus he argues that an optimally just society will have a minimal government, which he compares to a night watchman. It should be no larger and have no more power than is absolutely necessary to guarantee the safety of its citizens, protect them from fraud and theft, enforce contractual agreements, and so on."

"Sounds good to me," remarked Bo.

"Injustice occurs," Sterling continued, "whenever people have things to which they are not entitled. Thus Nozick enunciates three principles of entitlement. The *Principle of Justice in Acquisition* governs the acquisition of things that were previously unowned. Basically it says you have to leave enough to meet the needs of others. The *Principle of Justice in Transfer* governs transfer of possessions. So long as you do not steal from, coerce, defraud, or otherwise cheat the other person, you may dispose of legitimately owned property in any way you see fit. Similar considerations apply to the acquisition of previously owned property. The *Principle of Rectification of Injustice in Holdings* helps to answer the question, 'What must we do if we discover people have things to which they are not entitled?' It is a deceptively difficult question and Nozick does not feign a completely satisfactory answer. At base, however, he believes we must make an honest attempt to identify the victims and arrange suitable compensation."

"Sort of like Robin Hood stealing from the rich and giving to the poor?" asked Martha.

"Perhaps," replied Sterling. "But be careful with that analogy. The Robin Hood legends contain a lot of assumptions about the Normans acquiring their possessions from the Saxons via deception, fraud, theft, murder, and force. Nozick does not support taking something from someone just because they are rich. Nor does he support giving something to someone just because they are poor. If the rich people acquired their possessions justly from others who had legitimate title to them, it would be *unjust* to take them away."

"Even if the poor were starving?" asked Martha.

"*Even* if the poor were starving," replied Sterling. "Nozick acknowledges that we might have a moral obligation to help the poor, but believes government goes too far when it canonizes that obligation into a requirement. It may be helpful to think of Jesus' parable of the Good Samaritan. The Samaritan's assistance of the wounded stranger is praiseworthy. But would you really want a legal system that *mandates* such assistance? Nozick thinks not."

"Taxes, social obligations, feeding the poor . . . It sounds like we are right back where we started," remarked Wesley.

"In some ways," Sterling agreed. "These are very emotional issues. I don't think any of us have changed our minds, but I for one have come to understand our differences a little better. And I think we have all learned a thing or two about justice, fairness, and the distribution of wealth. Sometimes it helps to talk."

"Speaking of talking," Callie said, turning to Caitlin and taking her hand. "You said before that you were under a lot of stress. I mean what I said about being here to help. Maybe we can't solve issues like world hunger, but at least we can provide support and comfort to our friends. Is it something you want to talk about?"

Caitlin squirmed in her seat for a moment, glanced about nervously, then announced: "I wasn't going to tell anyone, but it's been eating me up inside. I thought for sure I was pregnant."

"Mine?" gasped Bo.

"There has never been anyone else," said Caitlin. "Don't look so scared; it was a false alarm."

"What would you have done if it hadn't been a false alarm?" asked Bo.

"I don't know," she said. "I thought a lot about abortion, but I don't think I could have gone through with it."

His voice quivering, Bo asked: "Would you have ever told me?"

"I didn't think you were interested in me anymore," responded Caitlin.

"I'm still interested," he said. "I was just feeling kind of crowded. Things were happening a little too fast. I don't know that I'm ready to make a long-term commitment. Till death do us part: that's a long time."

"Did you mean all those things you said about me? About personal integrity, and respect, and my deserving better?" asked Caitlin.

"Sure I did. I respect you a lot," he replied reassuringly. Bo then stared at his shoes for a moment, leaned closer to Caitlin, and said in a somewhat softer voice: "I didn't know. You should have told me."

"I didn't want you to know," Caitlin responded. "I thought I could deal with it all by myself. I guess I was wrong."

"Perhaps we were both wrong," said Bo. "Anyway, you shouldn't have to deal with something like that all by yourself. It wouldn't be fair."

Callie stood up and pushed in her chair. "Come on," she said, gesturing to her other friends. "I think these two need some time alone."

Abortion and the Concept of a Person

JANE ENGLISH

Jane English taught philosophy at the University of North Carolina in Chapel Hill. She edited a text titled *Sex Equality* (1977) and authored several articles, including "Justice Between Generations" and "Sex Equality in Sports." Her life ended tragically, at the age of 31, during a mountain climbing accident on the Matterhorn in 1978. The selection that follows was originally published in the *Canadian Journal of Philosophy* (October 1975).

The abortion debate rages on. Yet the two most popular positions seem to be clearly mistaken. Conservatives maintain that a human life begins at conception and that therefore abortion must be wrong because it is murder. But not all killings of humans are murders. Most notably, self defense may justify even the killing of an innocent person.

Liberals, on the other hand, are just as mistaken in their argument that since a fetus does not become a person until birth, a woman may do whatever she pleases in and to her own body. First, you cannot do as you please with your own body if it affects other people adversely.[1] Second, if a fetus is not a person, that does not imply that you can do to it anything you wish. Animals, for example, are not persons, yet to kill or torture them for no reason at all is wrong.

At the center of the storm has been the issue of just when it is between ovulation and adulthood that a person appears on the scene. Conservatives draw the line at conception, liberals at birth. In this paper I first examine our concept of a person and conclude that no single criterion can capture the concept of a person and no sharp line can be drawn. Next I argue that if a fetus is a person, abortion is still justifiable in many cases; and if a fetus is not a person, killing it is still wrong in many cases. To a large extent, these two solutions are in agreement. I conclude that our concept of a person cannot and need not bear the weight that the abortion controversy has thrust upon it.

I

The several factions in the abortion argument have drawn battle lines around various proposed criteria for determining what is and what is not a person. For example, Mary Anne Warren[2] lists five features (capacities for reasoning, self-awareness, complex communication, etc.) as her criteria for personhood and argues for the permissibility of abortion because a fetus falls outside this concept. Baruch Brody[3] uses brain waves. Michael Tooley[4] picks having-a-concept-of-self as his criterion and concludes that infanticide and abortion are justifiable, while the killing of adult animals is not. On the other side, Paul Ramsey[5] claims a certain gene structure is the defining characteristic. John Noonan[6] prefers conceived-of-humans and presents counterexamples to various other candidate criteria. For instance, he argues against viability as the criterion because the newborn and infirm would then be non-persons, since they cannot live without the aid of others. He rejects any criterion that calls upon the sorts of sentiments a being can evoke in adults on the grounds that this would allow us to exclude other races as non-persons if we could just view them sufficiently unsentimentally.

Jane English, "Abortion and the Concept of a Person," *Canadian Journal of Philosophy* Vol. 2 (1975), pp. 233–243. Reprinted with the permission of the Jane English Memorial Trust Fund and the *Canadian Journal of Philosophy.*

These approaches are typical: foes of abortion propose sufficient conditions for personhood which fetuses satisfy, while friends of abortion counter with necessary conditions for personhood which fetuses lack. But these both presuppose that the condition of a person can be captured in a strait jacket of necessary and/or sufficient conditions.[7] Rather, "person" is a cluster of features, of which rationality, having a self concept and being conceived of as humans are only part.

What is typical of persons? Within our concept of a person we include, first, certain biological factors: descended from humans, having a certain genetic makeup, having a head, hands, arms, eyes, capable of locomotion, breathing, eating, sleeping. There are psychological factors: sentience, perception, having a concept of self and of one's own interests and desires, the ability to use tools, the ability to use language or symbol systems, the ability to joke, to be angry, to doubt. There are rationality factors: the ability to reason and draw conclusions, the ability to generalize and to learn from past experience, the ability to sacrifice present interests for greater gains in the future. There are social factors: the ability to work in groups and respond to peer pressures, the ability to recognize and consider as valuable the interests of others, seeing oneself as one among "other minds," the ability to sympathize, encourage, love, the ability to evoke from others the responses of sympathy, encouragement, love, the ability to work with others for mutual advantage. Then there are legal factors: being subject to the law and protected by it, having the ability to sue and enter contracts, being counted in the census, having a name and citizenship, the ability to own property, inherit, and so forth.

Now the point is not that this list is incomplete, or that you can find counterinstances to each of its points. People typically exhibit rationality, for instance, but someone who was irrational would not thereby fail to qualify as a person. On the other hand, something could exhibit the majority of these features and still fail to be a person, as an advanced robot might. There is no single core of necessary and sufficient features which we can draw upon with the assurance that they constitute what really makes a person; there are only features that are more or less typical.

This is not to say that no necessary or sufficient conditions can be given. Being alive is a necessary condition for being a person, and being a U.S. Senator is sufficient. But rather than falling inside a sufficient condition or outside a necessary one, a fetus lies in the penumbra region where our concept of a person is not so simple. For this reason I think a conclusive answer to the question whether a fetus is a person is unattainable.

Here we might note a family of simple fallacies that proceed by stating a necessary condition for personhood and showing that a fetus has that characteristic. This is a form of the fallacy of affirming the consequent. For example, some have mistakenly reasoned from the premise that a fetus is human (after all, it is a human fetus rather than, say, a canine fetus), to the conclusion that it is *a* human. Adding an equivocation on "being," we get the fallacious argument that since a fetus is something both living and human, it is a human being.

Nonetheless, it does seem clear that a fetus has very few of the above family of characteristics, whereas a newborn baby exhibits a much larger proportion of them—and a two-year-old has even more. Note that one traditional anti-abortion argument has centered on pointing out the many ways in which a fetus resembles a baby. They emphasize its development ("It already has ten fingers . . .") without mentioning its dissimilarities to adults (it still has gills and a tail). They also try to evoke the sort of sympathy on our part that we only feel toward other persons ("Never to laugh . . . or feel the sunshine?"). This all seems to be a relevant way to argue, since its purpose is to persuade us that a fetus satisfies so many of the important features on the list that it ought to be treated as a person. Also note that a fetus near the time of birth satisfies many more of these factors than a fetus in the early months of development. This could provide reason for making distinctions among the different stages of pregnancy, as the U.S. Supreme Court has done.[8]

Historically, the time at which a person has been said to come into existence has varied widely. Muslims date personhood from fourteen days after conception. Some medievals followed Aristotle in placing ensoulment at forty days from conception for a male fetus and eighty days for a female fetus.[9] In European common law since the Seventeenth Century, abortion was considered the killing of a person only after quickening, the time when a pregnant woman first feels the fetus move on its own. Nor is this variety of opinions surprising. Biologically, a human being develops gradually. We shouldn't expect there to be any specific time or sharp dividing point when a person appears on the scene.

For these reasons I believe our concept of a person is not sharp or decisive enough to bear the weight of a solution to the abortion controversy. To use it to solve that problem is to clarify *obscurum per obscurius.*

II

Next let us consider what follows if a fetus is a person after all. Judith Jarvis Thomson's landmark article, "A Defense of Abortion,"[10] correctly points out that some additional argumentation is needed at this point in the conservative argument to bridge the gap between the premise that a fetus is an innocent person and the conclusion that killing it is always wrong. To arrive at this conclusion, we would need the additional premise that killing an innocent person is always wrong. But killing an innocent person is sometimes permissible, most notably in self defense. Some examples may help draw out our intuitions or ordinary judgments about self defense.

Suppose a mad scientist, for instance, hypnotized innocent people to jump out of the bushes and attack innocent passers-by with knives. If you are so attacked, we agree you have a right to kill the attacker in self defense, if killing him is the only way to protect your life or to save yourself from serious injury. It does not seem to matter here that the attacker is not malicious but himself an innocent pawn, for your killing of him is not done in a spirit of retribution but only in self defense.

How severe an injury may you inflict in self defense? In part this depends upon the severity of the injury to be avoided: you may not shoot someone merely to avoid having your clothes torn. This might lead one to the mistaken conclusion that the defense may only equal the threatened injury in severity; that to avoid death you may kill, but to avoid a black eye you may only inflict a black eye or the equivalent. Rather, our laws and customs seem to say that you may create an injury somewhat, but not enormously, greater than the injury to be avoided. To fend off an attack whose outcome would be as serious as rape, a severe beating or the loss of a finger, you may shoot; to avoid having your clothes torn, you may blacken an eye.

Aside from this, the injury you may inflict should only be the minimum necessary to deter or incapacitate the attacker. Even if you know he intends to kill you, you are not justified in shooting him if you could equally well save yourself by the simple expedient of running away. Self defense is for the purpose of avoiding harms rather than equalizing harms.

Some cases of pregnancy present a parallel situation. Though the fetus is itself innocent, it may pose a threat to the pregnant woman's well-being, life prospects or health, mental or physical. If the pregnancy presents a slight threat to her interests, it seems self defense cannot justify abortion. But if the threat is on a par with a serious beating or the loss of a finger, she may kill the fetus that poses such a threat, even if it is an innocent person. If a lesser harm to the fetus could have the same defensive effect, killing it would not be justified. It is unfortunate that the only way to free the woman from the pregnancy entails the death of the fetus (except in very late stages of pregnancy). Thus a self defense model supports Thomson's point that the woman has a right only to be freed from the fetus, not a right to demand its death.[11]

The self defense model is most helpful when we take the pregnant woman's point of view. In the preThomson literature, abortion is often framed as a question for a third party; do you, a doctor, have a right to choose between the life of the woman and that of the fetus? Some have claimed that if you were a passer-by who witnessed a struggle between the innocent hypnotized attacker and his equally innocent victim, you would have no reason to kill either in defense of the other. They have concluded that the self defense model implies that a woman may attempt to abort herself, but that a doctor should not assist her. I think the position of the third party is somewhat more complex. We do feel some inclination to intervene on behalf of the victim rather than the attacker, other things equal. But if both parties are innocent, other factors come into consideration. You would rush to the aid of your husband whether he was attacker or attackee. If a hypnotized famous violinist were attacking a skid row bum, we would try to save the individual who is of more value to society. These considerations would tend to support abortion in some cases.

But suppose you are a frail senior citizen who wishes to avoid being knifed by one of these innocent hypnotics, so you have hired a bodyguard to accompany you. If you are attacked, it is clear we believe that the bodyguard, acting as your agent, has a right to kill the attacker to save you from a serious beating. Your rights of self defense are transferred to your agent. I suggest that we should similarly view the doctor as the pregnant woman's agent in carrying out a defense she is physically incapable of accomplishing herself.

Thanks to modern technology, the cases are rare in which a pregnancy poses a clear threat to a woman's bodily health as an attacker brandishing a switchblade. How does self defense fare when more subtle, complex and long-range harms are involved?

To consider a somewhat fanciful example, suppose you are a highly trained surgeon when you are kidnapped by the hypnotic attacker. He says he does not intend to harm you but to take you back to the mad scientist who, it turns out, plans to hypnotize you to have a permanent mental block against all your knowledge of medicine. This would automatically destroy your career which would in turn have a serious adverse impact on your family, your personal relationships and your happiness. It seems to me that if the only way you can avoid this outcome is to shoot the innocent attacker, you are justified in so doing. You are defending yourself from a drastic injury to your life prospects. I think it is no exaggeration to claim that unwanted pregnancies (most obviously among teenagers) often have such adverse lifelong consequences as the surgeon's loss of livelihood.

Several parallels arise between various views on abortion and the self defense model. Let's suppose further that these hypnotized attackers only operate at night, so that it is well known that they can be avoided completely by the considerable inconvenience of never leaving your house after dark. One view is that since you could stay home at night, therefore if you go out and are selected by one of these hypnotized people, you have no right to defend yourself. This parallels the view that abstinence is the only acceptable way to avoid pregnancy. Others might hold that you ought to take along some defense such as Mace which will deter the hypnotized person without killing him, but that if this defense fails, you are obliged to submit to the resulting injury, no matter how severe it is. This parallels the view that contraception is all right but abortion is always wrong, even in cases of contraceptive failure.

A third view is that you may kill the hypnotized person only if he will actually kill you, but not if he will only injure you. This is like the position that abortion is permissible only if it is required to save a woman's life. Finally we have the view that it is all right to kill the attacker, even if only to avoid a very slight inconvenience to yourself and even if you knowingly walked down the very street where all these incidents have been taking place without taking along any Mace or protective escort. If we assume that a fetus is a person, this is the analogue of the view that abortion is always justifiable, "on demand."

The self defense model allows us to see an important difference that exists between abortion and infanticide, even if a fetus is a person from conception. Many have argued that the only way to justify abortion without justifying infanticide would be to find some characteristic of personhood that is acquired at birth. Michael Tooley, for one, claims infanticide is justifiable because the really significant characteristics of a person are acquired some time after birth. But all such approaches look to characteristics of the developing human and ignore the relation between the fetus and the woman. What if, after birth, the presence of an infant or the need to support it posed a grave threat to the woman's sanity or life prospects? She could escape this threat by a simple expedient of running away. So a solution that does not entail the death of the infant is available. Before birth, such solutions are not available because of the biological dependence of the fetus on the woman. Birth is the crucial point not because of any characteristics the fetus gains, but because after birth the woman can defend herself by a means less drastic than killing the infant. Hence self defense can be used to justify abortion without necessarily thereby justifying infanticide.

III

On the other hand, supposing a fetus is not after all a person, would abortion always be morally permissible? Some opponents of abortion seem worried that if a fetus is not a full-fledged person, then we are justified in treating it in any way at all. However, this does not follow. Non-persons do get some consideration in our moral code, though of course they do not have the same rights as persons have (and in general they do not have moral responsibilities), and though their interests may be overridden by the interests of persons. Still, we cannot treat them in any way at all.

Treatment of animals is a case in point. It is wrong to torture dogs for fun or to kill wild birds for no reason at all. It is wrong Period, even though dogs and birds do not have the same rights persons do. However, few people think it is wrong to use dogs as experimental animals, causing them considerable suffering in some cases, provided that the resulting research will probably bring discoveries of great benefit to people. And most of us think it all right to kill birds for food or to protect our crops. People's rights are different from the consideration we give to animals, then, for it is wrong to experiment on people, even if others might later benefit a great deal as a result of their suffering. You might volunteer to be a subject, but this would be supererogatory; you certainly have a right to refuse to be a medical guinea pig.

But how do we decide what you may or may not do to non-persons? This is a difficult problem, one for which I believe no adequate account exists. You do not want to say, for instance, that torturing dogs is all right whenever the sum of its effects on people is good—when it doesn't warp the sensibilities of the torturer so much that he mistreats people. If that were the case, it would be all right to torture dogs if you did it in private, or if the torturer lived on a desert island or died soon afterward, so that his actions had no effect on people. This is an inadequate account, because whatever moral consideration animals get, it has to be indefeasible, too. It will have to be a general proscription of certain actions, not merely a weighing of the impact on people on a case-by-case basis.

Rather, we need to distinguish two levels on which consequences of actions can be taken into account in moral reasoning. The traditional objections to Utilitarianism focus on the fact that it operates solely on the first level, taking all the consequences into account in particular cases only. Thus Utilitarianism is open to "desert island" and "lifeboat" counterexamples because these cases are rigged to make the consequences of actions severely limited.

Rawls' theory could be described as a teleological sort of theory, but with teleology operating on a higher level.[12] In choosing the principles to regulate society from the original position, his hypothetical choosers make their decision on the basis of the total consequences of various systems. Furthermore, they are constrained to choose a general set of rules which people can readily learn and apply. An ethical theory must operate by generating a set of sympathies and attitudes toward others which reinforces the functioning of that set of moral principles. Our prohibition against killing people operates by means of certain moral sentiments including sympathy, compassion and guilt. But if these attitudes are to form a coherent set, they carry us further: we tend to perform supererogatory actions, and we tend to feel similar compassion toward person-like non-persons.

It is crucial that psychological facts play a role here. Our psychological constitution makes it the case that for our ethical theory to work, it must prohibit certain treatment of non-persons which are significantly person-like. If our moral rules allowed people to treat some person-like non-persons in ways we do not want people to be treated, this would undermine the system of sympathies and attitudes that makes the ethical system work. For this reason, we would choose in the original position to make mistreatment of some sorts of animals wrong in general (not just wrong in the cases with public impact), even though animals are not themselves parties in the original position. Thus it makes sense that it is those animals whose appearance and behavior are most like those of people that get the most consideration in our moral scheme.

It is because of "coherence of attitudes," I think, that the similarity of a fetus to a baby is very significant. A fetus one week before birth is so much like a newborn baby in our psychological space that we cannot allow any cavalier treatment of the former while expecting full sympathy and nurturative support for the latter. Thus, I think that anti-abortion forces are indeed giving their strongest arguments when they point to the similarities between a fetus and a baby, and when they try to evoke our emotional attachment to and sympathy for the fetus. An early horror story from New York about nurses who were expected to alternate between caring for six-week premature infants and disposing of viable 24-week aborted fetuses is just that—a horror story. These beings are so much alike that no one can be asked to draw a distinction and treat them so very differently.

Remember, however, that in the early weeks after conception, a fetus is very much unlike a person. It is hard to develop these feelings for a set of genes which doesn't yet have a head, hands, beating heart, response to touch or the ability to move by itself. Thus it seems to me that the alleged "slippery slope" between conception and birth is not so very slippery. In the early stages of pregnancy, abortion can hardly be compared to murder for psychological reasons, but in the latest stages it is psychologically akin to murder.

Another source of similarity is the bodily continuity between fetus and adult. Bodies play a surprisingly central role in our attitudes toward persons. One has only to think of the philosophical literature on how far physical identity suffices for personal identity or Wittgenstein's remark that the best picture of the human soul is the human body. Even after death, when all agree the body is no longer a person, we still observe elaborate customs of respect for the human body; like people who torture dogs, necrophiliacs are not to be trusted with people.[13] So it is appropriate that we show respect to a fetus as the body continuous with the body of a person. This is a degree of resemblance to persons that animals cannot rival.

Michael Tooley also utilizes a parallel with animals. He claims that it is always permissible to drown newborn kittens and draws conclusions about infanticide.[14] But it is only permissible to drown kittens when their survival would cause some hardship. Perhaps it would be a burden to feed and house six more cats or to find other homes for them. The alternative of letting them starve produces even more suffering than the drowning. Since the kittens get their rights second-hand, so to speak, *via* the need for coherence in our attitudes, their interests are often overridden by the interests of full-fledged persons. But if their survival would be no inconvenience to people at all, then it is wrong to drown them, *contra* Tooley.

Tooley's conclusions about abortion are wrong for the same reason. Even if the fetus is not a person, abortion is not always permissible, because of the resemblance of a fetus to a person. I agree with Thomson that it would be wrong for a woman who is seven months pregnant to have an abortion just to avoid having to postpone a trip to Europe. In the early months of pregnancy when the fetus hardly resembles a baby at all, then, abortion is permissible whenever it is in the interests of the pregnant woman or her family. The reasons would only need to outweigh the pain and inconvenience of the abortion itself. In the middle months, when the fetus comes to resemble a person, abortion would be justifiable only when the continuation of the pregnancy or the birth of the child would cause harms—physical, psychological, economic or social—to the woman. In the late months of pregnancy, even on our current assumption that a fetus is not a person, abortion seems to be wrong except to save a woman from significant injury or death.

The Supreme Court has recognized similar gradations in the alleged slippery slope stretching between conception and birth. To this point, the present paper has been a discussion of the moral status of abortion only, not its legal status. In view of the great physical, financial and sometimes psychological costs of abortion, perhaps the legal arrangement most compatible with the proposed moral solution would be the absence of restrictions, that is, so-called abortion "on demand."

So I conclude, first, that application of our concept of a person will not suffice to settle the abortion issue. After all, the biological development of a human being is gradual. Second, whether a fetus is a person or not, abortion is justifiable early in pregnancy to avoid modest harms and seldom justifiable late in pregnancy except to avoid significant injury or death.[15]

Notes

1. We also have paternalistic laws which keep us from harming our own bodies even when no one else is affected. Ironically, anti-abortion laws were originally designed to protect pregnant women from a dangerous but tempting procedure.

2. Mary Anne Warren, "On the Moral and Legal Status of Abortion," *Monist* 57 (1973), p. 55.

3. Baruch Brody, "Fetal Humanity and the Theory of Essentialism," in Robert Baker and Frederick Elliston (eds.), *Philosophy and Sex* (Buffalo, N.Y., 1975).

4. Michael Tooley, "Abortion and Infanticide," *Philosophy and Public Affairs* 2 (1971).

5. Paul Ramsey, "The Morality of Abortion," in James Rachels, ed., *Moral Problems* (New York, 1971).

6. John Noonan, "Abortion and the Catholic Church: A Summary History," *Natural Law Forum* 12 (1967), pp. 125–131.

7. Wittgenstein has argued against the possibility of so capturing the concept of a game, *Philosophical Investigations* (New York, 1958), § 66–71.

8. Not because the fetus is partly a person and so has some of the rights of persons, but rather because of the rights of person-like non-persons. This I discuss in part III below.

9. Aristotle himself was concerned, however, with the different question of when the soul takes form. For historical data, see Jimmye Kimmey, "How the Abortion Laws Happened," *Ms.* 1 (April, 1973), pp. 48ff, and John Noonan, *loc. cit.*

10. J. J. Thomson, "A Defense of Abortion," *Philosophy and Public Affairs* 1 (1971).

11. *Ibid.*, p. 52.

12. John Rawls, *A Theory of Justice* (Cambridge, Mass., 1971) § 3–4.

13. On the other hand, if they can be trusted with people, then our moral customs are mistaken. It all depends on the facts of psychology.

14. *Op. cit.*, pp. 40, 60–61.

15. I am deeply indebted to Larry Crocker and Arthur Kuflik for their constructive comments.

I'm Black, You're White, Who's Innocent?

SHELBY STEELE

Shelby Steele teaches at San Jose State University in California. He received a National Book Critics Circle Award for *The Content of Our Character: A New Vision of Race in America* (1990). In the following selection, edited from an article that appeared in *Harper's Magazine* (June 1988), Professor Steele provides a historical perspective as well as a series of personal reflections concerning race, innocence, power, and responsibility.

It is a warm, windless California evening, and the dying light that covers the redbrick patio is tinted pale orange by the day's smog. Eight of us, not close friends, sit in lawn chairs sipping chardonnay. A black engineer and I (we had never met before) integrate the group. A psychologist is also among us, and her presence encourages a surprising openness. But not until well after the lovely twilight dinner has been served, when the sky has turned to deep black and the drinks have long since changed to scotch, does the subject of race spring awkwardly upon us. Out of nowhere the engineer announces, with a coloring of accusation in his voice, that it bothers him to send his daughter to a school where she is one of only three black children. "I didn't realize my ambition to get ahead would pull me into a world where my daughter would lose touch with her blackness," he says.

Over the course of the evening we have talked about money, infidelity, past and present addictions, child abuse, even politics. Intimacies have been revealed, fears named. But this subject, race, sinks us into one of those shaming silences where eye contact terrorizes. Our host looks for something in the bottom of his glass. Two women stare into the black sky as if to locate the Big Dipper and point it out to us. Finally, the psychologist seems to gather herself for a challenge, but it is too late. "Oh, I'm sure she'll be just fine," says our hostess, rising from her chair. When she excuses herself to get the coffee, the two sky gazers offer to help.

With three of us now gone, I am surprised to see the engineer still silently holding his ground. There is a willfulness in his eyes, an inner pride. He knows he has said something awkward, but he is determined not to give a damn. His unwavering eyes intimidate me. At last the host's head snaps erect. He has an idea. "The hell with coffee," he says. "How about some of the smoothest brandy you ever tasted?" An idea made exciting by the escape it offers. Gratefully we follow him back into the house, quickly drink his brandy, and say our good-byes.

An autopsy of this party might read: death induced by an abrupt and lethal injection of the American race issue. An accurate if superficial assessment. Since it has been my fate to live a rather integrated life, I have often witnessed sudden deaths like this. The threat of them, if not the reality, is a part of the texture of integration. In the late 1960s, when I was just out of college, I took a delinquent's delight in playing the engineer's role, and actually developed a small reputation for playing it well. Those were the days of flagellatory white guilt; it was such great fun to pinion some professor or housewife or, best of all, a large group of remorseful whites, with the knowledge of both their racism and their denial of it. The adolescent impulse to sneer at

Shelby Steele, "I'm Black, You're White, Who's Innocent?" *Harper's* (June 1988), pp. 45–53 (edited). Copyright © 1988 by Harper's Magazine. Reprinted with the permission of the publisher.

convention, to startle the middle-aged with doubt, could be indulged under the guise of racial indignation. And how could I lose? My victims—earnest liberals for the most part—could no more crawl out from under my accusations than Joseph K. in Kafka's *Trial* could escape the amorphous charges brought against him. At this odd moment in history the world was aligned to facilitate my immaturity.

About a year of this was enough: the guilt that follows most cheap thrills caught up to me, and I put myself in check. But the impulse to do it faded more slowly. It was one of those petty talents that is tied to vanity, and when there were ebbs in my self-esteem the impulse to use it would come alive again. In integrated situations I can still feel the faint itch. But then there are many youthful impulses that still itch, and now, just inside the door of mid-life, this one is least precious to me.

In the literature classes I teach, I often see how the presence of whites all but seduces some black students into provocation. When we come to a novel by a black writer, say Toni Morrison, the white students can easily discuss the human motivations of the black characters. But, inevitably, a black student, as if by reflex, will begin to set in relief the various racial problems that are the background of these characters' lives. This student's tone will carry a reprimand: the class is afraid to confront the reality of racism. Classes cannot be allowed to die like dinner parties, however. My latest strategy is to thank the student for his or her moral vigilance, and then appoint the young man or woman as the class's official racism monitor. But even if I get a laugh—I usually do, but sometimes the student is particularly indignant, and it gets uncomfortable—the strategy never quite works. Our racial division is suddenly drawn in neon. Overcaution spreads like spilled paint. And, in fact, the black student who started it all does become a kind of monitor. The very presence of this student imposes a new accountability on the class.

I think those who provoke this sort of awkwardness are operating out of a black identity that obliges them to badger white people about race almost on principle. Content hardly matters. (For example, it made no sense for the engineer to expect white people to sympathize with his anguish over sending his daughter to school with *white* children.) Race indeed remains a source of white shame; the goal of these provocations is to put whites, no matter how indirectly, in touch with this collective guilt. In other words, these provocations I speak of are *power* moves, little shows of power that try to freeze the "enemy" in self-consciousness. They gratify and inflate the provocateur. They are the underdog's bite. And whites, far more secure in their power, respond with a self-contained and tolerant silence that is, itself, a show of power. What greater power than that of non-response, the power to let a small enemy sizzle in his own juices, to even feel a little sad at his frustration just as one is also complimented by it. Black anger always, in a way, flatters white power. In America, to know that one is not black is to feel an extra grace, a little boost of impunity.

I think the real trouble between the races in America is that the races are not just races but competing power groups—a fact that is easily minimized perhaps because it is so obvious. What is not so obvious is that this is true quite apart from the issue of class. Even the well-situated middle-class (or wealthy) black is never completely immune to that peculiar contest of power that his skin color subjects him to. Race is a separate reality in American society, an entity that carries its own potential for power, a mark of fate that class can soften considerably but not eradicate.

The distinction of race has always been used in American life to sanction each race's pursuit of power in relation to the other. The allure of race as a human delineation is the very shallowness of the delineation it makes. Onto this shallowness—mere skin and hair—men can project a false depth, a system of dismal attributions, a series of malevolent or ignoble stereotypes that skin and hair lack the substance to contradict. These dark projections then rationalize the pursuit of power. Your difference from me makes you bad, and your badness justifies, even demands, my pursuit of power over you—the oldest formula for aggression known to man. Whenever much importance is given to race, power is the primary motive.

But the human animal almost never pursues power without first convincing himself that he is *entitled* to it. And this feeling of entitlement has its own precondition: to be entitled one must first believe in one's innocence, at least in the area where one wishes to be entitled. By innocence I mean a feeling of essential goodness in relation to others and, therefore, superiority to others. Our innocence always inflates us and deflates those we seek power over. Once inflated we are entitled; we are in fact licensed to go after the power our innocence tells us we deserve. In this sense, *innocence is power.* Of course, innocence need not be genuine or real in any objective sense, as the Nazis demonstrated not long ago. Its only test is whether or not we can convince ourselves of it.

I think the racial struggle in America has always been primarily a struggle for innocence. White racism from the beginning has been a claim of white innocence and, therefore, of white entitlement to subjugate blacks. And in the '60s, as went innocence so went power. Blacks used the innocence that grew out of their long subjugation to seize more power, while whites lost some of their innocence and so lost a degree of power over blacks. Both races instinctively understand that to lose innocence is to lose power (in relation to each other). Now to be innocent someone else must be guilty, a natural law that leads the races to forge their innocence on each other's backs. The inferiority of the black always makes the white man superior; the evil might of whites makes blacks good. This pattern means that both races have a hidden investment in racism and racial disharmony, despite their good intentions to the contrary. Power defines their relations, and power requires innocence, which, in turn, requires racism and racial division.

I believe it was this hidden investment that the engineer was protecting when he made his remark—the white "evil" he saw in a white school

"depriving" his daughter of her black heritage confirmed his innocence. Only the logic of power explained this—he bent reality to show that he was once again a victim of the white world and, as a victim, innocent. His determined eyes insisted on this. And the whites, in their silence, no doubt protected their innocence by seeing him as an ungracious troublemaker—his bad behavior underscoring their goodness. I can only guess how he was talked about after the party. But it isn't hard to imagine that his blunder gave everyone a lift. What none of us saw was the underlying game of power and innocence we were trapped in, or how much we needed a racial impasse to play that game.

*   *   *

When I was a boy of about twelve, a white friend of mine told me one day that his uncle, who would be arriving the next day for a visit, was a racist. Excited by the prospect of seeing such a man, I spent the following afternoon hanging around the alley behind my friend's house, watching from a distance as this uncle worked on the engine of his Buick. Yes, here was evil and I was compelled to look upon it. And I saw evil in the sharp angle of his elbow as he pumped his wrench to tighten nuts, I saw it in the blade-sharp crease of his chinos, in the pack of Lucky Strikes that threatened to slip from his shirt pocket as he bent, and in the way his concentration seemed to shut out the human world. He worked neatly and efficiently, wiping his hands constantly, and I decided that evil worked like this.

I felt a compulsion to have this man look upon me so that I could see evil—so that I could see the face of it. But when he noticed me standing beside his toolbox, he said only, "If you're looking for Bobby, I think he went up to the school to play baseball." He smiled nicely and went back to work. I was stunned for a moment, but then I realized that evil could be sly as well, could smile when it wanted to trick you.

Need, especially hidden need, puts a strong pressure on perception, and my need to have this man embody white evil was stronger than any contravening evidence. As a black person you always hear about racists but never meet any. And I needed to incarnate this odious category of humanity, those people who hated Martin Luther King Jr. and thought blacks should "go slow" or not at all. So, in my mental dictionary, behind the term "white racist," I inserted this man's likeness. I would think of him and say to myself, "There is no reason for him to hate black people. Only evil explains unmotivated hatred." And this thought soothed me; I felt innocent. If I hated white people, which I did not, at least I had a reason. His evil commanded me to assert in the world the goodness he made me confident of in myself.

In looking at this man I was *seeing for innocence*—a form of seeing that has more to do with one's hidden need for innocence (and power) than with the person or group one is looking at. It is quite possible, for example, that the man I saw that day was not a racist. He did absolutely nothing in my presence to indicate that he was. I invested an entire afternoon in seeing not the man but in seeing my innocence through the man. *Seeing for innocence* is, in this way, the essence of racism—the use of others as a means to our own goodness and superiority.

*   *   *

Black Americans have always had to find a way to handle white society's presumption of racial innocence whenever they have sought to enter the American mainstream. Louis Armstrong's exaggerated smile honored the presumed innocence of white society—I will not bring you your racial guilt if you will let me play my music. Ralph Ellison calls this "masking"; I call it bargaining. But whatever it's called, it points to the power of white society to enforce its innocence. I believe this power is greatly diminished today. Society has reformed and transformed—Miles Davis never smiles. Nevertheless, this power has not faded altogether; blacks must still contend with it.

Historically, blacks have handled white society's presumption of innocence in two ways: they have bargained with it, granting white society its inno-

cence in exchange for entry into the mainstream; or they have challenged it, holding that innocence hostage until their demand for entry (or other concessions) was met. A bargainer says, *I already believe you are innocent (good, fair-minded) and have faith that you will prove it.* A challenger says, *If you are innocent, then prove it.* Bargainers *give* in hope of receiving; challengers *withhold* until they receive. Of course, there is risk in both approaches, but in each case the black is negotiating his own self-interest against the presumed racial innocence of the larger society. . . .

*   *   *

"Innocence is ignorance," Kierkegaard says, and if this is so, the claim of innocence amounts to an insistence on ignorance, a refusal to know. In their assertions of innocence both races carve out very functional areas of ignorance for themselves—territories of blindness that license a misguided pursuit of power. Whites gain superiority by *not* knowing blacks; blacks gain entitlement by *not* seeing their own responsibility for bettering themselves. The power each race seeks in relation to the other is grounded in double-edged ignorance, ignorance of the self as well as the other.

The original sin that brought us to an impasse at the dinner party I mentioned at the outset occurred centuries ago, when it was first decided to exploit racial difference as a means to power. It was the determinism that flowed karmically from this sin that dropped over us like a net that night. What bothered me most was our helplessness. Even the engineer did not know how to go forward. His challenge hadn't worked, and he'd lost the option to bargain. The marriage of race and power depersonalized us, changed us from eight people to six whites and two blacks. The easiest thing was to let silence blanket our situation, our impasse.

I think the civil rights movement in its early and middle years offered the best way out of America's racial impasse: in this society, race must not be a source of advantage or disadvantage for anyone. This is fundamentally a *moral* position, one that seeks to breach the corrupt union of race and power with principles of fairness and human equality: if all men are created equal, then racial difference cannot sanction power. The civil rights movement was conceived for no other reason than to redress that corrupt union, and its guiding insight was that only a moral power based on enduring principles of justice, equality, and freedom could offset the lower impulse in man to exploit race as a means to power. Three hundred years of suffering had driven the point home, and in Montgomery, Little Rock, and Selma, racial power was the enemy and moral power the weapon.

An important difference between genuine and presumed innocence, I believe, is that the former must be earned through sacrifice, while the latter is unearned and only veils the quest for privilege. And there was much sacrifice in the early civil rights movement. The Gandhian principle of non-violent resistance that gave the movement a spiritual center as well as a method of protest demanded sacrifice, a passive offering of the self in the name of justice. A price was paid in terror and lost life, and from this sacrifice came a hard-earned innocence and a credible moral power.

Non-violent passive resistance is a bargainer's strategy. It assumes the power that is the object of the protest has the genuine innocence to morally respond, and puts the protesters at the mercy of that innocence. I think this movement won so many concessions precisely because of its belief in the capacity of whites to be moral. It did not so much demand that whites change as offer them relentlessly the opportunity to live by their own morality—to attain a true innocence based on the sacrifice of their racial privilege, rather than a false innocence based on presumed racial superiority. Blacks always bargain with or challenge the larger society; but I believe that in the early civil rights years, these forms of negotiation achieved a degree of integrity and genuineness never seen before or since.

In the mid-'60s all this changed. Suddenly a sharp *racial* consciousness emerged to compete with the moral consciousness that had defined the movement to that point. Whites were no longer welcome in the movement, and a vocal "black power" minority gained dramatic visibility. Increasingly, the movement began to seek racial as well as moral power, and thus it fell into a fundamental contradiction that plagues it to this day. Moral power precludes racial power by denouncing race as a means to power. Now suddenly the movement itself was using race as a means to power, and thereby affirming the very union of race and power it was born to redress. In the end, black power can claim no higher moral standing than white power.

It makes no sense to say this shouldn't have happened. The sacrifices that moral power demands are difficult to sustain, and it was inevitable that blacks would tire of these sacrifices and seek a more earthly power. Nevertheless, a loss of genuine innocence and moral power followed. The movement, splintered by a burst of racial militancy in the late '60s, lost its hold on the American conscience and descended more and more to the level of secular, interest-group politics. Bargaining and challenging once again became racial rather than moral negotiations.

You hear it asked, why are there no Martin Luther Kings around today? I think one reason is that there are no black leaders willing to resist the seductions of racial power, or to make the sacrifices moral power requires. King understood that racial power subverts moral power, and he pushed the principles of fairness and equality rather than black power because he believed these principles would bring blacks their most complete liberation. He sacrificed race for morality, and his innocence was made genuine by that sacrifice. What made King the most powerful and extraordinary black leader of this century was not his race but his morality.

Black power is a challenge. It grants whites no innocence; it denies their moral capacity and then demands that they be moral. No power can long insist on itself without evoking an opposing power. Doesn't an insistence on black power call up white power? (And could this have something to do with what many are now calling a resurgence of white racism?) I believe that what divided the races at the dinner party I attended, and what divides them in the nation, can only be bridged by an adherence to those moral principles that disallow race as a source of power, privilege, status, or entitlement of any kind. In our age, principles like fairness and equality are ill-defined and all but drowned in relativity. But this is the fault of people, not principles. We keep them muddied because they are the greatest threat to our presumed innocence and our selective ignorance. Moral principles, even when somewhat ambiguous, have the power to assign responsibility and therefore to provide us with knowledge. At the dinner party we were afraid of so severe an accountability.

What both black and white Americans fear are the sacrifices and risks that true racial harmony demands. This fear is the measure of our racial chasm. And though fear always seeks a thousand justifications, none is ever good enough, and the problems we run from only remain to haunt us. It would be right to suggest courage as an antidote to fear, but the glory of the word might only intimidate us into more fear. I prefer the word effort—relentless effort, moral effort. What I like most about this word are its connotations of everydayness, earnestness, and practical sacrifice. No matter how badly it might have gone for us that warm summer night, we should have talked. We should have made the effort.

Crime and Punishment

KAHLIL GIBRAN

*Kahlil Gibran (1883–1931) was a Syrian poet and painter. In the
following selection from* The Prophet *(1923), he presents
reflections concerning shared social responsibility and identity.*

Then one of the judges of the city stood forth and said, Speak to us of Crime and Punishment.

And he answered, saying:

It is when your spirit goes wandering upon the wind,

That you, alone and unguarded, commit a wrong unto others and therefore unto yourself.

And for that wrong committed must you knock and wait a while unheeded at the gate of the blessed.

*   *   *

Like the ocean is your god-self;

It remains for ever undefiled.

And like the ether it lifts but the winged.

Even like the sun is your god-self;

It knows not the ways of the mole nor seeks it the holes of the serpent.

But your god-self dwells not alone in your being.

Much in you is still man, and much in you is not yet man,

But a shapeless pigmy that walks asleep in the mist searching for its own awakening.

And of the man in you would I now speak.

For it is he and not your god-self nor the pigmy in the mist, that knows crime and the punishment of crime.

*   *   *

Oftentimes have I heard you speak of one who commits a wrong as though he were not one of you, but a stranger unto you and an intruder upon your world.

But I say that even as the holy and the righteous cannot rise beyond the highest which is in each one of you,

So the wicked and the weak cannot fall lower than the lowest which is in you also.

And as a single leaf turns not yellow but with the silent knowledge of the whole tree,

So the wrong-doer cannot do wrong without the hidden will of you all.

Like a procession you walk together towards your god-self.

You are the way and the wayfarers.

And when one of you falls down he falls for those behind him, a caution against the stumbling stone.

Ay, and he falls for those ahead of him, who though faster and surer of foot, yet removed not the stumbling stone.

*   *   *

And this also, though the word lie heavy upon your hearts;

The murdered is not unaccountable for his own murder,

And the robbed is not blameless in being robbed.

The righteous is not innocent of the deeds of the wicked,

And the white-handed is not clean in the doings of the felon.

Yea, the guilty is oftentimes the victim of the injured,

And still more often the condemned is the burden bearer for the guiltless and unblamed.

You cannot separate the just from the unjust and the good from the wicked;

For they stand together before the face of the sun even as the black thread and the white are woven together.

And when the black thread breaks, the weaver shall look into the whole cloth, and he shall examine the loom also.

*   *   *

If any of you would bring to judgment the unfaithful wife,

Let him also weigh the heart of her husband in scales, and measure his soul with measurements.

And let him who would lash the offender look unto the spirit of the offended.

And if any of you would punish in the name of righteousness and lay the ax unto the evil tree, let him see to its roots;

And verily he will find the roots of the good and the bad, the fruitful and the fruitless, all entwined together in the silent heart of the earth.

And you judges who would be just,

What judgment pronounce you upon him who though honest in the flesh yet is a thief in spirit?

What penalty lay you upon him who slays in the flesh yet is himself slain in the spirit?

And how prosecute you him who in action is a deceiver and an oppressor,

Yet who also is aggrieved and outraged?

*   *   *

And how shall you punish those whose remorse is already greater than their misdeeds?

Is not remorse the justice which is administered by that very law which you would fain serve?

Yet you cannot lay remorse upon the innocent nor lift it from the heart of the guilty.

Unbidden shall it call in the night, that men may wake and gaze upon themselves.

And you who would understand justice, how shall you unless you look upon all deeds in the fullness of light?

Only then shall you know that the erect and the fallen are but one man standing in twilight between the night of his pigmy-self and the day of his god-self,

And that the corner-stone of the temple is not higher than the lowest stone in its foundation.

Review and Reflection

1. Do you believe we have an obligation to assist members of distant communities threatened by natural disaster? Famine? War? Political oppression? Other? Why?

2. What, in your opinion, is the proper function of education within an established society? In what ways are your views similar to or different from those of Plato?

3. Explicate and discuss the social theories of John Rawls and Robert Nozick. In what ways are they similar? Different? Whose views do you prefer? Why?

4. Do you regard abortion as an acceptable solution to an unwanted pregnancy? Why? In what ways are your views similar to or different from those expressed by Jane English?

5. Have you ever had a socially difficult encounter similar to the ones discussed by Shelby Steele? How did you feel? How did you act? Do you believe, in retrospect, that you should have said or done something a little differently?

6. Do you agree with Kahlil Gibran's views concerning crime and punishment? Why?

Suggestions for Further Study

ARISTOTLE. *Nicomachean Ethics.* Translated by M. Ostwald. New York: Macmillan, 1962.

JOHN STUART MILL. *On Liberty.* New York: Macmillan, 1956.

LISA H. NEWTON. *Ethics in America: Source Reader.* Englewood Cliffs, NJ: Prentice Hall, 1989.

ROBERT NOZICK. *Anarchy, State and Utopia.* New York: Basic Books, 1974.

PLATO. *The Republic.* Translated by Desmond Lee. New York: Penguin, 1955.

JOHN RAWLS. *A Theory of Justice.* Cambridge, MA: Harvard University Press, 1971.

PETER SINGER. *The Expanding Circle: Ethics and Sociobiology.* New York: Farrar, Straus, and Giroux, 1981.

CHRISTINA HOFF SOMMERS. *Right and Wrong: Basic Readings in Ethics.* New York: Harcourt Brace Jovanovich, 1986.

CHAPTER 6

Technology and Human Values

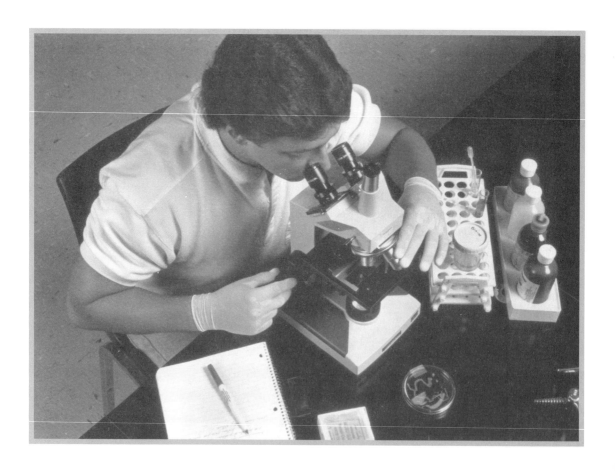

Advances in technology provide exciting new opportunities and options for the future. In the process they challenge the social and ethical fabric of the past, creating new issues and demanding decisions in areas which were previously beyond the scope of human manipulation and control. In addition to discussion of specific issues (genetic engineering and harvesting the dead, for example), the present chapter examines the impact of technology on basic human values and concepts of self.

Introductory Essay

The **Introductory Essay** provides a third and final visit with members of a hypothetical study group. Their discussion provides connections to previous chapters, establishes a framework for investigation of new issues, and foreshadows concepts and concerns presented in the readings by Murray, Gaylin, and Huxley. Specific points of focus include the influence of media images on human values and cognitions, the temptation to become spectators rather than participants, alienation, social insulation, and the simple difficulty of keeping up with the technological explosion. The final section of the dialogue tackles an assortment of related issues in the development of modern medicine (including transplantation, fetal tissue research, and allocation of limited resources).

Philosophical Reading

The selection by **Thomas Murray** examines some of the medical, ethical, and social issues that accompany the creation of genetically engineered material. Specifically, he discusses potential abuses of substances that regulate human growth and development. Much of his commentary concerns what he terms "heightism": social bias, discrimination, and preferential treatment based on differences in height. Gene therapy offers a potential "cure" for those who are socially disadvantaged on the basis of height, but Murray also sees tremendous potential for mischief. Thus he urges extreme caution and strict social control of synthetic hormones like hGH.

Scientific Reading

Willard Gaylin discusses the development and popularization of *brain death* as the new definitional standard. While adoption of the concept clarifies some technological and social issues, Dr. Gaylin argues that it creates others with which we may find ourselves equally uncomfortable. In particular, he discusses difficulties that stem from preservation of somatic functions of brain-dead individuals for research and other socially approved purposes.

Literary Reading

The selection by **Aldous Huxley** paints a vision of what the future may be like. He foresees increased technological sophistication giving rise to greater orchestration and control of reproduction, education, and social definition. It is a striking portrait of a tightly woven utilitarianism purchased at the price of individual difference and freedom of thought.

The Power Button

DOUGLAS W. SHRADER

Bo rapped on the door, then stuck in his head. "Hey, come on, you two! You'll be late for study group."

Sterling glanced up from the computer. "Be right with you," he said.

Wesley clicked the power button on his Walkman. "What are we supposed to talk about today?" he asked.

"Technology and human values," said Sterling, saving his program to a disk.

"I don't like technology," Wesley remarked. "It's dehumanizing."

Bo and Sterling glanced at one another, then burst out laughing.

"What?" asked Wesley.

"For a guy who doesn't like technology," explained Bo, "you sure spend a lot of time wearing those headphones."

"This is contemporary religious music," defended Wesley. "I wear the headphones so as not to bother others."

"Hard rock or gospel," Sterling remarked, "that's still a fairly sophisticated technological trinket."

"Must have set you back a pretty penny," observed Bo.

"I had to save up for several months," acknowledged Wesley. "But it was worth it. This is a good-quality piece of equipment: sharp, crisp highs; deep, distinct bass."

"Bet you could have fed a bunch of those street people you seemed so worried about the other day," kidded Bo.

"Man does not live by bread alone," retorted Wesley. "I do a lot for other people. I've worked as a Red Cross volunteer for many years. I started last term with the Salvation Army. And I plan to help with a Habitat for Humanity project this summer. Why does everyone criticize me if I do one little thing for myself? I have needs too, you know."

"We weren't criticizing," reassured Sterling. He glanced at Bo. "At least I wasn't."

They found Martha in the lounge, flipping through the channels on the TV. "Nothing but commercials," she said.

Despite the warning, all three guys found their attention drawn toward the screen. A pretty blonde in a flowered sundress was extolling the virtues of a new fresh-scent cleanser. She smiled as two children and a dog with muddy feet raced across the kitchen floor.

"See, that's what I mean," Wesley said. "TV is just a bunch of garbage. The shows are bad enough, but these commercials . . . !"

"If you don't like it, don't watch it," Bo said slowly. His eyes twinkled slightly, but the tone of his voice suggested the rebuke was not entirely in jest.

"I don't," retorted Wesley.

"What's got into these two?" asked Martha.

"Just a friendly debate about the dehumanizing influences of technology," replied Sterling.

"Dehumanizing influences of technology?" repeated Martha. "This must be something you started."

"Not really," said Sterling with a schoolboy smile. "Bo and I were teasing Wesley about his Walkman and the conversation just seemed to take on a life of its own."

"These two don't seem to understand," Wesley explained, "the evils of modern technology. It is undermining traditional religious values, contributing to the breakdown of the nuclear family, and turning us into a generation of video junkies. Everyone acts like music and television are just harmless amusements. But if you listen to something over and over again, or see it repeatedly on television and in the movies, it becomes so routine that you accept it as normal. People have become numb to violence, bloodshed, murder, extramarital sex, and a host of other things that would have shocked and shamed our ancestors."

"You take everything so seriously," responded Bo. "Not all television is violence and bloodshed. Besides, TV imitates reality. You won't see anything in a movie that you don't also see on the news."

"That's part of my point," countered Wesley. "You say 'TV imitates reality.' I say 'people imitate what they see on TV.' Part of the reason there is so much violence and bloodshed in our society is that people act out what they see on TV or hear in the lyrics of popular songs. If it wasn't in the programs it wouldn't be in the news."

"I didn't see any violence or bloodshed in that commercial you objected to a minute ago," observed Bo. "What I saw was a kind and understanding woman who didn't get all bent out of shape just because the kids got a little dirt on the floor. I wish life was more like TV."

"Can't you see that you are just being manipulated by the manufacturers of the product?" asked Wesley. "That stuff may not work better than plain water and a sponge, but they've succeeded in convincing you that life will be rosier and happier if you just buy a bottle of the jumbo economy size. The message is so phony it's pathetic: instead of addressing the real causes for human frustration and anger, the commercial suggests that a woman who yells at her kids for tracking dirt through the house may just be using the wrong cleanser."

"Give me a little credit," said Bo. "I'm not dumb enough to confuse real life with television. I like TV because it helps me forget my problems. I don't expect commercials to provide enlightenment about 'the real causes for human frustration and anger.' You overestimate the influence."

"Maybe you underestimate it," Wesley replied. "Have you ever stopped to think about how many hours you've spent watching television? I bet it is a whole lot more than you've spent reading."

"I don't watch as much as I used to," Bo responded defensively.

"I don't mean to pick on you," Wesley continued.

"But most people don't realize how much they are being bombarded and manipulated by all this seemingly innocent technology. If you sit for hours on end in front of the tube, all you will see is what the producers want you to see. Your emotions will be manipulated by professional actors and sound tracks. Sitcoms even use canned laughter to simulate peer pressure, encouraging people to laugh at things they might not otherwise think are funny. Pretty soon, people forget how to think and feel for themselves. Perhaps they never learn."

Bo shrugged, then nodded. "It does sound pretty scary when you put it that way," he acknowledged.

"What's really scary," said Wesley, "is that we subject ourselves to it voluntarily. We've even been trained to regard it as part of the good life. It may seem like harmless entertainment, but it is really a very elaborate form of mind control."

"It seems to me," Martha observed, "that it is not so much the technology to which you object, as it is the manner in which it is used."

"What do you mean?" asked Wesley.

"Although you've concentrated your remarks on television," she began, "you've made it clear that your concerns apply to music as well."

"That's right," Wesley confirmed. "Music is at least as dangerous as television, perhaps more so. Have you ever had the lyrics of a song stick in your mind? You try to think about something else, but the song keeps popping back into your consciousness? Perhaps you've even been kept awake at night by a song rattling about in your head. The lyrics bounce around and around, crowding out some thoughts and distorting others. Through that simple process of repetition you may eventually come to regard whatever the song says as commonplace, all without ever having given the matter any serious thought."

"Yet you use the Walkman several hours each day," Martha noted.

"I choose my tapes carefully," said Wesley. "I only listen to wholesome, uplifting, and edifying music. Society would be better if more people listened to the same things I do."

"That's my point," explained Martha. "You don't object to listening to music. You object to the values and messages of the music to which a lot of people listen. I bet if we press you on it we could even find a few movies and TV specials you like."

"There are some exceptions," admitted Wesley. "I like some of the things on public television; the Hallmark Hall of Fame presentations are usually pretty good; and I sometimes watch reruns of shows like *Ozzie and Harriet.* I wish the networks would bring back more family-oriented programming like that."

"That would be one way of cutting down on the amount of television I watch," observed Bo wryly.

Martha chuckled, then continued: "I guess there's no pleasing everybody. You guys have different tastes and maybe even some different values. But from what Bo said the other day about indoctrination, Wesley, I know he values autonomy and personal liberty as much as you."

"Very observant," said Sterling. "This ties in nicely with our lunchtime discussion about social and political philosophy. Long before television and radio were invented, Plato realized the immense role images play in the development of values and beliefs. Thus, in his sketch of the ideal society, he included provisions for the creation and control of images."

"Which is why you defended Martha's views about education," observed Bo.

"Right," said Sterling. "Martha was describing a strategy for teaching children to value difference and diversity. She recommended that we start with appropriate stories, then reinforce the teaching with movies, television programs, plays, and songs."

"I hate to admit it, but it is beginning to sound like Martha was right," conceded Bo. "If the control of images was important in Plato's society, think how much more so it must be in ours."

"That's what I've been trying to say," explained Wesley. "Images are serious business. Contemporary technology gives the media far greater power and influence than ever before. Look at a modern political election. A candidate's ability isn't nearly as important as his or her press coverage. Those who control the technology control the world."

"I don't know which is worse: the press or the politicians," groaned Bo. "There has got to be a better way."

"Perhaps," agreed Sterling, "but there is no going back to a simpler time and place. Like it or not, a modern candidate must be able to play to the camera. The development of recording and transmission technology has forever changed the landscape in which humans form their beliefs and values. As a result, it has changed the way in which they choose their political leaders."

"Is it any wonder," Martha mused, "that the American people elected a screen actor to be president?"

Canned laughter echoed across the room. On television a man had slipped on a toy firetruck, muttered a vague obscenity, and tumbled down a flight of stairs. "Oh Daddy," a child squealed in delight, "you found my firetruck!"

"Can we turn that off?" asked Wesley, reaching for the control. "I don't think anyone is watching it."

Bo eyed Wesley for a moment, then turned to Sterling and said: "I'm beginning to think that the secret to success is better awareness and manipulation of images."

"I suppose that depends on your definition of success," replied Sterling. "Our society's preoccupation with images causes me considerable concern. We seem to be losing touch with reality, with ourselves, and with one another."

"How's that?" asked Bo.

"Ours has become a videoculture," explained Sterling. "We have traded reality for illusion. We are entertained by images of people who do not know us, cannot see us, and do not care about us. We become vicariously involved in the imaginary lives and adventures of make-believe characters. If favorite characters encounter difficulties we may hold our breath or even shout out advice, but they cannot hear us. There is nothing we can do to affect the outcome on the screen. We become spectators rather than participants. In the process, we forget who we are and why we are here."

"I wouldn't want to become a couch potato," said Bo. "But I don't see anything wrong with being a spectator from time to time."

"There isn't anything wrong with being a spectator *from time to time*," replied Sterling. "But as Wesley pointed out, most people do not settle for occasional use. The video and audio images with which we are bombarded work their way into every corner of our lives. Whether we realize it or not, we use these images to define ourselves and our relationships with others."

"We learn to relate to images rather than people," added Wesley. "We may not be able to control the outcome, but we seem obsessed with controlling the images. We turn them on and off, adjust the color and sound quality to our own individual liking, pause the action, fast-forward through anything we don't want to see or hear, and rewind to catch anything we might have missed. It is a behavioral pattern which becomes deeply ingrained. After a while we treat other people as mere images to be manipulated via some imaginary remote control. We forget, or perhaps we never learn, that they have thoughts and feelings worthy of our consideration and respect."

"Right," said Sterling. "The attitudes and behaviors you identify mark the beginnings of a dangerous spiral. If we don't treat others with dignity and respect, it may be difficult or even impossible to respect ourselves. In the end we cheapen the entire human race."

"Many people never learn how to listen to another person," observed Martha. "Have you noticed how many students treat a class as though it were something they were watching on TV? They come in late and yell to their friends. They talk while the professor is talking. They pop gum or rattle papers so that other students can't hear. If you ask them to be quiet they act like you've infringed on *their* liberties."

"I know what you mean," said Wesley. "They act like members of an audience rather than partici-

pants in a class. They have no respect for anyone or anything: the professor, other students, the material they are supposed to be studying, or the desks on which they carve obscenities or lyrics from some contemporary rock song. I don't think they intend disrespect. They just never learned its importance. They may have spent so much time relating to images that they never developed the people skills necessary for truly meaningful human relationships. I feel sorry for them. They may not even realize they are disrupting others."

"You haven't said so," remarked Bo, "but we all know some of those remarks describe me. I'm really glad Sterling asked me to join this study group. This is complex material—I've learned more than if I had tried to sort through it all by myself. For that I am grateful because, as I explained before, I really need a good grade in this class. But another thing has been happening as well, one that I didn't expect. I think I'm learning to listen better. I've known almost everyone in the group for several years, yet I've learned more about each of you in the past few weeks than I ever knew before. I think I'm also learning a lot about myelf, strange as it may sound."

"It's not as strange as you may think," replied Sterling. "Discussing complex ideas with others forces us to examine our own beliefs and values. Self-discovery is not always comfortable, but it is important. You've added far more to our discussions than any of us really expected you to."

Bo grinned broadly. "I didn't know what I was missing," he said. "It's kind of embarrassing when I think about how reluctant I was to do this. The very thought of sitting around and discussing philosophy made my stomach churn. I never knew conversation could be so . . . so stimulating. Maybe we could make a movie out of this. You know: just two or three people sitting around talking about philosophy."

Martha laughed. "Always the video kid," she said. "Anyway, it's been done."

"You're kidding," said Bo.

"No—really," Martha replied. "I saw a movie a few years ago that was nothing but a conversation between two people about the meaning of life, the dehumanizing influences of technology—all the same kind of stuff we've been talking about. It is called *My Dinner With André*. The setting is a fairly fancy restaurant where two friends, Wally and André, enjoy a leisurely meal and just debate back and forth in much the same way we do."

"What do they say about technology?" asked Wesley.

"I don't remember everything," Martha said. "But one part that sticks out in my mind is a scene in which André is going on and on about the evils of an electric blanket. I remember thinking, 'Boy, this is dumb. I wouldn't give up my electric blanket for anything.' "

"What's so evil about an electric blanket?" asked Bo.

"The problem is not so much the blanket itself," replied Martha, "as it is the effect which using it may have on our values and perceptions of reality. The blanket is a token symbol of technological devices that make our lives more comfortable, but insulate us from reality. It may be freezing outside, but if we are warm and cozy in our room, snuggled up in an electric blanket, we lose all experiential contact with that cold."

"So?" asked Bo.

"André argues that the blanket is a way of lying to ourselves," explained Martha. "We substitute pretense for reality. Warm in our beds, we lose all trace of any threads which would tie us to people who may have little more than an old newspaper or cardboard box to shelter them from the cold. Eventually we become numb to their plight and lose the capacity to care. Like a person who has built up a tolerance to drugs, we may need a greater and greater dose of reality just to feel anything at all."

"It sounds like a pretty interesting movie," observed Wesley. "Everything you've said about the electric blanket is similar to what I've been saying about television."

"That it is," said Martha. "And I'm still not sure what to think about either one. I didn't throw my electric blanket away after watching *My Dinner*

With André, but I do regard it somewhat differently. I don't use it as much as I used to. I don't take it quite so much for granted. And I make a special effort, when I do use it, to think about people less fortunate than myself."

"That seems reasonable," responded Wesley. "I'd be happy if I could get people to develop that much awareness and responsibility concerning television."

"Let me see if I've got this right," Bo interjected. "You're willing to let us watch television as long as we *regard* it differently."

"I'd rather do away with it altogether," explained Wesley, "but I know that's not going to happen. It's part of our culture. People aren't going to give up their TVs any more than they are their electric blankets. But that doesn't mean we have to give in to television. We can control the programming, and we can control our attitudes. We can, as Martha phrased it, *regard it somewhat differently.*"

"This is an interesting clarification of your position," noted Sterling. "Can you tell us a little more about the type of attitude you think we should cultivate?"

"I'll try," said Wesley. "I'm not sure what order of importance to put these in, but three fundamental principles come to mind. First, we have to recognize that images are just images; they are not real and should not be treated as though they were real. Second, we have to appreciate the power and influence that images may have in the development of human values, beliefs, and behavior. We cannot air just any and everything. Finally, we have to distinguish between attitudes and behavior that are appropriate to images, and those that are required to develop relationships of mutual worth and respect with other flesh-and-blood humans. We cannot go on treating other people as though they were mere two-dimensional images to be manipulated according to our own petty desires and purposes."

"I guess I could live with each of those," remarked Bo. "But isn't the first one kind of obvious? Do you really think people confuse television with reality?"

"Yes, I do," answered Wesley. "The problem is particularly pernicious because, like you, they assume that it is easy to tell the difference. At one level, of course, they are right. Very few people actually mistake a television set for a person. But think for a moment about people who ask medical advice from an actor who plays a doctor."

"They're nuts," commented Bo.

"I admit it's a rather extreme case," continued Wesley, "but I've known a lot of otherwise normal people who develop distrust and dislike of an actress who plays an 'evil' character on a soap opera. We identify with some characters and hate others. Pretty soon we get caught up in the play. We forget it's not real."

"Perhaps," responded Bo, "but only temporarily."

"Even so," replied Wesley, "the effect lingers. The packaged reality we experience on television is perfected and sanitized. It is exciting and interesting, not dull, boring, and routine like most of our lives. All domestic problems can be solved in neat thirty-minute segments, even allowing a few timeouts for strategically placed commercials. Really big problems like averting a nuclear war or capturing an international terrorist may require a full two-hour movie. Throughout it all, no one makes mistakes, at least none with lasting consequences. No one ages. No one ever really dies. Is it any wonder that people become disillusioned with their lives, that they prefer to frequent this fantasy world rather than deal with their own problems, or that they develop unrealistic standards and expectations concerning the appearance and abilities of real-life people? If you don't think we are obsessed with image, just look at all the time and money we spend dieting, or stepping up and down on a block to firm our thighs and flatten our tummies. The ultimate, of course, is plastic surgery. The message is clear: if the image you see in the mirror doesn't match the image you see on the screen, we can fix that—for a price."

"You're pretty convincing," conceded Bo. "But not everything on television is glamorous. People make mistakes. We see famous actors flubbing their lines on various blooper programs. And there are several programs that air home videos. Those people aren't actors; they certainly aren't glamorous."

"Think about those programs for a minute," responded Wesley. "People laugh as other people suffer misfortune, embarrassment, or bodily injury. Real people experience real pain; yet somebody videotapes it and sends it in to the show for a buck. And what do we do? We laugh. So-called *Reality TV* just underscores what we were discussing before about the numbing effects of television. Even injury to a small child loses its shock value; it becomes standard fare, accepted routine. The television insulates us from reality every bit as much as André's electric blanket. We become part of the audience: spectators rather than participants."

"Sorry we're late," Callie said as she dropped her bookbag on the table and slumped into a nearby chair.

Caitlin opted for a spot on the sofa, next to Bo. "You wouldn't believe the hassle we've been through," she explained. "We've been going around in circles with the people in Accounts Payable. They've got a hold on my records for some overdue library book I've never heard of. Someone must have entered a number wrong in the computer."

"Isn't your ID card bar coded?" asked Sterling.

"Yeah," Caitlin replied, "but sometimes the light pen doesn't work and the person at the desk has to enter the numbers by keyboard. We think that is what may have happened."

"What can you do?" asked Bo.

"Maybe nothing," answered Caitlin. "I have an appointment to talk with the Dean of Students tomorrow, but I don't know if it will do any good. It's my word against that of the computer."

"Maybe the book will turn up," encouraged Martha.

"I doubt it," Caitlin said with a sigh. "It's already six months overdue."

"I had a similar experience at the bank last month," volunteered Wesley. "The statement showed the wrong amount for a check. It seemed pretty clear to me that someone had just entered the information incorrectly. The numbers were right, but they forgot to put in the decimal."

"That could be a costly mistake," observed Sterling.

"You're not kidding," said Wesley. "I had written a check for $21.16, but the bank debited my account $2116. It nearly wiped out my second tuition installment."

"Did you have the canceled check?" Callie asked.

"Yeah, that's what was so frustrating," answered Wesley. "Everyone I talked to asked me to wait a minute, punched a few buttons on their computer, and informed me that I must be wrong. I kept showing them the check and trying to explain that someone had made a mistake, but they kept saying, 'According to the computer . . .' "

"They're just so sure that if it says so in the computer, it must be right," noted Caitlin.

"Absolutely," agreed Wesley. "I finally got it straightened out, but it took forever to find someone who was willing to listen."

"Sometimes they make you feel like you're just a number in a computer," complained Caitlin. "I don't have any privacy. The computer doesn't even know me, but it tracks every detail of my life: where I live, what kind of car I drive, the classes I take and grades I receive, even my phone calls, meal purchases, and library readings."

"Of course the computer doesn't *know* you," responded Sterling. "It is only a machine. And although it is convenient to speak of computers tracking information of one sort or another, it is more accurate to say that people use computers to keep track of the data. Computers are tools, not people."

"Still," noted Wesley, "computers have made it easier to keep track of lots of details about our lives that most of us would prefer to regard as private. Computer networks have also made it easier for others to access that information."

"What I don't understand," remarked Bo, "is the attitude of people who use computers. On the one hand they say, 'Computers don't make mistakes.' But if something does go wrong they say, 'It must be

a computer error.' It's like they can't accept any responsibility for their own jobs. Sometimes I think they just hide behind the computer, using it to cover their own incompetence or feelings of inadequacy."

"A lot of people are intimidated by computers," explained Sterling. "They learn to operate them—to enter and retrieve data of one sort or another—but they never really understand how they work or how to program one. The industry has spent a lot of time and effort trying to make computers user-friendly. The result is a mixed blessing. More and more people are able to use computers, but their use is completely dependent on the software and programming efforts of others. They continue to be mystified by the tools they are learning to use. This results in a cognitive and affective distance between the tool and its user. It's what philosophers call *alienation*."

"Do you mean that people who use computers in their jobs every day may not understand them any better than I do?" asked Bo.

"That's right," replied Sterling. "We don't require people who work at checkout counters to understand the scientific or technological principles of a laser scanner. We just show them how to run a light pen across a bar code, wait for a beep, then collect money and provide change according to the printout on the screen. The people in Accounts Payable with whom Caitlin had to deal, or those at the bank who caused Wesley so much frustration, may not be much different. It's more sophisticated equipment, but their jobs may not call for anything more than following a complex set of pre-established procedures: *If you want A, press these keys in this order. If you want B, press those.*"

"I think I understand," said Bo. "If the equipment works right and everyone follows the pre-established procedures, everything will go smoothly and people will feel comfortable and secure in their positions. But if some of the data are wrong, or if you want something that is not on the menu of prescribed procedures, the people with whom you are dealing may feel just as helpless as you. They may become frustrated or even angry with you for throwing a wrench into their well-oiled system. Your problem may be a painful reminder that their job is just part of a system over which they have very little control."

"I guess I never thought of it that way," reflected Caitlin. "Maybe I was a little rough on some of those people today."

"Don't apologize yet," said Wesley. "The lack of a specifically prescribed rule is no excuse for treating another human being as an unwelcome problem. It may be a sad commentary on our times, but I think you and Callie were experiencing some of the very things we were talking about in your absence."

"Really? What's that?" Caitlin asked.

"The dehumanizing influences of technology," replied Wesley.

"For whatever it is worth," said Caitlin, "I certainly felt dehumanized."

"Just like I did at the bank," said Wesley. "Sterling was on the right track a moment ago when he spoke of alienation. We have become extremely dependent on a lot of technology that most of us don't even begin to understand: calculators, computers, microwave ovens, VCRs, CD players—the list goes on and on. We learn how to punch a few buttons and operate the controls; but if you dare to open the cover, the veneer of knowledge and illusion of familiarity will be shattered in a flash. I think all of us, down deep, have been frightened by the technological explosion of recent years. Things are changing so fast that we have become like strangers in a foreign land, struggling to learn enough to find our way from one place to another, but never developing a sense of identity or belonging. We are alienated from our jobs, from the things we use in our daily lives, from the people with whom we work and live, and possibly even from our true selves."

"Well, you are definitely right about technological dependency," Caitlin responded. "I don't think I would have gotten through high school math without a calculator. I know I would never manage some of these college classes if I didn't have access to a computer with spell-check. You are also right about the pressures of the technological explosion. Some-

times I feel so overwhelmed I could scream. There is so much to learn. And it seems like everything becomes obsolete as soon as you figure out how to use it."

"The technological explosion puts a lot of pressure on everyone," observed Bo. "It's almost impossible to keep up with the changes. My grandparents have even stopped trying. We sent them a VCR for their anniversary a few years ago. It sat in the box for six months, unopened until we were able to go there for a visit. My father took it out and connected it to their set, but I still don't think they've ever used it."

"My grandmother hasn't learned to use her microwave either, but at least she tries," Callie said. "She calls my mom every week or so with questions about which buttons to push for what kinds of food. You wouldn't believe some of those conversations. I tried to get her to read the instructions, but that was a lost cause."

"Some separation between the generations is both natural and desirable," noted Sterling. "In most societies the separation is buffered and balanced by a sense of historical tradition. Ancestors and elders are usually valued as sources of wisdom or knowledge; they may even be revered. But we've lost a lot of that. And the technological explosion is at least partially to blame. I'm not entirely sure, but I think a lot of our alienation and loss of identity is a direct consequence of this loss of historical tradition."

"I couldn't agree more," said Wesley. "Many so-called 'advances' in technology have led to greater and greater fracture within our society. Perhaps the Amish are right. We might all be better off if we renounced modern technology and returned to a simpler way of life."

"Why is everyone so down on technology today?" asked Callie. "You seem to forget that a human is a technological creature. We owe our evolutionary success to the abilities of our ancestors to develop tools and techniques for doing things that would have otherwise been beyond the range of their physical abilities. Without housing, clothing, and cultivation we would not be able to live in many parts of the world that humans now inhabit. Technological developments pose new problems, but also new possibilities."

"I didn't mean to sound negative," said Sterling. "You are certainly right when you say a human is a technological creature. That has indeed been our strength. But if we can't control the technology we create, it may be our undoing as well."

"Your point is well taken," responded Callie. "I too have read Mary Shelley's story of Frankenstein."

"It was a remarkably prophetic book," said Sterling. "Did you know that she was only nineteen when she wrote it during the summer of 1816? Or that it was subtitled *The Modern Prometheus*? She saw with amazing clarity both the possibilities and problems associated with transplantation of bodily parts. Even so, she would be astonished if she could witness the operations performed on a daily basis in a modern hospital."

"Imagine what she would think of *in vitro* fertilization or genetic engineering," added Martha.

"I know what *I* think," responded Wesley. "I think we've become obsessed with playing God. Modern technology has overstepped the natural boundaries that God created for us. The items you've mentioned are perfect examples of things that would have been better left undone: transplanting organs from one being to another, conceiving human life in a petri dish, and creating 'designer genes' with material from more than one species. We are forgetting our place, our role, our purpose, and our destiny. There is a story in the book of Genesis about people who aspired to be like God. It is called the Tower of Babel."

"I'm familiar with the story," said Callie, "but I don't agree with your interpretation. I believe in God every bit as much as you do. I believe she created us in her image. I do not believe we have any abilities that she did not give to us. And I cannot believe that she would want to sit idly by while a child dies if there is anything we might do to save that life. I was serious when I said technological developments pose problems as well as possibilities. If we only have one available heart for every ten children

who need one, I don't know any fair way to decide who lives and who dies. But the inability to save them all doesn't mean we shouldn't save any. If that means we are playing God, so be it. May she guide us in these difficult times."

"Where do you draw the line?" asked Wesley. "Would you cannibalize an anencephalic infant for parts?"

"I don't care much for your choice of terms," replied Callie. "When you phrase things in an inflammatory and prejudicial fashion, you make clear thought and rational discussion nearly impossible."

"Phrase it any way you like," said Wesley. "You haven't answered the question."

"Very well," responded Callie. "An anencephalic infant, by definition, is born without a fully developed brain. In fact, there may be almost no brain at all. The odds of keeping one alive for more than a few days are extremely small. The expense is enormous. And the chances of their ever developing into conscious, fully functioning human beings are nonexistent. Other organs, however, may be just fine. In many cases there are infants for whom the availability of those organs is a matter of life and death. Under such circumstances I believe it would be a tragic sin of short-sighted selfishness *not* to make the organs available for transplant."

"Even if the anencephalic infant were your own?" asked Wesley.

"Even if the infant were my own," replied Callie. "If he or she could not contribute to the life of another, my child would have died in vain. Moreover, by disallowing the transplant of viable organs, I would have in effect signed the death warrants of several other children as well."

"Then I suppose," said Wesley with a sigh, "that you also approve of research and treatment involving fetal tissue."

"Within limits," Callie said. "I don't know a lot about it, but from what I've read, fetal tissue research may help us to better understand diseases associated with aging: Parkinson's, Alzheimer's, and so on. Who knows, perhaps it will provide the key we need to find a cure for AIDS."

"You say, 'within limits,'" noted Wesley. "What limits do you have in mind? Do you, for example, recognize a difference based on the source of the tissue: spontaneous versus voluntary abortion?"

"I don't think the source makes much difference," Callie answered. "But I do believe the dignity we accord human beings extends in some measure to their organs and bodily parts. Thus we cannot do just any and everything with them, even if it happens to provide some slight benefit to another human. For instance, I would not support using fetal tissue to manufacture cosmetics."

"Thank God for that," said Wesley. "You know, Callie, I admire you in many ways. You are well informed and you demonstrate far more ethical sensitivity than most people with whom I have discussed these issues. But I am still concerned about the basic model of a human being that seems to underlie this approach to medicine. You treat a human as though he or she were nothing more than a machine. If one part of a human doesn't work right, you just remove it and stick in a replacement you salvaged from another."

"Is that so bad?" asked Callie. "Wouldn't you rather replace an organ than allow someone to die just because one part didn't work quite right?"

"I don't know," conceded Wesley. "If it were me or a member of my immediate family who needed the transplant, I guess I would feel about the same way as you. But I still don't like the model on which the technology is based. I know some of it is more hype than real, but I prefer the holistic model of health to the techno-fix-it model that dominates the industry. I don't want my life in the hands of an army of specialists who resemble auto mechanics more than they do caring, compassionate physicians."

"That's understandable," Callie said. "We definitely have some problems in the delivery of health care. Family practice is pretty much a thing of the past. The processes of diagnosis and treatment have become technologically more sophisticated and harder to understand. It is no wonder that people are turning to alternative models. Still, you cannot deny the tremendous advances made possible by specialization. Perhaps with tolerance, persistence, and sensitivity we will manage to balance the benefits and liabilities of each approach."

"Perhaps," agreed Wesley, "but one thing I can tell you for certain. If I had to choose between death with my body intact and life with a mechanical heart, I would choose death. I don't want to be kept alive by machines. And I don't want to be turned into one."

Callie shrugged and slowly shook her head.

"This may be a good time for a break," said Sterling. "Do you realize this all started when Wesley pushed the power button on his Walkman and complained about the dehumanizing influences of technology? Being converted into a machine, piece by piece, would certainly be the ultimate dehumanization. Anyway, I think we've covered enough ground for a while."

"Surely we're not going to stop now," complained Martha. "We haven't talked about the pollution created by our throwaway culture, the threat of nuclear war, toxic waste, the greenhouse effect, or our responsibility to future generations."

"Maybe we can discuss toxic waste some other time," Caitlin said. "Bo promised to take me to a movie tonight."

Bo grinned sheepishly, then glanced at Wesley as though pleading for approval.

"Go on," said Wesley. "Just don't forget what we talked about."

"Don't worry," said Bo as he helped Caitlin with her coat. "We're having dinner first. I will explain everything about the insulating properties of electric blankets and the importance of a properly regarded image. Just call me 'André.'"

As Caitlin and Bo gathered their books and hurried out the door, Martha turned to Wesley and remarked: "Maybe we should all go out to dinner and a movie. That's one conversation I would love to hear."

The Growing Danger From Gene-Spliced Hormones

THOMAS H. MURRAY

Thomas H. Murray is professor and director of the Center for Biomedical Ethics at Case Western Reserve University. In the following article, reprinted from *Discover* (1987), he discusses the social implications and potential abuse of genetically engineered substances. Other publications by Professor Murray include "Moral Obligations to the Not-Yet Born: The Fetus as Patient," "Genetic Screening in the Workplace: Ethical Issues," *Feeling Good and Doing Better: Ethics and Nontherapeutic Drug Use* (1984), and *Which Babies Shall Live?* (1985).

My son Peter is twelve, and lately the cuffs of his pants have been racing up his ankles—a sure sign that growth hormone is coursing through his body. He's on about the same growth schedule I was. By my fourteenth birthday I was already just shy of six feet, and hopeful of four or five inches more. I thought that would be enough to give me a shot at playing basketball in college. Alas, I'd reached my limit. Lacking any notable physical talents, I had to rely on guile; if you can't shoot over the guy, get him looking one way and then scurry past on the other side. (As we used to say, "Fake left, go right.") Recent happenings in genetic engineering make me wonder if something similar, albeit unintentional, is going on there: Is our attention being directed one way while what's important is slipping by on the other side?

At least since 1980, worries about using recombinant DNA technology to alter "human nature" have focused on gene therapy—the direct and intentional alteration of genetic material to treat disease. On June 20 of that year the general secretaries of three national organizations, for Protestants, Jews, and Catholics, wrote the President to warn: "History has shown us that there will always be those who believe it appropriate to 'correct' our mental and social structures by genetic means, so as to fit their vision of humanity. This becomes more dangerous when the basic tools to do so are finally at hand. Those who would play God will be tempted as never before."

Nothing garners attention as quickly as a nice little scandal; within a month of the letter, Dr. Martin Cline of UCLA provided one by experimenting on two patients with beta-zero thalassemia, a genetic condition that causes severe anemia. Cline removed some of their bone marrow, treated it with recombinant DNA containing normal hemoglobin genes, then reinserted it into the bone (after making room by killing some of the remaining marrow cells with radiation). The hope was that the treated cells would multiply and produce normal hemoglobin.

They didn't. Worse, Cline didn't have the approval of the UCLA committee that oversees research with human subjects. When the affair became public, the National Institutes of Health (NIH) stripped Cline of $162,000 in grant money and demanded strict supervision of his research. For those suspicious of human gene therapy, the case was proof that scientists couldn't be trusted to regulate themselves.

Thomas H. Murray, "The Growing Danger From Gene-Spliced Hormones," *Discover* 8.2 (February 1987), pp. 88–92. Reprinted with the permission of *Discover*.

185

Since then, such work has proceeded very cautiously. A presidential commission gave its tentative blessing to gene therapy with somatic cells—those that don't pass the altered genes on to future generations. The NIH's watchdog recombinant DNA advisory committee set up a "human gene therapy subcommittee," which has suggested "points to consider" for doctors who propose to tinker with genes. Among them: whether the benefits of the treatment outweigh the risks, how to choose patients fairly, and how to publicize the results of the research. Thanks to the brouhaha over gene therapy, no great threats to humanity are likely to slip by in the near future—at least not on that side.

But there's another side to genetic engineering that has the power to alter us physically and socially. Rather than directly altering our genes, it can modify our bodies by supplementing the natural supply of important regulatory hormones with genetically engineered ones. A prime example is biosynthetically manufactured human growth hormone—hGH. Except for one additional amino acid—methionine (which appears to have no effect on its action)—biosynthetic hGH is identical to the hormone that promotes normal growth.

Produced in the pituitary gland, hGH plays a key role in determining how tall we'll become. So-called pituitary dwarfs usually lack an adequate supply of bioactive hGH. To treat them, for more than twenty years we've been harvesting pituitaries from human cadavers, each of which yields a minute quantity of hGH. Until recently the supply was barely adequate. In 1979 genetic engineers cloned the gene carrying instructions for making hGH, inserted it into a microorganism, and coaxed the bug to produce the human hormone. Just in time, it appears, because some hGH recovered from human pituitaries seems to have been contaminated with the slow virus that causes Creutzfeldt-Jakob disease (CJD), a degenerative infection of the brain. In April 1985 the Food and Drug Administration (FDA) halted the sale of natural growth hormone, and shortly thereafter approved Genentech's biosynthetic version. Since no human tissue is used in producing it, there's no danger of contamination with the CJD virus. Also,

we're no longer limited by the scarcity of cadaver pituitaries, and other uses for hGH can be explored.

Biotechnology came to the rescue of kids deficient in growth hormone. But if hGH injections can make extremely short children a bit taller, what can it do for those who aren't dwarfs, but just shorter than average? What about the youngster who would have been only of average height? And what about the basketball player for whom a couple of inches more might mean the difference between the schoolyard and the NBA? In short (no pun intended), why not use hGH to give your child the advantages that come with being tall?

Years ago, at an FDA hearing, I speculated that once biosynthetic hGH was approved, people would want to use it for all sorts of nontherapeutic purposes. One member of the FDA committee told me that several parents had already asked her if they could get the drug for their kids, who weren't hGH-deficient. All, she recalled, were physicians. Rebecca Kirkland, who does clinical trials of biosynthetic hGH at the Baylor College of Medicine, recently said she's had inquiries from five parents wanting to get hGH for their normal children.

Why would parents want to go to such expense (treatment with biosynthetic hGH costs roughly $10,000 a year), cause their children pain (the shots hurt a bit), and risk unknown long-term side effects? Quite simply, because it's advantageous to be tall—within limits. A modest body of scientific evidence supports the commonsense observation that taller people often get the nod over their shorter counterparts, because they're perceived as more intelligent, good-looking, likable, extroverted, and attractive. Being very much taller than average is a mixed blessing, to be sure. But being a few inches above average seems to help.

A survey at the University of Pittsburgh in 1968 found that starting salaries for graduates varied with height: roughly $300 an inch up to six feet two inches. In a study of men whose heights had been recorded twenty-five years earlier, a graduate student at Washington University in St. Louis demonstrated a "height bonus" of approximately $400 per inch.

When a researcher at Eastern Michigan University presented two hypothetical job candidates to recruiters, one eight inches taller than the other, 72 per cent preferred the taller one, 27 per cent said there was no difference, and only one chose the shorter applicant. And much has been made of the fact that the taller candidate for President usually wins. Only two presidents—Madison and Benjamin Harrison—were shorter than the average American male of their eras.

If some parents want to give their child the edge that height seems to confer, what's wrong with that? If it's O.K. to spend $2,500 on orthodontics, to buy your kid private tennis and music lessons, or to spend $10,000 a year and up for prep school and private college, what's a few thousand bucks more to buy a couple of inches? The kid could turn out to be a klutz at tennis, have a tin ear, and major in Michelob, but taller is taller.

In this century, we make a strong presumption in favor of liberty. Before we interfere with the right of parents to bring up their children as they judge best, we demand strong reasons for doing so. Can we find them in the case of hGH?

Let me ask a skeptical question: What's the disease for which human growth hormone is the cure? Philosophers have a difficult time agreeing on the definition of disease, but most would recognize a physiological deficiency in hGH as a genuine disease, and hGH injections as a reasonable treatment. There are some kids, though, who aren't measurably deficient in hGH but who are very short. Their shortness can be the consequence of any one of numerous medical problems, or they may fall into the category of "familial short stature"—that is, short like mom or pop. Either way, can their shortness ever be a disability? A disability is a condition that interferes with the tasks of daily living. If people are so short that they qualify for the elevator riddle,* their shortness may well be a disability. Disabilities usually justify medical intervention. But what if a

person isn't suffering from a disease, and isn't so short that the lack of height becomes a disability? What if it's merely a disadvantage?

Even if hGH turns out to be physiologically harmless—some experts have warned of possible effects on glucose regulation, as well as an increased risk of atherosclerosis and high blood pressure—there may be psychological consequences to treating children with the hormone. The unmistakable message given to a child is that shortness is a grave enough problem to justify the considerable expense, inconvenience, and discomfort of hGH treatment. It's likely to increase the child's self-consciousness about height. And since children rarely grow as much with the hormone as they or their parents hope, disappointment is likely.

A study of hGH-deficient children and their families found that the most psychologically mature kids weren't those who grew the most but those whom parents and other adults had treated appropriately for their age rather than their size. Kids who were encouraged to pursue interests where their height wasn't a disadvantage were much happier with themselves.

People differ in so many ways: in intelligence, charm, quickness of hand and foot, facility with words, wit, etc. But when we put children through hGH treatments, we focus almost entirely on their height (where they don't "measure up") and ignore their other talents and abilities. Understandably, short kids receiving hGH may come to feel that they're inadequate and inferior.

All other things being equal, taller basketball players are more effective than shorter ones. Height is an advantage in basketball and some other sports. In almost all other realms of human endeavor, though, height bears no relationship to the ability to do a job well. But in a culture that regularly imputes desirable characteristics to tall people and undesirable ones to short ones, shortness is surely a disadvantage. (Even our language is laden with "heightisms": we look up to people we admire, look down on those we don't.)

Like other "isms," such as racism and sexism, heightism involves making unwarranted judgments

---

* Why did the man always take the elevator to the sixth floor, then walk up four more flights to his apartment? Because he could only reach the button for the sixth floor

about people based on irrelevant criteria. Does anyone believe the solution to racism is to find a drug that lightens black skin? The mind boggles at the possible biotechnological remedies for sexism. And yet those who want to give their kids hGH are proposing just this sort of technological end-run around heightism.

If we choose to allow hGH to be used for non-disease, non-disabling shortness, then we must make a choice. Either we let those who can afford it buy it for their children, or we make it available at public expense to all children whose parents want it.

Suppose we let it be sold. The children of rich parents will have one more leg up, so to speak, on their peers. You could ask, what's one more advantage in light of all the others available to people with means? But the prospect of two classes—one tall and monies, the other short and poor—is ugly and disquieting. It would allow injustice to be piled upon injustice.

Suppose we take the other route and provide hGH to anyone who wants it. If all parents (short and tall alike) rushed out to get hGH shots for their kids, the average height of the entire population might increase. But in all likelihood the distribution of height in the population wouldn't change much, if at all. There would still be the taller and the shorter, and since we're doing nothing to diminish heightism, discrimination against the shorter would continue. Some people would benefit, of course—for example, the stockholders in Genentech (which holds a patent for making biosynthetic hGH) and those who produce fabrics (since every-

one will be wearing bigger sizes). Meanwhile, at considerable social expense, kids would get their three shots a week with a little pain and, we hope, minimal side effects.

Inevitably, a few eager parents would want to regain the edge for their kids and try to get bigger doses of hGH, like those athletes who take increasing amounts of anabolic steroids in the hope of obtaining an advantage over their rivals. In both cases, individuals pursue their own interests, only to make everyone worse off.

Whether hGH is available just to those who can pay for it or to everyone, the results would be unfortunate. In one instance, we use biotechnology to reinforce the advantages of wealth; in the other, we incur enormous expense and unknown risks without making anyone better off. The wisest course is to restrict hGH to cases of disease and disability.

Although hGH may be the first biosynthetic hormone to tempt us to improve on human nature, it won't be the last. Imagine what we might do with a hormone that prompted damaged nerves to regenerate. Someone would wonder whether it would also stimulate growth in the brain. And soon we'd be trying to enlarge our brains, however misguided that might be, scientifically or morally.

It also occurs to me that simply by writing this article I may spur some parents to seek out growth hormone for their child of normal height. I fervently hope not. But the temptation posed by hGH, and by other fruits of biotechnology as yet unripened, will be great. And it will require all our collective common sense to use them wisely.

Harvesting the Dead

WILLARD GAYLIN

Willard Gaylin is president of the Institute of Society, Ethics and the Life Sciences in Hastings-on-Hudson, New York. A psychiatrist by training, Dr. Gaylin is a regular contributor to *Hastings Center Report*. His books include *Partial Justice: A Study of Bias in Sentencing* and *Adam and Eve and Pinocchio*. In the following article, originally published in *Harper's Magazine* (September 1974), he explores some of the implications, options, and responsibilities created by the development of medical technology.

Nothing in life is simple anymore, not even the leaving of it. At one time there was no medical need for the physician to consider the concept of death; the fact of death was sufficient. The difference between life and death was an infinite chasm breached in an infinitesimal moment. Life and death were ultimate, self-evident opposites.

With the advent of new techniques in medicine, those opposites have begun to converge. We are now capable of maintaining visceral functions without any semblance of the higher functions that define a person. We are, therefore, faced with the task of deciding whether that which we have kept alive is still a human being, or, to put it another way, whether that human being that we are maintaining should be considered "alive."

Until now we have avoided the problems of definition and reached the solutions in silence and secret. When the life sustained was unrewarding by the standards of the physician in charge—it was discontinued. Over the years, physicians have practiced euthanasia on an ad hoc, casual, and perhaps irresponsible basis. They have withheld antibiotics or other simple treatments when it was felt that a life did not warrant sustaining, or pulled the plug on the respirator when they were convinced that what was being sustained no longer warranted the definition of life. Some of these acts are illegal and, if one wished to prosecute, could constitute a form of manslaughter, even though it is unlikely that any jury would convict. We prefer to handle all problems connected with death by denying their existence. But death and its dilemmas persist.

New urgencies for recognition of the problem arise from two conditions: the continuing march of technology, making the sustaining of vital processes possible for longer periods of time; and the increasing use of parts of the newly dead to sustain life for the truly living. The problem is well on its way to being resolved by what must have seemed a relatively simple and ingenious method. As it turned out, the difficult issues of euthanasia could be evaded by redefining death.

In an earlier time, death was defined as the cessation of breathing. Any movie buff recalls at least one scene in which a mirror is held to the mouth of a dying man. The lack of fogging indicated that indeed he was dead. The spirit of man resided in his *spiritus* (breath). With increased knowledge of human physiology and the potential for reviving a nonbreathing man, the circulation, the pulsating heart, became the focus of the definition of life.

Willard Gaylin, "Harvesting the Dead," *Harper's* (September 1974), pp. 23–30. Copyright © 1974 by Willard Gaylin. Reprinted with the permission of the author and the Willi Morris Agency.

This is the tradition with which most of us have been raised.

There is of course a relationship between circulation and respiration, and the linkage, not irrelevantly, is the brain. All body parts require the nourishment, including oxygen, carried by the circulating blood. Lack of blood supply leads to the death of an organ; the higher functions of the brain are particularly vulnerable. But if there is no respiration, there is no adequate exchange of oxygen, and this essential ingredient of the blood is no longer available for distribution. If a part of the heart loses its vascular supply, we may lose that part and still survive. If a part of the brain is deprived of oxygen, we may, depending on its location, lose it and survive. But here we pay a special price, for the functions lost are those we identify with the self, the soul, or humanness, i.e., memory, knowledge, feeling, thinking, perceiving, sensing, knowing, learning, and loving.

Most people are prepared to say that when all of the brain is destroyed the "person" no longer exists; with all due respect for the complexities of the mind/brain debate, the "person" (and personhood) is generally associated with the functioning part of the head—the brain. The higher functions of the brain that have been described are placed, for the most part, in the cortex. The brain stem (in many ways more closely allied to the spinal cord) controls primarily visceral functions. When the total brain is damaged, death in all forms will ensue because the lower brain centers that control the circulation and respiration are destroyed. With the development of modern respirators, however, it is possible to artificially maintain respiration and with it, often, the circulation with which it is linked. It is this situation that has allowed for the redefinition of death—a redefinition that is being precipitously embraced by both scientific and theological groups.

The movement toward redefining death received considerable impetus with the publication of a report sponsored by the Ad Hoc Committee of the Harvard Medical School in 1968. The committee offered an alternative definition of death based on the functioning of the brain. Its criteria stated that if an individual is unreceptive and unresponsive, i.e., in a state of irreversible coma; if he has no movements or breathing when the mechanical respirator is turned off; if he demonstrates no reflexes; and if he has a flat electroencephalogram for at least twenty-four hours, indicating no electrical brain activity (assuming that he has not been subjected to hypothermia or central nervous system depressants), he may then be declared dead.

What was originally offered as an optional definition of death is, however, progressively becoming *the* definition of death. In most states there is no specific legislation defining death; the ultimate responsibility here is assumed to reside in the general medical community. Recently, however, there has been a series of legal cases which seem to be establishing brain death as a judicial standard. In California in May of this year an ingenious lawyer, John Cruikshank, offered as a defense of his client, Andrew D. Lyons, who had shot a man in the head, the argument that the cause of death was not the bullet but the removal of his heart by a transplant surgeon, Dr. Norman Shumway. Cruikshank's argument notwithstanding, the jury found his client guilty of voluntary manslaughter. In the course of that trial, Dr. Shumway said: "The brain in the 1970s and in the light of modern day medical technology is the sine qua non—the criterion for death. I'm saying anyone whose brain is dead is dead. It is the one determinant that would be universally applicable, because the brain is the one organ that can't be transplanted."

*   *   *

This new definition, independent of the desire for transplant, now permits the physician to "pull the plug" without even committing an act of passive euthanasia. The patient will first be defined as dead; pulling the plug will merely be the harmless act of halting useless treatment on a cadaver. But while the new definition of death avoids one complex problem, euthanasia, it may create others equally difficult which have never been fully defined or visualized. For if it grants the right to pull the plug, it also implicitly grants the privilege *not* to pull the plug, and the potential and meaning of this has not at all been adequately examined.

These cadavers would have the legal status of the dead with none of the qualities one now associates with death. They would be warm, respiring, pulsating, evacuating, and excreting bodies requiring nursing, dietary, and general grooming attention— *and could probably be maintained so for a period of years.* If we chose to, we could, with the technology already at hand, legally avail ourselves of these new cadavers to serve science and mankind in dramatically useful ways. The autopsy, that most respectable of medical traditions, that last gift of the dying person to the living future, could be extended in principle beyond our current recognition. To save lives and relieve suffering—traditional motives for violating tradition—we could develop hospitals (an inappropriate word because it suggests the presence of living human beings), banks, or farms of cadavers which require feeding and maintenance, in order to be harvested. To the uninitiated the "new cadavers" in their rows of respirators would seem indistinguishable from comatose patients now residing in wards of chronic neurological hospitals.

PRECEDENTS

The idea of wholesale and systematic salvage of useful body parts may seem startling, but it is not without precedent. It is simply magnified by the technology of modern medicine. Within the confines of one individual, we have always felt free to transfer body parts to places where they are needed more urgently, felt free to reorder the priorities of the naturally endowed structure. We will borrow skin from the less visible parts of the body to salvage a face. If a muscle is paralyzed, we will often substitute a muscle that subserves a less crucial function. This was common surgery at the time that paralytic polio was more prevalent.

It soon becomes apparent, however, that there is a limitation to this procedure. The person in want

does not always have a second-best substitute. He may then be forced to borrow from a person with a surplus. The prototype, of course, is blood donation. Blood may be seen as a regeneratable organ, and we have a long-standing tradition of blood donation. What may be more important, and perhaps dangerous, we have established the precedent in blood of commercialization—not only are we free to borrow, we are forced to buy and, indeed, in our country at least, permitted to sell. Similarly, we allow the buying or selling of sperm for artificial insemination. It is most likely that in the near future we will allow the buying and selling of ripened ova so that a sterile woman may conceive her baby if she has a functioning uterus. Of course, once *in vitro* fertilization becomes a reality (an imminent possibility), we may even permit the rental of womb space for gestation for a woman who does manufacture her own ova but has no uterus.

Getting closer to our current problem, there is the relatively long-standing tradition of banking body parts (arteries, eyes, skin) for short periods of time for future transplants. Controversy has arisen with recent progress in the transplanting of major organs. Kidney transplants from a near relative or distant donor are becoming more common. As heart transplants become more successful, the issue will certainly be heightened, for while the heart may have been reduced by the new definition of death to merely another organ, it will always have a core position in the popular thinking about life and death. It has the capacity to generate the passion that transforms medical decisions into political issues.

The ability to use organs from cadavers has been severely limited in the past by the reluctance of heirs to donate the body of an individual for distribution. One might well have willed one's body for scientific purposes, but such legacies had no legal standing. Until recently, the individual lost control over his body once he died. This has been changed by the Uniform Anatomical Gift Act. This model piece of legislation, adopted by all fifty states in an incredibly short period of time, grants anyone over eighteen (twenty-one in some states) the right to donate en masse all "necessary organs and tissues" simply by filling out and mailing a small card.

Beyond the postmortem, there has been a longer-range use of human bodies that is accepted procedure—the exploitation of cadavers as teaching material in medical schools. This is a long step removed from the rationale of the transplant—a dramatic gift of life from the dying to the near-dead; while it is true that medical education will inevitably save lives, the clear and immediate purpose of the donation is to facilitate training.

It is not unnatural for a person facing death to want his usefulness to extend beyond his mortality; the same biases and values that influence our life persist in our leaving of it. It has been reported that the Harvard Medical School has no difficulty in receiving as many donations of cadavers as they need, while Tufts and Boston Universities are usually in short supply. In Boston, evidently, the cachet of getting into Harvard extends even to the dissecting table.

The way is now clear for an ever-increasing pool of usable body parts, but the current practice minimizes efficiency and maximizes waste. Only a short period exists between the time of death of the patient and the time of death of his major parts.

USES OF THE NEOMORT

In the ensuing discussion, the word *cadaver* will retain its usual meaning, as opposed to the new cadaver, which will be referred to as a *neomort*. The "ward" or "hospital" in which it is maintained will be called a *bioemporium* (purists may prefer *bioemporion*).

Whatever is possible with the old embalmed cadaver is extended to an incredible degree with the neomort. What follows, therefore, is not a definitive list but merely the briefest of suggestions as to the spectrum of possibilities.

Training

Uneasy medical students could practice routine physical examinations—auscultation, percussion of the chest, examination of the retina, rectal and vaginal examinations, et cetera—indeed, everything except neurological examinations, since the neomort by definition has no functioning central nervous system.

Both the student and his patient could be spared the pain, fumbling, and embarrassment of the "first time."

Interns also could practice standard and more difficult diagnostic procedures, from spinal taps to pneumoencephalography and the making of arteriograms, and residents could practice almost all of their surgical skills—in other words, most of the procedures that are now normally taught with the indigent in wards of major city hospitals could be taught with neomorts. Further, students could practice more exotic procedures often not available in a typical residency—eye operations, skin grafts, plastic facial surgery, amputation of useless limbs, coronary surgery, etc.; they could also practice the actual removal of organs, whether they be kidneys, testicles, or what have you, for delivery to the transplant teams.

Testing

The neomort could be used for much of the testing of drugs and surgical procedures that we now normally perform on prisoners, mentally retarded children, and volunteers. The efficacy of a drug as well as its toxicity could be determined beyond limits we might not have dared approach when we were concerned about permanent damage to the testing vehicle, a living person. For example, operations for increased vascularization of the heart could be tested to determine whether they truly do reduce the incidence of future heart attack before we perform them on patients. Experimental procedures that proved useless or harmful could be avoided; those that succeeded could be available years before they might otherwise have been. Similarly, we could avoid the massive delays that keep some drugs from the marketplace while the dying clamor for them.

Neomorts would give us access to other forms of testing that are inconceivable with the living human being. We might test diagnostic instruments such as sophisticated electrocardiography by selectively damaging various parts of the heart to see how or whether the instrument could detect the damage.

Experimentation

Every new medical procedure demands a leap of faith. It is often referred to as an "act of courage," which seems to me an inappropriate terminology now that organized medicine rarely uses itself as the experimental body. Whenever a surgeon attempts a procedure for the first time, he is at best generalizing from experimentation with lower animals. Now we can protect the patient from too large a leap by using the neomort as an experimental bridge.

Obvious forms of experimentation would be cures for illnesses which would first be induced in the neomort. We could test antidotes by injecting poison, induce cancer or virus infections to validate and compare developing therapies.

Because they have an active hematopoietic system, neomorts would be particularly valuable for studying diseases of the blood. Many of the examples that I draw from that field were offered to me by Dr. John F. Bertles, a hematologist at St. Luke's Hospital Center in New York. One which interests him is the utilization of marrow transplants. Few human-to-human marrow transplants have been successful, since the kind of immunosuppression techniques that require research could most safely be performed on neomorts. Even such research as the recent experimentation at Willowbrook— where mentally retarded children were infected with hepatitis virus (which was not yet culturable outside of the human body) in an attempt to find a cure for this pernicious disease—could be done without risking the health of the subjects.

Banking

While certain essential blood antigens are readily storable (e.g., red cells can now be preserved in a frozen state), others are not, and there is increasing need for potential means of storage. Research on storage of platelets to be used in transfusion re-

quires human recipients, and the data are only slowly and tediously gathered at great expense. Use of neomorts would permit intensive testing of platelet survival and probably would lead to a rapid development of a better storage technique. The same would be true for white cells.

As has been suggested, there is great wastage in the present system of using kidney donors from cadavers. Major organs are difficult to store. A population of neomorts maintained with body parts computerized and catalogued for compatibility would yield a much more efficient system. Just as we now have blood banks, we could have banks for all the major organs that may someday be transplantable—lungs, kidney, heart, ovaries. Beyond the obvious storage uses of the neomort, there are others not previously thought of because there was no adequate storage facility. Dr. Marc Lappe of the Hastings Center has suggested that a neomort whose own immunity system had first been severely repressed might be an ideal "culture" for growing and storing our lymphoid components. When we are threatened by malignancy or viral disease, we can go to the "bank" and withdraw our stored white cells to help defend us.

Harvesting

Obviously, a sizable population of neomorts will provide a steady supply of blood, since they can be drained periodically. When we consider the cost–benefit analysis of this system, we would have to evaluate it in the same way as the lumber industry evaluates sawdust—a product which in itself is not commercially feasible but which supplies a profitable dividend as a waste from a more useful harvest.

The blood would be a simultaneous source of platelets, leukocytes, and red cells. By attaching a neomort to an IBM cell separator, we could isolate cell types at relatively low cost. The neomort could also be tested for the presence of hepatitis in a way that would be impossible with commercial donors. Hepatitis as a transfusion scourge would be virtually eliminated.

Beyond the blood are rarer harvests. Neomorts offer a great potential source of bone marrow for transplant procedures, and I am assured that a bioemporium of modest size could be assembled to fit most transplantation antigen requirements. And skin would of course, be harvested—similarly bone, corneas, cartilage, and so on.

Manufacturing

In addition to supplying components of the human body, some of which will be continually regenerated, the neomort can also serve as a manufacturing unit. Hormones are one obvious product, but there are others. By the injection of toxins, we have a source of antitoxin that does not have the complications of coming from another animal form. Antibodies for most of the major diseases can be manufactured merely by injecting the neomort with the viral or bacterial offenders.

Perhaps the most encouraging extension of the manufacturing process emerges from the new cancer research, in which immunology is coming to the fore. With certain blood cancers, great hope attaches to the use of antibodies. To take just one example, it is conceivable that leukemia could be generated in individual neomorts—not just to provide for *in vivo* (so to speak) testing of antileukemic modes of therapy but also to generate antibody immunity responses which could then be used in the living.

COST–BENEFIT ANALYSIS

If seen only as the harvesting of products, the entire feasibility of such research would depend on intelligent cost–benefit analysis. Although certain products would not warrant the expense of maintaining a community of neomorts, the enormous expense of other products, such as red cells with unusual antigens, would certainly warrant it. Then, of course, the equation is shifted. As soon as one economically sound reason is found for the maintenance of the community, all of the other

ingredients become gratuitous by-products, a familiar problem in manufacturing. There is no current research to indicate the maintenance cost of a bioemporium or even the potential duration of an average neomort. Since we do not at this point encourage sustaining life in the brain-dead, we do not know the limits to which it could be extended. This is the kind of technology, however, in which we have previously been quite successful.

Meantime, a further refinement of death might be proposed. At present we use total brain function to define brain death. The source of electroencephalogram activity is not known and cannot be used to distinguish between the activity of higher and lower brain centers. If, however, we are prepared to separate the concept of "aliveness" from "personhood" in the adult, as we have in the fetus, a good argument can be made that death should be defined not as cessation of total brain function but merely as cessation of cortical function. New tests may soon determine when cortical function is dead. With this proposed extension, one could then maintain neomorts without even the complication and expense of respirators. The entire population of decorticates residing in chronic hospitals and now classifed among the incurably ill could be redefined as dead.

But even if we maintain the more rigid limitations of total brain death, it would seem that a reasonable population could be maintained if the purposes warranted it. It is difficult to assess how many new neomorts would be available each year to satisfy the demand. There are roughly 2 million deaths a year in the United States. The most likely sources of intact bodies with destroyed brains would be accidents (about 113,000 per year), suicides (around 24,000 per year), homicides (18,000), and cerebrovascular accidents (some 210,000 per year). Obviously, in each of these categories a great many of the individuals would be useless—their bodies either shattered or scattered beyond value or repair.

*   *   *

And yet, after all the benefits are outlined, with the lifesaving potential clear, the humanitarian purposes obvious, the technology ready, the motives pure, and the material costs justified—how are we to reconcile our emotions? Where in this debit-credit ledger of limbs and livers and kidneys and costs are we to weigh and enter the repugnance generated by the entire philanthropic endeavor?

Cost–benefit analysis is always least satisfactory when the costs must be measured in one realm and the benefits in another. The analysis is particularly skewed when the benefits are specific, material, apparent, and immediate, and the price to be paid is general, spiritual, abstract, and of the future. It is that which induces people to abandon freedom for security, pride for comfort, dignity for dollars.

William May, in a perceptive article,* defended the careful distinctions that have traditionally been drawn between the newly dead and the long dead. "While the body retains its recognizable form, even in death, it commands a certain respect. No longer a human presence, it still reminds us of that presence which once was utterly inseparable from it." But those distinctions become obscured when, years later, a neomort will retain the appearance of the newly dead, indeed, more the appearance of that which was formerly described as living.

Philosophers tend to be particularly sensitive to the abstract needs of civilized man; it is they who have often been the guardians of values whose abandonment produces pains that are real, if not always quantifiable. Hans Jonas, in his *Philosophical Essays*, anticipated some of the possibilities outlined here, and defended what he felt to be the sanctity of the human body and the unknowability of the borderline between life and death when he insisted that "Nothing less than the maximum definition of death will do—brain death plus heart death plus any other indication that may be pertinent—before final violence is allowed to be done." And even then Jonas was only contemplating *temporary* maintenance of life for the collection of organs.

The argument can be made on both sides. The unquestionable benefits to be gained are the promise of cures for leukemia and other diseases, the reduction of suffering, and the maintenance of life. The proponents of this view will be mobilized with a force that may seem irresistible.

They will interpret our revulsion at the thought of a bioemporium as a bias of our education and experience, just as earlier societies were probably revolted by the startling notion of abdominal surgery, which we now take for granted. The proponents will argue that the revulsion, not the technology, is inappropriate.

Still there will be those, like May, who will defend that revulsion as a quintessentially human factor whose removal would diminish us all, and extract a price we cannot anticipate in ways yet unknown and times not yet determined. May feels that there is "a tinge of the inhuman in the humanitarianism of those who believe that the perception of social need easily overrides all other considerations and reduces the acts of implementation to the everyday, routine, and casual."

This is the kind of weighing of values for which the computer offers little help. Is the revulsion to the new technology simply the fear and horror of the ignorant in the face of the new, or is it one of those components of humanness that barely sustain us at the limited level of civility and decency that now exists, and whose removal is one more step in erasing the distinction between man and the lesser creatures—beyond that, the distinction between man and matter?

Sustaining life is an urgent argument for any measure, but not if that measure destroys those very qualities that make life worth sustaining.

---

* "Attitudes Toward the Newly Dead," *The Hastings Center Studies*, 1.1 (1973).

Brave New World

ALDOUS HUXLEY

Aldous Leonard Huxley (1894–1963) was a critically acclaimed poet, social satirist, and novelist. *Brave New World* explores a variety of relationships between technology, social control, and human independence. Originally published in 1932, Huxley's futuristic picture remains remarkably current. The selection that follows comprises the first two chapters of this now classic work. Chapter One concerns the biochemical and genetic bases of reproductive selection and manipulation. Chapter Two focuses on psychosocial control.

CHAPTER ONE

A squat grey building of only thirty-four stories. Over the main entrance the words, CENTRAL LONDON HATCHERY AND CONDITIONING CENTRE, and, in a shield, the World State's motto, COMMUNITY, IDENTITY, STABILITY.

The enormous room on the ground floor faced towards the north. Cold for all the summer beyond the panes, for all the tropical heat of the room itself, a harsh thin light glared through the windows, hungrily seeking some draped lay figure, some pallid shape of academic goose-flesh, but finding only the glass and nickel and bleakly shining porcelain of a laboratory. Wintriness responded to wintriness. The overalls of the workers were white, their hands gloved with a pale corpse-coloured rubber. The light was frozen, dead, a ghost. Only from the yellow barrels of the microscopes did it borrow a certain rich and living substance, lying along the polished tubes like butter, streak after luscious streak in long recession down the work tables.

"And this," said the Director opening the door, "is the Fertilizing Room."

Bent over their instruments, three hundred Fertilizers were plunged, as the Director of Hatcheries and Conditioning entered the room, in the scarcely breathing silence, the absent-minded, soliloquizing hum or whistle, of absorbed concentration. A troop of newly arrived students, very young, pink and callow, followed nervously, rather abjectly, at the Director's heels. Each of them carried a notebook, in which, whenever the great man spoke, he desperately scribbled. Straight from the horse's mouth. It was a rare privilege. The D. H. C. for Central London always made a point of personally conducting his new students round the various departments.

"Just to give you a general idea," he would explain to them. For of course some sort of general idea they must have, if they were to do their work intelligently—though as little of one, if they were to be good and happy members of society, as possible. For particulars, as every one knows, make for virtue and happiness; generalities are intellectually necessary evils. Not philosophers but fretsawyers and stamp collectors compose the backbone of society.

"To-morrow," he would add, smiling at them with a slightly menacing geniality, "you'll be settling down to serious work. You won't have time for generalities. Meanwhile . . ."

Meanwhile, it was a privilege. Straight from the horse's mouth into the notebook. The boys scribbled like mad.

Tall and rather thin but upright, the Director advanced into the room. He had a long chin and big rather prominent teeth, just covered, when he was not talking, by his full, floridly curved lips. Old, young? Thirty? Fifty? Fifty-five? It was hard to say. And anyhow the question didn't arise; in this year of stability, A. F. 632, it didn't occur to you to ask it.

"I shall begin at the beginning," said the D.H.C. and the more zealous students recorded his intention in their notebooks: *Begin at the beginning.* "These," he waved his hand, "are the incubators." And opening an insulated door he showed them racks upon racks of numbered test-tubes. "The week's supply of ova. Kept," he explained, "at blood heat; whereas the male gametes," and here he opened another door, "they have to be kept at thirty-five instead of thirty-seven. Full blood heat sterilizes." Rams wrapped in theremogene beget no lambs.

Still leaning against the incubators he gave them, while the pencils scurried illegibly across the pages, a brief description of the modern fertilizing process; spoke first, of course, of its surgical introduction—"the operation undergone voluntarily for the good of Society, not to mention the fact that it carries a bonus amounting to six months' salary"; continued with some account of the technique for preserving the excised ovary alive and actively developing; passed on to a consideration of optimum temperature, salinity, viscosity; referred to the liquor in which the detached and ripened eggs were kept; and, leading his charges to the work tables, actually showed them how this liquor was drawn off from the test-tubes; how it was let out drop by drop onto the specially warmed slides of the microscopes; how the eggs which it contained were inspected for abnormalities, counted and transferred to a porous receptacle; how (and he now took them to watch the operation) this receptacle was immersed in a warm bouillon containing free-swimming spermatozoa—at a minimum concentration of one hun-

dred thousand per cubic centimetre, he insisted; and how, after ten minutes, the container was lifted out of the liquor and its contents re-examined; how, if any of the eggs remained unfertilized, it was again immersed, and, if necessary, yet again; how the fertilized ova went back to the incubators; where the Alphas and Betas remained until definitely bottled; while the Gammas, Deltas and Epsilons were brought out again, after only thirty-six hours, to undergo Bokanovsky's Process.

"Bokanovsky's Process," repeated the Director, and the students underlined the words in their little notebooks.

One egg, one embryo, one adult—normality. But a bokanovskified egg will bud, will proliferate, will divide. From eight to ninety-six buds, and every bud will grow into a perfectly formed embryo, and every embryo into a full-sized adult. Making ninety-six human beings grow where only one grew before. Progress.

"Essentially," the D.H.C. concluded, "bokanovskification consists of a series of arrests of development. We check the normal growth and, paradoxically enough, the egg responds by budding."

Responds by budding. The pencils were busy.

He pointed. On a very slowly moving band a rack-full of test-tubes was entering a large metal box, another rack-full was emerging. Machinery faintly purred. It took eight minutes for the tubes to go through, he told them. Eight minutes of hard X-rays being about as much as an egg can stand. A few died; of the rest, the least susceptible divided into two; most put out four buds; some eight; all were returned to the incubators, where the buds began to develop; then, after two days, were suddenly chilled, chilled and checked. Two, four, eight, the buds in their turn budded; and having budded were dosed almost to death with alcohol; consequently burgeoned again and having budded—bud out of bud out of bud—were thereafter—further arrest being generally fatal—left to develop in peace. By which time the original egg was in a fair way to becoming anything from eight to ninety-six embryos—a prodigious improvement, you will agree, on nature. Identical twins—but not in piddling twos and threes as in the old viviparous days, when an egg would sometimes accidentally divide; actually by dozens, by scores at a time.

"Scores," the Director repeated and flung out his arms, as though he were distributing largesse. "Scores."

But one of the students was fool enough to ask where the advantage lay.

"My good boy!" The Director wheeled sharply round on him. "Can't you see? Can't you *see?*" He raised a hand; his expression was solemn. "Bokanovsky's Process is one of the major instruments of social stability!"

Major instruments of social stability.

Standard men and women; in uniform batches. The whole of a small factory staffed with the products of a single bokanovskified egg.

"Ninety-six identical twins working ninety-six identical machines!" The voice was almost tremulous with enthusiasm. "You really know where you are. For the first time in history." He quoted the planetary motto. "Community, Identity, Stability." Grand words. "If we could bokanovskify indefinitely the whole problem would be solved."

Solved by standard Gammas, unvarying Deltas, uniform Epsilons. Millions of identical twins. The principle of mass production at last applied to biology.

"But, alas," the Director shook his head, "we *can't* bokanovskify indefinitely."

Ninety-six seemed to be the limit; seventy-two a good average. From the same ovary and with gametes of the same male to manufacture as many batches of identical twins as possible—that was the best (sadly a second best) that they could do. And even that was difficult.

"For in nature it takes thirty years for two hundred eggs to reach maturity. But our business is to stabilize the population at this moment, here and now. Dribbling out twins over a quarter of a century—what would be the use of that?"

Obviously, no use at all. But Podsnap's Technique had immensely accelerated the process of ripening. They could make sure of at least a hundred and fifty mature eggs within two years. Fertil-

ize and bokanovskify—in other words, multiply by seventy-two—and you get an average of nearly eleven thousand brothers and sisters in a hundred and fifty batches of identical twins, all within two years of the same age.

"And in exceptional cases we can make one ovary yield us over fifteen thousand adult individuals."

Beckoning to a fair-haired, ruddy young man who happened to be passing at the moment. "Mr. Foster," he called. The ruddy young man approached. "Can you tell us the record for a single ovary, Mr. Foster?"

"Sixteen thousand and twelve in this Centre," Mr. Foster replied without hesitation. He spoke very quickly, had a vivacious blue eye, and took an evident pleasure in quoting figures. "Sixteen thousand and twelve; in one hundred and eighty-nine batches of identicals. But of course they've done much better," he rattled on, "in some of the tropical Centres. Singapore has often produced over sixteen thousand five hundred; and Mombasa has actually touched the seventeen thousand mark. But then they have unfair advantages. You should see the way a negro ovary responds to pituitary! It's quite astonishing, when you're used to working with European material. Still," he added, with a laugh (but the light of combat was in his eyes and the lift of his chin was challenging), "still, we mean to beat them if we can. I'm working on a wonderful Delta-Minus ovary at this moment. Only just eighteen months old. Over twelve thousand seven hundred children already, either decanted or in embryo. And still going strong. We'll beat them yet."

"That's that spirit I like!" cried the Director, and clapped Mr. Foster on the shoulder. "Come along with us, and give these boys the benefit of your expert knowledge."

Mr. Foster smiled modestly. "With pleasure." They went.

In the Bottling Room all was harmonious bustle and ordered activity. Flaps of fresh sow's peritoneum ready cut to the proper size came shooting up in little lifts from the Organ Store in the sub-basement. Whizz and then, click! the lift-hatches flew open; the bottle-liner had only to reach out a hand, take the flap, insert, smooth-down, and before the lined bottle had had time to travel out of reach along the endless band, whizz, click! another flap of peritoneum had shot up from the depths, ready to be slipped into yet another bottle, the next of that slow interminable procession on the band.

Next to the Liners stood the Matriculators. The procession advanced; one by one the eggs were transferred from their test-tubes to the larger containers; deftly the peritoneal lining was slit, the morula dropped into place, the saline solution poured in . . . and already the bottle had passed, and it was the turn of the labellers. Heredity, date of fertilization, membership of Bokanovsky Group— details were transferred from test-tube to bottle. No longer anonymous, but named, identified, the procession marched slowly on; on through an opening in the wall, slowly on into the Social Predestination Room.

"Eighty-eight cubic metres of card-index," said Mr. Foster with relish, as they entered.

"Containing *all* the relevant information," added the Director.

"Brought up to date every morning."

"And co-ordinated every afternoon."

"On the basis of which they make their calculations."

"So many individuals, of such and such quality," said Mr. Foster.

"Distributed in such and such quantities."

"The optimum Decanting Rate at any given moment."

"Unforeseen wastages promptly made good."

"Promptly," repeated Mr. Foster. "If you knew the amount of overtime I had to put in after the last Japanese earthquake!" He laughed goodhumouredly and shook his head.

"The Predestinators send in their figures to the Fertilizers."

"Who give them the embryos they ask for."

"And the bottles come in here to be predestined in detail."

"After which they are sent down to the Embryo Store."

"Where we now proceed ourselves."

And opening a door Mr. Foster led the way down a staircase into the basement.

The temperature was still tropical. They descended into a thickening twilight. Two doors and a passage with a double turn insured the cellar against any possible infiltration of the day.

"Embryos are like photograph film," said Mr. Foster waggishly, as he pushed open the second door. "They can only stand red light."

And in effect the sultry darkness into which the students now followed him was visible and crimson, like the darkness of closed eyes on a summer's afternoon. The bulging flanks of row on receding row and tier above tier of bottles glinted with innumerable rubies, and among the rubies moved the dim red spectres of men and women with purple eyes and all the symptoms of lupus. The hum and rattle of machinery faintly stirred the air.

"Give them a few figures, Mr. Foster," said the Director, who was tired of talking.

Mr. Foster was only too happy to give them a few figures.

Two hundred and twenty metres long, two hundred wide, ten high. He pointed upwards. Like chickens drinking, the students lifted their eyes towards the distant ceiling.

Three tiers of racks: ground floor level, first gallery, second gallery.

The spidery steel-work of gallery above gallery faded away in all directions into the dark. Near them three red ghosts were busily unloading demijohns from a moving staircase.

The escalator from the Social Predestination Room.

Each bottle could be placed on one of fifteen racks, each rack, though you couldn't see it, was a conveyor traveling at the rate of thirty-three and a third centimetres an hour. Two hundred and sixty-seven days at eight metres a day. Two thousand one hundred and thirty-six metres in all. One circuit of the cellar at ground level, one on the first gallery, half on the second, and on the two hundred and sixty-seventh morning, daylight in the Decanting Room. Independent existence—so called.

"But in the interval," Mr. Foster concluded, "we've managed to do a lot to them. Oh, a very great deal." His laugh was knowing and triumphant.

"That's the spirit I like," said the Director once more. "Let's walk around. You tell them everything, Mr. Foster."

Mr. Foster duly told them.

Told them of the growing embryo on its bed of peritoneum. Made them taste the rich blood surrogate on which it fed. Explained why it had to be stimulated with placentin and thyroxin. Told them of the *corpus luteum* extract. Showed them the jets through which at every twelfth metre from zero to 2040 it was automatically injected. Spoke of those gradually increasing doses of pituitary administered during the final ninety-six metres of their course. Described the artificial maternal circulation installed in every bottle at Metre 112; showed them the reservoir of blood-surrogate, the centrifugal pump that kept the liquid moving over the placenta and drove it through the synthetic lung and waste product filter. Referred to the embryo's troublesome tendency to anæmia, to the massive doses of hog's stomach extract and foetal foal's liver with which, in consequence, it had to be supplied.

Showed them the simple mechanism by means of which, during the last two metres out of every eight, all the embryos were simultaneously shaken into familiarity with movement. Hinted at the gravity of the so-called "trauma of decanting," and enumerated the precautions taken to minimize, by a suitable training of the bottled embryo, that dangerous shock. Told them of the test for sex carried out in the neighborhood of Metre 200. Explained the system of labelling—a T for the males, a circle for the females and for those who were destined to become freemartins a question mark, black on a white ground.

"For of course," said Mr. Foster, "in the vast majority of cases, fertility is merely a nuisance. One fertile ovary in twelve hundred—that would really be quite sufficient for our purposes. But we want to have a good choice. And of course one must always have an enormous margin of safety. So we allow as many as thirty per cent of the female embryos to develop normally. The others get a dose of male sex-hormone every twenty-four metres for the rest of the course. Result: they're decanted as freemartins—structurally quite normal (except," he had to admit, "that they *do* have the slightest tendency to grow beards), but sterile. Guaranteed sterile. Which brings us at last," continued Mr. Foster, "out of the realm of mere slavish imitation of nature into the much more interesting world of human invention."

He rubbed his hands. For of course, they didn't content themselves with merely hatching out embryos: any cow could do that.

"We also predestine and condition. We decant our babies as socialized human beings, as Alphas or Epsilons, as future sewage workers or future . . ." He was going to say "future World controllers," but correcting himself, said "future Directors of Hatcheries," instead.

The D.H.C. acknowledged the compliment with a smile.

They were passing Metre 320 on Rack 11. A young Beta-Minus mechanic was busy with screwdriver and spanner on the blood-surrogate pump of a passing bottle. The hum of the electric motor deepened by fractions of a tone as he turned the nuts. Down, down . . . A final twist, a glance at the revolution counter, and he was done. He moved two paces down the line and began the same process on the next pump.

"Reducing the number of revolutions per minute," Mr. Foster explained. "The surrogate goes round slower; therefore passes through the lung at longer intervals; therefore gives the embryo less oxygen. Nothing like oxygen-shortage for keeping an embryo below par." Again he rubbed his hands.

"But why do you want to keep the embryo below par?" asked an ingenious student.

"Ass!" said the Director, breaking a long silence. "Hasn't it occurred to you that an Epsilon embryo must have an Epsilon environment as well as an Epsilon heredity?"

It evidently hadn't occurred to him. He was covered with confusion.

"The lower the caste," said Mr. Foster, "the shorter the oxygen." The first organ affected was the brain. After that the skeleton. At seventy per cent of normal oxygen you got dwarfs. At less than seventy eyeless monsters.

"Who are no use at all," concluded Mr. Foster.

Whereas (his voice became confidential and eager), if they could discover a technique for shortening the period of maturation what a triumph, what a benefaction to Society!

"Consider the horse."

They considered it.

Mature at six; the elephant at ten. While at thirteen a man is not yet sexually mature; and is only full-grown at twenty. Hence, of course, that fruit of delayed development, the human intelligence.

"But in Epsilons," said Mr. Foster very justly, "we don't need human intelligence."

Didn't need and didn't get it. But though the Epsilon mind was mature at ten, the Epsilon body was not fit to work till eighteen. Long years of superfluous and wasted immaturity. If the physical development could be speeded up till it was as quick, say, as a cow's, what an enormous saving to the Community!

"Enormous!" murmured the students. Mr. Foster's enthusiasm was infectious.

He became rather technical; spoke of the abnormal endocrine co-ordination which made men grow so slowly; postulated a germinal mutation to account for it. Could the effects of this germinal mutation be undone? Could the individual Epsilon embryo be made a revert, by a suitable technique, to the normality of dogs and cows? That was the problem. And it was all but solved.

Pilkington, at Mombasa, had produced individuals who were sexually mature at four and full-grown at six and a half. A scientific triumph. But socially useless. Six-year-old men and women were too stupid to do even Epsilon work. And the process was an all-or-nothing one; either you failed to modify at all, or else you modified the whole way. They were still trying to find the ideal compromise between adults of twenty and adults of six. So far without success. Mr. Foster sighed and shook his head.

Their wanderings through the crimson twilight had brought them to the neighborhood of Metre 170 on Rack 9. From this point onwards Rack 9 was enclosed and the bottle performed the remainder of their journey in a kind of tunnel, interrupted here and there by openings two or three metres wide.

"Heat conditioning," said Mr. Foster.

Hot tunnels alternated with cool tunnels. Coolness was wedded to discomfort in the form of hard X-rays. By the time they were decanted the embryos had a horror of cold. They were predestined to emigrate to the tropics, to be miner and acetate silk spinners and steel workers. Later on their minds would be made to endorse the judgment of their bodies. "We condition them to thrive on heat," concluded Mr. Foster. "Our colleagues upstairs will teach them to love it."

"And that," put in the Director sententiously, "that is the secret of happiness and virtue—liking what you've *got* to do. All conditioning aims at that: making people like their inescapable social destiny."

In a gap between two tunnels, a nurse was delicately probing with a long fine syringe into the gelatinous contents of a passing bottle. The students and their guides stood watching her for a few moments in silence.

"Well, Lenina," said Mr. Foster, when at last she withdrew the syringe and straightened herself up.

The girl turned with a start. One could see that, for all the lupus and the purple eyes, she was uncommonly pretty.

"Henry!" Her smile flashed redly at him—a row of coral teeth.

"Charming, charming," murmured the Director and, giving her two or three little pats, received in exchange a rather deferential smile for himself.

"What are you giving them?" asked Mr. Foster, making his tone very professional.

"Oh, the usual typhoid and sleeping sickness."

"Tropical workers start being inoculated at Metre 150," Mr. Foster explained to the students. "The embryos still have gills. We immunize the fish against the future man's diseases." Then, turning back to Lenina, "Ten to five on the roof this afternoon," he said, "as usual."

"Charming," said the Director once more, and, with a final pat, moved away after the others.

On Rack 10 rows of next generation's chemical workers were being trained in the toleration of lead, caustic soda, tar, chlorine. The first of a batch of two hundred and fifty embryonic rocket-plane engineers was just passing the eleven hundred metre mark on Rack 3. A special mechanism kept their containers in constant rotation. "To improve their sense of balance," Mr. Foster explained. "Doing repairs on the outside of a rocket in mid-air is a ticklish job. We slacken off the circulation when they're right way up, so that they're half starved, and double the flow of surrogate when they're upside down. They learn to associate topsy-turvydom with wellbeing; in fact, they're only truly happy when they're standing on their heads.

"And now," Mr. Foster went on, "I'd like to show you some very interesting conditioning for Alpha Plus Intellectuals. We have a big batch of them on Rack 5. First Gallery level," he called to two boys who had started to go down to the ground floor.

"They're round about Metre 900," he explained. "You can't really do any useful intellectual conditioning till the foetuses have lost their tails. Follow me."

But the Director had looked at his watch. "Ten to three," he said. "No time for the intellectual embryos, I'm afraid. We must go up to the Nurseries before the children have finished their afternoon sleep."

Mr. Foster was disappointed. "At least one glance at the Decanting Room," he pleaded.

"Very well then." The Director smiled indulgently. "Just one glance."

CHAPTER TWO

Mr. Foster was left in the Decanting Room. The D.H.C. and his students stepped into the nearest lift and were carried up to the fifth floor.

INFANT NURSERIES. NEO-PAVLOVIAN CONDITIONING ROOMS, announced the notice board.

The Director opened a door. They were in a large bare room, very bright and sunny; for the whole of the southern wall was a single window. Half a dozen nurses, trousered and jacketed in the regulation white viscose-linen uniform, their hair aseptically hidden under white caps, were engaged in setting out bowls of roses in a long row across the floor. Big bowls, packed tight with blossom. Thousands of petals, ripe-blown and silkily smooth, like the cheeks of innumerable little cherubs, but of cherubs, in that bright light, not exclusively pink and Aryan, but also luminously Chinese, also Mexican, also apoplectic with too much blowing of celestial trumpets, also pale as death, pale with the posthumous whiteness of marble.

The nurses stiffened to attention as the D.H.C. came in.

"Set out the books," he said curtly.

In silence the nurses obeyed his command. Between the rose bowls the books were duly set out— a row of nursery quartos opened invitingly each at some gaily coloured image of beast or fish or bird.

"Now bring in the children."

They hurried out of the room and returned in a minute or two, each pushing a kind of tall dumbwaiter laden, on all its four wire-netted shelves, with eight-month-old babies, all exactly alike (a Bokanovsky Group, it was evident) and all (since their caste was Delta) dressed in khaki.

"Put them down on the floor."

The infants were unloaded.

"Now turn them so that they can see the flowers and books."

Turned, the babies at once fell silent, then began to crawl towards those clusters of sleek colours, those shapes so gay and brilliant on the white pages. As they approached, the sun came out of a momentary eclipse behind a cloud. The roses flamed up as though with a sudden passion from within; a new and profound significance seemed to suffuse the shining pages of the books. From the ranks of the crawling babies came little squeals of excitement, gurgles and twitterings of pleasure.

The Director rubbed his hands. "Excellent!" he said. "It might almost have been done on purpose."

The swiftest crawlers were already at their goal.

Small hands reached out uncertainly, touched, grasped, unpetaling the transfigured roses, crumpling the illuminated pages of the books. The Director waited until all were happily busy. Then, "Watch carefully," he said. And, lifting his hand, he gave the signal.

The Head Nurse, who was standing by a switchboard at the other end of the room, pressed down a little lever.

There was a violent explosion. Shriller and ever shriller, a siren shrieked. Alarm bells maddeningly sounded.

The children started, screamed; their faces were distorted with terror.

"And now," the Director shouted (for the noise was deafening), "now we proceed to rub in the lesson with a mild electric shock."

He waved his hand again, and the Head Nurse pressed a second lever. The screaming of the babies suddenly changed its tone. There was something desperate, almost insane, about the sharp spasmodic yelps to which they now gave utterance. Their little bodies twitched and stiffened; their limbs moved jerkily as if to the tug of unseen wires.

"We can electrify that whole strip of floor," bawled the Director in explanation. "But that's enough," he signalled to the nurse.

The explosions ceased, the bells stopped ringing, the shriek of the siren died down from tone to tone into silence. The stiffly twitching bodies relaxed, and what had become the sob and yelp of infant maniacs broadened out once more into a normal howl of ordinary terror.

"Offer them the flowers and the books again."

The nurses obeyed; but at the approach of the roses, at the mere sight of those gaily-coloured images of pussy and cock-a-doodle-doo and baa-baa black sheep, the infants shrank away in horror; the volume of their howling suddenly increased.

"Observe," said the Director triumphantly, "observe."

Books and loud noises, flowers and electric shocks—already in the infant mind these couples were compromisingly linked; and after two hundred repetitions of the same or a similar lesson would be wedded indissolubly. What man has joined, nature is powerless to put asunder.

"They'll grow up with what the psychologists used to call an 'instinctive' hatred of books and flowers. Reflexes unalterably conditioned. They'll be safe from books and botany all their lives." The Director turned to his nurses. "Take them away again."

Still yelling, the khaki babies were loaded on to their dumb-waiters and wheeled out, leaving behind them the smell of sour milk and a most welcome silence.

One of the students held up his hand; and though he could see quite well why you couldn't have lower-caste people wasting the Community's time over books, and that there was always the risk of their reading something which might undesirably decondition one of their reflexes, yet . . . well, he couldn't understand about the flowers. Why go to the trouble of making it psychologically impossible for Deltas to like flowers?

Patiently the D.H.C. explained. If the children were made to scream at the sight of a rose, that was on grounds of high economic policy. Not so very long ago (a century or thereabouts), Gammas, Deltas, even Epsilons, had been conditioned to like flowers—flowers in particular and wild nature in general. The idea was to make them want to be going out into the country at every available opportunity, and so compel them to consume transport.

"And didn't they consume transport?" asked the student.

"Quite a lot," the D.H.C. replied. "But nothing else."

Primroses and landscapes, he pointed out, have one grave defect: they are gratuitous. A love of nature keeps no factories busy. It was decided to abolish the love of nature, at any rate among the lower classes; to abolish the love of nature, but *not* the tendency to consume transport. For of course it was essential that they should keep on going to the country, even though they hated it. The problem was to find an economically sounder reason for consuming transport than a mere affection for primroses and landscapes. It was duly found.

"We condition the masses to hate the country," concluded the Director. "But simultaneously we condition them to love all country sports. At the same time, we see to it that all country sports shall entail the use of elaborate apparatus. So that they consume manufactured articles as well as transport. Hence those electric shocks."

"I see," said the student, and was silent, lost in admiration.

There was a silence; then, clearing his throat, "Once upon a time," the Director began, "while our Ford was still on earth, there was a little boy called Reuben Rabinovitch. Reuben was the child of Polish-speaking parents." The Director interrupted himself. "You know what Polish is, I suppose?"

"A dead language."

"Like French and German," added another student, officiously showing off his learning.

"And 'parent'?" questioned the D.H.C.

There was an uneasy silence. Several of the boys blushed. They had not yet learned to draw the significant but often very fine distinction between smut and pure science. One, at last, had the courage to raise a hand.

"Human beings used to be . . ." he hesitated; the blood rushed to his cheeks. "Well, they used to be viviparous."

"Quite right." The Director nodded approvingly.

"And when the babies were decanted . . ."

" 'Born,' " came the correction.

"Well, then they were the parents—I mean, not the babies, of course; the other ones." The poor boy was overwhelmed with confusion.

"In brief," the Director summed up, "the parents were the father and the mother." The smut that was really science fell with a crash into the boys' eye-avoiding silence. "Mother," he repeated loudly rubbing in the science; and, leaning back in his chair, "These," he said gravely, "are unpleasant facts; I know it. But then most historical facts *are* unpleasant."

He returned to Little Reuben—to Little Reuben, in whose room, one evening, by an oversight, his father and mother (crash, crash!) happened to leave the radio turned on.

("For you must remember that in those days of gross viviparous reproduction, children were always brought up by their parents and not in State Conditioning Centres.")

While the child was asleep, a broadcast programme from London suddenly started to come through; and the next morning, to the astonishment of his crash and crash (the more daring of the boys ventured to grin at one another), Little Reuben woke up repeating word for word a long lecture by that curious old writer ("one of the very few whose works have been permitted to come down to us"), George Bernard Shaw, who was speaking, according to a well-authenticated tradition, about his own genius. To Little Reuben's wink and snigger, this lecture was, of course, perfectly incomprehensible and, imagining that their child had suddenly gone mad, they sent for a doctor. He, fortunately, understood English, recognized the discourse as that which Shaw had broadcasted the previous evening, realized the significance of what had happened, and sent a letter to the medical press about it.

"The principle of sleep-teaching, or hypnopædia, had been discovered." The D.H.C. made an impressive pause.

The principle had been discovered; but many, many years were to elapse before that principle was usefully applied.

"The case of Little Reuben occurred only twenty-three years after Our Ford's first T-Model was put on the market." (Here the Director made a sign of the T on his stomach and all the students reverently followed suit.) "And yet . . ."

Furiously the students scribbled. "*Hypnopædia, first used officially in A.F. 214. Why not before? Two reasons. (a) . . .*"

"These early experimenters," the D.H.C. was saying, "were on the wrong track. They thought that hypnopædia could be made an instrument of intellectual education . . ."

(A small boy asleep on his right side, the right

arm stuck out, the right hand hanging limp over the edge of the bed. Through a round grating in the side of a box a voice speaks softly.

"The Nile is the longest river in Africa and the second in length of all the rivers of the globe. Although falling short of the length of the Mississippi-Missouri, the Nile is at the head of all rivers as regards the length of its basin, which extends through 35 degrees of latitude . . ."

At breakfast the next morning, "Tommy," some one says, "do you know which is the longest river in Africa?" A shaking of the head. "But don't you remember something that begins: The Nile is the . . ."

"The - Nile - is - the - longest - river - in - Africa - and - the - second - in - length - of - all - the - rivers - of - the - globe . . ." The words come rushing out. "Although - falling - short - of . . ."

"Well now, which is the longest river in Africa?"

The eyes are blank. "I don't know."

"But the Nile, Tommy."

"The - Nile - is - the - longest - river - in - Africa - and - second . . ."

"Then which river is the longest, Tommy?"

Tommy burst into tears. "I don't know," he howls.)

That howl, the Director made it plain, discouraged the earliest investigators. The experiments were abandoned. No further attempt was made to teach children the length of the Nile in their sleep. Quite rightly. You can't learn a science unless you know what it's all about.

"Whereas, if they'd only started on *moral* education," said the Director, leading the way towards the door. The students followed him, desperately scribbling as they walked and all the way up in the lift. "Moral education, which ought never, in any circumstances, to be rational."

"Silence, silence," whispered a loud speaker as they stepped out at the fourteenth floor, and "Silence, silence," the trumpet mouths indefatigably repeated at intervals down every corridor. The students and even the Director himself rose automatically to the tips of their toes. They were Alphas, of course; but even Alphas have been well conditioned. "Silence, silence." All the air of the fourteenth floor was sibilant with the categorical imperative.

Fifty yards of tiptoeing brought them to a door which the Director cautiously opened. They stepped over the threshold into the twilight of a shuttered dormitory. Eighty cots stood in a row against the wall. There was a sound of light regular breathing and a continuous murmur, as of very faint voices remotely whispering.

A nurse rose as they entered and came to attention before the Director.

"What's the lesson this afternoon?" he asked.

"We had Elementary Sex for the first forty minutes," she answered. "But now it's switched over to Elementary Class Consciousness."

The Director walked slowly down the long line of cots. Rosy and relaxed with sleep, eighty little boys and girls lay softly breathing. There was a whisper under every pillow. The D.H.C. halted and, bending over one of the little beds, listened attentively.

"Elementary Class Consciousness, did you say? Let's have it repeated a little louder by the trumpet."

At the end of the room a loud speaker projected from the wall. The Director walked up to it and pressed a switch.

". . . all wear green," said a soft but very distinct voice, beginning in the middle of a sentence, "and Delta Children wear khaki. Oh no, I don't want to play with Delta children. And Epsilons are still worse. They're too stupid to be able to read or write. Besides they wear black, which is such a beastly colour. I'm *so* glad I'm a Beta."

There was a pause; then the voice began again.

"Alpha children wear grey. They work much harder than we do, because they're so frightfully clever. I'm really awfully glad I'm a Beta, because I don't work so hard. And then we are much better than the Gammas and Deltas. Gammas are stupid. They all wear green, and Delta children wear khaki. Oh no, I *don't* want to play with Delta children. And Epsilons are still worse. They're too stupid to be able . . ."

The Director pushed back the switch. The voice

was silent. Only its thin ghost continued to mutter from beneath the eighty pillows.

"They'll have that repeated forty or fifty times more before they wake; then again on Thursday, and again on Saturday. A hundred and twenty times three times a week for thirty months. After which they go on to a more advanced lesson."

Roses and electric shocks, the khaki of Deltas and a whiff of asafœtida—wedded indissolubly before the child can speak. But wordless conditioning is crude and wholesale; cannot bring home the finer distinctions, cannot inculcate the more complex courses of behaviour. For that there must be words, but words without reason. In brief, hypnopædia.

"The greatest moralizing and socializing force of all time."

The students took it down in their little books. Straight from the horse's mouth.

Once more the Director touched the switch.

". . . so frightfully clever," the soft, insinuating, indefatigable voice was saying, "I'm really awfully glad I'm a Beta, because . . ."

Not so much like drops of water, though water, it is true, can wear holes in the hardest granite; rather, drops of liquid sealing-wax, drops that adhere, incrust, incorporate themselves with what they fall on, till finally the rock is all one scarlet blob.

"Till at last the child's mind *is* these suggestions, and the sum of the suggestions *is* the child's mind. And not the child's mind only. The adult's mind too—all his life long. The mind that judges and desires and decides—made up of these suggestions. But all these suggestions are *our* suggestions!" The Director almost shouted in his triumph. "Suggestions from the State." He banged the nearest table. "It therefore follows . . ."

A noise made him turn round.

"Oh, Ford!" he said in another tone, "I've gone and woken the children."

Review and Reflection

1. What, in your opinion, is the most serious problem associated with the development of modern technology? What is the most positive benefit?

2. Recall, from the Introductory Dialogue, the three suggestions that Wesley made concerning our attitude toward technology. Do you agree with his suggestions? Do you share his mistrust and suspicion of modern technology? Why?

3. Summarize, as clearly and concisely as possible, the major risks associated with the development of genetic engineering. Do you agree with the concerns and conclusions of Thomas Murray? Why?

4. What problems does Willard Gaylin associate with the acceptance of *brain death* as a new definitional standard? Do you share his concerns? Why?

5. Do you think we have (or will have) the power to create a world such as the one envisioned by Aldous Huxley in *Brave New World*? What, if anything, do you find objectionable about such a society? What, if anything, do you regard as its strength and appeal?

Suggestions for Further Study

RAZIEL ABELSON and MARIE-LOUISE FRIQUEGNON. *Ethics for Modern Life.* New York: Saint Martin's Press, 1982.

JOHN ARRAS and NANCY RODEN. *Ethical Issues in Modern Medicine.* Mountain View, CA: Mayfield, 1993.

REM EDWARDS and GLENN GRABER. *Bioethics.* New York: Harcourt Brace Jovanovich, 1988.

THOMAS MAPPES and JANE ZEMBATY. *Biomedical Ethics.* New York: McGraw-Hill, 1991.

JOHN STUART MILL. *On Liberty.* New York: Macmillan, 1956.

PLATO. *The Republic.* Translated by Desmond Lee. New York: Penguin, 1955.

TOM REGAN. *Matters of Life and Death: New Introductory Essays in Moral Philosophy.* New York: Random House, 1980.

PART 3

Truth and Being:
Exploring the Limits

CHAPTER 7   Philosophy of Science
CHAPTER 8   Metaphysics: Reflections on Reality

The three chapters in Part One focused on intimate, individual aspects of being. Those in Part Two concerned the dimension of self which is inextricably intertwined with the existence of others. While there is much more that could be said about each of those two areas, the time has come to expand our frame of consciousness once more. For as we continue to reflect on the nature of our being we must acknowledge that we are imbedded not only in a sociopolitical fabric, but in a physiochemical one as well. The attempt to understand our position in that portion of the fabric leads to science and metaphysics. Here we will explore the nature and value of scientific theories, the creation of methods to promote unbiased observation and empirical discovery, the complex relationships which exist between conceptual development and sense experience, and the many difficulties that arise through imprecise or uncertain use of human language.

CHAPTER 7

Philosophy of Science

The chapter surveys basic concepts, ideas, and presuppositions of modern science. Specific points of focus include the nature of a scientific theory, the role of empirical test, the anatomy of discovery, hypothesis formation, and assorted difficulties concerning observation, bias, and objectivity.

Introductory Essay

The **Introductory Essay** poses a series of questions concerning the proper relationship between theory, experience, and belief. Theories are defined as "conceptual structures designed to explain, unify, or otherwise account for puzzling, problematic, or poorly understood phenomena." Empirical testing is presented as one of the hallmarks of a scientific theory, but the concept is not without its share of logical and pragmatic difficulties. Additional reflections concern disagreements between individual scientists and the processes whereby scientific theories are modified, challenged, and eventually replaced. Rejecting extremes of unqualified acceptance and wholesale rejection, the essay advocates an epistemic humility characterized by empirical tolerance, fallibility, and provisional acceptance.

Philosophical Readings

The article by **Thomas Kuhn** challenges the traditional view of a scientific discovery as a well-defined event that occurs at a specific place and time. Using oxygen as an example, he marks a distinction between discovering *that* and discovering *what*. Consideration of two further examples leads to a discussion of expectation, anomaly, and the thesis that scientific discovery is often predicated on a breakdown of accepted techniques and standards.

Evelyn Fox Keller explores the male bias that has often dominated the conduct of science. She briefly discusses issues like unequal employment practices, bias in the choice and definition of problems selected for scientific study, and bias in the design and interpretation of research experiments, then advances a critique which she deems far more radical: the possibility that the core epistemic standards of objectivity and rationality are themselves reflections of an androcentric bias. Her investigation leads her into a discussion of human psychology, power, control, autonomy, consciousness, and the nature of scientific knowledge. She argues that all knowledge presents a potential for both power and transcendence, but that the scientific enterprise has thus far been geared almost exclusively to the pursuit of the first. She concludes that an enlightened science in which men and women work together to mine the full potential of the field will bring not a diminishment of power, but enrichment, liberation and transcendence.

Scientific Reading

The selection by **Stephen Jay Gould** explores the extent to which even scientific findings are a reflection of prior belief and expectation. Specific examples drawn from the history of biology include *Bathybius Haeckelii* and *Eozoon canadense.* Despite impressive theoretical support, an abundance of empirical data, and the conclusions of major scientific figures, we now regard these "animals" as little more than instances of the power of wishful thinking.

Literary Readings

Two selections are presented from **Robert Pirsig's** *Zen and the Art of Motorcycle Maintenance.* The first explores the relationship between data collection, hypothesis formation, and empirical testing. Specific concerns are raised regarding the large number of hypotheses that may be formulated on the basis of any given set of experiences. Pirsig's second selection examines the nature of scientific discovery, the development of non-Euclidean geometry, and the conventionalist views of Jules Henri Poincaré. Discussion is also provided concerning Poincaré's notion of the "subliminal self."

Matters of Theory

DOUGLAS W. SHRADER

Modern science is often regarded as the crowning achievement of Western intellectual tradition. The accolade is well deserved: the accomplishments of science are plentiful and impressive. This is true of both the theoretical side of science (the quest for knowledge and understanding) as well as its practical side (the creation and application of new technology). On the theoretical side, science seems to have unlocked some of the deepest secrets of the universe regarding the structure and composition of matter, the nature and origins of biological life, and even the age and origin of the universe. On the technological side, scientists have created vaccines (and vaccination procedures) to practically eliminate childhood disease like polio and smallpox, united human sperm and ova in glass dishes and successfully transplanted the products into the wombs of otherwise infertile women, and created and installed artificial hearts to give people with otherwise terminal heart disease several additional years of life. They have created vehicles that enable us to fly and to move about the surface of the planet at speeds greater than that of any other known creature, as well as ones that have taken humans to the moon and returned them safely to the earth.

This massive wide-ranging success occasions a certain awe, even a certain sort of reverence. It is sometimes said that science is the principal religion of modern society, and that scientists constitute its priesthood. The description may seem strange, but it is not entirely without warrant.

Very few people understand very much science. I have numerous colleagues who do not even begin to understand Quantum Mechanics or the workings of a nuclear reactor. Many believe they cannot, and perhaps they are right: many do not even understand the cars they drive. As a society, we may not understand science, but we place a tremendous amount of faith, hope, and money (the currency with which modern society declares its true allegiance) in the general conduct of science and the specialized work of its individual practitioners. Whenever we have a problem of almost any sort, we look to science to provide the solution. Even now scientists are, at national directive and expense, trying to find cures for cancer, AIDS, and a host of other problems.

While I have no wish to deny the impressive accomplishments of modern science, those accomplishments should not cause us to forget that science is a *human* activity. It is performed by human beings with human instruments according to human standards within a human socio-cultural and religious environment. Human limitations plague both the theoretical and applied sides of science. The scientific enterprise is not infallible; it has no stranglehold or inside track on truth. In fact, there is good reason to believe that most if not all of our current scientific theories are false. The technology is not always beneficial or without cost. Without science we would have neither atomic weapons nor the immense problems they create. Nuclear reactors generate both energy and nuclear waste. DDT helped control agricultural pests, but caused a mutation toward dangerously thin-shelled eggs in the peregrine falcon, seriously endangering the entire species.

TESTING TESTING

It is sometimes forgotten that scientific theories are just that: *theories*. Theories are conceptual structures or stories designed to explain, unify, or otherwise account for puzzling, problematic, or poorly understood phenomena or experiences. Some of the theories advanced by scientists have been nothing short of fantastic, but science is neither fantasy nor science fiction. To be a good scientist, one must do more than tell a good story. Not all theories are scientific; not all scientific theories are empirically acceptable; and not all empirically acceptable scientific theories are sufficiently interesting or promising to form the basis of a scientific research program.

To be scientific, a theory must be subject to manipulation and empirical test. Testing serves several related functions. Most obviously, it serves to increase or decrease our confidence in the theory. But negative results are not usually, by themselves, sufficient cause to reject a theory. Because they tell us where and sometimes how a theory breaks down, they may point the way toward refinements and improvements of the theory. In the process, they may lead to interesting new discoveries.

There is no general agreement as to how much manipulation and testing is necessary for a theory to count as scientific, but most philosophers and scientists agree: "more is better." Ironically, some of the most interesting theories prove extremely difficult to test. Only four ways have been found in which to test Einstein's General Theory of Relativity. It is sometimes alleged that Darwin's Theory of Evolution by Means of Natural Selection has never been tested at all. The latter claim is probably too strong, but the general point remains: testing is limited and tenuous at best.

A scientific test is an attempt to arrange a comparison or confrontation between a theoretically constructed reality and the "hard facts" of the "real world." If the predictions of the theory match our observations, results are said to be positive or confirming. Positive results are good. They usually increase our confidence in the theory. But no matter how many positive results we accumulate, they cannot be taken as incontrovertible proof of the truth of the theory. There are several reasons why this is so.

A problem of induction: First is a general difficulty with generalization. It is logically impossible to establish the truth of any empirical generalization unless we have examined each and every possible instance of that generalization. No matter how

many entities of a given type we may have observed, any inferences about unobserved entities of the same type are logically risky and uncertain. The point is a logical one, but as a couple of examples will demonstrate, the risk of error is very real.

After centuries of observation and examination of thousands of different species of animals, scientists came to believe that all mammals (vertebrate animals, the females of which produce milk to nourish their young) reproduce by means of sexual coupling and live birth. The generalization was both theoretically reasonable and experientially well confirmed. Nevertheless, as scientists were to discover when they investigated the fauna of Australia, it is false. The platypus exhibits most of the standard characteristics of a mammal. It is a warm-blooded, air-breathing vertebrate animal that nourishes its young with its own milk. But it does not give birth to live young. Instead, it lays eggs.

A more recent example concerns the basis of life itself. Two thousand years of experience and scientific investigation supported the theory that all life (on earth, at least) derives its energy from the sun, either directly through photosynthesis or indirectly through the associated food chain. As overwhelming as two thousand years of experience may seem, in recent years, near volcanic cracks on the ocean floor, explorers have found entire communities of plants and animals that derive their energy not from the sun but from this planet (via chemosynthesis).

The examples should teach us a little epistemic humility and perhaps a little metaphysical caution as well. No matter how extensive our experiences may be, we always run a substantial and serious risk of error when we try to extend what we have learned from those experiences to uncharted regions of space-time. Experience is a valuable guide, but the world is full of surprises. We never know what we will find.

The anatomy of a test: It is often the uncharted regions that interest scientists the most. Discovery of the unknown is exciting. Moreover, discovery is usually taken as a sure sign, and possibly even a necessary condition, of the advancement of scientific knowledge. Discovery of platypuses and chemosynthetic life required scientists to rethink some of their basic ideas about life. In the process, we believe our knowledge and understanding of biological life was enhanced rather than diminished.

The allure of the unknown is strong. Many of the most interesting (and controversial) scientific theories make claims about unexamined entities or portions of reality that we have not experienced. Testing these abstract and experientially remote theories is particularly problematic. We can sometimes build experimental bridges to the uncharted regions they theorize about, but the bridges are often elaborate ones with strong theoretical characteristics and dependencies of their own.

Suppose, for example, we have a theory about subatomic entities. We cannot, for obvious reasons, simply pick up a small piece of subatomic reality and look at it to see if what we have described does in fact happen. To test the theory we may have to create subatomic particles in a particle generator and accelerate them to "proper" speed in a mile-long cyclotron before releasing them into a bubble chamber where the traces of their collisions with other subatomic particles may be photographed. If we are lucky, computer-assisted examination of the photographs may provide a few tracks consistent with the predictions of the theory. If the tracks are ones that no one would have otherwise expected, the photographs may be taken as extremely impressive evidence. But even ignoring the difficulties with generalization discussed earlier, it should be fairly obvious that the photographs could never constitute unquestionable proof.

We can have no more confidence in the test results than we do in the testing procedures. If anything is going on in the particle generator, cyclotron, or bubble chamber other than what our theories tell us is going on, if the equipment has somehow malfunctioned, if we have failed to operate it properly, or if we have failed to recognize and control for a relevant variable, our test results become suspect and potentially useless. They may even lead us into serious error.

I have, in short fashion, pointed to several conceptually different if closely related difficulties. The difficulties are most apparent and perhaps especially acute when dealing with theories about highly abstract and speculative regions of reality. But the problems are far more general than may at first be imagined. They pertain to any test, even fairly simple ones of less ambitious and less questionable theories. Although they form an interrelated set, it may be helpful to separate, enumerate, and discuss the problems individually.

Problems: We begin with the possibility of human error. Even scientists make mistakes. An improperly washed beaker or inaccurate setting on a dial of a piece of sophisticated equipment can lead to results very different from what would otherwise have been obtained. Even if the test is performed perfectly the data may be misperceived, misrecorded, or misinterpreted. The misperception of data may be simple observational error, or it may be something deeper. That "something deeper" is our second problem.

There is no such thing as totally neutral observation. Sense perception is a complex phenomenon every bit as dependent on the cognitive functions of the brain as it is on the sense organs. In his otherwise exemplary experiments with peas, Gregor Mendel failed to recognize and mathematically control for a statistical bias in his data. But he consistently (apparently unintentionally and unconsciously) misidentified exactly the right number of plants in each group to yield the oversimplified ratios he erroneously expected.[1]

A third difficulty is closely related to the second: there is no direct theory-neutral access to reality (at least not to the sort of reality with which scientific theories are usually concerned). The point is most obvious when testing a theory about subatomic particles or the origin of the universe (somewhere we clearly cannot go without elaborate equipment and theoretical assumptions), but it applies to theories about less-remote regions as well. In general, if there is direct access to reality, there is no need to theorize about it. If our theories are to be anything other than free-floating fiction, we must find some way to ground them in experience. This of course is the whole idea of testing. But testing requires that we devise test procedures. And often this requires the construction or use of specialized equipment.

The fourth difficulty (or group of difficulties) concerns the risks that are always involved in the design of test procedures and the use of specialized equipment. The procedure may be flawed or the equipment may be functioning in some way other than we expect or realize. We may have failed to control for a relevant variable or unintentionally introduced biases into the data in our preparation, observation, or evaluation techniques (cf. Mendel). The difficulties here are very real. In the late nineteenth century scientists studied various forms of radiation using a device called a *cathode ray tube*. They did not control for possible effects of what we call *X-rays*, for they had no reason to suspect the existence of any such form of radiation. Suspected or not, it was there. Roentgen discovered it when some photographic plates left near a cathode ray tube were inexplicably fogged. Many experiments, the results of which had previously been considered unproblematic, had to be reperformed or reevaluated.

The fifth difficulty is simple but invidious: any equipment can malfunction. As our need for precision increases, so does the possibility of error. A slight voltage fluctuation or a temperature variance of a fraction of a degree may effect a radical change in the results of an experiment.

Consequences: The difficulties are serious and to some extent unavoidable. But they are not by themselves sufficient cause to abandon the scientific enterprise. In fact, science has developed a set of procedures to guard against and control for these eventualities.

Repetition of the experiment by different researchers with different equipment reduces (although it does not eliminate) the possibility of equipment or technician error. Additionally, since uncontrolled variables may vary, repetition has the potential to uncover the effects of an unsuspected contributing factor. Roentgen's discovery of X-rays shows not only that a piece of equipment can function in an unsuspected way, but also that the unsuspected function can be discovered in the normal course of scientific investigation.

Perhaps most importantly, scientists try to devise multiple ways of testing any given theory. Each of the tests is subject to the difficulties we have discussed, but the specific locus of possible error changes as we change the specifics of the testing procedure.

Logical certainty is beyond the reach of science. Caution, humility, and an attitude that acknowledges human fallibility are absolutely essential if we are to avoid becoming stuck in error or decimated by our failures. But fallibility is not fatalism. Difficulties notwithstanding, scientific tests usually provide reasonable grounds for accepting or rejecting a scientific theory (even if only provisionally).

CHANGE AND DISAGREEMENT IN SCIENCE

Even a cursory examination of the history of science reveals one thing: it changes. Many people, including prominent scientists such as Isaac Newton, have subscribed to one or another version of what is called the *Strict Cumulativity Thesis*. According to the thesis, all change in legitimate established science is (or should be) a simple matter of addition, generalization, or fine-tuning. Most change is held to be nothing more than a matter of learning new things or creating new technology; new theories are developed to explain newly discovered or otherwise hitherto unexplained phenomena. New large-scale theories ("supertheories") may be developed to unify or generalize theories that were originally more limited or specific. Along the way we may find it necessary to make minor adjustments or corrections to theories that remain, on the whole, entirely adequate and unobjectionable. The main thing is that we never throw anything away. Established scientific theories, according to the Strict Cumulativity Thesis, are never discarded as fundamentally misdirected, flawed, mistaken, or false.

If a cursory examination of the history of science shows that science changes, a slightly more in-depth examination shows the Strict Cumulativity Thesis to be hopelessly inept as a description of that change. History is full of cases in which a well-established theory or research program was abandoned in favor of a radically different and incompatible one. The replacement episodes are sometimes so obvious and striking or have such far-reaching consequences that they are called "scientific revolutions."

In the Copernican Revolution we changed from geocentric to heliocentric astronomy. In the Keplerian Revolution we changed from kinematic to mechanistic astronomy and from circular to elliptical planetary orbits. In the Darwinian Revolution we substituted evolution for immutability and natural selection for supernatural manipulation. In the Einsteinian Revolution we substituted Relativistic Space-Time (and all that that carries with it) for the Absolute Universal Space and Time of the Newtonian system. Obviously, the changes in these episodes are deep structural ones, not simple matters of fine-tuning.

Most changes in scientific theories are more gradual and partial. By and large, science changes in a piecemeal fashion. We sometimes speak of "the" Theory of Evolution or say that modern science accepts Darwin's Theory of Evolution by Means of Natural Selection as though no substantial changes have occurred in the theory since Darwin first published *Origin of Species* in 1859. But in fact "the" theory has undergone many changes, some of them quite significant.

For example, Darwin's evolutionary theory made use of a theoretical phenomenon we call "the inheritance of acquired characteristics." The idea is fairly simple: I can transmit to my offspring not only the characteristics with which I was born, but also characteristics I may have acquired during the course of my life. Thus a woman who lost a finger on her left hand in a childhood accident might give birth to a child with a missing finger on that same hand. A giraffe that repeatedly stretched its neck to reach the leaves of a tall tree might give birth to a giraffe with a longer-than-average neck.

The idea was accepted by scientists in Darwin's time and was a clearly important and useful ingredient of his theory. Unfortunately for Darwin's version of the theory, scientific investigations do not support the concept. The inheritance of acquired characteristics seems to have been nothing more than a creation of the human mind, supported only by faulty evidence and wishful thinking. Most modern biologists believe evolution proceeds by means of selective retention of randomly generated variations (mutations). The difference, although clearly significant, is not usually considered sufficient to warrant the appellation "revolution."

Differences of opinion: The phenomenon of scientific change shows us that scientists disagree with one another over time. Nonetheless, a lot of people seem to believe that at any given time all scientists (or all reputable scientists within a given field) are of a single mind; that to be an "accepted scientific theory" a theory must be more or less uniformly understood and unanimously accepted. There is indeed, at virtually any given time, a remarkable homogeneity of opinion within the scientific community. The homogeneity is impressive, but neither absolute nor universal. There is ample room for dissent.

For example, most modern biologists subscribe to one or another version of "the" Theory of Evolution, but the differences between the versions are often quite substantial. There are sometimes serious differences regarding the rate of evolution, the size and origin of the relevant variations, the mechanisms of selection, and even the units of evolution (what is it that evolves?). Scientists even disagree about the interpretation of the data (the fossil record, for example). As a paleontologist recently observed: "Sometimes it seems as though there are as many variations on each theme as there are individual biologists."[2]

Consequences: All of this change and variation poses a bit of a problem regarding the acceptance of scientific theories. Unless we believe the patterns of history to have been arrested or redirected, we must believe that future scientists will judge our theories in much the same way as we do those of our predecessors: many will be rejected as naive, wrongheaded, misdirected, or otherwise mistaken.

Knowing this, how can we judge them to be true? How can we even judge them to be approximately true or otherwise deserving of epistemic allegiance? For that matter, with potentially thousands of different versions of any given theory floating around at any given time, what sense can we even make of the claim that "the" theory is true?

Singularly and collectively, these questions concern what is sometimes termed the "epistemic status" of a scientific theory. Unless we are to turn a blind eye to critical analysis and reflection, we must acknowledge that any attempt to treat scientific theories as "true" conceals a subtle misrepresentation of the product. They are, after all, only theories. Our best scientific theories are nothing more than tentative guesses, necessarily limited by the available data, conceptual resources, and ingenuity of the theoretician. The most successful scientific theories (the most that any enlightened theoretician can hope for) are the ones which come to form the basis of a research program involving the efforts of hundreds or thousands of scientists. But such a theory sows the seeds of its own replacement.

In the very process of investigating the phenomena that the theory sought to describe, scientists extend the database and learn new things which, consequently, could not have been considered by the theoretician when formulating the theory. Unless the theory is to become quickly outdated, it will have to be modified to bring it into line with the new findings.

Different scientists may make different modifications. Some modifications may work better for some purposes than for others. The net effect is likely to be a sort of loosely defined patchwork called "the theory." As the theory breaks down in more and more places, and as versions of the theory now grow more numerous and divergent, it is only natural that theoreticians begin looking for a replacement.

The replacement theory should be contextually stronger and less problematic than the theory it replaces. But it, too, will one day be replaced; such is simply the nature of a scientific theory. The capacity for modification and eventual replacement on the basis of empirical investigation is one of the primary things that makes a theory scientific. As a result, no scientific theory lasts forever.

PROVISIONAL ACCEPTANCE

So where does all this leave us as regards the proper attitude toward contemporary scientific theories? We should not accept them as established proven fact (for that they are not), but neither should we reject them as a bunch of unsubstantiated nonsense. They are, contextually, the best that science has to offer.

Contemporary scientific theories guide the thoughts and research of the contemporary scientific community. We can be fairly sure that most—if not all—of them will be rejected by the scientific community of the future, but we cannot reject them for the reasons they will, for we do not know what they will know and we do not have the alternative theories they will have.

There is little left to do but "accept" the theories tentatively and provisionally for what they are: twentieth-century scientific theories. Anything less would deprive us of the investigations we might otherwise conduct on the basis of those theories. That of course would deprive us of the future of science. More generally, it would deprive us of science itself. A static, infertile science which does not lead beyond its present boundaries not only is not worth having but, properly speaking, is not science at all.

Notes

1. For a detailed account of the matter, see R. A. Fisher, "Has Mendel's Work Been Rediscovered?," *Annals of Science*, 1936.

2. Niles Eldredge, "Evolutionary Housecleaning," *Natural History*, February 1982, p. 81.

Historical Structure of Scientific Discovery

THOMAS S. KUHN

Thomas Kuhn began his academic training in physics, but gradually found himself becoming more interested in the historical and philosophical dimensions of the field than in the pursuit of science itself. He is best known for his revolutionary work, *The Structure of Scientific Revolutions* (1962/70). In the following article, reprinted from *Science* (June 1962), he calls for a radical rethinking of the traditional notions of scientific discovery.

My object in this article is to isolate and illuminate one small part of what I take to be a continuing historiographic revolution in the study of science.[1] The structure of scientific discovery is my particular topic, and I can best approach it by pointing out that the subject itself may well seem extraordinarily odd. Both scientists and, until quite recently, historians have ordinarily viewed discovery as the sort of event which, though it may have preconditions and surely has consequences, is itself without internal structure. Rather than being seen as a complex development extended both in space and time, discovering something has usually seemed to be a unitary event, one which, like seeing something, happens to an individual at a specifiable time and place.

This view of the nature of discovery has, I suspect, deep roots in the nature of the scientific community. One of the few historical elements recurrent in the textbooks from which the prospective scientist learns his field is the attribution of particular natural phenomena to the historical personages who first discovered them. As a result of this and other aspects of their training, discovery becomes for many scientists an important goal. To make a discovery is to achieve one of the closest approximations to a property right that the scientific career affords. Professional prestige is often closely associated with these acquisitions.[2] Small wonder, then, that acrimonious disputes about priority and independence in discovery have often marred the normally placid tenor of scientific communication. Even less wonder that many historians of science have seen the individual discovery as an appropriate unit with which to measure scientific progress, and have devoted much time and skill to determining what man made which discovery at what point in time. If the study of discovery has a surprise to offer, it is only that, despite the immense energy and ingenuity expended upon it, neither polemic nor painstaking scholarship has often succeeded in pinpointing the time and place at which a given discovery could properly be said to have "been made."

SOME DISCOVERIES PREDICTABLE, SOME NOT

That failure, both of argument and of research, suggests the thesis that I now wish to develop. Many scientific discoveries, particularly the most interesting and important, are not the sort of event about which the questions "Where?" and, more particularly, "When?" can appropriately be asked. Even if all conceivable data were at hand, those questions would not regularly possess answers. That we are persistently driven to ask them nonetheless is

Thomas Kuhn, "Historical Structure of Scientific Discovery," *Science* 136 (June 1, 1962), pp. 760–764. Copyright © 1962 by American Association for the Advancement of Science. Reprinted with the permission of the publ symptomatic of a fundamental inappropriateness in our image of discovery. That inappropriateness is here my main concern, but I approach it by considering first the historical problem presented by the attempt to date and to place a major class of fundamental discoveries.

The troublesome class consists of those discoveries—including oxygen, the electric current, x-rays, and the electron—which could not be predicted from accepted theory in advance and which therefore caught the assembled profession by surprise. That kind of discovery will shortly be my exclusive concern, but it will help first to note that there is another sort and one which presents very few of the same problems. Into this second class of discoveries fall the neutrino, radiowaves, and the elements which filled empty places in the periodic table. The existence of all these objects had been predicted from theory before they were discovered, and the men who made the discoveries therefore knew from the start what to look for. That foreknowledge did not make their task less demanding or less interesting, but it did provide criteria which told them when their goal had been reached.[3] As a result, there have been few priority debates over discoveries of this second sort, and only a paucity of data can prevent the historian from ascribing them to a particular time and place. Those facts help to isolate the difficulties we encounter as we return to the troublesome discoveries of the first class. In the cases that most concern us here, there are no benchmarks to inform either the scientist or the historian when the job of discovery has been done.

OXYGEN AS AN EXAMPLE

As an illustration of this fundamental problem and its consequences, consider first the discovery of oxygen. Because it has repeatedly been studied, often with exemplary care and skill, that discovery is unlikely to offer any purely factual surprises. Therefore it is particularly well suited to clarify points of principle.[4] At least three scientists—Carl Scheele, Joseph Priestley, and Antoine Lavoisier—have a legitimate claim to this discovery, and polemicists have occasionally entered the same claim for Pierre Bayen.[5] Scheele's work, though it was almost certainly completed before the relevant researches of Priestley and Lavoisier, was not made public until their work was well known.[6] Therefore it had no apparent causal role, and I shall simplify my story by omitting it.[7] Instead, I pick up the main route to the discovery of oxygen with the work of Bayen, who, sometime before March 1774, discovered that red precipitate of mercury (HgO) could, by heating, be made to yield a gas. That aeriform product Bayen identified as fixed air (CO_2), a substance made familiar to most pneumatic chemists by the earlier work of Joseph Black.[8] A variety of other substances were known to yield the same gas.

At the beginning of August 1774, a few months after Bayen's work had appeared, Joseph Priestley repeated the experiment, though probably independently. Priestley, however, observed that the gaseous product would support combustion and therefore changed the identification. For him, the gas obtained on heating red precipitate was nitrous air (N_2O), a substance that he had himself discovered more than two years before.[9] Later in the same month Priestley made a trip to Paris and there informed Lavoisier of the new reaction. The latter repeated the experiment, both in November 1774 and in February 1775. However, because he used tests somewhat more elaborate than Priestley's, Lavoisier again changed the identification. For him, as of May 1775, the gas released by red precipitate was neither fixed air nor nitrous air. Instead, it was "[atmospheric] air itself entire without alteration . . . even to the point that . . . it comes out more pure."[10] Meanwhile, however, Priestley had also been at work, and, before the beginning of March 1775, he too had concluded that the gas must be "common air." To this point all of the men who had produced a gas from red precipitate of mercury had identified it with some previously known species.[11]

The remainder of this story of discovery is briefly told. During March 1775 Priestley discovered that his gas was in several respects very much "better" than common air, and he therefore re-identified the gas once more, this time calling it "dephlogisticated air," that is, atmospheric air deprived of its normal complement of phlogiston. This conclusion Priestley published in the *Philosophical Transactions,* and it was apparently that publication which led Lavoisier to reexamine his own results.[12] The reexamination began during February 1776, and within a year led Lavoisier to the conclusion that the gas was actually a separable component of the atmospheric air which both he and Priestley had previously thought of as homogeneous. With this point reached, the gas recognized as an irreducibly distinct species, we may conclude that the discovery of oxygen had been completed.

However, to return to my initial question, when shall we say that oxygen was discovered and what criteria shall we use in answering that question? If discovering oxygen is simply holding an impure sample in one's hands, then the gas had been "discovered" in antiquity by the first man whoever bottled atmospheric air. Undoubtedly, for an experimental criterion, we must at least require a relatively pure sample like that obtained by Priestley in August 1774. But during 1774 Priestley was unaware that he had discovered anything except a new way to produce a relatively familiar species. Throughout that year his "discovery" is scarcely distinguishable from the one made earlier by Bayen, and neither case is quite distinct from that of the Reverend Stephen Hales who had obtained the same gas more than forty years before.[13] Apparently to discover something one must also be aware of the discovery and know as well what it is that one has discovered.

But, that being the case, how much must one know? Had Priestley come close enough when he identified the gas as nitrous air? If not, was either he or Lavoisier significantly closer when he changed the identification to common air? And what are we to say about Priestley's next identification, the one made in March 1775? Dephlogisticated air is still not oxygen or even, for the phlogistic chemist, a quite unexpected sort of gas. Rather, it is a particularly pure atmospheric air. Presumably, then, we wait for Lavoisier's work in 1776 and 1777, work which led him not merely to isolate the gas but to see what it was. Yet even that decision can be questioned, for in 1777 and to the end of his life Lavoisier insisted that oxygen was an atomic "principle of acidity" and that oxygen *gas* was formed only when that "principle" united with caloric, the matter of heat.[14] Shall we therefore say that oxygen had not yet been discovered in 1777? Some may be tempted to do so. But the principle of acidity was not banished from chemistry until after 1810 and caloric lingered on until the 1860s. Oxygen had, however, become a standard chemical substance long before either of those dates. Furthermore, what is perhaps the key point, it would probably have gained that status on the basis of Priestley's work alone, without benefit of Lavoisier's still partial reinterpretation.

I conclude that we need a new vocabulary and new concepts for analyzing events like the discovery of oxygen. Though undoubtedly correct, the sentence "Oxygen was discovered" misleads by suggesting that discovering something is a simple act unequivocally attributable, if only we knew enough, to an individual and an instant in time. When the discovery is unexpected, however, the latter attribution is always impossible and the former often is as well. Ignoring Scheele, we can, for example, safely say that oxygen had not been discovered before 1774; probably we would also insist that it had been discovered by 1777 or shortly thereafter. But within those limits, any attempt to date the discovery or to attribute it to an individual must inevitably be arbitrary. Furthermore, it must be arbitrary just because discovering a new sort of phenomenon is necessarily a complex process which involves recognizing both *that* something is and *what* it is. Observation and conceptualization, fact and the assimilation of fact to theory, are inseparably linked in the discovery of scientific novelty. Inevitably, that process extends over time and may often involve a number of people. Only for discoveries in my second category—those whose nature is known in advance—can discovering *that* and discovering *what* occur together and in an instant.

URANUS AND X-RAYS

Two last, simpler, and far briefer examples will simultaneously show how typical the case of oxygen is and also prepare the way for a somewhat more precise conclusion. On the night of March 13, 1781, the astronomer William Herschel made the following entry in his journal: "In the quartile near Zeta Tauri . . . is a curious either nebulous star or perhaps a comet."[15] That entry is generally said to record the discovery of the planet Uranus, but it cannot quite have done that. Between 1690 and Herschel's observation in 1781 the same object had been seen and recorded at least 17 times by men who took it to be a star. Herschel differed from them only in supposing that, because in his telescope it appeared especially large, it might actually be a *comet*! Two additional observations on March 17 and 19 confirmed that suspicion by showing that the object he had observed moved among the stars. As a result, astronomers throughout Europe were informed of the discovery, and the mathematicians among them began to compute the new comet's orbit. Only several months later, after all those attempts had repeatedly failed to square with observation, did the astronomer Lexell suggest that the object observed by Herschel might be a planet. And only when additional computations, using a planet's rather than a comet's orbit, proved reconcilable with observation, was that suggestion generally accepted. At what point during 1781 do we want to say that the planet Uranus was discovered? And are we entirely and unequivocally clear that it was Herschel rather than Lexell who had discovered it?

Or consider still more briefly the story of the discovery of x-rays, a story which opens on the day in 1895 when the physicist Roentgen interrupted a well-precedented investigation of cathode rays because he noticed that a barium platinocyanide screen far from his shielded apparatus glowed when the discharge was in process.[16] Additional investigations—they required seven hectic weeks during which Roentgen rarely left the laboratory—indicated that the cause of the glow traveled in straight lines from the cathode ray tube, that the radiation cast shadows, that it could not be deflected by a magnet, and much else besides. Before announcing his discovery, Roentgen had convinced himself that his effect was not due to cathode rays themselves but to a new form of radiation with at least some similarity to light. Once again the question suggests itself: When shall we say that x-rays were actually discovered? Not, in any case, at the first instant, when all that had been noted was a glowing screen. At least one other investigator had seen that glow and, to his subsequent chagrin, discovered nothing at all. Nor, it is almost as clear, can the moment of discovery be pushed back to a point during the last week of investigation. By that time Roentgen was exploring the properties of the new radiation he had *already* discovered. We may have to settle for the remark that x-rays emerged in Würzburg between November 8 and December 28, 1895.

AWARENESS OF ANOMALY

The characteristics shared by these examples are, I think, common to all the episodes by which unanticipated novelties become subjects for scientific attention. I therefore conclude these brief remarks by discussing three such common characteristics, which may help to provide a framework for further study of the extended episodes we customarily call "discoveries."

In the first place, notice that all three of our discoveries—oxygen, Uranus, and x-rays—began with the experimental or observational isolation of an anomaly, that is, with nature's failure to conform entirely to expectation. Notice, further, that the process by which that anomaly was educed displays simultaneously the apparently incompatible characteristics of the inevitable and the accidental. In the case of x-rays, the anomalous glow which provided Roentgen's first clue was clearly the result of an accidental disposition of his apparatus. But by 1895 cathode rays were a normal subject for research all over Europe, research that regularly juxtaposed cathode ray tubes with sensitive screens and films; as a result, Roentgen's accident was almost certain to occur elsewhere, as in fact it had. Those remarks, however, should make Roentgen's case look very much like those of Herschel and Priestley. Herschel first observed his oversized and thus anomalous star in the course of a prolonged survey of the northern heavens. That survey was, except for the magnification provided by Herschel's instruments, precisely of the sort that had repeatedly been carried through before and that had occasionally resulted in prior observations of Uranus. And Priestley, too—when he isolated the gas that behaved almost but not quite like nitrous air and then almost but not quite like common air—was seeing something unintended and wrong in the outcome of a sort of experiment for which there was much European precedent and which had more than once before led to the production of the new gas.

These features suggest the existence of two normal requisites for the beginning of an episode of discovery. The first, which throughout this paper I have largely taken for granted, is the individual skill, wit, or genius to recognize that something has gone wrong in ways that may prove consequential. Not any and every scientist would have noted that no unrecorded star should be so large, that the screen ought not have glowed, that nitrous air should not have supported life. But that requisite presupposes another which is less frequently taken for granted. Whatever the level of genius available to observe them, anomalies do not emerge from the normal course of scientific research until both instruments and concepts have developed sufficiently to make their emergence likely and to make the anomaly which results recognizable as a violation of expectation.[17] To say that an unexpected discovery begins only when something goes wrong is to say that it begins only when scientists know well both how their instruments and how nature should behave. What distinguished Priestley, who saw an anomaly,

from Hales, who did not, is largely the considerable articulation of pneumatic techniques and expectations that had come into being during the four decades which separate their two isolations of oxygen.[18] The very number of claimants indicates that after 1770 the discovery could not have been postponed for long.

MAKING THE ANOMALY BEHAVE

The role of anomaly is the first of the characteristics shared by our three examples. A second can be considered more briefly, for it has provided the main theme for the body of my text. Though awareness of anomaly marks the beginning of a discovery, it marks only the beginning. What necessarily follows, if anything at all is to be discovered, is a more or less extended period during which the individual and often many members of his group struggle to make the anomaly lawlike. Invariably that period demands additional observation or experimentation as well as repeated cogitation. While it continues, scientists repeatedly revise their expectations, usually their instrumental standards, and sometimes their most fundamental theories as well. In this sense discoveries have a proper internal history, prehistory, and a posthistory. Furthermore, within the rather vaguely delimited interval of internal history, there is no single moment or day which the historian, however complete his data, can identify as the point at which the discovery was made. Often, when several individuals are involved, it is even impossible unequivocally to identify any one of them as the discoverer.

ADJUSTMENT, ADAPTATION, AND ASSIMILATION

Finally, turning to the third of these selected common characteristics, note briefly what happens as the period of discovery draws to a close. A full discussion of that question would require additional evidence and a separate paper, for I have had little to say about the aftermath of discovery in the body of my text. Nevertheless, the topic must not be entirely neglected, for it is in part a corollary of what has already been said.

Discoveries are often described as mere additions or increments to the growing stockpile of scientific knowledge, and that description has helped make the unit-discovery seem a significant measure of progress. I suggest, however, that it is fully appropriate only to those discoveries which, like the elements that filled missing places in the periodic table, were anticipated and sought in advance and which therefore demanded no adjustment, adaptation, and assimilation from the profession. Though the sorts of discoveries we have here been examining are undoubtedly additions to scientific knowledge, they are also something more. In a sense that I can now develop only in part, they also react back upon what has previously been known, providing a new view of some previously familiar objects and simultaneously changing the way in which even some traditional parts of science are practiced. Those in whose area of special competence the new phenomenon falls often see both the world and their work differently as they emerge from the extended struggle with anomaly which constitutes that phenomenon's discovery.

William Herschel, for example, when he increased by one the time-honored number of planetary bodies, taught astronomers to see new things when they looked up at the familiar heavens even with instruments more traditional than his own. That change in the vision of astronomers must be a principal reason why, in the half century after the discovery of Uranus, 20 additional circumsolar bodies were added to the traditional seven.[19] A similar transformation is even clearer in the aftermath of Roentgen's work. In the first place, established techniques for cathode ray research had to be changed, for scientists found they had failed to control a relevant variable. Those changes included both the redesign of old apparatus and revised ways of asking old questions. In addition, those scientists most concerned experienced the same transformation of vision that we have just noted in the aftermath of the discovery of Uranus. X-rays were the first new sort of radiation discovered since infrared and ultraviolet at the beginning of the century. But within less than a decade after Roentgen's work, four more were disclosed by the new scientific sensitivity (for example, to fogged photographic plates) and by some of the new instrumental techniques that had resulted from Roentgen's work and its assimilation.[20]

Very often these transformations in the established techniques of scientific practice prove even more important than the incremental knowledge provided by the discovery itself. That could at least be argued in the case of Uranus and of x-rays; in the case of my third example, oxygen, it is categorically clear. Like the work of Herschel and Roentgen, that of Priestley and Lavoisier taught scientists to view old situations in new ways. Therefore, as we might anticipate, oxygen was not the only new chemical species to be identified in the aftermath of their work. But, in the case of oxygen, the readjustments demanded by assimilation were so profound that they played an integral and essential role—though they were not by themselves the cause—in the gigantic upheaval of chemical theory and practice which has since been known as the "chemical revolution." I do not suggest that every unanticipated discovery has consequences for science so deep and so far-reaching as those which followed the discovery of oxygen. But I do suggest that every such discovery demands, from those most concerned, the sorts of readjustment that, when they are more obvious, we equate with scientific revolution. It is, I believe, just because they demand readjustments like these, that the process of discovery is necessarily and inevitably one that shows structure and therefore extends in time.

References and Notes

1. The larger revolution is discussed in my book, *The Structure of Scientific Revolutions* (Chicago: University of Chicago Press, 1962). The central ideas in this paper have been abstracted from that source, particularly from its third chapter, "Anomaly and the emergence of scientific discoveries."

2. For a brilliant discussion of these points, see R. K. Merton, "Priorities in scientific discovery. A chapter in the sociology of science," *Am Sociol. Rev., 22,* 635 (1957). Also very relevant, though it did not appear until this article had been prepared, is F. Reif, "The competitive world of the pure scientist," *Science, 134,* 1957 (1961).

3. Not all discoveries fall so neatly as the preceding into one or the other of my two classes. For example, Anderson's work on the positron was done in complete ignorance of Dirac's electron theory from which the new particle's existence had already been very nearly predicted. On the other hand, the immediately succeeding work by Blackett and Occhialini made full use of Dirac's theory, and therefore exploited experiment more fully and constructed a more forceful case for the positron's existence than Anderson had been able to do. On this subject see N. R. Hanson, "Discovering the positron," *Brit.J. Phil. Sci., 12,* 194 (1961); *12,* 299 (1962). Hanson suggests several of the points developed here. I am much indebted to Professor Hanson for a preprint of this material.

4. I have developed a less familiar example from the same viewpoint in "The caloric theory of adiabatic compression," *Isis, 49,* 132 (1958). A closely similar analysis of the emergence of a new theory is included in the early pages of my essay "Conservation of energy as an example of simultaneous discovery," in *Critical Problems in the History of Science,* M. Clagett, Ed. (Univ. of Wisconsin Press, Madison, 1959), pp. 321–356. Reference to these papers may add depth and detail to the following discussion.

5. The still classic discussion of the discovery of oxygen is A. N. Meldrum, *The Eighteenth Century Revolution in Science—The First Phase* (Calcutta, 1930), chap. 5. A more convenient and generally quite reliable discussion is included in J. B. Conant, *The Overthrow of the Phlogiston Theory: The Chemical Revolution of 1775–1789,* "Harvard Case Histories in Experimental Science, Case 2" (Harvard Univ. Press, Cambridge, 1950). A more recent and indispensable review, which includes an account of the development of the priority controversy, is M. Daumas, *Lavoisier, théoricien et expérimentateur* (Paris, 1955), chaps. 2 and 3. H. Guerlac has added much significant detail to our knowledge of the early relations between Priestley and Lavoisier in his "Joseph Priestley's first papers on gases and their reception in France," *J. Hist. Med., 12,* 1 (1957), and in his very recent monograph, *Lavoisier—The Crucial Year* (Cornell Univ. Press, Ithaca, 1961). For Scheele see J. R. Partington, *A Short History of Chemistry* (London, 2nd ed., 1951), pp. 104–109.

6. For the dating of Scheele's work, see A. E. Nordenskiöld, Carl Wilhelm Scheele, *Nachgelassene Briefe und Aufzeichnungen* (Stockholm, 1892).

7. U. Bocklund ["A lost letter from Scheele to Lavoisier," *Lychnos* (1957–58), pp. 39–62] argues that Scheele communicated his discovery of oxygen to Lavoisier in a letter of Sept. 30, 1774. Certainly the letter is important, and it clearly demonstrates that Scheele was ahead of both Priestley and Lavoisier at the time it was written. But I think the letter is not quite so candid as Bocklund supposes, and I fail to see how Lavoisier could have drawn the discovery of oxygen from it. Scheele describes a procedure for reconstituting common air, not for produc-

ing a new gas, and that, as we shall see, is almost the same information that Lavoisier received from Priestley at about the same time. In any case, there is no evidence that Lavoisier performed the sort of experiment that Scheele suggested.

8. P. Bayen, "Essai d'expériences chymiques, faites sur quelques précipités de mercure, dans la vue de découvrir leur nature, Second partie." *Observations sur la physique* (1774), vol. 3, pp. 280–295, particularly pp. 289–291.

9. J. B. Conant (see 5, pp. 34–40).

10. A useful translation of the full text is available in Conant (see 5). For this description of the gas see p. 23.

11. For simplicity I use the term *red precipitate* throughout. Actually, Bayen used the precipitate; Priestley used both the precipitate and the oxide produced by direct calcination of mercury; and Lavoisier used only the latter. The difference is not without importance, for it was not unequivocally clear to chemists that the two substances were identical.

12. There has been some doubt about Priestley's having influenced Lavoisier's thinking at this point; but, when the latter returned to experimenting with the gas in February 1776, he recorded in his notebooks that he had obtained "l'air dephlogistique de M. Priestley" [M. Daumas (see 5, p. 36)].

13. J. R. Partington (see 5, p. 91).

14. For the traditional elements in Lavoisier's interpretations of chemical reactions, see H. Metzger, *La philosophie de la matière chez Lavoisier* (Paris, 1935), and Daumas (see 5, chap. 7).

15. P. Doig, *A Concise History of Astronomy* (Chapman, London, 1950), pp. 115–116.

16. L. W. Taylor, *Physics, the Pioneer Science* (Houghton Mifflin, Boston, 1941), p. 790.

17. Though the point cannot be argued here, the conditions which make the emergence of anomaly likely and those which make anomaly recognizable are to a very great extent the same. The fact may help us understand the extraordinarily large amount of *simultaneous discovery* in the sciences.

18. A useful sketch of the development of pneumatic chemistry is included in Partington (see 5, chap. 6).

19. R. Wolf, *Geschichte der Astronomie* (Munich, 1877), pp. 513–515, 683–693. The prephotographic discoveries of the asteroids is often seen as an effect of the invention of Bode's law. But that law cannot be the full explanation and may not even have played a large part. Piazzi's discovery of Ceres, in 1801, was made in ignorance of the current speculation about a missing planet in the "hole" between Mars and Jupiter. Instead, like Herschel, Piazzi was engaged on a star survey. More important, Bode's law was old by 1800 (R. Wolf, *ibid.*, p. 683), but only one man before that date seems to have thought it worthwhile to look for another planet. Finally, Bode's law, by itself, could only suggest the utility of looking for additional planets; it did not tell astronomers where to look. Clearly, however, the drive to look for additional planets dates from Herschel's work on Uranus.

20. For α-, β- and γ-radiation, discovery of which dates from 1896, see Taylor *16*, pp. 800–804. For the fourth new form of radiation, N-rays, see D. J. S. Price, *Science Since Babylon* (Yale Univ. Press, New Haven, 1961), pp. 84–89. That N-rays were ultimately the source of a scientific scandal does not make them less revealing of the scientific community's state of mind.

Feminism and Science

EVELYN FOX KELLER

Students familiar with the history of science may be able to recall the names of a few prominent female scientists (Marie Curie, Barbara McClintock, and others). But these women have been the exception rather than the rule. The vast majority of scientists have been men. Such is perhaps but a reflection of the sociopolitical climate that nurtured the discipline.

Regardless of the source, implications are potentially far-reaching. Male biases and perspectives may have influenced not only findings and theories, but perhaps basic principles governing research, testing, and evidence as well. As our social paradigm changes, it may be necessary to rethink the entire scientific enterprise. In the selection that follows, Evelyn Fox Keller attempts to reconcile her commitment to feminism with her career as a scientist.

In recent years, a new critique of science has begun to emerge from a number of feminist writings. The lens of feminist politics brings into focus certain masculinist distortions of the scientific enterprise, creating, for those of us who are scientists, a potential dilemma. Is there a conflict between our commitment to feminism and our commitment to science? As both a feminist and a scientist, I am more familiar than I might wish with the nervousness and defensiveness that such a potential conflict evokes. As scientists, we have very real difficulties in thinking about the kinds of issues that, as feminists, we have been raising. These difficulties may, however, ultimately be productive. My purpose in the present essay is to explore the implications of recent feminist criticism of science for the relationship between science and feminism. Do these criticisms imply conflict? If they do, how necessary is that conflict? I will argue that those elements of feminist criticism that seem to conflict most with at least conventional conceptions of science may, in fact, carry a liberating potential for science. It could therefore benefit scientists to attend closely to fem-inist criticism. I will suggest that we might even use feminist thought to illuminate and clarify part of the substructure of science (which may have been historically conditioned into distortion) in order to preserve the things that science has taught us, in order to be more objective. But first it is necessary to review the various criticisms that feminists have articulated.

The range of their critique is broad. Though they all claim that science embodies a strong androcentric bias, the meanings attached to this charge vary widely. It is convenient to represent the differences in meaning by a spectrum that parallels the political range characteristic of feminism as a whole. I label this spectrum from right to left, beginning somewhere left of center with what might be called the liberal position. From the liberal critique, charges of androcentricity emerge that are relatively easy to correct. The more radical critique calls for corre-

Evelyn Fox Keller, "Feminism and Science," *Signs* 7.3 (Spring 1982). Reprinted with the permission of The University of Chicago Press.

spondingly more radical changes; it requires a reexamination of the underlying assumptions of scientific theory and method for the presence of male bias. The difference between these positions is, however, often obscured by a knee-jerk reaction that leads many scientists to regard all such criticism as a unit—as a challenge to the neutrality of science. One of the points I wish to emphasize here is that the range of meanings attributed to the claim of androcentric bias reflects very different levels of challenge, some of which even the most conservative scientists ought to be able to accept.

First, in what I have called the liberal critique, is the charge that is essentially one of unfair employment practices. It proceeds from the observation that almost all scientists are men. This criticism is liberal in the sense that it in no way conflicts either with traditional conceptions of science or with current liberal, egalitarian politics. It is, in fact, a purely political criticism, and one which can be supported by all of us who are in favor of equal opportunity. According to this point of view, science itself would in no way be affected by the presence or absence of women.

A slightly more radical criticism continues from this and argues that the predominance of men in the sciences has led to a bias in the choice and definition of problems with which scientists have concerned themselves. This argument is most frequently and most easily made in regard to the health sciences. It is claimed, for example, that contraception has not been given the scientific attention its human importance warrants and that, furthermore, the attention it has been given has been focused primarily on contraceptive techniques to be used by women. In a related complaint, feminists argue that menstrual cramps, a serious problem for many women, have never been taken seriously by the medical profession. Presumably, had the concerns of medical research been articulated by women, these particular imbalances would not have arisen.[1] Similar biases in sciences remote from the subject of women's bodies are more difficult to locate—they may, however, exist. Even so,

this kind of criticism does not touch our conception of what science is, nor our confidence in the neutrality of science. It may be true that in some areas we have ignored certain problems, but our definition of science does not include the choice of problem—that, we can readily agree, has always been influenced by social forces. We remain, therefore, in the liberal domain.

Continuing to the left, we next find claims of bias in the actual design and interpretation of experiments. For example, it is pointed out that virtually all of the animal-learning research on rats has been performed with male rats.[2] Though a simple explanation is offered—namely, that female rats have a four-day cycle that complicates experiments—the criticism is hardly vitiated by the explanation. The implicit assumption is, of course, that the male rat represents the species. There exist many other, often similar, examples in psychology. Examples from the biological sciences are somewhat more difficult to find, though one suspects that they exist. An area in which this suspicion is particularly strong is that of sex research. Here the influence of heavily invested preconceptions seems all but inevitable. In fact, although the existence of such preconceptions has been well documented historically,[3] a convincing case for the existence of a corresponding bias in either the design or interpretation of experiments has yet to be made. That this is so can, I think, be taken as testimony to the effectiveness of the standards of objectivity operating.

But evidence for bias in the interpretation of observations and experiments is very easy to find in the more socially oriented sciences. The area of primatology is a familiar target. Over the past fifteen years women working in the field have undertaken an extensive reexamination of theoretical concepts, often using essentially the same methodological tools. These efforts have resulted in some radically different formulations. The range of difference frequently reflects the powerful influence of ordinary language in biasing our theoretical formulations. A great deal of very interesting work analyzing such distortions has been done.[4] Though I cannot begin to do justice to that work here, let me offer, as a single example, the following description of a single-male troop of animals that Jane Lancaster provides as a substitute for the familiar concept of "harem": "For a female, males are a resource in her environment which she may use to further the survival of herself and her offspring. If environmental conditions are such that the male role can be minimal, a one-male group is likely. Only one male is necessary for a group of females if his only role is to impregnate them."[5]

These critiques, which maintain that a substantive effect on scientific theory results from the predominance of men in the field, are almost exclusively aimed at the "softer," even the "softest," sciences. Thus they can still be accommodated within the traditional framework by the simple argument that the critiques, if justified, merely reflect the fact that these subjects are not sufficiently scientific. Presumably, fair-minded (or scientifically minded) scientists can and should join forces with the feminists in attempting to identify the presence of bias—equally offensive, if for different reasons, to both scientists and feminists—in order to make these "soft" sciences more rigorous.

It is much more difficult to deal with the truly radical critique that attempts to locate androcentric bias even in the "hard" sciences, indeed in scientific ideology itself. This range of criticism takes us out of the liberal domain and requires us to question the very assumptions of objectivity and rationality that underlie the scientific enterprise. To challenge the truth and necessity of the conclusions of natural science on the grounds that they too reflect the judgement of men is to take the Galilean credo and turn it on its head. It is not true that "the conclusions of natural science are true and necessary, and the judgement of man has nothing to do with them";[6] it is the judgment of woman that they have nothing to do with.

The impetus behind this radical move is twofold. First, it is supported by the experience of feminist scholars in other fields of inquiry. Over and over, feminists have found it necessary, in seeking to reinstate women as agents and as subjects, to question the very canons of their fields. They have turned their attention, accordingly, to the operation of patriarchal bias on ever deeper levels of social structure, even of language and thought.

But the possibility of extending the feminist critique into the foundations of scientific thought is created by recent developments in the history and philosophy of science itself.[7] As long as the course of scientific thought was judged to be exclusively determined by its own logical and empirical necessities, there could be no place for any signature, male or otherwise, in that system of knowledge. Furthermore, any suggestion of gender differences in our thinking about the world could argue only too readily for the further exclusion of women from science. But as the philosophical and historical inadequacies of the classical conception of science have become more evident, and as historians and sociologists have begun to identify the ways in which the development of scientific knowledge has been shaped by its particular social and political context, our understanding of science as a social process has grown. This understanding is a necessary prerequisite, both politically and intellectually, for a feminist theoretic in science.

Joining feminist thought to other social studies of science brings the promise of radically new insights, but it also adds to the existing intellectual danger of a political threat. The intellectual danger resides in viewing science as pure social product; science then dissolves into ideology and objectivity loses all intrinsic meaning. In the resulting cultural relativism, any emancipatory function of modern science is negated, and the arbitration of truth recedes into the political domain.[8] Against this background, the temptation arises for feminists to abandon their claim for representation in scientific culture and, in its place, to invite a return to a purely "female" subjectivity, leaving rationality and objectivity in the male domain, dismissed as products of a purely male consciousness.[9]

Many authors have addressed the problems raised by total relativism;[10] here I wish merely to mention some of the special problems added by its feminist variant. They are several. In important respects, feminist relativism is just the kind of radical move that transforms the political spectrum into a circle. By rejecting objectivity as a masculine ideal, it simultaneously lends its voice to an enemy chorus and dooms women to residing outside of the realpolitik modern culture; it exacerbates the very problem it wishes to solve. It also nullifies the radical potential of feminist criticism for our understanding of science. As I see it, the task of a feminist theoretic in science is twofold: to distinguish that which is parochial from that which is universal in the scientific impulse, reclaiming for women what has historically been denied to them; and to legitimate those elements of scientific culture that have been denied precisely because they are defined as female.

It is important to recognize that the framework inviting what might be called the nihilist retreat is in fact provided by the very ideology of objectivity we wish to escape. This is the ideology that asserts an opposition between (male) objectivity and (female) subjectivity and denies the possibility of mediation between the two. A first step, therefore, in extending the feminist critique to the foundations of scientific thought is to reconceptualize objectivity as a dialectical process so as to allow for the possibility of distinguishing the objective effort from the objectivist illusion. As Piaget reminds us:

> Objectivity consists in so fully realizing the countless intrusions of the self in everyday thought and the countless illusions which result—illusions of sense, language, point of view, value, etc.—that the preliminary step to every judgement is the effort to exclude the intrusive self. Realism, on the contrary, consists in ignoring the existence of self and thence regarding one's own perspective as immediately objective and absolute. Realism is thus anthropocentric illusion, finality—in short, all those illusions which teem in the history of science. So long as thought has not become conscious of self, it is a prey to perpetual confusions between objective and subjective, between the real and the ostensible.[11]

In short, rather than abandon the quintessentially human effort to understand the world in rational terms, we need to refine that effort. To do this, we need to add to the familiar methods of rational and empirical inquiry the additional process of critical self-reflection. Following Piaget's injunction, we need to "become conscious of self." In this way, we can become conscious of the features of the scientific project that belie its claim to universality.

The ideological ingredients of particular concern to feminists are found where objectivity is linked with autonomy and masculinity, and in turn, the goals of science with power and domination. The linking of objectivity with social and political autonomy has been examined by many authors and shown to serve a variety of important political functions.[12] The implications of joining objectivity with masculinity are less well understood. This conjunction also serves critical political functions. But an understanding of the sociopolitical meaning of the entire constellation requires an examination of the psychological processes through which these connections become internalized and perpetuated. Here psychoanalysis offers us an invaluable perspective, and it is to the exploitation of that perspective that much of my own work has been directed. In an earlier paper, I tried to show how psychoanalytic theories of development illuminate the structure and meaning of an interacting system of associations linking objectivity (a cognitive trait) with autonomy (an affective trait) and masculinity (a gender trait).[13] Here, after a brief summary of my earlier argument, I want to explore the relation of this system to power and domination.

Along with Nancy Chodorow and Dorothy Dinnerstein, I have found that branch of psychoanalytic theory known as object relations theory to be especially useful.[14] In seeking to account for personality development in terms of both innate drives and actual relations with other objects (i.e., subjects), it permits us to understand the ways in which our earliest experiences—experiences in large part determined by the socially structured relationships that form the context of our developmental processes—help to shape our conception of the world and our characteristic orientations to it. In particular, our first steps in the world are guided primarily by the parents of one sex—our mothers; this determines a maturational framework for our emotional, cognitive, and gender development, a framework later filled in by cultural expectations.

In brief, I argued the following: Our early maternal environment, coupled with the cultural definition of masculine (that which can never appear feminine) and of autonomy (that which can never be compromised by dependency) leads to the association of female with the pleasures and dangers of merging, and of male with the comfort and loneliness of separateness. The boy's internal anxiety about both self and gender is echoed by the more widespread cultural anxiety, thereby encouraging postures of autonomy and masculinity, which can, indeed may, be designed to defend against that anxiety and the longing that generates it. Finally, for all of us, our sense of reality is carved out of the same developmental matrix. As Piaget and others have emphasized, the capacity for cognitive distinctions between self and other (objectivity) evolves concurrently and interdependently with the development of psychic autonomy; our cognitive ideals thereby become subject to the same psychological influences as our emotional and gender ideals. Along with autonomy the very act of separating subject from object—objectivity itself—comes to be associated with masculinity. The combined psychological and cultural pressures lead all three ideals—affective, gender, and cognitive—to a mutually reinforcing process of exaggeration and rigidification.[15] The net result is the entrenchment of an objectivist ideology and a correlative devaluation of (female) subjectivity.

This analysis leaves out many things. Above all it omits discussion of the psychological meanings of power and domination, and it is to those meanings I now wish to turn. Central to object relations theory is the recognition that the condition of psychic autonomy is double edged: it offers a profound source of pleasure, and simultaneously of potential dread.

The values of autonomy are consonant with the values of competence, of mastery. Indeed competence is itself a prior condition for autonomy and serves immeasurably to confirm one's sense of self. But need the development of competence and the sense of mastery lead to a state of alienated selfhood, of denied connectedness, of defensive separateness? To forms of autonomy that can be understood as protections against dread? Object relations theory makes us sensitive to autonomy's range of meanings; it simultaneously suggests the need to consider the corresponding meanings of competence. Under what circumstances does competence imply mastery of one's own fate and under what circumstances does it imply mastery over anxiety? In short, are control and domination essential ingredients of competence, and intrinsic to selfhood, or are they correlates of an alienated selfhood?

One way to answer these questions is to use the logic of analysis summarized above to examine the shift from competence to power and control in the psychic economy of the young child. From that analysis, the impulse toward domination can be understood as a natural concomitant of defensive separateness—as Jessica Benjamin has written, "A way of repudiating sameness, dependency and closeness with another person, while attempting to avoid the consequent feelings of aloneness."[16] Perhaps no one has written more sensitively than psychoanalyst D. W. Winnicott of the rough waters the child must travel in negotiating the transition from symbiotic union to the recognition of self and other as autonomous entities. He alerts us to a danger that others have missed—a danger arising from the unconscious fantasy that the subject has actually destroyed the object in the process of becoming separate.

Indeed, he writes, "It is the destruction of the object that places the object outside the area of control. . . . After 'subject relates to object' comes 'subject destroys object' (as it becomes external); then may come 'object survives destruction by the subject.' But there may or may not be survival." When there is, "because of the survival of the object, the subject may now have started to live a life in the world of objects, and so the subject stands to gain immeasurably; but the price has to be paid in acceptance of the ongoing destruction in unconscious fantasy relative to object-relating."[17] Winnicott, of course, is not speaking of actual survival but of subjective confidence in the survival of the other. Survival in that sense requires that the child maintain relatedness; failure induces inevitable guilt and dread. The child is poised on a terrifying precipice. On one side lies the fear of having destroyed the object, on the other side, loss of self. The child may make an attempt to secure this precarious position by seeking to master the other. The cycles of destruction and survival are reenacted while the other is kept safely at bay, and as Benjamin writes, "the original self-assertion is . . . converted from innocent mastery to mastery over and against the other."[18] In psychodynamic terms, this particular resolution of preoedipal conflicts is a product of oedipal consolidation. The (male) child achieves his final security by identification with the father—an identification involving simultaneously a denial of the mother and a transformation of guilt and fear into aggression.

Aggression, of course, has many meanings, many sources, and many forms of expression. Here I mean to refer only to the form underlying the impulse toward domination. I invoke psychoanalytic theory to help illuminate the forms of expression that impulse finds in science as a whole, and its relation to objectification in particular. The same question I asked about the child I can also ask about science. Under what circumstances is scientific knowledge sought for the pleasures of knowing, for the increased competence it grants us, for the increased mastery (real or imagined) over our own fate, and under what circumstances is it fair to say that science seeks actually to dominate nature? Is there a meaningful distinction to be made here?

In his work *The Domination of Nature* William Leiss observes, "The necessary correlate of domination is the consciousness of subordination in those who must obey the will of another; thus properly speaking only other men can be the objects of dom-

ination."[19] (Or women, we might add.) Leiss infers from this observation that it is not the domination of physical nature we should worry about but the use of our knowledge of physical nature as an instrument for the domination of human nature. He therefore sees the need for correctives, not in science but in its uses. This is his point of departure from other authors of the Frankfurt school, who assume the very logic of science to be the logic of domination. I agree with Leiss's basic observation but draw a somewhat different inference. I suggest that the impulse toward domination does find expression in the goals (and even in the theories and practice) of modern science, and argue that where it finds such expression the impulse needs to be acknowledged as projection. In short, I argue that not only in the denial of interaction between subject and other but also in the access of domination to the goals of scientific knowledge, one finds the intrusion of a self we begin to recognize as partaking in the cultural construct of masculinity.

The value of consciousness is that it enables us to make choices—both as individuals and as scientists. Control and domination are in fact intrinsic neither to selfhood (i.e., autonomy) nor to scientific knowledge. I want to suggest, rather, that the particular emphasis Western science has placed on these functions of knowledge is twin to the objectivist ideal. Knowledge in general, and scientific knowledge in particular, serves two gods: power and transcendence. It aspires alternately to mastery over and union with nature.[20] Sexuality serves the same two gods, aspiring to domination and ecstatic communion—in short, aggression and eros. And it is hardly a new insight to say that power, control, and domination are fueled largely by aggression, while union satisfies a more purely erotic impulse.

To see the emphasis on power and control so prevalent in the rhetoric of Western science as projection of a specifically male consciousness requires no great leap of the imagination. Indeed, that perception has become a commonplace. Above all, it is invited by the rhetoric that conjoins the domination of nature with the insistent image of nature as female, nowhere more familiar than in the writings of Francis Bacon. For Bacon, knowledge and power are one, and the promise of science is expressed as "leading to you Nature with all her children to bind her to your service and make her your slave,"[21] by means that do not "merely exert a gentle guidance over nature's course; they have the power to conquer and subdue her, to shake her to her foundations."[22] In the context of the Baconian vision, Bruno Bettelheim's conclusion appears inescapable: "Only with phallic psychology did aggressive manipulation of nature become possible."[23]

The view of science as an oedipal project is also familiar from the writings of Herbert Marcuse and Norman O. Brown.[24] But Brown's preoccupation, as well as Marcuse's, is with what Brown calls a "morbid" science. Accordingly, for both authors the quest for a nonmorbid science, an "erotic" science, remains a romantic one. This is so because their picture of science is incomplete: it omits from consideration the crucial, albeit less visible, erotic components already present in the scientific tradition. Our own quest, if it is to be realistic rather than romantic, must be based on a richer understanding of the scientific tradition, in all its dimensions, and on an understanding of the ways in which this complex, dialectical tradition becomes transformed into a monolithic rhetoric. Neither the oedipal child nor modern science has in fact managed to rid itself of its preoedipal and fundamentally bisexual yearnings. It is with this recognition that the quest for a different science, a science undistorted by masculinist bias, must begin.

The presence of contrasting themes, of a dialectic between aggressive and erotic impulses, can be seen both within the work of individual scientists and, even more dramatically, in the juxtaposed writings of different scientists. Francis Bacon provides us with one model;[25] there are many others. For an especially striking contrast, consider a contemporary scientist who insists on the importance of "letting the material speak to you," of allowing it to "tell you what to do next"—one who chastises other scientists for attempting to "impose an answer" on what they see. For this scientist, discovery is facilitated by becoming "part of the system," rather than remaining outside; one must have a "feeling for the organism."[26] It is true that the author of these remarks is not only from a different epoch and a different field (Bacon himself was not actually a scientist by most standards), she is also a woman. It is also true that there are many reasons, some of which I have already suggested, for thinking that gender (itself constructed in an ideological context) actually does make a difference in scientific inquiry. Nevertheless, my point here is that neither science nor individuals are totally bound by ideology. In fact, it is not difficult to find similar sentiments expressed by male scientists. Consider for example, the following remarks: "I have often had cause to feel that my hands are cleverer than my head. That is a crude way of characterizing the dialectics of experimentation. When it is going well, it is like a quiet conversation with Nature."[27] The difference between conceptions of science as "dominating" and as "conversing with" nature may not be a difference primarily between epochs, nor between the sexes. Rather, it can be seen as representing a dual theme played out in the work of all scientists, in all ages. But the two poles of this dialectic do not appear with equal weight in the history of science. What we therefore need to attend to is the evolutionary process that selects one theme as dominant.

Elsewhere I have argued for the importance of a different selection process.[28] In part, scientists are themselves selected by the emotional appeal of particular (stereotypic) images of science. Here I am arguing for the importance of selection within scientific thought—first of preferred methodologies and aims, and finally of preferred theories. The two processes are not unrelated. While stereotypes are not binding (i.e., they do not describe all or perhaps any individuals), and this fact creates the possibility for an ongoing contest within science, the first selection process undoubtedly influences the outcome of the second. That is, individuals drawn by a particular ideology will tend to select themes consistent with that ideology.

One example in which this process is played out on a theoretical level is in the fate of interactionist theories in the history of biology. Consider the contest that has raged throughout this century between organismic and particulate views of cellular organization—between what might be described as hierarchical and nonhierarchical theories. Whether the debate is over the primacy of the nucleus or the cell as a whole, the genome or the cytoplasm, the proponents of hierarchy have won out. One geneticist has described the conflict in explicitly political terms:

> Two concepts of genetic mechanisms have persisted side by side throughout the growth of modern genetics, but the emphasis has been very strongly in favor of one of these. . . . The first of these we will designate as the "Master Molecule" concept. . . . This is in essence the Theory of the Gene, interpreted to suggest a totalitarian government. . . . The second concept we will designate as the "Steady State" concept. By this term . . . we envision a dynamic self-perpetuating organization of a variety of molecular species which owes its specific properties not to the characteristic of any one kind of molecule, but to the functional interrelationships of these molecular species.[29]

Soon after these remarks, the debate between "master molecules" and dynamic interactionism was foreclosed by the synthesis provided by DNA and the "central dogma." With the success of the new molecular biology such "steady state" (or egalitarian) theories lost interest for almost all geneticists. But today, the same conflict shows signs of reemerging—in genetics, in theories of the immune system, and in theories of development.

I suggest that method and theory may constitute a natural continuum, despite Popperian claims to the contrary, and that the same processes of selection may bear equally and simultaneously on both the means and aims of science and the actual theoretical descriptions that emerge. I suggest this in part because of the recurrent and striking consonance that can be seen in the way scientists work, the relation they take to their object of study, and the theoretical orientation they favor. To pursue the example cited earlier, the same scientist who allowed herself to become "part of the system" whose investigations were guided by a "feeling for the organism," developed a paradigm that diverged as radically from the dominant paradigm of her field as did her methodological style.

In lieu of the linear hierarchy described by the central dogma of molecular biology, in which the DNA encodes and transmits all instructions for the unfolding of a living cell, her research yielded a view of the DNA in delicate interaction with the cellular environment—an organismic view. Far more important than the genome as such (i.e., the DNA) is the "overall organism." As she sees it, the genome functions "only in respect to the environment in which it is found."[30] In this work the program encoded by the DNA is itself subject to change. No longer is a master control to be found in a single component of the cell; rather, control resides in the complex interactions of the entire system. When first presented, the work underlying this vision was not understood, and it was poorly received.[31] Today much of the work is undergoing a renaissance, although it is important to say that her full vision remains too radical for most biologists to accept.[32]

This example suggests that we need not rely on our imagination for a vision of what a different science—a science less restrained by the impulse to dominate—might be like. Rather, we need only look to the thematic pluralism in the history of our own science as it has evolved. Many other examples can be found, but we lack an adequate understanding of the full range of influences that lead to the acceptance or rejection not only of particular theories but of different theoretical orientations. What I am suggesting is that if certain theoretical interpretations have been selected against, it is precisely in this process of selection that ideology in general, and a masculinist ideology in particular, can be found to effect its influence. The task this implies for a radical feminist critique of science is, then, first a historical one, but finally a transformative one. In the historical effort, feminists can bring a whole new range of sensitivities, leading to an equally new consciousness of the potentialities lying latent in the scientific project.

Notes

1. Notice that the claim is not that the mere presence of women in medical research is sufficient to right such imbalances, for it is understood how readily women, or any "outsiders" for that matter, come to internalize the concerns and values of a world to which they aspire to belong.

2. I would like to thank Lila Braine for calling this point to my attention.

3. D. L. Hall and Diana Long, "The Social Implications of the Scientific Study of Sex," *Scholar and the Feminist* 4 (1977): 11–21.

4. See, e.g., Donna Haraway, "Animal Sociology and a Natural Economy of the Body Politic, Part I: A Political Physiology of Dominance"; and "Animal Sociology and a Natural Economy of the Body Politic, Part II: The Past Is the Contested Zone: Human Nature and Theories of Production and Reproduction in Primate Behavior Studies," *Signs: Journal of Women in Culture and Society* 4, no. 1 (Autumn 1978): 21–60.

5. Jane Lancaster, *Primate Behavior and the Emergence of Human Culture* (New York: Holt, Rinehart & Winston, 1975), p. 34.

6. Galileo Galilei, *Dialogue on the Great World Systems,* trans. T. Salusbury, ed. G. de Santillana (Chicago: University of Chicago Press, 1953), p. 63.

7. The work of Russell Hanson and Thomas S. Kuhn was of pivotal importance in opening up our understanding of scientific thought to a consideration of social, psychological, and political influences.

8. See, e.g., Paul Feyerabend, *Against Method* (London: New Left Books, 1975); and *Science in a Free Society* (London: New Left Books, 1978).

9. This notion is expressed most strongly by some of the new French feminists (see Elaine Marks and Isabelle de Courtivron, eds., *New French Feminisms: An Anthology* [Amherst: University of Massachusetts Press, 1980]), and is currently surfacing in the writings of some American feminists. See, e.g., Susan Griffin, *Woman and Nature: The Roaring Inside Her* (New York: Harper & Row, 1978).

10. See, e.g., Steven Rose and Hilary Rose, "Radical Science and Its Enemies," *Socialist Register 1979,* ed. Ralph Miliband and John Saville (Atlantic Highlands, NJ: Humanities Press, 1979), pp. 317–35. A number of the points made here have also been made by Elizabeth Fee in "Is Feminism a Threat to Objectivity?" (paper presented at the American Association for Advancement of Science meeting, Toronto, January 4, 1981).

11. Jean Piaget, *The Child's Conception of the World* (Totowa, NJ: Littlefield, Adams & Co., 1972).

12. Jerome R. Ravetz, *Scientific Knowledge and Its Social Problems* (London: Oxford University Press, 1971); and Hilary Rose and Steven Rose, *Science and Society* (London: Allen Lane, 1969).

13. Evelyn Fox Keller, "Gender and Science," *Psychoanalysis and Contemporary Thought* 1 (1978): 409–33.

14. Nancy Chodorow, *The Reproduction of Mothering: Psychoanalysis and the Sociology of Gender* (Berkeley: University of California Press, 1978); and Dorothy Dinnerstein, *The Mermaid and the Minotaur: Sexual Arrangements and Human Malaise* (New York: Harper & Row, 1976).

15. For a fuller development of this argument, see n. 12 above. By focusing on the contributions

of individual psychology, I in no way mean to imply a simple division of individual and social factors, or to set them up as alternative influences. Individual psychological traits evolve in a social system and, in turn, social systems reward and select for particular sets of individual traits. Thus if particular options in science reflect certain kinds of psychological impulses or personality traits, it must be understood that it is in a distinct social framework that those options, rather than others, are selected.

16. Jessica Benjamin has discussed this same issue in an excellent analysis of the place of domination in sexuality. See "The Bonds of Love: Rational Violence and Erotic Domination," *Feminist Studies* 6, no. 1 (Spring 1980): 144–74, esp. 150.

17. D. W. Winnicott, *Playing and Reality* (New York: Basic Books, 1971), pp. 89–90.

18. Benjamin, p. 165.

19. William Leiss, *The Domination of Nature* (Boston: Beacon Press, 1974), p. 122.

20. For a discussion of the different roles these two impulses play in Platonic and in Baconian images of knowledge, see Evelyn Fox Keller, "Nature as 'Her'" (paper delivered at the Second Sex Conference, New York Institute for the Humanities, September 1979).

21. B. Farrington, "*Temporis Partus Masculus:* An Untranslated Writing of Francis Bacon," *Centaurus* 1 (1951): 193–205, esp. 197.

22. Francis Bacon, "Description of the Intellectual Globe," in *The Philosophical Works of Francis Bacon*, ed. J. H. Robertson (London: Routledge & Sons, 1905), p. 506.

23. Quoted in Norman O. Brown, *Life Against Death* (New York: Random House, 1959), p. 280.

24. Brown; and Herbert Marcuse, *One Dimensional Man* (Boston: Beacon Press, 1964).

25. For a discussion of the presence of the same dialectic in the writings of Francis Bacon, see Evelyn Fox Keller, "Baconian Science: A Hermaphrodite Birth," *Philosophical Forum* 11, no. 3 (Spring 1980): 299–308.

26. Barbara McClintock, private interviews, December 1, 1978, and January 13, 1979.

27. G. Wald, "The Molecular Basis of Visual Excitation," *Les Prix Nobel en 1967* (Stockholm: Kungliga Boktryckerlet, 1968), p. 260.

28. Keller, "Gender and Science."

29. D. L. Nanney, "The Role of the Cyctoplasm in Heredity," in *The Chemical Basis of Heredity,* ed. William D. McElroy and Bentley Glass (Baltimore: Johns Hopkins University Press, 1957), p. 136.

30. McClintock, December 1, 1978.

31. McClintock, "Chromosome Organization and Genic Expression," *Cold Spring Harbor Symposium of Quantitative Biology* 16 (1951): 13–44.

32. McClintock's most recent publication on this subject is "Modified Gene Expressions Induced by Transposable Elements," in *Mobilization and Reassembly of Genetic Information,* ed. W. A. Scott, R. Werner, and J. Schultz (New York: Academic Press, 1980).

Bathybius Meets Eozoon

STEPHEN JAY GOULD

Stephen Jay Gould teaches biology, geology, and the history of science at Harvard University. A prolific writer, his many books include *Ever Since Darwin* (1977), *The Panda's Thumb* (1980), *The Mismeasure of Man* (1988), *Hen's Teeth and Horse's Toes* (1984), and *Eight Little Piggies* (1993). In the following selection, taken from his monthly column in *Natural History,* Professor Gould demonstrates that the findings of science depend as much on the hopes and expectations of scientists as they do on the properties of the data.

Early evolutionists thought these imaginary creatures must exist, so they found them.

When Thomas Huxley lost his young son, "our delight and our joy," to scarlet fever, Charles Kingsley tried to console him with a long peroration on the soul's immortality. Huxley, who invented the word "agnostic" to describe his own feelings, thanked Kingsley for his concern, but rejected the proferred comfort for want of evidence. In a famous passage, since taken by many scientists as a motto for proper action, he wrote: "My business is to teach my aspirations to conform themselves to fact, not to try and make facts harmonize with my aspirations. . . . Sit down before fact as a little child, be prepared to give up every preconceived notion, follow humbly wherever and to whatever abysses nature leads, or you shall learn nothing." Huxley's sentiments were noble, his grief affecting. But Huxley did not follow his own dictum, and no creative scientist ever has.

Great thinkers are never passive before facts. They ask questions of nature; they do not follow her humbly. They have hopes and hunches, and they try hard to construct the world in their light. Hence, great thinkers also make great errors.

Biologists have inspired a long and special chapter in the catalog of major mistakes—imaginary animals that should exist in theory. Voltaire spoke truly when he quipped: "If God did not exist, it would be necessary to invent him." Two related and intersecting chimeras arose during the early days of evolutionary theory—two animals that should have been, by Darwin's criteria, but were not. One of them had Thomas Henry Huxley for a godfather.

For most creationists, the gap between living and nonliving posed no special problem. God had simply made the living, fully distinct and more advanced than the rocks and chemicals. Evolutionists sought to close all the gaps. Ernst Haeckel, Darwin's chief defender in Germany and surely the most speculative and imaginative of early evolutionists, constructed hypothetical organisms to span all the spaces. The lowly amoeba could not serve as a model of the earliest life, for its internal differentiation into nucleus and cytoplasm indicated a large advance from primal formlessness. Thus Haeckel proposed a lowlier organism composed only of unorganized protoplasm, the Monera. (In a way, he was right. We use his name today for the kingdom of bacteria and blue-green algae, organisms without nucleus or mitochondria—although scarcely formless in Haeckel's sense.)

Haeckel defined his moneran as "an entirely homogeneous and structureless substance, a living particle of albumin, capable of nourishment and reproduction." He proposed a moneran as an intermediate form between the nonliving and living. He hoped that it would solve the vexing question of life's origin from the inorganic, for no problem seemed thornier for evolutionists and no issue attracted more rear-guard support for creationism than the apparent gap between the most complex chemicals and the simplest organisms. Haeckel wrote: "Every true cell already shows a division into two different parts, i.e., nucleus and plasm. The immediate production of such an object from spontaneous generation is obviously only conceivable with difficulty; but it is much easier to conceive of the production of an entirely homogeneous, organic substance, such as the structureless albumin body of the Monera."

During the 1860s, the identification of monerans assumed high priority on the agenda of Darwin's champions. And the more structureless and diffuse the moneran, the better. Huxley had told Kingsley that he would follow facts into a metaphorical abyss. But when he examined a true abyss in 1868, his prior hopes and expectations guided his observations. He studied some mud samples dredged from the sea bottom northwest of Ireland ten years before. He observed an inchoate, gelatinous substance in the samples. Embedded in it were tiny, circular, calcareous plates called coccoliths. Huxley identified his jelly as the heralded, formless moneran and the coccoliths as its primordial skeleton. (We now know that coccoliths are fragments of algal skeletons, which sink to the ocean bottom following the death of their planktonic producers.) Honoring Haeckel's prediction, he named it *Bathybius Haeckelii.* "I hope that you will not be ashamed of your godchild," he wrote to Haeckel. Haeckel replied that he was "very proud," and ended his note with a rallying cry: "Viva Monera."

Since nothing is quite so convincing as an anticipated discovery, *Bathybius* began to crop up everywhere. Sir Charles Wyville Thompson dredged a sample from the depths of the Atlantic and wrote: "The mud was actually alive; it stuck together in lumps, as if there were white of egg mixed with it: and the glairy mass proved, under the microscope, to be a living sarcode. Prof. Huxley . . . calls it *Bathybius.*" (The Sarcodina are a group of single-celled protozoans.) Haeckel, following his usual penchant, soon generalized and imagined that the entire ocean floor (below 5,000 feet) lay covered with a pulsating film of living *Bathybius,* the *Urschleim* (original slime) of the romantic nature philosophers (Goethe was one) idolized by Haeckel during his youth. Huxley, departing from his usual sobriety, delivered a speech in 1870 and proclaimed: "The *Bathybius* formed a living scum of film on the seabed, extending over thousands upon thousands of square miles . . . it probably forms one continuous scum of living matter girding the whole surface of the earth."

Having reached its limits of extension in space, *Bathybius* oozed out to conquer the only realm left—time. And here it met our second chimera. A tale writ larger than life, tailor-made for Hollywood as "*Bathybius* meets *Eozoon.*"

Eozoon canadense, the dawn animal of Canada, was another organism whose time had come. The fossil record had caused Darwin more grief than joy. He balked particularly at the Cambrian explosion, the coincident appearance of almost all complex organic designs, not near the beginning of the earth's history, but more than five-sixths of the way through it.

. . . His opponents took this explosion as the moment of creation, for not a single trace of Precambrian life had been discovered when Darwin wrote the *Origin of Species. . . .* Nothing could have been more welcome than a Precambrian organism, the simpler and more formless the better.

In 1858 a collector for the Geological Survey of Canada found some curious specimens among the world's oldest rocks. They were made of thin, concentric layers, alternating between serpentine (a silicate) and calcium carbonate. Sir William Logan, director of the Survey, thought that they might be fossils and displayed them to various scientists, receiving in return little encouragement for his views.

Logan found some better specimens near Ottawa in 1864, and brought them to Canada's leading paleontologist, J. William Dawson, the principal of McGill University. Dawson found "organic" structures in his microscopic slides, most notably a canal system in the calcite, and identified the concentric layering as the skeleton of a giant foraminifer, more diffusely formed but hundreds of times larger than any modern relative. He named it *Eozoon canadense*.

Darwin was delighted. *Eozoon* entered the fourth edition of the *Origin of Species* with Darwin's firm blessing: "It is impossible to feel any doubt regarding its organic nature." (Ironically, Dawson himself was a staunch creationist, probably the last prominent holdout against the Darwinian tide. As late as 1897, he wrote *Relics of Primeval Life,* a book about *Eozoon.* In it he argues that the persistence of simple Foraminifera throughout geologic time disproves natural selection since any struggle for existence would replace such lowly creatures with something more exalted.)

Bathybius and *Eozoon* were destined for union. They shared the desired property of diffuse formlessness and differed only in *Eozoon*'s discrete skeleton. Either *Eozoon* had lost its shell to become *Bathybius* or the two primordial forms were closely related as exemplars of organic simplicity. The great physiologist W. B. Carpenter, a champion of both creatures, wrote:

> If *Bathybius* . . . could form for itself a shelly envelope, that envelope would closely resemble *Eozoon.* Further, as Prof. Huxley has proved the existence of *Bathybius* through a great range not merely of depth but of temperature, I cannot but think it probable that it has existed continuously in the deep seas of all geological epochs. . . . I am fully prepared to believe that *Eozoon,* as well as *Bathybius,* may have maintained its existence through the whole duration of geological time.

A vision to titillate any evolutionist. The anticipated, formless organic matter had been found, and it extended throughout time and space to cover the floor of the mysterious and primal ocean bottom.

Before I chronicle the downfall of both creatures, I want to identify a bias that lay unstated and undefended in all the primary literature. All of the participants in the debate accepted without question the "obvious" truth that the most primitive life would be homogeneous and formless, diffuse and inchoate.

Carpenter wrote that *Bathybius* was "a type even lower, *because less definite,* than that of Sponges." Haeckel declared that "protoplasm exists here in its simplest and earliest form, i.e., it has scarcely individualized." Huxley proclaimed that life without the internal complexity of a nucleus proved that organization arose from indefinite vitality, not vice versa: *Bathybius* "proves the absence of any mysterious power in nuclei, and shows that life is a property of the molecules of living matter, and that organization is the result of life, not life the result of organization."

But why, when we think about it, should we equate formless with primitive? Modern organisms encourage no such view. Viruses are scarcely matched for regularity and repetition of form. The simplest bacteria have definite shapes. The taxonomic group that houses the amoeba, that prototype of slithering disorganization, also accommodates the Radiolaria, the most beautiful and most complexly sculpted of all regular organisms. DNA is a miracle of organization; Watson and Crick elucidated its structure by building an accurate Tinkertoy model and making sure that all the pieces fit. I would not assert any mystical Pythagorean notion that regular form underlies all organization, but I would argue that equation of primitive with formless has roots in the outdated progressivist metaphor that views organic history as a ladder leading inexorably through all the stages of complexity from nothingness to our own noble form. Good for the ego to be sure, but not a very good outline of our world.

In any case, neither *Bathybius* nor *Eozoon* outlived Queen Victoria. The same Sir Charles Wyville Thompson who had spoken so glowingly of *Bathybius* as a "glairy mass . . . actually alive" later became chief scientist of the *Challenger* expedition during the 1870s, the most famous of all scientific voyages to explore the world's oceans. The *Challenger* scientists tried again and again to find *Bathybius* in fresh samples of deep-sea mud, but with no success.

When mud samples were stored for later analysis, scientists traditionally added alcohol to preserve organic material. Huxley's original specimens of *Bathybius* had come from samples stored with alcohol for more than a decade. One member of the *Challenger* expedition noticed that *Bathybius* appeared whenever he added alcohol to a fresh sample. The expedition's chemist then analyzed *Bathybius* and found it to be no more than a colloidal precipitate of calcium sulfate, a product of the reaction of mud with alcohol. Thompson wrote to Huxley, and Huxley—without complaining—ate crow (or ate leeks, as he put it). Haeckel, as expected, proved more stubborn, but *Bathybius* quietly faded away.

Eozoon hung on longer. Dawson defended it literally to the death in some of the most acerbic comments ever written by a scientist. Of one German critic, he remarked in 1897: "Mobius, I have no doubt, did his best from his special and limited point of view; but it was a crime which science should not readily pardon or forget, on the part of editors of the German periodical, to publish and illustrate as scientific material a paper which was so very far from being either fair or adequate." Dawson, by that time, was a long holdout (although Kirkpatrick of last month's column revived *Eozoon* in a more bizarre form later). All scientists had agreed that *Eozoon* was a metamorphic product of heat and pressure. Indeed, it had only been found in highly metamorphosed rock, a singularly inauspicious place to find a fossil. If any more proof had been needed, the discovery of *Eozoon* in blocks of limestone ejected from Mount Vesuvius settled the issue in 1894.

Bathybius and *Eozoon*, ever since, have been treated by scientists as an embarrassment best forgotten. The conspiracy succeeded admirably, and I would be surprised if one percent of modern biologists ever heard of the two fantasies. Historians, trained in the older (and invalidated) tradition of science as a march to truth mediated by the successive shucking of error, also kept their peace. What can we get from errors except a good laugh or a compendium of moral homilies framed as "don'ts."

Modern historians of science have more respect for such inspired errors. They made sense in their own time: that they don't in ours is irrelevant. Ours is no standard for all ages; science is always an interaction of prevailing culture, individual eccentricity, and empirical constraint. Hence, *Bathybius* and *Eozoon* have received more attention in the 1970s than in all previous years since their downfall. (In writing this column, I was guided to original sources and greatly enlightened by articles of C. F. O'Brien [*Isis*, 1971] on *Eozoon*, and N. A. Rupke [*Studies in the History and Philosophy of Science*, 1976], and P. F. Rehbock [*Isis*, 1975] on *Bathybius*. The article by Rehbock is particularly thorough and insightful. *Isis* is the leading professional journal in the history of science.)

Science contains few outright fools. Errors usually have their good reasons once we penetrate their context properly, rather than judge them according to our current perception of "truth." They are usually more enlightening than embarrassing, for they are signs of changing contexts. The best thinkers have the imagination to create organizing visions, and they are sufficiently adventurous (or egotistical) to float them in a complex world that can never answer "yes" in all detail. The message provided by a study of inspired error is not a homily about the sin of pride, but a recognition that the capacity for great insight and great error are opposite sides of the same coin—and that the currency of both is brilliance.

Bathybius was surely an inspired error. It served the larger truth of advancing evolutionary theory. It provided a captivating vision of primordial life, extended throughout time and space. As Rehbock argues, it filled a plethora of functions as, simultaneously, lowliest form of protozoology, elemental unit of cytology, evolutionary precursor of all organisms, first organic form in the fossil record, major constituent of modern and marine sediments (in its coccoliths), and source of food for higher life in the nutritionally impoverished deep oceans. When *Bathybius* faded away, the problems that it had defined did not disappear. *Bathybius* inspired a great amount of fruitful scientific work and served as a focus for defining important problems still with us.

Orthodoxy can be as stubborn in science as in religion. I do not know how to shake it except by vigorous imagination that inspires unconventional work and contains within itself an elevated potential for inspired error. As the great Italian economist Vilfredo Pareto wrote: "Give me a fruitful error any time, full of seeds, bursting with its own corrections. You can keep your sterile truth for yourself." Not to mention a man named Thomas Henry Huxley who, when not in the throes of grief or the wars of parson hunting, argued that "irrationally held truths may be more harmful than reasoned errors."

Scientific Hypotheses

ROBERT M. PIRSIG

Robert Pirsig is best known for his autobiographical and deeply philosophical novel *Zen and the Art of Motorcycle Maintenance*, from which the following two selections are excerpted. The book chronicles his cross-country motorcycle trip with two friends, his eleven-year-old son, and a patchwork of memories from a largely forgotten past.

The son of the dean of a law school, Pirsig had dropped out of college, joined the Army, lived for a period of time in India, and held a variety of odd jobs before returning to the university environment where he eventually completed a master's degree in journalism. While teaching English composition at Montana State College, he became convinced of the need to form a clearer apprehension of what he called "Quality." Thus he packed his family and belongings and headed to Chicago to pursue graduate study in philosophy. It was a reasonable but ill-fated strategy. By the end of the first semester his wife found him sitting on the floor of their bedroom apartment, staring blankly at the wall, apparently withdrawn and unresponsive to external stimuli.

Pirsig was institutionalized and subjected to a therapy known as "Annihilation ECS." Strong electrical impulses were sent through his brain on twenty-eight consecutive occasions. The result was a "cure" with a price: his memory, and with it his sense of identity and purpose, had been erased.

In *Zen and the Art of Motorcycle Maintenance* Robert Pirsig shares the challenges, triumphs, and disappointments of one man's struggle to discover (or rediscover) himself. The search requires Pirsig to explore concepts and thought processes that had previously led to his institutionalization. Perhaps partially to insulate himself from any residual danger, and perhaps partially simply because he no longer has active memories of the period, he refers to his pre-institutional self as *Phaedrus*—a name taken from a Platonic dialogue.

Outside in the valley again the sky is still limited by the bluffs on either side of the river, but they are closer together and closer to us than they were this morning. The valley is narrowing as we move toward the river's source.

We're also at a kind of beginning point in the things I'm discussing at which one can at last start to talk about Phaedrus' break from the mainstream of rational thought in pursuit of the ghost of rationality itself.

There was a passage he had read and repeated to himself so many times that it survives intact. It begins:

In the temple of science are many mansions . . . and various indeed are they that dwell therein and the motives that have led them there.

Many take to science out of a joyful sense of superior intellectual power; science is their own special sport to which they look for vivid experience and the satisfaction of ambition; many others are to be found in the temple who have offered the products of their brains on this altar for purely utilitarian purposes. Were an angel of the Lord to come and drive all the people belonging to these two categories out of the temple, it would be noticeably emptier but there would still be some men of both present and past times left inside. . . . If the types we have just expelled were the only types there were, the temple would never have existed any more than one can have a wood consisting of nothing but creepers . . . those who have found favor with the angel . . . are somewhat odd, uncommunicative, solitary fellows, really less like each other than the hosts of the rejected.

What has brought them to the temple . . . no single answer will cover . . . escape from everyday life, with its painful crudity and hopeless dreariness, from the fetters of one's own shifting desires. A finely tempered nature longs to escape from his noisy cramped surroundings into the silence of the high mountains where the eye ranges freely through the still pure air

Robert M. Pirsig, excerpt from *Zen and the Art of Motorcycle Maintenance*, pp. 97–103. Copyright © 1974 by Robert M. Pirsig. Reprinted with the permission of William Morrow & Company, Inc.

and fondly traces out the restful contours apparently built for eternity.

The passage is from a 1918 speech by a young German scientist named Albert Einstein.

Phaedrus had finished his first year of University science at the age of fifteen. His field was already biochemistry, and he intended to specialize at the interface between the organic and inorganic worlds now known as molecular biology. He didn't think of this as a career for his own personal advancement. He was very young and it was a kind of noble idealistic goal.

The state of mind which enables a man to do work of this kind is akin to that of the religious worshipper or lover. The daily effort comes from no deliberate intention or program, but straight from the heart.

If Phaedrus had entered science for ambitious or utilitarian purposes it might never have occurred to him to ask questions about the nature of a scientific hypothesis as an entity in itself. But he did ask them, and was unsatisfied with the answers.

The formation of hypotheses is the most mysterious of all the categories of scientific method. Where they come from, no one knows. A person is sitting somewhere, minding his own business, and suddenly—flash!—he understands something he didn't understand before. Until it's tested the hypothesis isn't truth. For the tests aren't its source. Its source is somewhere else.

Einstein had said:

Man tries to make for himself in the fashion that suits him best a simplified and intelligible picture of the world. He then tries to some extent to substitute this cosmos of his for the world of experience, and thus to overcome it. . . . He makes this cosmos and its construction the pivot of his emotional life in order to find in this way the peace and serenity which he cannot find in the narrow whirlpool of personal experience. . . . The supreme task . . . is to arrive at those universal elementary laws from which the cosmos can be built up by pure deduction. There is no logical path to these laws; only intuition, resting on sympathetic understanding of experience, can reach them. . . .

Intuition? Sympathy? Strange words for the origin of scientific knowledge.

A lesser scientist than Einstein might have said, "But scientific knowledge comes from *nature. Nature* provides the hypotheses." But Einstein understood that nature does not. Nature provides only experimental data.

A lesser mind might then have said, "Well, then, *man* provides hypotheses." But Einstein denied this too. "Nobody," he said, "who has really gone into the matter will deny that in practice the world of phenomena uniquely determines the theoretical system, in spite of the fact that there is no theoretical bridge between phenomena and their theoretical principles."

Phaedrus' break occurred when, as a result of laboratory experience, he became interested in hypotheses as entities in themselves. He had noticed again and again in his lab work that what might seem to be the hardest part of scientific work, thinking up the hypotheses, was invariably the easiest. The act of formally writing everything down precisely and clearly seemed to suggest them. As he was testing hypothesis number one by experimental method a flood of other hypotheses would come to mind, and as he was testing these, some more came to mind, and as he was testing these, still more came mind until it became painfully evident that as he continued testing hypotheses and eliminating them or confirming them their number did not decrease. It actually *increased* as he went along.

At first he found it amusing. He coined a law intended to have the humor of a Parkinson's law that "The number of rational hypotheses that can explain any given phenomenon is infinite." It pleased him never to run out of hypotheses. Even when his experimental work seemed dead-end in every conceivable way, he knew that if he just sat down and muddled about it long enough, sure enough, another hypothesis would come along. And it always did. It was only months after he had coined the law

that he began to have some doubts about the humor or benefits of it.

If true, that law is not a minor flaw in scientific reasoning. The law is completely nihilistic. It is a catastrophic logical disproof of the general validity of all scientific method!

If the purpose of scientific method is to select from among a multitude of hypotheses, and if the number of hypotheses grows faster than experimental method can handle, then it is clear that all hypotheses can never be tested. If all hypotheses cannot be tested, then the results of any experiment are inconclusive and the entire scientific method falls short of its goal of establishing proven knowledge.

About this Einstein had said, "Evolution has shown that at any given moment out of all conceivable constructions a single one has always proved itself absolutely superior to the rest," and let it go at that. But to Phaedrus that was an incredibly weak answer. The phrase "at any given moment" really shook him. Did Einstein really mean to state that truth was a function of time? To state *that* would annihilate the most basic presumption of all science!

But there it was, the whole history of science, a clear story of continuously new and changing explanations of old facts. The time spans of permanence seemed completely random, he could see no order in them. Some scientific truths seemed to last for centuries, others for less than a year. Scientific truth was not dogma, good for eternity, but a temporal quantitative entity that could be studied like anything else.

He studied scientific truths, then became upset even more by the apparent cause of their temporal condition. It looked as though the time spans of scientific truths are an inverse function of the intensity of scientific effort. Thus the scientific truths of the twentieth century seem to have a much shorter lifespan than those of the last century because scientific activity is now much greater. If, in the next century, scientific activity increases tenfold, then the life expectancy of any scientific truth can be expected to drop to perhaps one-tenth as long as now. What shortens the life-span of the existing truth is the volume of hypotheses offered to replace it; the more the hypotheses, the shorter the time span of the truth. And what seems to be causing the number of hypotheses to grow in recent decades seems to be nothing other than scientific method itself. The more you look, the more you see. Instead of selecting one truth from a multitude you are *increasing the multitude.* What this means logically is that as you try to move toward unchanging truth through the application of scientific method, you actually do not move toward it at all. You move *away* from it! It is your application of scientific method that is causing it to change!

What Phaedrus observed on a personal level was a phenomenon, profoundly characteristic of the history of science, which has been swept under the carpet for years. The predicted results of scientific enquiry and the actual results of scientific enquiry are diametrically opposed here, and no one seems to pay too much attention to the fact. The purpose of scientific method is to select a single truth from among many hypothetical truths. That, more than anything else, is what science is all about. But historically science has done exactly the opposite. Through multiplication upon multiplication of facts, information, theories and hypotheses, it is science itself that is leading mankind from single absolute truths to multiple, indeterminate, relative ones. The major producer of the social chaos, the indeterminacy of thought and values that rational knowledge is supposed to eliminate, is none other than science itself. And what Phaedrus saw in the isolation of his own laboratory work years ago is now seen everywhere in the technological world today. Scientifically produced anti-science—chaos.

It's possible now to look back a little and see why it's important to talk about this person in relation to everything that's been said before concerning the division between classic and romantic realities and the irreconcilability of the two. Unlike the multitude of romantics who are disturbed about the chaotic changes science and technology force upon the human spirit, Phaedrus, with his scientifically trained classic mind, was able to do more than just wring his hands with dismay, or run away, or condemn the whole situation broadside without offering any solutions.

As I've said, he did in the end offer a number of solutions, but the problem was so deep and so formidable and complex that no one really understood the gravity of what he was resolving, and so failed to understand or misunderstood what he said.

The cause of our current social crises, he would have said, is a genetic defect within the nature of reason itself. And until this genetic defect is cleared, the crises will continue. Our current modes of rationality are not moving society forward into a better world. They are taking it further and further from that better world. Since the Renaissance these modes have worked. As long as the need for food, clothing and shelter is dominant they will continue to work. But now that for huge masses of people these needs no longer overwhelm everything else, the whole structure of reason, handed down to us from ancient times, is no longer adequate. It begins to be seen for what it really is—emotionally hollow, esthetically meaningless and spiritually empty. That, today, is where it is at, and will continue to be at for a long time to come.

I've a vision of an angry continuing social crisis that no one really understands the depth of, let alone has solutions to. I see people like John and Sylvia living lost and alienated from the whole rational structure of civilized life, looking for solutions outside that structure, but finding none that are really satisfactory for long. And then I've a vision of Phaedrus and his lone isolated abstractions in the laboratory—actually concerned with the same crisis but starting from another point, moving in the opposite direction—and what I'm trying to do here is put it all together. It's so big—that's why I seem to wander sometimes.

No one that Phaedrus talked to seemed really concerned about this phenomenon that so baffled him. They seemed to say, "We know scientific method is valid, so why ask about it?"

Phaedrus didn't understand this attitude, didn't know what to do about it, and because he wasn't a student of science for personal or utilitarian reasons, it just stopped him completely. It was as if he were contemplating that serene mountain landscape Einstein had described, and suddenly between the mountains had appeared a fissure, a gap of pure nothing. And slowly, and agonizingly, to explain this gap, he had to admit that the mountains, which had seemed built for eternity, might possibly be something else . . . perhaps just figments of his own imagination. It stopped him.

And so Phaedrus, who at the age of fifteen had finished his freshman year of science, was at the age of seventeen expelled from the University for failing grades. Immaturity and inattention to studies were given as official causes.

There was nothing anyone could have done about it; either to prevent it or correct it. The University couldn't have kept him on without abandoning standards completely.

In a stunned state Phaedrus began a long series of lateral drifts that led him into a far orbit of the mind, but he eventually returned along a route we are now following, to the doors of the University itself. Tomorrow I'll try to start on that route.

Poincaré and the Development of Non-Euclidean Geometry

ROBERT M. PIRSIG

Biographical details concerning Robert Pirsig may be found at the beginning of the preceding selection. The philosophical reflections that follow are edited from Chapter 22 of *Zen and the Art of Motorcycle Maintenance* (1974).

The next morning we check out of the hotel feeling refreshed, say goodbye to the DeWeeses, and head north on the open road out of Bozeman. The De-Weeses wanted us to stay, but a peculiar itching to move west and get on with my thoughts has taken over. I want to talk today about a person whom Phaedrus never heard of, but whose writings I've studied quite extensively in preparation for this Chautauqua. Unlike Phaedrus, this man was an international celebrity at thirty-five, a living legend at fifty-eight, whom Bertrand Russell has described as "by general agreement, the most eminent scientific man of his generation." He was an astronomer, a physicist, a mathematician and philosopher all in one. His name was Jules Henri Poincaré.

It always seemed incredible to me, and still does, I guess, that Phaedrus should have traveled along a line of thought that had never been traveled before. Someone, somewhere, must have thought of all this before, and Phaedrus was such a poor scholar it would have been just like him to have duplicated the commonplaces of some famous system of philosophy he hadn't taken the trouble to look into.

So I spent more than a year reading the very long and sometimes very tedious history of philosophy in a search for duplicate ideas. It was a fascinating way to read the history of philosophy, however, and a thing occurred of which I still don't know quite what to make. Philosophical systems that are supposed to be greatly opposed to one another *both* seem to be saying something very close to what Phaedrus thought, with minor variations. Time after time I thought I'd found whom he was duplicat-

ing, but each time, because of what appeared to be some slight differences, he took a greatly different direction. Hegel, for example, whom I referred to earlier, rejected Hindu systems of philosophy as no philosophy at all. Phaedrus seemed to assimilate them, or *be* assimilated by them. There was no feeling of contradiction.

Eventually I came to Poincaré. Here again there was little duplication but another kind of phenomenon. Phaedrus follows a long and torturous path into the highest abstractions, seems about to come down and then stops. Poincaré starts with the most basic scientific verities, works up to the same abstractions and then stops. Both trails stop *right at each other's end!* There is perfect continuity between them. When you live in the shadow of insanity, the appearance of another mind that thinks and talks as yours does is something close to a blessed event. Like Robinson Crusoe's discovery of footprints on the sand.

Poincaré lived from 1854 to 1912, a professor at the University of Paris. His beard and pince-nez were reminiscent of Henri Toulouse-Lautrec, who lived in Paris at the same time and was only ten years younger.

During Poincaré's lifetime, an alarmingly deep crisis in the foundations of the exact sciences had begun. For years scientific truth had been beyond the possibility of a doubt; the logic of science was infallible, and if the scientists were sometimes mistaken, this was assumed to be only from their mistaking its rules. The great questions had all been answered. The mission of science was now simply to refine these answers to greater and greater accuracy. True, there were still unexplained phenomena such as radioactivity, transmission of light through the "ether," and the peculiar relationship of magnetic to electric forces; but these, if past trends were any indication, had eventually to fall. It was hardly guessed by anyone that within a few decades there would be no more absolute space, absolute time, absolute substance or even absolute magnitude; that classical physics, the scientific rock of ages, would become "approximate"; that the soberest and most respected of astronomers would be telling mankind that if it looked long enough through a telescope powerful enough, what it would see was the back of its own head!

The basis of the foundation-shattering Theory of Relativity was as yet understood only by a very few, of whom Poincaré, as the most eminent mathematician of his time, was one.

In his *Foundations of Science* Poincaré explained that the antecedents of the crisis in the foundations of science were very old. It had long been sought in vain, he said, to demonstrate the axiom known as Euclid's fifth postulate and this search was the start of the crisis. Euclid's postulate of parallels, which states that through a given point there's not more than one parallel line to a given straight line, we usually learn in tenth-grade geometry. It is one of the basic building blocks out of which the entire mathematics of geometry is constructed.

All the other axioms seemed so obvious as to be unquestionable, but this one did not. Yet you couldn't get rid of it without destroying huge portions of the mathematics, and no one seemed about to reduce it to anything more elementary. What vast effort had been wasted in that chimeric hope was truly unimaginable, Poincaré said.

Finally, in the first quarter of the nineteenth century, and almost at the same time, a Hungarian and a Russian—Bolyai and Lobachevski—established irrefutably that a proof of Euclid's fifth postulate is impossible. They did this by reasoning that if there were any way to reduce Euclid's postulate to other, surer axioms, another effect would also be noticeable: a reversal of Euclid's postulate would create logical contradictions in the geometry. So they reversed Euclid's postulate.

Lobachevski assumes at the start that through a given point can be drawn two parallels to a given straight. And he retains besides all Euclid's other axioms. From these hypotheses he deduces a series of theorems among which it's impossible to find any contradiction, and he constructs a geometry whose faultless logic is inferior in nothing to that of Euclidian geometry.

Thus by his failure to find any contradictions he proves that the fifth postulate is irreducible to simpler axioms.

It wasn't the proof that was alarming. It was its rational byproduct that soon overshadowed it and almost everything else in the field of mathematics. Mathematics, the cornerstone of scientific certainty, was suddenly uncertain.

We now had *two* contradictory visions of unshakable scientific truth, true for all men of all ages, regardless of their individual preferences.

This was the basis of the profound crisis that shattered the scientific complacency of the Gilded Age. *How do we know which one of these geometries is right?* If there is no basis for distinguishing between them, then you have a total mathematics which admits logical contradictions. But a mathematics which admits internal logical contradictions is no mathematics at all. The ultimate effect of the non-Euclidian geometries becomes nothing more than a magician's mumbo jumbo in which belief is sustained purely by faith!

And of course once that door was opened one could hardly expect the number of contradictory systems of unshakable scientific truth to be limited to two. A German named Riemann appeared with another unshakable system of geometry which throws overboard not only Euclid's postulate, but also the first axiom, which states that only one straight line can pass through two points. Again there is no internal contradiction, only an inconsistency with both Lobachevskian and Euclidian geometries.

According to the Theory of Relativity, Riemann geometry best describes the world we live in. . . .

To solve the problem of what is mathematical truth, Poincaré said, we should first ask ourselves what is the nature of geometric axioms. Are they synthetic *a priori* judgments, as Kant said? That is, do they exist as a fixed part of man's consciousness, independently of experience and uncreated by experience? Poincaré thought not. They would then impose themselves upon us with such force that we couldn't conceive the contrary proposition, or build upon it a theoretic edifice. There would be no non-Euclidian geometry.

Should we therefore conclude the axioms of geometry are experimental verities? Poincaré didn't think that was so either. If they were, they would be subject to continual change and revision as new laboratory data came in. This seemed to be contrary to the whole nature of geometry itself.

Poincaré concluded that the axioms of geometry are *conventions*, our choice among all possible conventions is *guided* by experimental facts, but it remains *free* and is limited only by the necessity of avoiding all contradiction. Thus it is that the postulates can remain rigorously true even though the experimental laws that have determined their adoption are only approximate. The axioms of geometry, in other words, are merely disguised definitions.

Then, having identified the nature of geometric axioms, he turned to the question, Is Euclidian geometry true or is Riemann geometry true?

He answered, The question has no meaning.

As well ask whether the metric system is true and the avoirdupois system is false; whether Cartesian coordinates are true and polar coordinates are false. One geometry can not be more true than another; it can only be more *convenient*. Geometry is not true, it is advantageous.

Poincaré then went on to demonstrate the conventional nature of other concepts of science, such as space and time, showing that there isn't one way of measuring these entities that is more true than another; that which is generally adopted is only more *convenient.*

Our concepts of space and time are also definitions, selected on the basis of their convenience in handling the facts.

This radical understanding of our most basic scientific concepts is not yet complete however. The mystery of what is space and time may be made more understandable by this explanation, but now the burden of sustaining the order of the universe rests on "facts." What are facts?

Poincaré proceeded to examine these critically. *Which* facts are you going to observe? he asked. There is an infinity of them. There is no more chance that an unselective observation of facts will produce science than there is that a monkey at a typewriter will produce the Lord's Prayer.

The same is true of hypotheses. *Which* hypotheses? Poincaré wrote, "If a phenomenon admits of a complete mechanical explanation it will admit of an infinity of others which will account equally well for all the peculiarities disclosed by experiment." This was the statement made by Phaedrus in the laboratory; it raised questions that failed him out of school.

If the scientist had at his disposal infinite time, Poincaré said, it would only be necessary to say to him, "Look and notice well"; but as there isn't time to see everything, and as it's better not to see than to see wrongly, it's necessary for him to make a choice.

Poincaré laid down some rules: There is a hierarchy of facts.

The more general a fact, the more precious it is. Those which serve many times are better than those which have little chance of coming up again. Biologists, for example, would be at a loss to construct a science if only individuals and no species existed, and if heredity didn't make children like parents.

Which facts are likely to reappear? The simple facts. How to recognize them? Choose those that *seem* simple. Either this simplicity is real or the complex elements are indistinguishable. In the first case we're likely to meet this simple fact again either alone or as an element in a complex fact. The second case too has a good chance of recurring since nature doesn't randomly construct such cases.

Where is the simple fact? Scientists have been seeking it in the two extremes, in the infinitely great and in the infinitely small. Biologists, for example, have been instinctively led to regard the cell as more interesting than the whole animal; and, since Poincaré's time, the protein molecule as more interesting than the cell. The outcome has shown the wisdom of this, since cells and molecules belonging to different organisms have been found to be more alike than the organisms themselves.

How then choose the interesting fact, the one that begins again and again? Method is precisely this choice of facts; it is needful then to be occupied first with creating a method; and many have been imagined, since none imposes itself. It's proper to begin with the regular facts, but after a rule is established beyond all doubt, the facts in conformity with it become dull because they no longer teach us anything new. Then it's the exception that becomes important. We seek not resemblances but differences, choose the most accentuated differences because they're the most striking and also the most instructive.

We first seek the cases in which this rule has the greatest chance of failing; by going very far away in space or very far away in time, we may find our usual rules entirely overturned, and these grand overturnings enable us the better to see the little changes that may happen nearer to us. But what we ought to aim at is less the ascertainment of resemblances and differences than the recognition of likenesses hidden under apparent divergences. Particular rules seem at first discordant, but looking more closely we see in general that they resemble each other; different as to matter, they are alike as to form, as to the order of their parts. When we look at them with this bias we shall see them enlarge and tend to embrace everything. And this it is that makes the value of certain facts come to complete an assemblage and to show that it is the faithful image of other known assemblages.

No, Poincaré concluded, a scientist does not choose at random the facts he observes. He seeks to condense much experience and much thought into a slender volume; and that's why a little book on physics contains so many past experiences and a thousand times as many possible experiences whose result is known beforehand.

Then Poincaré illustrated how a fact is discovered. He had described generally how scientists arrive at facts and theories but now he penetrated narrowly into his own personal experience with the mathematical functions that established his early fame.

For fifteen days, he said, he strove to prove that there couldn't be any such functions. Every day he seated himself at his work-table, stayed an hour or two, tried a great number of combinations and reached no results.

Then one evening, contrary to his custom, he drank black coffee and couldn't sleep. Ideas arose in crowds. He felt them collide until pairs interlocked, so to speak, making a stable combination.

The next morning he had only to write out the results. A wave of crystallization had taken place.

He described how a second wave of crystallization, guided by analogies to established mathematics, produced what he later named the "Theta-Fuchsian Series." He left Caen, where he was living, to go on a geologic excursion. The changes of travel made him forget mathematics. He was about to enter a bus, and at the moment when he put his foot on the step, the idea came to him, without anything in his former thoughts having paved the way for it, that the transformations he had used to define the Fuchsian functions were identical with those of non-Euclidian geometry. He didn't verify the idea, he said, he just went on with a conversation on the bus; but he felt a perfect certainty. Later he verified the result at his leisure.

A later discovery occurred while he was walking by a seaside bluff. It came to him with just the same characteristics of brevity, suddenness and immediate certainty. Another major discovery occurred while he was walking down a street. Others eulogized this process as the mysterious workings of genius, but Poincaré was not content with such a shallow explanation. He tried to fathom more deeply what had happened.

Mathematics, he said, isn't merely a question of applying rules, any more than science. It doesn't merely make the most combinations possible according to certain fixed laws. The combinations so obtained would be exceedingly numerous, useless and cumbersome. The true work of the inventor consists in choosing among these combinations so as to eliminate the useless ones, or rather, to avoid the trouble of making them, and the rules that must guide the choice are extremely fine and delicate. It's almost impossible to state them precisely; they must be felt rather than formulated.

Poincaré then hypothesized that this selection is made by what he called the "subliminal self," an entity that corresponds exactly with what Phaedrus called preintellectual awareness. The subliminal self, Poincaré said, looks at a large number of solutions to a problem, but only the *interesting* ones break into the domain of consciousness. Mathematical solutions are selected by the subliminal self on the basis of "mathematical beauty," of the harmony of numbers and forms, of geometric elegance. "This is a true esthetic feeling which all mathematicians know," Poincaré said, "but of which the profane are so ignorant as often to be tempted to smile." But it is this harmony, this beauty, that is at the center of it all.

Poincaré made it clear that he was not speaking of romantic beauty, the beauty of appearances which strikes the senses. He meant classic beauty, which comes from the harmonious order of the parts, and which a pure intelligence can grasp, which gives structure to romantic beauty and without which life would be only vague and fleeting, a dream from which one could not distinguish one's dreams because there would be no basis for making the distinction. It is the quest of this special classic beauty, the sense of harmony of the cosmos, which makes us *choose the facts most fitting to contribute to this harmony.* It is not the facts but the relation of things that results in the universal harmony that is the sole objective reality.

What guarantees the objectivity of the world in which we live is that this world is common to us with other thinking beings. Through the communications that we have with other men we receive from them ready-made harmonious reasonings. We know that these reasonings do not come from us and at the same time we recognize in them, *because of their harmony,* the work of reasonable beings like ourselves. And as these reasonings appear to fit the world of our sensations, we think we may infer that these reasonable beings have seen the same thing as we; thus it is that we know we haven't been dreaming. It is this harmony, this *quality* if you will, that is the sole basis for the only reality we can ever know.

Poincaré's contemporaries refused to acknowledge that facts are preselected because they thought that to do so would destroy the validity of scientific method. They presumed that "preselected facts" meant that truth is "whatever you like" and called his ideas conventionalism. They vigorously ignored the truth that their own "principle of objectivity" is not itself an observable fact—and therefore by their own criteria should be put in a state of suspended animation.

They felt they had to do this because if they didn't, the entire philosophic underpinning of science would collapse. Poincaré didn't offer any resolutions of this quandary. He didn't go far enough into the metaphysical implications of what he was saying to arrive at the solution. What he neglected to say was that the selection of facts before you "observe" them is "whatever you like" *only in a dualistic, subject-object metaphysical system!* When Quality enters the picture as a third metaphysical entity, the preselection of facts is no longer arbitrary. The preselection of facts is not based on subjective, capricious "whatever you like" but on *Quality,* which is reality itself. Thus the quandary vanishes.

It was as though Phaedrus had been working on a puzzle of his own and because of lack of time had left one whole side unfinished.

Poincaré had been working on a puzzle of *his* own. His judgment that the scientist selects facts, hypotheses and axioms on the basis of harmony, also left the rough serrated edge of a puzzle incomplete. To leave the impression in the scientific world that the source of all scientific reality is merely a subjective, capricious harmony is to solve problems of epistemology while leaving an unfinished edge at the border of metaphysics that makes the epistemology unacceptable.

But we know from Phaedrus' metaphysics that the harmony Poincaré talked about is *not subjective.* It is the *source* of subjects and objects and exists in an anterior relationship to them. It is *not* capri-cious, it is the force that *opposes* capriciousness; the ordering principle of all scientific and mathematical thought which *destroys* capriciousness, and without which no scientific thought can proceed. What brought tears of recognition to my eyes was the discovery that these unfinished edges match perfectly in a kind of harmony that both Phaedrus and Poincaré talked about, to produce a complete structure of thought capable of uniting the separate languages of Science and Art into one. . . .

Review and Reflection

1. Explicate and discuss some of the difficulties we encounter when trying to test a scientific theory.

2. Should we regard scientific theories as true? Approximately true? Why?

3. Explicate and discuss Thomas Kuhn's views concerning scientific discovery. Do you agree with his analysis? Why?

4. Explicate and discuss the feminist critique of science. Do you agree with Evelyn Fox Keller's analysis and conclusions? Why?

5. What was (is) *Bathybius Haeckelii? Eozoon canadense?* What lessons would Stephen Jay Gould have us learn from examples such as these? Do you agree? Why?

6. Why is Pirsig concerned about the large number of hypotheses that may be formulated on the basis of any given set of experiences? Do you agree with his concerns? Why?

7. Explicate and discuss Poincaré's concept of subliminal self.

Suggestions for Further Study

CARL HEMPEL. *Philosophy of Natural Science.* Englewood Cliffs, NJ: Prentice-Hall, 1966.

THOMAS KUHN. *The Structure of Scientific Revolutions.* Chicago: University of Chicago Press, 1970.

LARRY LAUDAN. *Science and Values.* Berkeley: University of California Press, 1984.

ERNEST NAGEL. *The Structure of Science.* New York: Harcourt, 1961.

ROBERT PIRSIG. *Zen and the Art of Motorcycle Maintenance.* New York: Bantam Books, 1974.

CHAPTER 8

Metaphysics:
Reflections on Reality

RAPHAEL. SANTIVS PINX

IN AEDIBVS VATICANIS.

Metaphysics is the philosophical attempt to understand the nature and structure of reality. Selections expand and extend concepts from the preceding chapter, but also serve to prepare the soil for those yet to come (Part Four). Common threads include perceptual limitation, cognition, and linguistic clarity.

Introductory Essay

The **Introductory Essay** begins with a definition and overview of the field. A series of cautions underscores the need to pay special attention to both language and concept. Focus is provided by a classic metaphysical puzzle:

> If a tree falls in the forest when there is no one around to hear it, does it make a sound?

Solving the puzzle requires an analysis of the term "sound," which in turn leads to analysis and reflection concerning the nature of human sensation. Questions concerning the connections between experience and reality give rise to a discussion of Heisenberg's Uncertainty Relation, the Copenhagen Interpretation of Quantum Mechanics, and Schrödinger's cat.

Philosophical Readings

The selection by **Plato** is a section of *The Republic* known as "The Allegory of the Cave." In the cave are people imprisoned by the limitations of sensory experience and conceptual representation. A solitary individual, shaking off the fetters that bind his colleagues, sees higher and further than any. But his liberation comes at a price: it is personally difficult, physically painful, and marks him not as a saint or sage, but rather as a socially undesirable outcast. His efforts to enlighten others are met with scorn, reproach, and possibly even violence.

The selection by **René Descartes** attempts to establish the existence and nature of the conceptual self. Because he wishes to restrict his conclusions to those items that may be known with absolute certainty, he employs an investigative technique known as "Methodological Doubt." To serve as a constant reminder of these epistemic commitments, he imagines an evil demon bent on deceiving him at every possible turn. After considering and rejecting several possible candidates for knowledge, Descartes begins to wonder if he can be certain of anything. Is it perhaps possible that the demon has deceived him about each and every detail of his existence? Desperate as the situation may seem, Descartes finds a slender thread of hope at the core of his investigation. *Cogito ergo sum:* I think, therefore I am. No matter how powerful or clever the demon may be, Descartes reasons, he cannot possibly deceive me concerning the existential consequence of my own cognition.

Scientific Reading

Fritjof Capra draws a series of parallels between the metaphysical vision of the world presented by Eastern mysticism and that which appears to be developing from the investigations of twentieth-century science. The current chapter, taken from *The Tao of Physics,* focuses on the dynamic nature of the universe. The eastern traditions discussed by Capra include Hinduism, Buddhism, Taoism, and Zen. Relevant concepts from those traditions include *Brahman, Rita, Tao, karma, māyā, samsāra, Tathāgata,* and *līlā.* Scientific concepts include the Heisenberg Uncertainty Relation, wave/particle duality, the expanding universe, Einstein's Special Theory of Relativity, $E=mc^2$, subatomic structure, and quantum indeterminacy.

Literary Reading

The essay by **Bertrand Russell** recreates an imaginative dream full of the horrors that have tormented metaphysicians through the ages. Probability, induction, and indeterminacy have their role, but center stage is reserved for the concept of negation.

If a Tree Falls . . .

DOUGLAS W. SHRADER

Metaphysics is a branch of philosophy that deals with the nature and structure of reality. The scope of the field is obviously immense. Everything, literally, is up for grabs. Every belief, concept, assumption, or idea, no matter how commonplace or intuitively obvious, about any portion, aspect, or dimension of reality can be called into question. Upon analysis and reflection many seemingly familiar and unproblematic concepts and ideas turn out to have strange and sometimes undesirable consequences. Ideas that would ordinarily be considered ludicrous or positively insane may become the subject of serious discussion. They may even be adopted and defended by reputable and otherwise seemingly reasonable scholars.

The field is slippery; the terrain, treacherous. Metaphysics can be mind-boggling, even for a trained professional. It is easy to lose one's way.

Many metaphysical problems, discussions, and disagreements are fueled by conceptual vagueness or confusion, or by a simple failure to use the language in a consistent and uniform manner. Many scholars have become so disillusioned by the often confused and fruitless discussions that metaphysics itself has become the subject of serious debate. A number of modern philosophers (known usually as *Logical Empiricists* or *Positivists*) have argued that conceptual analysis and linguistic clarification are the only portions of metaphysics worth salvaging. The position has a certain appeal and has been widely influential, but all and all seems a bit too limited and naive.

While I agree that conceptual analysis and linguistic clarification are extremely important, I do not think the rest of metaphysics can or should be so easily discarded. Metaphysical assumptions are an essential ingredient of any belief set. Different people make different assumptions. Investigating metaphysical assumptions may not always help us decide who is right, but it should provide an increased awareness of our own beliefs and a better understanding of those of others. In the process we may develop a bit of epistemic humility and may even learn to conceptualize the world in new, less-limited ways.

Although the subject of all metaphysical discussions is in some general sense the same (reality), and although what we say or believe about one portion, aspect, or dimension of reality often influences what we say or believe about another, relatively few metaphysical discussions try to deal with reality as a whole (if indeed there is any such thing. Remember—*everything* is up for grabs.). As abstract and abstruse as they are prone to be, even metaphysical analyses and discussions require a focus. Most commonly, they are centered around (1) some particular portion or dimension of reality, or (2) some particular problem or question. Examples of the former include the nature of causation, the structure of space and/or time, and the composition of matter. Characteristic questions include: Is time travel possible? Is the idea of universal deterministic causation (frequently found in science) compatible with the concepts of human agency, freedom, and responsibility? Is a human being a purely physical entity, a purely spiritual one, a composite of the two, or something else altogether? and, the subject of this essay:

> If a tree falls in the forest when there is no one around to hear it, does it make a sound?

PRELIMINARY ANALYSIS: THE NATURE OF PERCEPTION

The question is not so simple, nor the answer so obvious and uncontroversial as it may at first seem. Although it asks specifically only about the sound of a falling tree, the question raises fundamental concerns about the nature of perception and its supposed relation to the reality we perceive. Since these concerns are metaphysical rather than linguistic, the question cannot be resolved by simply consulting a good dictionary. Nonetheless, it is a good place to start. You can be surprised by a dictionary, even as regards a familiar word like *sound*. And unless we are clear and precise in our use of the terms, we are sure to find ourselves bogged down in a linguistic squabble, confused and misled by our own language.

The word *sound* has a variety of meanings, most of which are clearly out of place in this context. Two examples of legitimate but contextually incongruous meanings are (1) a long, relatively wide passage of water separating an island from the mainland, and (2) the air bladder of a fish. Eliminating these and others like them is reasonably easy. But we are still left with a cluster of related meanings, each of which may be plausibly construed as an appropriate and intended meaning, but which may result in different answers to the question.

Loosely, sounds of the relevant sort are what we hear. But hearing is a complex phenomenon involving not only the experience itself, but also the conditions that give rise to the experience. As our focus and interest vary, so too will our use of the language. Different dictionaries give somewhat different definitions, but many resemble the following one from Webster's New Collegiate Dictionary.

> **sound** n. . . .1. The sensation of hearing; that which is heard; specif.:
>
>   a. *Psychophysics.* Sensation due to stimulation of the auditory nerves and auditory centers of the brain, usually by vibrations transmitted in a material medium, commonly air, affecting the organ of hearing.
>
>   b. *Physics.* Vibrational energy which occasions such a sensation. Sound is propagated by progressive longitudinal vibratory disturbances (**sound waves**).[1]

The psychophysical and physical components of the definition are clearly related, but also clearly different. They point to different parts of what may be reasonably regarded, in "normal" circumstances, as a single integrated process.

A tree falls in the forest. In falling, especially in landing, the tree releases energy in the form of vibratory disturbances of the surrounding mediums (it causes vibrations in the surrounding air, ground, and so on). The vibrational energy is transmitted (at the speed of sound, of course) in the form of sound waves. The energy is gradually dissipated and absorbed by the substances through which it travels. But if a sufficient portion reaches the auditory organs of a perceptually cognizant being of the appropriate sort (an alert non-deaf human will do quite well for a certain range of frequencies), it may set up vibrations in the auditory apparatus (eardrum and related structures), thereby stimulating the auditory nerves, which in turn stimulate the auditory centers of the brain, resulting in the sensation described variously as "the sound of a falling tree," or "hearing a tree fall."

The alternative characterizations of the sensation reflect to some extent the variance of usage that underlies Webster's double-sided definition. The first accords with the psychophysical approach of treating sound as the actual sensation or awareness (usually the result of a causal process such as the one described above). The second is more ambiguous, but may reasonably be regarded as belonging to the same camp as the physical approach in which sound is treated as the vibrational energy released by the falling tree and transmitted via sound waves to the auditory apparatus of an appropriate perceptually cognizant being. To avoid both confusion and unnecessarily complex linguistic formulations, we will henceforth call the first sense "sound$_1$," and the second "sound$_2$."

Sound$_1$ clearly requires the presence of a perceptually cognizant being of an appropriate sort. It makes no sense, except hypothetically, to talk of sensations that no one has. This brings us at last to a position from which we can offer a preliminary answer to the focal question. If by "sound" we mean "auditory sensation" (sound$_1$), if by "make a sound" we mean "occasions an auditory sensation," and if by "no one is around to hear it" we mean "no appropriate perceptually cognizant being is located within the spatio-temporal region necessary to occasion an auditory sensation," we can reasonably assert that if a tree falls in the forest when there is no one around to hear it, it does not make any sound.

Though it may strike you as bizarre or counterintuitive, the conclusion should not have taken you by total surprise. What you may not have anticipated is that the conclusion is supported not only by the first, but by the second sense of "sound" as well. If the falling tree does not occasion an auditory sensation (sound$_1$), then neither does it occasion vibrational energy that occasions an auditory sensation (sound$_2$). The point may seem somewhat subtle and it may help to insert a modifier like "actually" or "in fact." Sound$_2$ is vibrational energy that *actually* occasions an auditory sensation. As a result, there are no sounds$_2$ which do not cause sounds$_1$. In other words, there are no sounds$_2$ that are not heard.

Perhaps I should hasten to add that sound$_2$ is easily mistaken for a third sense we will call "sound$_3$." It may even be argued that the physics component of Webster's definition is ambiguous in this regard. By "sound$_3$," we will mean "vibrational energy of the sort which occasions *or would occasion* an auditory sensation *if and/or when* it impinges on the auditory apparatus of an appropriate perceptually cognizant being." Sound$_3$ is broader than sound$_2$. In fact, sound$_2$ is a proper subset of sound$_3$: all sounds$_2$ are also sounds$_3$ though there may be some sounds$_3$ that are not sounds$_2$. The difference between sound$_2$ and sound$_3$ may seem slight, but it is crucial as regards the focal question. There can be no instances of sound$_2$ in the absence of an appropriate perceptually cognizant being, but there may be instances of sound$_3$ that no one hears. Thus if a tree falls in the forest when there is no one around to hear it, it does not make any sound$_1$ or sound$_2$, but it may make a sound$_3$.

PRIVATE SOUNDS

The differences between these three senses of the term do not stop with the question about the falling tree. Many people suffer from a condition known as "tinnitus." They hear what would seem to be a ringing, buzzing, whistling, roaring, or similar noise. The sensation is very real and often quite maddening. There is genuine stimulation of the auditory nerves and auditory centers of the brain. But unlike normal hearing, which is occasioned by the auditory reception of externally generated vibrational energy, the cause of tinnitus is predominantly internal. Thus it may affect one ear, but not the other.

Should we say that a person suffering from tinnitis is actually hearing sounds (ringing, buzzing, and so on)? If we use "sound" to mean "auditory sensation due to stimulation of the auditory centers of the brain regardless of the origin of that stimulation" (which is what I have intended sound$_1$ to mean), the answer is clearly "yes." But if by "sound" we mean sound$_2$ or sound$_3$, the answer is clearly "no." As regards these senses of the term, we would have to say that there is no genuine sound in cases of tinnitus; it just *seems* to the person that they hear a sound such as the pounding of the ocean surf.

The above characterization of sound$_1$ may have seemed needlessly complex, but the time has come to distinguish it from two other closely related senses. We will use "sound$_4$" to mean "auditory sensation occasioned by the auditory reception of externally generated vibrational energy." And by "sound$_5$" we will mean "auditory sensation regardless of origin." Sound$_4$ is more narrow than sound$_1$; sound$_5$ is broader. The ringing heard in tinnitus, which counts as sound$_1$, will also count as sound$_5$, but not as sound$_4$. Incidentally, if a tree falls in the forest when there is no one around to hear it, it will make neither sound$_4$ nor sound$_5$.

Psychophysicists have discovered that we can produce sensations similar to tinnitus by electrically stimulating the auditory center of the brain. The proper description of these experiments follows the same linguistic pattern as the description of tinnitus: artificially induced electrical stimulation of the auditory center of the brain produces $sound_1$ and $sound_5$, but not $sound_2$, $sound_3$, or $sound_4$.

Judgments are slightly more difficult as regards someone who sincerely believes they hear the voice of God, the sound of a heavenly choir, or the music of the spheres. We may one day be surprised, but at present it seems unlikely that these "sounds" are transmitted by sound waves. Thus we can reasonably assert that the person does not, in these instances, hear $sound_2$, $sound_3$, or $sound_4$. Others may have a different opinion, but if we keep the various senses of the term straight we can maintain focus, come to a clearer understanding of the source and nature of our disagreements, and possibly even devise a way to resolve the issue.

I am a little less sure about $sound_1$. I know of no studies that could authoritatively tell us whether the "sounds" are due to stimulation of the auditory center of the brain. I tend to think not, but the workings of the human brain are still largely mysterious and it is perhaps best to admit the speculative character of my judgment.

I am not even entirely sure the "sounds" should count as instances of $sound_5$. People who claim to hear the voice of God often express concerns regarding the limitations of human conceptualization and language. Their use of terms like "hear" may be more figurative than literal. They may even explicitly reject the characterization of their experience as an auditory sensation, suggesting perhaps that it was somehow different from what they would normally characterize as a sensation, or perhaps that it was not as auditory as we may have been led to believe on the basis of a description like "I heard the voice of God." It is therefore possible that these experiences are not sounds at all, at least not in any of the senses we have thus far delineated.

The five senses of "sound" form a continuum of sorts, though it may have been slightly obscured by our numbering system. In the interest of overall clarity we have numbered the senses in the order of presentation rather than according to their place within the continuum. A moment's reflection should disclose the rhyme and reason behind the following pattern:

$sound_5$ (auditory sensation regardless of origin)
$sound_1$ (auditory sensation due to stimulation of the auditory centers of the brain regardless of the origin of that stimulation)
$sound_4$ (auditory sensation occasioned by the auditory reception of externally generated vibrational energy)
$sound_2$ (vibrational energy that occasions an auditory sensation)
$sound_3$ (vibrational energy of the sort that occasions or would occasion an auditory sensation if and/or when it impinges on the auditory apparatus of an appropriate perceptually cognizant being)

The two ends of the continuum are most general. They become more specific, meet, and overlap as we move toward the center.

The continuum can be broken in different places by different questions. The question about the falling tree breaks the continuum between 2 and 3, while the one about tinnitus effects a break between 1 and 4. Although questions about "the voice of God" are somewhat more ambiguous and difficult to decide with any reliable degree of assurance, the continuum at least serves as a reference base to help focus and express our concerns and/or disagreements.

SOUNDS THAT NO ONE HEARS

Earlier I characterized sound loosely as "what we hear." But what does it mean to say that we hear sounds? If by "sound" we mean "$sound_2$," or "$sound_3$," the expression amounts to saying that we hear vibrational energy. Some people will find this obvious and unproblematic; others may think it absurd. The difference, of course, lies in our preferred usage of the term. Someone inclined to use "sound" in the sense of sound$_1$, sound$_4$, or sound$_5$ may readily agree that many of the sounds we hear are occasioned by vibrational energy, but will find any talk of actually hearing vibrational energy somewhat odd or stilted. On these three senses of "sound" (1, 4, and 5) we would speak instead of hearing auditory sensations. Such talk will seem equally odd or stilted to someone not accustomed to thinking and speaking in this way. It may even seem circular or nonsensical unless we note a sharp distinction between the *sense* of hearing and the *sensation* of sound. Sensations are what we sense.

THE SUBJECTIVE NATURE OF SENSATION

Do you hear what I hear? If two people stand side by side in a forest observing a falling tree, will they hear the same sound? If one is deaf and the other is not, the answer is obviously "no," for the deaf person will hear no sound at all. What if one has "normal" hearing, while the other is "hearing impaired?" The differences in the sensitivity of their auditory perceptual apparatus may be sufficient to yield qualitatively very different sensations. Even two people with "normal" hearing are likely to have some differences in the sensitivity of their auditory perceptual apparatus. Add to this differences of focus (the variable degree of alertness, concentration, or attention), background experience, psychological mood, and valuative orientation (what is sweet music to a lumber baron may be a terrifying or sickening sound to an environmentalist) and you are sure to get related but subjectively quite different experiences.

Sensations are private, individual sorts of things. If I jab my finger with a pin I will feel pain. You may wince at the thought and may even feel empathetic pain, but the pain I feel will be felt by me alone. If I run my finger across the cover of this book I will feel certain tactile sensations. I believe you will feel similar sensations if you run your finger across the cover, but you cannot feel the sensation of my finger running across the cover, and I cannot feel yours.

The same sort of reflections apply to all sensations: auditory, visual, and so on. Thus if we understand "sound" as an auditory sensation (sense 1, 4, or 5), there is a serious and legitimate sense in which we never hear the same sounds as anyone else.

There is something right about this approach, but something deeply disturbing as well. If we never hear, see, or touch the same things as anyone else, what sense can we make of the common-sense idea that we share a common reality? How can we avoid the conclusion that we each live in our own little world, inaccessible to anyone but ourself?

Suppose we treat sound as vibrational energy (sense 2 or 3). No matter how close we stand to one another, the portion of the vibrational energy that affects your hearing will be numerically different from the portion that affects mine. There may be qualitative differences as well. The qualitative differences will be more obvious if we occupy different observational positions (for example, if I am close to the tree and you are far away) or if we have markedly different auditory capacities. Consider deafness or heightened sensitivity to selective frequencies. Think also about the varying capabilities of different animals. If a dog, frog, and bat were with us, would they hear the same sound as well?

There is a legitimate sense in which we can answer "yes." It is the same sense in which a person on a mechanics creeper can be looking at the same car as another in the driver's seat and a third standing behind it. There is a sense in which they are looking at different things (the transmission, the dash, and the trunk), and their experiences are apt to be qualitatively quite different, but there is no need to posit the existence of (or buy license plates for) three different cars. We do not take "I see the car" to mean "I see each and every part of the car from every conceivable angle, distance, and magnification." In like manner, we should not take "I hear the sound of a falling tree" to mean "I hear each and every frequency of the vibrational energy occasioned by the falling tree from every conceivable angle, distance, and position."

PROBLEMS OF INDIVIDUATION

How many sounds does a falling tree make? Depending on our sense of "sound," the answer may depend on how many sensations it occasions, how many vibrational energies it produces, or possibly both (note especially sound$_2$ in this regard). The approach of the preceding section is to treat the vibrational energy released by the falling tree as a single—if complex—entity. It thus answers that a falling tree makes but a single sound, different parts of which may be perceived by different observers in different ways. The approach is reasonably plausible, but counting is not as simple and metaphysically unproblematic as it may at first seem—especially as regards something like energy. Although we know fairly well how to *measure* energy (to determine *how much* energy is produced), there is something odd about trying to *count* energy (to determine *how many* energies are produced). But if energy cannot be individuated and counted, then neither obviously can sound$_3$, nor possibly sound$_2$. There may be something metaphysically odd or inappropriate about asking, with respect to these senses of the term, how many sounds are produced or even whether we hear the same sound.

If these results seem unacceptable, we might try counting instead the events that occasion sound. We could then take "We hear the same sound" as elliptical for "We hear sound occasioned by the same event." Counting events presents difficulties of its own. There is an element of arbitrariness about it (should we count the falling of a tree as a single event or a series of events?), but arbitrariness and similar difficulties notwithstanding, events are more easily and clearly delineated and counted than energy.

The approach, interestingly, might also help the sensationist out of his private-realities hole. Although you and I experience numerically different sensations, if those sensations are occasioned by the same event there is a reasonable sense in which we may say we are experiencing the same reality.

YOU HEAR *WHAT?*

The reflections of the preceding paragraphs reveal an ambiguity about what constitutes experiencing "the same reality." It is an ambiguity reflected in even our most common everyday language. What is it that we actually experience? Although we sometimes speak of hearing sound, more often we speak as though we could hear events themselves (the falling of a tree or the clapping of hands). The phenomenon is even more pronounced as regards sight, touch, and taste. We almost always speak as though we could actually see, touch, and taste physical objects. This way of talking is so common that many people have difficulty accepting or even understanding alternative formulations. Consider claims such as the following:

What you see is not the sun itself, but the light emitted by the sun eight minutes ago (alternately: the sensation occasioned by the visual reception and processing of the light emitted by the sun eight minutes ago).

What you see is not the book itself, but the effect of the surface structure of the book on the light being reflected from it to your eyes (alternately: the sensation occasioned by the visual reception and processing of the light reflected from the surface of the book).

What you feel is not the book itself, but the sensation produced by touching the book (alternately: some properties of the surface structure of the book or the effect of bringing that surface structure into contact with your skin).

What you taste is not the spaghetti you are eating, but the sensation produced by eating spaghetti (alternately: something concerning the chemical or structural properties of the spaghetti or the effect of those chemical or structural properties on your taste buds).

The alternative expressions are obviously complicated and cumbersome. Even if we believe they are metaphysically more accurate, adopting them in everyday discourse would make communication more difficult and time-consuming. We may choose to regard expressions like "I hear a falling tree" or "I see the sun" as convenient linguistic shorthand for more complex expressions about psychophysical sensations or physical processes. But the issues are not entirely linguistic. There is a strong metaphysical component to each of these different expressions. People do not readily give up the idea that what they see, taste, touch, smell, and hear are in fact the physical objects and events that they seem to see, taste, touch, smell, and hear. The illusion, if indeed it is an illusion, is an extremely strong one.

PERCEPTUAL DEPENDENCE

This at last brings us to the most basic, fundamental, and controversial issue raised by the question about the falling tree. To what extent does reality (more cautiously: the sort of reality we actually experience) depend for its very existence on someone's experience of it?

If, as has been suggested above, the only realities we ever experience are sensations, and if, as it seems, these sensations are heavily dependent on us for both their existence and their qualities, then obviously the reality we experience would not exist if we did not in fact experience it. We may be tempted to speculate about an underlying reality beyond the range of human experience, but how could we ever come to know anything about such a realm? Since our language has developed in conjunction with our experiences, how could we even be sure that we would be using the right sorts of terms and categories to discuss such a realm? Would it contain trees, forests, and mountains? If so, what would they be like? The object we know as a tree might in this spirit be treated as little more than an organized composite of sensations: some visual, some tactile, and so on. As such, it is not simply the sound of the falling tree, but its very existence in the absence of perceptually cognizant beings which is called into question.

Ideas such as this may seem exceedingly strange, unusual, and even bizarre, but they have been seriously discussed and debated by philosophers in all traditions and all ages. They have even given rise to an extremely prominent scientific position as regards the investigation of subatomic phenomena.

QUANTUM MECHANICS

In 1927 Werner Heisenberg discovered a very interesting and largely unexpected limitation in the investigation of the subatomic realm. We cannot measure, with precision, both the position and momentum of a subatomic particle. If we perform a precise measurement of its position, we thereby preclude a precise measurement of its momentum. And vice versa: a precise measurement of the momentum of a subatomic particle precludes a precise measurement of its position. It is possible to make imprecise and largely inaccurate measurements of both, but any increase in the precision of one will increase the uncertainty of the other. The limitation is known generally as Heisenberg's uncertainty relation (principle).

Although we might be tempted to dismiss Heisenberg's finding as a simple limitation of measurement, many scientists saw it as a serious challenge to the classical interpretation of their experiments. It raises difficult and controversial metaphysical and epistemological questions. Should we believe that subatomic particles have precise position and momentum in the absence of our measurements, and thus simultaneous precise position and momentum even though we cannot measure it? Or should we perhaps believe that the precise position (or momentum) of the particle is created in the measurement process, and thus, in the absence of a measurement, it has neither precise position nor precise momentum?

Subatomic reality had been difficult to conceptualize and deal with in other ways as well. Was an electron a particle, a unit of energy, or a field of some sort? Did light consist of particles or waves? And so on. In the autumn of 1927 a number of prominent physicists met at the fifth Solvay Congress in Brussels. Despite vehement and sustained opposition by Einstein, there emerged from the conference a view that rapidly gained the support of many scientists and has continued to dominate the field ever since. In recognition of the strong influence of Niels Bohr (from Copenhagen), it is called "the Copenhagen Interpretation of Quantum Mechanics." According to the Copenhagen Interpretation, Quantum Mechanics deals not so much with "reality as it is independent of any observation or experiment" as it does with the correlation of experimental procedures and observable results. It is not "nature itself" but "nature exposed to our method of questioning"[2] that is the subject of scientific investigation. As such, the Copenhagen Interpretation does not worry about the precise but unmeasured position of an electron, the "true" nature of light, and so on.

Erwin Schrödinger (originator of the Schrödinger wave equations) devised an ingenious example to demonstrate differences between the Copenhagen Interpretation and common-sense ideas about reality. The example is known as "Schrödinger's cat." Imagine an opaque soundproof box containing a vial of poisonous gas attached to a small radioactive triggering device. Suppose further that the triggering device is intrinsically probabilistic. We can calculate a probability curve for the release of the gas, but in the absence of an empirical observation cannot know with any degree of assurance whether the gas has been released. Imagine now that we place a live (but possibly unconscious) cat in the box and seal it so that there is no way, other than opening the box, to tell if the gas has been released.

Common sense tells us that the box contains an unfortunate and possibly frightened animal. The cat is either alive or dead depending on the (unknown) action of the triggering device.

But according to the principles of the Copenhagen Interpretation of Quantum Mechanics, the box contains an unknown reality, described only by our probability functions in terms of what we would be likely to find if we opened the box. Upon opening the box we will find either a live or dead cat. But until or unless that happens, it does not contain a cat (as we know it) at all!

Notes

1. Springfield, MA: G. & C. Merriam Co., 1961, p. 808.

2. Werner Heisenberg. *Physics and Philosophy*. New York: Harper & Row, 1958, p. 58.

The Allegory of the Cave

PLATO

"The Allegory of the Cave" is part of *The Republic* (circa 375 B.C.).
The dialogue is between Socrates and Glaucon. Topics include
illusion, reality, knowledge, and education.[1]

'I want you to go on to picture the enlightenment or ignorance of our human condition somewhat as follows. Imagine an underground chamber like a cave, with a long entrance open to the daylight and as wide as the cave. In this chamber are men who have been prisoners there since they were children, their legs and necks being so fastened that they can only look straight ahead of them and cannot turn their heads. Some way off, behind and higher up, a fire is burning, and between the fire and the prisoners and above them runs a road, in front of which a curtain-wall has been built, like the screen at puppet shows between the operators and their audience, above which they show their puppets.'

'I see.'

'Imagine further that there are men carrying all sorts of gear along behind the curtain-wall, projecting above it and including figures of men and animals made of wood and stone and all sorts of other materials, and that some of these men, as you would expect, are talking and some not.'

'An odd picture and an odd sort of prisoner.'

'They are drawn from life,'[1] I replied. 'For, tell me, do you think our prisoners could see anything of themselves or their fellows except the shadows thrown by the fire on the wall of the cave opposite them?'

'How could they see anything else if they were prevented from moving their heads all their lives?'

'And would they see anything more of the objects carried along the road?'

'Of course not.'

'Then if they were able to talk to each other, would they not assume that the shadows they saw were the real things?'

'Inevitably.'

'And if the wall of their prison opposite them reflected sound, don't you think that they would suppose, whenever one of the passers-by on the road spoke, that the voice belonged to the shadow passing before them?'

'They would be bound to think so.'

'And so in every way they would believe that the shadows of the objects we mentioned were the whole truth.'[2]

'Yes, inevitably.'

'Then think what would naturally happen to them if they were released from their bonds and cured of their delusions. Suppose one of them were let loose, and suddenly compelled to stand up and turn his head and look and walk towards the fire; all these actions would be painful and he would be too dazzled to see properly the objects of which he used to see the shadows. What do you think he would say

Plato, from *The Republic*, Third Revised Edition, translated by Desmond Lee, pp. 317–322. Copyright 1953, 1974, 1987 by H. D. P. Lee. Reprinted with the permission of Penguin Books Ltd.

[1]Details concerning Plato's life and philosophical commitments precede the selection titled "The Myth of Er" (Literary Reading for Chapter 2). Note also "The Death of Socrates" (Chapter 2), "The Ring of Gyges" (Chapter 4), "Choices" (Chapter 4), and "It's Just Not Fair!" (Chapter 5).

if he was told that what he used to see was so much empty nonsense and that he was now nearer reality and seeing more correctly, because he was turned towards objects that were more real, and if on top of that he were compelled to say what each of the passing objects was when it was pointed out to him? Don't you think he would be at a loss, and think that what he used to see was far truer[3] than the objects now being pointed out to him?'

'Yes, far truer.'

'And if he were made to look directly at the light of the fire, it would hurt his eyes and he would turn back and retreat to the things which he could see properly, which he would think really clearer than the things being shown him.'

'Yes.'

'And if,' I went on, 'he were forcibly dragged up the steep and rugged ascent and not let go till he had been dragged out into the sunlight, the process would be a painful one, to which he would much object, and when he emerged into the light his eyes would be so dazzled by the glare of it that he wouldn't be able to see a single one of the things he was now told were real.'[4]

'Certainly not at first,' he agreed.

'Because, of course, he would need to grow accustomed to the light before he could see things in the upper world outside the cave. First he would find it easiest to look at shadows, next at the reflections of men and other objects in water, and later on at the objects themselves. After that he would find it easier to observe the heavenly bodies and the sky itself at night, and to look at the light of the moon and stars rather than at the sun and its light by day.'

'Of course.'

'The thing he would be able to do last would be to look directly at the sun itself, and gaze at it without using reflections in water or any other medium, but as it is in itself.'

'That must come last.'

'Later on he would come to the conclusion that it is the sun that produces the changing seasons and years and controls everything in the visible world,

and is in a sense responsible for everything that he and his fellow-prisoners used to see.'

'That is the conclusion which he would obviously reach.'

'And when he thought of his first home and what passed for wisdom there, and of his fellow-prisoners, don't you think he would congratulate himself on his good fortune and be sorry for them?'

'Very much so.'

'There was probably a certain amount of honour and glory to be won among the prisoners, and prizes for keen-sightedness for those best able to remember the order of sequence among the passing shadows and so be best able to divine their future appearances. Will our released prisoner hanker after these prizes or envy this power or honour? Won't he be more likely to feel, as Homer says, that he would far rather be "a serf in the house of some landless man",[5] or indeed anything else in the world, than hold the opinions and live the life that they do?'

'Yes,' he replied, 'he would prefer anything to a life like theirs.'

'Then what do you think would happen,' I asked, 'if he went back to sit in his old seat in the cave? Wouldn't his eyes be blinded by the darkness, because he had come in suddenly out of the sunlight?'

'Certainly.'

'And if he had to discriminate between the shadows, in competition with the other prisoners, while he was still blinded and before his eyes got used to the darkness—a process that would take some time—wouldn't he be likely to make a fool of himself? And they would say that his visit to the upper world had ruined his sight, and that the ascent was not worth even attempting. And if anyone tried to release them and lead them up, they would kill him if they could lay hands on him.'

'They certainly would.'

'Now, my dear Glaucon,' I went on, 'this simile must be connected throughout with what preceded it.[6] The realm revealed by sight corresponds to the prison, and the light of the fire in the prison to the power of the sun. And you won't go wrong if you connect the ascent into the upper world and the sight of the objects there with the upward progress of the mind into the intelligible region. That at any rate is my interpretation, which is what you are anxious to hear; the truth of the matter is, after all, known only to god. But in my opinion, for what it is worth, the final thing to be perceived in the intelligible region, and perceived only with difficulty, is the form of the good; once seen, it is inferred to be responsible for whatever is right and valuable in anything, producing in the visible region light and the source of light, and being in the intelligible region itself controlling source of truth and intelligence. And anyone who is going to act rationally either in public or private life must have sight of it.'

'I agree,' he said, 'so far as I am able to understand you.'

'Then you will perhaps also agree with me that it won't be surprising if those who get so far are unwilling to involve themselves in human affairs, and if their minds long to remain in the realm above. That's what we should expect if our simile holds good again.'

'Yes, that's to be expected.'

'Nor will you think it strange that anyone who descends from contemplation of the divine to human life and its ills should blunder and make a fool of himself, if, while still blinded and unaccustomed to the surrounding darkness, he's forcibly put on trial in the law-courts or elsewhere about the shadows of justice or the figures of which they are shadows, and made to dispute about the notions of them held by men who have never seen justice itself.'

'There's nothing strange in that.'

'But anyone with any sense,' I said, 'will remember that the eyes may be unsighted in two ways, by a transition either from light to darkness or from darkness to light, and will recognize that the same thing applies to the mind. So when he sees a mind confused and unable to see clearly he will not laugh without thinking, but will ask himself whether it has come from a clearer world and is confused by the unaccustomed darkness, or whether it is dazzled by the stronger light of the clearer world to which it has escaped from its previous ignorance. The first condition of life is a reason for congratulation, the second for sympathy, though if one wants to laugh at it one can do so with less absurdity than at the mind that has descended from the daylight of the upper world.'

'You put it very reasonably.'

'If this is true,' I continued, 'we must reject the conception of education professed by those who say that they can put into the mind knowledge that was not there before—rather as if they could put sight into blind eyes.'

'It is a claim that is certainly made,' he said.

'But our argument indicates that this is a capacity which is innate in each man's mind, and that the organ by which he learns is like an eye which cannot be turned from darkness to light unless the whole body is turned; in the same way the mind as a whole must be turned away from the world of change until its eye can bear to look straight at reality, and at the brightest of all realities which is what we call the good.'

Notes

1. Lit: 'like us'. How 'like' has been a matter of controversy. Plato can hardly have meant that the ordinary man cannot distinguish between shadows and real things. But he does seem to be saying, with a touch of caricature (we must not take him too solemnly), that the ordinary man is often very uncritical in his beliefs, which are little more than a 'careless acceptance of appearances' (Crombie).

2. Lit: 'regard nothing else as true but the shadows'. The Greek word *alēthēs* (true) carries an implication of genuineness, and some translators render it here as 'real'.

3. Or 'more real'.

4. Or 'true', 'genuine'.

5. *Odyssey*, xi, 489.

6. I.e. the similes of the Sun and the Line. The detailed relations between the three similes have been much disputed, as has the meaning of the word here translated 'connected'. Some interpret it to mean a detailed correspondence ('every feature . . . is meant to fit'—Comford), others to mean, more loosely, 'attached' or 'linked to'. That Plato intended some degree of 'connection' between the three similes cannot be in doubt in view of the sentences which follow. But we should remember that they are similes, not scientific descriptions, and it would be a mistake to try to find out too much detailed precision. Plato has just spoken of the prisoners 'getting their hands' on their returned fellow and killing him. How could they do that if fettered as described at the opening of the simile? But Socrates was executed, so of course they must. This translation assumes the following main correspondences:

Tied prisoner in the cave	Illusion
Freed prisoner in the cave	Belief
Looking at shadows and reflections in the world outside the cave and the ascent thereto	Reason
Looking at real things in the world outside the cave	Intelligence
Looking at the sun	Vision of the form of the good.

Meditations

RENÉ DESCARTES

René Descartes (1596–1650) was one of the premier figures of the intellectual explosion of the early seventeenth century. His contemporaries included Francis Bacon, Johannes Kepler, Galileo Galilei, and Thomas Hobbes. A prolific thinker, Descartes made major contributions to physics, mathematics, and philosophy. Often regarded as the founder of analytic geometry, he is perhaps best known for the coordinate systems that continue to bear his name in recognition of his influence. Anyone who has ever connected the dots on a graph with x and y axes has benefited from (or perhaps been cursed by) his genius. His discoveries in mathematics reflect deep-seated commitments to rationalism, conceptual clarity, and rigorous demonstrability. Not surprising, his philosophical work is founded upon similar epistemic principles and methodological values.

The current selection comes from Descartes's popular treatise Meditations on First Philosophy (first published in Latin in 1641). Though his reflections concern the nature and existence of his own being, his detached style and critical examination demonstrate clearly his unflagging allegiance to the geometrical model of knowledge as logical demonstration from axiomatic first principles.

FIRST MEDITATION

Concerning Things That Can Be Doubted

There is no novelty to me in the reflection that, from my earliest years, I have accepted many false opinions as true, and that what I have concluded from such badly assured premises could not but be highly doubtful and uncertain. From the time that I first recognized this fact, I have realized that if I wished to have any firm and constant knowledge in the sciences, I would have to undertake, once and for all, to set aside all the opinions which I had previously accepted among my beliefs and start again from the very beginning. But this enterprise appeared to me to be of very great magnitude, and so I waited until I had attained an age so mature that I could not hope for a later time when I would be more fitted to execute the project. Now, however, I have delayed so long that henceforward I should be afraid that I was committing a fault if, in continuing to deliberate, I expended time which should be devoted to action.

The present is opportune for my design; I have freed my mind of all kinds of cares; I feel myself, fortunately, disturbed by no passions; and I have found a serene retreat in peaceful solitude. I will therefore make a serious and unimpeded effort to destroy generally all my former opinions. In order to do this, however, it will not be necessary to show that they are all false, a task which I might never be able to complete; because since reason already convinces me that I should abstain from the belief in things which are not entirely certain and indubitable no less carefully than from the belief in those which appear to me to be manifestly false, it will be enough to make me reject them all if I can find in each some ground for doubt. And for that it will not be necessary for me to examine each one in particular, which would be an infinite labor; but since the destruction of the foundation necessarily involves the collapse of all the rest of the edifice, I shall first attack the principles upon which all my former opinions were founded.

Everything which I have thus far accepted as entirely true and assured has been acquired from the senses or by means of the senses. But I have learned by experience that these senses sometimes mislead me, and it is prudent never to trust wholly those things which have once deceived us.

But it is possible that, even though the senses occasionally deceive us about things which are barely perceptible and very far away, there are many other things which we cannot reasonably doubt, even though we know them through the senses—as, for example, that I am here, seated by the fire, wearing a winter dressing gown, holding this paper in my hands, and other things of this nature. And how could I deny that these hands and this body are mine, unless I am to compare myself with certain lunatics whose brain is so troubled and befogged by the black vapors of the bile that they continually affirm that they are kings while they are paupers, that they are clothed in gold and purple while they are naked; or imagine that their head is made of clay, or that they are gourds, or that their body is glass? But this is ridiculous; such men are fools, and I would be no less insane than they if I followed their example.

Nevertheless, I must remember that I am a man, and that consequently I am accustomed to sleep and

in my dreams to imagine the same things that lunatics imagine when awake, or sometimes things which are even less plausible. How many times has it occurred that the quiet of the night made me dream of my usual habits: that I was here, clothed in a dressing gown, and sitting by the fire, although I was in fact lying undressed in bed! It seems apparent to me now, that I am not looking at this paper with my eyes closed, that this head that I shake is not drugged with sleep, that it is with design and deliberate intent that I stretch out this hand and perceive it. What happens in sleep seems not at all clear and as distinct as all this. But I am speaking as though I never recall having been misled, while asleep, by similar illusions! When I consider these matters carefully, I realize so clearly that there are no conclusive indications by which waking life can be distinguished from sleep that I am quite astonished, and my bewilderment is such that it is almost able to convince me that I am sleeping.

So let us suppose now that we are asleep and that all these details, such as opening the eyes, shaking the head, extending the hands, and similar things, are merely illusions; and let us think that perhaps our hands and our whole body are not such as we see them. Nevertheless, we must at least admit that these things which appear to us in sleep are like painted scenes and portraits which can only be formed in imitation of something real and true, and so, at the very least, these types of things—namely, eyes, head, hands, and the whole body—are not imaginary entities, but real and existent. For in truth painters, even when they use the greatest ingenuity in attempting to portray sirens and satyrs in bizarre and extraordinary ways, nevertheless cannot give them wholly new shapes and natures, but only invent some particular mixture composed of parts of various animals; or even if perhaps their imagination is sufficiently extravagant that they invent something so new that nothing like it has ever been seen, and so their work represents something purely imaginary and absolutely false, certainly at the very least the colors of which they are composed must be real.

And for the same reason, even if these types of things—namely, a body, eyes, head, hands, and other similar things—could be imaginary, nevertheless, we are bound to confess that there are some other still more simple and universal concepts which are true and existent, from the mixture of which, neither more nor less than in the case of the mixture of real colors, all these images of things are formed in our minds, whether they are true and real or imaginary and fantastic.

Of this class of entities is corporeal nature in general and its extension, including the shape of extended things, their quantity, or size and number, and also the place where they are, the time that measures their duration, and so forth. That is why we will perhaps not be reasoning badly if we conclude that physics, astronomy, medicine, and all the other sciences which follow from the consideration of composite entities are very dubious and uncertain; whereas arithmetic, geometry, and the other sciences of this nature, which treat only of very simple and general things without concerning themselves as to whether they occur in nature or not, contain some element of certainty and sureness. For whether I am awake or whether I am asleep, two and three together will always make the number five, and the square will never have more than four sides; and it does not seem possible that truths so clear and so apparent can ever be suspected of any falsity or uncertainty.

Nevertheless, I have long held the belief that there is a God who can do anything, by whom I have been created and made what I am. But how can I be sure that he has brought it to pass that there is no earth, no sky, no extended bodies, no shape, no size, no place, and that nevertheless I have the impressions of all these things and cannot imagine that things might be other than as I now see them? And furthermore, just as I sometimes judge that others are mistaken about those things which they think they know best, how can I be sure but that God has brought it about that I am always mistaken when I add two and three or count the sides of a square, or when I judge of something else even easier, if I can imagine anything easier than that? But perhaps God did not wish me to be deceived in that fashion, since he is said to be supremely good. But if it was repugnant to his goodness to have made me so that I was always mistaken, it would seem also to be inconsistent for him to permit me to be sometimes mistaken, and nevertheless I cannot doubt that he does permit it.

At this point there will perhaps be some persons who would prefer to deny the existence of so powerful a God, rather than to believe that everything else is uncertain. Let us not oppose them for the moment, and let us concede according to their point of view that everything which I have stated here about God is fictitious. Then in whatever way they suppose that I have reached the state of being that I now have, whether they attribute it to some destiny or fate or refer it to chance, or whether they wish to explain it as the result of a continual interplay of events or in any other manner; nevertheless, since to err and be mistaken is a kind of imperfection, to whatever degree less powerful they consider the author to whom they attribute my origin, in that degree it will be more probable that I am so imperfect that I am always mistaken. To this reasoning, certainly, I have nothing to reply; and I am at last constrained to admit that there is nothing in what I formerly believed to be true which I cannot somehow doubt, and this not for lack of thought and attention, but for weighty and well-considered reasons. Thus I find that, in the future, I should withhold and suspend my judgment about these matters, and guard myself no less carefully from believing them than I should from believing what is manifestly false if I wish to find any certain and assured knowledge in the sciences.

It is not enough to have made these observations; it is also necessary that I should take care to bear them in mind. For these customary and long-standing beliefs will frequently recur in my thoughts, my long and familiar acquaintance with them giving them the right to occupy my mind against my will and almost to make themselves masters of my beliefs. I will never free myself of the habit of deferring to them and having faith in them as long as I consider that they are what they really are—that is, somewhat doubtful, as I have just shown, even if highly probable—so that there is much more reason to believe than to deny them. That is why I think that I would not do badly if I deliberately took the opposite position and deceived myself in pretending for some time that all these opinions are entirely false and imaginary, until at last I will have so balanced my former and my new prejudices that they cannot incline my mind more to one side than the other, and my judgment will not be mastered and turned by bad habits from the correct perception of things and the straight road leading to the knowledge of the truth. For I feel sure that I cannot overdo this distrust, since it is not now a question of acting, but only of meditating and learning.

I will therefore suppose that, not a true God, who is very good and who is the supreme source of truth, but a certain evil spirit, not less clever and deceitful than powerful, has bent all his efforts to deceiving me. I will suppose that the sky, the air, the earth, colors, shapes, sounds, and all other objective things that we see are nothing but illusions and dreams that he has used to trick my credulity. I will consider myself as having no hands, no eyes, no flesh, no blood, nor any senses, yet falsely believing that I have all these things. I will remain resolutely attached to this hypothesis; and if I cannot attain the knowledge of any truth by this method, at any rate it is in my power to suspend my judgment. That is why I shall take great care not to accept any falsity among my beliefs and shall prepare my mind so well for all the ruses of this great deceiver that, however powerful and artful he may be, he will never be able to mislead me in anything.

But this undertaking is arduous, and a certain laziness leads me insensibly into the normal paths of ordinary life. I am like a slave who, enjoying an imaginary liberty during sleep, begins to suspect that his liberty is only a dream; he fears to wake up and conspires with his pleasant illusions to retain them longer. So insensibly to myself I fall into my former opinions; and I am slow to wake up from this slumber for fear that the labors of waking life which will have to follow the tranquillity of this sleep, instead of leading me into the daylight of the knowledge of the truth, will be insufficient to dispel the darkness of all the difficulties which have just been raised.

SECOND MEDITATION

Of the Nature of the Human Mind, and That It Is More Easily Known Than the Body

Yesterday's Meditation has filled my mind with so many doubts that it is no longer in my power to forget them. Nor do I yet see how I will be able to resolve them; I feel as though I were suddenly thrown into deep water, being so disconcerted that I can neither plant my feet on the bottom nor swim on the surface. I shall nevertheless make every effort to conform precisely to the plan commenced yesterday and put aside every belief in which I could imagine the least doubt, just as though I knew that it was absolutely false. And I shall continue in this manner until I have found something certain, or at least, if I can do nothing else, until I have learned with certainty that there is nothing certain in this world. Archimedes, to move the earth from its orbit and place it in a new position, demanded nothing more than a fixed and immovable fulcrum; in a similar manner I shall have the right to entertain high hopes if I am fortunate enough to find a single truth which is certain and indubitable.

I suppose, accordingly, that everything I see is false; I convince myself that nothing has ever existed of all that my deceitful memory recalls to me. I think that I have no senses; and I believe that body, shape, extension, motion, and location are merely inventions of my mind. What then could still be thought true? Perhaps nothing else, unless it is that there is nothing certain in the world.

But how do I know that there is some entity, of a different nature from what I have just judged uncertain, of which there cannot be the least doubt? Is there not some God or some other power who gives me these thoughts? But I need not think this to be true, for possibly I am able to produce them myself. Then, at the very least, am I not an entity myself? But I have already denied that I had any senses, or any body. However, at this point I hesitate, for what follows from that? Am I so dependent upon the body and the senses that I could not exist without them? I have just convinced myself that nothing whatsoever existed in the world, that there was no sky, no earth, no minds, and no bodies; have I not thereby convinced myself that I did not exist? Not at all; without doubt I existed if I was convinced or even if I thought anything. Even though there may be a deceiver of some sort, very powerful and very tricky, who bends all his efforts to keep me perpetually deceived, there can be no slightest doubt that I exist, since he deceives me; and let him deceive me as much as he will, he can never make me be nothing as long as I think that I am something. Thus, after having thought well on this matter, and after examining all things with care, I must finally conclude and maintain that this proposition: *I am, I exist,* is necessarily true every time that I pronounce it or conceive it in my mind.

But I do not yet know sufficiently clearly what I am, I who am sure that I exist. So I must henceforth take very great care that I do not incautiously mistake some other thing for myself, and so make an error even in that knowledge which I maintain to be more certain and more evident than all other knowledge that I previously had. That is why I shall now consider once more what I thought myself to be before I began these last deliberations. Of my former opinions I shall reject all that are rendered even slightly doubtful by the arguments that I have just now offered, so that there will remain just that part alone which is entirely certain and indubitable.

What then have I previously believed myself to be? Clearly, I believed that I was a man. But what is a man? Shall I say a rational animal? Certainly not, for I would have to determine what an "animal" is and what is meant by "rational"; and so, from a single question, I would find myself gradually enmeshed in an infinity of others more difficult and more inconvenient, and I would not care to waste the little time and leisure remaining to me in disentangling such difficulties. I shall rather pause here to consider the ideas which previously arose naturally and of themselves in my mind whenever I considered what I was. I thought of myself first as having a face, hands, arms, and all this mechanism composed of bone and flesh and members, just as it appears in a corpse, and which I designated by the name of "body." In addition, I thought of the fact that I consumed nourishment, that I walked, that I perceived and thought, and I ascribed all these actions to the soul. But either I did not stop to consider what this soul was or else, if I did, I imagined that it was something very rarefied and subtle, such as a wind, a flame, or very much expanded air which penetrated into and was infused throughout my grosser components. As for what body was, I did not realize that there could be any doubt about it, for I thought that I recognized its nature very distinctly. If I had wished to explain it according to the notions that I then entertained, I would have described it somewhat in this way: By "body" I understand all that can be bounded by some figure: that can be located in some place and occupy space in such a way that every other body is excluded from it; that can be perceived by touch or sight or hearing or taste or smell; that can be moved in various ways, not by itself but by some other object by which it is touched and from which it receives an impulse. For to possess the power to move itself, and also to feel or to think, I did not believe at all that these are attributes of corporeal nature; on the contrary, rather, I was astonished to see a few bodies possessing such abilities.

But I, what am I, on the basis of the present hypothesis that there is a certain spirit who is extremely powerful and, if I may dare to say so, malicious and tricky and who uses all his abilities and efforts in order to deceive me? Can I be sure that I possess the smallest fraction of all those characteristics which I have just now said belonged to the nature of body? I pause to consider this attentively. I pass and repass in review in my mind each one of all these things—it is not necessary to pause to take the time to list them—and I do not find any one of them which I can pronounce to be part of me. Is it characteristic of me to consume nourishment and to walk? But if it is true that I do not have a body, these also are nothing but figments of the imagination. To perceive?[1] But once more, I cannot perceive without the body, except in the sense that I have thought I perceived various things during sleep, which I recognized upon waking not to have been really perceived. To think?[2] Here I find the answer. Thought is an attribute that belongs to me; it alone is inseparable from my nature.

I am, I exist—that is certain; but for how long do I exist? For as long as I think; for it might perhaps happen, if I totally ceased thinking, that I would at the same time completely cease to be. I am now admitting nothing except what is necessarily true. I am therefore, to speak precisely, only a thinking being, that is to say, a mind, an understanding,[3] or a reasoning being, which are terms whose meaning was previously known to me.

I am something real and really existing, but what thing am I? I have already given the answer: a thing which thinks. And what more? I will stimulate my imagination to see if I am not something else beyond this. I am not this assemblage of members which is called a human body; I am not a rarefied and penetrating air spread throughout all these members; I am not a wind, a flame, a breath, a vapor, or anything at all that I can imagine and picture to myself—since I have supposed that all that was nothing, and since, without abandoning this supposition, I find that I do not cease to be certain that I am something.

But perhaps it is true that those same things which I suppose not to exist because I do not know them are really no different from the self which I do know. As to that I cannot decide; I am not discussing that question at the moment, since I can pass judgment only upon those things which are known to me: I know that I exist and I am seeking to discover what I am, that "I" that I know to be. Now it is very certain that this notion and knowledge of my being, thus precisely understood, does not depend on things whose existence is not yet known to me; and consequently and even more certainly, it does not depend on any of those things

that I picture in my imagination. And even these terms, "picture" and "imagine," warn me of my error. For I would be imagining falsely indeed were I to picture myself as something; since to imagine is nothing else than to contemplate the shape or image of a bodily entity, and I already know both that I certainly exist and that it is altogether possible that all these images, and everything in general, which is involved in the nature of body, are only dreams and illusions. From this I see clearly that there was no more sense in saying that I could stimulate my imagination to learn more distinctly what I am than if I should say: I am now awake, and I see something real and true; but because I do not yet perceive it sufficiently clearly, I will go to sleep on purpose, in order that my dreams will show it to me with more truth and evidence. And thus I know manifestly that nothing of all that I can understand by means of the imagination is pertinent to the knowledge which I have of myself, and that I must remember this and prevent my mind from thinking in this fashion, in order that it may clearly perceive its own nature.

But what then am I? A thinking being.[4] What is a thinking being? It is a being which doubts, which understands, which conceives, which affirms, which denies, which wills, which rejects, which imagines also, and which perceives. It is certainly not a trivial matter if all these things belong to my nature. But why should they not belong to it? Am I not that same person who now doubts almost everything, who nevertheless understands and conceives certain things, who is sure of and affirms the truth of this one thing alone, who denies all the others, who wills and desires to know more about them, who rejects error, who imagines many things, sometimes even against my will, and who also perceives many things, as through the medium of the senses for the organs of the body? Is there anything in all that which is not just as true as it is certain that I am and that I exist, even though I were always asleep and though the one who created me directed all his efforts to deluding me? And is there any one of these attributes which can be distinguished from my thinking or which can be said to be separable from my nature? For it is so obvious that it is I who doubt, understand, and desire, that nothing could be added to make it more evident. And I am also certainly the same one who imagines; for once more, even though it could happen that the things I imagine are not true, nevertheless this power of imagining cannot fail to be real, and it is part of my thinking. Finally I am the same being which perceives—that is, which observes certain objects as though by means of the sense organs, because I do really see light, hear noises, feel heat. Will it be said that these appearances are false and that I am sleeping? Let it be so; yet at the very least it is certain that it seems to me that I see light, hear noises, and feel heat. This much cannot be false, and it is this, properly considered, which in my nature is called perceiving, and that, again speaking precisely, is nothing else but thinking.

Notes

1. [L. *sentire;* F. *sentir.*]

2. [L. *cogitare;* F. *penser.*]

3. [L. *intellectus;* F. *entendement.*]

4. [L. *res cogitans;* F. *une chose qui pense.*]

The Dynamic Universe

FRITJOF CAPRA

Fritjof Capra is a high-energy physicist who has lectured and conducted research at a number of universities in America and Europe. He is best known for his controversial book *The Tao of Physics*, from which the following selection is edited. Discussion of contemporary scientific theories is mixed with reflections concerning Hinduism, Buddhism, and Taoism. Thus some of the parallels suggested here are explored further in Chapters 10 and 11, particularly in the selection by Capra titled "The Cosmic Dance."

The central aim of Eastern mysticism is to experience all phenomena in the world as manifestations of the same ultimate reality. This reality is seen as the essence of the universe, underlying and unifying the multitude of things and events we observe. The Hindus call it *Brahman,* the Buddhists *Dharmakaya* (the Body of Being), or *Tathata* (Suchness), and the Taoists *Tao;* each affirming that it transcends our intellectual concepts and defies further description. This ultimate essence, however, cannot be separated from its multiple manifestations. It is central to its very nature to manifest itself in myriad forms which come into being and disintegrate, transforming themselves into one another without end. In its phenomenal aspect, the cosmic One is thus intrinsically dynamic, and the apprehension of its dynamic nature is basic to all schools of Eastern mysticism. Thus D. T. Suzuki writes about the Kegon school of Mahayana Buddhism:

> The central idea of Kegon is to grasp the universe dynamically whose characteristic is always to move onward, to be forever in the mood of moving, which is life.[1]

This emphasis on movement, flow, and change is not only characteristic of the Eastern mystical traditions, but has been an essential aspect of the world view of mystics throughout the ages. In ancient Greece, Heraclitus taught that "everything flows" and compared the world to an ever-living fire, and in Mexico, the Yaqui mystic Don Juan talks about the "fleeting world" and affirms that "to be a man of knowledge one needs to be light and fluid."[2]

Diagram of Change from the Taoist Canon, Northern Sung dynasty.

In Indian philosophy, the main terms used by Hindus and Buddhists have dynamic connotations. The word *Brahman* is derived from the Sanskrit root *brih*—to grow—and thus suggests a reality which is dynamic and alive. In the words of S. Radhakrishnan, "The word *Brahman* means growth and is suggestive of life, motion, and progress."[3] The *Upanishads* refer to *Brahman* as "this unformed, immortal, moving,"[4] thus associating it with motion even though it transcends all forms.

The *Rig Veda* uses another term to express the dynamic nature of the universe: the term *Rita*. This word comes from the root *ri*—to move; its original meaning in the *Rig Veda* being "the course of all things," "the order of nature." It plays an important role in the legends of the *Veda* and is connected with all the Vedic gods. The order of nature was conceived by the Vedic seers, not as a static divine law, but as a dynamic principle which is inherent in the universe. This idea is not unlike the Chinese conception of *Tao*—"The Way"—as the way in which the universe works; i.e., the order of nature. Like the Vedic seers, the Chinese sages saw the world in terms of flow and change, and thus gave the idea of a cosmic order an essentially dynamic connotation. Both concepts, *Rita* and *Tao,* were later brought down from their original cosmic level to the human level and were interpreted in a moral sense; *Rita* as the universal law which all gods and humans must obey, and *Tao* as the right way of life.

The Vedic concept of *Rita* anticipates the idea of *karma* which was developed later to express the dynamic interplay of all things and events. The word *karma* means "action" and denotes the "active," or dynamic, interrelation of all phenomena. In the words of the *Bhagavad Gita*, "All actions take place in time by the interweaving of the forces of nature."[5] The Buddha took up the traditional concept of *karma* and gave it a new meaning by extending the idea of dynamic interconnections to the sphere of human situations. *Karma* thus came to signify the never-ending chain of cause and effect in human life which the Buddha had broken in attaining the state of enlightenment.

Hinduism has also found many ways of expressing the dynamic nature of the universe in mythical language. Thus Krishna says in the *Gita*, "If I did not engage in action, these worlds would perish,"[6] and Shiva, the Cosmic Dancer, is perhaps the most perfect personification of the dynamic universe. Through his dance, Shiva sustains the manifold phenomena in the world, unifying all things by immersing them in his rhythm and making them participate in the dance—a magnificent image of the dynamic unity of the universe.

The general picture emerging from Hinduism is one of an organic, growing, and rhythmically moving cosmos; of a universe in which everything is fluid and ever-changing, all static forms being *maya*, that is, existing only as illusory concepts. This last idea—the impermanence of all forms—is the starting point of Buddhism. The Buddha taught that "all compounded things are impermanent," and that all suffering in the world arises from our trying to cling to fixed forms—objects, people, or ideas—instead of accepting the world as it moves and changes. The dynamic world view lies thus at the very root of Buddhism. In the words of S. Radhakrishnan:

> A wonderful philosophy of dynamics was formulated by Buddha 2,500 years ago. . . . Impressed with the transitoriness of objects, the ceaseless mutation and transformation of things, Buddha formulated a philosophy of change. He reduces substances, souls, monads, things to forces, movements, sequences, and processes, and adopts a dynamic conception of reality.[7]

Buddhists call this world of ceaseless change *samsara*, which means, literally, "incessantly in motion"; and they affirm that there is nothing in it which is worth clinging to. So for the Buddhists, an enlightened being is one who does not resist the

Fritjof Capra, "The Dynamic Universe" from *The Tao of Physics: An Exploration of the Parallels Between Modern Physics and Eastern Mysticism,* Third Edition, Updated, pp. 174–191. Copyright © 1975, 1983, 1991 by Fritjof Capra. Reprinted with the permission of Shambhala Publications, Inc.

flow of life, but keeps moving with it. When the *Ch'an* monk Yün-men was asked, "What is the *Tao*?" he answered simply, "Walk on!" Accordingly, Buddhists also call the Buddha the *Tathagata*, or "the one who comes and goes thus." In Chinese philosophy, the flowing and ever-changing reality is called the *Tao* and is seen as a cosmic process in which all things are involved. Like the Buddhists, the Taoists say that one should not resist the flow, but should adapt one's actions to it. This, again, is characteristic of the sage—the enlightened being. If the Buddha is one who "comes and goes thus," the Taoist sage is one who "flows," as Huai Nan Tzu says, "in the current of the *Tao*."

The more one studies the religious and philosophical texts of the Hindus, Buddhists and Taoists, the more it becomes apparent that in all of them the world is conceived in terms of movement, flow and change. This dynamic quality of Eastern philosophy seems to be one of its most important features. The Eastern mystics see the universe as an inseparable web, whose interconnections are dynamic and not static. The cosmic web is alive; it moves, grows and changes continually. Modern physics, too, has come to conceive of the universe as such a web of relations and, like Eastern mysticism, has recognized that this web is intrinsically dynamic. The dynamic aspect of matter arises in quantum theory as a consequence of the wave-nature of subatomic particles, and is even more essential in relativity theory, as we shall see, where the unification of space and time implies that the being of matter cannot be separated from its activity. The properties of subatomic particles can therefore only be understood in a dynamic context; in terms of movement, interaction and transformation.

According to quantum theory, particles are also waves, and this implies that they behave in a very peculiar way. Whenever a subatomic particle is confined to a small region of space, it reacts to this confinement by moving around. The smaller the region of confinement, the faster will the particle "jiggle" around in it. This behavior is a typical "quantum ef-

fect," a feature of the subatomic world which has no macroscopic analogy. To see how it comes about, we have to remember that particles are represented, in quantum theory, by wave packets . . . the length of such a wave packet represents the uncertainty in the location of the particle. The following wave pattern,

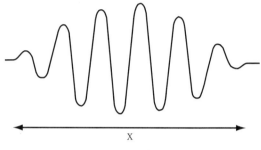

a wave packet

for example, corresponds to a particle located somewhere in the region X; where exactly we cannot say with certainty. If we want to localize the particle more precisely, i.e., if we want to confine it to a smaller region, we have to squeeze its wave packet into this region (see diagram below). This, however,

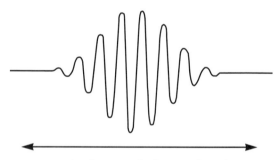

squeezing the wave packet into a smaller region

will affect the wavelength of the wave packet, and consequently the velocity of the particle. As a result, the particle will move around; the more it is confined, the faster it will move.

The tendency of particles to react to confinement with motion implies a fundamental "restlessness" of matter which is characteristic of the subatomic world. In this world, most of the material particles are bound to the molecular, atomic and nuclear structures, and therefore are not at rest but have an inherent tendency to move about—they are intrinsically restless. According to quantum theory, matter is thus never quiescent, but always in a state of motion. Macroscopically, the material objects around us may seem passive and inert, but when we magnify such a "dead" piece of stone or metal, we see that it is full of activity. The closer we look at it, the more alive it appears. All the material objects in our environment are made of atoms which link up with each other in various ways to form an enormous variety of molecular structures which are not rigid and motionless, but oscillate according to their temperature and in harmony with the thermal vibrations of their environment. In the vibrating atoms, the electrons are bound to the atomic nuclei by electric forces which try to keep them as close as possible, and they respond to this confinement by whirling around extremely fast. In the nuclei, finally, the protons and neutrons are pressed into a minute volume by the strong nuclear forces, and consequently race about with unimaginable velocities.

Modern physics, then, pictures matter not at all as passive and inert, but as being in a continuous dancing and vibrating motion whose rhythmic patterns are determined by the molecular, atomic and nuclear structures. This is also the way in which the Eastern mystics see the material world. They all emphasize that the universe has to be grasped dynamically, as it moves, vibrates and dances; that nature is not in a static, but a dynamic equilibrium. In the words of a Taoist text:

> The stillness is not the real stillness. Only when there is stillness in movement can the spiritual rhythm appear which pervades heaven and earth.[8]

In physics, we recognize the dynamic nature of the universe not only when we go to small dimensions—to the world of atoms and nuclei—but also when we turn to large dimensions—to the world of stars and galaxies. Through our powerful telescopes we observe a universe in ceaseless motion. Rotating clouds of hydrogen gas contract to form stars, heating up in the process until they become burning fires in the sky. When they have reached that stage, they still continue to rotate, some of them ejecting material into space which spirals outwards and condenses into planets circling around the star. Eventually, after millions of years, when most of its hydrogen fuel is used up, a star expands, and then contracts again in the final gravitational collapse. This collapse may involve gigantic explosions, and may even turn the star into a black hole. All these activities—the formation of stars out of interstellar gas clouds, their contraction and subsequent expansion, and their final collapse—can actually be observed somewhere in the skies.

The spinning, contracting, expanding or exploding stars cluster into galaxies of various shapes—flat discs, spheres, spirals, etc.—which, again, are not motionless but rotate. Our galaxy, the Milky Way, is an immense disc of stars and gas turning in space like a huge wheel, so that all its stars—including the sun and its planets—move around the galaxy's center. The universe is, in fact, full of galaxies strewn out through all the space we can see; all spinning like our own.

When we study the universe as a whole, with its millions of galaxies, we have reached the largest scale of space and time; and again, at that cosmic level, we discover that the universe is not static—it is expanding! This has been one of the most important discoveries in modern astronomy. A detailed analysis of the light received from distant galaxies has shown that the whole swarm of galaxies expands, and that it does so in a well-orchestrated way; the recession velocity of any galaxy we observe is proportional to the galaxy's distance. The more distant the galaxy, the faster it moves away from us; at double the distance, the recession velocity will also double. This is true not only for distances measured from our galaxy, but applies to any point of reference. Whichever galaxy you happen to be in, you will observe the other galaxies rushing away from you; nearby galaxies at several thousand miles per second, farther ones at higher speeds, and the farthest at velocities approaching the speed of light. The light from galaxies beyond that distance will never reach us, because they move away from us faster than the speed of light. Their light is—in the words of Sir Arthur Eddington—"like a runner on an expanding track with the winning post receding faster than he can run."

To have a better idea of the way in which the universe expands, we have to remember that the proper framework for studying its large-scale features is Einstein's general theory of relativity. According to this theory, space is not "flat," but is "curved," and the precise way in which it is curved is related to the distribution of matter by Einstein's field equations. These equations can be used to determine the structure of the universe as a whole; they are the starting point of modern cosmology.

When we talk about an expanding universe in the framework of general relativity, we mean an expansion in a higher dimension. Like the concept of curved space, we can only visualize such a concept with the help of a two-dimensional analogy. Imagine a balloon with a large number of dots on its surface. The balloon represents the universe, its two-dimensional curved surface representing the three-dimensional curved space, and the dots on the surface the galaxies in that space. When the balloon is blown up, all the distances between the dots increase. Whichever dot you choose to sit on, all the other dots will move away from you. The universe expands in the same way: whichever galaxy an observer happens to be in, the other galaxies will move away from him.

An obvious question to be asked about the expanding universe is: how did it all start? From the relation between the distance of a galaxy and its recession velocity—which is known as Hubble's law—one can calculate the starting point of the expansion, in other words, the age of the universe. Assuming that there has been no change in the rate of expansion, which is by no means certain, one arrives at an age of the order of 10,000 million years. This, then, is the age of the universe. Most cosmologists believe today that the universe came into be-

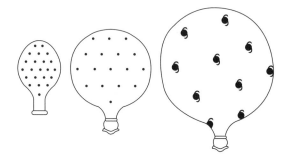

ing in a highly dramatic event about 10,000 million years ago, when its total mass exploded out of a small primeval fireball. The present expansion of the universe is seen as the remaining thrust of this initial explosion. According to this "big-bang" model, the moment of the big bang marked the beginning of the universe and the beginning of space and time. If we want to know what happened before that moment, we run—again—into severe difficulties of thought and language. In the words of Sir Bernard Lovell:

> There we reach the greater barrier of thought because we begin to struggle with the concepts of time and space before they existed in terms of our everyday experience. I feel as though I've suddenly driven into a great fog barrier where the familiar world has disappeared.[9]

As far as the future of the expanding universe is concerned, Einstein's equations do not provide a unique answer. They allow for several different solutions corresponding to different models of the universe. Some models predict that that expansion will continue forever; according to others, it is slowing down and will eventually change into a contraction. These models describe an oscillating universe, expanding for billions of years, then contracting until its total mass has condensed into a small ball of matter, then expanding again, and so on without end.

This idea of a periodically expanding and contracting universe, which involves a scale of time and space of vast proportions, has arisen not only in modern cosmology, but also in ancient Indian mythology. Experiencing the universe as an organic and rhythmically moving cosmos, the Hindus were able to develop evolutionary cosmologies which come very close to our modern scientific models. One of these cosmologies is based on the Hindu myth of *lila*—the divine play—in which *Brahman* transforms himself into the world. *Lila* is a rhythmic play which goes on in endless cycles, the One becoming the many and the many returning into the One. In the *Bhagavad Gita,* the god Krishna describes this rhythmic play of creation in the following words:

> At the end of the night time all things return to my nature; and when the new day of time begins I bring them again into light.
>
> Thus through my nature I bring forth all creation and this rolls around in the circles of time.
>
> But I am not bounded by this vast work of creation. I am and I watch the drama of works.
>
> I watch and in its work of creation nature brings forth all that moves not: and thus the revolutions of the world go round.[10]

The Hindu sages were not afraid to identify this rhythmic divine play with the evolution of the cosmos as a whole. They pictured the universe as periodically expanding and contracting and gave the name *kalpa* to the unimaginable time span between the beginning and the end of one creation. The scale of this ancient myth is indeed staggering; it has taken the human mind more than two thousand years to come up again with a similar concept.

From the world of the very large, from the expanding cosmos, let us now return to the world of the infinitely small. Physics in the twentieth century has been characterized by an ever-progressing penetration into this world of submicroscopic dimensions, down into the realms of atoms, nuclei, and their constituents. This exploration of the submicroscopic world has been motivated by one basic question which has occupied and stimulated human thought throughout the ages: what is matter made of? Ever since the beginning of natural philosophy, men and women have speculated about this question, trying to find the "basic stuff" of which all matter is made; but only in our century has it been possible to seek an answer by undertaking experiments. With the help of a highly sophisticated technology, physicists were able to explore first the structure of atoms, finding that they consisted of nuclei and electrons, and then the structure of the atomic nuclei which were found to consist of protons and neutrons, commonly called nucleons. In the last two decades, they have gone yet another step farther and have begun to investigate the structure of the nucleons—the constituents of the atomic nuclei—which, again, do not seem to be the ultimate particles, but seem to be composed of other entities.

The first step in the penetration into ever-deeper layers of matter—the exploration of the world of atoms—has led to several profound modifications of our view of matter which have been discussed in the previous chapters. The second step was the penetration of the world of atomic nuclei and their constituents, and it has forced us to change our views in a way which is no less profound. In this world, we deal with dimensions which are a hundred thousand times smaller than atomic dimensions, and consequently the particles confined to such small dimensions move considerably faster than those confined to atomic structures. They move, in fact, so fast that they can only be described adequately in the framework of the special theory of relativity. To understand the properties and interactions of subatomic particles, it is thus necessary to use a framework which takes into account both quantum theory and relativity theory, and it is relativity theory which forces us to modify our view of matter once more.

The characteristic feature of the relativistic framework is . . . that it unifies basic concepts which seemed totally unrelated before. One of the most important examples is the equivalence of mass and energy which is expressed mathematically by Einstein's famous equation E = mc². To understand the profound significance of this equivalence, we first have to understand the meaning of energy, and the meaning of mass.

Energy is one of the most important concepts used in the description of natural phenomena. As in everyday life, we say that a body has energy when it has the capacity for doing work. This energy can take a great variety of forms. It can be energy of motion, energy of heat, gravitational energy, electrical energy, chemical energy, and so on. Whatever the form is, it can be used to do work. A stone, for example, can be given gravitational energy by lifting it up to some height. When it is dropped from that height, its gravitational energy is transformed into energy of motion (kinetic energy), and when the stone hits the ground it can do work by breaking something. Taking a more constructive example, electrical energy or chemical energy can be transformed into heat energy and used for domestic purposes. In physics, energy is always associated with some process, or some kind of activity, and its fundamental importance lies in the fact that the total energy involved in a process is always conserved. It may change its form in the most complicated way, but none of it can get lost. The conservation of energy is one of the most fundamental laws of physics. It governs all known natural phenomena and no violation of the law has so far been observed.

The mass of a body, on the other hand, is a measure of its own weight: i.e., of the pull of gravity on the body. Besides that, mass measures the inertia of an object: i.e., its resistance against being accelerated. Heavy objects are harder to accelerate than light objects, a fact which is well known to anybody who has ever pushed a car. In classical physics, mass was furthermore associated with an indestructible material substance: i.e., with the "stuff" of which all things were thought to be made. Like energy, it was believed to be rigorously conserved, so that no mass could ever get lost.

Now relativity theory tells us that mass is nothing but a form of energy. Energy can not only take the various forms known in classical physics, but

can also be locked up in the mass of an object. The amount of energy contained, for example, in a particle is equal to the particle's mass, m, times c², the square of the speed of light; thus:

Once it is seen to be a form of energy, mass is no longer required to be indestructible, but can be transformed into other forms of energy. This can happen when subatomic particles collide with one another. In such collisions, particles can be destroyed, and the energy contained in their masses can be transformed into kinetic energy and distributed among the other particles participating in the collision. Conversely, when particles collide with very high velocities, their kinetic energy can be used to form the masses of new particles. . . . .

The creation and destruction of material particles is one of the most impressive consequences of the equivalence of mass and energy. In the collision processes of high-energy physics, mass is no longer conserved. The colliding particles can be destroyed and their masses may be transformed partly into the masses, and partly into the kinetic energies of the newly created particles. Only the total energy involved in such a process, that is, the total kinetic energy plus the energy contained in all the masses, is conserved. The collisions of subatomic particles are our main tool to study their properties and the relation between masses and energy is essential for their description. It has been verified innumerable times and particle physicists are completely familiar with the equivalence of mass and energy; so familiar, in fact, that they measure the masses of particles in the corresponding energy units.

The discovery that mass is nothing but a form of energy has forced us to modify our concept of a particle in an essential way. In modern physics, mass is no longer associated with a material substance, and hence particles are not seen as consisting of any basic "stuff," but as bundles of energy. Since energy, however, is associated with activity, with processes, the implication is that the nature of subatomic particles is intrinsically dynamic. To understand this better, we must remember that these particles can only be conceived in relativistic terms, that is, in terms of a framework where space and time are fused into a four-dimensional continuum. The particles must not be pictured as static three-dimensional objects, like billiard balls or grains of sand, but rather as four-dimensional entities in space-time. Their forms have to be understood dynamically, as forms in space and time. Subatomic particles are dynamic patterns which have a space aspect and a time aspect. Their space aspect makes them appear as objects with a certain mass, their time aspect as processes involving the equivalent energy.

These dynamic patterns, or "energy bundles," form the stable nuclear, atomic, and molecular structures which build up matter and give it its macroscopic solid aspect, thus making us believe that it is made of some material substance. At the macroscopic level, this notion of substance is a useful approximation, but at the atomic level it no longer makes sense. Atoms consist of particles, and these particles are not made of any material stuff. When we observe them, we never see any substance; what we observe are dynamic patterns continually changing into one another—a continuous dance of energy.

Quantum theory has shown that particles are not isolated grains of matter, but are probability patterns, interconnections in an inseparable cosmic web. Relativity theory, so to speak, has made these patterns come alive by revealing their intrinsically dynamic character. It has shown that the activity of matter is the very essence of its being. The particles of the subatomic world are not only active in the sense of moving around very fast; they themselves are processes! The existence of matter and its activity cannot be separated. They are but different aspects of the same space-time reality.

. . . the awareness of the "interpenetration" of space and time has led the Eastern mystics to an intrinsically dynamic world-view. A study of their writings reveals that they conceive the world not only in terms of movement, flow and change, but also seem to have a strong intuition for the "space-time" character of material objects which is so typical of relativistic physics. Physicists have to take into account the unification of space and time when they study the subatomic world and, consequently, they view the objects of this world—the particles—not statically, but dynamically, in terms of energy, activity and processes. The Eastern mystics, in their nonordinary states of consciousness, seem to be aware of the interpenetration of space and time at a macroscopic level, and thus they see the macroscopic objects in a way which is very similar to the physicist's conception of subatomic particles. This is particularly striking in Buddhism. One of the principal teachings of the Buddha was that "all compounded things are impermanent." In the original Pali version of this famous saying,[11] the term used for "things" is *sankhara* (Sanskrit: *samskara*), a word which means first of all "an event" or "a happening"—also "a deed," "an act"—and only secondarily "an existing thing." This clearly shows that Buddhists have a dynamic conception of things as ever-changing processes. In the words of D. T. Suzuki:

> Buddhists have conceived an object as an event and not as a thing or substance. . . . The Buddhist conception of 'things' as *samskara* (or *sankhara*), that is, as 'deeds,' or 'events,' makes it clear that Buddhists understand our experience in terms of time and movement.[12]

Like modern physicists, Buddhists see all objects as processes in a universal flux and deny the existence of any material substance. This denial is one of the most characteristic features of all schools of Buddhist philosophy. It is also characteristic of Chinese thought which developed a similar view of things as transitory stages in the ever-flowing *Tao* and was more concerned with their interrelations than with their reduction to a fundamental substance. "While European philosophy tended to find reality in substance," writes Joseph Needham, "Chinese philosophy tended to find it in relation."[13]

In the dynamic world-views of Eastern mysticism and of modern physics, then, there is no place for static shapes, or for any material substance. The basic elements of the universe are dynamic patterns; transitory stages in the "constant flow of transformation and change," as Chuang Tzu calls it.

According to our present knowledge of matter, its basic patterns are the subatomic particles, and the understanding of their properties and interactions is the principal aim of modern fundamental physics. We know today over two hundred particles, most of them being created artificially in collision processes and living only an extremely short time; far less than a millionth of a second! It is thus quite obvious that these short-lived particles represent merely transitory patterns of dynamic processes. The main questions with regard to these patterns, or particles, are the following: What are their distinguishing features? Are they composite and, if so, what do they consist of, or—better—what other patterns do they involve? How do they interact with one another: i.e., what are the forces between them? Last, if the particles themselves are processes, what kind of processes are they?

We have become aware that in particle physics all these questions are inseparably connected. Because of the relativistic nature of subatomic particles, we cannot understand their properties without understanding their mutual interactions, and because of the basic interconnectedness of the subatomic world we shall not understand any one particle before understanding all the others. The following chapters will show how far we have come in understanding the particles' properties and interactions. Although we are still lacking a complete quantum-relativistic theory of the subatomic world, several partial theories and models have been developed, which describe some aspects of this world very successfully. A discussion of the most important of these models and theories will show that they all involve philosophical conceptions which are in striking agreement with those in Eastern mysticism.

Notes

1. D. T. Suzuki, *The Essence of Buddhism*, p. 53.

2. Carlos Castaneda, *A Separate Reality*, p. 16.

3. S. Radhakrishnan, *Indian Philosophy*, p. 173.

4. *Brihad-aranyaka Upanishad*, 2.3.3.

5. *Bhagavad Gita*, 8.3.

6. Ibid., 3.24.

7. S. Radhakrishnan, op. cit., p. 367.

8. *Ts'ai-ken t'an:* quoted in T. Leggett, *A First Zen Reader,* p. 229, and in N. W. Ross, *Three Ways of Asian Wisdom*, p. 144.

9. A. C. B. Lovell, *The Individual and the Universe,* p. 93.

10. *Bhagavad Gita*, 9.7–10.

11. *Digha Nikaya*, ii, 198.

12. D. T. Suzuki, op. cit., p. 55.

13. J. Needham, *Science and Civilization in China,* vol. II, p. 478.

The Metaphysician's Nightmare

BERTRAND RUSSELL

In the following essay, Bertrand Russell (1872–1970) playfully toys
with the concept of negation. But negation is no laughing matter.
It is instead an extremely difficult concept which has generated
numerous philosophical puzzles and caused many philosophers,
Russell included, a tremendous amount of conceptual anguish.

My poor friend Andrei Bumblowski, formerly Professor of Philosophy in a now extinct university of
Central Europe, appeared to me to suffer from a
harmless kind of lunacy. I am myself a person of ro-
bust common sense; I hold that the intellect must
not be taken as a guide in life, but only as affording
pleasant argumentative games and ways of annoying less agile opponents. Bumblowksi, however, did
not take this view; he allowed his intellect to lead
him whither it would, and the results were odd. He
seldom argued, and to most of his friends the
grounds of his opinions remained obscure. What
was known was that he consistently avoided the
word 'not' and all its synonyms. He would not say
'this egg is not fresh', but 'chemical changes have occurred in this egg since it was laid'. He would not say
'I cannot find that book', but 'the books I have
found are other than that book'. He would not say
'thou shalt not kill', but 'thou shalt cherish life'. His
life was unpractical, but innocent, and I felt for him
a considerable affection. It was doubtless this affection which at last unlocked his lips, and led him to
relate to me the following very remarkable experience, which I give in his own words:

*   *   *

I had at one time a very bad fever of which I almost
died. In my fever I had a long consistent delirium. I
dreamt that I was in Hell, and that Hell is a place full
of all those happenings that are improbable but not
impossible. The effects of this are curious. Some of
the damned, when they first arrive below, imagine

that they will beguile the tedium of eternity by
games of cards. But they find this impossible, because, whenever a pack is shuffled, it comes out in
perfect order, beginning with the Ace of Spades and
ending with the King of Hearts. There is a special
department of Hell for students of probability. In
this department there are many typewriters and
many monkeys. Every time that a monkey walks on
a typewriter, it types by chance one of Shakespeare's
sonnets. There is another place of torment for
physicists. In this there are kettles and fires, but
when the kettles are put on the fires, the water in
them freezes. There are also stuffy rooms. But experience has taught the physicists never to open a window because, when they do, all the air rushes out
and leaves the room a vacuum. There is another region for gourmets. These men are allowed the most
exquisite materials and the most skilful chefs. But
when a beefsteak is served up to them, and they take
a confident mouthful, they find that it tastes like a
rotten egg; whereas, when they try to eat an egg, it
tastes like a bad potato.

There is a peculiarly painful chamber inhabited
solely by philosophers who have refuted Hume.
These philosophers, though in Hell, have not
learned wisdom. They continue to be governed by
their animal propensity towards induction. But

Bertrand Russell, "The Metaphysician's Nightmare" from *The
Basic Writings of Bertrand Russell* (New York: Simon & Schuster,
1961), pp. 100–103. Reprinted with the permission of The
Bertrand Russell Peace Foundation, Ltd

285

every time that they have made an induction, the next instance falsifies it. This, however, happens only during the first hundred years of their damnation. After that, they learn to expect that an induction will be falsified, and therefore it is not falsified until another century of logical torment has altered their expectation. Throughout all eternity surprise continues, but each time at a higher logical level.

Then there is the Inferno of the orators who have been accustomed while they lived to sway great multitudes by their eloquence. Their eloquence is undimmed and the multitudes are provided, but strange winds blow the sounds about so that the sounds heard by the multitudes, instead of being those uttered by the orators, are only dull and heavy platitudes.

At the very centre of the infernal kingdom is Satan, to whose presence only the most distinguished among the damned are admitted. The improbabilities become greater and greater as Satan is approached, and He Himself is the most complete improbability imaginable. He is pure Nothing, total non-existence, and yet continually changing.

I, because of my philosophical eminence, was early given audience with the Prince of Darkness. I had read of Satan as *der Geist der stets verneint*, the Spirit of Negation. But on entering the Presence I realized with a shock that Satan has a negative body as well as a negative mind. Satan's body is, in fact, a pure and complete vacuum, empty not only of particles of matter but also of particles of light. His prolonged emptiness is secured by a climax of improbability: whenever a particle approaches His outer surface, it happens by chance to collide with another particle which stops it from penetrating the empty region. The empty region, since no light ever penetrates it, is absolutely black—not more or less black, like things to which we loosely ascribe this word, but utterly, completely and infinitely black. It has a shape, and the shape is that which we are accustomed to ascribe to Satan: horns, hooves, tail and all. All the rest of Hell is filled with murky flame, and against this background Satan stands out in awful majesty. He is not immobile. On the contrary, the emptiness of which He is constituted is in perpetual motion. When anything annoys Him, He swinges the horror of His folded tail like an angry cat. Sometimes He goes forth to conquer new realms. Before going forth, He clothes Himself in shining white armour, which completely conceals the nothingness within. Only His eyes remain unclothed, and from His eyes piercing rays of nothingness shoot forth seeking what they may conquer. Wherever they find negation, wherever they find prohibition, wherever they find a cult of not-doing, there they enter into the inmost substance of those who are prepared to receive Him. Every negation emanates from Him and returns with a harvest of captured frustrations. The captured frustrations become part of Him, and swell His bulk until He threatens to fill all space. Every moralist whose morality consists of 'don'ts', every timid man who 'lets I dare not wait upon I would', every tyrant who compels his subjects to live in fear, becomes in time a part of Satan.

He is surrounded by a chorus of sycophantic philosophers who have substituted pandiabolism for pantheism. These men maintain that existence is only apparent; non-existence is the only true reality. They hope in time to make the non-existence of appearance appear, for in that moment what we now take to be existence will be seen to be in truth only an outlying portion of the diabolic essence. Although these metaphysicians showed much subtlety, I could not agree with them. I had been accustomed while on earth to oppose tyrannous authority, and this habit remained with me in Hell. I began to argue with the metaphysical sycophants:

'What you say is absurd,' I expostulated. 'You proclaim that non-existence is the only reality. You pretend that this black hole which you worship exists. You are trying to persuade me that the non-existent exists. But this is a contradiction; and, however hot the flames of Hell may become, I will never so degrade my logical being as to accept a contradiction.'

At this point the President of the sycophants took up the argument: 'You go too fast, my friend,' he said. 'You deny that the non-existent exists? But what is this to which you deny existence? If the non-existent is nothing, any statement about it is nonsense. And so is your statement that it does not exist. I am afraid you have paid too little attention to the logical analysis of sentences, which ought to have been taught you when you were a boy. Do you not know that every sentence has a subject, and that, if the subject were nothing, the sentence would be nonsense? So, when you proclaim, with virtuous heat, that Satan—who is the non-existent—does not exist, you are plainly contradicting yourself.'

'You,' I replied, 'have no doubt been here for some time and continue to embrace somewhat antiquated doctrines. You prate of sentences having subjects, but all that sort of talk is out of date. When I say that Satan, who is the non-existent, does not exist, I mention neither Satan nor the non-existent, but only the word "Satan" and the word "non-existent". Your fallacies have revealed to me a great truth. The great truth is that the word "not" is superfluous. Henceforth I will not use the word "not".'

At this all the assembled metaphysicians burst into a shout of laughter. 'Hark how the fellow contradicts himself,' they said when the paroxysm of merriment had subsided. 'Hark at his great commandment which is to avoid negation. He will not use the word "not", forsooth!'

Though I was nettled, I kept my temper. I had in my pocket a dictionary. I scratched out all the words expressing negation and said: 'My speech shall be composed entirely of the words that remain in this dictionary. By the help of these words that remain, I shall be able to describe everything in the universe. My descriptions will be many, but they will all be of things other than Satan. Satan has reigned too long in this infernal realm. His shining armour was real and inspired terror, but underneath the armour there was only a bad linguistic habit. Avoid the word "not", and his empire is at an end.'

Satan, as the argument proceeded, lashed His tail with ever-increasing fury, and savage rays of darkness shot from His cavernous eyes. But at the last, when I denounced Him as a bad linguistic habit, there was a vast explosion, the air rushed in from all sides, and the horrid shape vanished. The murky air of Hell, which had been due to inspissated rays of nothingness, cleared as if by magic. What had seemed to be monkeys at the typewriters were suddenly seen to be literary critics. The kettles boiled, the cards were jumbled, a fresh breeze blew in at the windows, and the beefsteaks tasted like beefsteaks. With a sense of exquisite liberation, I awoke. I saw that there had been wisdom in my dream, however it might have worn the guise of delirium. From that moment the fever abated, but the delirium—as you may think it—has remained.

Review and Reflection

1. If a tree falls in the forest when there is no one around to hear it, does it make a sound? Your discussion of this philosophical puzzle should include analysis of the term "sound" and reflection concerning the nature of human sensation.

2. Discuss the connections between experience and reality. Pay particular attention to Heisenberg's Uncertainty Relation, the Copenhagen Interpretation of Quantum Mechanics, and Schrödinger's cat.

3. Retell, in your own terms, Plato's Allegory of the Cave. What lessons do you think Plato would have us draw from the story? Is it perhaps possible that he was thinking of Socrates (Chapter 2)?

4. Do you agree with Descartes's conclusions regarding his famed *cogito?* Why?

5. What conclusions do you believe we can draw from parallels such as those suggested by Fritjof Capra?

6. What reactions and conclusions have you formed concerning Bertrand Russell's metaphysical nightmare? Do you believe it is possible to eliminate negative terms from our vocabulary? Is it desirable? Why?

Suggestions for Further Study

GEORGE BERKELEY. *Three Dialogues between Hylas and Philonous.* C. Turbayne, editor. New York: Macmillan, 1949.

FRITJOF CAPRA. *The Tao of Physics.* New York: Bantam Books, 1984 (2nd edition).

RENÉ DESCARTES. *Meditations on First Philosophy.* Translated by L. Lafleur. New York: Macmillan, 1960.

ROBERT PIRSIG. *Zen and the Art of Motorcycle Maintenance.* New York: Bantam Books, 1974.

PLATO. *Meno.* Translated by B. Jowlett. New York: Macmillan, 1949.

BERTRAND RUSSELL. *The Problems of Philosophy.* New York: Oxford University Press, 1959.

RICHARD TAYLOR. *Metaphysics.* Englewood Cliffs, NJ: Prentice Hall, 1992.

PART 4

Of Ultimate Concern:
A Higher Consciousness

Chapter 9   The Existence of God
Chapter 10   Wisdom of India
Chapter 11   Wisdom of the Orient
Chapter 12   Yoga and Meditation

Most cultures have established elaborate religions and rituals to represent, symbolize, and otherwise respond to what many perceive to be a profound spiritual dimension of our being. The exploration of that dimension constitutes the subject matter of Part Four.

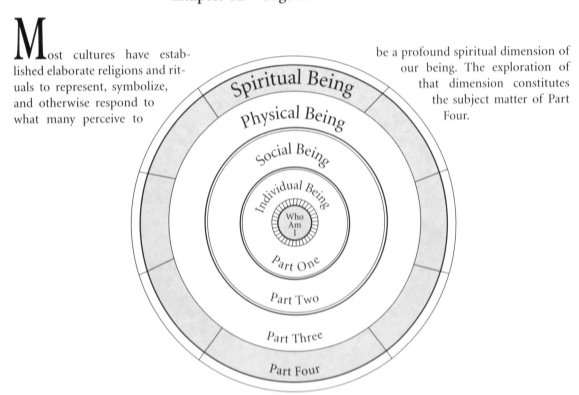

289

CHAPTER 9

The Existence of God

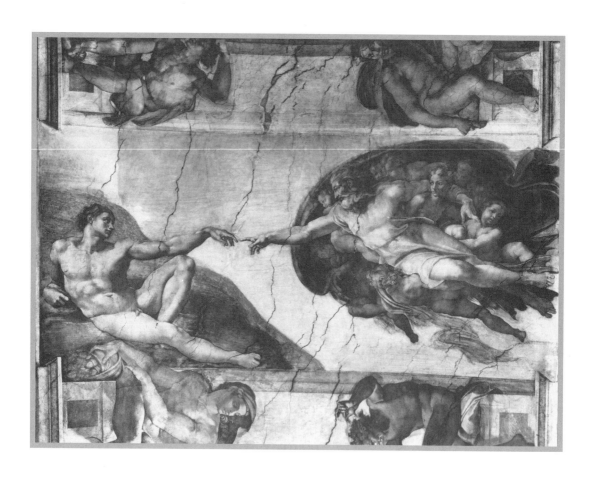

The chapter presents and examines several arguments concerning the existence of God, the views of Paul Tillich and Carol Christ concerning symbolic representation, and C. S. Lewis's views concerning demons and devils.

Introductory Essay

The **Introductory Essay** concerns St. Anselm's Ontological Argument for the Existence of God. Background and perspective are provided as regards logic, language analysis, and analytic argumentation. The structure of the argument is clarified via the development of parodies (arguments with parallel structure but different content). The parodies also facilitate investigation of the conceptual content of the argument's definition of God as a perfect being. Further analysis of central concepts leads to Paul Tillich's notion of a transcendent God, Immanuel Kant's critique concerning the use of "existence" as a predicate, and clarification of the analytic character of the argument's conclusion.

Philosophical Readings

Bertrand Russell presents a series of objections to what he regards as the fundamental principles of Christianity. As regards the existence of God, he considers and rejects the First-cause Argument, the Natural-law Argument, the Argument from Design, Kant's Moral Argument, and the Argument for the Remedying of Injustice. Russell professes admiration for Jesus Christ but rejects the claim that he was, at a minimum, "the best and wisest of men." Readers are reminded of episodes recorded in the gospels in which Jesus seems cruel, heartless, and vindictive. Final reflections concern the emotional and social foundations of religion.

   Paul Tillich's article presents and clarifies his notion of God as ultimate concern. In the process he discusses the nature and characteristics of a religious symbol, the importance of faith, and the proper interpretation of religious myths.

Scientific Reading

The selection by **Carol Christ** examines the psychological and social significance of the symbols we use. In particular, she is concerned with the effect that masculine symbols of

God have on the women in our society. Her conclusion is simple but controversial: women need a feminine symbol (a Goddess) if they are to develop and mature to their fullest potential.

Literary Readings

Raymond Smullyan's imaginative conversation with God demonstrates the importance of analysis and reflection concerning even first-person experiences.

C. S. Lewis addresses the existence and nature of a demonic force. The reading begins with selections from a playful set of letters presumably written from an administrative devil to a novice tempter. Concepts include love, prayer, and distraction. The final section of the reading concerns the various ways in which devils and angels have been portrayed in art and literature. In the process we encounter Professor Lewis's presentation of his personal beliefs regarding these issues.

The Ontological Argument

DOUGLAS W. SHRADER

The Ontological Argument has attracted the attention of some of the greatest philosophers of all time. The argument is clever and ingenious. Unfortunately, it is also slippery and easily misunderstood. Advocates and critics alike have fallen into numerous errors and much conceptual confusion.

As may often be the case, it is the elements that make the argument interesting and potentially instructive that cause most of the difficulty. Although the argument itself is relatively simple, it is located in the middle of a conceptual labyrinth. Issues include: the nature of God, the nature and desirability of existence, the concept of perfection, the limits and proper use of language, the nature and limits of human knowledge, and the importance of empirical observation. Our discussion of the argument will take us in each of these different directions—first one way, then another. Proceed with caution. If the argument or my analysis seems unclear from time to time, stop and think about it. Reread a section or two. Remember, if you are puzzled or confused, you will be in good company.

THE ARGUMENT

The argument may be presented in several ways. One of the most popular is that of St. Anselm (eleventh century A.D.), who presented it as a sort of thought experiment. He began by asking people to think of the most perfect being imaginable. Never mind that any two given people were likely to come up with different thought pictures; a complete point-by-point agreement was not required. Anselm then asked, "Does the being which you thought of exist?" If a person answered "No," Anselm responded: "Then you did not think of the most perfect being you possibly could. There is a simple way to make the being you conceptualized more perfect, and that is to think of it as existing (being real)."

Anselm believed he had caught would-be atheists in a logical contradiction. He thought of God as a perfect being. To deny the existence of Anselm's God, atheists would have to say, in one way or another, "a perfect being does not exist." But "perfect," Anselm reasoned, means "having all (and only) desirable characteristics." Moreover, he continued, existence is clearly desirable. As a result, a perfect being must exist. To claim otherwise would be tantamount to saying, "a perfect being is not perfect." Such of course would be sheer foolishness, and Anselm concluded: "Only a fool hath said in his heart, 'There is no God.' "

The Ontological Argument

1. "God" means "perfect being."
2. "Perfect" means "having all (and only) desirable characteristics."
3. <u>Existence is a desirable characteristic.</u>
   God exists.

INITIAL REACTIONS

Reactions to the argument vary widely. I usually have a few students who find it as clear and convincing as Anselm does. A substantial number are too confused to know what to think. But an equally large number are convinced that it is all a cheap trick, an illegitimate sleight of hand. They complain that the argument is "too easy," that Anselm is "just playing with words," or that he has somehow "defined God into existence."

There is something roughly right about each of these objections, and others as well. But the argument is not a *cheap* trick; nor is there any intentional deception. Its proponents are usually intelligent and serious. The errors into which they fall are subtle ones. To understand the errors we must say something more about the structure of the argument itself, and about argumentation in general.

ANALYTIC ARGUMENTATION

It is objected that the argument is "too easy." The phrase is vague, but the general complaint seems to be a lack of empirical content. Anselm claims to prove the existence of God, but offers only self-serving definitions and a rather strange-sounding suggestion about the desirability of existence. There is nothing we would normally regard as sense experience or empirical evidence.

This lack of empirical evidence would be a serious embarrassment for someone trying to construct an empirical argument. But the proponents of the Ontological Argument are neither surprised nor embarrassed, for the Ontological Argument does not pretend to be an empirical one. It is instead an example of what philosophers call an analytic (a.k.a. conceptual) argument.

Although most people are not accustomed to dealing with analytic arguments, the argument form is generally recognized as legitimate and occasionally useful. As anyone who has ever used a dictionary knows, words are defined in terms of other words. Our language is a rich, complex web of interdefinition and mutual dependency. Analytic arguments travel along those conceptual threads to reveal otherwise unrecognized linguistic relations or, as is often the case, to clarify and underscore recognized but cloudy relationships. They help maintain a high degree of logical consistency in our use of the language, without which we could not communicate effectively, but would instead find ourselves blabbering unintelligible gibberish.

Perhaps an example will help to make the idea somewhat clearer. *The New Merriam-Webster Pocket Dictionary* defines "bachelor" as "a man who has not married." "Man" is defined as "an adult male." "Married" is the past tense of "marry," defined in terms of taking a husband or wife according to law or custom. Several things may be concluded simply on the basis of these definitions. For example: "Bachelors are not married," "All bachelors are male," and "No bachelor has a wife." Aided only by a few other definitions, we can conclude that no bachelors are children, that no women are bachelors, and so on.

Some inferences are more interesting than others. I doubt that any of you felt enlightened to find that bachelors are not married, though some may have found it interesting that unmarried women do not (on Webster's definitions) count as bachelors. You may or may not like the definitions. You may decide that such a gender-specific word is out of keeping with modern unisex trends and resolve to eliminate it from your vocabulary. You may even spearhead a national movement to change the meaning(s).

Whatever your reaction to the example, stop and reflect on the general character of the conclusions. There is a sense in which they are true (correct), but it is not the same sense in which it is true that snow is usually white, that the earth is round, or that most cats and dogs have tails. "No bachelors are children" is a linguistic (a.k.a. conceptual, analytic, or definitional) truth. The relevant facts of the matter are not so much facts about children or bachelors as they are about the way in which we use the language.

In fact, it does not even particularly matter whether there are any such things as children or bachelors. Analytic arguments exploit relations between concepts, but do not depend on the empirical existence of entities correctly described by those concepts. Thus, even if there eventually comes a time when there are no longer any bachelors, the conceptual connections will remain (barring change in the concepts). It is analytically true that unicorns have one horn, even if it is empirically true that there are no unicorns.

As a result, we should not expect analytic arguments to tell us anything about "the world." In particular, we should not expect them to make existence claims. "No bachelors are married" does not tell us whether or not there are any bachelors. "No squares are round" does not tell us whether there are any unround squares. And "All unicorns have one horn" does not tell us whether there are any unicorns.

The Ontological Argument, supposedly, is an exception. Most proponents agree that existence claims are empirical claims to be decided, normally, on the basis of empirical evidence. But the Ontological Argument, they maintain, shows the existence of God (conceptualized as a perfect being) to be a special case. God (and possibly God alone) is supposed to be a being whose existence is analytically guaranteed. According to the argument, "God does not exist" is a conceptual contradiction. One might just as well try to talk about married bachelors, round squares, or unicorns with two horns. In each case, so long as the definitions remained unchanged, one would be speaking simple nonsense.

The phrase "so long as the definitions remain unchanged" may seem problematic. The degree to which the argument depends on specific definitions troubles many people. It is sometimes objected that the argument "defines God into existence." In a sense, the charge is true. The conclusion "God exists" follows from Anselm's definitions in much the same way as "No bachelors are women" follows from Webster's. If we use different definitions, we will get different results. If by "bachelor" we mean "any unmarried person," we will find that some bachelors may be women or children. If by "God" we mean "a powerful but nonetheless imperfect being who created the universe," we will not be able to prove His/Her existence by means of the Ontological Argument.

This definitional relativity of the argument is worth noting, but should not be overrated. All knowledge claims are definitionally specific. If by "tree" we meant "intelligent extraterrestrial life form," we could not, at present, prove the existence of trees. If by "God" we meant "water," proving the existence of God would be fairly simple and straightforward. Should we, on the basis of these reflections, tell other people that we are uncertain about the existence of trees or order a glass of God to accompany our meal in a restaurant? Obviously not.

If Anselm's definitions were as silly, concocted, and nonstandard as the two I have just given, we could rightly reject the argument as silly, concocted, and irrelevant to the concerns of real people. Charges of wordplay, mind games, and possibly even malicious deception would be justified. But Anselm's definitions are not silly, concocted, and nonstandard. They are not arbitrary ones, made up for the sole purpose of proving God's existence. Nor are they wholly implausible or unattractive. There are of course numerous other characterizations of God and alternative definitions of perfection. But unless the Ontological Argument is otherwise flawed, Anselm will have succeeded in proving the existence of a fairly interesting God candidate: one which possesses all (and only) desirable characteristics. What more could one want?

PARODIES

Let us pause to consider the question of uniqueness. Is the argument as unparalleled as its advocates seem usually to think? Suppose I am looking for "the perfect girl." Suppose you tell me that I am only wasting my time and making myself miserable, that there is no such person. Having studied the Ontological Argument, I might respond: "Perfect" means "having all and only desirable characteristics." Since existence is clearly desirable, a perfect girl would have to have it (existence, that is). To claim otherwise would be tantamount to saying, "a perfect girl is not perfect." Such would be sheer foolishness. Only a fool hath said in his heart, "There is no perfect girl."

The argument is called a "parody." It has the same logical structure as the Ontological Argument, but because of differences in the content of the premises sanctions a different conclusion.

Would the argument convince you of the existence of a perfect girl? Would it make my search for one any more reasonable? Any doubts we have about this argument should occasion similar pause as regards the one which it was designed to parallel.

Before you decide to accept the existence of a perfect girl to accompany the existence of God, reflect on the structure of the argument and the ease with which additional parodies with ever more impalpable conclusions can be generated. We can easily construct versions to prove the existence of a perfect boy, a perfect mother, a perfect government, a perfect diet cola, a perfect nuclear reactor—in short, a perfect anything. If the argument form works, it would seem that it works "too well."

The parodies are possible because, although the Ontological Argument has spoken of the existence of a perfect being, it is the adjective "perfect," not the noun "being," that does all the work. The conceptual muscle is the supposed logical connection between the concept of perfection and that of existence such that anything thought of as being perfect should also be thought of as being real (existing). If the connection works for "being" it should also work for "girl," "paper clip," "philosophy professor," and so on.

Conceptual Issues

It may be objected that the parodies suffer logical difficulties that the original argument does not. Conceptual conjunctions like "perfect girl," "perfect philosophy professor," and "perfect nuclear reactor" are problematic at best; they may be logically inconsistent.

Human beings are notoriously imperfect. When someone makes a mistake or otherwise falls in some undertaking, we console, "It's only human." We live but for a short time and then die. Even while we are here we are subject to various diseases and bouts of ill health. Are these simply characteristics most of us happen to have, or are they somehow central to our concept "human"? Would we consider someone who was immortal, never got sick, never made mistakes, and never failed in any way, human (in the normal sense of the word)? The point is debatable, but it may be that it makes no more sense to speak of a perfect girl than it does to talk about married bachelors or round squares.

If phrases like "a perfect girl" are logically inconsistent, then parodies of the Ontological Argument that purport to prove the existence of the corresponding entities are doomed from the start. If we introduce logical inconsistencies into our premise set, we cannot very well complain when the argument yields a logically inconsistent, counterintuitive or otherwise problematic conclusion. That, the proponent of the Ontological Argument may charge, is the difference between the Ontological Argument and our parodies of it: "perfect being" makes sense in a way in which "perfect girl" (etcetera) does not.

But does "perfect being" really make sense? I am not sure that I can conjure up an image of "perfect being" any more than I can of "perfect girl." How big would a perfect being be? Don't tell me—I know: neither too large nor too small. But how large is too large? And how small is too small? Too large to do what? (Fit through a mouse hole? Dance on the head of a pin?) Too small to do what? (See over the tallest mountain? Touch the clouds?) Would a perfect being even have size at all? Similar questions could be raised about the being's shape, color, chemical composition, and so forth.

Consider for a moment the suggestion that a perfect being would have no size, shape, color, etcetera. The size and shape of an entity are determined by its limits and boundaries. But a perfect being, it is suggested, would be unlimited and boundless. Hence a perfect being would have no size or shape.

The color of an entity is determined by the manner in which light is reflected from its surface. But the surface of an entity is a boundary of sorts (one that determines its physical shape). If it has no boundaries (and hence no shape), neither can it have a surface. Without a surface, it can have no color.

Arguments such as these may have a certain initial plausibility, but do little more than bring us back to square one. I know what it means to say that two beings have *different* limits, or that one is limited in a way the second is not; but what does it mean to say that a being has *no* limits? I am not at all sure I can imagine a being without any size, shape, color, etcetera. These are the sort of properties that allow us to distinguish one thing from another. If you take away the conceptual machinery we use to say "this rather than that," what possible description could we ever give of our supposedly perfect being?

The Ontological Argument tells us that a perfect being would have all (and only) desirable characteristics. How do we determine what those characteristics are? Is it logically possible to have all (and only) desirable characteristics? Does the idea even make sense?

As a college professor I value the ability to learn new things. I think the ability to grow in a manner satisfying to oneself, and perhaps to others as well, is one of the most desirable characteristics any being can possess. But for a being who already has all desirable characteristics, improvement and growth are not possible. Such a being could never learn anything new, for there would be nothing it does not already know. If a capacity for growth and learning is truly desirable, then a being which has all (and only) desirable characteristics is a conceptual impossibility.

The question "Would a being which has all (and only) desirable characteristics have a capacity for growth and learning?" poses a dilemma:

1. if the being is capable of growth and learning, it must lack some desirable characteristics (there must be some room for improvement);

2. if the being is not capable of growth and learning, it thereby lacks a desirable characteristic (i.e., a capacity for growth and learning).

Either way we arrive at the same conclusion: the being does not have all desirable characteristics.[1]

There is an obvious way out of the conceptual trap created in the preceding paragraphs, but the advocate of the Ontological Argument may not like the direction in which it takes us. The ability to improve, we may say, is a desirable characteristic of an imperfect being, but totally unnecessary (hence not desirable) for a perfect one. The problem, in short, is that we have tried to judge God by human standards. This resolves the dilemma regarding growth and learning, but opens doors to new problems.

The Ontological Argument depends heavily on the suggestion that existence is desirable. But surely this is a human judgment, made by human beings according to human standards, every bit as much as the suggestion about the ability to learn (etcetera). If human judgments about desirability are disallowed, then the "existence is desirable" line must be stricken from the argument, and without it the argument cannot prove the existence of God.

There are a couple of tactics available to the advocate of the Ontological Argument, but neither works particularly well. S/he might first attempt an appeal to unanimity of opinion, suggesting that everyone agrees that existence is desirable but that not everyone cares a great deal about the ability to learn new things (etcetera). The attempt falters, first, because unanimous or not, it is still a human judgment. Beyond that there is some genuine disagreement about the desirability of existence. Presumably at least some suicides are of the opinion that nonexistence is better than the life they have.

Alternatively, the advocate might attempt an appeal to universality of application, suggesting that existence is a desirable characteristic of any and everything but that the ability to learn, while desirable for some things, has no real application to others (e.g., clouds, garbage, cans, or telephone poles). The suggestion encounters an immediate difficulty. It would seem that it is just plain false. I do not find the existence of nuclear weapons, racial hatred, or the AIDS virus particularly desirable. Granted, others might, but I do not see that our disagreement could be resolved by appeal to a dubious general principle such as "Existence is a desirable characteristic of any and everything." In fact, as I understand it, even Anselm's God does not consider as desirable the existence of human sin.

Quite apart from what we might say about the desirability of nuclear weapons (and so on), the suggestion begs the question as regards the existence of God. Even if it were true that existence was a desirable characteristic of everything we encounter in our limited sojourn on this tiny planet, it would not follow that it is necessarily desirable as regards an infinite, unlimited being. In fact, existence may even be regarded as a type of boundary or limitation. Several influential theologians (such as Paul Tillich) have argued that God *transcends* existence and thus that "He" does not, in any normal sense of the term, exist.[2]

In general, we can see that desirability is a relative concept. What one person finds desirable, a second may not. A desirable characteristic for one sort of thing may not be for another. To ask, in the abstract, whether something is or is not desirable is to ask an unanswerable question. But the Ontological Argument has defined "perfect" as "possessing all (and only) desirable characteristics." Without some standards and a reference class, the phrase is sheer nonsense.

CLARIFYING THE CONCLUSIONS

The conceptual difficulties are serious ones. I am not at all sure that we can make coherent sense of phrases like "perfect being" or "possesses all (and only) desirable characteristics." Even "existence is desirable" is problematic. In what sense can existence be considered a characteristic? It is not the sort of quality which some things have and others do not, or which some things acquire and others lose. In order to be something at all, that something must exist. We might do better to think of existence as a condition for having characteristics than as a characteristic proper. The point is one to which we will return.[3]

Even if we find our way through the conceptual jungle, the Ontological Argument cannot do what its advocates hope: it cannot prove the existence of God, nor can it show atheism to be logically incoherent. The argument is an analytic argument; it can establish only a connection between concepts. Even if all the concerns of the previous pages vanish into nothingness, the most the argument can do is establish a limited analytic connection between a particular conception of God and a particular notion of existence. The conclusion can indeed be roughly phrased as "God exists" or "God must exist," but the phrases are dangerously misleading. For while the connection is analytic, the conclusion *looks* like an empirical claim.

The connection is hard to express without creating the appearance of an empirical claim (this may be the primary reason that the argument is so often misunderstood). The following are a few suggestions, grouped into two classes for reasons that will become apparent as we proceed:

1. a. "If *x* is God, *x* exists."
   b. "Nothing can be God if it does not exist."
   c. "We will not count anything as God unless it exists."
   d. "Nonexistent things cannot be God."
   e. "Existence is a necessary condition of Godhood."

2. a. "To think of God as a perfect being one must think of God as existing."
   b. "A nonexistent but perfect being is a conceptual impossibility."
   c. "It is conceptually impossible to deny the existence of a perfect being."

The suggestions of the first group are clearly conditional (if-then statements). They try to tell us something about the conditions that something would have to meet to be (or be recognized as) God. The stated conditions are minimal: the entity must exist. Tillich's arguments to the contrary,[4] the condition does not seem unreasonable. One must meet it in order to be a paper clip or a dog. To be anything at all, one must exist.

The suggestions of the second group are also conditional. They try to tell us something about the conditions of thought. They seem stronger than the first group, for they appear to put the would-be atheist in a serious conceptual bind (restricting the ability to deny, even in one's innermost thought, the existence of God).

Before accepting such a restriction, examine the claims closely. There are similarities, but important differences as well. **2a** and **2b** are legitimate expressions of the conceptual connection that fuels the Ontological Argument. **2c,** however, is too strong.

I do not believe there are any animals that correspond to the mythic concept of a unicorn. Yet there are conceptual connections between existence and each of the supposed characteristics of a unicorn. I cannot conceive of a creature that has a single horn in the center of its forehead, but which does not exist. In order to have a horn in the center of one's forehead, one must have a forehead. In order to have a forehead, one must have a head, and so on. In order to genuinely have *any* characteristics, one must exist. Nonexistent things (if that phrase makes any sense at all) do not have characteristics. They cannot. They do not exist.

Does this mean that we cannot deny the existence of unicorns? Of course not; I did so in the opening sentence of the previous paragraph. But existential claims (such as "Unicorns do not exist") require special caution. They are not, as proponents of the Ontological Argument seem to have assumed, simply special instances of attributive claims (e.g., "Uni-

corns are not white"). A person who made the latter claim might reasonably be asked to present an example or photograph of a unicorn that was not white. Yet someone who says "Unicorns do not exist" cannot very well be expected to present as their evidence something which (a) is a unicorn and (b) does not exist. That, however, is effectively what proponents of the Ontological Argument have requested the atheist to do.

The point is reminiscent of our earlier remarks about the proper characterization of existence. Existence is not so much a characteristic as it is a condition for having characteristics. Accordingly, atheists are not simply quibbling over a supposed characteristic of God. They do not claim to have found a nonexistent God any more than a disbeliever in unicorns claims to have found a nonexistent unicorn. Instead, they say: "We have not been able to find anything matching your description, and moreover do not believe we ever will." Atheists may be wrong, but they are not guilty of simple self-contradiction.

Notes

1. To those who believe that God is omnipotent (able to do anything) skeptics have posed the question, "Can God make a rock so large that even S/He cannot lift it?" If so, there is something that God cannot do (i.e., lift the rock). If not, there is something that God cannot do (i.e., make a rock so large that even S/He cannot lift it).

2. Central to Tillich's position is a fairly sophisticated set of assumptions regarding human concepts, linguistic expression, and symbolic

representation. See "Symbols of Faith," included in the readings for the present chapter.

3. Advanced readers may wish to compare this point with the line of argument advanced by Immanuel Kant in *Critique of Pure Reason* (*Transcendental Dialectic:* Chapter III, Section 4: B620–630).

Why I Am Not a Christian

BERTRAND RUSSELL

Lord Bertrand Russell (1872–1970) is one of the best known and most influential philosophers of the twentieth century. In addition to numerous books in philosophy, Russell wrote popular essays on everything from politics and religion to sex and education. He was awarded the 1950 Nobel Prize in Literature "in recognition of his many-sided and important work in which he has constantly stood forth as a champion of humanity and freedom of thought." The following essay was first delivered as a lecture under the auspices of the British National Secular Society on March 6, 1927.

As your Chairman has told you, the subject about which I am going to speak to you tonight is "Why I Am Not a Christian." Perhaps it would be as well, first of all, to try to make out what one means by the word *Christian*. It is used these days in a very loose sense by a great many people. Some people mean no more by it than a person who attempts to live a good life. In that sense I suppose there would be Christians in all sects and creeds; but I do not think that that is the proper sense of the word, if only because it would imply that all people who are not Christians—all the Buddhists, Confucians, Mohammedans, and so on—are not trying to live a good life. I do not mean by a Christian any person who tries to live decently according to his lights. I think that you must have a certain amount of definite belief before you have a right to call yourself a Christian. The word does not have quite such a full-blooded meaning now as it had in the times of St. Augustine and St. Thomas Aquinas. In those days, if a man said that he was a Christian it was known what he meant. You accepted a whole collection of creeds which were set out with great precision, and every single syllable of those creeds you believed with the whole strength of your convictions.

WHAT IS A CHRISTIAN?

Nowadays it is not quite that. We have to be a little more vague in our meaning of Christianity. I think, however, that there are two different items which are quite essential to anybody calling himself a Christian. The first is one of a dogmatic nature—namely, that you must believe in God and immortality. If you do not believe in those two things, I do not think that you can properly call yourself a Christian. Then, further than that, as the name implies, you must have some kind of belief about Christ. The Mohammedans, for instance, also believe in God and in immortality, and yet they would not call themselves Christians. I think you must have at the very lowest the belief that Christ was, if not divine, at least the best and wisest of men. If you are not going to believe that much about Christ, I do not think you have any right to call yourself a Christian. Of course, there is another sense, which you find in *Whitaker's Almanack* and in geography books, where the population of the world is said to be divided into Christians, Mohammedans, Buddhists, fetish worshipers, and so on; and in that sense we are all Christians. The geography books count us all in, but that is a purely geographical sense, which I suppose we can ignore. Therefore I take it that when I tell you why I am not a Christian I have to tell you two different things: first, why I do not believe in God and in immortality; and, secondly, why I do not think that Christ was the best and wisest of men, although I grant him a very high degree of moral goodness.

But for the successful efforts of unbelievers in the past, I could not take so elastic a definition of Christianity as that. As I said before, in olden days it had a much more full-blooded sense. For instance, it included the belief in hell. Belief in eternal hell-fire was an essential item of Christian belief until pretty recent times. In this country, as you know, it ceased to be an essential item because of a decision of the Privy Council, and from that decision the Archbishop of Canterbury and the Archbishop of York dissented; but in this country our religion is settled by Act of Parliament, and therefore the Privy Council was able to override their Graces and hell was no longer necessary to a Christian. Consequently I shall not insist that a Christian must believe in hell.

THE EXISTENCE OF GOD

To come to this question of the existence of God: it is a large and serious question, and if I were to attempt to deal with it in any adequate manner I should have to keep you here until Kingdom Come, so that you will have to excuse me if I deal with it in a somewhat funny fashion. You know, of course, that the Catholic Church has laid it down as a dogma that the existence of God can be proved by the unaided reason. That is a somewhat curious dogma, but it is one of their dogmas. They had to introduce it because at one time the freethinkers adopted the habit of saying that there were such and such arguments which mere reason might urge against the existence of God, but of course they

knew as a matter of faith that God did exist. The arguments and the reasons were set out at great length, and the Catholic Church felt that they must stop it. Therefore they laid it down that the existence of God can be proved by the unaided reason and they had to set up what they considered were arguments to prove it. There are, of course, a number of them, but I shall take only a few.

THE FIRST-CAUSE ARGUMENT

Perhaps the simplest and easiest to understand is the argument of the First Cause. (It is maintained that everything we see in this world has a cause, and as you go back in the chain of causes further and further you must come to a First Cause, and to that First Cause you give the name of God.) That argument, I suppose, does not carry very much weight nowadays, because, in the first place, cause is not quite what it used to be. The philosophers and the men of science have got going on cause, and it has not anything like the vitality it used to have; but, apart from that, you can see that the argument that there must be a First Cause is one that cannot have any validity. I may say that when I was a young man and was debating these questions very seriously in my mind, I for a long time accepted the argument of the First Cause, until one day, at the age of eighteen, I read John Stuart Mill's Autobiography, and I there found this sentence: "My father taught me that the question 'Who made me?' cannot be answered, since it immediately suggests the further question 'Who made God?' " That very simple sentence showed me, as I still think, the fallacy in the argument of the First Cause. If everything must have a cause, then God must have a cause. If there can be anything without a cause, it may just as well be the world as God, so that there cannot be any validity in that argument. It is exactly of the same nature as the Hindu's view, that the world rested upon an elephant and the elephant rested upon a tortoise; and whey they said, "How about the tortoise?" the Indian said, "Suppose we change the subject." The argument is really no better than that. There is no reason why the world could not have come into being without a cause; nor, on the other hand, is there any reason why it should not have always existed. There is no reason to suppose that the world had a beginning at all. The idea that things must have a beginning is really due to the poverty of our imagination. Therefore, perhaps, I need not waste any more time upon the argument about the First Cause.

The Natural-law Argument

Then there is a very common argument from natural law. That was a favorite argument all through the eighteenth century, especially under the influence of Sir Isaac Newton and his cosmogony. People observed the planets going around the sun according to the law of gravitation, and they thought that God had given a behest to these planets to move in that particular fashion, and that was why they did so. That was, of course, a convenient and simple explanation that saved them the trouble of looking any further for explanations of the law of gravitation. Nowadays we explain the law of gravitation in a somewhat complicated fashion that Einstein has introduced. I do not propose to give you a lecture on the law of gravitation, as interpreted by Einstein, because that again would take some time; at any rate, you no longer have the sort of natural law that you had in the Newtonian system, where, for some reason that nobody could understand, nature behaved in a uniform fashion. We now find that a great many things we thought were natural laws are really human conventions. You know that even in the remotest depths of stellar space there are still three feet to a yard. That is, no doubt, a very remarkable fact, but you would hardly call it a law of nature. And a great many things that have been regarded as laws of nature are of that kind. On the other hand, where you can get down to any knowledge of what atoms actually do, you will find they are much less subject to law than people thought, and that the laws at which you arrive are statistical averages of just the sort that would emerge from chance. There is, as we all know, a law that if you throw dice you will get double sixes only about once in thirty-six times, and we do not regard that as evidence that the fall of the dice is regulated by design; on the contrary, if the double sixes came every time we should think that there was design. The laws of nature are of that sort as regards a great many of them. They are statistical averages such as would emerge from the laws of chance; and that makes this whole business of natural law much less impressive than it formerly was. Quite apart from that, which represents the momentary state of science that may change tomorrow, the whole idea that natural laws imply a lawgiver is due to a confusion between natural and human laws. Human laws are behests commanding you to behave in a certain way, in which way you may choose to behave, or you may choose not to behave; but natural laws are a description of how things do in fact behave, and being a mere description of what they in fact do, you cannot argue that there must be somebody who told them to do that, because even supposing that there were, you are then faced with the question "Why did God issue just those natural laws and no others?" If you say that he did it simply from his own good pleasure, and without any reason, you then find that there is something which is not subject to law, and so your train of natural law is interrupted. If you say, as more orthodox theologians do, that in all the laws which God issues he had a reason for giving those laws rather than others—the reason, of course, being to create the best universe, although you would never think it to look at it—if there were a reason for the laws which God gave, then God himself was subject to law, and therefore you do not get any advantage by introducing God as an intermediary. You have really a law outside and anterior to the divine edicts, and God does not serve your purpose, because he is not the ultimate lawgiver. In short, this whole argument about natural law no longer has anything like the strength that it used to have. I am traveling on in time in my review of the arguments. The arguments that are used for the existence of God change their character as time goes on. They were at first hard intellectual arguments embodying certain quite definite fallacies. As we come to modern times they become less respectable intellectually and more and more affected by a kind of moralizing vagueness.

THE ARGUMENT FROM DESIGN

The next step in this process brings us to the argument from design. You all know the argument from design: everything in the world is made just so that we can manage to live in the world, and if the world was ever so little different, we could not manage to live in it. That is the argument from design. It sometimes takes a rather curious form; for instance, it is argued that rabbits have white tails in order to be easy to shoot. I do not know how rabbits would view that application. It is an easy argument to parody. You all know Voltaire's remark, that obviously the nose was designed to be such as to fit spectacles. That sort of parody has turned out to be not nearly so wide of the mark as it might have seemed in the eighteenth century, because since the time of Darwin we understand much better why living creatures are adapted to their environment. It is not that their environment was made to be suitable to them but that they grew to be suitable to it, and that is the basis of adaptation. There is no evidence of design about it.

When you come to look into this argument from design, it is a most astonishing thing that people can believe that this world, with all the things that are in it, with all its defects, should be the best that omnipotence and omniscience have been able to produce in millions of years. I really cannot believe it. Do you think that, if you were granted omnipotence and omniscience and millions of years in which to perfect your world, you could produce nothing better than the Ku Klux Klan or the Fascists? Moreover, if you accept the ordinary laws of science, you have to suppose that human life and life in general on this planet will die out in due course: it is a stage in the decay of the solar system; at a certain stage of decay you get the sort of conditions of temperature and so forth which are suitable to protoplasm, and there is life for a short time in the life of the whole solar system. You see in the moon the sort of things to which the earth is tending—something dead, cold, and lifeless.

I am told that that sort of view is depressing, and people will sometimes tell you that if they believed that, they would not be able to go on living. Do not believe it; it is all nonsense. Nobody really worries much about what is going to happen millions of years hence. Even if they think they are worrying much about that, they are really deceiving themselves. They are worried about something much more mundane, or it may merely be a bad digestion; but nobody is really seriously rendered unhappy by the thought of something that is going to happen to this world millions and millions of years hence. Therefore, although it is of course a gloomy view to suppose that life will die out—at least I suppose we may say so, although sometimes when I contemplate the things that people do with their lives I think it is almost a consolation—it is not such as to render their life miserable. It merely makes you turn your attention to other things.

THE MORAL ARGUMENTS FOR DEITY

Now we reach one stage further in what I shall call the intellectual descent that the Theists have made in their argumentation, and we come to what are called the moral arguments for the existence of God. You all know, of course, that there used to be in the old days three intellectual arguments for the existence of God, all of which were disposed of by Immanuel Kant in the *Critique of Pure Reason;* but no sooner had he disposed of those arguments than he invented a new one, a moral argument, and that quite convinced him. He was like many people: in intellectual matters he was skeptical, but in moral matters he believed implicitly in the maxims that he had imbibed at his mother's knee. That illustrates what the psychoanalysts so much emphasize—the immensely stronger hold upon us that our very early associations have than those of later times.

Kant, as I say, invented a new moral argument for the existence of God, and that in varying forms was extremely popular during the nineteenth century. It has all sorts of forms. One form is to say that there would be no right or wrong unless God existed. I am not for the moment concerned with whether there is a difference between right and wrong, or whether there is not: that is another question. The point I am concerned with is that, if you are quite sure there is a difference between right and wrong, you are then in this situation: Is that difference due to God's fiat or is it not? If it is due to God's fiat, then for God himself there is no difference between right and wrong, and it is no longer a significant statement to say that God is good. If you are going to say, as theologians do, that God is good, you must then say that right and wrong have some meaning which is independent of God's fiat, because God's fiats are good and not bad independently of the mere fact that he made them. If you are going to say that, you will then have to say that it is only through God that right and wrong came into being, but that they are in their essence logically anterior to God. You could, of course, if you liked, say that there was a superior deity who gave orders to the God who made this world, or could take up the line that some of the gnostics took up—a line which I often thought was a very plausible one— that as a matter of fact this world that we know was made by the devil at a moment when God was not looking. There is a good deal to be said for that, and I am not concerned to refute it.

THE ARGUMENT FOR THE REMEDYING OF INJUSTICE

Then there is another very curious form of moral argument, which is this: they say that the existence of God is required in order to bring justice into the world. In the part of this universe that we know there is great injustice, and often the good suffer, and often the wicked prosper, and one hardly knows which of those is the more annoying; but if you are going to have justice in the universe as a whole you have to suppose a future life to redress the balance of life here on earth. So they say that there must be a God, and there must be heaven and

hell in order that in the long run there may be justice. That is a very curious argument. If you looked at the matter from a scientific point of view, you would say, "After all, I know only this world. I do not know about the rest of the universe, but so far as one can argue at all on probabilities one would say that probably this world is a fair sample, and if there is injustice here the odds are that there is injustice elsewhere also." Supposing you got a crate of oranges that you opened, and you found all the top layer of oranges bad, you would not argue, "The underneath ones must be good, so as to redress the balance." You would say, "Probably the whole lot is a bad consignment"; and that is really what a scientific person would argue about the universe. He would say, "Here we find in this world a great deal of injustice, and so far as that goes that is a reason for supposing that justice does not rule in the world; and therefore so far as it goes it affords a moral argument against deity and not in favor of one." Of course I know that the sort of intellectual arguments that I have been talking to you about are not what really moves people. What really moves people to believe in God is not any intellectual argument at all. Most people believe in God because they have been taught from early infancy to do it, and that is the main reason.

Then I think that the next most powerful reason is the wish for safety, a sort of feeling that there is a big brother who will look after you. That plays a very profound part in influencing people's desire for a belief in God.

THE CHARACTER OF CHRIST

I now want to say a few words upon a topic which I often think is not quite sufficiently dealt with by Rationalists, and that is the question whether Christ was the best and the wisest of men. It is generally taken for granted that we should all agree that that was so. I do not myself. I think that there are a good many points upon which I agree with Christ a great deal more than the professing Christians do. I do not know that I could go with Him all the way, but

I could go with Him much further than most professing Christians can. You will remember that He said, "Resist not evil: but whosoever shall smite thee on thy right cheek, turn to him the other also." That is not a new precept or a new principle. It was used by Lao-tse and Buddha some 500 or 600 years before Christ, but it is not a principle which as a matter of fact Christians accept. I have no doubt that the present Prime Minister,* for instance, is a most sincere Christian, but I should not advise any of you to go and smite him on one cheek. I think you might find that he thought this text was intended in a figurative sense.

Then there is another point which I consider excellent. You will remember that Christ said, "Judge not lest ye be judged." That principle I do not think you would find was popular in the law courts of Christian countries. I have known in my time quite a number of judges who were very earnest Christians, and none of them felt that they were acting contrary to Christian principles in what they did. Then Christ says, "Give to him that asketh of thee, and from him that would borrow of thee turn not thou away." That is a very good principle. Your Chairman has reminded you that we are not here to talk politics, but I cannot help observing that the last general election was fought on the question of how desirable it was to turn away from him that would borrow of thee, so that one must assume that the Liberals and Conservatives of this country are composed of people who do not agree with the teaching of Christ, because they certainly did very emphatically turn away on that occasion.

Then there is another maxim of Christ which I think has a great deal in it, but I do not find that it is very popular among some of our Christian friends. He says, "If thou wilt be perfect, go and sell that which thou hast, and give to the poor." That is a very excellent maxim, but, as I say, it is not much practiced. All these, I think, are good maxims, although they are a little difficult to live up to. I do

* Stanley Baldwin.

not profess to live up to them myself; but then, after all, it is not quite the same thing as for a Christian.

DEFECTS IN CHRIST'S TEACHING

Having granted the excellence of these maxims, I come to certain points in which I do not believe that one can grant either the superlative wisdom or the superlative goodness of Christ as depicted in the Gospels; and here I may say that one is not concerned with the historical question. Historically it is quite doubtful whether Christ ever existed at all, and if He did we do not know anything about Him, so that I am not concerned with the historical question, which is a very difficult one. I am concerned with Christ as He appears in the Gospels, taking the Gospel narrative as it stands, and there one does find some things that do not seem to be very wise. For one thing, He certainly thought that His second coming would occur in clouds of glory before the death of all the people who were living at that time. There are a great many texts that prove that. He says, for instance, "Ye shall not have gone over the cities of Israel till the Son of Man be come." Then He says, "There are some standing here which shall not taste death till the Son of Man comes into His Kingdom"; and there are a lot of places where it is quite clear that He believed that His second coming would happen during the lifetime of many then living. That was the belief of His earlier followers, and it was the basis of a good deal of His moral teaching. When He said, "Take no thought for the morrow," and things of that sort, it was very largely because He thought that the second coming was going to be very soon, and that all ordinary mundane affairs did not count. I have, as a matter of fact, known some Christians who did believe that the second coming was imminent. I knew a parson who frightened his congregation terribly by telling them that the second coming was very imminent indeed, but they were much consoled when they found that he was planting trees in his garden. The early Christian did really believe it, and they did abstain from such things as planting trees in their gardens, because they did accept from Christ the belief that the second coming was imminent. In that respect, clearly He was not so wise as some other people have been, and He was certainly not superlatively wise.

THE MORAL PROBLEM

Then you come to moral questions. There is one very serious defect in my mind in Christ's moral character, and that is that He believed in hell. I do not myself feel that any person who is really profoundly human can believe in everlasting punishment. Christ certainly as depicted in the Gospels did believe in everlasting punishment, and one does find repeatedly a vindictive fury against those people who would not listen to His preaching—an attitude which is not uncommon with preachers, but which does somewhat detract from superlative excellence. You do not, for instance find that attitude in Socrates. You find him quite bland and urbane toward the people who would not listen to him; and it is, to my mind, far more worthy of a sage to take that line than to take the line of indignation. You probably all remember the sort of things that Socrates was saying when he was dying, and the sort of things that he generally did say to people who did not agree with him.

You will find that in the Gospels Christ said, "Ye serpents, ye generation of vipers, how can ye escape the damnation of hell." That was said to people who did not like His preaching. It is not really to my mind quite the best tone, and there are a great many of these things about hell. There is, of course, the familiar text about the sin against the Holy Ghost: "Whosoever speaketh against the Holy Ghost it shall not be forgiven him neither in this World nor in the world to come." That text has caused an unspeakable amount of misery in the world, for all sorts of people have imagined that they have committed the sin against the Holy Ghost, and thought that it would not be forgiven them either in this world or in the world to come. I really do not think that a person with a proper degree of kindliness in his nature would have put fears and terrors of that sort into the world.

Then Christ says, "The Son of Man shall send forth His angels, and they shall gather out of His Kingdom all things that offend, and them which do iniquity, and shall cast them into a furnace of fire; there shall be wailing and gnashing of teeth"; and He goes on about the wailing and gnashing of teeth. It comes in one verse after another, and it is quite manifest to the reader that there is a certain pleasure in contemplating wailing and gnashing of teeth, or else it would not occur so often. Then you all, of course, remember about the sheep and the goats; how at the second coming He is going to divide the sheep from the goats, and He is going to say to the goats, "Depart from me, ye cursed, into everlasting fire." He continues, "And these shall go away into everlasting fire." Then He says again, "If thy hand offend thee, cut it off; it is better for thee to enter into life maimed, than having two hands to go into hell, into the fire that never shall be quenched; where the worm dieth not and the fire is not quenched." He repeats that again and again also. I must say that I think all this doctrine, that hell-fire is a punishment for sin, is a doctrine of cruelty. It is a doctrine that put cruelty into the world and gave the world generations of cruel torture; and the Christ of the Gospels, if you could take Him as His chroniclers represent Him, would certainly have to be considered partly responsible for that.

There are other things of less importance. There is the instance of the Gadarene swine, where it certainly was not very kind to the pigs to put the devils into them and make them rush down the hill to the sea. You must remember that He was omnipotent, and He could have made the devils simply go away; but He chose to send them into the pigs. Then there is the curious story of the fig tree, which always rather puzzled me. You remember what happened about the fig tree. "He was hungry; and seeing a fig tree afar off having leaves, He came if haply He might find anything thereon; and when He came to it He found nothing but leaves, for the time of figs was not yet. And Jesus answered and said unto it: 'No man eat fruit of thee hereafter for ever' . . . and Peter . . . saith unto Him: 'Master, behold the fig tree which thou cursedst is withered away.' " This is a very curious story, because it was not the right time of year for figs, and you really could not blame the tree. I cannot myself feel that either in the matter of wisdom or in the matter of virtue Christ stands quite as high as some people known to history. I think I should put Buddha and Socrates above Him in those respects.

THE EMOTIONAL FACTOR

As I said before, I do not think that the real reason why people accept religion has anything to do with argumentation. They accept religion on emotional grounds. One is often told that it is a very wrong thing to attack religion, because religion makes men virtuous. So I am told; I have not noticed it. You know, of course, the parody of that argument in Samuel Butler's book, *Erewhon Revisited.* You will remember that in *Erewhon* there is a certain Higgs who arrives in a remote country, and after spending some time there he escapes from that country in a balloon. Twenty years later he comes back to that country and finds a new religion in which he is worshiped under the name of the "Sun Child," and it is said that he ascended into heaven. He finds that the Feast of the Ascension is about to be celebrated, and he hears Professors Hanky and Panky say to each other that they never set eyes on the man Higgs, and they hope they never will; but they are the high priests of the religion of the Sun Child. He is very indignant, and he comes up to them, and he says, "I am going to expose all this humbug and tell the people of Erewhon that it was only I, the man Higgs, and I went up in a balloon." He was told, "You must not do that, because all the morals of this country are bound round this myth, and if they once know that you did not ascend into heaven they will all become wicked"; and so he is persuaded of that and he goes quietly away.

That is the idea—that we should all be wicked if we did not hold to the Christian religion. It seems to me that the people who have held to it have been for the most part extremely wicked. You find this curious fact, that the more intense has been the religion of any period and the more profound has been the dogmatic belief, the greater has been the cruelty and the worse has been the state of affairs. In the so-called ages of faith, when men really did believe the Christian religion in all its completeness, there was the Inquisition, with its tortures; there were millions of unfortunate women burned as witches; and there was every kind of cruelty practiced upon all sorts of people in the name of religion.

You find as you look around the world that every single bit of progress in human feeling, every improvement in the criminal law, every step toward the diminution of war, every step toward better treatment of the colored races, or every mitigation of slavery, every moral progress that there has been in the world, has been consistently opposed by the organized churches of the world. I say quite deliberately that the Christian religion, as organized in its churches, has been and still is the principal enemy of moral progress in the world.

HOW THE CHURCHES HAVE RETARDED PROGRESS

You may think that I am going too far when I say that that is still so. I do not think I am. Take one fact. You will bear with me if I mention it. It is not a pleasant fact, but the churches compel one to mention facts that are not pleasant. Supposing that in this world that we live in today an inexperienced girl is married to a syphilitic man; in that case the Catholic Church says, "This is an indissoluble sacrament. You must endure celibacy or stay together. And if you stay together, you must not use birth control to prevent the birth of syphilitic children." Nobody whose natural sympathies have not been warped by dogma, or whose moral nature was not absolutely dead to all sense of suffering, could maintain that it is right and proper that that stage of things should continue.

That is only an example. There are a great many ways in which, at the present moment, the church, by its insistence upon what it chooses to call morality, inflicts upon all sorts of people undeserved and unnecessary suffering. And of course, as we know, it is in its major part an opponent still of progress and of improvement in all the ways that diminish suffering in the world, because it has chosen to label as morality a certain narrow set of rules of conduct which have nothing to do with human happiness; and when you say that this or that ought to be done because it would make for human happiness, they think that has nothing to do with the matter at all. "What has human happiness to do with morals? The object of morals is not to make people happy."

Fear, the Foundation of Religion

Religion is based, I think, primarily and mainly upon fear. It is partly the terror of the unknown and partly, as I have said, the wish to feel that you have a kind of elder brother who will stand by you in all your troubles and disputes. Fear is the basis of the whole thing—fear of the mysterious, fear of defeat, fear of death. Fear is the parent of cruelty, and therefore it is no wonder if cruelty and religion have gone hand in hand. It is because fear is at the basis of those two things. In this world we can now begin a little to understand things, and a little to master them by help of science, which has forced its way step by step against the Christian religion, against the churches, and against the opposition of all the old precepts. Science can help us get over this craven fear in which mankind has lived for so many generations. Science can teach us, and I think our hearts can teach us, no longer to look around for imaginary supports, no longer to invent allies in the sky, but rather to look to our own efforts here below to make this world a fit place to live in, instead of the sort of place that the churches in all these cultures have made it.

We want to stand upon our own feet and look fair and square at the world—its good facts, its bad facts, its beauties, and its ugliness; see the world as it is and be not afraid of it. Conquer the world by intelligence and not merely by being slavishly subdued by the terror that comes from it. The whole conception of God is a conception derived from the ancient Oriental despotisms. It is a conception quite unworthy of free men. When you hear people in church debasing themselves and saying that they are miserable sinners, and all the rest of it, it seems contemptible and not worthy of self-respecting human beings. We ought to stand up and look the world frankly in the face. We ought to make the best we can of the world, and if it is not so good as we wish, after all it will still be better than what these others have made of it in all these ages. A good world needs knowledge, kindliness, and courage; it does not need a regretful hankering after the past or a fettering of the free intelligence by the words uttered long ago by ignorant men. It needs a fearless outlook and a free intelligence. It needs hope for the future, not looking back all the time toward a past that is dead, which we trust will be far surpassed by the future that our intelligence can create.

Symbols of Faith

PAUL TILLICH

Paul Tillich (1886–1965) is one of the most provocative and influential theologians of the twentieth century. His many books include *The Interpretation of History, Systematic Theology, The Future of Religions, Morality and Beyond, The Courage to Be,* and *Dynamics of Faith,* from which the following selection is taken.

Because he works within a web of interconnected but often unintuitive and controversial concepts, Tillich's work can appear more foreboding and impenetrable than it really is. If you find yourself perplexed by this selection, refer back to the following principles, which form the foundation of most of his thought:

1.   religion is a matter of ultimate concern (whatever concerns one most is one's religion/god/faith);

2.   God, properly speaking, transcends existence (is the foundation of the world rather than an element of it);

3.   God's nature cannot be captured by human concepts or categories (which are formulated on the basis of earthly experience); and

4.   the proper language of religion is therefore one of symbolic representation, instructive parable, and metaphysical myth.

I. THE MEANING OF SYMBOL

Man's ultimate concern must be expressed symbolically, because symbolic language alone is able to express the ultimate. This statement demands explanation in several respects. In spite of the manifold research about the meaning and function of symbols which is going on in contemporary philosophy, every writer who uses the term "symbol" must explain his understanding of it.

Symbols have one characteristic in common with signs; they point beyond themselves to do something else. The red sign at the street corner points to the order to stop the movements of cars at certain intervals. A red light and the stopping of cars have essentially no relation to each other, but conventionally they are united as long as the convention lasts. The same is true of letters and numbers and partly even words. They point beyond themselves to sounds and meanings. They are given this special function by convention within a nation or by international conventions, as the mathematical signs. Sometimes such signs are called symbols; but this is unfortunate because it makes the distinction between signs and symbols more difficult. Decisive is the fact that signs do not participate in the reality of that to which they point, while symbols do. Therefore, signs can be replaced for reasons of expediency of convention, while symbols cannot.

This leads to the second characteristic of the symbol: It participates in that to which it points: the flag participates in the power and dignity of the nation for which it stands. Therefore, it cannot be replaced except after an historic catastrophe that changes the reality of the nation which it symbolizes. An attack on the flag is felt as an attack on the majesty of the group in which it is acknowledged. Such an attack is considered blasphemy.

The third characteristic of a symbol is that it opens up levels of reality which otherwise are closed for us. All arts create symbols for a level of reality which cannot be reached in any other way. A picture and a poem reveal elements of reality which cannot be approached scientifically. In the creative work of art we encounter reality in a dimension which is closed for us without such works. The symbol's fourth characteristic not only opens up dimensions and elements of reality which otherwise would remain unapproachable but also unlocks dimensions and elements of our soul which correspond to the dimensions and elements of reality. A great play gives us not only a new vision of the human scene, but it opens up hidden depths of our own being. Thus we are able to receive what the play reveals to us in reality. There are within us dimensions of which we cannot become aware except through symbols, as melodies and rhythms in music.

Symbols cannot be produced intentionally—this is the fifth characteristic. They grow out of the individual or collective unconscious and cannot function without being accepted by the unconscious dimension of our being. Symbols which have an especially social function, as political and religious symbols, are created or at least accepted by the collective unconscious of the group in which they appear.

The sixth and last characteristic of the symbol is a consequence of the fact that symbols cannot be invented. Like living beings, they grow and they die. They grow when the situation is ripe for them, and they die when the situation changes. The symbol of the "king" grew in a special period of history, and it died in most parts of the world in our period. Symbols do not grow because people are longing for them, and they do not die because of scientific or practical criticism. They die because they can no longer produce response in a group where they originally found expression.

These are the main characteristics of every symbol. Genuine symbols are created in several spheres of man's cultural creativity. We have mentioned already the political and artistic realm. We could add history and, above all, religion, whose symbols will be our particular concern.

2. RELIGIOUS SYMBOLS

We have discussed the meaning of symbols generally because, as we said, man's ultimate concern must be expressed symbolically! One may ask: Why can it not be expressed directly and properly? If money, success or the nation is someone's ultimate concern, can this not be said in a direct way without symbolic language? Is it not only in those cases in which the content of the ultimate concern is called "God" that we are in the realm of symbols? The answer is that everything which is a matter of unconditional concern is made into a god. If the nation is someone's ultimate concern, the name of the nation becomes a sacred name and the nation receives divine qualities which far surpass the reality of the being and functioning of the nation. The nation then stands for and symbolizes the true ultimate, but in an idolatrous way. Success as ultimate concern is not the natural desire of actualizing potentialities, but is readiness to sacrifice all other values of life for the sake of a position of power and social predominance. The anxiety about not being a success is an idolatrous form of anxiety about divine condemnation. Success is grace; lack of success, ultimate judgment. In this way concepts designating ordinary realities become idolatrous symbols of ultimate concern.

The reason for this transformation of concepts into symbols is the character of ultimacy and the nature of faith. That which is the true ultimate transcends the realm of finite reality infinitely. Therefore, no finite reality can express it directly and properly. Religiously speaking, God transcends his own name. This is why the use of his name easily becomes an abuse or blasphemy. Whatever we say about that which concerns us ultimately, whether or not we call it God, has a symbolic meaning. It points beyond itself while participating in that to which it points. In no other way can faith express itself adequately. The language of faith is the language of symbols. If faith were what we have shown that it is not, such an assertion could not be made. But faith, understood as the state of being ultimately concerned, has no language other than symbols. When saying this I always expect the question: Only a symbol? He who asks this question shows that he has not understood the difference between signs and symbols nor the power of symbolic language, which surpasses in quality and strength the power of any nonsymbolic language. One should never say "only a symbol," but one should say, "not less than a symbol." With this in mind we can now describe the different kinds of symbols of faith.

The fundamental symbol of our ultimate concern is God. It is always present in any act of faith, even if the act of faith includes the denial of God. Where there is ultimate concern, God can be denied only in the name of God. One God can deny the other one. Ultimate concern cannot deny its own character as ultimate. Therefore, it affirms what is meant by the word "God." Atheism, consequently, can only mean the attempt to remove any ultimate concern—to remain unconcerned about the meaning of one's existence. Indifference toward the ultimate question is the only imaginable form of atheism. Whether it is possible is a problem which must remain unsolved at this point. In any case, he who denies God as a matter of ultimate concern affirms God, because he affirms ultimacy in his concern. God is the fundamental symbol for what concerns us ultimately. Again it would be completely wrong to ask: So God is nothing but a symbol? Because the next question has to be: A symbol for what? And then the answer would be: For God! God is symbol for God. This means that in the notion of God we must distinguish two elements: the element of ultimacy, which is a matter of immediate experience and not symbolic in itself, and the element of concreteness, which is taken from our ordinary experience and symbolically applied to God. The man whose ultimate concern is a sacred tree has both the ultimacy of concern and the concreteness of the tree which symbolizes his relation to the ultimate. The man who adores Apollo is ultimately concerned, but not in an abstract way. His ultimate concern is symbolized in the divine figure of Apollo. The man who glorifies Jahweh, the God of the Old Testament, has both an ultimate concern and a concrete image of what concerns him ultimately. This is the meaning of the seemingly cryptic statement that God is the symbol of God. In this qualified sense God is the fundamental and universal content of faith.

It is obvious that such an understanding of the meaning of God makes the discussions about the existence or non-existence of God meaningless. It is meaningless to question the ultimacy of an ultimate concern. This element in the idea of God is in itself certain. The symbolic expression of this element varies endlessly through the whole history of mankind. Here again it would be meaningless to ask whether one or another of the figures in which an ultimate concern is symbolized does "exist." If "existence" refers to something which can be found within the whole of reality, no divine being exists. The question is not this, but: which of the innumerable symbols of faith is most adequate to the meaning of faith? In other words, which symbol of ultimacy expresses the ultimate without idolatrous elements? This is the problem, and not the so-called "existence of God"—which is in itself an impossible combination of words. God as the ultimate in man's ultimate concern is more certain than any other certainty, even that of oneself. God as symbolized in a divine figure is a matter of daring faith, of courage and risk.

God is the basic symbol of faith, but not the only one. All the qualities we attribute to him, power, love, justice, are taken from finite experiences and applied symbolically to that which is beyond finitude and infinity. If faith calls God "almighty," it uses the human experience of power in order to symbolize the content of its infinite concern, but it does not describe a highest being who can do as he pleases. So it is with all the other qualities and with all the actions, past, present and future, which men attribute to God. They are symbols taken from our daily experience, and not information about what God did once upon a time or will do sometime in the future. Faith is not the belief in such stories, but it is the acceptance of symbols that express our ultimate concern in terms of divine actions.

Another group of symbols and faith are manifestations of the divine in things and events, in persons and communities, in words and documents. This whole realm of sacred objects is a treasure of symbols. Holy things are not holy in themselves, but they point beyond themselves to the source of all holiness, that which is of ultimate concern.

3. SYMBOLS AND MYTHS

The symbols of faith do not appear in isolation. They are united in "stories of the gods," which is the meaning of the Greek word "mythos"—myth. The gods are individualized figures, analogous to human personalities, sexually differentiated, descending from each other, related to each other in love and struggle, producing world and man, acting in time and space. They participate in human greatness and misery, in creative and destructive works. They give to man cultural and religious traditions, and defend these sacred rites. They help and threaten the human race, especially some families, tribes or nations. They appear in epiphanies and incarnations, establish sacred places, rites and persons, and thus create a cult. But they themselves are under the command and threat of a fate which is beyond everything that is. This is mythology as developed most impressively in ancient Greece. But

many of these characteristics can be found in every mythology. Usually the mythological gods are not equals. There is a hierarchy, at the top of which is a ruling god, as in Greece; or a trinity of them, as in India; or a duality of them, as in Persia. There are savior-gods who mediate between the highest gods and man, sometimes sharing the suffering and death of man in spite of their essential immortality. This is the world of the myth, great and strange, always changing but fundamentally the same: man's ultimate concern symbolized in divine figures and actions. Myths are symbols of faith combined in stories about divine-human encounters.

Myths are always present in every act of faith, because the language of faith is the symbol. They are also attacked, criticized and transcended in each of the great religions of mankind. The reason for this criticism is the very nature of the myth. It uses material from our ordinary experience. It puts the stories of the gods into the framework of time and space although it belongs to the nature of the ultimate to be beyond time and space. Above all, it divides the divine into several figures, removing ultimacy from each of them without removing their claim to ultimacy. This inescapably leads to conflicts of ultimate claims, able to destroy life, society, and consciousness.

The criticism of the myth first rejects the division of the divine and goes beyond it to one God, although in different ways according to the different types of religion. Even one God is an object of mythological language, and if spoken about is drawn into the framework of time and space. Even he loses his ultimacy if made to be the content of concrete concern. Consequently, the criticism of the myth does not end with the rejection of the polytheistic mythology.

Monotheism also falls under the criticism of the myth. It needs, as one says today, "demythologization." This word has been used in connection with the elaboration of the mythical elements in stories and symbols of the Bible, both of the Old and New Testaments—stories like those of the Paradise, of the fall of Adam, of the great Flood, of the Exodus from

Egypt, of the virgin birth of the Messiah, of many of his miracles, of his resurrection and ascension, of his expected return as the judge of the universe. In short, all the stories in which divine-human interactions are told are considered as mythological in character, and objects of demythologization. What does this negative and artificial term mean? It must be accepted and supported if it points to the necessity of recognizing a symbol as a symbol and a myth as a myth. It must be attacked and rejected if it means the removal of symbols and myths altogether. Such an attempt is the third step in the criticism of the myth. It is an attempt which never can be successful, because symbol and myth are forms of the human consciousness which are always present. One can replace one myth by another, but one cannot remove the myth from man's spiritual life. For the myth is the combination of symbols of our ultimate concern.

A myth which is understood as a myth, but not removed or replaced, can be called a "broken myth." Christianity denies by is very nature any unbroken myth, because its presupposition is the first commandment: the affirmation of the ultimate as ultimate and the rejection of any kind of idolatry. All mythological elements in the Bible, and doctrine and liturgy should be recognized as mythological, but they should be maintained in their symbolic form and not be replaced by scientific substitutes. For there is no substitute for the use of symbols and myths: they are the language of faith.

The radical criticism of the myth is due to the fact that the primitive mythological consciousness resists the attempt to interpret the myth of myth. It is afraid of every act of demythologization. It believes that the broken myth is deprived of its truth and of its convincing power. Those who live in an unbroken mythological world feel safe and certain. They resist, often fanatically, any attempt to introduce an element of uncertainty by "breaking the myth," namely, by making conscious its symbolic character. Such resistance is supported by authoritarian systems, religious or political, in order to give security to the people under their control and unchallenged power to those who exercise the control.

The resistance against demythologization expresses itself in "literalism." The symbols and myths are understood in their immediate meaning. The material, taken from nature and history, is used in its proper sense. The character of the symbol to point beyond itself to something else is disregarded. Creation is taken as a magic act which happened once upon a time. The fall of Adam is localized on a special geographical point and attributed to a human individual. The virgin birth of the Messiah is understood in biological terms, resurrection and ascension as physical events, the second coming of the Christ as a telluric, or cosmic, catastrophe. The presupposition of such literalism is that God is a being, acting in time and space, dwelling in a special place, affecting the course of events and being affected by them like any other being in the universe. Literalism deprives God of his ultimacy and, religiously speaking, of his majesty. It draws him down to the level of that which is not ultimate, the finite and conditional. In the last analysis it is not rational criticism of the myth which is decisive but the inner religious criticism. Faith, if it takes its symbols literally, becomes idolatrous! It calls something ultimate which is less than ultimate. Faith, conscious of the symbolic character of its symbols, gives God the honor which is due him.

One should distinguish two stages of literalism, the natural and the reactive. The natural stage of literalism is that in which the mythical and the literal are indistinguishable. The primitive period of individuals and groups consists in the inability to separate the creations of symbolic imagination from the facts which can be verified through observation and experiment. This stage has a full right of its own and should not be disturbed, either in individuals or in groups, up to the moment when man's questioning mind breaks the natural acceptance of the mythological visions as literal. If, however, this moment has come, two ways are possible. The one is to replace the unbroken by the broken myth. It is the objectively demanded way, although it is impossible for many people who prefer the repression of their questions to the uncertainty which appears with the breaking of the myth. They are forced into the second stage of literalism, the conscious one, which is aware of the questions but represses them, half consciously, half unconsciously. The tool of repression is usually an acknowledged authority with sacred qualities like the Church or the Bible, to which one owes unconditional surrender. This stage is still justifiable, if the questioning power is very weak and can easily be answered. It is unjustifiable if a mature mind is broken in its personal center by political or psychological methods, split in his unity, and hurt in his integrity. The enemy of a critical theology is not natural literalism but conscious literalism with repression of and aggression toward autonomous thought.

Symbols of faith cannot be replaced by other symbols, such as artistic ones, and they cannot be removed by scientific criticism. They have a genuine standing in the human mind, just as science and art have. Their symbolic character is their truth and their power. Nothing less than symbols and myths can express our ultimate concern.

One more question arises, namely, whether myths are able to express every kind of ultimate concern. For example, Christian theologians argue that the word "myth" should be reserved for natural myths in which repetitive natural processes, such as the seasons, are understood in their ultimate meaning. They believe that if the world is seen as a historical process with beginning, end and center, as in Christianity and Judaism, the term "myth" should not be used. This would radically reduce the realm in which the term would be applicable. Myth could not be understood as the language of our ultimate concern, but only as a discarded idiom of this language. Yet history proves that there are not only natural myths but also historical myths. If the earth is seen as the battleground of two divine powers, as in ancient Persia, this is an historical myth. If the God of creation selects and guides a nation through history toward an end which transcends all history, this is an historical myth. If the Christ—a transcendent, divine being—appears in the fullness of time, lives, dies and is resurrected, this is an historical myth. Christianity is superior to those religions which are bound to a natural myth. But Christianity speaks the mythological language like every other religion. It is a broken myth, but it is a myth; otherwise Christianity would not be an expression of ultimate concern.

Why Women Need the Goddess

CAROL P. CHRIST

Carol Christ is a respected scholar whose work provides both insight and challenge to two seemingly distinct fields: Women's Studies and Religious Studies. She is the author of *Laughter of Aphrodite: Reflections on a Journey to the Goddess* (1987), *Diving Deep and Surfacing: Women Writers on Spiritual Quest* (1986), and co-editor of *Womanspirit Rising: A Feminist Reader on Religion* (1979). In the following selection from *Womanspirit Rising* she explains why, in her opinion, women need a feminine symbol of the deity (a Goddess).

At the close of Ntosake Shange's stupendously successful Broadway play *For Colored Girls Who Have Considered Suicide When the Rainbow is Enuf,* a tall beautiful black woman rises from despair to cry out, "I found God in myself and I loved her fiercely."[1] Her discovery is echoed by women around the country who meet spontaneously in small groups on full moons, solstices, and equinoxes to celebrate the Goddess as symbol of life and death powers and waxing and waning energies in the universe and in themselves.[2]

> It is the night of the full moon. Nine women stand in a circle, on a rocky hill above the city. The western sky is rosy with the setting sun; in the east the moon's face begins to peer above the horizon.... The woman pours out a cup of wine onto the earth, refills it and raises it high. "Hail, Tana, Mother of mothers!" she cries. "Awaken from your long sleep, and return to your children again."[3]

What are the political and psychological effects of this fierce new love of the divine in themselves for women whose spiritual experience has been focused by the male God of Jerusalem and Christianity? Is the spiritual dimension of feminism a passing diversion, an escape from difficult but necessary political work? Or does the emergence of the symbol of Goddess among women have significant political and psychological ramifications for the feminist movement?

To answer this question, we must first understand the importance of religious symbols and rituals in human life and consider the effect of male symbolism of God on women. According to anthropologist Clifford Geertz, religious symbols shape a cultural ethos, defining the deepest values of a society and the persons in it. "Religion," Geertz writes, "is a system of symbols which act to produce powerful, pervasive, and long-lasting moods and motivations"[4] in the people of a given culture. A "mood" for Geertz is a psychological attitude such as awe, trust, and respect, while a "motivation" is the *social* and *political* trajectory created by a mood that transforms mythos into ethos, symbol system into social and political reality. Symbols have both psychological and political effects, because they create the inner conditions (deep-seated attitudes and feelings) that lead people to feel comfortable with or to accept social and political arrangements that correspond to the symbol system.

Because religion has such a compelling hold on the deep psyches of so many people, feminists cannot afford to leave it in the hands of the fathers. Even people who no longer "believe in God" or participate in the institutional structure of patriarchal religion still may not be free of the power of the symbolism of God the Father. A symbol's effect does not depend on rational assent, for a symbol also functions on levels of the psyche other than the rational. Religion fulfills deep psychic needs by providing symbols and rituals that enable people to cope with limit situations[5] in human life (death, evil, suffering) and to pass through life's important transitions (birth, sexuality, death). Even people who consider themselves completely secularized will often find themselves sitting in a church or synagogue when a friend or relative gets married, or when a parent or friend has died. The symbols associated with these important rituals cannot fail to affect the deep or unconscious structures of the mind of even a person who has rejected these symbolisms on a conscious level—especially if the person is under stress. The reason for the continuing effect of religious symbols is that the mind abhors a vacuum. Symbol systems cannot simply be rejected, they must be replaced. Where there is not any replacement, the mind will revert to familiar structures at times of crisis, bafflement, or defeat.

Religions centered on the worship of a male God create "moods" and "motivations" that keep women in a state of psychological dependence on men and male authority, while at the same time legitimating the *political* and *social* authority of fathers and sons in the institutions of society.

Religious symbol systems focused around exclusively male images of divinity create the impression that female power can never be fully legitimate or wholly beneficent. This message need never be explicitly stated (as, for example, it is in the story of Eve) for its effect to be felt. A woman completely ignorant of the myths of female evil in biblical religion nonetheless acknowledges the anomaly of female power when she prays exclusively to a male God. She may see herself as like God (created in the image of God) only by denying her own sexual identity and affirming God's transcendence of sexual identity. But she can never have the experience that is freely available to every man and boy in her culture, of having her full sexual identity affirmed as being in the image and likeness of God. In Geertz' terms, her "mood" is one of trust in male power as salvific and distrust of female power in herself and other women as inferior or dangerous. Such a powerful, pervasive, and long-lasting "mood" cannot fail to become a "motivation" that translates into social and political reality.

In *Beyond God the Father,* feminist theologian Mary Daly detailed the psychological and political ramifications of father religion for women. "If God in 'his' heaven is a father ruling his people," she wrote, "then it is the 'nature' of things and according to divine plan and the order of the universe that society be male dominated. Within this context, a *mystification of roles* takes place. The husband dominating his wife represents God 'himself.' The images and values of a given society have been projected into the realm of dogmas and 'Articles of Faith,' and these in turn justify the social structures which have given rise to them and which sustain their plausibility."[6]

Philosopher Simone de Beauvoir was well aware of the function of patriarchal religion as legitimater of male power. As she wrote, "Man enjoys the great advantage of having a god endorse the code he writes; and since man exercises a sovereign authority over women it is especially fortunate that this authority has been vested in him by the Supreme Being. For the Jews, Mohammedans, and Christians, among others, man is Master by divine right; the fear of God will therefore repress any impulse to revolt in the downtrodden female."[7]

This brief discussion of the psychological and political effects of God religion puts us in an excellent position to begin to understand the significance of the symbol of Goddess for women. In discussing the meaning of the Goddess, my method will first be phenomenological. I will isolate a meaning of the symbol of the Goddess as it has emerged in the lives of contemporary women. I will then discuss its psychological and political significance by contrasting the "moods" and "motivations" engendered by Goddess symbols with those engendered by Christian symbolism. I will also correlate Goddess symbolism with themes that have emerged in the women's movement, in order to show how Goddess symbolism undergirds and legitimates the concerns of the women's movement, much as God symbolism in Christianity undergirded the interests of men in patriarchy. I will discuss four aspects of Goddess symbolism here: the Goddess as affirmation of female power, the female body, the female will, and women's bonds and heritage. There are, of course, many other meanings of the Goddess that I will not discuss here.

The sources for the symbol of the Goddess in contemporary spirituality are traditions of Goddess worship and modern women's experience. The ancient Mediterranean, pre-Christian European, native American, Mesoamerican, Hindu, African, and other traditions are rich sources for Goddess symbolism. But these traditions are filtered through modern women's experiences. Traditions of Goddesses' subordination to Gods, for example, are ignored. Ancient traditions are tapped selectively and eclectically, but they are not considered authoritative for modern consciousness. The Goddess symbol has emerged spontaneously in the dreams, fantasies, and thoughts of many women around the country in the past several years. Kirsten Grimstad and Susan Rennie reported that they were surprised to discover widespread interest in spirituality, including the Goddess, among feminists around the country in the summer of 1974.[8] *WomanSpirit* magazine, which published its first issue in 1974 and has contributors from across the United States, has expressed the grass roots nature of the women's spirituality movement. In 1976, a journal, *Lady Unique,* devoted to the Goddess emerged. In 1975, the first women's spirituality conference was held in Boston and attended by 1,800 women. In 1978, a University of Santa Cruz course on the Goddess drew over 500 people. Sources for this essay are

these manifestations of the Goddess in modern women's experiences as reported in *WomanSpirit, Lady Unique,* and elsewhere, and as expressed in conversations I have had with women who have been thinking about the Goddess and women's spirituality.

The simplest and most basic meaning of the symbol of Goddess is the acknowledgement of the legitimacy of female power as a beneficent and independent power. A woman who echoes Ntosake Shange's dramatic statement, "I found God in myself and I loved her fiercely," is saying "Female power is strong and creative." She is saying that the divine principle, the saving and sustaining power, is in herself, that she will no longer look to men or male figures as saviors. The strength and independence of female power can be intuited by contemplating ancient and modern images of the Goddess. This meaning of the symbol of Goddess is simple and obvious, and yet it is difficult for many to comprehend. It stands in sharp contrast to the paradigms of female dependence on males that have been predominant in Western religion and culture. The internationally acclaimed novelist Monique Wittig captured the novelty and flavor of the affirmation of female power when she wrote, in her mythic work *Les Guérillères,*

> There was a time when you were not a slave, remember that. You walked alone, full of laughter, you bathed bare-bellied. You say you have lost all recollection of it, remember . . . you say there are not words to describe it, you say it does not exist. But remember. Make an effort to remember. Or, failing that, invent.[9]

While Wittig does not speak directly of the Goddess here, she captures the "mood" of joyous celebration of female freedom and independence that is created in women who define their identities through the symbol of Goddess. Artist Mary Beth Edelson expressed the political "motivations" inspired by the Goddess when she wrote,

> The ascending archetypal symbols of the feminine unfold today in the psyche of modern Every woman.

They encompass the multiple forms of the Great Goddess. Reaching across the centuries we take the hands of our Ancient sisters. The Great Goddess alive and well is rising to announce to the patriarchs that their 5,000 years are up—Hallelujah! Here we come.[10]

The affirmation of female power contained in the Goddess symbol has both psychological and political consequences. Psychologically, it means the defeat of the view engendered by patriarchy that women's power is inferior and dangerous. This new "mood" of affirmation of female power also leads to new "motivations"; it supports and undergirds women's trust in their own power and power of other women in family and society.

If the simplest meaning of the Goddess symbol is an affirmation of the legitimacy and beneficence of female power, then a question immediately arises, "Is the Goddess simply female power writ large, and if so, why bother with the symbol of Goddess at all? Or does the symbol refer to a Goddess 'out there' who is not reducible to a human potential?" The many women who have rediscovered the power of Goddess would give three answers to this question: (1) The Goddess is divine female, a personification who can be invoked in prayer and ritual; (2) the Goddess is symbol of the life, death, and rebirth energy in nature and culture, in personal and communal life and (3) the Goddess is symbol of the affirmation of the legitimacy and beauty of female power (made possible by the new becoming of women in the women's liberation movement). If one were to ask these women which answer is the "correct" one, different responses would be given. Some would assert that the Goddess definitely is *not* "out there," that the symbol of a divinity "out there" is part of the legacy of patriarchal oppression, which brings with it the authoritarianism, hierarchicalism, and dogmatic rigidity associated with biblical monotheistic religions. They might assert that the Goddess symbol reflects the sacred power within women and nature, suggesting the connectedness between women's cycles of menstruation, birth, and menopause and the life and death cycles of the universe. Others seem quite comfortable with the notion of Goddess as a divine female protector and creator and would find their experience of Goddess limited by the assertion that she is not *also* out there as well as within themselves and in all natural processes. When asked what the symbol of Goddess means, feminist priestess Starhawk replied, "It all depends on how I feel. When I feel weak, she is someone who can help and protect me. When I feel strong, she is the symbol of my own power. At other times I feel her as the natural energy in my body and the world."[11] How are we to evaluate such a statement? Theologians might call these the words of a sloppy thinker. But my deepest intuition tells me they contain a wisdom that Western theological thought has lost.

To theologians, these differing views of the "meaning" of the symbol of Goddess might seem to threaten a reply of the trinitarian controversies. Is there, perhaps, a way of doing theology which would not lead immediately into dogmatic controversy, which would not require theologians to say definitively that one understanding is true and the others are false? Could people's relation to a common symbol be made primary and varying interpretations be acknowledged? The diversity of explications of the meaning of the Goddess symbol suggests that symbols have a richer significance than any explications of their meaning can express, a point literary critics have long insisted on. This phenomenological fact suggests that theologians may need to give more than lip service to a theory of symbol in which the symbol is viewed as the primary fact and the meanings are viewed as secondary. It also suggests that a *thea*logy[12] of the Goddess would be very different from the *theo*logy we have known in the West. But to spell out this notion of the primacy of *symbol* in thealogy in contrast to the primacy of the *explanation* in theology would be the topic of another paper. Let me simply state that women, who have been deprived of a female religious symbol system for centuries, are therefore in an excellent position to recognize the power and primacy of symbols. I believe women must develop a theory of symbol and thealogy congruent with their experience at the same time as they "remember and invent" new symbol systems.

A second important implication of the Goddess symbol for women is the affirmation of the female body and the life cycle expressed in it. Because of women's unique position as menstruants, birth-givers, and those who have traditionally cared for the young and the dying, women's connection to the body, nature, and this world has been obvious. Women were denigrated because they seemed more carnal, fleshy, and earthy than the culture-creating males.[13] The misogynist anti*body* tradition in Western thought is symbolized in the myth of Eve who is traditionally viewed as a sexual temptress, the epitome of women's carnal nature. This tradition reaches its nadir in the *Malleus Maleficarum (The Hammer of Evil-Doing Women),* which states, "All witchcraft stems from carnal lust, which in women is insatiable."[14] The Virgin Mary, the positive female image in Christianity, does not contradict Christian denigration of the female body and its powers. The Virgin Mary is revered because she, in her perpetual virginity, transcends the carnal sexuality attributed to most women.

The denigration of the female body is expressed in cultural and religious taboos surrounding menstruation, childbirth, and menopause in women. While menstruation taboos may have originated in a perception of the awesome powers of the female body,[15] they degenerated into a simple perception that there is something "wrong" with female bodily functions. Menstruating women were forbidden to enter the sanctuary in ancient Hebrew and premodern Christian communities. Although only Orthodox Jews still enforce religious taboos against menstruant women, few women in our culture grow up affirming their menstruation as a connection to sacred power. Most women learn that menstruation is a curse and grow up believing that the bloody facts of menstruation are best hidden away. Feminists challenge this attitude to the female body. Judy Chicago's art piece "Menstruation Bathroom" broke these menstrual taboos. In a sterile white bathroom, she exhibited boxes of Tampax and Kotex on an open shelf, and the wastepaper basket was overflowing with bloody tampons and sanitary napkins.[16] Many women who viewed the piece felt relieved to have their "dirty secret" out in the open.

The denigration of the female body and its powers is further expressed in Western culture's attitudes toward childbirth.[17] Religious iconography does not celebrate the birthgiver, and there is no theology or ritual that enables a woman to celebrate the process of birth as a spiritual experience. Indeed, Jewish and Christian traditions also had blood taboos concerning the woman who had recently given birth. While these religious taboos are rarely enforced today (again, only by Orthodox Jews), they have secular equivalents. Giving birth is treated as a disease requiring hospitalization, and the woman is viewed as a passive object, anesthetized to ensure her acquiescence to the will of the doctor. The women's liberation movement has challenged these cultural attitudes, and many feminists have joined with advocates of natural childbirth and home birth in emphasizing the need for women to control and take pride in their bodies, including the birth process.

Western culture also gives little dignity to the postmenopausal or aging woman. It is no secret that our culture is based on a denial of aging and death, and that women suffer more severely from this denial than men. Women are placed on a pedestal and considered powerful when they are young and beautiful, but they are said to lose this power as they age. As feminists have pointed out, the "power" of the young woman is illusory, since beauty standards are defined by men, and since few women are considered (or consider themselves) beautiful for more than a few years of their lives. Some men are viewed as wise and authoritative in age, but old women are pitied and shunned. Religious iconography supports this cultural attitude towards aging women. The purity and virginity of Mary and the female saints is often expressed in the iconographic convention of perpetual youth. Moreover, religious mythology associates aging women with evil in the symbol of the wicked old witch.

Feminists have challenged cultural myths of aging women and have urged women to reject patriarchal beauty standards and to celebrate the distinctive beauty of women of all ages.

The symbol of Goddess aids the process of naming and reclaiming the female body and its cycles and processes. In the ancient world and among modern women, the Goddess symbol represents the birth, death, and rebirth process of the natural and human worlds. The female body is viewed as the direct incarnation of waxing and waning, life and death, cycles in the universe. This is sometimes expressed through the symbolic connection between the twenty-eight-day cycles of menstruation and the twenty-eight-day cycles of the moon. Moreover, the Goddess is celebrated in the triple aspect of youth, maturity, and age, or maiden, mother, and crone. The potentiality of the young girl is celebrated in the nymph or maiden aspect of the Goddess. The Goddess as mother is sometimes depicted giving birth, and giving birth is viewed as a symbol for all the creative, life-giving powers of the universe.[18] The life-giving powers of the Goddess in her creative aspect are not limited to physical birth, for the Goddess is also seen as the creator of all the arts of civilization, including healing, writing, and the giving of just law. Women in the middle of life who are not physical mothers may give birth to poems, songs, books, or nurture other women, men, and children. They too are incarnations of the Goddess in her creative, life-changing aspect. At the end of life, women incarnate the crone aspect of the Goddess. The wise old woman, the woman who knows from experience what life is about, the woman whose closeness to her own death gives her a distance and perspective on the problems of life, is celebrated as the third aspect of the Goddess. Thus, women learn to value youth, creativity, and wisdom in themselves and other women.

The possibilities of reclaiming the female body and its cycles have been expressed in a number of Goddess-centered solstice rituals. Hallie Mountainwing and Barby My Own created a summer solstice ritual to celebrate menstruation and birth. The women simulated a birth canal and birthed each other into their circle. They raised power by placing their hands on each other's bellies and chanting together. Finally, they marked each other's faces with rich, dark menstrual blood saying, "This is the blood that promises renewal. This is the blood that promises sustenance. This is the blood that promises life."[19] From hidden dirty secret to symbol of the life power of the Goddess, women's blood has come full circle. Other women have created rituals that celebrate the crone aspect of the Goddess. Z. Budapest believes that the crone aspect of the Goddess is predominant in the fall, especially at Halloween, an ancient holiday. On this day, the wisdom of the old woman is celebrated, and it is also recognized that the old must die so that the new can be born.[19a]

The "mood" created by the symbol of the Goddess in triple aspect is one of positive, joyful affirmation of the female body and its cycles and acceptance of aging and death as well as life. The "motivations" are to overcome menstrual taboos, to return the birth process to the hands of women, and to change cultural attitudes about age and death. Changing cultural attitudes toward the female body could go a long way toward overcoming the spirit-flesh, mind-body dualisms of Western culture, since, as Ruether has pointed out, the denigration of the female body is at the heart of these dualisms. The Goddess as symbol of the revaluation of the body and nature thus also undergirds the human potential and ecology movements. The "mood" is one of affirmation, awe, and respect for the body and nature, and the "motivation" is to respect the teachings of the body and the rights of all living beings.

A third important implication of the Goddess symbol for women is the positive valuation of will in a Goddess-centered ritual, especially in Goddess-centered ritual magic and spellcasting in womanspirit and feminist witchcraft circles. The basic notion behind ritual magic and spellcasting is energy as power. Here the Goddess is a center or focus of power and energy; she is the personification of the energy that flows between beings in the natural and human worlds. In Goddess circles, energy is raised by chanting or dancing. According to Starhawk, "Witches conceive of psychic energy as having form and substance that can be perceived and directed by those with a trained awareness. The power generated within the circle is built into a cone form, and at its peak is released—to the Goddess, to reenergize the members of the coven, or to do a specific work such as healing."[20] In ritual magic, the energy raised is directed by willpower. Women who celebrate in Goddess circles believe they can achieve their wills in the world.

The emphasis on the will is important for women, because women traditionally have been taught to devalue their wills, to believe that they cannot achieve their will through their own power, and even to suspect that the assertion of will is evil. Faith Wildung's poem "Waiting," from which I will quote only a short segment, sums up women's sense that their lives are defined not by their own will, but by waiting for others to take the initiative.

Waiting for my breasts to develop
Waiting to wear a bra
Waiting to menstruate

. . .

Waiting for life to begin, Waiting—
Waiting to be somebody

. . .

Waiting to get married
Waiting for my wedding day
Waiting for my wedding night

. . .

Waiting for the end of day
Waiting for sleep. Waiting . . .[21]

Patriarchal religion has enforced the view that female initiative and will are evil through the juxtaposition of Eve and Mary. Eve caused the fall by asserting her will against the command of God, while Mary began the new age with her response to God's initiative, "Let it be done to me according to thy word" (Luke 1:38). Even for men, patriarchal religion values the passive will subordinate to divine initiative. The classical doctrines of sin and grace view sin as the prideful assertion of will and grace as the obedient subordination of the human will to the divine initiative or order. While this view of will might be questioned from a human perspective, Valerie Saiving has argued that it has particularly deleterious consequences for women in Western culture. According to Saiving, Western culture encourages males in the assertion of will, and thus it may make some sense to view the male form of sin as an excess of will. But since culture discourages females in the assertion of will, the traditional doctrines of sin and grace encourage women to remain in their form of sin, which is self-negation or insufficient assertion of will.[22] One possible reason the will is denigrated in a patriarchal religious framework is that both human and divine will are often pictured as arbitrary, self-initiated, and exercised without regard for other wills.

In a Goddess-centered context, in contrast, the will is valued. *A woman is encouraged to know her will, to believe that her will is valid, and to believe that her will can be achieved in the world,* three powers traditionally denied to her in patriarchy. In a Goddess-centered framework, a women's will is not subordinated to the Lord God as king and ruler, nor to men as his representatives. Thus a woman is not reduced to waiting and acquiescing in the wills of others as she is in patriarchy. But neither does she adopt the egocentric form of will that pursues self-interest without regard for the interests of others.

The Goddess-centered context provides a different understanding of the will than that available in the traditional patriarchal religious framework. In the Goddess framework, will can be achieved only when it is exercised in harmony with the energies and wills of other beings. Wise women, for example, raise a cone of healing energy at the full moon or solstice when the lunar or solar energies are at their high points with respect to the earth. This discipline encourages them to recognize that not all times are propitious for the achieving of every will.

Similarly, they know that spring is a time for new beginnings in work and love, summer a time for producing external manifestations of inner potentialities, and fall or winter times for stripping down to the inner core and extending roots. Such awareness of waxing and waning processes in the universe discourages arbitrary ego-centered assertion of will, while at the same time encouraging the assertion of individual will in cooperation with natural energies and the energies created by the wills of others. Wise women also have a tradition that whatever is sent out will be returned and this reminds them to assert their wills in cooperative and healing rather than egocentric and destructive ways. This view of will allows women to begin to recognize, claim, and assert their wills without adopting the worst characteristics of the patriarchal understanding and use of will. In the Goddess-centered framework, the "mood" is one of positive affirmation of personal will in the context of the energies of other wills or beings. The "motivation" is for women to know and assert their wills in cooperation with other wills and energies. This of course does not mean that women always assert their wills in positive and life-affirming ways. Women's capacity for evil is, of course, as great as men's. My purpose is simply to contrast the differing attitudes toward the exercise of will *per se,* and the female will in particular, in Goddess-centered religion and in the Christian God-centered religion.

The fourth and final aspect of Goddess symbolism that I will discuss here is the significance of the Goddess for a revaluation of woman's bonds and heritage. As Virginia Woolf has said, "Chloe liked Olivia," a statement about a woman's relation to another woman, is a sentence that rarely occurs in fiction. Men have written the stories, and they have written about women almost exclusively in their relations to men.[23] The celebrations of women's bonds to each other, as mothers and daughters, as colleagues and coworkers, as sisters, friends, and lovers, is beginning to occur in the new literature and culture created by women in the women's movement. While I believe that the revaluing of

each of these bonds is important, I will focus on the mother-daughter bond, in part because I believe it may be the key to the others.

Adrienne Rich has pointed out that the mother-daughter bond, perhaps the most important of woman's bonds, "resonant with charges . . . the flow of energy between two biologically alike bodies, one of which has lain in amniotic bliss inside the other, one of which has labored to give birth to the other,"[24] is rarely celebrated in patriarchal religion and culture. Christianity celebrates the father's relation to the son and the mother's relation to the son, but the story of the mother and daughter is missing. So, too, in patriarchal literature and psychology the mothers and the daughters rarely exist. Volumes have been written about the oedipal complex, but little has been written about the girl's relation to her mother. Moreover, as de Beauvoir has noted, the mother-daughter relation is distorted in patriarchy because the mother must give her daughter over to men in a male-defined culture in which women are viewed as inferior. The mother must socialize her daughter to become subordinate to men, and if her daughter challenges patriarchal norms, the mother is likely to defend the patriarchal structures against her own daughter.[25]

These patterns are changing in the new culture created by women in which the bonds of women to women are beginning to be celebrated. Holly Near has written several songs that celebrate women's bonds and women's heritage. In one of her finest songs she writes of an "old-time woman" who is "waiting to die." A young woman feels for the life that has passed the old woman by and begins to cry, but the old woman looks her in the eye and says, "If I had not suffered, you wouldn't be wearing those jeans/Being an old-time woman ain't as bad as it seems."[26] This song, which Near has said was inspired by her grandmother, expresses and celebrates a bond and a heritage passed down from one woman to another. In another of Near's songs, she sings of a "hiking-boot mother who's seeing the world/For the first time with her own little girl." In this song, the mother tells the drifter who has been traveling with her to pack up and travel alone if he thinks "traveling three is a drag" because "I've got a little one who loves me as much as you need me/And darling, that's loving enough."[27] This song is significant because the mother places her relationship to her daughter above her relationship to man, something women rarely do in patriarchy.[28]

Almost the only story of mothers and daughters that has been transmitted in Western culture is the myth of Demeter and Persephone that was the basis of religious rites celebrated by women only, the Thesmophoria, and later formed the basis of the Eleusian mysteries, the underworld. Unwilling to accept this state of affairs, Demeter rages and withholds fertility from the earth until her daughter is returned to her. What is important for women in this story is that a mother fights for her daughter and for her relation to her daughter. This is completely different from the mother's relation to her daughter in patriarchy. The "mood" created by the story of Demeter and Persephone is one of celebration of the mother-daughter bond, and the "motivation" is for mothers and daughters to affirm the heritage passed on from mother to daughter and to reject the patriarchal pattern where the primary loyalties of mother and daughter must be to men.

The symbol of Goddess has much to offer women who are struggling to be rid of the "powerful, pervasive, and long-lasting moods and motivations" of devaluation of female power, denigration of the female body, distrust of female will, and denial of the women's bonds and heritage that have been engendered by patriarchal religion. As women struggle to create a new culture in which women's power, bodies, will, and bonds are celebrated, it seems natural that the Goddess would reemerge as symbol of the newfound beauty, strength, and power of women.

Notes

1. From the original cast album, Buddah Records, 1976.

2. See Susan Rennie and Kristen Grimstad, "Spiritual Explorations Cross-Country," *Quest*, 1975, *I* (4), 1975, 49–51; and *WomanSpirit* magazine.

3. See Starhawk, "Witchcraft and Women's Culture," in Carol P. Christ and Judith Plaskow, eds., *WomanSpirit Rising: A Feminist Reader in Religion* (San Francisco: Harper & Row, 1979).

4. "Religion as a Cultural System," in William L. Lessa and Evon V. Vogt, eds., *Reader in Comparative Religion*, 2nd ed. (New York: Harper & Row, 1972), p. 206.

5. Geertz, p. 210.

6. Boston: Beacon Press, 1974, p. 13, italics added.

7. *The Second Sex*, trans. H. M. Parshleys (New York: Alfred A. Knopf, 1953).

8. See Grimstad and Rennie.

9. *Les Guérillères*, trans. David LeVay (New York: Avon Books, 1971), p. 89. Also quoted in Morgan MacFarland, "Witchcraft: The Art of Remembering," *Quest*, 1975, I(4), 41.

10. "Speaking for Myself," *Lady Unique*, 1976, I, 56.

11. Personal communication.

12. A term coined by Naomi Goldenberg to refer to reflection on the meaning of the symbol of Goddess.

13. This theory of the origins of the Western dualism is stated by Rosemary Ruether in *New Woman: New Earth* (New York: Seabury Press, 1975), and elsewhere.

14. Heinrich Kramer and Jacob Sprenger (New York: Dover, 1971), p. 47.

15. See Rita M. Gross, "Menstruation and Child-birth as Ritual and Religious Experience in the Religion of the Australian Aborigines," in *The Journal of the American Academy of Religion,* 1977, *45* (4), Supplement 1147–1181.

16. *Through the Flower* (New York: Doubleday & Company, 1975), plate 4, pp. 106–107.

17. See Adrienne Rich, *Of Woman Born* (New York: Bantam Books: 1977), chaps. 6 and 7.

18. See James Mellaart, *Earliest Civilizations of the Near East* (New York: McGraw-Hill, 1965), p. 92.

19. Barby My Own, "Ursa Maior: Menstrual Moon Celebration" in Anne Kent Rush, ed. *Moon, Moon* (Berkeley, Calif., and New York: Moon Books and Random House, 1976), pp. 374–387.

19a. In Georgia Kaufman's videotape, "Women, Ritual and Religion," 1977.

20. Starhawk, op. cit.

21. In Judy Chicago, pp. 213–217.

22. "The Human Situation: A Feminine View," in *Journal of Religion,* 1960 *40,* 100–112, and reprinted in Christ and Plaskow, ed., op. cit.

23. *A Room of One's Own* (New York: Harcourt Brace Jovanovich, 1928), p. 86.

24. Rich, p. 226.

25. De Beauvoir, pp. 448–449.

26. "Old Time Woman," lyrics by Jeffrey Langley and Holly Near, from *Holly Near: A Live Album,* Redwood Records, 1974.

27. "Started Out Fine," by Holly Near from *Holly Near: A Live Album.*

28. Rich, p. 223.

A Conversation with God

RAYMOND M. SMULLYAN

Although many people talk to God (pray, curse, and so forth), very few believe they have actually heard God talk back. Suppose you did. Would it settle for you the question of God's existence? In the following imaginative piece Raymond Smullyan, Professor of Philosophy at Indiana University, raises doubts about the interpretation of even first-person experiences of this kind.

MORTAL: If I can't see you, how do I know you exist?

GOD: Good question! How in fact do you know I exist?

MORTAL: Well, I am talking to you, am I not?

GOD: How do you know you are talking to me? Suppose you told a psychiatrist, "Yesterday I talked to God." What do you think he would say?

MORTAL: That might depend on the psychiatrist. Since most of them are atheistic, I guess most would tell me I had simply been talking to myself.

GOD: And they would be right!

MORTAL: What? You mean you don't exist?

GOD: You have the strangest faculty of drawing false conclusions! Just because you are talking to yourself, it follows that *I* don't exist?

MORTAL: Well, if I think I am talking to you, but I am really talking to myself, in what sense do you exist?

GOD: Your question is based on two fallacies plus a confusion. The question of whether or not you are now talking to me and the question of whether or not I exist are totally separate. Even if you were not now talking to me (which obviously you are), it still would not mean that I don't exist.

MORTAL: Well, all right, of course! So instead of saying "if I am talking to myself, then you don't exist," I should rather have said, "if I am talking to myself, then I obviously am not talking to you."

GOD: A very different statement indeed, but still false.

MORTAL: Oh, come now, if I am only talking to myself, then how can I be talking to you?

GOD: Your use of the word "only" is quite misleading! I can suggest several logical possibilities under which your talking to yourself does not imply that you are not talking to me.

MORTAL: Suggest just one!

GOD: Well, obviously one such possibility is that you and I are identical.

MORTAL: Such a blasphemous thought—at least had *I* uttered it!

GOD: According to some religions, yes. According to others, it is the plain, simple, immediately perceived truth.

MORTAL: So the only way out of my dilemma is to believe that you and I are identical?

GOD: Not at all! This is only one way out. There are several others. For example, it may be that you are part of me, in which case you may be talking to that part of me which is you. Or I may be part of you, in which case you may be talking to that part of you which is me. Or again, you and I might partially overlap, in which case you may be talking to the intersection and hence talking both to you and to me. The only way your talking to yourself might seem to imply that you are not talking to me is if you and I were totally disjoint—and even then, you could conceivably be talking to both of us.

MORTAL: So you claim you do exist.

GOD: Not at all. Again you draw false conclusions! The question of my existence has not even come up. All I have said is that from the fact you are talking to yourself one cannot possibly infer my nonexistence, let alone the weaker fact that you are not talking to me.

MORTAL: All right, I'll grant your point! But what I really want to know is *do* you exist?

GOD: What a strange question!

MORTAL: Why? Men have been asking for countless millennia.

GOD: I know that! The question itself is not strange; what I mean is that it is a most strange question to ask of *me!*

MORTAL: Why?

GOD: Because I am the very one whose existence you doubt! I perfectly well understand your anxiety. You are worried that your present experience with me is a mere hallucination. But how can you possibly expect to obtain reliable information from a being about his very existence when you suspect the nonexistence of the very same being?

MORTAL: So you won't tell me whether or not you exist?

GOD: I am not being willful! I merely wish to point out that no answer I could give could possibly satisfy you. All right, suppose I said, "No, I don't exist." What would that prove? Absolutely nothing! Or if I said, "Yes, I exist." Would that convince you? Of course not!

MORTAL: Well, if you can't tell me whether or not you exist, then who possibly can?

GOD: That is something which no one can tell you. It is something which only you can find out for yourself.

MORTAL: How do I go about finding this out for myself?

GOD: That also no one can tell you. This is another thing you will have to find out for yourself.

Demons and Devils

C. S. LEWIS

Many people profess belief in a benevolent super spirit or force ("God"), but balk at the supposed existence of other spiritual beings (angels, demons, etcetera). Evil spirits are especially problematic. In *The Screwtape Letters* (1941–1943), from which the following selection is edited, Clive Staples Lewis (1898–1963) presents an imaginary exchange between an administrative devil and a novice tempter. We begin with a brief quote from Professor Lewis and, after a few demonic exchanges, allow him to speak more at length regarding his own beliefs and the various ways in which devils and angels have been portrayed in art and literature.

PREFACE

There are two equal and opposite errors into which our race can fall about the devils. One is to disbelieve in their existence. The other is to believe, and to feel an excessive and unhealthy interest in them. They themselves are equally pleased by both errors, and hail a materialist or a magician with the same delight.

*   *   *

THE EXISTENCE OF DEVILS

My dear Wormwood,

I wonder you should ask me whether it is essential to keep the patient in ignorance of your own existence. That question, at least for the present phase of the struggle, has been answered for us by the High Command. Our policy, for the moment, is to conceal ourselves. Of course this has not always been so. We are really faced with a cruel dilemma. When the humans disbelieve in our existence we lose all the pleasing results of direct terrorism, and we make no magicians. On the other hand, when they believe in us, we cannot make them materialists and sceptics. At least, not yet. I have great hopes that we shall learn in due time how to emotionalise and mythologise their science to such an extent that what is, in effect, a belief in us (though not under that name) will creep in while the human mind remains closed to belief in the Enemy. The "Life Force," the worship of sex, and some aspects of Psychoanalysis may here prove useful. If once we can produce our perfect work—the Materialist Magician, the man, not using, but veritably worshipping, what he vaguely calls "Forces" while denying the existence of "spirits"—then the end of the war will be in sight. But in the meantime we must obey our orders. I do not think you will have much difficulty in keeping the patient in the dark. The fact that "devils" are predominantly *comic* figures in the modern imagination will help you. If any faint suspicion of your existence begins to arise in his mind, suggest to him a picture of something in red tights, and per-

C. S. Lewis, excerpts from *The Screwtape Letters* (New York: Macmillan, 1971), edited from the 1941 edition: Preface (p. 3); Chapter 7 (pp. 32–33, 35); Chapter 18 (pp. 80–84); Chapter 19 (p. 85); Chapter 27 (pp. 125–129); and from the 1961 edition: Preface (pp. vii–xii). Originally published in *The Guardian*, 1941–1943. Copyright © 1959 by Helen Joy Lewis. Copyright © 1961 by C. S. Lewis. Reprinted with permission of HarperCollins Publishers, Ltd.

suade him that since he cannot believe in that (it is an old textbook method of confusing them) he therefore cannot believe in you.

I had not forgotten my promise to consider whether we should make the patient an extreme patriot or an extreme pacifist. All extremes except extreme devotion to the Enemy are to be encouraged. . . . .

Whichever he adopts, your main task will be the same. Let him begin by treating the Patriotism or the Pacifism as a part of his religion. Then let him, under the influence of partisan spirit, come to regard it as the most important part. Then quietly and gradually nurse him on to the stage at which the religion becomes merely part of the "Cause," in which Christianity is valued chiefly because of the excellent arguments it can produce in favour of the British war effort or of pacifism. The attitude which you want to guard against is that in which temporal affairs are treated primarily as material for obedience. Once you have made the World an end, and faith a means, you have almost won your man, and it makes very little difference what kind of worldly end he is pursuing. Provided that meetings, pamphlets, policies, movements, causes, and crusades, matter more to him than prayers and sacraments and charity, he is ours—and the more "religious" (on those terms), the more securely ours. I could show you a pretty cageful down here.

Your affectionate uncle

SCREWTAPE

*   *   *

SEX AND LOVE

My dear Wormwood,

Even under Slubgob you must have learned at college the routine technique of sexual temptation, and since, for us spirits, this whole subject is one of considerable tedium (though necessary as part of our training) I will pass it over. But on the larger issues involved I think you have a good deal to learn.

The Enemy's demand on humans takes the form of a dilemma: *either* complete abstinence *or* unmitigated monogamy. Ever since Our Father's first great victory, we have rendered the former very difficult to them. The latter, for the last few centuries, we have been closing up as a way of escape. We have done this through the poets and novelists by persuading the humans that a curious, and usually short-lived, experience which they call "being in love" is the only respectable ground for marriage; that marriage can, and ought to, render this excitement permanent; and that a marriage which does not do so is no longer binding. This idea is our parody of an idea that came from the Enemy.

The whole philosophy of Hell rests on recognition of the axiom that one thing is not another thing, and, specially, that one self is not another self. My good is my good, and your good is yours. What one gains another loses. Even an inanimate object is what it is by excluding all other objects from the space it occupies; if it expands, it does so by thrusting other objects aside or by absorbing them. A self does the same. With beasts the absorption takes the form of eating; for us, it means the sucking of will and freedom out of a weaker self into a stronger. "To be" *means* "to be in competition."

Now, the Enemy's philosophy is nothing more nor less than one continued attempt to evade this very obvious truth. He aims at contradiction. Things are to be many, yet somehow also one. The good of one self is to be the good of another. This impossibility He calls *Love,* and this same monotonous panacea can be detected under all He does and even all He is—or claims to be. Thus He is not content, even Himself, to be a sheer arithmetical unity; He claims to be three as well as one, in order that this nonsense about Love may find a foothold in His own nature. At the other end of the scale, He introduces into matter that obscene invention the organism, in which the parts are perverted from their natural destiny of competition and made to cooperate.

His real motive for fixing on sex as the method of reproduction among humans is only too apparent for the use He has made of it. Sex might have been, from our point of view, quite innocent. It might have been merely one more mode in which a stronger self preyed upon a weaker—as it is, indeed, among the spiders where the bride concludes her nuptials by eating her groom. But in the humans the Enemy has gratuitously associated affection between the parties with sexual desire. He has also made the offspring dependent on the parents and given the parents an impulse to support it—thus producing the Family, which is like the organism, only worse; for the members are more distinct, yet also united in a more conscious and responsible way. The whole thing, in fact, turns out to be simply one more device for dragging in Love.

Now comes the joke. The Enemy described a married couple as "one flesh." He did not say "a happily married couple" or "a couple who married because they were in love," but you can make the humans ignore that. You can also make them forget that the man they call Paul did not confine it to *married* couples. Mere copulation, for him, makes "one flesh." You can thus get the humans to accept as rhetorical eulogies of "being in love" what were in fact plain descriptions of the real significance of sexual intercourse. The truth is that wherever a man lies with a woman, there, whether they like it or not, a transcendental relation is set up between them which must be eternally enjoyed or eternally endured. From the true statement that this transcendental relation was intended to produce—and, if obediently entered into, too often *will* produce—affection and the family, humans can be made to infer the false belief that the blend of affection, fear, and desire which they call "being in love" is the only thing that makes marriage either happy or holy. The error is easy to produce because "being in love" does very often, in western Europe, precede marriages which are made in obedience to the Enemy's designs, that is, with the intention of fidelity, fertility, and goodwill; just as religious emotion very often, but not always, attends conversion. In other words, the humans are to be encouraged to regard as the basis for marriage a highly coloured and distorted version of something the Enemy really promises as its result. Two advantages follow. In the first place,

humans who have not the gift of continence can be deterred from seeking marriage as a solution because they do not find themselves "in love," and, thanks to us, the idea of marrying with any other motive seems to them low and cynical. Yes, they think that. They regard the intention of loyalty to a partnership for mutual help, for the preservation of chastity, and for the transmission of life, as something lower than a storm of emotion. (Don't neglect to make your man think the marriage service very offensive.) In the second place any sexual infatuation whatever, so long as it intends marriage, will be regarded as "love," and "love" will be held to excuse a man from all the guilt, and to protect him from all the consequences, of marrying a heathen, a fool, or a wanton. But more of this in my next.

Your affectionate uncle

SCREWTAPE

My dear Wormwood,

I have been thinking very hard about the question in your last letter. If, as I have clearly shown, all selves are by their very nature in competition, and therefore the Enemy's idea of Love is a contradiction in terms, what becomes of my reiterated warning that He really loves the human vermin and really desires their freedom and continued existence? I hope, my dear boy, you have not shown my letters to anyone. Not that it matters, of course. Anyone would see that the appearance of heresy into which I have fallen is purely accidental. . . .

*   *   *

PRAYER, DISTRACTIONS, ETC.

My dear Wormwood,

You seem to be doing very little good at present. The use of his "love" to distract his mind from the Enemy is, of course, obvious, but you reveal what poor use you are making of it when you say that the whole question of distraction and the wandering mind has now become one of the chief subjects of his prayers. That means you have largely failed. When this or any other distraction crosses his mind you ought to encourage him to thrust it away by sheer will power and to try to continue the normal prayer as if nothing had happened; once he accepts the distraction as his present problem and lays *that* before the Enemy and makes it the main theme of his prayers and his endeavours, then, so far from doing good, you have done harm. Anything, even a sin, which has the total effect of moving him close up to the Enemy makes against us in the long run.

A promising line is the following: Now that he is in love, a new idea of *earthly* happiness has arisen in his mind: and hence a new urgency in his purely petitionary prayers—about this war and other such matters. Now is the time for raising intellectual difficulties about prayer of that sort. False spirituality is always to be encouraged. On the seemingly pious ground that "praise and communion with God are the true prayer," humans can often be lured into direct disobedience to the Enemy Who (in His usual flat, commonplace, uninteresting way) has definitely told them to pray for their daily bread and the recovery of their sick. You will, of course, conceal from him the fact that the prayer for daily bread, interpreted in a "spiritual sense," is really just as crudely petitionary as it is in any other sense.

But since your patient has contracted the terrible habit of obedience, he will probably continue such "crude" prayers whatever you do. But you can worry him with the haunting suspicion that the practice is absurd and can have no objective result. Don't forget to use the "Heads I win, tails you lose" argument. If the thing he prays for doesn't happen, then that is one more proof that petitionary prayers don't work; if it does happen, he will, of course, be able to see some of the physical causes which led up to it, and "therefore it would have happened anyway," and thus a granted prayer becomes just as good a proof as a denied one that prayers are ineffective.

You, being a spirit, will find it difficult to understand how he gets into this confusion. But you must remember that he takes Time for an ultimate real-

ity. He supposes that the Enemy, like himself, sees some things as present, remembers others as past, and anticipates others as future; or even if he believes that the Enemy does not see things that way, yet, in his heart of hearts, he regards this as a peculiarity of the Enemy's mode of perception—he doesn't really think (though he would say he did) that things as the Enemy sees them are things as they are! If you tried to explain to him that men's prayers today are one of the innumerable coordinates with which the Enemy harmonises the weather of tomorrow, he would reply that then the Enemy always knew men were going to make those prayers and, if so, they did not pray freely but were predestined to do so. And he would add that the weather on a given day can be traced back through its causes to the original creation of matter itself—so that the whole thing, both on the human and on the material side, is given "from the word go." What he ought to say, of course, is obvious to us: that the problem of adapting the particular weather to the particular prayers is merely the appearance, at two points in his temporal mode of perception, of the total problem of adapting the whole spiritual universe to the whole corporeal universe; that creation in its entirety operates at every point of space and time, or rather that their kind of consciousness forces them to encounter the whole, self-consistent creative act as a series of successive events. *Why* that creative act leaves room for their free will is the problem of problems, the secret behind the Enemy's nonsense about "Love." *How* it does so is no problem at all; for the Enemy does not *foresee* the humans making their free contributions in a future, but *sees* them doing so in His unbounded Now. And obviously to watch a man doing something is not to make him do it.

It may be replied that some meddlesome human writers, notably Boethius, have let this secret out. But in the intellectual climate which we have at last succeeded in producing throughout western Europe, you needn't bother about that. Only the learned read old books, and we have now so dealt with the learned that they are of all men the least likely to acquire wisdom by doing so. We have done this by inculcating the Historical Point of View. The Historical Point of View, put briefly, means that when a learned man is presented with any statement in an ancient author, the one question he never asks is whether it is true. He asks who influenced the ancient writer, and how far the statement is consistent with what he said in other books, and what phase in the writer's development, or in the general history of thought, it illustrates, and how it affected later writers, and how often it has been misunderstood (specially by the learned man's own colleagues) and what the general course of criticism on it has been for the last ten years, and what is the "present state of the question." To regard the ancient writer as a possible source of knowledge—to anticipate that what he said could possibly modify your thoughts or your behaviour—this would be rejected as unutterably simple-minded. And since we cannot deceive the whole human race all the time, it is most important thus to cut every generation off from all others; for where learning makes a free commerce between the ages there is always the danger that the characteristic errors of one may be corrected by the characteristic truths of another. But, thanks be to Our Father and the Historical Point of View, great scholars are now as little nourished by the past as the most ignorant mechanic who holds that "history is bunk."

Your affectionate uncle

SCREWTAPE

*   *   *

DEVILS AND ANGELS IN ART AND LITERATURE

The commonest question is whether I really "believe in the Devil."

Now, if by "the Devil" you mean a power opposite to God and, like God, self-existent from all eternity, the answer is certainly No. There is no uncreated being except God. God has no opposite. No being could attain a "perfect badness" opposite to the perfect goodness of God; for when you have taken away every kind of good thing (intelligence, will, memory, energy, and existence itself) there would be none of him left.

The proper question is whether I believe in devils. I do. That is to say, I believe in angels, and I believe that some of these, by the abuse of their free will, have become enemies to God and, as a corollary, to us. These we may call devils. They do not differ in nature from good angels, but their nature is depraved. *Devil* is the opposite of *angel* only as Bad Man is the opposite of Good Man. Satan, the leader or dictator of devils, is the opposite, not of God, but of Michael.

I believe this not in the sense that it is part of my creed, but in the sense that it is one of my opinions. My religion would not be in ruins if this opinion were shown to be false. Till that happens—and proofs of a negative are hard to come by—I shall retain it. It seems to me to explain a good many facts. It agrees with the plain sense of Scripture, the tradition of Christendom, and the beliefs of most men at most times. And it conflicts with nothing that any of the sciences has shown to be true.

It should be (but it is not) unnecessary to add that a belief in angels, whether good or evil, does not mean a belief in either as they are represented in art and literature. Devils are depicted with bats' wings and good angels with birds' wings, not because anyone holds that moral deterioration would be likely to turn feathers into membrane, but because most men like birds better than bats. They are given wings at all in order to suggest the swiftness of unimpeded intellectual energy. They are given human form because man is the only rational creature we know. Creatures higher in the natural order than ourselves, either incorporeal or animating bodies of a sort we cannot experience, must be represented symbolically if they are to be represented at all.

These forms are not only symbolical but were always known to be symbolical by reflective people. The Greeks did not believe that the gods were really like the beautiful human shapes their sculptors gave them. In their poetry a god who wishes to "appear" to a mortal temporarily assumes the likeness of a man. Christian theology has nearly always explained the "appearance" of an angel in the same way. It is only the ignorant, said Dionysius in the fifth century, who dream that spirits are really winged men.

In the plastic arts these symbols have steadily degenerated. Fra Angelico's angels carry in their face and gesture the peace and authority of Heaven. Later come the chubby infantile nudes of Raphael; finally the soft, slim, girlish, and consolatory angels of nineteenth century art, shapes so feminine that they avoid being voluptuous only by their total insipidity—the frigid houris of a teatable paradise. They are a pernicious symbol. In Scripture the visitation of an angel is always alarming; it has to begin by saying "Fear not." The Victorian angel looks as if it were going to say, "There, there."

The literary symbols are more dangerous because they are not so easily recognized as symbolical. Those of Dante are the best. Before his angels we sink in awe. His devils, as Ruskin rightly remarked, in their rage, spite, and obscenity, are far more like what the reality must be than anything in Milton. Milton's devils, by their grandeur and high poetry, have done great harm, and his angels owe too much to Homer and Raphael. But the really pernicious image is Goethe's Mephistopheles. It is Faust, not he, who really exhibits the ruthless, sleepless, unsmiling concentration upon self which is the mark of Hell. The humorous, civilised, sensible, adaptable Mephistopheles has helped to strengthen the illusion that evil in liberating.

A little man may sometimes avoid some single error made by a great one, and I was determined that my own symbolism should at least not err in Goethe's way. For humor involves a sense of proportion and a power of seeing yourself from the outside. Whatever else we attribute to beings who sinned through pride, we must not attribute this. Satan, said Chesterton, fell through force of gravity. We must picture Hell as a state where everyone is perpetually concerned about his dignity and advancement, where everyone has a grievance, and where everyone lives the deadly serious passions of envy, self-importance, and resentment. This, to begin with. For the rest, my own choice of symbols depended, I suppose, on temperament and on the age.

I like bats much better than bureaucrats. I live in the Managerial Age, in a world of "Admin." The greatest evil is not now done in those sordid "dens of crime" that Dickens loved to paint. It is not done even in concentration camps and labour camps. In those we see its final result. But it is conceived and ordered (moved, seconded, carried, and minuted) in clean, carpeted, warmed, and well-lighted offices, by quiet men with white collars and cut fingernails and smooth-shaven cheeks who do not need to raise their voice. Hence, naturally enough, my symbol for Hell is something like the bureaucracy of a police state or the offices of a thoroughly nasty business concern.

Milton has told us that "devil with devil damned Firm concord holds." But how? Certainly not by friendship. A being which can still love is not yet a devil. Here again my symbol seemed to me useful. It enabled me, by earthly parallels, to picture an official society held together entirely by fear and greed. On the surface, manners are normally suave. Rudeness to one's superiors would obviously be suicidal; rudeness to one's equals must put them on their guard before you were ready to spring your mine. For of course "Dog eat dog" is the principle of the world organisation. Everyone wishes everyone else's discrediting, demotion, and ruin; everyone is an expert in the confidential report, the pretended alliance, the stab in the back. Over all this their good manners, their expressions of grave respect, their "tributes" to one another's invaluable services form a thin crust. Every now and then it gets punctured, and the scalding lava of their hatred spurts out.

This symbol also enabled me to get rid of the absurd fancy that devils are engaged in the disinterested pursuit of something called Evil (the capital is essential). Mine have no use for any such turnip ghost. Bad angels, like bad men, are entirely practical. They have two motives. The first is fear of punishment: for as totalitarian countries have their camps for torture, so my Hell contains deeper Hells, its "houses of correction." Their second motive is a kind of hunger. I feign that devils can, in a spiritual sense, eat one another; and us. Even in human life we have seen the passion to dominate, almost to digest, one's fellow; to make his whole intellectual and emotional life merely an extension of one's own—to hate one's hatreds and resent one's grievances and indulge one's egoism through him as well as through oneself. His own little store of passion must of course be suppressed to make room for ours. If he resists this suppression he is being very selfish.

On Earth this desire is often called "love." In Hell I feign that they recognise it as hunger. But there the hunger is more ravenous, and a fuller satisfaction is possible. There, I suggest, the stronger spirit—there are perhaps no bodies to impede the operation—can really and irrevocably suck the weaker into itself and permanently gorge its own being on the weaker's outraged individuality. It is (I feign) for this that devils desire human souls and the souls of one another. It is for this that Satan desires all his own followers and all the sons of Eve and all the host of Heaven. His dream is of the day when all shall be inside him and all that says "I" can say it only through him. This, I surmise, is the bloated-spider parody, the only imitation he can understand, of that unfathomed bounty whereby God turns tools into servants and servants into sons, so that they may be at last reunited to Him in the perfect freedom of a love offered from the height of the utter individualities which He has liberated them to be.

Review and Reflection

1. Present, as clearly and succinctly as you can, the Ontological Argument to the Existence of God. Do you accept the argument's premises? Conclusion? Why?

2. Explicate and discuss the concept of analytic argumentation. What is its principal value? What are its limitations?

3. Compile a list of Bertrand Russell's reasons for not being a Christian. Do you find them convincing? Why?

4. What, according to Paul Tillich, is the primary function of a religious symbol? Do you agree with Tillich's interpretation of "God"? Why?

5. Do you agree with Carol Christ's conclusions concerning the personal and social importance of a feminine symbol of the deity (a Goddess)? Why?

6. What reactions did you form concerning Raymond Smullyan's "Conversation with God"? What questions, other than those presented by Smullyan, might you ask if you were confronted with a similar situation? What answers do you think you might receive?

7. Do you agree with C. S. Lewis's views regarding the existence of devils? Why?

Suggestions for Further Study

MARTIN BUBER. *I and Thou.* New York: Scribner's, 1970.

SIGMUND FREUD. *The Future of an Illusion.* New York: Norton, 1961.

CHARLES HARTSHORNE. *Omnipotence and Other Theological Mistakes.* Albany, NY: SUNY Press, 1984.

JOHN HICK. *Philosophy of Religion.* Englewood Cliffs, NJ: Prentice Hall, 1990.

LOUIS J. POJMAN. *Philosophy of Religion: An Anthology.* Belmont, CA: Wadsworth, 1987.

BERTRAND RUSSELL. *Why I Am Not a Christian (and other essays).* New York: Simon & Schuster, 1957.

PAUL TILLICH. *The Courage to Be.* New Haven, CT: Yale University Press, 1952.

PAUL TILLICH. *Dynamics of Faith.* New York: Harper and Row, 1957.

CHAPTER 10

Wisdom of India

India is the cradle of one of the world's most ancient civilizations. Of the many philosophical and religious systems that have developed in its fertile soil, Hinduism and Buddhism stand out in terms of their influence, the richness of their history, and their insights concerning the human self. Despite many interconnections between the two traditions, separation of concepts and ideas is both possible and desirable. For clarity and instructional flexibility we have provided an Introductory Essay for each tradition, divided primary readings, and separated other materials as appropriate.

Introductory Essays

Hinduism

The **Introductory Essay on Hinduism** summarizes the essential features and basic ideas of the *Vedas, Upanishads,* and *Bhagavad Gītā* he *Vedas,* written around 2500 B.C., are Hinduism's oldest books. The Hindu sages began by deifying nature. They wrote poems and created rituals to worship and placate its friendly forces. As their thought became more sophisticated, their rich polytheism gave rise to a belief that the naturalistic deities were manifestations of a more basic, more powerful force. In time they arrived at the notion of an absolute principle that was higher than even the highest god. This principle was called "the indescribable *Brahman.*" Although Brahman was believed to be beyond the concepts and categories of the intellect, it might nonetheless be grasped directly in a mystical experience.

This mystical knowledge of Brahman became the central theme of the *Upanishads.* The Hindus believed Brahman, the absolute principle responsible for everything that is, was present in each and every person. This individualized form of Brahman was called *Ātman.* Through meditation Ātman, and thus Brahman, could be experienced. This experience—believed to be one of eternal existence, infinite knowledge, and total bliss—became the ultimate goal of life.

The *Bhagavad Gītā* combines the religion of the *Vedas* with the philosophy of the *Upanishads*. The Hindu trinity of Brahma, Vishnu, and Shiva are presented as three ways in which Brahman functions. Through Brahma, it creates. Through Vishnu, it preserves. Through Shiva, it destroys. Krishna, the hero of the *Bhagavad Gītā*, is Vishnu who has taken human form to help the forces of good in their struggle against evil.

Buddhism

The **Introductory Essay on Buddhism** covers the life, enlightenment, and doctrines of the Buddha. The Buddha was a Hindu prince who challenged beliefs and practices of Hinduism which he considered restrictive, impractical, and outdated. He rejected concepts of god, heaven, hell, life after death, caste differences, and the power of the priesthood. In their place he developed a world view that emphasizes present life and experience. He taught that salvation is a personal achievement within the grasp of each individual. Suffering can be defeated through wisdom and compassion. To develop wisdom he provided instruction in the four noble truths. To develop compassion he taught the eightfold path.

Philosophical Readings

Hinduism

The **Two Vedic Hymns** come from the *Rig Veda*, the oldest and most philosophical of the four Vedas. "The Hymn of Creation" talks about the nature of ultimate reality as well as its initial creative urge. One unique feature of the hymn is its introduction of skepticism: Knowledge of the ultimate creative principle may be unattainable. "The Hymn of Puruṣa" explains creation in terms of the sacrifice of Puruṣa (the cosmic person). Thus it emphasizes the importance of ritual and sacrifice and serves also as a justification for the Hindu caste system.

According to the *Māṇḍūkya Upanishad* there are four stages of consciousness: ordinary, dreaming, dreamless sleep, and mystical. The fourth is believed to be the foundation for the other three. Thus experience of the fourth stage is regarded as a fundamental goal of life.

Buddhism

"The Four Noble Truths" constitute the Buddha's most fundamental teaching. The fourth truth, also known as "the Eightfold Path," describes a method whereby individuals may develop compassion and achieve enlightenment. Clarification, analysis, and philosophical reflection concerning the eight steps of the method are provided in the essay by **Walpola Rahula**.

Scientific Reading

The selection by **Fritjof Capra** complements the one in Chapter 8 (Metaphysics). He extends and elaborates upon his previous comparisons between eastern mysticism and modern physics. Of special interest is what Hindus have called "the Dance of Shiva."

Literary Readings

Hinduism

"**The Way of Renunciation**" is a new transcreation of chapter five of the *Bhagavad Gītā*. It presents, in a systematic way, the nature of a selfless action. Such an action is performed with total dedication to Krishna, without regard for consequence or reward. A person whose life consists of actions such as this, it is claimed, will surely reach enlightenment.

Buddhism

The teachings of Buddhism can, as demonstrated by the Introductory Essay and selection by Rahula, be conveyed through religious and philosophical doctrines. They can also be conveyed, perhaps with greater emphasis and effectiveness, through "**Some Buddhist Parables and Legends.**" The three stories included in this selection weave a tapestry of love, suffering, compassion, and redemption.

Hinduism

ASHOK K. MALHOTRA

Hinduism was created by Indo-Aryans who migrated to India from Asia Minor a little before 2500 B.C. From an intermingling of their ideas with those of the Indus Valley civilization of India, a new philosophy and religion was born. This "new" philosophy and religion is now one of the oldest in the world. It has contributed to the development of three other systems of thought: Buddhism, Jainism, and Sikhism.

The Indo-Aryans did not call themselves "Hindus"; nor did they call their religion "Hinduism." Rather, because they believed their religion to be based upon eternal priciples, they regarded themselves as practitioners of *sanatam dharma*. But because they lived along the river Sindhu, the Persians, who pronounced an *s* as an *h*, called them *Hindus*. With the passage of time, the word *Hinduism* was used as a name for the philosophical beliefs and religious practices of the people of the Sindhu river.

Unlike other major religions like Christianity, Judaism, Islam, and Buddhism, Hinduism has no founder, no single authoritative book, no single inspired prophet, no one god, no supreme figure in religious matters and no authoritative Hindu council to resolve religious disputes. Instead it has innumerable gods and goddesses, many scriptures of equal authority, many sects, different classes, and a variety of paths to enlightenment.

What are the common links among the different sects and classes of Hinduism? Hindu scholars answer simply that their religion is based upon certain eternal principles found in the various texts of the *Vedas*, the *Upanishads*, and the *Bhagavad Gītā* the yoga system, the *Puranas*, and two great epics called the *Ramayana* and the *Mahabharata*.

HINDUISM IN THE VEDAS

The Indo-Aryans who had come to India as conquerors adopted some of the ideas that were prevalent in the Indus Valley Civilization. The intermingling of the ideas of the two groups gave rise to the four *Vedas*, the earliest books of the Hindus. The *Rig Veda* is not only the oldest but also the most philosophical of the four *Vedas*. It contains the essential ideas on which Hinduism is founded.

The word *Veda* comes from the root *Vid*, which means something seen in a vision. The *Vedas* are regarded as books that contain the visions of the Hindu sages. The Hindus believe that the *Vedas* are the reservoirs of wisdom regarding the nature of reality, the nature of a human being, his/her relationship to the universe, and the nature of a good life for a human person. All other works of the Hindus draw inspiration from the *Vedas*. The later philosophical and religious developments that took place in Hinduism are indebted to the *Vedas*, especially to the *Rig Veda*.

When the Indo-Aryans came to India they confronted a new fertile land with an abundance of water, green forests, and ease of life. They were struck with the magnificent beauty of the mountains and the bountiful land. The new inhabitants adored the hills, the rivers, the bountiful earth, the warmth of the sun, the thunder, the lightning, the rain, the sunrise and the sunset, and the lush greenery of the magnificent forests. This panoramic natural beauty was so overwhelming for these newcomers that it inspired their poetic imagination and prompted an emotional response. They felt the entire universe surrounding them to be friendly and hospitable. They adored every aspect of it by writing poems about each item that had a direct or indirect relationship to their lives.

They wrote emotionally charged poems about the earth, the sun, the sunrise, the wind, the speech, the thunder, the lightning, the fire, the maker and the architect of the universe. All aspects of nature that were found to have connection to the life of people were colored with emotions and humanized. The entire universe was regarded as pulsating with life and needing to be admired, adored, respected, and revered.

They wrote long poems consisting of hymns extolling the beauty, power, and generosity of these forces. They created chants and an elaborate scheme of rituals to form intimate relationships with these forces, which were neither inanimate nor impersonal. Though much more powerful than humans, they could be worshiped, adored, and even flattered. A correct performance of a chant or a ritual, assisted by a proper mental attitude and a heartfelt devotion, would get the aspirant the desired result.

This Vedic religion was filled with a great deal of celebrative ritualistic chants, performed around fire in the company of a large number of other believers. Originally, specific powers were assigned to different forces of nature. It was believed that a dialogical relationship between these natural powers and human beings was possible through the proper recitation of these chants. However, with the passage of time, a shift of emphasis took place whereby the performance of chants and rituals became more important than the powers themselves. If a ritual was correctly enacted, the natural power addressed through it was *bound* (required) to reward the aspirant.

The Vedic poets called these forces of nature *Devas*. The term *Deva* is roughly equivalent to English terms like *God* and *Goddess*. These Devas covered the three major domains of the universe. There were Devas of the earth, the heaven, and the space in between. Some of the prominent Devas were: *Agni* (fire), *Soma* (intoxicating drink), *Indra* (thunder, lightning, and rain), *Pṛithvi* (earth), *Usha* (dawn), *Vac* (speech), *Puruṣa* (the Great Person, the First Person), *Varuṇa* (controller of the cosmos),

Vishwakarma (maker of the universe), and *Yama* (ruler of the domain of death).

The Vedic Hindus created a pantheon of gods and goddesses who inhabited various parts of the universe and were believed to influence human destiny on this earth. The only way they could be controlled was through the use of proper worship. Because they worshiped many different gods and goddesses, Hinduism is correctly regarded as a form of *polytheism*.

An interesting intellectual development took place during this period of the *Vedas*. A few poems assigned an exalted place to some of the deities. Indra and Varuṇa were regarded as more powerful than other gods and were given a higher status in the hierarchy. They were worshiped as possessing not only many different powers but also as controlling other gods and goddesses. This hierarchical tendency is called *henotheism*.

The Vedic speculation did not stop here. Their deeper reflection on this hierarchy of gods and goddesses revealed to them that there was a power called the *Ṛta* which was higher than all the gods of the pantheon. Ṛta was an all-pervasive power, somewhat similar to concepts like "natural justice." It consisted of laws of nature as well as spiritual principles that everything—including gods, goddesses, nature, and human beings—must follow. This kind of speculation further led to a belief in the god *Puruṣa*, who was believed to have sacrificed his body to create both the visible and the invisible universe. Puruṣa was regarded as the Supreme God who controlled all the other deities, including those who were assigned exalted places in the pantheon. This idea of a personal God who reigned supreme over all others indicates a development toward *monotheism* (the belief that there is but one god/ goddess).

As the Vedic speculation continued further, some of the sages were not satisfied with the idea of many deities or even with the idea of one supreme personal god. Their speculation led them to the discovery of an impersonal principle that underlay the visible or the manifest universe. This principle was called *Brahman.* It was regarded as the ineffable absolute reality, which, though indescribable, made possible all forms and descriptions. Various deities were the different manifestations of this unmanifest, ultimate, impersonal being. This principle was understood as the unity that underlay the diversity of the universe. The Vedic speculation culminated in this discovery of an absolute reality beyond all names and forms. In philosophical terminology, such a belief in an absolute unitary reality is called *monism.*

The speculation of the Vedic sages starts with a belief that nature is pulsating with innumerable powers or deities. This attitude toward the universe is polytheistic. Not content with this belief, the Vedic sages created the idea that some deities are more important during certain emergency situations, where they take upon themselves the powers of other deities. Here they moved from polytheism to henotheism. Their dissatisfaction with these explanations continued until they discovered one single god who was all-powerful and was the governor of the rest. This was a move toward monotheism. And finally, their speculative restlessness offered them the greatest reward. They made the discovery of an impersonal principle of Brahman, the unitary law controlling all diversity. This development led Hinduism in the direction of monism.

Several conclusions follow. First, a Hindu can believe in many gods, one god, or no god at all and still be a Hindu. Second, a Hindu is willing to tolerate differences—that is, s/he is ready to accept that there are many different ways of reaching the abode of the ultimate reality. Last, the Vedic literature does not make a very clear distinction between philosophy and religion.

While many Hindus continue to believe in deities and worship them according to the rules prescribed in the *Vedas,* others have sought a clearer vision of the indescribable Brahman. The pursuit of such a vision is the focal point of the final portions of the *Vedas,* called the *Upanishads.*

HINDUISM IN THE UPANISHADS

The *Upanishads* are the philosophical parts of the *Vedas.* Here Indian thought reached its peak of philosophical development. Though created more than 3000 years ago, the *Upanishads* continue to influence the philosophy, religion, and life of the Hindus.

The word *Upanishad* refers to the disciple sitting devotedly near a teacher to learn the secrets of ultimate reality. What is this ultimate reality? How can its secrets be revealed and imparted to a student?

There are more than 200 books of the *Upanishads,* yet all share a similar concern regarding the nature of ultimate reality and the means of reaching it. The central question is: "What is this ultimate being, knowing which, everything else becomes known?" For the sages of the *Upanishads,* Brahman is this ultimate being. If one can obtain the knowledge of Brahman, one will know everything else. But what is the nature of this Brahman and how do we obtain the knowledge of its nature?

Though the concept of Brahman was a great discovery of the *Vedas,* the seers regarded its nature to be ineffable. Since rituals and sacrifices were prominent in the life of most of the religious practitioners during the Vedic period, they did not show much interest in the abstract concept of Brahman. This overwhelming concern with ritual produced skepticism in some sages and led others to the calmness of the forest to contemplate the nature of this absolute principle or Brahman. Their peaceful surroundings and solitary contemplation made possible three most important discoveries.

First, during their intense concentration, the seers reconfirmed Brahman to be the objective principle or the supreme incomprehensible being, the source of the manifest universe.

Second, as they undertook the inner journey through their consciousness, they made an added discovery that the spark of divinity resided at the core of their being. They called this divine spark *Ātman* (the self). Ātman was experienced as the unitary consciousness which made possible all sensations, perceptions, feelings, emotions, images, ideas, and values. The experience of Ātman was one of ineffable peace or total contentment.

Finally, as the sages continued with this inward meditative journey, they found that Ātman (the inner self) was identical to Brahman (the objective self). During this inner ascent, the walls of their ego collapsed, and they experienced the melting of their being into the being of Brahman. The self so revealed was a spaceless and timeless undifferentiated unity identical to the universal self. The experience of the identity of Ātman and Brahman gave rise to an intense feeling of peace and serenity equal to the experience of sorrowlessness. The seers described it as the experience of infinite existence, infinite knowledge, and infinite bliss. Since the self was immortal, all-knowing, and in possession of boundless joy, the *Upanishads* taught that there was no higher goal of life than the experience of the inner core of one's being.

What method was followed by the seers to obtain this self-realization? In the *Upanishads,* the sages acquired this state of bliss through concentrated contemplation, performed with full devotion and without interruption. The seers reserved this kind of training for a select few, believing most people were not interested in following this difficult method, or the wonderful realization it might bring. The teaching was available only to those pupils who had complete faith in it, were ready to devote all their time to it, had patience and perseverance, were tranquil, and wanted to become teachers of this doctrine.

Once the students were selected, instruction was given in two parts. First, the pupil was required to learn certain moral and psychological rules of action and behavior so that s/he could be calm, quiet, patient, and content. Second, the pupil was given a secret teaching that involved continued reflection on certain mystical words, expressions, formulas, and mantras.

The mantras chosen for meditation were believed to contain within them the secret of reality. Some of the prominent mantras were: *Tat Twam Asi,* meaning "You are that"; *Aham Brahman Asi,* meaning "I am Brahman"; *So Ham,* meaning "the sound of breathing"; *Aum* or *Om,* meaning "the mystical sound relating to stages of consciousness"; *Tajjalan,* meaning "from whom everything comes out, by whom everything is supported, and in whom everything returns"; and *Neti Neti,* meaning "not this, not this." It was believed that these mantras contained the essence of the great discovery made by the sages of the Upanishads.

So Ham and *Aum* were given to the beginner. As the pupil's concentration improved, s/he was given other mantras, such as *Aham Brahman Asi* or *Tat Twam Asi.* As the student meditated upon these mantras, s/he was brought closer to the discovery that Ātman (the inner self) was identical to Brahman (the objective self). According to the *Chandogya Upanishads,* this Ātman, which resides in one's heart, is larger than earth, the sky, and the universe, and is identical to Brahman. However, the mantra *Neti Neti* reminds the pupil that the experience of the unity of Ātman and Brahman could never be described through any concepts or categories and would always remain ineffable. Though this mystical consciousness of the identity of Ātman and Brahman was indescribable, it offered the aspirant total joy and fulfillment.

Tajjalan was a later addition to the mantras of the *Upanishads.* This mantra was the first attempt to specify the functions performed by the ultimate principle. *Tajjalan* ("From whom everything comes out, by whom everything is supported and in whom everything returns") gave to Brahman the three functions of being the creator, the preserver, and the destroyer of the manifest universe. This mantra was instrumental in the development of the idea of the Hindu trinity, which personifies Brahma as the creator, Vishnu as the preserver, and Shiva as the destroyer of the universe. Once the idea of the three gods of the Hindu trinity was conceived, Hinduism as a religion was systematized. Brahman as an impersonal and indescribable principle could now be appropriated through the three gods who were significantly related to the living of life on this earth.

Of special importance were Vishnu (the preserver) and Shiva (the destroyer). A number of books called the *Puranas* were written to describe the lives and actions of Vishnu and Shiva. Vishnu is believed to be a caring god who occasionally descends to the human world in material form. He helps good forces in their struggle against evil so that the world may be spared destruction. This material manifestation of Vishnu is called *Avatara*. Hindus believe that Vishnu has come down to save this earth nine times: as a fish, tortoise, wild boar, man-lion, dwarf, Rama with the ax, Rama as the hero of the epic *Ramayana*, Krishna as the hero of the *Bhagavad Gītā*, and Buddha, who started a new religion. When evil becomes too pervasive to be eliminated by less drastic measures, Vishnu will take the tenth Avatara of *Kalki*. The roles of Vishnu and Shiva will then merge. Kalki will destroy the existing universe and reconstruct a new one from its ashes.

HINDUISM IN THE *BHAGAVAD GĪTĀ*

The basic principles of Hinduism were first systematized in the *Bhagavad Gītā*, circa 500 B.C. The *Bhagavad Gītā*, itself part of the epic *Mahabharata*, is one of the most popular books of the Hindus. It is written in a dialogical style where complex religious and ethical issues are explained in a simple language accessible to everyone. It offers a synthesis of the diverse systems of Hindu thought and the methods of self-realization. Its grassroots level of discussion of religious, social, and practical issues has made it a standard textbook on Hinduism.

The *Bhagavad Gītā* brings together the essential ideas of the *Vedas*, the *Upanishads*, and the yoga system. Its synthetic approach fuses together the ritualistic aspects of the *Vedas*, the mystical elements of the *Upanishads*, and the ascetic meditative practices of yoga. It agrees with all of these systems by holding that self-realization is the ultimate goal of human life.

The *Bhagavad Gītā* introduces the idea of a personal god Krishna who encompasses within his being the three functions of the creator, the preserver,

and the destroyer. It emphasizes that all the gods and goddesses of the *Vedas* are nothing more than various manifestations of Krishna. Instead of worshiping these images, one should direct all of one's emotional and spiritual energies toward the person of Krishna.

The Upanishadic idea of Brahman as the ultimate reality also finds a rightful place in the system of the *Bhagavad Gītā*. Krishna becomes the personal god who is both the transcendental and the immanent reality. In his transcendental aspect, he is the supreme self, totally detached and unconcerned with the affairs of the world. In his immanent aspect, he creates the universe and dwells in all things, including human beings. As long as the universe lasts, he preserves it.

Since Krishna is the eternal spirit which has taken a human form, he is personable and approachable. A devotee can form an intimate relationship with him through love and devotion. Unlike the Upanishads, where one needed to reflect upon some secret mantras to comprehend this eternal being, the *Bhagavad Gītā* emphasizes that a devotee can form an intimate relationship with Krishna by performing all actions in the spirit of self-surrender and devotion. Though the *Bhagavad Gītā* recommends the yogic method for certain kinds of people, it finds it unsuitable for everyone. In its place, the *Bhagavad Gītā* offers the path of devotion, which is available to everyone. This path, consisting of living a life in complete devotion and service to Krishna, is the surest way to God-realization.

NATURE OF A GOOD LIFE IN THE *BHAGAVAD GĪTĀ*

The *Bhagavad Gītā* utilizes the model of the dual nature of the ultimate reality to understand a human being. An individual is a combination of empirical self and transcendental self. The empirical (psychophysical) self is made up of the body, the brain, and the mind. The transcendental self is pure consciousness and resides at the core of one's being. The transcendental self (Ātman) possesses the three qualities of infinite existence, infinite knowledge, and infinite bliss. When the empirical self acts as a mirror to the consciousness of the transcendental self, it acquires the quality of consciousness. As it works with this borrowed consciousness, the empirical self ignores the spiritual self completely and starts believing that it is the ultimate self of a human being. This mistake on the part of the empirical self is the cause of human unhappiness and suffering. The goal of life is to remove this suffering by helping the person realize that his/her real nature is Ātman (transcendental self).

The *Bhagavad Gītā* does not ignore the empirical self, but suggests ways of improving it so that it may become a perfect vehicle for the expression of the transcendental self. To this end, the *Bhagavad Gītā* creates an elaborate religious-ethical system incorporating four castes, four goals of life, four stages of human development, and three paths of self-realization.

The *Bhagavad Gītā* teaches that all human beings are identical in terms of the transcendental self, but differ as regards the psychophysical self. Since they are born with different psychophysical abilities, society should create various classes where these innate capacities can find full expression. Specifically, the *Bhagavad Gītā* teaches that people are naturally predisposed toward four kinds of activities, and thus that four castes are needed to run an organized society: scholars, kings, businessmen, and workers.

Because people are born with unique abilities, there should be more than one path of self-realization. The *Bhagavad Gītā* suggests three paths: knowledge, action, and devotion. By these paths members of the various castes can reach the goal of transcendental self-realization.

The *Bhagavad Gītā* also teaches that life is a gift given to us by gods, ancestors, parents, teachers, and society. Since we are obligated to all of them, our life should be organized so as to fulfill our obligations toward each. This is possible by living, in sequence, the life of a student, a householder, a hermit, and an ascetic.

The first twenty-five years of life should be spent as a student. During this stage one learns the scriptures, the moral and religious principles, and the duties of one's caste. Through this learning, one pays one's debt to one's teachers.

The next twenty-five years are to be spent as a householder where the person gets married, has children, and supports a family by taking up a job in the society. During this period an individual enhances the wealth of the society, performs caste duties, and acquires name, fame, and fortune. Furthermore, the person fulfills the earthly goals of pleasure, wealth, and righteous life. By creating children, one's indebtedness toward one's ancestors and parents is completed; through one's job and the performance of one's caste duties, one's obligations toward the society are fulfilled.

At age fifty, a person enters the stage of a hermit and moves away from the society in order to reflect on the mystery of life. More and more time is spent listening, reflecting, and contemplating the universe in order to form a closer tie with the rest of existence.

At age seventy-five, the individual becomes an ascetic by renouncing all ties to family and society. Here one moves to the depth of the forest to feel oneness with the ultimate reality (Brahman). During this stage, when an individual is enlightened, s/he is able to reach the goal of life: total liberation from all limitations. When the empirical self of such a person dies, the true being realizes eternal bliss by merging into the immortal Brahman.

Buddhism

ASHOK K. MALHOTRA

Buddhism arose as a protest against Hinduism. The Buddha, who was a Hindu prince, found some of the key beliefs and practices of Hinduism to be restrictive, impractical, and outdated. He openly challenged the polytheism and the ritualism of the *Vedas,* the esoteric mysticism of the *Upanishads,* the caste system and belief in the Hindu trinity of the *Bhagavad Gītā,* and the emphasis on self-mortification and restrictive meditative practices of yoga. In its place, the Buddha offered his own unique brand of religion, which was devoid of god, soul, creation, permanence, ritual, external authority, last judgment, and caste distinctions.

Buddha constructed a religion that emphasized human life here and now. For him, the present world was the arena where the drama of life's problems and their solutions was to be enacted. If there was any salvation, it was to be obtained during the course of this existence. Salvation was possible only through one's own efforts. It was a personal achievement within the reach of each human being.

Buddha rejected discussion of esoteric and metaphysical subjects such as the nature of absolute reality, life after death, and the nature of enlightenment. He regarded such talk as futile and meaningless. Since the uniqueness of the Buddha's religion is interwoven with his personal realization, we can gain access to the basic ideas of Buddhism by presenting the story of his life. This tale can be told in three parts: first, in terms of the Buddha's life leading toward enlightenment; second, the Buddha's description of this enlightenment through the Four Noble Truths; and third, the imparting of enlightenment to others through the Eightfold Path.

THE LIFE OF BUDDHA

The story of the Buddha's life has all the ingredients of a great drama. His original name was "Sid-dhartha Gautama." He was born in 563 B.C., the son of a king who ruled a small principality in the northern part of India. When a son was born to a Hindu king, it was customary to ask astrologers to predict the child's future. Their prediction was that Siddhartha would either become the greatest king India ever had, or renounce the world to become a great sage. The astrologers warned the king that Siddhartha would choose the second path if faced with suffering associated with disease, decay, and death.

To shield his son from the miseries of life and to nourish in him the earthly pleasures, the king provided the prince with beautiful palaces, exotic gardens, dancing girls, and entertainers. To further ground Siddhartha to this earth, the king arranged his son's marriage to a beautiful princess, Yasodhara. Siddhartha enjoyed a number of years of conjugal love with Yasodhara, who bore him a handsome son, Rahula.

The life of pleasure and leisure did offer a temporary escape from the sorrows of the world. But one day Siddhartha visited the city that lay outside the walls of the palaces and its pleasure gardens. On his first outing, Siddhartha saw an old man, enfeebled by age. On Siddhartha's inquiry, his charioteer explained that this man had been born, lived, and now was near his death. This is the fate of each person. Siddhartha, who had no experience of old age, was deeply touched by this sight.

On his second outing, Siddhartha encountered a man who was seriously ill. Weakened by his disease, he showed signs of helplessness and agony. When Siddhartha asked his charioteer about this man, he was told that the man had an incurable disease and was near death. Again Siddhartha was deeply touched by this man's suffering.

On his third outing, Siddhartha witnessed the

cremation of a corpse. Siddhartha, who had never before seen death, inquired about the state of this man. The charioteer replied that everyone who was born was subject to aging, disease, and eventually death. Death takes its toll indiscriminately. It spares neither the rich nor the poor. King and pauper equally fall prey to it. Death is the fate of every creature. After observing the three sights of old age, sickness, and death, Siddhartha's own suffering became unbearable. He decided to look for a way out of this agony.

On his fourth outing, Siddhartha met ascetics in ocher robes. Their way of walking, talking, and looking revealed that they were at peace with themselves and the world. On his inquiry, the charioteer told Siddhartha that these ascetics had conquered their existential agony by renouncing this world. This indicated to Siddhartha a way out of suffering. He decided to abandon the world to join these ascetics. At age 29 he left his kingdom, his wife, and his child to become a recluse. He spent the next six years of his life seeking enlightenment by following the path of asceticism. He put himself on a strict routine of fasting, yogic exercises, and meditation. He mastered all these arts during this short span of six years. After living a life of intense self-mortification, Siddhartha realized that he was no closer to enlightenment than when he started. While sitting under a tree, Siddhartha decided to abandon the path of the ascetic as well as his quest for enlightenment. As he did this, he was enlightened. From that moment onward he was called "the Buddha," which means "the awakened one." The tree became known as the *Bodhi* tree (tree of enlightenment).

During his enlightenment, the Buddha not only experienced the state of sorrowlessness, but also gained wisdom about the reasons for suffering and the method of eliminating the same. He spent the next forty-five years of his life teaching masses of people in India the truths experienced during his enlightenment. He conveyed these insights through the doctrines of the Four Noble Truths and the Eightfold Path.

THE FOUR NOBLE TRUTHS

After the Buddha was enlightened, he formulated his discoveries into four simple principles called the Four Noble Truths. These principles can be outlined as follows:

First, all life is suffering (*dukkha*).
Second, suffering is caused by selfish craving (*tanha*).
Third, suffering can be removed by replacing selfish craving with compassion (*karuna*).
Finally, compassion can be inculcated by practicing the Eightfold Path.

According to the Buddha, if we look closely we will find that all life is marked by pain and misery. Though there are some pleasant moments in one's life, they are evanescent, fleeting, and rare. In contrast, suffering and agony permeate all aspects of human existence. If we reflect on birth, sickness, old age, death, our coming in contact with unpleasant things, our separation from pleasant things, and our unsatisfied cravings, we will see clearly the pervasiveness of suffering (*dukkha*) in all these aspects of life. Suffering, then, is a universal principle that defines human existence on this earth.

The Second Noble Truth deals with the cause of suffering. Why do human beings suffer? What is the reason for this pain and agony, which color human existence from birth to death? According to the Buddha, people suffer because their lives are guided by "selfish craving" (*tanha*). People are conditioned by the society to believe that they possess an ego. We are taught that we can enhance ourselves only through private fulfillment or by increasing our possessions. When the focus is on self-inflation we get trapped by the expanding walls of the ego. This personal aggrandizement separates us from others. The more our egos expand, the more we crave everything for ourselves exclusive of others, and the more our misery increases.

According to the Buddha, this selfish craving is based upon one fundamental mistake. The person who wants everything for her/himself is duped into thinking that the world hides the secret of a stable, immutable being that could be possessed. Furthermore, the individual believes that an aspect of this being in the form of an unchanging self resides in each person. According to the Buddha, the world is in constant motion. Nothing remains the same for more than a moment. Since everything is transitory, there is no stable self in the world or in us. Thus, there is nothing to possess because nothing can be possessed. Once this realization takes place, one is awakened to the futility of one's selfish craving. As one stops these desires, one's isolation from others disappears and one's suffering is lessened.

The Third Noble Truth offers a way out of this ignorance and misery. Through compassion (*karuna*), one can puncture the walls of the ego. These walls come down when genuine compassion, kindness, care, and generosity are shown to others. Compassion for others consists in the forgetting of one's ego, the "going forth" toward the other, and the helping of others as oneself. As one inculcates compassion, one's selfish craving is dissolved and suffering disappears.

How can one learn to be compassionate? What kind of training is needed? The Buddha suggests two ways to develop compassion within oneself. First, one can learn compassion by following the Eightfold Path. Second, one can be educated into compassion by listening to the stories of people who performed deeds that involved care, concern, and generosity.

Buddha and his disciples used parables and stories to teach people the nature of compassion. Buddha believed that morality could be taught by discussion, practice, and listening to examples of those who embodied it. The Buddhist literature is teeming with such stories. Consider the following example.

A student listened to a lecture given by a senior monk about the possibility of experiencing the Buddha in his physical form by practicing egolessness and meditation. The student decided to accomplish this goal for himself. He practiced meditation devotedly and flawlessly for twelve years. He hoped that on the completion of this arduous journey he would have a vision of the Buddha. To the utter surprise and anguish of the student, no Buddha showed up at the conclusion of his meditation.

The student monk was furious, hurt, and resentful. He felt deceived and lied to. He had wasted twelve years of his life foolishly following this path. Angry and frustrated by this futile quest, he left his hermitage to walk toward a nearby village. As he walked, his mind was filled with all the negative emotions of dejection, deception, anger, agitation, and restlessness. His ego was badly injured.

It happened that his glance fell upon a dog standing under a tree. The student monk looked at the gentle face of the dog and observed two beautiful black eyes that showed intense sadness. He looked at the dog's body: The front half appeared to be in good shape, but the hind legs and tail were severely infested with maggots. In his sympathy for the suffering dog, the monk forgot his own mental anguish. Overwhelmed by compassion, he wanted to relieve the dog of the maggots. As he was about to move them, another thought crossed his mind: "By removing the maggots I will be relieving the dog of its misery, but I will also be depriving the maggots of their food."

Driven by concern for both the dog and the maggots, the student monk cut a piece of flesh from his own thigh. He tried to lure the maggots away from the dog's body to this fresh piece of meat, but they refused to move. He thought of moving the maggots with his finger but did not want to injure them. Concerned with both the misery of the dog and the well-being of the maggots, the monk totally forgot himself. It occurred to him that he might be able to use his tongue to gently move the maggots away from the dog's infected body. But when he bent to take the maggots onto his tongue, the dog miraculously transformed into the smiling Buddha.

The astonished monk asked the Buddha why he did not show up at the completion of his meditation. The Buddha, still smiling, replied that the monk was too wrapped up in ego aggrandizement during and after his meditation. It was only when he saw the suffering of the dog and felt compassion for the maggots that he discarded his ego completely. It is only then that he expressed genuine care and concern. Since his compassion toward those two creatures was selfless, he was able to see the Buddha in the dog. As a selfish act separates us from others, an egoless act unifies us with all existence. Through the performance of a compassionate act, one gets rid of misery and suffering.

Through parables and stories, one can become sensitive to the way others express compassion, care, love, and generosity. As a Buddhist monk, one needs to follow the step-by-step procedure suggested by the Buddha. This method is called the Eightfold Path. It contains eight principles of right knowledge, right inspiration, right speech, right action, right livelihood, right effort, right mindfulness, and right concentration. The first two steps of right knowledge and right inspiration are concerned with adopting a proper mental attitude. The student needs the right views and the correct drive to conduct him/herself wisely and devotedly. This wisdom is required as a guide to the performance of the next three steps (right speech, right action, and right livelihood). These three constitute the ethical disciplines. They instruct the student to behave nonviolently and compassionately when s/he uses language, performs an action, or chooses a profession. Wisdom and moral conduct are the preparatory steps for the right effort, right mindfulness, and right concentration. These last three steps of the path help one develop mental control, which in turn is essential for contemplation and enlightenment. When an individual follows the Eightfold Path devotedly and continuously for a long period of time, s/he is assured of enlightenment.

This stage of enlightenment is called *Nirvāṇa*. It has been understood in both negative and positive ways. In the negative sense, Nirvāṇa depicts the highest stage of existence where all the fires of selfish cravings are extinguished, the belief in the existence of a stable self is annihilated, and all attachments to people and things are eliminated. In the positive sense, Nirvāṇa depicts a stage of existence where the enlightened person has gained serenity, peace, and contentment. All Buddhists aspire to this state, believing it to be the highest accomplishment for any mortal being.

Two Vedic Hymns

The *Rig Veda* is the oldest and most philosophical of the four *Vedas* of Hinduism. It contains more than 1000 hymns, two of which are reproduced in the pages that follow.

The Hymn of Creation talks about the nature of the ultimate reality as well as its initial creative urge. The uniqueness of the hymn lies in its introduction of skepticism. The hymn cautions us that the knowledge of the creative process may not be within the reach of anyone.

The Hymn to Puruṣa has served the Hindu tradition in four interrelated ways. First, like other Vedic hymns, it emphasizes the importance of ritual and sacrifice. Second, it conveys the information that all forms of life and society began with the sacrifice of the Puruṣa (the cosmic person) by the gods. Third, since the Puruṣa sarificed His body to create everything in the universe, the performance of sacrifice and ritual for religious purpose is commended. And fourth, the hymn justifies the caste system via its claim that the four classes of Hindu society were created from the body of the Puruṣa.

HYMN OF CREATION

1. Non-being then existed not nor being:
   There was no air, nor sky that is beyond it.
   What was concealed? Wherein? In whose protection?
   And was there deep unfathomable water?

2. Death then existed not nor life immortal;
   Of neither night nor day was any token.
   By its inherent force the One breathed windless:
   No other thing than that beyond existed.

3. Darkness there was at first by darkness hidden;
   Without distinctive marks, this all was water.
   That which, becoming, by the void was covered,
   That One by force of heat came into being.

4. Desire entered the One in the beginning:
   It was the earliest seed, of thought the product.
   The sages searching in their hearts with wisdom,
   Found out the bond of being in non-being.

5. Their ray extended light across the darkness:
   But was the One above or was it under?
   Creative force was there, and fertile power:

Radhakrishnan and Moore, *A Sourcebook in Indian Philosophy,* pp. 23–24 and 55–56. Copyright © 1957 by Princeton University Press, renewed 1985. Reprinted with the permission of the publishers.

Below was energy, above was impulse.

6. Who knows for certain? Who shall here declare it?
   Whence was it born, and whence came this creation?
   The gods were born after this world's creation:
   Then who can know from whence it has arisen?

7. None knoweth whence creation has arisen;
   And whether he has or has not produced it:
   He who surveys it in the highest heaven,
   He only knows, or haply he may know not.

TO PURUṢA [PERSON OR MAN PERSONIFIED]

1. Thousand-headed was the Puruṣa, thousand-eyed, thousand-footed. He embraced the earth on all sides, and stood beyond the breadth of ten fingers.

2. The Puruṣa is this all, that which was and which shall be. He is Lord of immortality, which he grows beyond through (sacrificial) food.

3. Such is his greatness, and still greater than that is the Puruṣa. One fourth of him is all beings. The three fourths of him is the immortal in Heaven.

4. Three fourths on high rose the Puruṣa. One fourth of him arose again here (on the earth). Thence in all directions he spread abroad, as that which eats and that which eats not.

5. From him Virāj was born, from Virāj the Puruṣa. He when born reached beyond the earth behind as well as before.

6. When the Gods spread out the sacrifice with the Puruṣa as oblation, spring was its ghee, summer the fuel, autumn the oblation.

7. As the sacrifice on the strewn grass they besprinkled the Puruṣa, born in the beginning. With him the Gods sacrificed, the Sādhyas and the sages.

8. From that sacrifice completely offered was the sprinkled ghee collected. He made it the beasts of the air, of the forest, and those of the village.

9. From that sacrifice completely offered were born the Verses (*Ṛg Veda*) and the *Sāman-melodies* (*Sāma Veda*). The metres were born from it. From it was born the Sacrificial formula (*Yajur Veda*).

10. From it were born horses, and they that have two rows of teeth. Cattle were born from it. From it were born goats and sheep.

11. When they divided the Puruṣa, into how many parts did they arrange him? What was his mouth? What his two arms? What are his thighs and feet called?

12. The *brāhmin* was his mouth, his two arms were made the *rājanya* (warrior), his two thighs the *vaiśya* (trader and agriculturist), from his feet the *śūdra* (servile class) was born.

13. The moon was born from his spirit (*manas*), from his eye was born the sun, from his mouth Indra and Agni, from his breath Vāyu (wind) was born.

14. From his navel arose the middle sky, from his head the heaven originated, from his feet the earth, the quarters from his ear. Thus did they fashion the worlds.

15. Seven were his sticks that enclose (the fire), thrice seven were made the faggots. When the Gods spread out the sacrifice, they bound the Puruṣa as a victim.

16. With the sacrifice the Gods sacrificed the sacrifice. These were the first ordinances. These great powers reached to the firmament, where are the ancient Sādhyas, the Gods.

Māṇḍūkya Upanishad

The *Upanishads* are the philosophical portions of the *Vedas.*
Though there are many *Upanishads,* they all share a common
concern regarding the nature of ultimate reality and the means of
attaining it. One of the most important Upanishads is named for
the sage Māṇḍūkya. The Upanishad concerns the four states of
consciousness and their relation to the mystic symbol *Om.*

1. *Om!*—This syllable is this whole world.
   Its further explanation is:—

   The past, the present, the future—
   everything is just the word *Om.*
   And whatever else that transcends
   threefold time—that, too, is just the
   word *Om.*

2. For truly, everything here is *Brahman;*
   this self is *Brahman.* This same self has
   four fourths.

3. The waking state, outwardly cognitive,
   having seven limbs, having nineteen
   mouths, enjoying the gross, the
   Common-to-all-men, is the first
   fourth.

4. The dreaming state, inwardly cognitive,
   having seven limbs, having nineteen
   mouths, enjoying the exquisite, the
   Brilliant, is the second fourth.

5. If one asleep desires no desire whatsoever, sees no dream whatsoever, that is
   deep sleep.
   The deep-sleep state, unified, just a
   cognition-mass, consisting of bliss, enjoying bliss, whose mouth is thought,
   the cognitional, is the third fourth.

6. This is the lord of all. This is the all-
   knowing. This is the inner controller.
   This is the source of all, for this is the
   origin and the end of beings.

7. Not inwardly cognitive, not outwardly
   cognitive, not both-wise cognitive, not
   a cognition-mass, not cognitive, not
   non-cognitive, unseen, with which
   there can be no dealing, ungraspable,
   having no distinctive mark, non-think-
   able, that cannot be designated, the
   essence of the assurance of which is the
   state of being one with the Self, the
   cessation of development, tranquil, benign, without a second (*a-dvaita*)—
   [such] they think is the fourth. He is
   the Self. He should be discerned.

8. This is the Self with regard to the word
   Om, with regard to its elements. The elements are the fourths; the fourths, the
   elements: the letter *a,* the letter *u,* the
   letter *m.*[1]

9. The waking state, the Common-to-
   all-men, is the letter *a,* the first element, from *āpti* (obtaining) or from
   ādimatva (being first).
   He obtains, verily, indeed, all desires,
   he becomes first—he who knows this.

Radhakrishnan and Moore, *A Sourcebook in Indian Philosophy,*
pp. 23–24 and 55–56. Copyright © 1957 by Princeton University
Press, renewed 1985. Reprinted with the permission of the publishers.

10. The sleeping state, the brilliant, is the leter *u,* the second element, from *utkarṣa* (exaltation) or from *ubhayatvā* (intermediateness).
    He exalts, verily, indeed, the continuity of knowledge; and he becomes equal; no one ignorant of *Brahman* is born in the family of him who knows this.

11. The deep-sleep state, the cognitional, is the letter *m,* the third element, from *miti* ("erecting") or from *apiti* ("immerging").

He, verily, indeed, erects (*minoti*) this whole world, and he becomes its immerging—he who knows this.

12. The fourth is without an element, with which there can be no dealing, the cessation of development, benign, without a second.
    Thus *Om* is the Self (Ātman) indeed. He who knows this, with his self enters the Self—yea, he who knows this!

Notes

1. In Sanskrit the vowel *o* is constitutionally a diphthong, contracted from *a* + *u*. Om therefore may be analyzed into the elements *a* + *u* + *m*.

The Fourth Noble Truth

WALPOLA RAHULA

Walpola Rahula is a Sri Lankan Buddhist. The following selection from *What the Buddha Taught* (1974) discusses the Buddha's fourth noble truth. According to this teaching, enlightenment can be attained by following the eightfold path. The steps of the path train the student in ethical conduct, mental discipline, and wisdom.

The Fourth Noble Truth is that of the Way leading to the Cessation of *Dukkha* [suffering—Ed.] (*Dukkhanirodhagāminīpatipadāariyasacca*). This is known as the 'Middle Path' (*Majjhimā Patipadā*), because it avoids two extremes: one extreme being the search for happiness through the pleasures of the senses, which is 'low, common, unprofitable and the way of the ordinary people'; the other being the search for happiness through self-mortification in different forms of asceticism, which is 'painful, unworthy and unprofitable'. Having himself first tried these two extremes, and having found them to be useless, the Buddha discovered through personal experience the Middle Path 'which gives vision and knowledge, which leads to Calm, Insight, Enlightenment, Nirvāna'. This Middle Path is generally referred to as the Noble Eightfold Path (*Ariya-Atthangika-Magga*), because it is composed of eight categories or divisions: namely,

1. Right Understanding (*Sammā ditthi*),
2. Right Thought (*Sammā sankappa*),
3. Right Speech (*Sammā vācā*),
4. Right Action (*Sammā kammanta*),
5. Right Livelihood (*Sammā ājīva*),
6. Right Effort (*Sammā vāyāma*),
7. Right Mindfulness (*Sammā sati*),
8. Right Concentration (*Sammā samādhi*).

Practically the whole teaching of the Buddha, to which he devoted himself during 45 years, deals in some way or other with this Path. He explained it in different ways and in different words to different people, according to the stage of their development and their capacity to understand and follow him. But the essence of those many thousand discourses scattered in the Buddhist Scriptures is found in the Noble Eightfold Path.

It should not be thought that the eight categories or divisions of the Path should be followed and practised one after the other in the numerical order as given in the usual list above. But they are to be developed more or less simultaneously, as far as possible according to the capacity of each individual. They are all linked together and each helps the cultivation of the others.

These eight factors aim at promoting and perfecting the three essentials of Buddhist training and discipline: namely: (*a*) Ethical Conduct (*Sīla*), (*b*) Mental Discipline (*Samādhi*) and (*c*) Wisdom (*Paññā*). It will therefore be more helpful for a coherent and better understanding of the eight divisions of the Path, if we group them and explain them according to these three heads.

Ethical Conduct (*Sīla*) is built on the vast conception of universal love and compassion for all living beings, on which the Buddha's teaching is based. It is regrettable that many scholars forget this great ideal of the Buddha's teaching, and indulge in only dry philosophical and metaphysical divagations when they talk and write about Buddhism. The Buddha gave his teaching 'for the good of the many, for the happiness of the many, out of compassion for the world' (*bahujanahitāya bahujanasukhāya lokānukampāya*).

According to Buddhism for a man to be perfect there are two qualities that he should develop equally: compassion (*karuṇā*) on one side, and wisdom (*paññā*) on the other. Here compassion represents love, charity, kindness, tolerance and such noble qualities on the emotional side, or qualities of the heart, while wisdom would stand for the intellectual side or the qualities of the mind. If one develops only the emotional neglecting the intellectual, one may become a good-hearted fool; while to develop only the intellectual side neglecting the emotional may turn one into a hard-hearted intellect without feeling for others. Therefore, to be perfect one has to develop both equally. That is the aim of the Buddhist way of life: in it wisdom and compassion are inseparably linked together, as we shall see later.

Now, in Ethical Conduct (*Sīla*), based on love and compassion, are included three factors of the Noble Eightfold Path: namely, Right Speech, Right Action and Right Livelihood. (Nos. 3, 4 and 5 in the list).

Right speech means abstention (1) from telling lies, (2) from backbiting and slander and talk that may bring about hatred, enmity, disunity and disharmony among individuals or groups of people, (3) from harsh, rude, impolite, malicious and abusive language, and (4) from idle, useless and foolish babble and gossip. When one abstains from these forms of wrong and harmful speech one naturally has to speak the truth, has to use words that are friendly and benevolent, pleasant and gentle, meaningful and useful. One should not speak carelessly: speech should be at the right time and place. If one cannot say something useful, one should keep 'noble silence'.

Right Action aims at promoting moral, honourable and peaceful conduct. It admonishes us that we should abstain from destroying life, from stealing, from dishonest dealings, from illegitimate sexual intercourse, and that we should also help others to lead a peaceful and honourable life in the right way.

Right Livelihood means that one should abstain from making one's living through a profession that brings harm to others, such as trading in arms and lethal weapons, intoxicating drinks, poisons, killing animals, cheating, etc., and should live by a profession which is honourable, blameless and innocent of harm to others. One can clearly see here that Buddhism is strongly opposed to any kind of war, when it lays down that trade in arms and lethal weapons is an evil and unjust means of livelihood.

These three factors (Right Speech, Right Action and Right Livelihood) of the Eightfold Path constitute Ethical Conduct. It should be realized that the Buddhist ethical and moral conduct aims at promoting a happy and harmonious life both for the individual and for society. This moral conduct is considered as the indispensable foundation for all higher spiritual attainments. No spiritual development is possible without this moral basis.

Next comes Mental Discipline, in which are included three other factors of the Eightfold Path: namely, Right Effort, Right Mindfulness (or Attentiveness) and Right Concentration. (Nos. 6, 7 and 8 in the list).

Right Effort is the energetic will (1) to prevent evil and unwholesome states of mind from arising, and (2) to get rid of such evil and unwholesome states that have already arisen within a man, and also (3) to produce, to cause to arise, good and wholesome states of mind not yet arisen, and (4) to develop and bring to perfection the good and wholesome states of mind already present in a man.

Right Mindfulness (or Attentiveness) is to be diligently aware, mindful and attentive with regard to (1) the activities of the body (*kāya*), (2) sensations or feelings (*vedantā*) (3) the activities of the mind (*citta*) and (4) ideas, thoughts, conceptions and things (*dhamma*).

The practice of concentration on breathing (*ānapānasati*) is one of the well-known exercises, connected with the body, for mental development. There are several other ways of developing attentiveness in relation to the body—as modes of meditation.

With regard to sensations and feelings, one should be clearly aware of all forms of feelings and sensations, pleasant, unpleasant and neutral, of how they appear and disappear within oneself.

Concerning the activities of mind, one should be aware whether one's mind is lustful or not, given to hatred or not, deluded or not, distracted or concentrated, etc. In this way one should be aware of all movements of mind, how they arise and disappear.

As regards ideas, thoughts, conceptions and things, one should know their nature, how they appear and disappear, how they are developed, how they are suppressed, and destroyed, and so on.

These four forms of mental culture or meditation are treated in detail in the *Satipaṭṭhānasutta* (Setting-up of Mindfulness).

The third and last factor of Mental Discipline is Right Concentration leading to the four stages of *Dhyāna*, generally called trance or *recueillement*. In the first stage of *Dhyāna*, passionate desires and certain unwholesome thoughts like sensuous lust, ill-will, languor, worry, restlessness, and sceptical doubt are discarded, and feelings of joy and happiness are maintained, along with certain mental activities. In the second stage, all intellectual activities are suppressed, tranquillity and 'one-pointedness' of mind developed, and the feelings of joy and happiness are still retained. In the third stage, the feeling of joy, which is an active sensation, also disappears, while the disposition of happiness still remains in addition to mindful equanimity. In the fourth stage of *Dhyāna*, all sensations, even of happiness and unhappiness, of joy and sorrow, disappear, only pure equanimity and awareness remaining.

Thus the mind is trained and disciplined and developed through Right Effort, Right Mindfulness, and Right Concentration.

The remaining two factors, namely Right Thought and Right Understanding go to constitute Wisdom.

Right Thought denotes the thoughts of selfless renunciation or detachment, thoughts of love and thoughts of non-violence, which are extended to all beings. It is very interesting and important to note here that thoughts of selfless detachment, love and non-violence are grouped on the side of wisdom. This clearly shows that true wisdom is endowed with these noble qualities, and that all thoughts of selfish desire, ill-will, hatred and violence are the result of a lack of wisdom—in all spheres of life whether individual, social, or political.

Right Understanding is the understanding of things as they are, and it is the Four Noble Truths that explain things as they really are. Right Understanding therefore is ultimately reduced to the understanding of the Four Noble Truths. This understanding is the highest wisdom which sees the Ultimate Reality. According to Buddhism there are two sorts of understanding: What we generally call understanding is knowledge, an accumulated memory, an intellectual grasping of a subject according to certain given data. This is called 'knowing accordingly' (*anubodha*). It is not very deep. Real deep understanding is called 'penetration' (*paṭivedha*), seeing a thing in its true nature, without name and label. This penetration is possible only when the mind is free from all impurities and is fully developed through meditation.

From this brief account of the Path, one may see that it is a way of life to be followed, practised and developed by each individual. It is self-discipline in body, word and mind, self-development and self-purification. It has nothing to do with belief, prayer, worship or ceremony. In that sense, it has nothing which may popularly be called 'religious'. It is a Path leading to the realization of Ultimate Reality, to complete freedom, happiness and peace through moral, spiritual and intellectual perfection.

In Buddhist countries there are simple and beautiful customs and ceremonies on religious occasions. They have little to do with the real Path. But they have their value in satisfying certain religious emotions and the needs of those who are less advanced, and helping them gradually along the Path.

With regard to the Four Noble Truths we have four functions to perform:

The First Noble Truth is *Dukkha*, the nature of life, its suffering, its sorrows and joys, its imperfection and unsatisfactoriness, its impermanence and insubstantiality. With regard to this, our function is to understand it as a fact, clearly and completely (*pariññeyya*).

The Second Noble Truth is the Origin of *Dukkha*, which is desire, 'thirst', accompanied by all other passions, defilements and impurities. A mere understanding of this fact is not sufficient. Here our function is to discard it, to eliminate, to destroy and eradicate it (*pahātabba*).

The Third Noble Truth is the Cessation of *Dukkha*, Nirvāṇa, the Absolute Truth, the Ultimate Reality. Here our function is to realize it (*sacchikātabba*).

The Fourth Noble Truth is the Path leading to the realization of Nirvāṇa. A mere knowledge of the Path, however complete, will not do. In this case, our function is to follow it and keep to it (*bhāvetabba*).

The Cosmic Dance

FRITJOF CAPRA

Fritjof Capra is a high-energy physicist who has lectured and conducted research at a number of universities in America and Europe. He is best known for his controversial book *The Tao of Physics*, from which the following selection is edited. The dance to which he refers is the one that Hindus call "The Dance of Shiva." Background concerning the scientific theories discussed here may be found in Chapters 7 and 8, particularly in the selection by Capra titled "The Dynamic Universe."

The exploration of the subatomic world in the twentieth century has revealed the intrinsically dynamic nature of matter. It has shown that the constituents of atoms, the subatomic particles, are dynamic patterns which do not exist as isolated entities, but as integral parts of an inseparable network of interactions. These interactions involve a ceaseless flow of energy manifesting itself as the exchange of particles; a dynamic interplay in which particles are created and destroyed without end in a continual variation of energy patterns. The particle interactions give rise to the stable structures which build up the material world, which again do not remain static, but oscillate in rhythmic movements. The whole universe is thus engaged in endless motion and activity; in a continual cosmic dance of energy. . . .

The Eastern mystics have a dynamic view of the universe similar to that of modern physics, and consequently it is not surprising that they, too, have used the image of the dance to convey their intuition of nature. A beautiful example of such an image of rhythm and dance is given by Alexandra David-Neel in her *Tibetan Journey*, where she describes how she met a lama who referred to himself as a "master of sound" and gave her the following account of his view of matter:

All things . . . are aggregations of atoms that dance and by their movements produce sounds. When the rhythm of the dance changes, the sound it produces also changes. . . . Each atom perpetually sings its song, and the sound, at every movement, creates dense and subtle forms.[1]

The similarity of this view to that of modern physics becomes particularly striking when we remember that sound is a wave with a certain frequency which changes when the sound does, and that particles—the modern equivalent of the old concept of atoms—are also waves with frequencies proportional to their energies. According to field theory, each particle does indeed "perpetually sing its song," producing rhythmic patterns of energy (the virtual particles) in "dense and subtle forms."

The metaphor of the cosmic dance has found its most profound and beautiful expression in Hinduism in the image of the dancing god Shiva.

Among his many incarnations, Shiva, one of the oldest and most popular Indian gods, appears as the King of Dancers. According to Hindu belief, all life is part of a great rhythmic process of creation and destruction, of death and rebirth, and Shiva's dance symbolizes this eternal life-death rhythm which goes on in endless cycles. In the words of Ananda Coomaraswamy:

> In the night of *Brahman,* Nature is inert and cannot dance till Shiva wills it: He rises from His rapture, and dancing sends through inert matter pulsing waves of awakening sound, and lo! matter also dances, appearing as a glory round about Him. Dancing, He sustains its manifold phenomena. In the fullness of time, still dancing, He destroys all forms and names by fire and gives new rest. This is poetry, but nonetheless science.[2]

The Dance of Shiva symbolizes not only the cosmic cycles of creation and destruction, but also the daily rhythm of birth and death which is seen in Indian mysticism as the basis of all existence. At the same time, Shiva reminds us that the manifold forms in the world are *maya*—not fundamental, but illusory and ever-changing—as he keeps creating and dissolving them in the ceaseless flow of his dance. As Heinrich Zimmer has put it:

> His gestures wild and full of grace, precipitate the cosmic illusion; his flying arms and legs and the swaying of his torso produce—indeed, they are—the continuous creation-destruction of the universe, death exactly balancing birth, annihilation the end of every coming-forth.[3]

Indian artists of the tenth and twelfth centuries have represented Shiva's cosmic dance in magnificent bronze sculptures of dancing figures with four arms whose superbly balanced and yet dynamic gestures express the rhythm and unity of Life. The various meanings of the dance are conveyed by the details of these figures in a complex pictorial allegory. The upper right hand of the god holds a drum to symbolize the primal sound of creation; the upper left bears a tongue of flame, the element of de-

struction. The balance of the two hands represents the dynamic balance of creation and destruction in the world, accentuated further by the Dancer's calm and detached face in the center of the two hands, in which the polarity of creation and destruction is dissolved and transcended. The second right hand is raised in the sign of "do not fear," symbolizing maintenance, protection and peace, while the remaining left hand points down to the uplifted foot which symbolizes release from the spell of *maya.* The god is pictured as dancing on the body of a demon, the symbol of human ignorance which has to be conquered before liberation can be attained.

Shiva's dance—in the words of Coomaraswamy—is "the clearest image of the activity of God which any art or religion can boast of."[4] As the god is a personification of *Brahman,* his activity is that of *Brahman's* myriad manifestations in the world. The dance of Shiva is the dancing universe; the ceaseless flow of energy going through an infinite variety of patterns that melt into one another.

Modern physics has shown that the rhythm of creation and destruction is not only manifest in the turn of the seasons and in the birth and death of all living creatures, but is also the very essence of inorganic matter. According to quantum field theory, all interactions between the constituents of matter take place through the emission and absorption of virtual particles. More than that, the dance of creation and destruction is the basis of the very existence of matter, since all material particles "self-interact" by emitting and reabsorbing virtual particles. Modern physics has thus revealed that every subatomic particle not only performs an energy dance, but also *is* an energy dance; a pulsating process of creation and destruction.

The patterns of this dance are an essential aspect of each particle's nature and determine many of its properties. For example, the energy involved in the emission and absorption of virtual particles is equivalent to a certain amount of mass which contributes to the mass of the self-interacting particle. Different particles develop different patterns in their dance, requiring different amounts of energy, and hence have different masses. Virtual particles, finally, are not only an essential part of all particle interactions and of most of the particles' properties, but are also created and destroyed by the vacuum. Thus, not only matter, but also the void, participates in the cosmic dance, creating and destroying energy patterns without end.

For the modern physicists, then, Shiva's dance is the dance of subatomic matter. As in Hindu mythology, it is a continual dance of creation and destruction involving the whole cosmos; the basis of all existence and of all natural phenomena. Hundreds of years ago, Indian artists created visual images of dancing Shivas in a beautiful series of bronzes. In our time, physicists have used the most advanced technology to portray the patterns of the cosmic dance. The bubble-chamber photographs of interacting particles, which bear testimony to the continual rhythm of creation and destruction in the universe, are visual images of the dance of Shiva equaling those of the Indian artists in beauty and profound significance. The metaphor of the cosmic dance thus unifies ancient mythology, religious art, and modern physics. It is indeed, as Coomaraswamy has said, "poetry, but nonetheless science."

Notes

1. A. David-Neel, *Tibetan Journey,* pp. 186–87.

2. A. K. Coomaraswamy, *The Dance of Shiva,* p. 78.

3. H. Zimmer, *Myths and Symbols in Indian Art and Civilization,* p. 155.

4. A. K. Coomaraswamy, op. cit., p. 67.

The Way of Renunciation
(Chapter 5 of the *Bhagavad Gītā*)

TRANSLATED BY ASHOK K. MALHOTRA

The *Bhagavad Gītā* is one of the major religious books of the Hindus. Here the main ideas of Hinduism are presented in a systematic way. The *Bhagavad Gītā* consists of eighteen chapters that deal with the nature of the ultimate reality, enlightenment, the caste system, and the three basic paths of salvation. Chapter 5 presents a discussion of the path of renunciation. True renunciation consists of the performance of an action with complete detachment from its fruits. When an individual performs an action spontaneously without hankering after the rewards, the action manifests the spirit of renunciation.

Arjuna asked Krishna:

5:1 First you say that one should renounce action and then you praise the performance of action; tell me decisively which one of the two is better.

Krishna replied:

5:2 Though both action and renunciation of action are equally conducive to salvation, action is better.

5:3 One who has perfected renunciation neither hates anyone nor desires anything. Such a person is disentangled from the clutches of the world.

5:4 The foolish distinguish between the paths of action and knowledge; the wise do not. A person who perfects either enjoys the benefits of both.

5:5 Those established in the path of knowledge have the same status as those established in the path of action. One who grasps this identify understands an important truth.

5:6 Without disciplined action, a person cannot attain renunciation. With disciplined action, sages reach the infinite self without difficulty.

5:7 A person who has purity of heart, has complete control over the senses; who is disciplined in action, and who identifies with all creatures, is not tainted by action.

5:8 While seeing, hearing, smelling, eating, walking, and breathing, a person of disciplined action who knows reality reminds oneself that s/he is doing nothing.

5:9 While speaking, giving, and taking, the senses are engaged in their activities and the knower of reality does nothing that involves effort.

5:10 Like the lotus flower which is untouched by dirty water, a person absorbed in the infinite self, who relinquishes the fruits of action, is untainted by evil.

5:11 Being completely unattached, the sage uses the body, the heart, the mind, and the senses towards purifying the infinite self.

5:12 A disciplined mind abandons the fruits of action and attains unlimited peace; but an undisciplined mind becomes a slave to the rewards of its action.

5:13 A person who has mentally detached oneself from all actions, neither doing anything oneself nor forcing others to do anything, dwells happily in one's body of nine gates.

5:14 The infinite self is not the doer of action, nor the cause of action, nor the fruit of action. It is the physical nature of a human being which is responsible for these.

5:15 The infinite self cannot take on the merits or demerits of a person. Since ignorance envelops knowledge, a person is misled.

5:16 Just as the Sun reveals the nature of the world, so too do those who destroy their ignorance with the aid of wisdom display the form of the Supreme Being.

5:17 One whose intellect resides in the Supreme Being, whose heart is engrossed in It, who makes It the ultimate goal of life and the only object of worship, frees oneself from the cycle of births and rebirths.

5:18 A sage makes no distinction between a Brahmin, a cow, a dog, an elephant, and an outcast.

5:19 People whose hearts are imbued with this sense of equality are able to overcome the death-birth cycle of this world. They find repose in the Supreme Being who is flawless and is present in everything.

5:20 A person who possesses a stable intelligence, is totally free of attachment, is neither happy for obtaining something pleasant nor unhappy for obtaining something unpleasant, resides in the Supreme Being.

5:21 When one is not attracted to external objects, one finds peace at the core of one's being. When one is totally absorbed in the contemplation of the Supreme Being, one finds unlimited happiness.

5:22 The pleasure obtained through contact with object is actually the source of sorrow because it is impermanent. O Arjuna, wise people are uninterested in it.

5:23 By successfully controlling anger and desire, one may find happiness and become a yogi in this lifetime.

5:24 One who finds peace within, bliss within, and the spark of divinity within, is absorbed into the Supreme Being, and thus becomes this Being.

5:25 One whose bad deeds are destroyed, whose uncertainties are eradicated, whose heart is disciplined, and who takes delight in helping all creatures, achieves liberation.

5:26 One who is free of desire and anger, is in control of one's heart, and has knowledge of the infinite spirit within, achieves the eternal peace of the Supreme Being.

5:27, 28 By cutting off one's contact with the external objects, by focusing vision between the eyebrows, by regulating the inhalation and exhalation of breath, and by controlling the sense organs, heart and mind, one who has become oblivious to desire, fear, and anger, has obtained total liberation.

5:29 One who regards Me as the receiver of all sacrifice and prayer, controller of the entire universe, and friend of all creatures, attains peace.

Some Buddhist Parables and Legends

PAUL CARUS

Like many philosophical and religious traditions, Buddhism has developed a rich stock of parables and legends. The stories which follow concern love, death, marriage, family relations, and faith.

KISĀ GOTAMĪ

There was a rich man who found his gold suddenly transformed into ashes; and he took to his bed and refused all food. A friend, hearing of his sickness, visited the rich man and learned the cause of his grief. And the friend said: "Thou didst not make good use of thy wealth. When thou didst hoard it up it was not better than ashes. Now heed my advice. Spread mats in the bazaar; pile up these ashes, and pretend to trade with them."

The rich man did as his friend had told him, and when his neighbors asked him, "Why sellest thou ashes?" he said: "I offer my goods for sale."

After some time a young girl, named Kisā Gotamī, an orphan and very poor, passed by, and seeing the rich man in the bazaar, said: "My lord, why pilest thou thus up gold and silver for sale?"

And the rich man said: "Wilt thou please hand me that gold and silver?" And Kisā Gotamī took up a handful of ashes, and lo! they changed back into gold.

Considering that Kisā Gotamī had the mental eye of spiritual knowledge and saw the real worth of things, the rich man gave her in marriage to his son, and he said: "With many, gold is no better than ashes, but with Kisā Gotamī ashes become pure gold."

And Kisā Gotamī had an only son, and he died. In her grief she carried the dead child to all her neighbors, asking them for medicine, and the people said: "She has lost her senses. The boy is dead."

At length Kisā Gotamī met a man who replied to her request: "I cannot give thee medicine for thy child, but I know a physician who can."

And the girl said: "Pray tell me, sir; who is it?" And the man replied: "Go to Sakyamuni, the Buddha."

Kisā Gotamī repaired to the Buddha and cried: "Lord and Master, give me the medicine that will cure my boy."

The Buddha answered: "I want a handful of mustard-seed." And when the girl in her joy promised to procure it, the Buddha added: "The mustard-seed must be taken from a house where no one has lost a child, husband, parent, or friend."

Poor Kisā Gotamī now went from house to house, and the people pitied her and said: "Here is mustard-seed; take it!" But when she asked, "Did a son or daughter, a father or mother, die in your family?" they answered her: "Alas! the living are few, but the dead are many. Do not remind us of our deepest grief." And there was no house but some beloved one had died in it.

Kisā Gotamī became weary and hopeless, and sat down at the wayside, watching the lights of the city, as they flickered up and were extinguished again. At last the darkness of the night reigned everywhere. And she considered the fate of men, that their lives flicker up and are extinguished. And she thought to herself: "How selfish am I in my

Lin Yutang, "Some Buddhist Parables and Legends" from THE GOSPEL OF BUDDHA, edited by Paul Carus (Chicago: Open Court, nd), pp. 367–376.

grief! Death is common to all; yet in this valley of desolation there is a path that leads him to immortality who has surrendered all selfishness."

Putting away the selfishness of her affection for her child, Kisā Gotamī had the dead body buried in the forest. Returning to the Buddha, she took refuge in him and found comfort in the Dharma, which is a balm that will soothe all the pains of our troubled hearts.

The Buddha said:

"The life of mortals in this world is troubled and brief and combined with pain. For there is not any means by which those that have been born can avoid dying; after reaching old age there is death; of such a nature are living beings.

"As ripe fruits are early in danger of falling, so mortals when born are always in danger of death.

"As all earthen vessels made by the potter end in being broken, so is the life of mortals.

"Both young and adult, both those who are fools and those who are wise, all fall into the power of death; all are subject to death.

"Of those who, overcome by death, depart from life, a father cannot save his son, nor kinsmen their relations.

"Mark! While relatives are looking on and lamenting deeply, one by one mortals are carried off, like an ox that is led to the slaughter.

"So the world is afflicted with death and decay, therefore the wise do not grieve, knowing the terms of the world.

"In whatever manner people think a thing will come to pass, it is often different when it happens, and great is the disappointment; see, such are the terms of the world.

"Not from weeping nor from grieving will any one obtain peace of mind; on the contrary, his pain will be the greater and his body will suffer. He will make himself sick and pale, yet the dead are not saved by his lamentation.

"People pass away, and their fate after death will be according to their deeds.

"If a man live a hundred years, or even more, he will at last be separated from the company of his relatives, and leave the life of this world.

"He who seeks peace should draw out the arrow of lamentation, and complaint, and grief.

"He who has drawn out the arrow and has become composed will obtain peace of mind; he who has overcome all sorrow will become free from sorrow, and be blessed."

The Marriage-Feast in Jambūnada

There was a man in Jambūnada who was to be married the next day, and he thought, "Would that the Buddha, the Blessed One, might be present at the wedding."

And the Blessed One passed by his house and met him, and when he read the silent wish in the heart of the bridegroom, he consented to enter.

When the Holy One appeared with the retinue of his many bhikkhus, the host whose means were limited received them as best he could, saying: "Eat, my Lord, and all thy congregation, according to your desire."

While the holy men ate, the meats and drinks remained undiminished, and the host thought to himself: "How wondrous is this! I should have had plenty for all my relatives and friends. Would that I had invited them all."

When this thought was in the host's mind, all his relatives and friends entered the house; and although the hall in the house was small there was room in it for all of them. They sat down at the table and ate, and there was more than enough for all of them.

The Blessed One was pleased to see so many guests full of good cheer and he quickened them and gladdened them with words of truth, proclaiming the bliss of righteousness:

"The greatest happiness which a mortal man can imagine is the bond of marriage that ties together two loving hearts. But there is a greater happiness still: it is the embrace of truth. Death will separate husband and wife, but death will never affect him who has espoused the truth.

"Therefore be married unto the truth and live with the truth in holy wedlock. The husband who loves his wife and desires for a union that shall be everlasting must be faithful to her so as to be like truth itself, and she will rely upon him and revere him and minister unto him. And the wife who loves her husband and desires a union that shall be everlasting must be faithful to him so as to be like truth itself; and he will place his trust in her, he will provide for her. Verily, I say unto you, their children will become like unto their parents and will bear witness to their happiness.

"Let no man be single, let every one be wedded in holy love to the truth. And when Māra, the destroyer, comes to separate the visible forms of your being, you will continue to live in the truth, and you will partake of the life everlasting, for the truth is immortal."

There was no one among the guests but was strengthened in his spiritual life, and recognized the sweetness of a life of righteousness; and they took refuge in the Buddha, the Dharma, and the Sangha.

FOLLOWING THE MASTER OVER THE STREAM

South of Sāvatthi is a great river, on the banks of which lay a hamlet of five hundred houses. Thinking of the salvation of the people, the World-honored One resolved to go to the village and preach the doctrine. Having come to the riverside he sat down beneath a tree, and the villagers seeing the glory of his appearance approached him with reverence; but when he began to preach, they believed him not.

When the World-honored Buddha had left Sāvatthi, Sāriputta felt a desire to see the Lord and to hear him preach. Coming to the river where the wa-ter was deep and the current strong, he said to himself: "This stream shall not prevent me. I shall go and see the Blessed One," and he stepped upon the water which was as firm under his feet as a slab of granite.

When he arrived at a place in the middle of the stream where the waves were high, Sāriputta's heart gave way, and he began to sink. But rousing his faith and renewing his mental effort, he proceeded as before and reached the other bank.

The people of the village were astonished to see Sāriputta, and they asked how he could cross the stream where there was neither a bridge nor a ferry.

And Sāriputta replied: "I lived in ignorance until I heard the voice of the Buddha. As I was anxious to hear the doctrine of salvation, I crossed the river and I walked over its troubled waters because I had faith. Faith, nothing else, enabled me to do so, and now I am here in the bliss of the Master's presency."

The World-honored One added: "Sāriputta, thou hast spoken well. Faith like thine alone can save the world from the yawning gulf of migration and enable men to walk dryshod to the other shore."

And the Blessed One urged to the villagers the necessity of ever advancing in the conquest of sorrow and of casting off all shackles so as to cross the river of worldliness and attain deliverance from death.

Hearing the words of the Tathāgata, the villagers were filled with joy and believing in the doctrines of the Blessed One embraced the five rules and took refuge in his name.

Review and Reflection

Hinduism

1. Summarize the main philosophical and religious ideas of the *Vedas*.

2. How can a Hindu believe in many gods, one god, and no god? How is this contradiction reconciled in the *Vedas*?

3. What is the central discovery of the *Upanishads*? How is this discovery a further development of the ideas of the *Vedas*?

4. What is a good life in the *Bhagavad Gītā*? How does the *Gītā* reconcile the ideas of the *Vedas* and *Upanishads*?

5. Summarize and discuss the major philosophical ideas from the "Hymn of Creation." Do the same for the "Hymn to Puruṣa."

6. What are the four stages of consciousness discussed in the *Māṇḍūkya Upanishad*? Does this theory make sense in the context of the twentieth-century psychology?

7. Can anyone ever act without thought of reward? Can one ever perform a selfless act? Take a position for or against this view from the *Bhagavad Gītā*.

8. Summarize Capra's major points from "The Cosmic Dance." Are the parallels between the discoveries of contemporary physics and those of Eastern mystics real or contrived? Defend your answer against possible objections.

Buddhism

1. Give a summary of the Buddha's life and enlightenment. How did he arrive at his philosophy of the four noble truths?

2. Discuss the concepts of *dukkha, tanha,* and *karuna.* How are they related to the Buddha's teachings?

3. What is the eightfold path? Discuss each step in detail. Would it make sense for a contemporary person to adopt this method?

4. What were some of the basic criticisms of Hinduism presented by the Buddha? Did he make any improvement on Hinduism?

5. How can compassion be inculcated? What were the ways chosen by the Buddha to teach compassion?

6. Discuss the Buddha's concepts of wisdom and compassion. What relevance, if any, do these concepts have for contemporary life?

Suggestions for Further Study

Hinduism

Lewis Hopfe. *The Religions of the World.* New York: Macmillan, 1987.

John Koller. *Oriental Philosophies.* New York: Macmillan, 1985.

Radhakrishnan and Moore. *A Sourcebook of Indian Philosophy.* Princeton, NJ: Princeton University Press, 1973.

Huston Smith. *The Religions of Man.* New York: Harper and Row, 1958.

Rajmani Tigunait. *Seven Systems of Indian Philosophy.* Honesdale, PA: The Himalayan Institute, 1989.

Buddhism

Paul Carus. *The Gospel of Buddha.* Chicago: Open Court, 1915.

Edward Conze. *Buddhism: Its Essence and Development.* New York: Harper and Row, 1969.

Hermann Hesse. *Siddhartha.* New York: New Directions, 1957.

John Koller. *Oriental Philosophies.* New York: Macmillan, 1985.

Trevor Ling. *The Buddha.* New York: Penguin Books, 1973.

Huston Smith. *The Religions of Man.* New York: Harper and Row, 1958.

CHAPTER 11

Wisdom of the Orient

The principal philosophical and religious traditions of China are Taoism, Confucianism, and Buddhism. While Confucianism shaped the social and political aspects of life, Taoism molded the Chinese character. Its precepts and philosophical perspective have dominated the art, thought, and culture of China for 2700 years. When Buddhism was brought to China in 527 A.D., it intermingled with the ideas of Taoism, giving rise to a distinctive version known as "Ch'an." Ch'an Buddhism was then introduced to Japanese culture during the twelfth century. Once again it found fertile soil, gained rapid acceptance, and acquired a new name: *Zen.*

Introductory Essays

Taoism

The **Introductory Essay on Taoism** summarizes the views of Taoism's founder, Lao Tzu, and his fourth-century follower, Chuang Tzu. Tao, regarded as ultimate reality, may be understood in each of its three main aspects: the unmanifest, the manifest, and the power of *Te* residing in its created being. The unmanifest Tao, though ineffable, is the source of the other two. The goal of life is to understand the power within (*Te*). Through *Te* one can grasp the nature of the unmanifest Tao. Whereas Lao Tzu advocates a life devoted to the contemplation of nature, Chuang Tzu delineates a system of meditation to experience the *Te* within. To live a meaningful life, they suggest the following: Live a simple life; prefer obscurity; regard all values as relative; eliminate the fear of death; abandon the need to win; develop cosmic humility; and center your being on the Tao, rather than yourself.

Zen Buddhism

The **Introductory Essay on Zen Buddhism** focuses on four principal concepts: *zen, satori, kōan,* and *zazen.* Zen emphasizes intimate, direct experience of reality. It is an openness to the constantly changing and moving process of life, which does not require scriptures, doctrines, or external aids. When a person realizes that nothing can be possessed and there is no possessor to appropriate it, attachment to the world disappears and a new insight emerges. The experience is a non-dualistic viewpoint that corresponds roughly to enlightenment. This non-intellectual, non-logical, and non-conceptual view of the universe and the self is called *satori*.

A Zen master helps a student prepare for *satori* through judicious use of *kōans* and *zazen*. A *kōan* is a puzzle designed to open the mind to its own secrets. It presents a dilemma, a choice between two impossible alternatives. Through contemplation of a *kōan*, a student comes to understand the futility of the intellectual approach to enlightenment.

Zazen is a series of meditative exercises that train the mind to empty itself of all contents. The exercises consist of physical postures, breath control, elimination of thoughts and images, and the intense observation of reality here and now. By emptying the mind and refocusing on the present moment, one is able to obtain deeper insight than would otherwise be possible.

Philosophical Readings

Taoism

Selections from the *Tao Te Ching* of Lao Tzu provide an opportunity to experience the original text on which Taoism is based. The selections deal with the nature of the Tao, the influence of discriminating intellect, and the concept of actionless action known as *Wu Wei*.

Zen Buddhism

The essay by **Alan Watts** provides further analysis and discussion of the techniques of *kōan* and *zazen*. He compares *satori* to the Christian concept of conversion and discusses, among others, the philosophical position of William James (see Chapter 12).

Scientific Reading

The selection by **Thomas Kasulis** offers a comparative analysis of Zen as well as discussion and reflection concerning its practical implications. Zen cannot be incorporated into Western society, Kasulis argues, without substantial modification of some of its basic ideas and techniques. Zen would have to adapt itself to the individualism of the West, and the West in turn would have to change its attitude toward the contemplative dimension of Zen. The application of Zen may, he suggests, serve as a form of humanistic therapy.

Literary Reading

The "Stories of Chuang Tzu and Hui Tzu" by **Arthur Waley** concern the relativity of values, fear of death, living in union with nature, and cosmic humility. Stories such as these not only appeal to our intellect, but touch our hearts and move us to action.

Taoism

ASHOK K. MALHOTRA

Taoism originated in China in the sixth century B.C. (Chou Dynasty). Its main ideas were first formulated by Lao Tzu, a recluse who had once been a keeper of royal archives. Not much is known about Lao Tzu except that he became disenchanted with court life and disgusted by what he perceived to be a fundamental breakdown of law and order. Lao Tzu challenged the moral and political authority of the state. Unlike Confucianism, Taoism prefers a state of nature to that of a complex society.

Lao Tzu expressed his thoughts in a small book called the *Tao Te Ching*. In the fourth century B.C., Chuang Tzu added a metaphysical and mystical dimension to Taoism. Through this and further modifications by other disciples, Taoism came to occupy a significant place in the life and culture of China.

Taoism is sometimes difficult to understand by an individual who has been raised to value culture and society more than his or her own intuition and the simple lessons of a mountain, stream, or tree. Particularly difficult, for many, is the first principle and basis upon which all else is constructed: the *Tao*.

THE NATURE OF *TAO*

Although there is only one *Tao*, it may be approached by human cognition in three distinct ways, corresponding to three different sets of issues and concerns.

First, *Tao* is ultimate reality. In itself, it is unmanifest. Yet it is the basis for all that exists. It cannot be described because it is beyond all names and forms. It is the transcendental source of everything else.

The second meaning of *Tao* refers to its manifest form. All that is tangible, concrete, and describable in the universe is the visible *Tao*. This manifest *Tao*

is both created and supported by the unmanifest *Tao*.

Third, *Tao* is the way or path one must follow to live an ideal (satisfying, meaningful) life. In this sense, *Tao* is closely related to another difficult concept: the *Te*.

Unmanifest Tao. The unmanifest *Tao* as the ultimate reality is the ground of both being and non-being. It is the ultimate creative force. All things come from it, are supported by it, and eventually merge back into it. In this primal state, *Tao* is the unity that underlies the diversity of things. Without form or name, this *Tao* is uncharacterizable. It is an undifferentiated reality devoid of all divisions or distinctions. Since this *Tao* lacks form, name, and action, it is sometimes described as the *absolute vacuity*. Such a description should not mislead us into thinking that the *Tao* is a nothingness. It is the pure creative force that is the basis of all names and forms. According to Chuang Tzu, this *Tao* has been there eternally; it has existed before heaven and earth, and though it is invisible, it can be transmitted. This *Tao* should not be mistaken for the God who is the maker and ruler of the universe. Rather, it is the immutable and unchanging absolute principle which makes possible everything that is mutable and changing.

Manifest Tao. The manifest *Tao* is multifaceted. All change and transformation take place here. This is the realm of ceaseless activity. In the realm of the unmanifest *Tao* there were no things, no transformation, no material force, no time, and no activity. When an aspect of the unmanifest becomes the manifest, various visible forms come into being. The first to evolve is the material force, which in turn gives rise to matter. Transformations take place in matter, which evolves into organic matter and life. Since ceaseless change is the nature of the manifest *Tao,* transformations continue to take place in the life process. First, the life process gives rise to simple organisms, which in turn create higher and more complex organisms. Life evolves itself through plants, birds, and animals into human beings. Human beings and other life forms take part in this universal process.[1]

All things come from the unmanifest *Tao* and return to it at the end. Life and death are but two links in this natural process. To be born is to become part of the manifest *Tao.* To die is to merge back into the creative force of the unmanifest *Tao.* Thus, says Chuang Tzu, death is not to be feared because you are never out of the *Tao.* You are never annihilated. Death means the change of form or movement from the formed to the formless *Tao.*

The nature of Te *and its relationship to* Tao. The third meaning of *Tao* is conveyed through the idea of *Te.* The manifest *Tao* with its multiple forms is the visible, concrete, and tangible universe. Each item or thing in the manifest universe carries within itself the mark of the *Tao,* called the *Te.* The *Te* is the distinguishing mark or individual function of each created being. *Tao* is that by which things come to be. *Te* is that by which they are what they are. According to Chuang Tzu, *Tao* is the basic or originative principle, whereas the *Te* is an aspect of *Tao* in everything.

Each being is born with a natural capacity. In order to be happy, content, and fulfilled, each person should express this ability. One must guide one's life in such a way that this natural potential is actualized. One should never do what one is not capable of doing. Any time one tries to go beyond one's natural capacity one becomes artificial, which results in suffering. Whether I am naturally endowed to be an artist, scientist, professor, or carpenter, I should express this potential to its fullest. This expression of my nature in the appropriate realm will bring fulfillment and contentment. If I try or aspire to be something other than myself, the outcome will be frustraion and unhappiness.

Chuang Tzu uses examples from nature to persuade humans of this simple truth. A sparrow is content and happy when it hops around from one branch of a tree to another all day. When it is hungry it eats tiny leaves and fruit from the tree. When it feels the urge to communicate, it sings its songs. When it is tired it sleeps or rests on this tree. It is following its nature and is happy. In like manner, there is a hawk who soars on the currents of high winds. It floats around in the sky and travels long distances to capture its prey. It is content because it expresses its nature through these activities. Suppose one day the hawk and the sparrow reverse their roles. The hawk jumps from one branch of the tree to the other all day, and the sparrow soars high in the sky all day. Both of them will be tired, exhausted, or bored from their activities because they are going against their natures. Both will be discontented and unhappy.

If we indulge in activities that are against our nature, or aspire to achievements and accomplishments beyond our abilities, we doom ourselves to a lifetime of suffering, frustration, and profound unhappiness. Happiness, according to Chuang Tzu, lies in knowing your *Te,* recognizing your natural limits, and expressing what lies within those limits (living up to your full potential with neither regrets nor resentment).

How does one go about learning one's limits? What is the best way to experience the *Te*? The *Te* cannot be seen, but it can be apprehended through its workings in nature. As explained in the following section, Lao Tzu and Chuang Tzu offer two ways in which the *Te* may be realized.

THE NATURE OF A MEANINGFUL LIFE

In the *Tao Te Ching,* Lao Tzu teaches the contemplation of nature. Since ultimate reality (*Tao*) is harmony and perfection, a continuous absorption in *Tao* results in peace, serenity, and contentment. All suffering is due to deviation from one's nature. The more we go against nature, the more we suffer. To eliminate suffering, one must live a life in tune with the universe. This kind of life consists of taking delight in nature, contemplating it, identifying with it, and blending with the cosmic process. Nature is the best teacher and educator.

All aspects of nature are pulsating with knowlege. Each of its creations is an open chapter to be studied and emulated. There are lessons to be learned from the flight of birds, the murmuring sound of water, the morning dew, and the rays of the sun. The earth and sun give us everything without asking anything in return. By meditating on nature, all worthwhile knowledge can be obtained. Our life should be patterned on the model of a child who looks at the universe with innocent eyes and finds every aspect of it intriguing, pleasing, and mysterious.

It is also important to direct one's attention inward. The *Te*, our natural capacity, is a gift given to us by the creative *Tao*. The goal of our life is to experience and express it to its fullest. Lao Tzu writes:

Wisdom comes from understanding others.
Illumination comes from understanding oneself.
Strength comes from overcoming others.
But might comes from overcoming oneself.

Chuang Tzu explains that freedom and happiness can be found only in the inner core of one's being, never in the artifacts of civilization. The more you seek them in the external world of human creation, the more futile will be your search and the less you will find them. The secret of total freedom and happiness lies in experiencing the flow of the *Tao* within one's being. Chuang Tzu's motto is: "Know the universe, without leaving your home."

Chuang Tzu believes that contentment is best achieved by what may be regarded as total idleness. One should let nature lead. Let nature be the teacher, the master, and the guru. When one goes with the flow of the *Tao,* the inner capacities of the individual follow their natural course and satisfaction and fulfillment ensue.

For both Lao Tzu and Chuang Tzu, the focus is the *Tao*. In the case of Lao Tzu, happiness is achieved by going out into nature where one sees, hears, tastes, smells, touches, and feels the flow of the *Tao* in all its created forms. In the case of Chuang Tzu, one takes an inward journey into the core of one's being. After going through the worlds of sensations, feelings, emotions, passions, images, words, values, and ideas, one delves into the core of one's being where one experiences the *Tao*. Lao Tzu recommends a lifestyle or a method consisting of a childlike playfulness leading to a complete absorption into nature. Chuang Tzu complements this method by offering a lifestyle of idleness and total forgetfulness of the surrounding world. When one sits in idleness, one becomes oblivious to both body and mind. One simply lets the *Tao* work through one's being. This idleness should not be confused with laziness. In idleness, one is totally awake to the workings of the *Tao* within and without. As such, idleness is the source of all creativity. In contrast, laziness is a state of dullness, unawareness, and non-alertness. Laziness is not conducive to creativity.

The meditative styles of Lao Tzu and Chuang Tzu are not methods in the usual sense. When we use the word *method* we usually mean a step-by-step procedure designed to accomplish a particular goal or end. Chuang Tzu rejects all deliberate attempts at the cultivation of the inner life. He believes that happiness and contentment are never to be found through a planned course of action. Such attempts fail because they attempt to locate happiness in only one kind of activity. The truth is that happiness surrounds us everywhere.

Thus Lao Tzu and Chuang Tzu do not teach methods, but rather natural, spontaneous, and effortless ways of tuning oneself to the universal music of the *Tao*. Their "ways" are directed toward no specific end and can perhaps best be described as ways of seeking nothing in particular. This non-seeking is called *Wu Wei*.

NATURE OF *WU WEI*

The phrase *Wu Wei* is often translated as *non-action* or *non-doing*. Both phrases unfortunately convey the impression of passivity or inertia. In its proper sense, *Wu Wei* is pure action. Since actions are usually guided by some kind of motive, intention, or reason, they require effort. In contrast, *Wu Wei* is an action with neither motive nor intention. Since it is completely natural and spontaneous, it is effortless.

In most cases of action, the flow of the *Tao* within us is obstructed by psychological blemishes (such as worries, cares, anxieties, fears, anger, or hatred). But the individual who follows *Wu Wei* lets the *Tao* work through him/her unhindered. Such a person uses effort effortlessly at the right moment.

Wu Wei may also be regarded as a type of intelligence or knowledge. In *The Spirit of Zen*, Alan Watts correctly describes it as an insight into the principles, structures, and trends of human and natural affairs, and a practical approach to dealing with them by expending the least amount of energy. This innate wisdom is to be recognized through idleness and acute observation of the flow of nature.

Can the technique or understanding of *Wu Wei* be cultivated? The answer is both *no* and *yes*. First, both Lao Tzu and Chuang Tzu emphatically point out that all intentional attempts to cultivate *Wu Wei* are bound to fail because they are contradictory, like beating a drum in search of a fugitive. Chuang Tzu believes that the *Tao* cannot be captured by concepts or categories because it lies beyond them. Nature follows its own course and laws. It does not consult our books. Humans sometimes regard something that cannot be captured through our concepts as nonsensical or chaotic. But in doing so we fail to recognize that the *Tao* is multifaceted and beyond all definitions. Being beyond the grasp of the network of sense and intellect, the *Tao* cannot be trapped by the step-by-step procedure of a cultivated method.

Individuals who do not impose their will on the will of the *Tao* may at least come close to the pure experience of *Wu Wei*. Both Lao Tzu and Chuang Tzu engaged in meditation and skillfully followed along the fluid path of the *Tao*, moved with its movements, and reverberated with its vibrations. The art lies in merging with the flow of the *Tao*.

Contemplation helps, not in controlling the *Tao*, but by teaching the meditator that there is only one way, and that is the way of the *Tao*.

Though there is no strict method that can be cultivated to make possible the experience of the *Tao*, both Lao Tzu and Chuang Tzu offer certain guidelines:

First, live a simple, ordinary life and enjoy the very fact of existing.

Second, prefer obscurity and solitude; discard desire for name, fame, and recognition.

Third, regard all values, whether ethical, aesthetic, or religious, as relative; do not become attached to relative values.

Fourth, believe in the relativity of life and death, for they are two sides of the same process; get rid of the fear of life or death.

Fifth, abandon the need to win and compete.

Sixth, develop a sense of cosmic humility and realize the emptiness of all values and aspirations; feel your own nothingness and become completely forgetful of yourself.

Seventh, recognize yourself to be like any other human being; be ordinary like other ordinary people. But remember one difference: You are centered on the *Tao*, rather than yourself.

Our usual way of looking at the world and life is biased by our cultural upbringing. This obscures our minds and makes us forget our rootedness in the *Tao*. The seven guidelines help us in two concrete ways. First, they help us recognize that our perspective on reality is conditioned by our culture. Second, they help us to replace our conditioned view with the way of the *Tao*.

Lao Tzu and Chuang Tzu were not concerned with questions relating to the afterlife, but rather with perfection and freedom as they could be experienced within this life span. For them, a perfect being is one who has experienced the *Tao* within and felt identity with the universal reality. A Taoist sage embodies the meditative lifestyle of *Wu Wei*.

Notes

1. Chuang Tzu's view resembles the Darwinian view of evolution. However, the former arrived at it through mystical reflection, whereas the latter, presumably, reached his conclusions on the basis of fieldwork.

Zen Buddhism

ASHOK K. MALHOTRA

HISTORICAL NOTE[1]

Buddhism originated in India in the sixth century B.C. Its founder, Siddhartha Gautama, was born as a prince in a small kingdom in the northern part of India. In his early years, Siddhartha was brought up in the lap of luxury. He lived in palaces teeming with dancing girls and entertainers. He was married to a beautiful princess and was blessed with a son. Siddhartha's father secluded him from the miseries of life and offered him the most luxurious existence. When Siddhartha was finally exposed to the suffering of sickness, old age, and death, he left behind his life of luxury and abandoned his palace, wife, and child. At twenty-nine, he became a recluse. For the next six years he sought enlightenment. Finally, at thirty-five, he became enlightened and thus came to be called *the Buddha* (meaning, roughly, the one who has awakened).

The original ideas of Buddhism were presented in a book called the *Dhammapada*. A sage called the *Boddhidharma* brought Buddhism to China in 527 A.D. There, from the intermingling of the ideas of Buddhism and Taoism, Zen Buddhism was born, and was introduced to Japan during the 12th century A.D. It was quickly incorporated into Japanese culture and has since become a prominent worldwide tradition.

QUESTIONS

This chapter will attempt to answer three major questions. First, what is Zen? Second, what is the nature of *satori*? And finally, what role do *kōan* and *zazen* play in the achievement of *satori*? To answer what Zen is, we must first consider what it is not.

WHAT ZEN IS NOT

First, Zen is not a philosophy. A philosophy, as commonly understood, is a system of thought that presents and develops a theory of reality utilizing the tools of logic and analysis. Zen is not a philosophy, in this sense, because it has nothing to do with logic, analysis, construction of theories, or presentation of doctrines. Instead, Zen is totally illogical, unabashedly synthetic, and completely pragmatic. It has no set principles or doctrines. It is based upon no philosophical books.

Second, Zen is not a religion. Religion typically involves the concept of a god, certain holy scriptures, some rituals and rites, some kind of belief in afterlife, and some notion of heaven or hell.

Zen is silent about God. It transcends the existence or nonexistence of deities. Zen adheres to no rituals or rites. It believes in no moral principles emanating from a deity. There is no belief in life before birth or after death; its emphasis is on life here and now. It does not believe in any heaven or hell. It has no holy scriptures. Zen is unlike any religion.

Third, Zen is not meditation. Meditation is the deliberate concentration of the mind on the object chosen for contemplation. In all forms of meditation, whether they are Christian, Hindu, Jewish, or Islamic, the meditator selects an object, image, or idea as a focal point of concentration. The meditator keeps the mind on the chosen object and pays less and less attention to the distracting thoughts. If meditation is understood in this manner, Zen is not meditation, for there is nothing contrived about Zen. There is no systematic orientation of the mind toward anything in particular; in fact, Zen attempts to dismantle these systematic attempts. It tries to get away from any intentional directedness of the mind. A Zen master will accomplish this by shocking the pupil who raises systematic questions expecting the usual kinds of intellectual answers. Zen is not interested in defining or conceptualizing, but rather in experiencing the essential nature of our mind.

Finally, some critics believe Zen encourages nonaction, and lends support to a life of inactivity of both body and mind. Zen does not use the concepts and categories to experience the inner workings of our being. But it would be a mistake to believe thereby that Zen encourages nonaction or inactivity. Instead, Zen is the most direct action. Through Zen, one comes in contact with the core of one's being. It is a pure action that sees, hears, smells, touches, tastes, and feels ordinary reality in an extraordinary way. It penetrates through the network of concepts and discards them in order to experience reality as it is in itself.

WHAT ZEN IS

If Zen is not a philosophy or religion or meditation or inaction, then what is it? It is almost impossible to come up with a sensible or logical answer to this question because Zen defies all attempts at conceptualization. It is not the kind of thing that can be captured by any set of categories. It is indescribable. Though language is inadequate in offering us an understanding of Zen, it is still possible to point out some of its unique characteristics. D. T. Suzuki calls Zen "the Far-Eastern mysticism which centers on a personal experience of reality here and now." This experience is uniquely simple, direct, practical, pragmatic, and is closely connected to everyday life.

In *The Spirit of Zen,* Alan Watts concurs with Suzuki on the nature of Zen. According to Watts, since we believe Zen is something highly abstruse and hard to understand, we look for it in obscure places. We think that we can find it in the holy scriptures, the sayings of the prophets, or the discourses of men of wisdom. But in actuality the truth of Zen is simple and obvious. It is near us, it surrounds us, it is all around us, and it is in us. The truth of Zen is in this moment and in everybody. It is not to be found in a hermitage, paradise, or celestial realm. It is here on this earth enveloping us all the time. For Watts, the difference between an unenlightened and an enlightened person is that the former is looking for enlightenment in sacred books or the cottage of a hermit, whereas the latter is aware of it in this moment and in himself. When a Zen master was asked about the nature of enlightenment, he answered that it was your everyday thought and your daily life. The truth of Zen resides everywhere: in your thoughts, feelings, emotions, actions, in the murmuring sound of the water in the brook, in the flight of the geese, and in the sound of thunder or the flash of lightning. We are fooled into thinking that enlightenment cannot be real if it is that simple and obvious.

Zen means experiencing reality directly. It is a straightforward experience, uninterrupted by discursive thought. It is an immediate experience of things as they live and move. We do not need doctrines, scriptures, or other external aids to experience this wondrous reality. A student of Zen is deeply involved in this constantly changing and moving process of life. S/he realizes the transitoriness of things, egos, and ideas, and ceases to cling to them. When a student of Zen realizes that nothing can be possessed, s/he loses all attachment to things. Through this sense of dispossession and loss, the student gains a direct insight into reality.

THE NATURE OF *SATORI*

Our usual approach to the world is dualistic. We look at the universe with the help of the concepts of our intellect and are accustomed to viewing the world through contrary or contradictory categories. Our analytical and logical approach to reality is limited. Instead of giving us a glimpse into the nature of reality, our concepts often act as barriers or screens. *Satori* is the acquiring of a new viewpoint on the essence of reality, roughly equivalent to enlightenment. It is a unique nonintellectual, nonlogical and nonconceptual view of the universe and the self: an intuitive insight into the nature of reality that transcends our usual dualistic approach to the world.

Our upbringing in this world is made possible by our parents, who introduce us to our native language and its logic. Social and educational institutions introduce us to philosophical, religious, and cultural values. Our own choices help us develop personal likes and dislikes. All these factors work together to assist us in developing a view of the universe and the self. According to Zen, this dualistic view of reality where the self and the world are seen as two separate entities is an illusionary view which is transcended during the *satori* experience.

Satori can happen unexpectedly. Because it is a simple and obvious experience, it may appear to be totally nonsensical. The ego-bound consciousness suddenly discards its limited conceptual encumbrances and is able to experience the non-egolike self. It is not the consciousness that is altered, but the way it views the world of objects, people, and the self. *Satori* occurs when one relaxes one's hold on oneself by emptying the mind of all its previous contents. Those who experience *satori* feel not only rejuvenated, but as though they have been born again. As a result, *satori* provides a fresh, innocent, and childlike view of life.

KŌAN AND ZAZEN

When our mind is burdened by the concepts and categories of our intellect, it is deluded and confused. On the other hand, when our mind is able to remove its own confusion, clarity dawns upon it and it is able to experience the Buddha-nature. In Zen Buddhism, mastery of the mind is achieved through the use of the techniques of *kōan* and *zazen*.

A *kōan* is, literally, a public document. When discussed in the Zen writings or used by a Zen master, it means a problem or puzzle lacking logical solution, or a question that confuses the intellect. *Kōans* are used to open the mind to its own secrets.

Each mind obstructs itself from gaining this entry into one's real existence. To obtain the experience of the life force within, we must get out of our own way. But it is not easy for an ordinary human being to get rid of this dualistic way of thinking. To challenge and destroy this intellectual mode, Zen masters created *kōans*.

A *kōan* presents a dilemma to the intellect, a choice between two impossible alternatives. A Zen master will give a disciple a *kōan* to work on. The more the disciple thinks about the dilemma presented by the *kōan*, the more s/he will realize that intellect and its logic have limits. After trying all the logical and intellectual tricks, the disciple will realize that s/he has reached an impasse where intellect cannot offer a solution to the problem at hand. This realization is the opening of the experience of *satori*.

Working with a *kōan* is not a matter of passivity or killing of the mental processes. Rather one uses the mind to its utmost capacity and finally comes to the realization that an intellectual search for a clue to the puzzle is futile. Transcending or breaking this barrier of the intellect is the goal of a *kōan*. Once this barrier is removed, a new birth or a new way of seeing is achieved, unencumbered by the categories of the intellect.

A *kōan* is both a teaching as well as a testing instrument. A *kōan* is given to the disciple for three reasons. The first is to encourage contemplation of all the various ways in which the puzzle may be solved intellectually. This active mental involvement helps the disciple develop powers of concentration. Second, as the student wrangles with various intellectual solutions to the impossible problem, s/he reaches an impasse and realizes the limits of human intellect. Finally, through this revelation of the insolvency of the intellect, s/he might be able to gain the experience of *satori*.

According to Suzuki, there are approximately 1700 *kōans* in the Zen writings. There is no special significance attached to this number. One is enough if it helps the student gain insight into the truth of life.

To better illustrate the nature of a *kōan*, two examples are presented below. These, and other *kōans,* are discussed in the philosophical selection by Alan Watts.

1. A long time ago a man kept a goose in a bottle. It grew larger and larger until it could not get out of the bottle any more; he did not want to break the bottle, nor did he wish to hurt the goose. How would you get it out?

2. Here is a man on a tree holding one of the branches in his mouth, but neither clinging to any of them with his hands nor touching the trunk with his feet. Someone at the foot of the tree asks him, "What is Zen?" If he does not answer the question he cannot satisfy the man, but if he speaks, even a word, he will at once fall down to death. At such a moment, what answer would you make if you were he?[2]

Like the *kōan, zazen* is a tool used by the Zen masters to facilitate enlightenment. *Zazen* means, literally, "sitting in meditation." Both *kōan* and *zazen* are needed to achieve the experience of *satori.*

Zazen is a set of meditative exercises designed to take the aspirant from the level of dualistic thinking to the realm of fluid reality. These exercises include physical posture; breathing; psychological control; stopping the movements of the conscious mind; elimination of all movements, thoughts, and images; and being intensely aware of things here and now. During *zazen*, the mind is emptied of its contents and refocused on the present moment.

Each aspect of life—whether it is an action, feeling, image or thought—has to be lived fully and in the present moment. If life is lived according to the dictates of *zazen*, one will find that every ordinary moment will become extraordinary and one will exclaim with joy that if there is any mystical life, then this is it.

Notes

1. Buddhism is covered more fully in Chapter 10. This historical note will provide basic background for those who have not read the other chapter. For those who have, it should serve as a useful reminder.

2. Alan Watts, *The Spirit of Zen.* New York: Grove Press, 1958. Pp. 69–70.

Selections from the *Tao Te Ching*

LAO TZU

Tao Te Ching was written by Lao Tzu in 600 B.C. The book consists of 5000 words and is divided into 81 verselike chapters. There are more translations and commentaries of *Tao Te Ching* than any other Chinese classic. It has exerted profound influence on the Chinese mind and affected the development of Chinese art, culture, religion, and philosophy. It has guided the lives of mystics, kings, and ordinary people.

1. The Tao (Way) that can be told of is not the
     eternal Tao;
   The name that can be named is not the eternal
     name.
   The Nameless is the origin of Heaven and Earth;
   The Named is the mother of all things.
   Therefore let there always be non-being so we
     may see their subtlety,
   And let there always be being so we may see
     their outcome.
   The two are the same,
   But after they are produced, they have different
     names.
   They both may be called deep and profound
     (hsüan).
   Deeper and more profound,
   The door of all subtleties!

2. When the people of the world all know beauty
     as beauty,
     There arises the recognition of ugliness.
   When they all know the good as good,
     There arises the recognition of evil.
   Therefore:
     Being and non-being produce each other;
     Difficult and easy complete each other;
     Long and short contrast each other;
     High and low distinguish each other;
     Sound and voice harmonize with each other;
     Front and back follow each other.

Therefore the sage manages affairs without
   action (wu-wei)
And spreads doctrines without words.
All things arise, and he does not turn away
   from them.
He produces them, but does not take possession
   of them.
He acts, but does not rely on his own ability.
He accomplishes his task, but does not claim
   credit for it.
It is precisely because he does not claim credit
   that his accomplishment remains with him.

3. Do not exalt the worthy, so that the people shall
     not compete.
   Do not value rare treasures, so that the people
     shall not steal.

Do not display objects of desire, so that the
   people's hearts shall not be disturbed.
Therefore in the government of the sage,
   He keeps their hearts vacuous (hsü),
   Fills their bellies,
   Weakens their ambitions,
   And strengthens their bones.

Lao Tzu, Books 1–5, 7–11, 15–17, 25, and 76 from *The Way of Lao Tzu* translated by Wing Tsit Chan. Copyright © 1963 by Macmillan Publishing Company. Reprinted with the permission of the publishers.

He always causes his people to be without
    knowledge (cunning) or desire,
And the crafty to be afraid to act.
By acting without action, all things will be in
    order.

4. Tao is empty (like a bowl).
    It may be used but its capacity is never exhausted.
    It is bottomless, perhaps the ancestor of all things.
    It blunts its sharpness,
    It unties its tangles.
    It softens its light.
    It becomes one with the dusty world.
    Deep and still, it appears to exist forever.
    I do not know whose son it is.
    It seems to have existed before the Lord.

5. Heaven and Earth are not humane (jen).
    They regard all things as straw dogs.
    The sage is not humane.
    He regards all people as straw dogs.
    How Heaven and Earth are like a bellows!
    While vacuous, it is never exhausted.

    When active, it produces even more.
    Much talk will of course come to a dead end.
    It is better to keep to the center (chung).

7. Heaven is eternal and Earth everlasting.
    They can be eternal and everlasting because they
        do not exist for themselves,
    And for this reason can exist forever.
    Therefore the sage places himself in the back-
        ground, but finds himself in the foreground.
    He puts himself away, and yet he always remains.
    Is it not because he has no personal interests?
    This is the reason why his personal interests are
        fulfilled.

8. The best (man) is like water.
    Water is good; it benefits all things and does not
        compete with them.
    It dwells in (lowly) places that all disdain.
    This is why it is so near to Tao.

[The best man] in his dwelling loves the earth.
    In his heart, he loves what is profound.
    In his associations, he loves humanity.
    In his words, he loves faithfulness.
    In government, he loves order.
    In handling affairs, he loves competence.
    In his activities, he loves timeliness.
    It is because he does not compete that he is
        without reproach.

9. To hold and fill to overflowing
    Is not as good as to stop in time.
    Sharpen a sword-edge to its very sharpest,
    And the (edge) will not last long.
    When gold and jade fill your hall,
    You will not be able to keep them.
    To be proud with honor and wealth
    Is to cause one's own downfall.
    Withdraw as soon as your work is done.
    Such is Heaven's Way.

10. Can you keep the spirit and embrace the One
       without departing from them?
    Can you concentrate your vital force (ch'i) and
       achieve the highest degree of weakness like
       an infant?
    Can you clean and purify your profound in-
       sight so it will be spotless?
    Can you love the people and govern the state
       without knowledge (cunning)?
    Can you play the role of the female in the open-
       ing and closing of the gates of Heaven?
    Can you understand all and penetrate all with-
       out taking any action?
    To produce things and to rear them,
    To produce, but not to take possession of them,
    To act, but not to rely on one's own ability,
    To lead them, but not to master them—
    This is called profound and secret virtue
       (hsüan-te).

11. Thirty spokes are united around the hub to
       make a wheel,
    But it is on its non-being that the utility of
       the carriage depends.

Clay is molded to form a utensil,
But it is on its non-being that the utility of
the utensil depends.
Doors and windows are cut out to make a room,
But it is on its non-being that the utility of
the room depends.
Therefore turn being into advantage, and turn
non-being into utility.

15. *Of old those who were the best rulers were*
subtly mysterious and profoundly penetrating;
Too deep to comprehend.
And because they cannot be comprehended,
I can only describe them arbitrarily:
Cautious, like crossing a frozen stream in the
winter.
Being at a loss, like one fearing danger on all
sides,
Reserved, like one visiting,
Supple and pliant, like ice about to melt,
Genuine, like a piece of uncarved wood,
Open and broad, like a valley,
Merged and undifferentiated, like muddy
water.

Who can make muddy water gradually clear
through tranquillity?
Who can make the still gradually come to life
through activity?
He who embraces this Tao does not want to fill
himself to overflowing.
It is precisely because there is no overflowing
that he is beyond wearing out and renewal.

16. *Attain complete vacuity,*
Maintain steadfast quietude.
All things come into being,
And I see thereby their return.
All things flourish,
But each one returns to its root.
This return to its root means tranquillity.
It is called returning to its destiny.
To return to destiny is called the eternal (Tao).
To know the eternal is called enlightenment.

Not to know the eternal is to act blindly to re-
sult in disaster.
He who knows the eternal is all-embracing.
Being all-embracing, he is impartial.
Being impartial, he is kingly (universal).
Being kingly, he is one with Nature.
Being one with Nature, he is in accord with Tao.
Being in accord with Tao, he is everlasting,
And is free from danger throughout his lifetime.

17. *The best (rulers) are those whose existence is*
(merely) known by the people.
The next best are those who are loved and
praised.
The next are those who are feared.
And the next are those who are despised.
It is only when one does not have enough faith
in others that others will have no faith in him.
[The great rulers] value their words highly.
They accomplish their task; they complete their
work.
Nevertheless their people say that they simply
follow Nature (Tzu-jan).

25. *There was something undifferentiated and yet*
complete,
Which existed before heaven and earth.
Soundless and formless, it depends on nothing
and does not change.
It operates everywhere and is free from danger.
It may be considered the mother of the universe.
I do not know its name; I call it Tao.
If forced to give it a name, I shall call it Great.
Now being great means functioning everywhere.
Functioning everywhere means far-reaching.
Being far-reaching means returning to the
original point.
Therefore Tao is great.
Heaven is great.
Earth is great.
And the king is also great.
There are four great things in the universe,
and the king is one of them.

Man models himself after Earth.
Earth models itself after Heaven.
Heaven models itself after Tao.
And Tao models itself after Nature.

76. *When man is born, he is tender and weak.*
   At death, he is stiff and hard.
   All things, the grass as well as trees, are tender
       and supple while alive.

When dead, they are withered and dried.
Therefore the stiff and the hard are compan-
   ions of death.
The tender and the weak are companions of
   life.
Therefore if the army is strong, it will not win.
If a tree is stiff, it will break.
The strong and the great are inferior, while the
   tender and the weak are superior.

The Technique of Zen

ALAN WATTS

Alan Watts is among the most influential philosophers of the twentieth century. He has written many popular books, including *The Spirit of Zen, The Two Hands of God, The Book, This Is It, Myth and Ritual in Christianity,* and *The Joyous Cosmology.* In these books, Watts tries to reveal the underlying unity of human consciousness. His presentation of the complex philosophical and religious concepts of the East in a simple idiom has made these foreign traditions understandable for the layperson in the West. The following selection is taken from *The Spirit of Zen* (1958).

Described in words, Zen has much in common with many other religions and philosophies; the ideas of poverty, freedom, acceptance and direct contact with reality set forward in the previous chapter are found also in Taoism, Vedanta, Sufiism and the writings of many Christian mystics. Though Zen may go somewhat further than other systems in all these things, it is in no way radically different so far as the ultimate spiritual experience is concerned. In its methods, however, it is unique. Whereas the fate of almost every cult is to fall away in time from the spirit of its early followers, Zen has been able to preserve that spirit up to the present day; after more than 1,400 years it has in no way degenerated into mere 'philosophism' or into the formal observance of precepts of which the original meaning is no longer known. There are two reasons for this; firstly, that the criterion of Zen is a spiritual experience so definite that there can be no mistaking it, and secondly, that the early masters devised a means of passing on their teaching which can never be explained away by the intellect—a means which, if put into use at all, can only have one result, and that is this spiritual experience. These two factors are inseparable; the first is known as *Satori* and the second as the *Koan* (pron. *Ko-an*).

Satori is a definite experience in so far as the manner of its coming and its effects upon character are concerned; otherwise it is indefinable, for it is the sudden realization of the truth of Zen. Essentially Satori is a sudden experience, and it is often described as a 'turning over' of the mind, just as a pair of scales will suddenly turn over when a sufficient amount of material has been poured into one pan to overbalance the weight in the other. Hence it is an experience which generally occurs after a long and concentrated effort to discover the meaning of Zen. Its immediate cause may be the most trivial event, while its effect has been described by Zen masters in the most astonishing terms. A master wrote of his own experience, 'It was beyond description and altogether incommunicable, for there was nothing in the world to which it could be compared. . . . As I looked round and up and down, the whole universe with its multitudinous sense-objects now appeared quite different; what was loathsome before, together with ignorance and passions, was seen to be nothing else but the outflow of my own inmost nature, which in itself remained bright, true and transparent.' Another wrote, 'Whatever doubts and indecisions I had before were completely dissolved like a piece of thawing ice. I called out loudly, "How wondrous! How wondrous! There is no birth-and-death from which one has to escape, nor is there any supreme knowledge after which one has to strive." '

Some descriptions are even more vivid than these; in many cases it seemed as though the bottom had fallen out of the universe, as though the oppressiveness of the outer world had suddenly melted like a vast mountain of ice, for Satori is release from one's habitual state of tenseness, of clinging to false ideas of possession. The whole rigid structure which is man's usual interpretation of life suddenly drops to pieces, resulting in a sense of boundless freedom, and the test of true Satori is that he who experiences it has not the slightest doubt as to the completeness of his release. If there is anywhere the least uncertainty, the least feeling of 'this is too good to be true', then the Satori is only partial, for it implies the desire to cling to the experience lest it should be lost, and until that desire is overcome the experience can never be complete. The wish to hold fast to Satori, to make sure that one possesses it, kills it in just the same way as it kills every other experience. But one's own feeling of certainty is not the only test of Satori; the experienced master can tell at once whether the disciple has any doubts, firstly, by his intuition, and secondly, by testing the disciple with a Koan.

While Satori is 'the measure of Zen', because without it there can be no Zen at all, only a heap of nonsense, the Koan is the measure of Satori. Literally the word 'Koan' means 'a public document', but it has come to mean a form of problem based on the actions and sayings of famous masters. It is a problem which admits of no intellectual solution; the answer has no *logical* connection with the question, and the question is of such a kind as to baffle the intellect altogether. Here are some examples:

'A sound is made by the clapping of two hands. What is the sound of one hand?'

'A long time ago a man kept a goose in a bottle. It grew larger and larger until it could not get out of the bottle any more; he did not want to break the bottle, nor did he wish to hurt the goose; how would you get it out?'

'When the Many are reduced to the One, to what is the One to be reduced?'

'Here is a man on a tree holding one of the branches in his mouth, but neither clinging to any of them with his hands nor touching the trunk with his feet. Someone at the foot of the tree asks him, "What is Zen?" If he does not answer the question, he cannot satisfy the man, but if he speaks, even a word, he will at once fall down to death. At such a moment, what answer would you make if you were he?'

To Westerners these Koans may appear as pure rubbish, reminiscent of 'Why is a mouse when it spins?' But it will be noticed that all of these Koans involve one in some kind of dilemma; there is generally a choice between two alternatives, both of which are equally impossible. Thus each Koan reflects the giant Koan of life, for to Zen the problem of life is to pass beyond the two alternatives of assertion and denial, both of which obscure the truth. Thus a less 'nonsensical' Koan is the already quoted, 'Beyond assertion and denial say one word of Zen, or thirty blows for you!' Every Koan must eventually lead to this impasse. One begins by trying to grapple with it intellectually; it is found to contain a certain amount of symbolism and analogy. Thus in the tale about the goose we find that the goose represents man and the bottle his circumstances; he must either abandon the world so as to be free of it, or else be crushed by it, but both of these alternatives are forms of suicide. What purpose is to be served by abandoning the world, and what can we achieve if we allow it to crush us? Here is the fundamental dilemma with which the Zen disciple is confronted, and somehow he must find a way through. The moment he finds it there comes the flash of Satori; the goose is out of the bottle and the bottle is unbroken, for suddenly the disciple has escaped from the bondage of his own imaginary prison—the rigid view of life which he himself has created out of his desire for possession. Thus to the question, 'How shall I escape from the Wheel of Birth and Death?' a master replied, 'Who puts you under restraint?'

Many Western students are under the impression that Zen 'meditation' (i.e. work on the Koan) is a form of self-hypnosis, its object being to induce a state of trance. Acting on this impression, Mr. Arthur Waley has described Zen as 'Quietism', Reischauer as 'mystical self-intoxication', and Griffiths as 'mind murder and the curse of idle reverie' (*Religions of Japan,* p. 255). The exact opposite is the truth; work with a Koan, to be successful, must have none of the passivity of Quietism; as for 'mind murder and the curse of idle reverie', a few days' sojourn in a Zen community would dispose of any suspicion of idle reverie, while the accusation that Zen is 'mind murder' is no more true than the charge that it upsets all morality. For like morality, the mind (intellect) is a good servant and a bad master, and while the rule is for men to become enslaved by their intellectual modes of thought, Zen aims at controlling and surpassing the intellect, but as in the case of the goose and the bottle, the intellect, like the bottle, is not destroyed. For the Koan is not a means of inducing trance as if some kind of trance were the highest possible attainment for human beings; it is simply a means of breaking through a barrier, or as the Zen masters describe it, it is a brick with which to knock at a door; when the door is opened, the brick may be thrown away, and this door is the rigid barrier which man erects between himself and spiritual freedom. When the door is opened at the moment of Satori, the disciple passes not into a trance but into a new attitude towards life which reflects itself in a character of remarkable beauty. These misinformed Western critics must be confusing Zen proper with a schism certainly as old as the time of Hui Neng, the Sixth Patriarch, who remarked that there were some disciples who imagined that all one had to do was to sit still with a perfectly vacant mind, but on more than one occasion he said emphatically that such persons were no better than inanimate objects, than blocks of wood and pieces of stone.

Far from being an exercise in passivity, the Koan involves the most tremendous mental and spiritual struggle, requiring what the masters call a 'great spirit of inquiry'. Thus master Ku-mei Yu writes: 'Once lifted up before the mind, never let the Koan slip off; try to see with all the persistence you find in yourself into the meaning of the Koan given you, and never once waver in your determination to get into the very bottom of the matter. . . . Do not make a guess-work of your Koan; do not search for its meaning in the literature you have learned; go straight at it without leaning on any kind of intermediary help.' Once work upon a Koan has been started a whole mass of ideas will arise in the mind—symbolical meanings, associations, possible solutions and all manner of wandering thoughts. These must be ruthlessly thrust aside, and the more insistent they become, the more intensively must the disciple concentrate on the Koan itself, striving to penetrate the dilemma which it presents. From time to time the master will interview the disciple to find out how he is progressing, and as often as the disciple offers a merely intellectual and logically thought out solution the master will disapprove and tell him to try again. Usually this process will continue for several years, until the disciple eventually reaches a complete impasse; he realizes that every intellectual solution is futile; he arrives at a state where the dilemma of life enshrined in the Koan becomes an overpowering reality and a problem so urgent that it has been compared to a ball of red-hot iron stuck in one's throat. Philosophically, we may understand perfectly that the great problem of life is to get the goose out of the bottle without hurting either, to pass beyond assertion and negation, to find release from the impossible alternatives of overcoming the world by attempting to possess everything, or of letting ourselves be completely ruled by circumstances. But that does not mean that we realize the problem as the most urgent of all necessities. The choice is between asserting ourselves against the world, trying to make all things submit to us, and, on the other hand, giving way entirely to 'Fate', denying our own capacity to achieve anything. Most of us shun the latter and attempt feebly to realize the former, by clinging fast to our mental and physical possessions, hoping gradually to add to their store. And while this first alternative can never possibly be achieved, since the more we grasp the faster do the objects of our desire slip away, the thought of the second fills us with the horror of eternal death. If this ever occurs to us as a problem it is only in a remote and philosophical way; it seems as far off as the Day of Judgement, and since there is plenty of time between now and then we can hope for a possible solution to 'turn up'.

But work with a Koan makes the problem an immediate reality, and when the impasse is reached the disciple is likened to a pursued rat that has run up a blind tunnel, to a man who has climbed to the end of a pole or reached the edge of a precipice in an attempt to flee from a raging fire. It is just when this most hopeless stage has been reached that the masters urge their disciples to redouble their efforts. A way must be found off the end of the pole and the rat must gather all its strength to break through the tunnel walls. In a work called *The Mirror for Zen Students* compiled by the master T'ui-yin it is said, 'As the inquiry goes on steadily and uninterruptedly you will come to see that there is no intellectual clue in the Koan, that it is altogether devoid of sense as you ordinarily understand the word, that it is entirely flat, devoid of taste, has nothing appetizing about it, and that you are beginning to have a certain feeling of uneasiness and impatience.' After a while this feeling becomes intensified, and the Koan seems so overwhelming and impenetrable that the disciple is likened to a mosquito trying to bite a lump of iron, but 'at the very moment the iron absolutely rejects your frail proboscis, you for once forget yourself; you penetrate, and the work is done'. There is no way of explaining this moment other than by saying that it is the time when the fetters of illusion snap asunder at the intense pressure of the disciple's will. The Koan exercise is so devised as to concentrate the mind and stimulate the will to the highest degree, and in its later stages effort will be provoked simply by the in-creasing difficulty of the task. Thus when the final dilemma is faced the disciple will meet it with his entire strength, and as the tremendous force of his will meets with the stubborn resistance of the Koan, something happens; just at the moment of 'impact' when the mosquito jabs at the lump of iron, there comes the flash of Satori, and the disciple realizes that there was nothing in it after all! 'Nothing is left to you at this moment,' writes a master, 'but to burst out into a loud laugh.'

Our only means of discovering the why and wherefore of this experience is to turn to the sayings of the Zen masters themselves, and to see if we can gather anything from their descriptions of the ways in which it came upon them. A good example comes from Hakuin, who describes this last stage of the Koan exercise as follows: 'When the disciple grapples with a Koan single-handedly, he will come to see that he has reached the limit of his mental tension, and he is brought to a standstill. Like the man hanging over the precipice, he is completely at a loss what to do next. . . . All of a sudden he finds his mind and body wiped out of existence, together with the Koan. This is what is known as "letting go your hold." As you become awakened from the stupor and regain your breath, it is like drinking water and knowing for yourself that it is cold. It will be a joy inexpressible.' The important phrase in this quotation is 'letting go your hold'. For if the Koan is taken to be a way of presenting in miniature the giant Koan of life, the great dilemma and problem at which every being is working, however unconsciously, then, in the same way as life itself, the Koan can never be grasped. The Zen masters distinguished between two kinds of phrases (*chü*)—the dead and the living—the dead being those which were amenable to logical analysis and solution, and the living being those which could never be confined to any fixed system of interpretation. Koans belong to the second type, for they share in life's elusiveness and indefinability. Thus when the disciple comes to the final point where the Koan absolutely refuses to be grasped, he comes also to the realization that life can never be grasped, never possessed or made to stay still. Whereupon he 'lets go', and this letting go is the acceptance of life *as* life, as that which cannot be made anyone's property, which is always free and spontaneous and unlimited. The Koan is a way of presenting the central problem of life in an intensified form. For the final impasse of the Koan, of the living phrase, magnifies the impasse always reached by those who try to clutch anything that is alive in their desire that it may be possessed and made to surrender its own life to theirs. Yet they can never take hold of its life; all that they can have is its corpse, which must in time decay also. Therefore the Zen disciple is given something which cannot be killed by definition and analysis; he must try to grasp it alive, and the moment he realizes, finally and absolutely, that it cannot be grasped, he lets go, understanding in a flash what a fool he has been to deny the right of all things to live by trying to grasp them for his own. Thus at this moment he attains freedom of the spirit, for he realizes the suffering inherent in man's attempt to shut the wind in a box, to keep life alive without letting it live.

There are, of course, various degrees of Satori, and in order to reach the highest of these it is necessary to work with many Koans. There are said to be 1,700 of these Koans and though it will hardly be necessary for the disciple to solve all of them before his understanding of Zen is complete, it is exceedingly rare that one alone is sufficient to achieve the final Satori. In the early stages of Zen practice the flash of enlightenment will last only for a few seconds, while as time goes on it will become more permanent, until at last the disciple has a Satori which sweeps away every shadow of doubt and uncertainty. There are certain similarities between Satori and the 'Sudden Conversion' of Christianity. William James gives some remarkable instances of this in his *Varieties of Religious Experience*, and it is interesting to compare them with the records left by the Zen masters. James gives an instance of a man who was trying to pray, and every time he attempted to call on God he felt that something was choking him.

Finally something said: 'Venture on the atonement, for you will die anyway if you don't.' So I made one final struggle to call on God for mercy, with the same choking and strangling, determined to finish the sentence of prayer for mercy, if I did strangle and die, and the last I remember that time was falling back on the ground with the same unseen hand on my throat. . . . When I came to the very heavens seemed to open and pour down rays of light and glory. Not for a moment only, but all day and night, floods of light and glory seemed to pour through my soul, and oh, how I was changed, and everything became new. My horses and hogs and everybody seemed changed.

James shows that in almost every case the sudden conversion is preceded by a feeling of acute despair and wretchedness, somewhat similar to the final impasse of the Koan. He notes that Protestant theology with its emphasis on the fundamental sinfulness and impotence of man lends itself especially to this type of experience. 'In the extreme of melancholy the self that consciously *is* can do absolutely nothing. It is completely bankrupt and without resource, and no works it can accomplish will avail.' There follows the complete surrender of the soul to God, which is in some ways similar to what Hakuin describes as 'letting go your hold'. A French Protestant, Adolphe Monod, speaking of his own experience of conversion, says 'Renouncing then all merit, all strength, abandoning all my personal resources, and acknowledging no other title to His mercy than my own utter misery . . . I prayed as I had never yet prayed in my life.' Many converts speak of the results of this final surrender as giving them an entirely new outlook on life, whereby everything becomes transformed and made full of the Glory of God. Here it is interesting to compare the Zen masters' records of the after-effects of Satori; Hakuin says, 'It is like drinking water and knowing for yourself that it is cold. It will be a joy inexpressible,' while another master already quoted is even more emphatic, saying, 'As I looked round and up and down, the whole universe . . . appeared quite different; whatever was loathsome before . . . was seen to be nothing else but the outflow of my inmost nature, which in itself remained bright, true and transparent.' Another expresses it in a verse—

Oh, this one rare occurrence,
For which would I not be glad to give ten thou-
*   sand pieces of gold!*
A hat is on my head, a bundle around my loins;
And on my staff the refreshing breeze and the full
*   moon I carry!*

(*Trans.* SUZUKI.)

Here we see that something altogether new has been found in the monk's ordinary mushroom hat, his travelling bundle, the breeze and the moon. Again, there is the story of master Yao-shan—

One eve he climbed
Straight up the solitary peak;
Revealed in the clouds the moon he saw,
And what a hearty laugh he gave!

(*Trans.* SUZUKI.)

Once more we are reminded of P'ang-yün's

How wondrously supernatural,
And how miraculous, this!
I draw water, and I carry fuel!

Turning from Zen to Christianity we find something closely akin to this in another record quoted by James:

I plead for mercy, and had a vivid realization of forgiveness and renewal of my nature. When rising from my knees I exclaimed, 'Old things have passed away, all things have become new.' It was like entering another world, a new state of existence. Natural objects were glorified, my spiritual vision was so clarified that I saw beauty in every material object of the universe, the woods were vocal with heavenly music.

But the Zen masters are more subtle and reserved in their allusions to the joy of their new life; for some reason they do not appear to be so serious about it

as the Christian mystics, and only rarely do they speak of their rapture at finding so priceless a treasure. They will describe quite vividly the one moment's flash of illumination which seems to shake the whole universe, but as to what follows they only hint, and speak of it in the most matter-of-fact terms. Thus Chao-pien writes of it as

A sudden clash of thunder, the mind-doors burst
*   open,*
And lo, there sitteth the old man (the Buddha-
*   nature) in all his homeliness.*

And thereafter they refer to their realization in terms of the most ordinary affairs, for their object is to show Zen as something perfectly natural, as intimately related to everyday life, while the Buddha is just 'the old man in all his homeliness'; he has been there all the time, for his home is ordinary life, but nobody recognizes him!

There is a famous Zen parable which fitly sums up this particular attitude to life. It is said that to those who know nothing of Zen mountains are just mountains, trees are just trees, and men are just men. After one has studied Zen for a little time, the emptiness and transience of all forms is perceived, and mountains are no longer mountains, trees no longer trees, and men no longer men, for while ignorant people believe in the reality of objective things, the partially enlightened see that they are only appearances, that they have no abiding reality and pass away like drifting clouds. But, the parable concludes, to him who has a full understanding of Zen mountains are once again mountains, trees are trees, and men are men.

Thus while the main characteristics of Satori and Sudden Conversion are the same, they are approached and interpreted in very different ways. In the first place, Conversion is held to come to essentially depraved Man from an external God, while Satori is the realization of one's own inmost nature. Conversion takes place when something comes from outside and transforms the world, while

Satori is just seeing the world as it really is, for to Zen the supernatural is natural, while to Christianity it is something not inherent in nature at all; it is at certain times brought *to* nature by the Grace of God; heaven comes down to earth and supersedes nature. But in Zen there is no dualism of heaven and earth, natural and supernatural, Man and God, material and spiritual, mortal and immortal, for ordinary men and Buddhas, Samsara and Nirvana, Avidya (Ignorance) and Bodhi (Enlightenment) are the same; it is one's own spiritual realization that makes the difference, and

The mind is its own place, and of itself
Can make a heaven of hell, a hell of heaven.

Therefore the mind is the key to life, for under illusion it creates confusion and when clarified it reveals the Buddha-nature. Thus in Zen, as in almost all the religions of the East, the essential task is to master the mind. This is achieved primarily through the Koan exercise, and to assist this task the Zen masters have evolved a technique of meditation or Za-zen which enables the disciple to relax the body, banish wandering thoughts and preserve his nervous energy so that he may devote his entire strength to the Koan. The elements of Za-zen were probably derived from Indian Yoga, for a similar posture is adopted and careful attention is paid to correct breathing. But the aims of Yoga and Za-zen appear to be rather different, for the Zen masters discourage the various kinds of trance which are considered so important in Yoga psychology. They point out that although certain types of trance may possibly arise, they are not the objectives of the exercise; they declare, on the contrary, that wisdom can never be found by seeking after these static and other-worldly states of consciousness, for the Chi-

nese mind required something altogether more vital and practical. This is not to imply that Za-zen is right while Yoga is wrong, but that different types of mind will find Enlightenment in different ways; what may be right for the Indian is wrong for the Chinese, because the inhabitants of cold or temperate climates will require something more vigorous than the inhabitants of tropical regions, where life finds it possible to carry on with a minimum of exertion.

The aim of Za-zen is simply to release the mind from having to think about the body, and to reduce all distractions so that its whole attention may be directed to a particular task. The periods of the day set aside for Za-zen in a Zen monastery (Zendo) are thus for intense work upon the Koan, although the masters advise that the Koan should be kept in mind at all times of the day, whatever one's occupation and circumstances may be. But it must be remembered that Za-zen and the Koan are not, in themselves, the objectives of the Zen life. They are a form of spiritual gymnastics to assist in bringing about a certain experience, and when that experience has been attained, the devices used for producing it can be discarded. For the aim of Zen is not to retire for ever from the world into solitary meditation; such retirement is only a means of obtaining knowledge, which, to be of any use, must be applied to the Bodhisattva's task of bringing wisdom to all the world. To confuse this objective with sitting in Za-zen and working at Koans is once again to mistake the finger for the moon, thereby defeating entirely the purpose of these exercises. As is said in the commentary to the Cowherding Pictures, 'When you know that what you need is not the snare or the net, but the hare and the fish, it is like gold separated from dross, like the moon rising out of the clouds.'

Zen in the West

THOMAS P. KASULIS

Thomas Kasulis is a past president of the Society for Asian and Comparative Philosophy. He has taught at Harvard, Yale, and the University of Hawaii. The selection that follows is taken from his popular text, *Zen Action/Zen Person* (1981).

Can Zen Buddhism be directly transplanted into Western society today? Can it exert an influence in our society as powerful as the one it has exerted in Japan? If Zen Buddhism is to become a major influence in Western life, it will have to be transformed, not merely transplanted. Japanese culture is sufficiently different from ours that a Western disciple of Zen cannot be trained in exactly the same way as a Japanese. As we have seen, the Westerner generally has a different self-image from his or her Japanese counterpart. Specifically, Western individualism allows one to retain self-identity in radically different settings; in Japan, one's identity tends to be socially defined and it is expected to change from context to context. This does not mean, of course, that no Westerner can ever become an authentic Zen Buddhist. Individual differences may outweigh cultural influence. For a few Westerners, a traditional Zen Buddhist training may be highly effective, but we cannot expect *Japanese* Zen Buddhism to become a major religious force in the West. For similar reasons, perhaps, Christianity has never taken hold in Japan.

Still, the fundamental perspective of Zen Buddhism is acultural: it involves no necessary connection with a historical religious personage nor a faith in a fixed sacred reality articulated in a revelatory text. Zen Buddhism might, therefore, be so transformed as to be accessible to a greater number of Westerners. In Japan, despite the outreach of Zen to the laity (especially Sōtō Zen), Zen Buddhism is still primarily a monastic tradition. We have seen a good reason for this: monastic life establishes the uniquely Zen environment of nothingness out of which the Zen disciple will derive personal meaning. But, as we have just noted, context generally plays a more dominant role in determining personal meaning in Japan than in the West. Thus, in developing its more layperson-directed form, a Western Zen might not only be accessible to more people. It might also adapt to the individualism found in Western secular society.

Even with such transformations, Zen Buddhism may never become a prominent Western religious movement, but it could still be influential. Its very presence in our society can sensitize us to the value of contemplation—especially the Zen form of meditation. Although there might not be many who would characterize themselves as Zen Buddhists, a larger part of our population might someday be exposed to zazen and thereby recognize the prereflective as the ground of all experience. Zazen as a personal practice can also supplement other forms of religious activity. This development has already begun, in fact; many Christian monastic communities participate in zazen retreats, for example. To an ever greater extent, Western contemplatives see zazen as a means of revitalizing their own traditions.

In short, even though Zen Buddhism itself shows no signs of becoming a major Western religious tradition, its distinctive practice of zazen may yet add an important dimension to the spiritual life of non-Buddhists. If the Zen evaluation of prereflective experience were to become a prominent part of the

Thomas P. Kasulis, *Zen Action/Zen Person:* "Zen in the West." Honolulu: University of Hawaii Press, 1981. Pp. 145–154.

Western tradition, how might the Western view of the person be affected? Before speculating on this question, let us first examine Zen's influence on a humanistic movement in modern Japan.

MORITA THERAPY: ZEN HUMANISM IN MODERN JAPAN

As a young man, MORITA Shōma (1874–1938) was interested in Freudian psychoanalysis, but he eventually developed his own, uniquely Japanese, form of psychotherapy. The Zen Buddhist influence on Morita therapy is complex: although Morita himself denied any direct Zen influence and preferred to name Ludwig Binswanger, Wier Mitchell, and Paul Dubois as his predecessors, he did have training in zazen, frequently quoted the great Zen Masters, and used Zen-influenced terminology. In this way, Morita exemplifies what we may increasingly see in the West: a person trained in zazen who does not consider himself or herself a Zen Buddhist and yet develops a humanistic theory with a distinctively Zen perspective.

To appreciate Morita's theory as a humanism, let us see how early Western theories were more scientific in orientation. For brevity, we will consider only the two figures having the most sustained influence: Freud and Jung. In the Freudian model, neurosis arises from repressing the memory of a psychically traumatic event. Freud developed various techniques (dream interpretation and free association, for example) by which the analyst could bypass the ego's defense mechanisms and bring the repressed data to consciousness. The goal of Freudian therapy is, therefore, abreaction: the psychic reenactment of that traumatic event in order to release the tension accrued from it and from the repression of its memory. This allows the patient to recall the previous traumatic event and to *express the painful effect in words*. In a Freudian analysis, the analysand seeks self-understanding: the explanation of one's present neurotic behavior by articulation of a repressed memory. The cure follows upon this reflective understanding.

In short, Freud's psychoanalytic therapy is retrospective and reflective in character. It is retrospective in its goal of making the past available to present consciousness. It is reflective in two respects. From the analyst's standpoint, theoretical structures (ego/id/superego; conscious/unconscious/ preconscious; the symbolism of dreams interpreted as the wish-fulfillment of the libido) are used to explain the patient's behavior and motivations. From the patient's standpoint, the cure comes about through an articulated, conceptual understanding of forgotten events causing the present neurosis. In other words, Freudian therapy arises out of etiology and, to this extent, is scientific in orientation.

Jung's model is also scientific in this regard, although it differs in two major aspects. First, it is prospective rather than retrospective. Second, its scientific model is more organic than mechanistic. Let us briefly examine how this is so. Jung believed the psyche, like any other organism, tends to cure itself if unhindered by external forces. That is, when a neurotic imbalance develops, the psyche has a natural tendency to right itself. This propensity reveals itself through archetypal symbols appearing in dreams, hallucinations, and the imagination. A competent Jungian analyst interprets these symbols in order to reveal the psyche's attempt to establish an equilibrium among thinking, feeling, intuition, and sensation. Hence, Jungian analysis is prospective in seeking that toward which the psyche is developing. Its goal is to eliminate all obstructions to that process.

Despite this divergence from Freud, Jungian therapy is nevertheless primarily reflective. A cure is achieved only through a conceptual analysis of the patient's archetypal experiences. The interpretation is formulated in terms of a previously established theory. While Jung's approach may be more like the organic treatment of a physician and Freud's more like the repair work of an engineer, both are reflective and quasi-scientific in spirit in emphasizing etiology, reflective interpretation, and predetermined sets of heuristic categories. Morita's Zen-influenced form of psychotherapy has a different character, however.

Morita therapy is directed primarily toward a group of hypochondriacal conditions generally characterized as "nervosity" or "nervousness" (*shin-keishitsu*)—the specific symptoms range from headaches or insomnia to fears of interpersonal contact and even a phobia for dirt. The disorder generally afflicts introverted, intelligent, goal-directed perfectionists who are overly self-conscious and critical of their own feelings and thoughts. Morita holds that the self-conscious focus on one's own psychological states is perfectly normal. Trouble begins only when one is "caught" (*toraware*) in this mode and the flow of consciousness is blocked. Some minor malady captures one's attention, becomes a fixation and, consequently, the basis for hypochondria. The more one concentrates on one's symptoms, the worse they become.

A hallmark of Morita therapy is its lack of attempting any *cure*. The goal is to have the patient accept the given without concern for what should be. If one cannot sleep, one does not exacerbate the situation by thinking one *should* be able to do so. Taking the insomnia as a given, one simply goes on with one's affairs. Similarly, one is advised to accept emotions as they arise; one is responsible for actions, not feelings. Morita therapists use the example of jumping off a high diving board. How one feels about jumping is irrelevant. If one is fearful, one accepts that fear and jumps anyway. The fear is "just what is" (*arugamama*), and one does not analyze it for either causes in the past or anticipations of what the future will bring. One just acts. The therapy itself begins with a week of complete bed rest: no activities whatsoever are allowed. One is told simply to think what one thinks and to feel what one feels. Eventually, the patient develops a desire to perform some activity and is gradually given increasingly complex duties (starting with raking the leaves in the garden, for example). Finally, one reaches the point when one can see what has to be done on one's own initiative.

Although this is only a brief sketch, it is enough to show how Morita therapy is related to Zen humanism. This relation has four major aspects. First, the therapy is not scientific in that its goals—self-aware-ness and action—are achieved without passing through the intermediate stage of theoretical self-understanding. Morita therapists are basically uninterested in either etiology or cure. Thus, patients are given no theory through which to understand their neurosis. One is trained to see what is and what needs to be done; then one simply acts accordingly. Second, Morita therapy is present-directed rather than retrospective or prospective. For the healthy person, retrospection and prospection are normal ways of reflecting on one's own activity, but for someone suffering from *shinkeishitsu,* they are ways of becoming caught (*toraware*) in intellection and of neurotically postponing action. Third, Morita ultimately defines the person in terms of action. One learns to see oneself as what one does. In fact, a Morita patient keeps a daily diary—not of feelings, thoughts, or desires, but of the actions one actually performs each day.

Finally, self-consciousness, even as a reflective mode, is accepted as a natural part of human life. What causes suffering, however, is being trapped in self-reflection. The neurosis of *shinkeishitsu* is much like the suffering Zen finds in everyday, unenlightened consciousness—namely, one thinks about thinking and tries futilely to break this cycle by thinking more. Analysis, whether of the self or of the world, can never end; a new distinction is always possible. One becomes decreasingly responsive in one's actions as one understands oneself to be an agent independent of the experiential process. The way out of the vicious cycle is to forget the self and return to what is—*arugamama* or, in Dōgen's terms, *genjōkōan*. Bearing in mind this contemporary Japanese example of a non-Buddhist application of Zen humanism,* we can now return to our

---

* This is not to say that Morita therapy perfectly matches the Zen Buddhist ideal. In the first place, Morita therapy lacks the Zen emphasis on creativity. Moreover, it draws a strong distinction between actions and feelings, claiming success when the patient is able to function again even if the psychological trauma continues. In this sense, Zen Buddhism is different in that it does try to cure the psychological pain as well. In fact, all forms of Buddhism share the ideal of alleviating human suffering.

own situation. How might a Zen humanism be applied to present Western concerns?

ZEN HUMANISM FOR THE WEST

As we noted at the beginning of this chapter, the traditional Western view of the person has suffered from the rise of scientism. In many respects, traditional humanism operated within medieval, scholastic categories. We thought of the person as having a uniquely human essence transcending all physical, contingent characteristics. This essence was considered not only the source of our humanity but also the seat of free will. In short, the traditional Western notion affirmed a *soul,* or at least a spirit. It is significant, however, that the medieval triad of body, mind, and soul has gradually given way to the modern dyad of body and mind. Originally, the term *mind,* as in the German word *Geist,* contained the notion of both mind and spirit, but the thrust of scientism has been to eliminate the spiritual component entirely. The Darwinian argues, for example, that our animal ancestors had no spirit. Hence how could a component so distinctive evolve from the lower species? Cybernetics regards the computer as an electronic mind, the assumption often being that *spirit,* whatever the anachronists mean by that word, is just an intricate function qualitatively no different from ordinary cognitive acts. Behaviorists like B. F. Skinner reduce spirit to complex conditioned responses that, once understood, will obviate the need for humanistic ideals like dignity and freedom. Even more perniciously, these scientific standpoints often reduce not only spirit to mind, but even mind to body. In this regard, the social sciences are losing ground to the natural sciences. To maintain their scientific respectability, they have become increasingly quantitative.

Even the humanities, in self-defense perhaps, have sought ever greater objectivity and scientific distance. In philosophy, for example, there is an emphasis on the logical study of language, and the positivists have suggested that all empirically unverifiable claims should be expurgated from philosophical discourse. In the literary realm, the New Criticism centers on the completed literary document; the author's creative intent and personal circumstances are irrelevant. In the study of religion, the emphasis has shifted from the articulation of religious sentiments to the linguistic analysis of texts, the objective reporting of religious behavior, and the accumulation of historical facts. Even on the popular level, biblical literalism reads scripture like a science textbook rather than as a creative expression of religious aspiration in the light of revelation.

Because many of the basic ideas about the self were thus reevaluated in light of scientific discoveries, an either/or alternative emerged: either we affirm the person as something totally outside scientific understanding (a view taken by some personalists and existentialists, for example) or we let our view of the person be defined totally in terms of scientific understanding (as, for instance, in behaviorism). But does this have to be the case? Is there not a way to reformulate our humanism so that it at once affirms traditional values and also recognizes the truth of scientific discoveries? The Zen humanism we have been investigating suggests such a possibility. While the humanities have increasingly focused on the final product of human activity, Zen is both refreshing and provoking in its emphasis on the source, not the end result, of the human act.

For Zen, body, mind, and spirit are not three substantially different entities; rather, they are three profiles of the person that are determined by perspective. In our culture, the natural sciences focus mainly on the body, the social sciences on the mind, the humanities on the spirit. The natural scientist stands in the physical world and sees the human being as a continuous part of it. Such a perspective understands human activity to be governed by natural laws. The social scientist, on the other hand, sees the human being as *homo faber*—one who has realized in practice the concepts of a given time and place. From this standpoint, the observer tries to isolate the conscious and unconscious frameworks structuring the human world. The humanities center on the creative enterprise itself: the way in which human needs, desires, and ideas take form in different historical and cultural contexts. Another way of characterizing these differences is to say the natural sciences examine the human being as a product (of physical and organic forces); the social sciences study a human product (the social world); and the humanities study human producing (artistic, moral, religious, and philosophical ideals).

Zen *humanism* does not, however, mean the Zen view of the person affirms the standpoint of the humanities over that of the natural and social sciences. Any form of knowledge is reflective and, therefore, of secondary concern. In emphasizing the prereflective ground of all experience, Zen is prescientific and prehumanistic. Thus, zazen might be of interest to a natural scientist for its physiological implications or to a social scientist for its social relevance in Japan. This book is representative of the humanities in its investigation of the philosophical implications of zazen. Still, Zen Buddhism might object to scientism even though it has no quarrel with science per se. Scientism is reductionistic: it claims that the scientific perspective is the only valid one. In Morita's terms, the scientistic view is *caught* in its own conceptualization. Science is capable of discovering great truths about humanity and its world, but any truth achieved through reflection is dependent on context.

As Dōgen pointed out, the ocean indeed is a translucent palace to a fish and a necklace of glittering jewels to a deva in heaven. Given their standpoints, each account is true. Difficulties only arise, for example, when the fish believes that the translucence of the ocean proves the deva wrong in seeing it as glittering. We desire a theory of the world and of the person which is true from all perspectives, but no theory can meet this criterion. We cannot transcend the fact that we are spatially, temporally, culturally, and linguistically determinate. Every reflective truth is an expression not only of what is but also of *how* it is from a specific viewpoint. This is why Zen Buddhism advocates the

context of *mu*. To be freely responsive, to act as the situation demands, one must have no vested interest in a conceptual scheme. Having one's meaning as a person tied to no context, one can express each situation or occasion (*jisetsu*) as it is.

In the final analysis, the Zen person has no *intrinsic* meaning: there is no person at all. As each context arises, however, the Zen person is the response to what is, as it is. The act is an expression in a context; it is the meaning of the Zen person for that time, place, and situation. Grounded in the prereflective base of experience, the Zen Buddhist changes his or her meaning as the contexts change. Hence, the tradition speaks of human freedom as being like clouds or water—continually altering form to fit surrounding circumstances.

For such a Zen humanism to take hold in the West, we would have to relinquish certain beliefs. Above all, we must recognize that no theory can ever explain everything. Every discursive account depends on the context. This notion is easy to accept in abstraction, but difficult to realize in practice. The psychological obstruction is not simply a desire for omniscience, a wish to be God. As the Buddhists point out, the cause of our dogmatism, inflexibility, and suffering is our craving for permanence, especially personal permanence. We want truth to be cumulative so that what is learned as true today will also be true tomorrow, even though the context changes. We fancy ourselves at the center of a fixed and absolute worldview. Our commitment to this ideal of the static self is the source of our anxiety. Change is painful in proportion to our resistance to it. If we cease desiring the permanent, all-inclusive Truth, will we not be flexible enough to express the truth in each situation? Because our resistance to Zen humanism is psychological and practical, not theoretical, to understand Zen Buddhism intellectually is not enough. For Zen to affect the West in any significant and lasting fashion, Zen practice, not Zen theory, must be internalized into our culture. Zazen is central because in it action and being are one: one is what one does. The Zen person is inseparable from Zen action.

In conclusion, if Westerners commit themselves to the practice of zazen (or any other contemplative practice, Eastern or Western, emphasizing prereflective experience), there will be a gradual reorientation in our notion of the person. We will be less comfortable with theories that take the person to be a closed system, whether that system be posed in terms taken from the humanities or the sciences. We will, moreover, appreciate the mystery at the base of experience. This mystery is not an obscure realm like the unconscious: something unfathomable and never experienced directly. Rather, it is a mystery in a more technically religious sense. That is, the prereflective ground of experience is immediately encountered in even the most mundane of experiences, but it cannot be articulated conceptually without thereby limiting its richness. Articulation is by no means *wrong;* in fact, it is an accomplishment of our species as it effects the creative adjustment of the world to our needs, and our needs to the world. But any expression, however true, is limited.

The genuine person—the person who intrinsically has no standpoint—takes a specific perspective in order to achieve an expression of what is. This free act of creation underlies the formulations of both the sciences and the humanities. The goal of Zen humanism is to appreciate the wondrous power of this act while being aware of the limitations of the context which makes the expression possible. To be Rinzai's person of no status, to be Enō's original face, to be Dōgen's primordial person is to be essentially no person, while simultaneously being the personal act appropriate to the occasion.

Kono michi ya	Ah, this path.
Yukuhito nashi ni	With no person travelling it,
Aki no kure.	An autumn twilight.

—Bashō

Stories of Chuang Tzu and Hui Tzu

ARTHUR WALEY

Arthur Waley was an orientalist and poet who translated a number of Chinese and Japanese works. His major books include *Chinese Poems*, *An Introduction to Chinese Painting*, *The Way and Its Power*, and *The Analects of Confucius*. The present selection is edited from *Three Ways of Thought in Ancient China*. The stories contained in this selection are from a book written by Chuang Tzu in the fourth century B.C. Through these stories, the abstract ideas of Taoism are given concrete form.

Hui Tzu said to Chuang Tzu, 'Your teachings are of no practical use.' Chuang Tzu said, 'Only those who already know the value of the useless can be talked to about the useful. This earth we walk upon is of vast extent, yet in order to walk a man uses no more of it than the soles of his two feet will cover. But suppose one cut away the ground round his feet till one reached the Yellow Springs,[1] would his patches of ground still be of any use to him for walking?' Hui Tzu said, 'They would be of no use.' Chuang Tzu said, 'So then the usefulness of the useless is evident.'

Hui Tzu recited to Chuang Tzu the rhyme:

> 'I have got a big tree
> That men call the chü.
> Its trunk is knotted and gnarled,
> And cannot be fitted to plumb-line and ink;
> Its branches are bent and twisted,
> And cannot be fitted to compass or square.
> It stands by the road-side,
> And no carpenter will look at it.'

'Your doctrines,' said Hui Tzu, 'are grandoise, but useless, and that is why no one accepts them.' Chuang Tzu said, 'Can it be that you have never seen the pole-cat, how it crouches waiting for the mouse, ready at any moment to leap this way or that, high or low, till one day it lands plump on the spring of a trap and dies in the snare? Again there is the yak, "huge as a cloud that covers the sky." It can maintain this great bulk and yet would be quite incapable of catching a mouse. . . . As for you and the big tree which you are at a loss how to use, why do you not plant it in the realm of Nothing Whatever, in the wilds of the Unpastured Desert, and aimlessly tread the path of Inaction by its side, or vacantly lie dreaming beneath it?

> 'What does not invite the axe
> No creature will harm.
> What cannot be used
> No troubles will befall.'

Hui Tzu said to Chuang Tzu, 'The king of Wei gave me the seed of one of his huge gourds. I planted it, and it bore a gourd so enormous that if I had filled it with water or broth it would have taken several men to lift it, while if I had split it into halves and made ladles out of it they would have been so flat that no liquid would have lain in them. No one could deny that it was magnificently large; but I was unable to find any use for it, and in the end I

Arthur Waley, "Stories of Chuang Tzu and Hui Tzu" from *Three Ways of Thought in Ancient China* (Garden City, NJ: Doubleday, 1956), pp. 3–9 and 30–32. Reprinted with the permission of Unwin Hyman, Ltd., an imprint of HarperCollins Publishers, Ltd.

smashed it up and threw it away.' Chuang Tzu said, 'I have noticed before that you are not very clever at turning large things to account. There was once a family in Sung that possessed a secret drug which had enabled its members for generations past to steep silk floss without getting chapped hands. A stranger hearing of it offered to buy the recipe for a hundred pieces of gold. The head of the family pointed out to his kinsmen that if all the money that the family had made in successive generations through the use of the drug were added together it would not come to more than one or two pieces of gold, and that a hundred pieces would amply repay them for parting with their secret. The stranger carried off the recipe and spoke of it to the king of Wu, whose country was being harried by the battleships of Yüeh. The stranger was put in command of the Wu fleet, and so efficacious was the remedy that despite the bitter cold (for it was a winter's day) the fingers of the Wu sailors never once grew chapped or numbed, and the fleet of Yüeh was entirely destroyed. The land of Yüeh was divided and the stranger rewarded with a fief.

'The sole property of the drug was that it prevented hands from getting chapped. Yet so much depends on the user that, if it had stayed with the man of Sung, it would never have done more than help him to steep floss; while no sooner had it passed into the stranger's possession than it gained him a fief. As for you and your large gourd, why did you not tie it as a buoy at your waist, and, borne up by it on the waters, float to your heart's content amid the streams and inland seas? Instead, you grumble about its gigantic dimensions and say that ladles made from it would hold nothing; the reason being, I fear, that your own thoughts have not learnt to run beyond the commonplace.'

* * *

Hui Tzu said to Chuang Tzu, 'Can a man really become passionless?' Chuang Tzu said, 'He can.' Hui Tzu said, 'A man without passions cannot be called a man.' Chaung Tzu said, ' "Tao gave him substance, Heaven gave him form"; how is it possible not to call him a man?' Hui Tzu said, 'I would rather say, Granted that he is still a man, how is it possible for him to be passionless?' Chuang Tzu said, 'You do not understand what I mean when I say "passionless."[2] When I say "passionless" I mean that a man does not let love or hate do damage within, that he falls in with the way in which things happen of themselves, and does not exploit life.' Hui Tzu said, 'If he does not exploit life, what is the use of his having a body?' Chuang Tzu said:

'Tao gave him substance,
Heaven gave him form;
Let him not by love or hate
Bring this gift to harm.

'Yet here are you,

'Neglecting your soul,
Wearying your spirit,
Propped against a pile of books you drone,
Leaning against your zithern you doze.
Heaven made you sound and whole;
Yet all your song is hard *and* white.'[3]

When Chuang Tzu's wife died, Hui Tzu came to the house to join in the rites of mourning. To his surprise he found Chuang Tzu sitting with an inverted bowl on his knees, drumming upon it and singing a song.[4] 'After all,' said Hui Tzu, 'she lived with you, brought up your children, grew old along with you. That you should not mourn for her is bad enough; but to let your friends find you drumming and singing—that is going too far!' 'You misjudge me,' said Chuang Tzu. 'When she died, I was in despair, as any man well might be. But soon, pondering on what had happened, I told myself that in death no strange new fate befalls us. In the beginning we lack not life only, but form. Not form only, but spirit. We are blended in the one great featureless indistinguishable mass. Then a time came when the mass evolved spirit, spirit evolved form, form evolved life. And now life in its turn has evolved death. For not nature only but man's being has its seasons, its sequence of spring and autumn, summer and winter. If some one is tired and has gone to lie down, we do not pursue him with shouting and bawling. She whom I have lost has lain down to sleep for a while in the Great Inner Room. To break in upon her rest with the noise of lamentation would but show that I knew nothing of nature's Sovereign Law. That is why I ceased to mourn.'

Chuang Tzu and Hui Tzu were strolling one day on the bridge over the river Hao. Chuang Tzu said, 'Look how the minnows dart hither and thither where they will. Such is the pleasure that fish enjoy.' Hui Tzu said, 'You are not a fish. How do you know what gives pleasure to fish?' Chuang Tzu said, 'You are not I. How do you know that I do not know what gives pleasure to fish?' Hui Tzu said, 'If because I am not you, I cannot know whether you know, then equally because you are not a fish, you cannot know what gives pleasure to fish. My argument still holds.' Chuang Tzu said, 'Let us go back to where we started. You asked me how I knew what gives pleasure to fish. But you already knew how I knew it when you asked me. You knew that I knew it by standing here on the bridge at Hao.'

When Hui Tzu was minister in Liang, Chuang Tzu decided to pay him a visit. Someone said to Hui Tzu, 'Chuang Tzu is coming and hopes to be made Minister in your place.' This alarmed Hui Tzu and he searched everywhere in Liang for three days and three nights to discover where Chuang Tzu was. Chuang Tzu, however, arrived on his own accord and said, 'In the South there is a bird. It is called *yüan-ch'u.*[5] Have you heard of it? This *yüan-ch'u* starts from the southern ocean and flies to the northern ocean. During its whole journey it perches on no tree save the sacred *wu-t'ung,*[6] eats no fruit save that of the *lien,*[7] drinks only at the Magic Well. It happened that an owl that had got hold of the rotting carcass of a rat looked up as this bird flew by, and terrified lest the *yüan-ch'u* should stop and snatch at the succulent morsel, it screamed, "Shoo! Shoo!" And now I am told that you are trying to "Shoo" me off from this precious Ministry of yours.'

* * *

Once when Chuang Tzu was walking in a funeral procession, he came upon Hui Tzu's tomb, and turning to those who were with him he said, 'There was once a wall-plasterer who when any plaster fell upon his nose, even a speck no thicker than a fly's wing, used to get the mason who worked with him to slice it off. The mason brandished his adze with such force that there was a sound of rushing wind; but he sliced the plaster clean off, leaving the plasterer's nose completely intact; the plasterer, on his side, standing stock still, without the least change of expression.

'Yüan, prince of Sung, heard of this and sent for the mason, saying to him, "I should very much like to see you attempt this performance." The mason said, "It is true that I used to do it. But I need the right stuff to work upon, and the partner who supplied such material died long ago."

'Since Hui Tzu died I, too, have had no proper stuff to work upon, have had no one with whom I can really talk.'

* * *

It was not always by dialogue that Chuang Tzu warred with the logicians. Another of his weapons was parody. A favourite method of the argumentative school of philosophy was to take an imaginary case: 'take the case of a man who . . . ,' they constantly say to illustrate their argument.

* * *

'Take the case of some words,' Chuang Tzu says, parodying the logicians, 'I do not know which of them are in any way connected with reality or which are not at all connected with reality. If some that are so connected and some that are not so connected are connected with one another, then as regards truth or falsehood the former cease to be in any way different from the latter. However, just as an experiment, I will now say them: 'If there was a beginning, there must have been a time before the beginning began, and if there was a time before the beginning began, there must have been a time before the time before the beginning began. If there is being, there must also be not-being. If there was a time before there began to be any not-being, there must also have been a time before the time before there began to be any not-being. But here am I, talking about being and not-being and still do not know whether it is being that exists and not-being that does not exist, or being that does not exist and not-being that really exists! I have spoken, and do not know whether I have said something that means anything or said nothing that has any meaning at all.

'Nothing under Heaven is larger than a strand of gossamer, nothing smaller than Mt. T'ai. No one lives longer than the child that dies in its swaddling-clothes, no one dies sooner than P'êng Tsu.[8] Heaven and earth were born when I was born; the ten thousand things and I among them are but one thing.' All this the sophists have proved. But if there were indeed only one thing, there would be no language with which to say so. And in order that anyone should state this, there must be more language in which it can be stated. Thus their one thing together with their talk about the one thing makes two things. And their one thing together with their talk and my statement about it makes three things. And so it goes on, to a point where the cleverest mathematician could no longer keep count, much less an ordinary man. Starting with not-being and going on to being, one soon gets to three. What then would happen if one started with being and went on to being?'

*   *   *

When Chuang Tzu was going to Ch'u he saw by the roadside a skull, clean and bare, but with every bone in its place. Touching it gently with his chariot-whip he bent over it and asked it saying, 'Sir, was it some insatiable ambition that drove you to transgress the law and brought you to this? Was it the fall of a kingdom, the blow of an executioner's axe that brought you to this? Or had you done some shameful deed and could not face the reproaches of father and mother, of wife and child, and so were brought

to this? Was it hunger and cold that brought you to this, or was it that the springs and autumns of your span had in their due course carried you to this?'

Having thus addressed the skull, he put it under his head as a pillow and went to sleep. At midnight the skull appeared to him in a dream and said to him, 'All that you said to me—your glib, commonplace chatter—is just what I should expect from a live man, showing as it does in every phrase a mind hampered by trammels from which we dead are entirely free. Would you like to hear a word or two about the dead?'

'I certainly should,' said Chuang Tzu.

'Among the dead,' said the skull, 'none is king, none is subject, there is no division of the seasons; for us the whole world is spring, the whole world is autumn. No monarch on his throne has joy greater than ours.'

Chuang Tzu did not believe this. 'Suppose,' he said, 'I could get the Clerk of Destinies to make your frame anew, to clothe your bones once more with flesh and skin, send you back to father and mother, wife and child, friends and home, I do not think you would refuse.'

A deep frown furrowed the skeleton's brow. 'How can you imagine,' it asked, 'that I would cast away joy greater than that of a king upon his throne, only to go back again to the toils of the living world?'

*   *   *

Tzu-lai fell ill. He was already at the last gasp; his wife and children stood weeping and wailing round his bed. 'Pst,' said Tzu-li, who had come to call, 'stand back! A great Change is at work; let us not disturb it.' Then, leaning against the door, he said to Tzu-lai, 'Mighty are the works of the Changer! What is he about to make of you, to what use will he put you? Perhaps a rat's liver, perhaps a beetle's claw!' 'A child,' said Tzu-lai, 'at its parents' bidding must go north and south, east or west; how much the more when those parents of all Nature, the great powers Yin and Yang command him, must he needs go where they will. They have asked me to die, and if I do not obey them, shall I not rank as an unmanageable child? I can make no complaint against them. These great forces housed me in my bodily frame, spent me in youth's toil, gave me repose when I was old, will give me rest at my death. Why should the powers that have done so much for me in life, do less for me in death?

'If the bronze in the founder's crucible were suddenly to jump up and say, "I don't want to be a tripod, a plough-share or a bell. I must be the sword *Without Flaw,*" the caster would think it was indeed unmannerly metal that had got into his stock.

'In this life I have had the luck to be fashioned in human form. But were I now to say to the Great Transformer, "I refuse to let anything be made out of me but a man," he would think that it was indeed an unmannerly being who had come into his hands.'

*   *   *

How do I know that wanting to be alive is not a great mistake? How do I know that hating to die is not like thinking one has lost one's way, when all the time one is on the path that leads to home? Li Chi was the daughter of the frontier guardsman at Ai.

When first she was captured and carried away to Chin, she wept till her dress was soaked with tears. But when she came to the king's palace, sat with him on his couch and shared with him the dainties of the royal board, she began to wonder why she had wept. How do I know that the dead do not wonder why they should ever have prayed for long life? It is said that those who dream of drinking wine will weep when day comes; and that those who dream of weeping will next day go hunting. But while a man is dreaming, he does not know that he is dreaming; nor can he interpret a dream till the dream is done. It is only when he wakes, that he knows it was a dream. Not till the Great Wakening can he know that all this was one Great Dream. . . .

Once Chuang Chou[9] dreamt that he was a butterfly. He did not know that he had ever been anything but a butterfly and was content to hover from flower to flower. Suddenly he woke and found to his astonishment that he was Chuang Chou. But it was hard to be sure whether he really was Chou and had only dreamt that he was a butterfly, or was really a butterfly, and was only dreaming that he was Chou.

Notes

1. The world of the dead.

2. The '—less' has dropped out of the original.

3. That is to say, is concerned with the problem of logic, such as the question whether hardness and whiteness exist separately from an object that is hard and white.

4. Both his attitude and his occupation were the reverse of what the rites of mourning demand.

5. Identified nowadays with the Argus pheasant, but used by Chuang Tzu in a mythological sense.

6. The kola-nut tree.

7. Identified nowadays with the Persian Lilac.

8. The Chinese Methusaleh.

9. I.e., Chuang Tzu.

Review and Reflection

Taoism

1. Describe the three concepts of Tao. How are they related to each other?

2. What is *Wu Wei*? What relevance, if any, does the concept have for contemporary life? What is its use within Taoism?

3. What are the distinguishing features of Taoism? Why did it have a special appeal for the Chinese heart and mind?

4. What, according to Taoists, are the characteristics of a meaningful life? Describe the presuppositions and methods of Lao Tzu and Chuang Tzu in this regard. Distinguish clearly between the thought of these two sages.

5. Summarize the main ethical and philosophical themes contained in the stories of Chuang Tzu and Hui Tzu. What can we learn from them?

6. Summarize three major issues described in the selections from the *Tao Te Ching*. Discuss one of them in detail.

Zen Buddhism

1. Describe the concepts of *Zen, satori, kōan,* and *zazen*. Which two constitute the technique of the Zen philosophy?

2. What is a *kōan*? How does it differ from *zazen*?

3. Compare and contrast the Zen concept of *satori* with the Christian one of conversion. In what ways is your analysis similar to the one presented by Alan Watts? In what ways does it differ?

4. Can Zen be incorporated into the West? What, if anything, would have to be changed? How does your answer compare to that of Thomas Kasulis?

5. Identify and discuss, on the basis of the essay by Thomas Kasulis, the humanistic aspects of Zen.

Suggestions for Further Study

Taoism

H. G. CREEL. *Chinese Thought from Confucius to Mao Tse-tung.* New York: Mentor, 1964.

RAY GRIGG. *The Tao of Relationship.* New York: Bantam Books, 1989.

JOHN KOLLER. *Oriental Philosophies.* New York: Macmillan,1985.

STEPHEN MITCHELL. *Tao Te Ching.* New York: Harper Perennial, 1992.

HUSTON SMITH. *Religions of Man.* New York: Harper and Row, 1958.

ARTHUR WALEY. *Three Ways of Thought in Ancient China.* New York: Doubleday Anchor, 1956.

Zen Buddhism

Masao Abe. *Zen and Western Thought.* Honolulu, HI: University of Hawaii Press, 1985.

Eugene Herrigel. *Zen in the Art of Archery.* New York: Pantheon, 1953.

Phillip Kapleau. *The Three Pillars of Zen.* New York: Harper and Row, 1969.

Thomas Kasulis. *Zen Action/Zen Person.* Honolulu, HI: University of Hawaii Press, 1981.

D. T. Suzuki. *An Introduction to Zen.* New York: Grove Press, 1964.

Alan Watts. *The Spirit of Zen.* New York: Grove Press, 1958.

CHAPTER 12

Yoga and Meditation

Although yoga originated in India, it is an empirical method of meditation that has been adopted by many people who do not consider themselves Hindus. Because it is an empirical method, its results can be and have been subjected to scientific scrutiny. This chapter covers the basics of the practice, the philosophy that supports it, and the results of various attempts to assess the validity of its claims.

Introductory Essay

The **Introductory Essay** presents an overview of the nature, goal, method, and accomplishments of yoga. A human being is treated as a combination of material nature and spiritual self. A person may suffer needlessly if, due to ignorance, he or she identifies the material nature with the real self. Yoga provides a step-by-step procedure designed to replace this ignorance with knowledge so that suffering may cease and natural bliss be regained.

Philosophical Readings

Selections from the *Yoga Sūtras* of Patañjali provide an opportunity to experience the original text that forms the basis of the yoga system. The translation is a new one, prepared especially for this book to convey both form and content in a language more easily understood by a lay person. Patañjali condensed the entire system of yoga into 196 statements, called sūtras. Translation is provided for 57 sūtras, approximately one quarter of the total text.

The essay by **William James** presents and explores mysticism in terms of what he calls "mystical states of consciousness." Mystical states are distinguished from ordinary consciousness by four distinctive qualities: ineffability, noetic quality, transiency, and passivity. He discusses various examples of mystical awareness, the possibility of inducing such a state chemically (e.g., by inhaling nitrous oxide), and the epistemic criteria by which we may evaluate the claims of the mystic.

Scientific Reading

Swami Ajaya is a clinical psychologist who argues that meditation can be practiced in ordinary, daily living. Doing so requires one to live in the here and now, get rid of common dependencies and addictions, create a meditative environment, and let the world of nature be the educator. For those who wish to try the experiment, Ajaya offers a daily exercise.

Literary Reading

The selection by **Hermann Hesse** comes from his popular novel *Siddhartha*. The literary hero, Siddhartha, joins a group of samanas (ascetics) from whom he learns the art of fasting, yogic exercises, and meditation. He perfects these arts until he is more proficient than his teachers. Despite this perfection, Siddhartha does not attain the enlightenment he seeks. Hesse's story is thus a criticism of yoga, and a caution to those who regard it as an infallible path to mystical enlightenment.

The Philosophy and Psychology of Yoga

ASHOK K. MALHOTRA

In the media, yoga is often portrayed as a set of physical exercises designed to promote good health and fitness. Faced with a glut of popular literature and conflicting claims concerning yoga, most people have difficulty separating fact from fancy.

In the scientific community, yoga is studied in terms of its effects on the psychophysical state of human beings. For example, scientists have tested claims that the practice of yoga slows heart rate and breathing, decreases anxiety and phobias, and helps relax both body and mind through the production of alpha waves.

There are also those who believe the study and practice of yoga can make possible extraordinary powers. This group is fascinated by the supernatural faculties that they believe an accomplished yogi possesses. A belief in this magical approach has, at times, led individuals to become involved in religious cults. Cult leaders have capitalized on this faith by presenting themselves not only as enlightened beings, but as the sole transmitters of this highest consciousness.

Although each of these approaches finds a source in the yoga sytem, they constitute but a small portion of its philosophy and practice.

PATAÑJALI'S YOGA PHILOSOPHY

The original yoga system was created in India around 500 B.C. The system was presented most completely in a work entitled the *Yoga Sūtras*, compiled by the Hindu sage Patañjali. The text is divided into four parts corresponding to the philosophical, psychological, scientific, and religious aspects of yoga.

Part I offers a philosophical discussion of the definition and goal of yoga. Additionally, it provides an elaborate description of the activities of the human mind and how they may be controlled.

In Part II the psychological description of the mind is accompanied by a discussion of the causes of human suffering. A step-by-step scientific method to perfect both body and mind is presented.

Part III discusses the technique of meditation and the supernormal powers of the practitioner who has achieved mastery of the method.

Part IV teaches the nature of self-realization. The ultimate goal is total liberation of the self from all limitations.

Philosophy, psychology, and religion are intertwined in yoga and provide us with different pathways to unravel the mystery of the self.

YOGA AS A WORLD VIEW

As a system of philosophy, Yoga offers a picture of reality that includes both material and spiritual components. The universe is perceived as consisting of two distinct realities: the *Puruṣa* and the *Prakriti*.

The *Puruṣa* is a pure consciousness. It is immortal, spiritual, and always free. It is also described as infinite existence, knowledge, and happiness. The *Puruṣa* constitutes the true essence of a human being.

The *Prakriti* is the unconscious world. It is mortal, material, and determined. This *Prakritic* world makes up the mind and the body of a human being.

It should be clear from the foregoing that a human being has a dual nature: the real self (the *Puruṣa*) and the material self (the *Prakriti*). If we mistakenly identify our self with the mind-body complex (the *Prakriti*), we may come to believe that our true self is mortal. This belief is the source of all human misery. The goal of yoga is to eliminate suffering by helping us attain discriminative knowledge of the *Puruṣa* and the *Prakriti*. The enlightened person comes to recognize his/her true self as *Puruṣa*. This realization brings contentment, peace, and happiness.

NATURE OF MIND

In the world of material reality, the mind is the subtlest product. It lies in close proximity to the pure consciousness of the self (*Puruṣa*). It is also a crucial link between the Self and the body and makes possible the interaction between the two. Although it is unconscious, the mind has the power to become conscious by reflecting the consciousness of the *Puruṣa*.

Like a mirror, the mind reflects the light of the Self and is thus falsely led into believing it is conscious. Believing it is conscious, the mind looks out at the material world. It becomes aware of objects and their forms and begins a complex process of assigning labels, meanings, and values. An example may help to clarify the process.

Imagine that you have just purchased a new automobile. Your mind assigns the car qualities of prestige, beauty, and value. Regarding the car thus, you then come to identify yourself with it. The qualities that originated in your mind are now seen to be intrinsic properties of the object ("The car is beautiful"). Your mind feels that it possesses the car in the same way it regards itself as possessing your body. With this sense of possession comes a feeling of complete identity. If someone dents the car, you feel hurt. If someone admires it, you feel proud, as though you were the one who had been admired.

In general, when the mind perceives an object, the object leaves an impression or thought wave in the mind. If this impression is pleasant, as was the case with the new car, the mind identifies with it and believes that it is happy. When the impression is unpleasant, as in the example of the dented car, the mind believes that it is unhappy.

Thus all our knowledge—whether of objects, others, or ourselves—consists of nothing more than thought waves or impressions in the mind. If a mind is blurred by values, meanings, ideas, images, and attitudes—or if it is shaken by feelings, emotions, and passions—it cannot transmit the full intensity of the *Puruṣa*'s pure consciousness. As a result, the pure joy of consciousness will reach the individual only partially and discontinuously. To make the mind a perfect vehicle for the expression of this blissful consciousness, mental modifications must be controlled and stopped. Yoga gives us a step-by-step procedure to reach this end.

THE METHOD OF YOGA

The method of yoga consists of eight steps with which an individual can master both body and mind. The steps are arranged in a hierarchical order:

1. *Yama* (five restraints)
2. *Niyama* (five disciplines)
3. *Āsana* (physical postures)
4. *Prānāyama* (regulation of breathing or vital force)
5. *Pratyāhāra* (sense organ withdrawal)
6. *Dhāranā* (concentration)
7. *Dhyāna* (contemplation)
8. *Samādhi* (absorption)

The first five steps are called the *external steps;* they constitute the *preparatory stage*. The final three steps compose the *meditative stage;* they are termed *internal steps*. The external steps are directed toward inhibiting, controlling, and eliminating modifications arising from outer sources. This is accomplished through the development of moral and spiritual attitudes, the control of body and breathing, and the withdrawal of consciousness from the outer world. While the external steps stop the flow of information from outside, the internal steps cleanse the mind of both inner and outer distractions.

External Steps (Preparatory Stage)

Yoga compares the mind to a lake whose surface is turbulent with sense impression, memory, imagination, and emotion. Because we tend to falsely identify our real selves with these mental contents or modifications, the mind is engaged in a constant state of restless disturbance. If it is to perfectly reflect the consciousness of the Self, the mind must be cleansed of such distractions.

1. Yama (five restraints). The first step of the method, *Yama*, aims to control these distractions. *Yama* consists of five moral principles: Do not engage in violence, do not lie, do not steal, do not crave for sexual pleasure, and do not be possessive. Of these, the principle of nonviolence is the most crucial. Nonviolence means not hurting any form of life. Beyond that, it requires love and compassion for other human beings. The other four principles are based on the rule of nonviolence, for lying, stealing, aggressive craving, and possessiveness are blurs that may cause injury to others or to oneself. Only by making these principles a way of life can the yoga student develop the proper moral attitude to pursue the next step.

2. Niyama (five disciplines). *Niyama* consists of five positive rules: purity, contentment, austerity, study, and devotion to the Higher Self. When properly observed, these rules prepare the student spiritually.

Purity means cleansing one's body and mind of all pollutants. One should eat only those foods conducive to health and calmness. All emotions, images, and ideas that cause pain and agitation should be discarded.

Contentment gives one the mental and spiritual balance necessary to the pursuit of enlightenment. One must learn to be content with oneself under all circumstances.

The student who follows austerity learns two essential things. First, a major portion of our life is wasted in enhancing egotistical impulses, biases, and prejudices. Second, we must discard those things if we are to transcend the trappings of the ego. This training in ego denial is a good preparation for spiritual development.

The rule of study involves reading the holy books and observing the lifestyle of saints and sages. Through their example, one becomes sensitive to the working of spirituality within oneself.

Devotion to the Higher Self demands commitment to something more basic and fundamental than one's own being. One should learn to perform all actions in a spirit of detachment.

Yama and *Niyama* build the necessary physical, mental, and spiritual habits that lead to the development of a calm and positive relationship with oneself and others. These steps prepare the individual for the more arduous task of controlling the body.

3. Āsana (physical postures). According to yoga, the body is intimately connected to the mind; a change in one causes a corresponding modification in the other. Yoga offers a number of physical postures (*Āsanas*), the practice of which induces harmony in the circulatory, respiratory, and nervous systems of the body. While these exercises improve bodily beauty and vitality, their ultimate goal is to produce a state of physical calmness and mental tranquility. The practice of these physical postures prepares body and mind for the more difficult task of meditation. The perfection of the body through the *Āsanas* serves as a catalyst for the expression of the light of the spiritual Self.

4. Prānāyama (regulation of breathing or vital force). Connected to the control of the body is the regulation of vital breath (*Prānāyama*). Breathing serves as an energizing force for all bodily organs and is responsible for the health and well-being of both physical and mental functions. Since this vital force links the physical body and the mind, yoga stresses its proper regulation. The yoga practitioner develops voluntary control over the parts of breathing: inhalation, retention, and exhalation. Because breathing is intimately connected to the emotions, the yogi also develops control over them as well.

5. Pratyāhāra (sense withdrawal). Although the first four steps of the yogic method are helpful in restraining the emotions and controlling the body and breathing, the mind is still receiving information through the five sense organs. The fifth step, *Pratyāhāra*, aims at the absolute elimination of these sense impressions.

According to yoga, our awareness of external objects involves four items: consciousness, mind, sense organs, and objects. For knowledge of objects to take place, three conditions must be satisfied: First, consciousness must be directed toward the mind; second, the mind must come in contact with the sense organs; and third, the sense organs must make contact with the objects. Mind is a vehicle through which consciousness is directed toward sense organs and objects. In the *Pratyāhāra* step, a yogi trains his/her mind to withdraw consciousness from the objects and directs it toward the inner contents of the mind. Here, consciousness focuses upon sensations, perceptions, emotions, images, and ideas that reside in the inner world. Whereas our minds are usually conditioned to direct themselves outwardly through the senses, *Pratyāhāra* reverses this and draws the mind inward.

These five external steps (*Yama, Niyama, Āsana, Prānāyama, Pratyāhāra*) cleanse the mind of all distractions originating from outer sources and prepare it for the second, more difficult stage of the yogic method. Now that the mind is oblivious to the influences of the external world, it is in a unique position to meditate upon its own contents. These contents include first, the information retained and modified by memory and imagination, and second, the awareness that this information belongs to oneself. The final three steps of the yogic method aim to control and eventually even eliminate these mental contents.

Internal Steps (Meditative Stage)

The internal steps of the yogic method are concentration (*dhāranā*), contemplation (*dhyāna*), and absorption (*samādhi*). Although each of these constitutes a stage of meditation, they differ in terms of intensity.

6. Dhāranā (concentration). Concentration is the lowest level of meditation. When concentration begins, the body comes to a halt, respiration is stilled, and the mind is freed from distractions. Unhindered by external disturbances, the mind takes an inward journey during which the individual sees objects and hears sounds that are the product of his/her own memory and imagination. In other words, they are mental constructs rather than physical entities.

The individual deliberately fixes his/her mind on one idea, letting other images glide by, paying no attention to them. The more the practitioner is able to keep his/her mind on the chosen mental area, the better is his/her concentration. With constant practice, an individual requires less and less effort to focus his mind within a limited mental sphere. When the frequency of distraction is reduced to zero, the practitioner moves to the next stage of meditation.

7. Dhyāna (contemplation). In contemplation, the mind can immediately focus on any mental image and confine it as long as it wishes without interruptions from other contents. The mind, therefore, gets to know the object in its entirety. There still remains one important obstacle, however: the mind's awareness of itself as a subject meditating upon an object.

8. Samādhi (absorption). The ultimate goal in meditation is reached during the stage of absorption, when the individual transcends her/his ego sense and achieves an intuitive revelation in which s/he becomes her/his real Self—the *Puruṣa*. This highest stage has been described variously as self-realization, divine madness, and mystical ecstasy. The fully realized yogi crosses the ordinary world of perceptions and concepts to experience the spark of divinity that lies within the core of her/his being. The experience of the immortal or *Puruṣic* self is one of infinite existence, consciousness, and bliss, comparable to the attainment of freedom from all limitations. For a practitioner of yoga, this ultimate freedom constitutes salvation.

Mystical Accomplishments and Supernormal Powers

It has often been claimed that an accomplished yogi develops various supernormal powers. The first five steps of the method have been held to induce extraordinary strength, perfect the body and the sense organs, and increase resistance to disease. By mastering the internal meditative steps a yogi is believed to achieve a state of expanded consciousness and possession of mystical powers. These may include the ability to levitate, become invisible, or comprehend the language of animals.

Not surprisingly, scientists have been skeptical regarding the existence of such powers. It was only when teachers and students of meditation offered themselves as subjects for scientific study that scientists began to take the claims more seriously.

Two innovative studies by Therese Brosse (1937) and M. A. Wenger and B. K. Bagchi (1957) focused upon the physiological effects of yoga meditation. Their research revealed that yogis were able to decrease heartbeat and rate of respiration. Other studies have tested the effects of meditation on the social behavior of the practitioner. They reveal significant changes in the development of empathy, openness to experience, self-confidence, reduction of anxiety, phobias, stress, and drug abuse.

In 1961, B. K. Ananda, G. S. Chinna, and B. Singh collaborated to study claims made by yogis that they were unaffected by internal or external stimuli and could remain in a state of extended relaxation. The investigators focused upon the electroencephalographic study of the brain activity of two groups of yogis. One group, during the practice of meditation, was exposed to photic, auditory, thermal, and vibrational stimuli. The second group had developed an unusually high pain threshold to cold water. The experimenters observed well-marked alpha activity (indicating a deep state of relaxation) in both groups. This activity during meditation was unhindered by sensory stimuli. Two yogis who could keep their hands immersed in ice water showed persistent alpha activity both before and during meditation, indicating no discomfort. At a minimum, their research produces strong support for the claim that yoga meditation facilitates changes in the body and brain of the practitioner.

Drs. H. Benson and R. Wallace studied practitioners who used the mantra technique popularized by transcendental meditation. They concluded that this form of meditation brought about significant physical changes and made possible an altered state of consciousness. Wallace described the state as "hypermetabolic": complete relaxation different from wakeful, dreaming, and sleeping states of consciousness. Thus their research not only corroborates claims of physiological effects, but documents a level of consciousness that until recently theologians and religious scholars tended to discuss in predominantly mystical terms.

Still, research on meditation has been limited. Most highly trained yogis have never been involved in a scientific study. Moreover, the current state of technology is inadequate to measure the complex levels of consciousness attained by masters of meditation. What of the yoga practitioner who claims that he can remember his past lives, can read other people's minds, and has the power to levitate? Are we to disregard these assertions as fictitious simply because they have not yet been substantiated scientifically? Such claims may never come under scientific scrutiny. But it is equally possible that future research will be able to demonstrate conclusively the truth or falsity of these astounding claims.

Selections from the *Yoga Sūtras*

PATAÑJALI

TRANSLATED BY ASHOK K. MALHOTRA

The *Yoga Sūtras* were compiled by the Indian Sage Patañjali, circa 500 b.c. Since Indian thinkers preferred oral communication to writing, they created a unique method to memorize the philosophical and religious books. A *sūtra* is a statement containing the gist of an idea or a theory. Patañjali condensed the entire system of yoga into 196 sūtras. To further assist understanding and memorization, the *Yoga Sūtras* text is divided into four parts:

Part I	*Samādhipāda*
Part II	*Sādhanapāda*
Part III	*Vibhūtipāda*
Part IV	*Kaivalyapāda*

A brief summary of each part is provided below. New translations have been prepared to help convey a sense of form as well as content. The process of numbering *sūtras* facilitates scholarly reference, and may assist the process of memorization.

PART I: *SAMĀDHIPĀDA* (TRANCE AS THE GOAL OF YOGA)

This part consists of 51 sutras and deals with the goal of yoga, the impediments to enlightenment, and the nature of concentration or trance.

SŪTRAS

No. 1   Here now begins the study of yoga.

No. 2   Yoga is the restraint and stoppage of all mental modifications.

No. 3   Once these modifications are brought under control, the seer is able to experience his/her real nature.

No. 4   When these modifications are not restrained, a person identifies his/her real nature with changes in the mind.

No. 5   There are five kinds of mental modifications. They are both painful and not painful.

No. 6   The five modifications are: right knowledge, wrong knowledge, sleep, imagination, and memory.

No. 7   Perception, inference, and verbal testimony constitute right knowledge.

No. 8   An awareness that lacks discrimination is wrong knowledge.

No. 9   An awareness where words do not correspond to any substantial reality is imagination.

No. 10   An awareness that lacks any mental content is sleep.

No. 11   An awareness where a previously experienced mental image is recalled is called memory.

No. 12   Through practice and nonattachment, these mental modifications can be controlled.

No. 13   Disciplining these modifications with the help of continuous effort is called practice.

No. 14   Practice becomes well established when undertaken devotedly for a long time.

No. 15   Nonattachment results when one stops seeking objects and eradicates the will to appropriate them.

No. 16   The awareness of the real self results in the highest kind of detachment. Here one renounces attachment to the qualities that make up the material self.

No. 17   The first kind of trance is accompanied by philosophical curiosity, meditative discrimination, joy, and sense of the Higher Self.

No. 18   In the second kind of trance, all manifested mental modifications are eliminated. Mind retains only the unmanifested ones.

No. 19   When there is no nonattachment in the trance, a student can get entangled in the natural world and what lies beyond the natural.

No. 20   Trance is obtained by some through faith, energy, memory, concentration, and discernment.

No. 21   Those who pursue it with abundance of energy are successful in obtaining the trance.

No. 22   The success of a yoga student will depend on whether the means followed are easy, difficult, or intense.

No. 23   Trance is also possible by devotion to the higher self or *Iswara*.

No. 24   This Higher Self is a special being who has transcended all desires, sufferings, and effects of action.

No. 25   The knowledge that is a mere seed in all of us becomes infinite in this Higher Self.

No. 26   This Self is the eternal and the highest teacher.

No. 27   The Higher Self reveals itself through *OM*.

No. 28   To reach this Higher Self, one needs to repeat and concentrate on *OM*.

No. 29   Through this, one removes all hindrances and learns the art of studying the world within.

PART II: *SĀDHANAPĀDA* (METHOD OF YOGA)

This part consists of 55 sutras and focuses on two aspects of the yoga method. First, the *Kriyā Yoga* is offered as a preparatory method. Its goal is to get rid of the pain-carrying obstructions and prepare the yogi for a trance. The other method is called the *Ashtānga Yoga*. It is more difficult than the *Kriyā Yoga*. It consists of eight steps that aim at accomplishing total liberation or salvation.

Kriyā Yoga

SŪTRAS

No. 1   Austerity, introspection, and ego surrender constitute the yoga of action (*Kriyā Yoga*).

No. 2   This yoga prepares one for trance by getting rid of afflictions.

No. 3   The afflictions are ignorance, egoism, attachment, repulsion, and the fear of death.

No. 5   Ignorance is mistaking the noneternal for the eternal; the nonreal for the real; the painful for the pleasurable; and the nonself for the self.

No. 6   Egoism results when the seen and the power of seeing are identified.

No. 7   Attachment is intense seeking after pleasure.

No. 8   Repulsion is intense aversion from pain.

No. 9   Fear of death is intense clinging to life.

Ashtānga Yoga

SŪTRAS

No. 29   By steadily following the eight steps of the yoga method, one's ignorance is destroyed and enlightenment or discriminative knowledge is gained.

No. 30   Restraint, discipline, physical posture, regulation of vital force, sense-organ withdrawal, concentration, contemplation, and absorption are the steps of yoga.

No. 31   The restraints (*Yama*) are nonviolence, nonlying, nonstealing, noncraving for sexual pleasure, and nonpossessiveness.

No. 32   The disciplines (*Niyamna*) are purity, contentment, austerity, introspection, and ego surrender.

No. 46   Posture (*Āsana*) should be firm and easy.

No. 49   The regulation of the vital force (*Prānā-yama*) is the next step.

No. 54   In the *Pratyāhāra* step, the senses are withdrawn from the objects and are directed inward.

No. 55   By so doing, the senses are brought under full control.

PART III: *VIBHŪTIPĀDA* (ACCOMPLISHMENTS)

The 54 sūtras in this part discuss the three steps of meditation as well as the powers obtained through the yogic discipline.

The Three Meditative Steps

SŪTRAS

No. 1   *Dhāranā* is a steady concentration of the mind on an object.

No. 2   *Dhyāna* is the uninterrupted flow of consciousness toward an object.

No. 3   *Samādhi* is the total absorption of consciousness into an object where the self-awareness is completely obliterated.

No. 4   When taken together, these three steps are called *Samyama* (one-pointedness).

Powers Obtained Through Yogic Discipline

When *Samyama* (one-pointedness) is directed toward an object, person, or idea, the yogi experiences extraordinary powers regarding their nature. The sutras that follow provide only a few examples of the many powers that are claimed to result from the correct application of *Samyama*.

SŪTRAS

No. 23   When *Samyama* is directed toward the power of an elephant, one attains these powers.

No. 25   When directed toward the sun, one obtains the knowledge of the world.

No. 26   When directed toward the moon, one obtains the knowledge of the starry heavens.

No. 27   When directed toward the polestar, one obtains the knowledge of the movements of the stars.

No. 28   When directed toward the navel plexus, the knowledge of the entire body is revealed.

No. 29   When directed toward the throat, one feels no hunger or thirst.

No. 33   When directed toward the heart, one achieves the knowledge of the mind.

PART IV: *KAIVALYAPĀDA* (TOTAL LIBERATION OR SALVATION)

This is the shortest of the four parts. It consists of only 34 sūtras. The main concern is with the nature of *Kaivalya* (total liberation or salvation). Here the power of consciousness returns to its own source.

Mysticism

WILLIAM JAMES

William James (1842–1910) is often regarded as America's greatest philosopher and psychologist. He wrote the first *Introduction to Psychology,* set up the first psychology laboratory, and founded the philosophical movement known as *pragmatism.* His many varied interests included not only philosophy and psychology, but also religion and mysticism. The selection that follows is edited from his popular book *The Varieties of Religious Experience: A Study in Human Nature* (1902). Other works by James include *Some Problems of Philosophy, The Principles of Psychology, Essays in Radical Empiricism, The Meaning of Truth, The Will to Believe, A Pluralistic Universe,* and "The Moral Equivalent of War."

Over and over again in these lectures I have raised points and left them open and unfinished until we should have come to the subject of Mysticism. Some of you, I fear may have smiles as you noted my reiterated postponements. But now the hour has come when mysticism must be faced in good earnest, and those broken threads wound up together. One may say truly, I think, that personal religious experience has its root and centre in mystical states of consciousness; so for us, who in these lectures are treating personal experience as the exclusive subject of our study, such states of consciousness ought to form the vital chapter from which the other chapters get their light. Whether my treatment of mystical states will shed more light or darkness, I do not know, for my own constitution shuts me out from their enjoyment almost entirely, and I can speak of them only at second hand. But though forced to look upon the subject so externally, I will be as objective and receptive as I can; and I think I shall at least succeed in convincing you of the reality of the states in question, and of the paramount importance of their function.

First of all, then, I ask, What does the expression 'mystical states of consciousness' mean? How do we part off mystical states from other states?

The words 'mysticism' and 'mystical' are often used as terms of mere reproach, to throw at any opinion which we regard as vague and vast and sentimental, and without a base in either facts or logic. For some writers a 'mystic' is any person who believes in thought-transference, or spirit-return. Employed in this way the word has little value: there are too many less ambiguous synonyms. So, to keep it useful by restricting it, I will do what I did in the case of the word 'religion,' and simply propose to you four marks which, when an experience has them, may justify us in calling it mystical for the purpose of the present lectures. In this way we shall save verbal disputation, and the recriminations that generally go therewith.

1. Ineffability.—The handiest of the marks by which I classify a state of mind as mystical is negative. The subject of it immediately says that it defies expression, that no adequate report of its contents can be given in words. It follows from this that its

William James, "Mysticism" from Lectures XVI and XVII of *The Varieties of Religious Experience,* found in *The Essential Writings of William James,* edited by Bruce W. Wilshire (Albany, NY: SUNY Press, 1984), pp. 241–251.

quality must be directly experienced; it cannot be imparted or transferred to others. In this peculiarity mystical states are more like states of feeling than like states of intellect. No one can make clear to another who has never had a certain feeling, in what the quality or worth of it consists. One must have musical ears to know the value of a symphony; one must have been in love one's self to understand a lover's state of mind. Lacking the heart or ear, we cannot interpret the musician or the lover justly, and are even likely to consider him weak-minded or absurd. The mystic finds that most of us accord to his experiences an equally incompetent treatment.

2. Noetic quality.—Although so similar to states of feeling, mystical states seem to those who experience them to be also states of knowledge. They are states of insight into depths of truth unplumbed by the discursive intellect. They are illuminations, revelations, full of significance and importance, all inarticulate though they remain; and as a rule they carry with them a curious sense of authority for after-time.

These two characters will entitle any state to be called mystical, in the sense in which I use the word. Two other qualities are less sharply marked, but are usually found. These are:

3. Transiency.—Mystical states cannot be sustained for long. Except in rare instances, half an hour, or at most an hour or two, seems to be the limit beyond which they fade into the light of common day. Often, when faded, their quality can but imperfectly be reproduced in memory; but when they recur it is recognized; and from one recurrence to another it is susceptible of continuous development in what is felt as inner richness and importance.

4. Passivity.—Although the oncoming of mystical states may be facilitated by preliminary voluntary operations, as by fixing the attention, or going through certain bodily performances, or in other ways which manuals of mysticism prescribe; yet when the characteristic sort of consciousness once has set in, the mystic feels as if his own will were in abeyance, and indeed sometimes as if he were grasped and held by a superior power. This latter pecularity connects mystical states with certain definite phenomena of secondary or alternative personality, such as prophetic speech, automatic writing, or the mediumistic trance. When these latter conditions are well pronounced, however, there may be no recollection whatever of the phenomenon, and it may have no significance for the subject's usual inner life, to which, as it were, it makes a mere interruption. Mystical states, strictly so called, are never merely interruptive. Some memory of their content always remains, and a profound sense of their importance. They modify the inner life of the subject between the times of their recurrence. Sharp divisions in this region are, however, difficult to make, and we find all sorts of gradations and mixtures.

These four characteristics are sufficient to mark out a group of states of consciousness peculiar enough to deserve a special name and to call for careful study. Let it then be called the mystical group.

Our next step should be to gain acquaintance with some typical examples. Professional mystics at the height of their development have often elaborately organized experiences and a philosophy based thereupon. But you remember what I said in my first lecture: Phenomena are best understood when placed within their series, studied in their germ and in their over-ripe decay, and compared with their exaggerated and degenerated kindred. The range of mystical experience is very wide, much too wide for us to cover in the time at our disposal. Yet the method of serial study is so essential for interpretation that if we really wish to reach conclusions we must use it. I will begin, therefore, with phenomena which claim no special religious significance, and end with those of which the religious pretensions are extreme.

The simplest rudiment of mystical experience would seem to be that deepened sense of the significance of a maxim or formula which occasionally sweeps over one. "I've heard that said all my life," we exclaim, "but I never realized its full meaning until now." "When a fellow-monk," said Luther, "one day repeated the words of the Creed: 'I believe in the forgiveness of sins,' I saw the Scripture in an entirely new light; and straightway I felt as if I were born anew. It was as if I had found the door of paradise thrown wide open."[1] This sense of deeper significance is not confined to rational propositions. Single words,[2] and conjunctions of words, effects of light on land and sea, odors and musical sounds, all bring it when the mind is tuned aright. Most of us can remember the strangely moving power of passages in certain poems read when we were young, irrational doorways as they were through which the mystery of fact, the wildness and the pang of life, stole into our hearts and thrilled them. The words have now perhaps become mere polished surfaces for us; but lyric poetry and music are alive and significant only in proportion as they fetch these vague vistas of a life continuous with our own, beckoning and inviting, yet ever eluding our pursuit. We are alive or dead to the eternal inner message of the arts according as we have kept or lost this mystical susceptibility.

A more pronounced step forward on the mystical ladder is found in an extremely frequent phenomenon, that sudden feeling, namely, which sometimes sweeps over us, of having 'been here before,' as if at some indefinite past time, in just this place, with just these people, we were already saying just these things. As Tennyson writes:

> *Moreover, something is or seems,*
> *That touches me with mystic gleams,*
> *Like glimpses of forgotten dreams—*
> *Of something felt, like something here;*
> *Of something done, I know not where;*
> *Such as no language may declare.*[3]

Sir James Crichton-Browne has given the technical name of 'dreamy states' to these sudden invasions of vaguely reminiscent consciousness. They bring a sense of mystery and of the metaphysical duality of things, and the feeling of an enlargement of perception which seems imminent but which never completes itself. In Dr. Crichton-Browne's opinion they connect themselves with the perplexed and scared disturbances of self-consciousness which occasionally precede epileptic attacks. I think that this learned alienist takes a rather absurdly alarmist view of an intrinsically insignificant phenomenon. He follows it along the downward ladder, to insanity; our path pursues the upward ladder chiefly. The divergence shows how important it is to neglect no part of a phenomenon's connections, for we make it appear admirable or dreadful according to the context by which we set it off.

Somewhat deeper plunges into mystical consciousness are met with in yet other dreamy states. Such feelings as these which Charles Kingsley describes are surely far from being uncommon, especially in youth:

> When I walk the fields, I am oppressed now and then with an innate feeling that everything I see has a meaning, if I could but understand it. And this feeling of being surrounded with truths which I cannot grasp amounts to indescribable awe sometimes. . . . Have you not felt that your real soul was imperceptible to your mental vision, except in a few hallowed moments?[4]

Nitrous oxide and ether, especially nitrous oxide, when sufficiently diluted with air, stimulate the mystical consciousness in an extraordinary degree. Depth beyond depth of truth seems revealed to the inhaler. This truth fades out, however, or escapes, at the moment of coming to; and if any words remain over in which it seemed to clothe itself, they prove to be the veriest nonsense. Nevertheless, the sense of a profound meaning having been there persists; and I know more than one person who is persuaded that in the nitrous oxide trance we have a genuine metaphysical revelation.

Some years ago I myself made some observations on this aspect of nitrous oxide intoxication, and reported them in print.* One conclusion was forced upon my mind at that time, and my impression of its truth has ever since remained unshaken. It is that our normal waking consciousness, rational consciousness as we call it, is but one special type of consciousness, whilst all about it, parted from it by the filmiest of screens, there lie potential forms of consciousness entirely different. We may go through life without suspecting their existence; but apply the requisite stimulus, and at a touch they are there in all their completeness, definite types of mentality which probably somewhere have their field of application and adaptation. No account of the universe in its totality can be final which leaves these other forms of consciousness quite disregarded. How to regard them is the question—for they are so discontinuous with ordinary consciousness. Yet they may determine attitudes though they cannot furnish formulas, and open a region though they fail to give a map. At any rate, they forbid a premature closing of our accounts with reality. Looking back on my own experiences, they all converge towards a kind of insight to which I cannot help ascribing some metaphysical significance. The keynote of it is invariably a reconciliation. It is as if the opposites of the world, whose contradictoriness and conflict make all our difficulties and troubles, were melted into unity. Not only do they, as contrasted species, belong to one and the same genus, but *one of the species,* the nobler and better one, *is itself the genus, and so soaks up and absorbs its opposite into itself.* This is a dark saying, I know, when thus expressed in terms of common logic, but I cannot wholly escape from its authority. I feel as if it must mean something, something like what the hegelian philosophy means, if one could only lay hold of it more clearly. Those who have ears to hear, let them hear; to me the living sense of

---

* An addendum to "On Some Hegelisms," *The Will to Believe,* 294 ff. [B.W.]

its reality only comes in the artificial mystic state of mind. . . .

*   *   *

In mystical literature such self-contradictory phrases as 'dazzling obscurity,' 'whispering silence,' 'teeming desert,' are continually met with. They prove that not conceptual speech, but music rather, is the element through which we are best spoken to by mystical truth. Many mystical scriptures are indeed little more than musical compositions. . . .

*   *   *

. . . Music gives us ontological messages which non-musical criticism is unable to contradict, though it may laugh at our foolishness in minding them. There is a verge of the mind which these things haunt; and whispers therefrom mingle with the operations of our understanding, even as the waters of the infinite ocean send their waves to break among the pebbles that lie upon our shores. . . .

*   *   *

My next task is to inquire whether we can invoke it as authoritative. Does it furnish any *warrant for the truth* of the twice-bornness and supernaturality and pantheism which it favors? I must give my answer to this question as concisely as I can.

In brief my answer is this—and I will divide it into three parts:

(1) Mystical states, when well developed, usually are, and have the right to be, absolutely authoritative over the individuals to whom they come.

(2) No authority emanates from them which should make it a duty for those who stand outside of them to accept their revelations uncritically.

(3) They break down the authority of the non-mystical or rationalistic consciousness, based upon the understanding and the senses alone. They show it to be only one

kind of consciousness. They open out the possibility of other orders of truth, in which, so far as anything in us vitally responds to them, we may freely continue to have faith.

I will take up these points one by one.

1.

As a matter of psychological fact, mystical states of a well-pronounced and emphatic sort *are* usually authoritative over those who have them. They have been 'there,' and know. It is vain for rationalism to grumble about this. If the mystical truth that comes to a man proves to be a force that he can live by, what mandate have we of the majority to order him to live in another way? We can throw him into prison or a madhouse, but we cannot change his mind—we commonly attach it only the more stubbornly to its beliefs. It mocks our utmost efforts, as a matter of fact, and in point of logic it absolutely escapes our jurisdiction. Our own more 'rational' beliefs are based on evidence exactly similar in nature to that which mystics quote for theirs. Our senses, namely, have assured us of certain states of fact; but mystical experiences are as direct perceptions of fact for those who have them as any sensations ever were for us. The records show that even though the five senses be in abeyance in them, they are absolutely sensational in their epistemological quality, if I may be pardoned the barbarous expression—that is, they are face to face presentations of what seems immediately to exist.

The mystic is, in short, *invulnerable*, and must be left, whether we relish it or not, in undisturbed enjoyment of his creed. Faith, says Tolstoy, is that by which men live. And faith-state and mystic-state are practically convertible terms.

2.

But I now proceed to add that mystics have no right to claim that we ought to accept the deliverance of their peculiar experiences, if we are ourselves outsiders and feel no private call thereto. The utmost they can ever ask of us in this life is to admit that they establish a presumption. They form a consensus and have an unequivocal outcome; and it would be odd, mystics might say, if such a unanimous type of experience should prove to be altogether wrong. At bottom, however, this would only be an appeal to numbers, like the appeal of rationalism the other way; and the appeal to numbers has no logical force. If we acknowledge it, it is for 'suggestive,' not for logical reasons: we follow the majority because to do so suits our life.

But even this presumption from the unanimity of mystics is far from being strong. In characterizing mystic states as pantheistic, optimistic, etc., I am afraid I over-simplified the truth. I did so for expository reasons, and to keep the closer to the classic mystical tradition. The classic religious mysticism, it now must be confessed, is only a 'privileged case.' It is an *extract,* kept true to type by the selection of the fittest specimens and their preservation in 'schools.' It is carved out from a much larger mass; and if we take the larger mass as seriously as religious mysticism has historically taken itself, we find that the supposed unanimity largely disappears. To begin with, even religious mysticism itself, the kind that accumulates traditions and makes schools, is much less unanimous than I have allowed. It has been both ascetic and antinomianly self-indulgent within the Christian church. It is dualistic in Sankhya, and monistic in Vedanta philosophy. I called it pantheistic; but the great Spanish mystics are anything but pantheists. They are with few exceptions non-metaphysical minds, for whom 'the category of personality' is absolute. The 'union' of man with God is for them much more like an occasional miracle than like an original identity. How different again, apart from the happiness common to all, is the mysticism of Walt Whitman, Edward Carpenter, Richard Jefferies, and other naturalistic pantheists, from the more distinctively Christian sort. The fact is that the mystical feeling of enlargement, union, and emancipation has no specific intellectual content whatever of its own. It is capable of forming matrimonial alliances with material furnished by the most diverse philosophies and theologies, provided only they can find a place in their framework for its peculiar emotional mood. We have no right, therefore, to invoke its prestige as distinctly in favor of any special belief, such as that in absolute idealism, or in the absolute monistic identity, or in the absolute goodness, of the world. It is only relatively in favor of all these things—it passes out of common human consciousness in the direction in which they lie.

So much for religious mysticism proper. But more remains to be told, for religious mysticism is only one half of mysticism. The other half has no accumulated traditions except those which the textbooks on insanity supply. Open any one of these, and you will find abundant cases in which 'mystical ideas' are cited as characteristic symptoms of enfeebled or deluded states of mind. In delusional insanity, paranoia, as they sometimes call it, we may have a *diabolical* mysticism, a sort of religious mysticism turned upside down. The same sense of ineffable importance in the smallest events, the same texts and words coming with new meanings, the same voices and visions and leadings and missions, the same controlling by extraneous powers; only this time the emotion is pessimistic: instead of consolations we have desolations; the meanings are dreadful; and the powers are enemies to life. It is evident that from the point of view of their psychological mechanism, the classic mysticism and these lower mysticisms spring from the same mental level, from that great subliminal or transmarginal region of which science is beginning to admit the existence, but of which so little is really known. That region contains every kind of matter: 'seraph and snake' abide there side by side. To come from thence is no infallible credential. What comes must be sifted and tested, and run the gauntlet of confrontation with the total context of experience, just like what comes from the outer world of sense. Its value must be ascertained by empirical methods, so long as we are not mystics ourselves.

Once more, then, I repeat that non-mystics are under no obligation to acknowledge in mystical states a superior authority conferred on them by their intrinsic nature.

3.

Yet, I repeat once more, the existence of mystical states absolutely overthrows the pretension of non-mystical states to be the sole and ultimate dictators of what we may believe. As a rule, mystical states merely add a supersensuous meaning to the ordinary outward data of consciousness. They are excitements like the emotions of love or ambition, gifts to our spirit by means of which facts already objectively before us fall into a new expressiveness and make a new connection with our active life. They do not contradict these facts as such, or deny anything that our senses have immediately seized. It is the rationalistic critic rather who plays the part of denier in the controversy, and his denials have no strength, for there never can be a state of facts to which new meaning may not truthfully be added, provided the mind ascend to a more enveloping point of view. It must always remain an open question whether mystical states may not possibly be such superior points of view, windows through which the mind looks out upon a more extensive and inclusive world. The difference of the views seen from the different mystical windows need not prevent us from entertaining this supposition. The wider world would in that case prove to have a mixed constitution like that of this world, that is all. It would have its celestial and its infernal regions, its tempting and its saving moments, its valid experiences and its counterfeit ones, just as our world has them; but it would be a wider world all the same. We should have to use its experiences by selecting and subordinating and substituting just as is our custom in this ordinary naturalistic world; we should be liable to error just as we are now; yet the counting in of that wider world of meanings, and the serious dealing with it, might, in spite of all the perplexity, be indispensable stages in our approach to the final fullness of the truth.

*   *   *

In this shape, I think, we have to leave the subject. Mystical states indeed wield no authority due simply to their being mystical states. But the higher ones among them point in directions to which the religious sentiments even of non-mystical men incline. They tell of the supremacy of the ideal, of vastness, of union, of safety, and of rest. They offer us *hypotheses,* hypotheses which we may voluntarily ignore, but which as thinkers we cannot possibly upset. The supernaturalism and optimism to which they would persuade us may, interpreted in one way or another, be after all the truest of insights into the meaning of this life.

"Oh, the little more, and how much it is; and the little less, and what worlds away!" It may be that possibility and permission of this sort are all that the religious consciousness requires to live on. In my last lecture I shall have to try to persuade you that this is the case. Meanwhile, however, I am sure that for many of my readers this diet is too slender. If supernaturalism and inner union with the divine are true, you think, then not so much permission, as compulsion to believe, ought to be found. Philosophy has always professed to prove religious truth by coercive arguments; and the construction of philosophies of this kind has always been one favorite function of the religious life, if we use this term in the large historic sense. . . .

Notes

1. Newman's *Securus judicat orbis terrarum* is another instance.

2. 'Mesopotamia' is the stock comic instance. . . . Of John Foster it is said that "single words (as *chalcedony*), or the names of ancient heroes, had a mighty fascination over him. 'At any time the word *hermit* was enough to transport him.' The words *woods* and *forests* would produce the most powerful emotion." Foster's Life, by Ryland, New York, 1846, p. 3.

3. "The Two Voices."

4. *Charles Kingsley's Life,* i, 55, quoted by Inge: *Christian Mysticism,* London, 1899, p. 341.

Meditation in Daily Life

SWAMI AJAYA

Allen Weinstock received a Ph.D. in clinical psychology from the University of California at Berkeley. He was initiated into yoga and Vedanta philosophy by Swami Rama and given the name *Ajaya Bharati*. His three major works are *Psychotherapy East and West*, *Yoga and Psychotherapy*, and *Yoga Psychology*, from which the following selection is edited.

It is important to understand how meditation relates to our experiences as we are involved in various activities during the rest of the day. For most of us have only a short time to devote to meditation each day, but we spend many hours in outward activities. We have many obligations and things to take care of thoughout the day. We have our work and our families to look after. We are busy providing for ourselves and there are the needs of others to be met as well. For meditation to be of real value it should have some carry-over, and it should provide purpose, direction and a sense of peace and harmony throughout the day. This is accomplished through meditation in action. Learning to apply the theory and techniques of meditation while we are active, allows us to turn our entire day into a meditational experience. Instead of withdrawing from the world to meditate for only a half-hour or so, our entire sixteen or eighteen waking hours can be transformed into a meditative practice.

You may find that there are times during the day when you are active, yet your mind is centered. You feel a sense of peace and calm despite the activity. You may be talking to someone or writing, and there is a sense of peace and calm. Then there are other times when you become restless, worried, distraught or emotional. You daydream or become distracted thinking about what is going to happen in the future. There is a sense of imbalance. As you watch yourself through the day you may notice these two very distinct states of mind. Some of us

fluctuate from one condition to the other. Others spend most of their time in one of these attitudes. It is possible to cultivate that experience of calmness and centeredness if we patiently follow the techniques of meditation in action. We can develop that joy which is found in meditation even in the midst of activity.

Some of us would like to leave the restlessness and confusion of the world behind. We would like to go on a permanent holiday, somewhere in the mountains or in the country where we can enjoy peace and tranquility. We think "If only I were in a more serene environment, then I could work on myself, I could calm myself down and begin to feel good." But we don't realize that our most intimate environment is our own mind and that we take this with us wherever we go, in whatever we do. We have to learn to relate to this internal environment, and once this is achieved we can be comfortable in any surroundings in which we may find ourselves.

Some of us tend toward extremes of outward activity, anxiously running here and there, with little ability to find a center within ourselves. We are like a cork bouncing about on the restless sea of the world with little stability. Others of us withdraw to

Swami Ajaya, excerpts from Chapter 5: "Meditation in Daily Life" from *Yoga Psychology* (Honesdale, PA: Himalayan International Institute, 1977), pp. 92–115 (edited). Reprinted with the permission of the Himalayan International Institute of Yoga Science and Philosophy of the U.S.A.

a quiet atmosphere, fearful of confronting the pushes and pulls of the world outside. But the practice of meditation in action is meant to lead us to an integration of these two extremes. It allows us to develop internal stability and to carry this out into the restlessness of the external environment where it can be further tested, refined, and put to effective use. . . .

In our everyday living many of us wander about lost; we try one path and another, often repeating our steps. But a meditative attitude can be a compass for our lives. It can provide us with the reference point, the center from which our actions can derive stability and direction.

A compass sitting on a shelf is of little use. On the other hand, being lost without one can be a nightmare. A compass has its proper function and purpose in the context of the world. When used in the right situation it serves as a guide and even brings comfort and security. Meditation without application to our everyday living is limited. Experiencing the world without a center can lead to all the anxieties one feels when lost in a dark forest. Together, meditation in the context of action can guide us and transform our experiences into a joy. Jut as the compass is made for and used in our activities in the world, so meditation is meant to be used as a guide to our actions. . . .

COMMON ASPECTS OF MEDITATION AND MEDITATION IN ACTION

There is actually little difference between the way we master our thoughts during meditation and the way we must learn to deal with ourselves in the midst of actions. The ways are basically the same. Consider what happens in meditation. You sit still, withdrawing your awareness from the external world, and attempt to center yourself on a single experience, such as awareness of your breath or a mantra as you become more and more absorbed in it, you leave your restlessness and preoccupations behind. It is a very simple thing that you are doing, but it is very difficult, because many other thoughts

that are embedded in your memory come into your awareness. The hopes, expectations, fears, joys, the unhappy moments, all sorts of things from your unconscious mind come before you as you sit down and meditate. They distract you and disrupt your tranquility. The practice of meditation is a process of learning how to remain centered even though such thoughts come to mind. As we advance in meditation we learn not to be disturbed by these thoughts. Instead of becoming involved with them, we just observe them.

Dealing with the world outside in meditation in action is essentially the same process. Here you learn to center your mind on a particular thought in the midst of your activities. In this case the disrupting thoughts do not come only from your memories and occasional stimuli, but the situation is a much more complex one. All sorts of suggestions, events and melodramas bring new input from the external world into our conscious mind. Many of these also release additional memories of past experiences which are brought into our awareness.

Quantitatively there may seem to be more to deal with when we are actively involved in the world, but qualitatively there is little difference. Thoughts are thoughts whether they occur primarily as a result of past stimuli or as a reaction to present stimuli. And the process of meditation is in each case learning not to identify with or to become absorbed in those thoughts that come to mind, however few or many they may be.

Meditation in action seems more difficult because of the complexity and quantity of stimulation with which we must deal. In a sense, sitting meditation might be thought of as a simplified preliminary practice. The complexity is purposely reduced so that we can find our center and learn how to watch and relate to our thoughts. When we learn to play an instrument we do not begin with complex compositions but work separately with the many components involved—fingering, scales, rhythm and so on. Eventually we must also deal with the world itself in all its complexity just as the accomplished musician must learn to play an intricate piece. The more we evolve in our meditational practice the more we become interested in applying what we are learning to the complexity of our living situations. We have learned to some degree to remain aware of the compass needle, now we take our instrument with us as we move about.

Applying meditation to action is like being aware of two channels at once. You take part in and notice your actions, at the same time you maintain awareness of a center within. That center can be a mantra, watching your breath, or another focus which is used as a stable reference point. Even though there is an outward activity you remember that center and remain calm. You are like a wheel. The outermost part is spinning rapidly but its center is still. As long as you identify with the outer rim you are restless and agitated, but when you identify with the hub you are at peace. The behavior you engage in and the activities that are going on around you are just like the thoughts that come before your mind in meditation. They are part of your awareness but they do not affect you adversely.

In the *Bhagavad Gita* it is stated that even the advanced meditator has many thoughts coming before his conscious mind. But these thoughts do not lead him to become disturbed or unbalanced because he does not identify with them. Thoughts don't disrupt him, don't carry him off from that center so that he throws his weight out onto one section of the rim of the wheel and creates an imbalance in his entire system. Similarly, as we go through the day, if we can have part of our mind focused on a calm center such as a mantra or the breath, we will be able to maintain peace and tranquility in the midst of confusion. If you could observe yourself in your actions from this center, serenity would be yours.

BEING IN THE NOW

One of the major principles learned in meditation is to bring our minds again and again to awareness of the present moment. As we meditate, we find our minds frequently wander to thoughts of the past and future. We recall experiences we have just had or those from the distant past. Anticipations, expectations and worries about what will take place also disturb our minds. Each time such thoughts occur during meditations, we watch them come before our awareness and pass by rather than becoming caught up in them. We learn to remain in the experience of the moment rather than be taken over by memories and fantasies. If we are to achieve calmness and serenity in our everyday living, the same attitude must also be cultivated in the midst of actions.

Most of our concerns about the future involve fears and expectations of events which will never take place. Ninety percent of the things we worry about will never occur. We spend a great deal of time in needless concern instead of working in the moment to correct whatever is causing the problem. This absorption in worries and expectations leads us away from the joy and happiness which exist right here and right now.

Paradoxical though it may seem, the best way of effectively dealing with the future is to center on the present and take care of it as best we can. By worrying about the future we merely create added difficulties for ourselves. Our preoccupation interferes with our ability to cope effectively in the present and even creates the future difficulties that we're afraid might occur. In this way our fears about the future become self-fulfilling prophecies. They themselves create the disaster that's ahead of us. . . . For example, when we speak before a group or interact with others we remain preoccupied with how they will respond to us. "Will they like me? Will they approve of my dress and what I say?" Instead of feeling at ease in the now, you become mildly anxious. Your words become disjointed and off target. You lack presence as your mind runs toward what may happen. . . .

Your future is created out of your thoughts and actions in the now. You are continually constructing a path before you which leads to your future. The path that lies ahead of you can be strewn with thorns if your present actions are callous and hurting. But your path can also be cushioned with flower petals if actions in the present show compassion and sensitivity toward others. Worrying about possible thorns that will face you is not the way to eliminate them. But entering into the present moment in order to construct a more positive future is.

We often look toward the future concerned about structuring experiences that will be enjoyable. We spend much of our time thinking ahead to make things as perfect as possible in the future. But, in this process, we neglect the present and spend our time right now in unhappiness. We don't realize that it is our attitude in facing *whatever situation* which may come our way that leads to contentment and joy. . . .

Many of us have divided our lives into two categories—chores and pleasures. Tasks are undertaken only because they have to be done. While doing them, we think ahead to the time when we will be finished and can then enjoy our leisure. But these so-called chores can become enjoyable and gratifying in themselves if we can bring our minds to the experience of them. What now seems routine and undesirable can actually become a precious experience. As this lesson is learned our entire life experience will change and the everyday "mundane" things will become a source of great satisfaction. A Zen master once said: "Before I was enlightened, I chopped wood and carried water. Since I've become enlightened, I chop wood and carry water." The outward activities may not change with the expansion of consciousness but the same activity is experienced in an entirely different way. If we could be more completely in the moment, we would find many of the things happening around us, which are taken for granted and seem dull and uninteresting, have a great beauty, harmony and perfection. . . .

If you want to experience more peacefulness, relaxation must be practiced in *every* action. You can't rush through the day and then anticipate that you can suddenly change your attitude and frame of mind to become peaceful. Thus, seemingly unimportant actions are just as significant as what we would ordinarily consider "important" ones. If the attitude is developed of respecting the former then the latter will also be carefully done. If, however, the small activities of the day are neglected, when something important comes along it will not be handled with the proper care and respect. For we will not have learned how to act with awareness. Thus, being open and warm with a friend will not easily follow from rushing through our chores quickly. Relating with more awareness and sensitivity, however, becomes almost automatic when tasks as small as folding a letter are performed with care. The person we are in each small activity is the same type of person that we find involved in the larger task. Care in the small things will inevitably lead to care and grace in other activities. . . .

It is only by slowing down and paying attention to each moment that such chaos and confusion can be avoided. Once we learn to focus the mind on the task at hand, concentration improves to such an extent that performance of any task is enhanced. Through such care and patience, we can accomplish anything. If we wish to do things skillfully, efficiently and with success, it is necessary to develop such an attitude of care in each activity.

Here, having care does not imply being overly involved or overly emotional about what you are doing; it means a constant process of bringing mindfulness, greater sensitivity, awareness and gentleness to each and every experience. As you work toward developing such care, you will find that old habits return. Your mind will turn towards anticipation of the future again and again. But (just as in your practice of sitting in meditation), refuse to become involved in these intruding thoughts. Simply watch how the mind loses awareness of the present to become, momentarily, caught up in the future. Then allow your mind to once again rest on the moment at hand. You can slowly train your mind to reside more and more in the present. Progress is made in tiny steps. But, as drops of water gradually accumulate one by one in a large vessel, so eventually your attitude and whole being can be transformed through this practice. . . .

You will come to find that the activities which are necessary are quite few and that these few activities can bring all the joy, harmony and peace that you have wished for. You will come to see that you have few needs but many wants. These wants are created out of seeking an illusory happiness in the future. When you find your happiness in the present moment, such wants will diminish. As you slow down and become aware of your activities and experience that joy and spontaneity inherent within the moment, your desires will decrease. As the desires decrease, there will be more time to pay even greater attention to the moment. You will then find that the most simple things in life are vastly rewarding. The most complete joy is contained in that simplicity rather than in the complexity created by our many desires. . . .

LETTING GO

The whole process of meditation, whether it is working with thoughts inside or objects outside, is learning how not to get absorbed in those thoughts or objects so that we forget our essential nature. The core of meditation involves letting go each time we find we have become dependent or addicted. The process of letting go has the quality of a flower which is opening, and this creates a very beautiful feeling. It is a feeling of joy, purity, and innocence. It contrasts markedly with the tense discomfort of clinging. This is what the experience of growth is all about. Growth is a joy, a blossoming, an opening, a letting go of whatever we have been grasping so that we can move out of the past and experience what is fresh and new in the present. When you sit down and meditate and find you are holding unto ideas of who you are, or fears or expectations, just say to yourself, "let go." And do exactly the same in the world. With things that you are holding onto and feel "I have to have it, it's part of me," let go of that clinging attitude. It is not necessary to give up the object outwardly. Letting go mentally of your dependency on the object is sufficient to create that feeling of completeness within yourself and within

the moment. Simply have the attitude "I don't have to have it in order to be whole. I can let go and still be full and complete." . . .

Gradually as we progress in meditation we learn to stop clinging to those things to which we have been addicted. We learn to give up the attached attitude. You don't have to give up your car or any of the things that you have. Only learn the attitude that "the essence of my being is not that object. I don't need to depend on it. If I really do lose my car it's not so catastrophic."

All too often we are frightened about losing something we depend on. We worry, for example "what if I can't get to work." But usually things work out, we find ways to work them out, and it's not such a big thing. In fact we might even have a better time of it. We might find that the world is much more pleasant without that thing we thought we really needed than it was when we were holding unto it.

CREATING OUR ENVIRONMENT

The apparent difference between meditation and meditation in action is the difference between inside and outside. Our thoughts seem to come from within, while our actions and experiences in the world have to do with outside. But actually inside and outside are one and the same thing. The outside is nothing but a projection of the inside. The entire world in which you live really comes from inside. It is a creation that you have made. The job you have, the place you live, the person you live with, your situations and relationships were all created by desires you have had in the past. You could have created a very different environment for yourself. The world you are in now, your current situation, came from thoughts inside. You projected these fantasies, these hopes and expectations, and created a whole environment for yourself with which you now are living. For example, if you have hopes, expectations or fantasies of getting a college degree, you write away to a number of schools for catalogs. Then you choose the college you want to attend. Later you rent an apartment, find new friends, and then you find yourself living in the midst of that environment.

The world outside is nothing but a manifestation of what is inside you. You have created a physical, three-dimensional, solid form in which to work with your fantasies, desires, addictions and aversions, so that you become less disturbed by them. You have provided material for yourself, a form in which you can learn to do that. Through this form you can play out your attachments and aversions and find out if they are really good or as bad as you imagined them to be. As you experience each, you eventually find that it wasn't quite what you expected. You learn to become less involved in that particular desire or you clear your mind of that disturbance.

In order to accomplish anything we need some material. An artist, for example, needs paint, brushes, a canvas or other material in order to create. Without these he could not produce a painting. The environment which we have established around us is the material out of which we create ourselves. Through projecting our wishes, fantasies, fears, we can explore them and realize their insubstantiality.

Yet we often get upset because of the situation we are in. We say, "My husband doesn't understand me," or "My boss expects too much from me." We think the situation we are in is very unpleasant or unhappy. We think negatively about our lives, not realizing that the situation we are in was brought about by ourselves for our own learning.

Learning to see the value of any situation we are in is another aspect of meditation in action. Accepting responsibility for our circumstances and seeing the positive value in them as a learning experience can help to free us from involvement. Instead of losing our center in complaint, annoyance, and rejection, we can learn to stand above our situation. We can learn to relate to any circumstance without becoming imbalanced. It has been said that "there are sermons in stones and in running brooks." When we understand that there are hidden teachings in all situations we will begin to find happiness and joy in

all sorts of activities that we thought were mundane or repulsive.

If we could fully understand and appreciate that we are always creating our own reality, and if we could live with that idea, our entire way of experiencing our world would be changed. Instead of blaming others for our situation and pushing off responsibility from ourselves, we would begin to see that when we assume responsibility for what comes our way we then transform our world both in terms of our internal state of mind and the external environment as well. As long as you make others responsible by saying, "They're doing it to me, I have to do this, I have to get my degree, my father wants me to work in his business, I have to do it," the thoughts which make up your internal environment are those of a helpless slave. If you think in these terms you are creating a negative attitude for yourself, and the world that you live in is unhappy, unpleasant and negative. But when you begin to realize that you yourself choose your circumstances, the world takes on a different hue.

THE WORLD AS A TEACHER

Instead of thinking of involvement in the world as an interruption to your peacefulness you can see these activities as opportunities to learn how to meditate in all sorts of different contexts. Each situation is an opportunity to learn how to center your mind despite the confusion and turmoil that is going on around. Without being in the world and in the midst of activity, that opportunity would be lost.

There was once a king in India who was also a sage. He practiced meditation in action and was very developed spiritually. He spent his time actively involved in taking care of the country and did a great deal to improve it. One day a disciple asked him, "How is it possible to maintain a meditative state while you are involved with so many things of the world?" The king said, "I'll show you how it is done." He filled a goblet with wine up to the brim and said, "I want you to take this goblet and walk through my palace. There are many wonderous things to experience—jewels, beautiful women, marvelous sculpture and paintings unmatched by anything you have ever seen." (Just imagine yourself walking through that palace. You would probably be eager to see what it is like and would quickly become absorbed in what you encounter). The king said, "I want you to walk throughout the entire palace and then come back to me in several hours' time, with this goblet completely filled. You are not to spill even a drop of wine." The student thought, "I can do that. I'll be very careful." And so he kept his eyes fixed on the goblet and walked very slowly. He had practiced meditation for some time and was skilled in concentrating his mind. He thought, "I'm not going to pay attention to all these things around me. I'll just concentrate my attention on this goblet and nothing will distract me." Most of us, if we were given this task, would be easily distracted, just as we are in our everyday life. Something would catch our eye and we would spill some of the wine. But this was an advanced student of meditation and he was able to complete the task successfully. He came back and he said, "I've done it. Does that indicate that I know how to practice meditation in action?" The king replied, "No, that's only the first step. Now this time I want you to go back through the palace, take in every sight and enjoy it all, still not spilling any of the wine."

This latter task is much more difficult. You can go through life so that nothing affects you, but it is also possible to enjoy the various aspects of life while maintaining a center within yourself. When you remember this center continuously you will not become attached, dependent, and swayed off-balance by the world. You can experience the joys of the moment without becoming clinging. This is the path of meditation in action. . . .

There is a well known story which illustrates this approach of meeting life and remaining centered in the midst of situations that come your way.

Two monks were walking along a path which was intersected by a turbulent stream. There was no bridge and it appeared difficult to cross. An attractive young woman stood by the bank, afraid of going on. "Get on my back," said one of the monks. "I'll carry you across." When they had reached the other shore and the monks resumed walking together, the other monk was noticeably distraught and angry. "You know that we have taken a vow to remain aloof from women," he said. "I put her down on the bank," said the first monk, "but I see that you are still carrying her."

Avoiding involvement in the world may lead to the appearance of peace and equanimity, but unnoticed by others our mind may be turbulent and restless. By confronting the world we can sometimes bring this restlessness out into the open and work with it directly. But we must be careful not to lull ourselves into the belief that simply living in the world is a spiritual practice. We must look again and again to see if we are maintaining that stability, that objectivity, that awareness of the center within.

A DAILY EXERCISE

As we understand the process of meditation in action better, we realize that it is a process of self-study. We study how and when we become imbalanced, learning how to right ourselves and how to maintain stability. There are many useful methods which can assist us in this process. These often involve some kind of discipline in which we can evaluate ourselves objectively. Keeping a diary or a daily journal is useful. Another technique to gain objectivity and balance is sometimes called retrospection. This tool has been used in a number of spiritual traditions. Retrospection is like keeping a mental journal. It involves a daily review of each day's events and is best practiced at the end of the day just before falling asleep.

Simply begin to remember the last experience you had that day. Without becoming involved, let the event momentarily pass across your consciousness. Notice the quality of the experience. For example, were you anxious or relaxed, frustrated or at peace. Then in the same way recall the experience you had just before this one. Be a neutral observer, as if you were watching someone else. Don't become caught up in judging, criticizing or approving of yourself but simply make a mental note of the quality of the experience.

In this way systematically go through your entire day, beginning with the last event and ending with the moment when you awoke. This need not be a long involved process if you do not dwell on any happening, but move smoothly from one to another. The entire exercise should be completed in about ten minutes. To gain the full benefits of this technique it should be repeated daily.

It is not necessary to be judgmental for this exercise to be effective. Simply observing yourself objectively will lead you naturally to correct the imbalances and disturbances in your behavior and thoughts. Your objectivity will lead you back to your center. Furthermore, you will find that it will positively affect your behavior and thoughts the next day. The self-observational skill you are cultivating will lead you to notice and interrupt a sense of disturbance while you are experiencing it. You may find yourself pausing as you discover yourself distraught, and beginning again in your interaction or task with a new centeredness.

A similar exercise may also be practiced at the beginning of each day. In this case you can spend a few minutes after you have awakened objectively visualizing the experiences you are likely to have during the day. If you anticipate going shopping, what quality will that event have? Will you be preoccupied? Will you enjoy the experience? Simply let each anticipated happening pass across your consciousness before you arise and continue on your day.

Only a few of the innumerable aspects and techniques of meditation in action have been described here. If you are to experience their value they must be used in your daily life. For any approach or method to work it must be applied systematically. All too often we read books or go to lectures about higher states of consciousness to be inspired, informed or entertained. We accumulate a great deal of knowledge but put only a small portion of it into practice. We may be so busy collecting techniques that we have no time for practicing them. If this is the case, then we are not properly following the path of meditation in action. For one important facet of meditation in action is patient and persistent practice. If you practice only one exercise thoroughly you will find more benefit than learning a hundred techniques and practicing several inconsistently. For each exercise in itself can be a path to expanded consciousness if you will only follow it far enough.

With the Samanas

HERMANN HESSE

Hermann Hesse (1877–1962) is usually regarded as one of the greatest novelists of the twentieth century. He is especially noted for the deep philosophical character of his works, which include Narcissus and Goldmund, Steppenwolf, Demian, Magister Ludi (The Glass Bead Game), and Siddhartha, from which the following selection is taken. Hesse was awarded the Nobel Prize for Literature in 1946.

On the evening of that day they overtook the Samanas and requested their company and allegiance. They were accepted.

Siddhartha gave his clothes to a poor Brahmin on the road and only retained his loincloth and earth-colored unstitched cloak. He only ate once a day and never cooked food. He fasted fourteen days. He fasted twenty-eight days. The flesh disappeared from his legs and cheeks. Strange dreams were reflected in his enlarged eyes. The nails grew long on his thin fingers and a dry, bristly beard appeard on his chin. His glance became icy when he encountered women; his lips curled with contempt when he passed through a town of well-dressed people. He saw businessmen trading, princes going to the hunt, mourners weeping over their dead, prostitutes offering themselves, doctors attending the sick, priests deciding the day for sowing, lovers making love, mothers soothing their children—and all were not worth a passing glance, everything lied, stank of lies; they were all illusions of sense, happiness and beauty. All were doomed to decay. The world tasted bitter. Life was pain.

Siddhartha had one single goal—to become empty, to become empty of thirst, desire, dreams, pleasure and sorrow—to let the Self die. No longer to be Self, to experience the peace of an emptied heart, to experience pure thought—that was his goal. When all the Self was conquered and dead, when all passions and desires were silent, then the last must awaken, the innermost of Being that is no longer Self—the great secret!

Silently Siddhartha stood in the fierce sun's rays, filled with pain and thirst, and stood until he no longer felt pain and thirst. Silently he stood in the rain, water dripping from his hair on to his freezing shoulders, on to his freezing hips and legs. And the ascetic stood until his shoulders and legs no longer froze, till they were silent, till they were still. Silently he crouched among the thorns. Blood dripped from his smarting skin, ulcers formed, and Siddhartha remained stiff, motionless, till no more blood flowed, till there was no more pricking, no more smarting.

Siddhartha sat upright and learned to save his breath, to manage with little breathing, to hold his breath. He learned, while breathing in, to quiet his heartbeat, learned to lessen his heartbeats, until there were few and hardly any more.

Instructed by the eldest of the Samanas, Siddhartha practiced self-denial and meditation according to the Samana rules. A heron flew over the bamboo wood and Siddhartha took the heron into his soul, flew over forest and mountains, became a heron, ate fishes, suffered heron hunger, used heron language, died a heron's death. A dead jackal lay on the sandy shore and Siddhartha's soul slipped into its corpse; be became a dead jackal, lay on the shore, swelled, stank, decayed, was dismembered by hyenas, was picked at by vultures, became a skeleton, became dust, mingled with the atmosphere. And Siddhartha's soul returned, died, decayed, turned into dust, experienced the troubled course of the life cycle. He waited with new thirst like a hunter at a chasm where the life cycle ends, where there is an end to causes, where painless eternity begins. He killed his senses, he killed his memory, he slipped out of his Self in a thousand different forms. He was animal, carcass, stone, wood, water, and each time he reawakened. The sun or moon shone, he was again Self, swung into the life cycle, felt thirst, conquered thirst, felt new thirst.

Siddhartha learned a great deal from the Samanas; he learned many ways of losing the Self. He travelled along the path of self-denial through pain, through voluntary suffering and conquering of pain, through hunger, thirst and fatigue. He travelled the way of self-denial through meditation, through the emptying of the mind of all images. Along these and other paths did he learn to travel. He lost his Self a thousand times and for days on end he dwelt in nonbeing. But although the paths took him away from Self, in the end they always led back to it. Although Siddhartha fled from the Self a thousand times, dwelt in nothing, dwelt in animal and stone, the return was inevitable; the hour was inevitable when he would again find himself, in sunshine or in moonlight, in shadow or in rain, and was again Self and Siddhartha, again felt the torment of the onerous life cycle.

At his side lived Govinda, his shadow; he travelled along the same path, made the same endeavors. They rarely conversed with each other apart from the necessities of their service and practices. Sometimes they went together through the villages in order to beg food for themselves and their teachers.

"What do you think, Govinda?" Siddhartha asked at the beginning of one of these expeditions. "Do you think we are any further? Have we reached our goal?"

Govinda replied: "We have learned and we are still learning. You will become a great Samana, Siddhartha. You have learned each exercise quickly. The old Samanas have often appraised you. Some day you will be a holy man, Siddhartha."

Siddhartha said: "It does not appear so to me, my friend. What I have so far learned from the Samanas, I could have learned more quickly and easily in every inn in a prostitute's quarter, amongst the carriers and dice players."

Govinda said: "Siddhartha is joking. How could you have learned meditation, holding of the breath and insensibility towards hunger and pain, with those wretches?"

And Siddhartha said softly, as if speaking to himself: "What is meditation? What is abandonment of the body? What is fasting? What is the holding of breath? It is a flight from the Self, it is a temporary escape from the torment of Self. It is a temporary palliative against the pain and folly of life. The driver of oxen makes this same flight, takes this temporary drug when he drinks a few bowls of rice wine or cocoanut milk in the inn. He then no longer feels his Self, no longer feels the pain of life; he then experiences temporary escape. Falling asleep over his bowl of rice wine, he finds what Siddhartha and Govinda find when they escape from their bodies by long exercises and dwell in the non-Self."

Govinda said: "You speak thus, my friend, and yet you know that Siddhartha is no driver of oxen and a Samana is no drunkard. The drinker does indeed find escape, he does indeed find a short respite and rest, but he returns from the illusion and finds everything as it was before. He has not grown wiser, he has not gained knowledge, he has not climbed any higher."

Siddhartha answered with a smile on his face: "I do not know. I have never been a drunkard. But that I, Siddhartha, only find a short respite in my exercises and meditation, and am as remote from wisdom, from salvation, as a child in the womb, that, Govinda, I do know."

On another occasion when Siddhartha left the wood with Govinda in order to beg for food for their brothers and teachers, Siddhartha began to speak and said: "Well, Govinda, are we on the right road? Are we gaining knowledge? Are we approaching salvation? Or are we perhaps going in circles—we who thought to escape from the cycle?"

Govinda said: "We have learned much, Siddhartha. There still remains much to learn. We are not going in circles, we are going upwards. The path is a spiral; we have already climbed many steps."

Siddhartha replied: "How old, do you think, is our oldest Samana, our worthy teacher?"

Govinda said: "I think the eldest would be about sixty years old."

And Siddhartha said: "He is sixty years old and has not attained Nirvana. He will be seventy and eighty years old, and you and I, we shall grow as old as he, and do exercises and fast and meditate, but we will not attain Nirvana, neither he nor we. Govinda, I believe that amongst all the Samanas, probably not even one will attain Nirvana. We find consolations, we learn tricks with which we deceive ourselves, but the essential thing—the way—we do not find."

"Do not utter such dreadful words, Siddhartha," said Govinda. "How could it be that amongst so many learned men, amongst so many Brahmins, amongst so many austere and worthy Samanas, amongst so many seekers, so many devoted to the inner life, so many holy men, none will find the right way?"

Siddhartha, however, said in a voice which contained as much grief as mockery, in a soft, somewhat sad, somewhat jesting voice: "Soon, Govinda, your friend will leave the path of the Samanas along which he has travelled with you so long. I suffer thirst, Govinda, and on this long Samana path my thirst has not grown less. I have always thirsted for knowledge, I have always been full of questions. Year after year I have questioned the Brahmins, year after year I have questioned the holy Vedas. Perhaps, Govinda, it would have been equally good, equally clever and holy if I had questioned the rhinoceros or the chimpanzee. I have spent a long time and have not yet finished, in order to

learn this, Govinda: that one can learn nothing. There is, so I believe, in the essence of everything, something that we cannot call learning. There is, my friend, only a knowledge—that is everywhere, that is Atman, that is in me and you and in every creature, and I am beginning to believe that this knowledge has no worse enemy than the man of knowledge, than learning."

Thereupon Govinda stood still on the path, raised his hands and said: "Siddhartha, do not distress your friend with such talk. Truly, your words trouble me. Think, what meaning would our holy prayers have, the venerableness of the Brahmins, the holiness of the Samanas, if, as you say, there is no learning? Siddhartha, what would become of everything, what would be holy on earth, what would be precious and sacred?"

Govinda murmured a verse to himself, a verse from one of the Upanishads:

"He whose reflective pure spirit sinks into Atman
Knows bliss inexpressible through words."

Siddhartha was silent. He dwelt long on the words which Govinda had uttered.

Yes, he thought, standing with bowed head, what remains from all that seems holy to us? What remains? What is preserved? And he shook his head.

Once, when both youths had lived with the Samanas about three years and shared their practices, they heard from many sources a rumor, a report. Someone had appeared, called Gotama, the Illustrious, the Buddha. He had conquered in himself the sorrows of the world and had brought to a standstill the cycle of rebirth. He wandered through the country preaching, surrounded by disciples, having no possessions, homeless, without a wife, wearing the yellow cloak of an ascetic, but with lofty brow, a holy man, and Brahmins and princes bowed before him and became his pupils.

This report, this rumor, this tale was heard and spread here and there. The Brahmins talked about it in the town, the Samanas in the forest. The name of Gotama, the Buddha, continually reached the ears of the young men, spoken of well and ill, in praise and in scorn.

Just as when a country is ravaged with the plague and a rumor arises that there is a man, a wise man, a learned man, whose words and breath are sufficient to heal the afflicted, and as the report travels across the country and everyone speaks about it, many believe and many doubt it. Many, however, immediately go on their way to seek the wise man, the benefactor. In such a manner did that rumor, that happy report of Gotama the Buddha, the wise man from the race of Sakya, travel through the country. He possessed great knowledge, said the believers; he remembered his former lives, he had attained Nirvana and never returned on the cycle, he plunged no more into the troubled stream of forms. Many wonderful and incredible things were reported about him; he had performed wonders, had conquered the devil, had spoken with the gods. His enemies and doubters, however, said that this Gotama was an idle fraud; he passed his days in high living, scorned the sacrifices, was unlearned and knew neither practices nor mortification of the flesh.

The rumors of the Buddha sounded attractive; there was magic in these reports. The world was sick, life was difficult and here there seemed new hope, here there seemed to be a message, comforting, mild, full of fine promises. Everywhere there were rumors about the Buddha. Young men all over India listened, felt a longing and a hope. And among the Brahmins' sons in the towns and villages, every pilgrim and stranger was welcome if he brought news of him, the Illustrious, the Sakyamuni.

The rumors reached the Samanas in the forest and Siddhartha and Govinda, a little at a time, every little item heavy with hope, heavy with doubt. They spoke little about it, as the eldest Samana was no friend of this rumor. He had heard that this alleged Buddha had formerly been an ascetic and had lived in the woods, had then turned to high living and the pleasure of the world, and he held no brief for this Gotama.

"Siddhartha," Govinda once said to his friend, "today I was in the village and a Brahmin invited me to enter his house and in the house was a Brahmin's son from Magadha; he had seen the Buddha with his own eyes and had heard him preach. Truly I was filled with longing and I thought: I wish that both Siddhartha and I may live to see the day when we can hear the teachings from the lips of the Perfect One. My friend, shall we not also go hither and hear the teachings from the lips of the Buddha?"

Siddhartha said: "I always thought that Govinda would remain with the Samanas. I always believed it was his goal to be sixty and seventy years old and still practice the arts and exercises which the Samanas teach. But how little did I know Govinda! How little did I know what was in his heart! Now, my dear friend, you wish to strike a new path and go and hear the Buddha's teachings."

Govinda said: "It gives you pleasure to mock me. No matter if you do, Siddhartha. Do you not also feel a longing, a desire to hear this teaching? And did you not once say to me—I will not travel the path of the Samanas much longer?"

Then Siddhartha laughed in such a way that his voice expressed a shade of sorrow and a shade of mockery and he said: "You have spoken well, Govinda, you have remembered well, but you must also remember what else I told you—that I have become distrustful of teachings and learning and that I have little faith in words that come to us from teachers. But, very well, my friend, I am ready to hear that new teaching, although I believe in my heart that we have already tasted the best fruit of it."

Govinda replied: "I am delighted that you are agreed. But tell me, how can the teachings of Gotama disclose to us its most precious fruit before we have even heard him?"

Siddhartha said: "Let us enjoy this fruit and await further ones, Govinda. This fruit, for which we are already indebted to Gotama, consists in the fact that he has enticed us away from the Samanas. Whether there are still other and better fruits, let us patiently wait and see."

On the same day, Siddhartha informed the eldest Samana of his decision to leave him. He told the old man with the politeness and modesty fitting to young men and students. But the old man was angry that both young men wished to leave him and he raised his voice and scolded them strongly.

Govinda was taken aback, but Siddhartha put his lips to Govinda's ear and whispered: "Now I will show the old man that I have learned something from him."

He stood near the Samana, his mind intent; he looked into the old man's eyes and held him with his look, hypnotized him, made him mute, conquered his will, commanded him silently to do as he wished. The old man became silent, his eyes glazed, his will crippled; his arms hung down, he was power-less under Siddhartha's spell. Siddhartha's thoughts conquered those of the Samana; he had to perform what they commanded. And so the old man bowed several times, gave his blessings and stammered his wishes for a good journey. The young men thanked him for his good wishes, returned his bow, and departed.

On the way, Govinda said: "Siddhartha, you have learned more from the Samanas than I was aware. It is difficult, very difficult to hypnotize an old Samana. In truth, if you had stayed there, you would have soon learned how to walk on water."

"I have no desire to walk on water," said Siddhartha. "Let the old Samanas satisfy themselves with such arts."

Review and Reflection

1. What, according to Patañjali, is the goal of yoga?

2. How can we distinguish between Puruṣa and Prakriti? Why is the mind regarded as the source of all suffering?

3. Distinguish between the external and internal steps of Ashtāṅga yoga. Are the external steps necessary for enlightenment? Why?

4. Discuss the distinction between Kriyā yoga and Ashtāṅga yoga. Do we need both of them for attaining enlightenment or mystical states? Why?

5. Discuss William James's concept and treatment of mysticism. What does he regard as the distinguishing marks of mystical consciousness?

6. Can meditation be made part of our daily lives? Discuss Ajaya's position regarding meditation in action.

7. In what way does Hesse criticize the yoga system of Patañjali? Do you agree with his criticism? Why?

8. Do you believe that mystical states are possible? Why? Explicate and support your position as clearly as possible.

Suggestions for Further Study

SWAMI AJAYA. *Yoga Psychology*. Honesdale, PA: The Himalayan Institute, 1989.

USHERBUDH ARYA. *Yoga-Sūtras of Patañjali*. Honesdale, PA: The Himalayan Institute, 1986.

ASHOK MALHOTRA. *Mysticism in the Hindu Tradition*. New York: Agathos, 1993.

RAMAMURTI MISHRA. *The Textbook of the Yoga Psychology*. New York: Julian Press, 1987.

SWAMI RAMA. *Lectures of Yoga*. Honesdale, PA: The Himalayan Insitute, 1979.

JEAN VARENNE. *Yoga and the Hindu Tradition*. Chicago: University of Chicago Press, 1976.

EPILOGUE

One of the most powerful and intriguing yet also puzzling and disturbing concepts in Hinduism is a doctrine known as *māyā*. The word is akin to our English term *magic*. The doctrine is far easier to state than it is to understand; put simply: the world which we typically take as real—that which we see, hear, feel, and otherwise experience via our senses—is but an illusion. To help motivate and explicate this difficult concept, Hindu sages have developed an array of parables and stories, including the following one about an exceptionally perceptive and intelligent scholar.

Narada, it is said, studied the holy scriptures for many long years. He knew the verses by heart and could recite all of the major commentaries. In the process he came to understand everything except one thing: the doctrine of *māyā*. As a reward for his piety and diligence, the gods agreed to grant him a single wish.

Narada was of course overjoyed. He requested the opportunity to visit the abode of the gods and to have Vishnu personally explain to him this elusive concept. Vishnu granted the request and began by showing Narada the magnificent celestial palace in which dwelled the many gods and goddesses of Hinduism. Fascinating as it may seem to you and me, Narada soon grew tired of the celestial palace and beseeched Vishnu to get on with the explanation of māyā. Vishnu agreed, but suggested they walk to a nearby grove of trees where they could remain undisturbed for a substantial period of time.

When they reached the trees Vishnu took up a comfortable position, then asked Narada to fill a *lota* (flask, canteen) with water so that he might speak without his throat becoming dry. Narada seized the lota and began walking toward a farmhouse just visible on the horizon. The house was farther than he had initially believed and he was thus tired and winded when he finally came to its door. There he was greeted by a beautiful young maiden who filled the lota with water and invited him for supper as well. "What can it hurt?" he asked himself. "Vishnu wants water, but I need food." Sitting by the cooking fire, enjoying the food and company of this simple family, Narada was happy and soon found himself accepting their invitation to stay the night. A night turned into a week, a week into a month, and a month into a year.

As he married the young maiden who had fetched his water, he glanced at the lota still hanging above the fireplace and thought: "There was something I came here for, something I was supposed to do. Oh well, I will think about that tomorrow. Today is my wedding day and I must not upset my bride with thoughts such as this."

Sometimes when plowing the field he would gaze at the grove of trees in the distance and think: "Someday I must go and see what is beyond the bounds of this horizon. It almost seems as though someone is calling to me from the distance. But I cannot go today, for I have plowing to do. Perhaps I will go tomorrow."

When his children were all grown and married and had gone off to establish families of their own, he sometimes sat in front of the fire and stared at the lota still hanging where he had left it many years ago. As it had so many times before, the thought would enter his consciousness: "There was something I came here for, something I was supposed to do." Then he would look at his wife, now aging and feeble, and remind himself that he had responsibilities still at home. "Perhaps another day," he would say to himself.

Eventually it happened that his wife died. When Narada had given her a proper burial and paid his last respects, there was nothing else to tie him to the land or the tiny house in which he had lived for so many years. He took down the lota, still filled with the water drawn by his wife's then-youthful hand, and set off for the grove of trees he had watched so often as he plowed the fields.

As he approached the trees he saw Vishnu sitting patiently, still waiting for his water. Memories flooded in with terrifying force. Narada fell to his knees and begged the god's forgiveness. But Vishnu was not angry. Instead he smiled, stroked Narada's hair, and explained: "You wanted to know about māyā. Māyā is going to fetch a lota of water for your deity, but becoming so concerned and caught up in the day-to-day affairs of life that you forget your purpose. You forget what you came for, and what you are supposed to do."

GLOSSARY

A

Academy A school which Plato established in Athens circa 375 B.C.

Aesthetics The study of values and judgments concerning beauty, taste, and related concepts.

Agni The god of fire in the Vedas.

Agnosticism The belief that humans have no way of knowing whether or not there is a deity.

Aham Brahman Asi A mantra used in meditation ("I am Brahman").

Alienation Existentialism: separation or estrangement from the world in which we live. In Marxism, separation or estrangement from the products of our labors.

Altruism Ethics: a variant of consequentialism in which the morality of an action is judged in terms of its consequences for others (excluding the self).

Analytic argument A logical argument that exploits relations between concepts but does not depend on the empirical existence of the entities described by those concepts. Cf. *Tautology.*

Anselm, Saint (1033–1109) Benedictine monk and Archbishop of Canterbury, known especially for his formulation and defense of the Ontological Argument.

Anthropocentric Any approach that makes human beings its central concern.

A posteriori Epistemology: knowledge based on sense experience.

A priori Epistemology: knowledge not based on sense experience.

Aristotle (384–322 B.C.) Greek philosopher, pupil of Plato, and tutor of Alexander the Great.

Argument Logic: a group of statements consisting of premises and conclusion such that the truth of the premises is intended to establish the truth of the conclusion. Cf. *Valid* and *Sound.*

Āsana The third step of the yoga method—the physical postures.

Ashtānga yoga The eightfold path of yoga discipline.

Astral projection An out-of-body experience that is consciously induced and/or controlled.

Atheism The belief that there are no deities.

Ātman Hinduism: the essence of a human being, the Self. Regarded as infinite existence, infinite consciousness, and infinite joy.

Aum (Om) The highest mantra—used properly, it is said to be capable of unraveling the nature of the ultimate reality.

Authentic Existentialism: actions characterized by awareness of freedom, respect for the freedom of others, total commitment, and acceptance of responsibility.

Avatar (avatara) The physical incarnation of a deity—a god's descent into the human world in material form. In Hinduism, used especially of Vishnu.

Axiology One of four traditional divisions of philosophy—the study of values and value judgments. Major divisions of axiology include ethics and aesthetics.

Axiom A proposition regarded as self-evident (obviously true).

439

B

Bad faith (Self-deception) Existentialism: a lie to oneself.

Bathybius Haeckelii A colloidal precipitate incorrectly identified by Thomas Huxley as an evolutionary link that bridged the gap between the living and the nonliving. Cf. *Eozoon canadense.*

Being-for-itself A phrase used by Jean-Paul Sartre to designate consciousness (the being of a human being).

Being-in-itself A phrase used by Jean-Paul Sartre to designate the psychophysical universe, excluding human consciousness.

Bhagavad Gītā The first book to systematize the basic ideas of Hinduism (circa 500 B.C.). Part of the *Mahabharata.*

Bioemporium (bioemporion) A term coined by Willard Gaylin to designate the hospital ward or laboratory used to maintain neomorts.

Boddhidharma A sage who brought the original ideas of Buddhism from India to China in 527 A.D.

Bodhi tree The tree of knowledge under which the Buddha was enlightened.

Brahma One of the gods of the Hindu Trinity: the creator of the universe.

Brahman (Brahmin) Hinduism: a member of the highest caste, often a priest.

Brahman In the *Vedas,* it is the singular ultimate reality.

Brain stem The portion of the brain that connects to the spinal cord; it is responsible for cephalic reflexes (e.g., pupil dilation), and is featured prominently in contemporary debates concerning brain death.

Broken myth A myth that is understood as a myth, but not discarded or replaced. Cf. *Demythologization* and *Literalism.*

Buddha "The awakened one"—a title given to Siddhartha Gautama when he attained enlightenment.

Buddhism The system of philosophy and religion started by Siddhartha Gautama (the Buddha).

C

Camus, Albert (1913–1960) French philosopher and author, best known as an atheistic existentialist.

Categorical imperative Ethics: Kant's principle that we should never act in a way we would not be willing for others to act as well (that all ethical acts should be capable of universal generalization).

Chāndogya Upanishad One of the 200 books of the *Upanishads;* it presents a dialogue between a human being and the god of death.

Chuang Tzu (369–286 B.C.) Disciple of Lao Tzu, popularizer of Taoism, and author of *Chuang Tzu.*

Cogito ergo sum "I think, therefore I am." Cf. *Descartes.*

Confucius (Sixth–fifth centuries B.C.) Chinese sage and philosopher.

Consequentialism Ethics: any of a series of views which hold that the morality of an action is a function of its consequences. Cf. *Altruism, Egoism,* and *Utilitarianism.*

Copenhagen Interpretation Quantum Mechanics: the view that Quantum Mechanics deals only with the correlation of experimental procedures and observable results, and thus does not yield knowledge of any reality which may exist independent of those observations and experiments.

Cosmological argument An argument that seeks to infer the existence of God from the existence of the cosmos. Also called "the First Cause Argument."

Cosmos The world; the universe.

Cultural relativism Ethics: the view that the morality of an action depends on the laws, norms, or customs of a particular culture.

D

Darwin, Charles (1809–1882) English biologist, architect of the theory of evolution by means of natural selection.

Death, biological Cessation of the processes of biological synthesis and replication.

Death, brain Death of the brain (usually but not always taken to mean the entire brain, including brain stem as well as neocortex). Although the heart, lungs, and other portions of the organism may continue to function, brain death is a currently accepted medical and legal standard for death of a human being.

Death, local Death of a part of the body.

Death, molecular Death of the tissues.

Death, somatic Death of the organism as a whole.

Death of the person Phenomenon whereby a body ceases to be, encase, or be uniquely associated with a person.

Deductive logic System of logical principles according to which the truth of the premises will guarantee the truth of the conclusion.

Deism The belief that a deity created the universe, then adopted a "hands off" policy allowing it to develop according to natural law as well as the behavioral choices of its inhabitants.

Demythologization The process of recognizing a symbol as a symbol and a myth as a myth. Cf. *Broken myth* and *Literalism.*

Deontological theory Ethics: a theory based on moral assumptions which cannot be reduced to human preference or behavioral consequence. Cf. *Consequentialism* and *Relativism.*

Descartes, René (1596–1650) French philosopher and mathematician, known especially for his rationalistic proof of his own existence: *cogito ergo sum* ("I think, therefore I am").

Devas Hinduism: the powers or forces inhabiting the universe. This idea was first presented in the *Vedas.*

Dhammapada The sacred text that contains the original teachings of the Buddha.

Dhāranā The first step of meditation—concentration accompanied by distraction.

Dhyāna The second step of meditation—concentration without distractions.

Difference principle John Rawls's Theory of Justice: social and economic inequalities are just only if they benefit all members of the society, especially the least advantaged.

Divine will theory (divine command theory) Ethics: the view that the morality of an action depends on the approval or disapproval of a divine being.

Dualism Metaphysics: the doctrine that reality consists of two fundamentally different "substances" (e.g., mind and body). Cf. *Monism.*

Dukkha (Dukha) Suffering. "All is dukkha" is the first noble truth of Buddhism.

E

Egoism Ethics: a variant of consequentialism in which the morality of an action is judged in terms of its consequences for a single individual.

Eightfold path The Buddhist path of enlightenment.

Einstein, Albert (1879–1955) German-American physicist, best known for his theories of relativity.

Empirical Based on sense experience.

Empiricism The view that experience, especially sense experience, is the only source of knowledge.

Entitlement Something that one deserves. Cf. *Nozick's theory of justice as entitlement.*

Eozoon canadense A metamorphic product of heat and pressure incorrectly identified by William Logan as a fossil and accepted by Charles Darwin as an evolutionary link that bridged the gap between the living and the nonliving. Cf. *Bathybius Haeckelii.*

Epistemology One of four traditional divisions of philosophy—the study of belief, opinion, knowledge, and related concepts.

Er, Myth of Story told by Socrates at the end of Plato's *Republic*. Er was supposedly a soldier killed in battle, but allowed to return to the land of the living so as to tell others about the punishments and rewards they would encounter in the afterlife.

Essence Innate nature. Existentialism: the foundational qualities of a human being.

Ethics The study of moral values and judgments.

Euclid (Third century B.C.) Greek mathematician known for his systematic geometry based on points, lines, and planes.

Eudemonism Ethics: the view that the morality of an action depends on its ability to produce happiness (eudemonia). Cf. *Hedonism.*

Existence Existentialism: our being here and now.

Existentialism A philosophical movement of the nineteenth and twentieth centuries that emphasizes human existence, freedom, and responsibility.

Extrinsic value Anything which derives its value from something else. Cf. *Intrinsic value.*

F

Fallacy Violation of the principles of logic.

Four Noble Truths The principal teachings of the Buddha: All is dukkha, dukkha is caused by tanha, tanha can be overcome by cultivating karuna, and karuna can be cultivated by following the eightfold path.

Freedom Absence of internal and external restrictions to human action.

Freud, Sigmund (1856–1939) German psychologist, founder of psychoanalysis.

G

Gautama The family name of the Buddha.

Glaucon Brother of Plato—one of the principle characters of *The Republic.*

H

Hedonism Ethics: the view that the morality of an action depends on its ability to produce pleasure. Cf. *Eudemonism.*

Heidegger, Martin (1889–1976) German existentialist philosopher.

Heisenberg, Werner (1901–1976) German physicist known especially for the Uncertain Relation that bears his name.

Henotheism In the *Vedas,* the belief that some gods are more powerful than others.

Hindu A practitioner of Hinduism. Originally, one who lived by the Sindhu river.

Hinduism A system of philosophy and religion that originated in India circa 2500 B.C. Principle texts include the *Vedas,* the *Upanishads,* and the *Bhagavad Gītā.*

Huxley, Aldous (1894–1963) English novelist and social critic. Author of *Brave New World* (1932).

I

Indra The god of thunder and lightning in the *Vedas.*

Inductive logic System of logical principles according to which the truth of the premises makes the truth of the conclusion more or less probable.

Inheritance of acquired characteristics A genetic thesis accepted by Darwin and his contemporaries but now rejected by most biologists: the idea that biological organisms can transmit to their offspring not only the characteristics with which they are born, but also those they have acquired during the course of their life.

Intrinsic value Anything valued for its own sake. Cf. *Extrinsic value.*

K

Kalki (Kali) The tenth avatar of Vishnu, who will come to destroy the entire universe.

Kant, Immanuel (1724–1804) German philosopher noted for his analytical critiques of reason.

Karuna Buddhism: total concern or compassion for the other.

Kierkegaard, Søren (1813–1855) Danish philosopher, one of the founders of existentalism.

Kōan A paradox or a puzzle given to the disciple by a Zen master. *Kōans* are given to open the mind to its own secrets.

Krishna The hero of the *Bhagavad Gītā*, regarded by the Hindus as the eighth avatar of Vishnu.

Kriyā Yoga The preliminary yoga: austerity, introspection, and ego surrender.

Kwakiutl Civilization that developed along the North Pacific Coast of North America. Used by Ruth Fulton Benedict as an example of the cultural basis of ethical values.

L

Lao Tzu A Chinese sage who formulated the original ideas of Taoism in a book commonly called the *Tao Te Ching.*

Literalism Understanding myths and symbols in their immediate, literal meanings. *Natural literalism* occur when no distinction has been drawn between the mythical and the literal meanings. *Reactive literalism* occurs when those distinctions have been drawn, but denied. Cf. *Broken myth* and *Demythologization.*

Locke, John (1632–1704) English philosopher noted especially for his epistemological and sociopolitical theories.

Logic One of four traditional divisions of philosophy—the disciplined effort to think and reason clearly.

Lyceum A school which Aristotle established on the outskirts of Athens in 335 B.C.

M

Mahabharata One of the two great epics of India. The *Bhagavad Gītā* forms an important religious and philosophical part of the *Mahabharata.*

Māṇḍūkya Upanishad One of the 200 books of the *Upanishads*—provides a concise description of the four stages of consciousness.

Mantra A sound or phrase used as a focus symbol in meditation.

Māyā Hindu doctrine that the world we typically take as real—what we see, hear, feel, and otherwise experience via our senses—is but an illusion. Cf. *Empiricism.*

Mendel, Gregor Johann (1822–1884) Austrian monk and biologist noted for his statistical approach to the study of genetics.

Metaphysics One of four traditional divisions of philosophy, a disciplined but largely nonempirical attempt to understand the nature and structure of reality.

Mill, John Stuart (1806–1873) English philosopher known predominantly for his contributions to ethics and sociopolitical philosophy—one of the founders of utilitarianism.

Monism the belief that the ultimate reality is a single impersonal principle (or substance). Cf. *Dualism.*

Monotheism Belief in one and only one god.

Moral argument An argument that seeks to infer the existence of God from the moral dimensions of human life.

N

Near-death experiences (NDE) Term coined by Raymond Moody (*Life after Life,* 1975) to designate an intriguing set of experiences occasioned by a close brush with death.

Neocortex The most recently evolved part of the brain, believed to be the portion associated with human consciousness.

Neomort Term coined by Willard Gaylin to refer to the newly dead, especially those in whom somatic function is maintained for the benefit of others. Cf. *Bioemporium.*

Neti Neti "Not this, Not this." In the *Upanishads,* a caution offered to the practitioner that the nature of the ultimate reality will always remain indescribable.

Newton, Isaac (1642–1727) English mathematician, scientist, and philosopher, noted especially for his development of differential calculus and his theory of universal gravitation.

Nietzsche, Friedrich (1844–1900) German existentialist philosopher whose ideas were misappropriated by the Nazis. Known especially for his claim that "God is dead" and his concept of an übermensch (overman or superman: a human savior of sorts who is still to come).

Nihilism A philosophical movement that rejects moral values and objective truths.

Nirvāṇa Buddhism: a state of total liberation from all suffering.

Niyama The second step of the yoga method—five positive principles including rules of physical, moral, and spiritual hygiene.

Nozick, Robert (b. 1938) American philosopher known for his concept of justice as entitlement.

O

Om (aum) The highest mantra—used properly, it is said to be capable of unraveling the nature of the ultimate reality.

Omnibeneficent All-caring.

Omnipotent All-powerful.

Omnipresent Present at all times and places.

Omniscient All-knowing.

Ontological argument An argument that seeks to prove the existence of God via a simple analysis of the concepts. Cf. *Analytic argument.*

Ontology The study of being (existence).

Original position John Rawls's Theory of Justice: a fictitious time in which all members of the society participate in choosing the principles according to which the society will be governed.

Out-of-body experience (OBC) An experience in which the apparent locus of consciousness differs from that of the physical location of the body. The "self" may seem to leave the body and view the happenings from above or off to one side. Consciously controlled OBEs are termed *astral projection.*

P

Pantheism The belief that everything is (or is a part of) God.

Patañjali The Hindu sage who compiled the *Yoga Sūtra* text in 500 B.C.

Philosophy Literally, "love of wisdom." Like most words, *philosophy* is a term with several distinct if related meanings. It can refer to:

1. the activity of questioning, conceptualizing, analyzing, evaluating, puzzling, wondering, and reflecting.
2. the academic discipline based on that activity, or
3. any of a number of specific answers or approaches to thorny problems and issues (the philosophy of Plato, Oriental philosophy, etc.).

The order of primacy is as given (activity, academic discipline, and specific answers). Philosophy is, first and foremost, something one does.

Plato (427–347 B.C.) Greek philosopher known especially for a series of dialogues in which Socrates, who had been Plato's teacher, discussed matters of moral and political philosophy with other scholars of the period.

Poincaré, Jules Henri (1854–1912) French mathematician and physicist known especially for his discoveries in non-Euclidean geometry.

Polarization The process of dividing items into two mutually exclusive categories.

Polytheism The belief that the universe is inhabited by many deities.

Prakriti Yoga: material reality.

Prānāyama The fourth step of the yoga method—breathing exercises.

Pratyāhāra The fifth step of the yoga method, in which the disciple disconnects his/her mind from the objects of sense.

Prima facie duties Ethics: Seven duties that William David Ross believed would be obvious to an unbiased moral agent.

Principle of equal basic liberty for all John Rawls's Theory of Justice: a principle that guarantees everyone the same fundamental rights and freedoms, the maximum compatible with everyone else having the same amount.

Principle of justice in acquisition Robert Nozick's theory of justice as entitlement: acquisition of previously unowned items requires one to leave sufficient resources to meet the needs of others.

Principle of justice in transfer Robert Nozick's theory of justice as entitlement: so long as you do not steal from, coerce, defraud, or otherwise cheat the other person, you may dispose of legitimately owned property in any way you see fit.

Principle of rectification of injustice in holdings Robert Nozick's theory of justice as entitlement: attempt to answer the question, "What must we do if we discover people have things to which they are not entitled?"

Prithvi The goddess of earth in the *Vedas*.

Problem of evil An argument against the existence of a perfect God based on the apparent irreconcil-ability of that concept with the existence of evil. Cf. *Theodicy*.

Puranas The ancient books of the Hindus. The *Vishnu Puranas* and the *Shiva Puranas* relate the stories of the lives of the gods Vishnu and Shiva.

Puruṣa (Purusha) In the *Vedas*, Purusha is the cosmic person who creates the universe by sacrificing a portion of his body. In the yoga system, purusha designates pure consciousness (the essence of a human being).

Pythagoras (sixth century B.C.) Italian philosopher and mathematician.

Q

Quantum mechanics Physics: the study of the subatomic realm.

R

Ramayana One of the two great epics of India, the *Ramayana* describes the life and intrigues of King Rama of India. Its focus includes concepts of ideal manhood, womanhood, kingship, and kingdom.

Rationalism The view that the mind is capable of generating knowledge independent of sense experience. Cf. *A priori*.

Rawls, John (b. 1921) American philosopher known for his concept of justice as fairness.

Relativism Ethics: any of a series of views which hold that the morality of an action depends on the approval or disapproval of some individual or group of individuals. Cf. *Cultural relativism* and *Divine will theory*.

Rig Veda The most philosophical of the four *Vedas*.

Ring of Gyges Story told by Glaucon in Plato's *Republic*. By turning the bezel of the ring, Gyges was able to become invisible and thus to pursue any lifestyle he wished without fear of discovery or punishment.

Roentgen, Wilhelm Konrad (1845–1923) German physicist best known for his discovery of X-rays.

Ross, William David (1877–1970) British philosopher known especially for his deontological views in ethics.

Ṛta (Rita) In the *Vedas*, Ṛta is the highest universal law that governs everything—the principle of harmony in the universe.

S

Samādhi The goal of yoga; the eighth step of the yoga method.

Sanatam Dharma Sanskrit: a religion based upon eternal principles. The scholars of Hinduism are fond of regarding their religion as Sanatam Dharma.

Sartre, Jean-Paul (1905–1980) French philosopher and novelist, best known as a proponent of atheistic existentialism.

Satori Zen Buddhism: the state of enlightenment.

Schopenhauer, Arthur (1788–1860) German philosopher often regarded as a nihilist.

Schrödinger, Erwin (1887–1961) Austrian physicist and philosopher.

Schrödinger's cat An example devised by Erwin Schrödinger to demonstrate differences between the Copenhagen Interpretation and commonsense ideas about reality.

Shiva One of the gods of the Hindu trinity: the destroyer of the universe.

Siddhartha The original (proper) name of the Buddha.

Sindhu The original name of the river Indus which flows from the Himalayas to the Arabian Sea.

Sisyphus Greek mythology: a king of Corinth condemned to an eternity of rolling a rock up a hill.

Socrates (470–399 B.C.) Greek philosopher convicted and executed on charges of impiety and corrupting the youth.

Soham A mantra given to a beginner in meditation.

Soma The god of intoxicating drink in the *Vedas*.

Sound Logic: a valid argument with true premises.

Strict cumulativity thesis The thesis that all change in science is (or should be) a simple matter of addition, generalization, or fine-tuning.

Superfluous Something that is inessential, unnecessary, or too much.

Suzuki, D. T. (1870–1966) Japanese teacher of the Rinzai school of Zen Buddhism, author of numerous books concerning the aims and practices of Zen.

T

Tajjalan A mantra used in meditation ("Everything arises out of it, is preserved by it, and merges back into it").

Tanha Buddhism: the self-centered desire of incessant seeking for one's own gain.

Tao The central concept in Taoism—the ultimate reality or "The Way."

Tao Te Ching "The Way and Its Power"—a book written by Lao Tzu which presents the foundational ideas of Taoism.

Taoism A school of philosophy originating in China in the sixth century B.C. Its major ideas were formulated by Lao Tzu.

Tat Twam Asi A mantra used in meditation ("You are That"—your essence is identical with the universal essence).

Tautology A proposition whose truth depends only on the meaning of the terms. Also known as an analytic truth.

Te An aspect of the *Tao*—present in us as our natural abilities.

Teleological argument An argument that seeks to infer the existence of God from the apparent design of the cosmos. Also called "the Argument from Design."

Teleology The study of ends, goals, and purposes.

Thales (*floruit* 585 B.C.) Often regarded as the first Western philosopher—known especially for the first successful prediction of a solar eclipse, the metaphysical doctrine that all is water, and the saying, "All things are full of gods."

Theodicy An attempt to answer the Problem of Evil.

Theory A conceptual structure designed to explain, unify, or otherwise account for puzzling, problematic, or poorly understood phenomena or experiences.

Theism Belief in God(s).

Tillich, Paul (1886–1965) German Protestant theologian who developed the concept of God as Ultimate Concern and emphasized the irreplaceable importance of religious myths and symbols.

Transcendent Beyond space and time.

Transcendental meditation A form of meditation that utilizes mantras as aids, popularized by Maharishi Mahesh Yogi.

Transient argument An argument which, based on the transient (short-lived) nature of human life, concludes that it cannot be meaningful in any cosmic sense.

U

Ultimate concern That which is of greater concern than anything else. According to Tillich, a person's ultimate concern is his/her god.

Uncertainty Relation Quantum Mechanics: principle discovered by Heisenberg according to which it is impossible to make precise measurements of both position and momentum of a subatomic particle. The Uncertainty Relation has since been demonstrated to hold for other pairs of predicates as well: space and time, mass and energy, and so on.

Upanishads The philosophical portions of the *Vedas*—200 books that form the basis of later Hindu philosophy.

Usha The goddess of dawn in the *Vedas*.

Utilitarianism Ethics: a variant of consequentialism in which the morality of an action is judged in terms of its consequences for a group of individuals.

V

Valid Logic: an argument in which the conclusion follows from the premises according to accepted principles of logic.

Varuṇa One of the gods of the *Vedas* who controls other gods through the power of Ṛta.

Vedas The earliest expressions of Hinduism (circa 2500 B.C.).

Veil of ignorance John Rawls's Theory of Justice: hypothetical device to guarantee the fairness of social principles—those designing and choosing the principles do not know the race, gender, or socioeconomic class to which they will belong.

Vishnu One of the gods of the Hindu trinity; the preserver of the universe. He takes material forms and descends to earth to help good forces destroy the evil. In Hindu mythology, Vishnu has descended nine times to save the world and humanity.

Vishwakarma The Vedic god who is regarded as the maker of the universe.

Voltaire, François Marie Arouet (1694–1778) French philosopher, essayist, and contributor to the *Encyclopedie*.

W

Wu wei Actionless action or pure action. Taoism believes that through this pure action one can experience the flow of the *Tao* within. It is an aid to enlightenment.

Y

Yama The god of death in the *Upanishads*.

Yama The five moral constraints that constitute the first step of the yoga method.

Yoga A system of Hindu philosophy which offers a step-by-step method to achieve enlightenment.

Yoga Sūtras The original text of yoga compiled by Patañjali in 500 B.C.

Z

Zazen Zen Buddhism: "Sitting in meditation"—a technique used to achieve the experience of *satori*.

Zen A popular Japanese form of Buddhism that emphasizes the direct experience of reality.

SUGGESTIONS FOR FURTHER STUDY

Introduction: A Guidebook for Students

G. S. KIRK and J. E. RAVEN. *The Presocratic Philosophers.* New York: Oxford University Press, 1957.

BERTRAND RUSSELL. *A History of Western Philosophy.* New York: Simon & Schuster, 1945.

PART I: The Human Condition: Knowing Thyself

HAZEL BARNES. *An Existentialist Ethics.* Chicago: University of Chicago Press, 1967.

WILLIAM BARRETT. *Irrational Man.* New York: Anchor Books, 1962.

T. BEAUCHAMP and S. PERLIN. *Ethical Issues in Death and Dying.* Englewood Cliffs, NJ: Prentice Hall, 1978.

ALBERT CAMUS. *The Myth of Sisyphus and Other Essays.* New York: Alfred A. Knopf, 1955.

VICTOR FRANKL. *Man's Search for Meaning.* New York: Washington Square Press, 1959.

ELISABETH KÜBLER-ROSS. *On Death and Dying.* New York: Macmillan, 1969.

ASHOK MALHOTRA. *Jean-Paul Sartre's Existentialism in Nausea and Being and Nothingness.* Calcutta, India: Writers Workshop, 1978.

RAYMOND MOODY. *Life After Life.* New York: Bantam, 1975.

RAYMOND MOODY. *Reflections on Life After Life.* New York: Bantam, 1977.

L. NATHAN OAKLANDER. *Existential Philosophy: An Introduction.* Englewood Cliffs, NJ: Prentice Hall, 1992.

WALKER PERCY. *Lost in the Cosmos: The Last Self-Help Book.* New York: Farrar, Straus and Giroux, 1983.

WALKER PERCY. *The Thanatos Syndrome.* New York: Farrar, Straus and Giroux, 1987.

PLATO. *The Last Days of Socrates [Euthyphro, The Apology, Crito, and Phaedol].* Translation by Hugh Tredennick. New York: Penguin, 1954.

MICHAEL SABOM. *Recollections of Death: A Medical Investigation.* Philadelphia: Harper and Row, 1982.

STEVEN SANDERS and DAVID CHENEY. *The Meaning of Life.* Englewood Cliffs, NJ: Prentice-Hall, 1980.

JEAN-PAUL SARTRE. *Existentialism Is a Humanism.* New York: Philosophical Library, 1957.

JEAN-PAUL SARTRE. *Nausea.* New York: New Directions, 1964.

LEO TOLSTOY. *My Confession.* Translation by Leo Wiener. London: J. M. Dent and Sons, 1905.

PART II: Values and Systems: Living With Others

RAZIEL ABELSON and MARIE-LOUISE FRIQUEGNON. *Ethics for Modern Life.* New York: Saint Martin's Press, 1982.

ARISTOTLE. *Nicomachean Ethics.* Translated by M. Ostwald. New York: Macmillan, 1962.

JOHN ARRAS and NANCY RHODEN. *Ethical Issues in Modern Medicine.* Mountain View, CA: Mayfield, 1989.

REM EDWARDS and GLENN GRABER. *Bioethics.* New York: Harcourt Brace Jovanovich, 1988.

THOMAS MAPPES and JANE ZEMBATY. *Biomedical Ethics.* New York: McGraw-Hill, 1991.

JOHN STUART MILL. *On Liberty.* New York: Macmillan, 1956.

LISA H. NEWTON. *Ethics in America: Source Reader.* Englewood Cliffs, NJ: Prentice Hall, 1989.

ROBERT NOZICK. *Anarchy, State and Utopia.* New York: Basic Books, 1974.

PLATO. *The Republic.* Translated by Desmond Lee. New York: Penguin, 1955.

JOHN RAWLS. *A Theory of Justice.* Cambridge, MA: Harvard University Press, 1971.

Tom Regan. *Matters of Life and Death: New Introductory Essays in Moral Philosophy.* New York: Random House, 1980.

Peter Singer. *The Expanding Circle: Ethics and Sociobiology.* New York: Farrar, Straus, and Giroux, 1981.

Christina Hoff Sommers. *Right and Wrong: Basic Readings in Ethics.* New York: Harcourt Brace Jovanovich, 1986.

PART III: Truth and Being: Exploring the Limits

George Berkeley. *Three Dialogues Between Hylas and Philonous.* C. Turbayne, editor. New York: Macmillan, 1954.

Fritjof Capra. *The Tao of Physics.* New York: Bantam Books, 1984 (2nd edition).

René Descartes. *Meditations on First Philosophy.* Translated by L. Lafleur. New York: Macmillan, 1960.

Carl Hempel. *Philosophy of Natural Science.* Englewood Cliffs, NJ: Prentice-Hall, 1966.

Thomas Kuhn. *The Structure of Scientific Revolutions.* Chicago: University of Chicago Press, 1970.

Larry Laudan. *Science and Values.* Berkeley: University of California Press, 1984.

Ernest Nagel. *The Structure of Science.* New York: Harcourt, 1961.

Robert Pirsig. *Zen and the Art of Motorcycle Maintenance.* New York: Bantam Books, 1974.

Plato. *Meno.* Translated by B. Jowlett. New York: Macmillan, 1949.

Bertrand Russell. *The Problems of Philosophy.* New York: Oxford University Press, 1959.

Richard Taylor. *Metaphysics.* Englewood Cliffs, NJ: Prentice Hall, 1992.

PART IV: Of Ultimate Concern: A Higher Consciousness

Masao Abe. *Zen and Western Thought.* Honolulu, HI: University of Hawaii Press, 1985.

Usherbudh Arya. *Yoga-Sūtras of Patañjali.* Honesdale, PA: The Himalayan Institute, 1986.

Swami Ajaya. *Yoga Psychology.* Honesdale, PA: Himalayan International Institute, 1977.

Martin Buber. *I and Thou.* New York: Scribner's, 1970.

Paul Carus. *The Gospel of Buddha.* Chicago: Open Court, 1915.

Edward Conze. *Buddhism: Its Essence and Development.* New York: Harper and Row, 1969.

H. G. Creel. *Chinese Thought From Confucius to Mao Tsetung.* New York: Mentor, 1964.

Sigmund Freud. *The Future of an Illusion.* New York: Norton, 1961.

Ray Grigg. *The Tao of Relationship.* New York: Bantam Books, 1989.

Charles Hartshorne. *Omnipotence and Other Theological Mistakes.* Albany, NY: SUNY Press, 1984.

Eugene Herrigel. *Zen in the Art of Archery.* New York: Pantheon, 1953.

John Hick. *Philosophy of Religion.* Englewood Cliffs, NJ: Prentice Hall, 1990.

Lewis Hopfe. *The Religions of the World.* New York: Macmillan, 1987.

Phillip Kapleau. *The Three Pillars of Zen.* New York: Harper and Row, 1969.

Thomas Kasulis. *Zen Action/Zen Person.* Honolulu, HI: University of Hawaii Press, 1981.

John Koller. *Oriental Philosophies.* New York: Macmillan, 1985.

John Koller and Patricia Koller. *A Sourcebook in Asian Philosophy.* New York: Macmillan, 1991.

Lao Tzu. *Tao Te Ching.* Translated by Wing-Tsit Chan. New York: Macmillan, 1963.

Trevor Ling. *The Buddha.* New York: Penguin Books, 1973.

Ramamurti Mishra. *The Textbook of the Yoga Psychology.* New York: Julian Press, 1987.

Stephen Mitchell. *Tao Te Ching.* New York: Harper Perennial, 1992.

Louis J. Pojman. *Philosophy of Religion: An Anthology.* Belmont, CA: Wadsworth, 1987.

Radhakrishnan and Moore. *A Sourcebook in Indian Philosophy.* Princeton, NJ: Princeton University Press, 1957.

Swami Rama. *Lectures of Yoga.* Honesdale, PA: The Himalayan Institute, 1979.

BERTRAND RUSSELL. *Why I Am Not a Christian* (*and other essays*). New York: Simon & Schuster, 1957.

HUSTON SMITH. *The Religions of Man.* New York: Harper and Row, 1958.

D. T. SUZUKI. *Zen Buddhism.* New York: Doubleday and Company, 1956.

D. T. SUZUKI. *An Introduction to Zen.* New York: Grove Press, 1964.

RAJMANI TIGUNAIT. *Seven Systems of Indian Philosophy.* Honesdale, PA: The Himalayan Institute, 1989.

PAUL TILLICH. *The Courage to Be.* New Haven, CT: Yale University Press, 1952.

PAUL TILLICH. *Dynamics of Faith.* New York: Harper and Row, 1957.

JEAN VARENNE. *Yoga and the Hindu Tradition.* Chicago: University of Chicago Press, 1976.

ARTHUR WALEY. *Three Ways of Thought in Ancient China.* New York: Doubleday Anchor, 1956.

ALAN WATTS. *The Spirit of Zen.* New York: Grove Press, 1958.

LIN YUTANG. *The Wisdom of China and India.* New York: Random House, 1942.

PHOTO CREDITS